THE CAMBRIDGE C(
TACITL

Tacitus is universally recognised as ancient
his account of the Roman Empire in the first century AD has been fundamental in shaping the modern perception of Rome and its emperors. This *Companion* provides a new, up-to-date and authoritative assessment of his work and influence that will be invaluable for students and non-specialists as well as of interest to established scholars in the field. First situating Tacitus within the tradition of Roman historical writing and his own contemporary society, it goes on to analyse each of his individual works and then discuss key topics such as his distinctive authorial voice and his views of history and freedom. It ends by tracing Tacitus' reception, beginning with the transition from manuscript to printed editions, describing his influence on political thought in early modern Europe, and concluding with his significance in the twentieth century.

A complete list of books in the series is at the back of the book

THE CAMBRIDGE
COMPANION TO
TACITUS

EDITED BY
A. J. WOODMAN

*Gildersleeve Professor of Classics,
University of Virginia*

CAMBRIDGE
UNIVERSITY PRESS

CAMBRIDGE UNIVERSITY PRESS
Cambridge, New York, Melbourne, Madrid, Cape Town, Singapore,
São Paulo, Delhi, Dubai, Tokyo

Cambridge University Press
The Edinburgh Building, Cambridge CB2 8RU, UK

Published in the United States of America by Cambridge University Press, New York

www.cambridge.org
Information on this title: www.cambridge.org/9780521697484

© Cambridge University Press 2009

This publication is in copyright. Subject to statutory exception
and to the provisions of relevant collective licensing agreements,
no reproduction of any part may take place without the written
permission of Cambridge University Press.

First published 2009

Printed in the United Kingdom at the University Press, Cambridge

A catalogue record for this publication is available from the British Library

Library of Congress Cataloguing in Publication data
The Cambridge companion to Tacitus / [edited by] A. J. Woodman.
  p. cm. – (Cambridge companions to literature)
  ISBN 978-0-521-87460-1 (Hardback)
  1. Tacitus, Cornelius–Criticism and interpretation.
  I. Woodman, A. J. (Anthony John), 1945–
    PA6716.C36 2009
    878'.0109–dc22   2009035037

ISBN 978-0-521-87460-1 Hardback
ISBN 978-0-521-69748-4 Paperback

Cambridge University Press has no responsibility for the persistence or
accuracy of URLs for external or third-party internet websites referred to in
this publication, and does not guarantee that any content on such websites is,
or will remain, accurate or appropriate.

*To the memory of
Ronald Martin*

CONTENTS

List of Contributors		*page* x
Preface		xv
	Introduction A. J. WOODMAN	1

PART I: CONTEXTS

1	From the annalists to the *Annales*: Latin historiography before Tacitus A. M. GOWING	17
2	Tacitus and the contemporary scene A. J. WOODMAN	31

PART II: TEXTS

3	The *Agricola* A. R. BIRLEY	47
4	The *Germania* as literary text RICHARD F. THOMAS	59
5	The faces of eloquence: the *Dialogus de oratoribus* SANDER M. GOLDBERG	73
6	Fission and fusion: shifting Roman identities in the *Histories* RHIANNON ASH	85
7	The Tiberian hexad CHRISTINA SHUTTLEWORTH KRAUS	100

CONTENTS

8	*Hamlet* without the prince? The Claudian *Annals* S. J. V. MALLOCH	116
9	'Is dying so very terrible?' The Neronian *Annals* E. E. KEITEL	127

PART III: TOPICS

10	Tacitus' personal voice CHRISTOPHER PELLING	147
11	Tacitus as a historian MIRIAM T. GRIFFIN	168
12	*Res olim dissociabiles*: emperors, senators and liberty S. P. OAKLEY	184
13	Style and language S. P. OAKLEY	195
14	Speeches in the *Histories* D. S. LEVENE	212
15	Warfare in the *Annals* D. S. LEVENE	225

PART IV: TRANSMISSION

16	From manuscript to print R. H. MARTIN	241
17	Tacitus and political thought in early modern Europe, c. 1530–c. 1640 ALEXANDRA GAJDA	253
18	Gibbon and Tacitus PAUL CARTLEDGE	269
19	A dangerous book: the reception of the *Germania* C. B. KREBS	280
20	Tacitus and the twentieth-century novel MARTHA MALAMUD	300
21	Tacitus' Syme MARK TOHER	317

CONTENTS

Chronological table   330
Abbreviations and bibliography   332
Index locorum   357
General index   361

CONTRIBUTORS

RHIANNON ASH is Fellow and Tutor in Classics at Merton College, Oxford. Her interests lie in Roman historiography, above all Tacitus. She has published a range of articles in this area, as well as a monograph, *Ordering Anarchy: Armies and Leaders in Tacitus' Histories* (1999), and a commentary, *Tacitus: Histories Book II* (2007).

A. R. BIRLEY was Professor of Ancient History at the Universities of Manchester (1974–90) and Düsseldorf (1990–2002), and is now Honorary Professor in the Department of Classics and Ancient History at the University of Durham. His publications include biographies of the emperors Hadrian, Marcus Aurelius and Septimius Severus, several books on Roman Britain, and a new translation, with introduction and commentary, of Tacitus' *Agricola* and *Germania* for the series Oxford World's Classics (1999). He has been Chair of the Trustees of the Vindolanda Trust since 1996.

PAUL CARTLEDGE is A.G. Leventis Professor of Greek Culture at the University of Cambridge, and Hellenic Parliament Global Distinguished Professor (visiting) at New York University. He is the author, co-author, editor and co-editor of over twenty books on many aspects of Greek history and historiography, with a special focus on Sparta. His engagement with Tacitus dates back to his undergraduate years at Oxford (1965–9); that with Gibbon dates particularly from the bicentenary in 1976 of the original publication of the first volume of the *Decline and Fall*.

ALEXANDRA GAJDA is a lecturer in Early Modern History at the University of Birmingham. She is preparing a monograph on Robert Devereux, 2nd earl of Essex, and political culture in late Elizabethan England.

SANDER M. GOLDBERG is Professor of Classics at the University of California, Los Angeles. His research centres on Roman performative arts, particularly drama and oratory, in their literary and social context. His published work includes *The Making of Menander's Comedy* (1980), *Understanding Terence* (1986), *Epic in Republican Rome* (1995) and *Constructing Literature in the Roman Republic* (2005). From 1991 to 1995 he was editor of the *Transactions of the American Philological Association*.

A. M. GOWING is Professor and Chair of Classics at the University of Washington in Seattle, where he has been on the faculty since 1988, after receiving his PhD from Bryn Mawr College. His chief interests lie in the area of Roman historiography and literature, especially of the imperial period; his most recent book is *Empire and Memory: The Representation of the Roman Republic in Imperial Culture* (2005).

MIRIAM T. GRIFFIN is Emeritus Fellow in Ancient History of Somerville College, Oxford. She is the author of *Seneca: A Philosopher in Politics* (1976; reissued with Postscript, 1992), *Nero: The End of a Dynasty* (1984) and (with E.M. Atkins) *Cicero: On Duties* (1991). She is currently working on a study of Seneca's *De Beneficiis*.

E. E. KEITEL has taught at the University of Massachusetts since 1980. She has written many articles on Tacitus and with Jane Crawford has edited a school text of Cicero's *Pro Caelio* (forthcoming).

CHRISTINA SHUTTLEWORTH KRAUS is Professor of Classics at Yale University; in the past she has taught at the University of Oxford, University College London and New York University. Her primary research interests are in commentaries and Latin historiography. She is currently working (with A.J. Woodman) on a commentary on Tacitus' *Agricola* for the Cambridge Greek and Latin Classics series.

C. B. KREBS is an Assistant Professor at Harvard University. He is the author of *Negotiatio Germaniae: Tacitus' Germania und Enea Silvio Piccolomini, Giannantonio Campano, Conrad Celtis und Heinrich Bebel* (2005) and is currently finishing a study of the reception of the *Germania* from the 15th to the 20th century. He has written articles mostly on Greek and Roman historians and the classical tradition, on which he also co-chairs a seminar at Harvard's Humanities Center.

D. S. LEVENE is Professor of Classics at New York University. He has published a variety of works on Latin historiography and rhetoric, including *Religion in Livy* (1993); among his current projects is a book on Livy and the Hannibalic War.

LIST OF CONTRIBUTORS

MARTHA MALAMUD is Associate Professor of Classics at the University at Buffalo (State University of New York) and co-editor of the classics journal *Arethusa*.

S. J. V. MALLOCH has recently held appointments at the Universities of Munich and Cambridge and is currently a lecturer in Roman history at the University of Nottingham. He has published on the history and historiography of early imperial Rome, and is now finishing an edition of Tacitus, *Annals* 11.

R. H. MARTIN was Emeritus Professor of Classics at the University of Leeds and author of commentaries on Terence's *Phormio* (1959) and *Adelphoe* (1976) and Books 5–6 of Tacitus' *Annals* (2001). He wrote *Tacitus* (1981, revised 1994) and with A.J.Woodman produced commentaries on *Annals* Books 3 (1996) and 4 (1989 and often reprinted). He also edited and translated the fifteenth-century *Epitome margaritae castigatae eloquentiae* of Traversagni (1971).

S. P. OAKLEY has taught in the Universities of Cambridge and Reading and is currently Kennedy Professor of Latin at the University of Cambridge and Fellow of Emmanuel College. His principal publications are *The Hill-forts of the Samnites* (1995) and *A Commentary on Livy, Books VI–X* (1997–2005). He is currently working on the manuscript traditions of several Latin prose authors. Professor Oakley is a Fellow of the British Academy.

CHRISTOPHER PELLING is Regius Professor of Greek at the University of Oxford. His books include a commentary on Plutarch's *Life of Antony* (1988), *Literary Texts and the Greek Historian* (2000) and *Plutarch and History* (2002); he also edited *Characterization and Individuality in Greek Literature* (1990) and *Greek Tragedy and the Historian* (1997). He is currently finishing a commentary on Plutarch's *Life of Caesar,* which will appear in the Clarendon Ancient History series. Professor Pelling is a Fellow of the British Academy.

RICHARD F. THOMAS taught at Harvard, Cincinnati and Cornell before returning to Harvard in 1987, where he is Professor of Greek and Latin; he has served as Chair of the Department of the Classics and as Director of Graduate Studies and of Undergraduate Studies; presently he is co-chair of the seminar on 'The civilizations of Greece and Rome' at Harvard's Humanities Center. He has served as Director of the American Philological Association and as Trustee of the Vergilian Society, of which he is currently a Director. He has published a monograph *Lands and*

Peoples in Roman Poetry: The Ethnographical Tradition (1982), a two-volume text and commentary on Virgil's *Georgics* (1988) and a collection of his articles on the subject of Virgilian allusion, *Reading Virgil and his Texts* (1999). His recent work includes *Virgil and the Augustan Reception* (2001), two co-edited volumes, *Classics and the Uses of Reception* (2006) and *Bob Dylan's Performance Artistry* (*Oral Tradition* 22.1, 2007), and a forthcoming commentary on Horace, *Odes* 4 for the series Cambridge Greek and Latin Classics.

MARK TOHER is the Frank Bailey Professor of Classics at Union College in Schenectady, New York. He is the author of articles and essays on topics in Greek and Roman history and historiography, and along with Kurt Raaflaub he co-edited *Between Republic and Empire: Interpretations of Augustus and His Principate* (1990). He is presently at work on an edition of the life of Augustus by Nicolaus of Damascus.

A. J. WOODMAN is Basil L. Gildersleeve Professor of Classics at the University of Virginia and Emeritus Professor of Latin at the University of Durham. He is author of two volumes of commentary on Velleius Paterculus (1977, 1983), *Rhetoric in Classical Historiography* (1988), *Latin Historians* (1997, with C.S. Kraus), *Tacitus Reviewed* (1998), and also two annotated translations: *Tacitus: The Annals* (2004, revised 2008) and *Sallust: Catiline's War, The Jugurthine War, Histories* (2007). With R.H. Martin he has produced commentaries on Tacitus' *Annals*, Books 3 (1996) and 4 (1989 and often reprinted). He is co-editor of *Quality and Pleasure in Latin Poetry* (1974), *Creative Imitation and Latin Literature* (1979), *Poetry and Politics in the Age of Augustus* (1984), *Past Perspectives: Studies in Greek and Roman Historical Writing* (1986), *Author and Audience in Latin Literature* (1992), *Tacitus and the Tacitean Tradition* (1993) and *Traditions and Contexts in the Poetry of Horace* (2002). Currently he is co-authoring (with C.S. Kraus) a commentary on Tacitus' *Agricola* for the series Cambridge Greek and Latin Classics, and co-editing volumes of essays on Catullus (with I.M. Le M. Du Quesnay) and on first-century AD poetry and historiography (with J.F. Miller).

PREFACE

Who seeks the companionship of a *Companion*? One answer seems to be certain: such a book will be read and consulted by students, whether graduates or undergraduates or (as the time-honoured phrase has it) those in 'the upper forms of schools'. If this is true, it appears to follow that the book will also be read by those who teach these students: that is to say, professional classicists of one sort or another. It is to be hoped that *Companions* will also have an appeal for the more general reader, and contributors to this *Companion* have certainly been asked to keep such readers in mind; but they have also been encouraged to pursue their own ideas and not necessarily to be content with a mere summary of the available scholarship. The aim of the book is to provide a practical demonstration of current work on Tacitus as written by experts.

Although the book covers a wide range of topics, the limitations of space or the prejudices of the editor or the refusals of importuned contributors mean that it cannot be completely comprehensive and some readers may be disappointed to find little or no treatment of an expected or favourite theme. If the *Annals* is thought to receive disproportionate coverage, the reason is that it is Tacitus' greatest and most influential work. Although efforts have been made to avoid overlap between one chapter and another, in a book of this kind it is inevitable that contributors will sometimes cover the same ground or resort to the same passages of text. While readers should be prepared to make allowances in such cases, it should not be assumed that one contributor will take the same view as the next or that contributors will interpret a given passage in the same way.

I am most grateful to Michael Sharp for the suggestion that I should edit *The Cambridge Companion to Tacitus*. In the course of editing I have taken advice from various friends and colleagues, including Susan Brigden, Andrew Feldherr, Miriam Griffin, Chris Kraus, Quentin Skinner, Richard Williams, Peter Wiseman and Blair Worden; I owe an especial debt of gratitude to Salvador Bartera, Anna Chahoud and David Levene. Above all I am grateful to the contributors, whose company has made the production of this *Companion* such a pleasurable, if protracted, experience.

　Lovers of Tacitus will be sad to learn that this book contains the final contribution to Tacitean scholarship by Ronald Martin, who passed away in the summer of 2008 in his ninety-third year. His scholarly career began during the war in Newcastle upon Tyne at King's College (as the University was then called), where G.B.A. Fletcher pointed him towards Tacitean study and in particular towards the work of Löfstedt and his followers. Ronald published his first paper on Tacitus in 1946 and for more than sixty years thereafter played a leading role in Tacitean scholarship. He was, in the words of F.R.D. Goodyear, 'of all scholars the most deeply versed in the intricacies of Tacitus' style', and his *Tacitus* (1981) is commonly accepted as the best introduction to the author. Modest and unassuming, he was an unfailing source of advice and good judgement to generations of friends and colleagues, not least the editor of this volume. He leaves, as one of his fellow contributors has said, 'a remarkable legacy' and will be greatly missed.

Charlottesville   A.J.W.

A. J. WOODMAN

Introduction

In the year 17 the Cheruscan chief Arminius, revered as a founding figure by Germans of later ages and commemorated in the nineteenth century by massive monuments in the Teutoburg Forest and Minnesota,[1] was engaged in exchanging insults with his rival, Maroboduus. This, at least, is what we are told by Tacitus, who says that Arminius called Maroboduus 'a fugitive and inexperienced in battle, one who had been protected by his lair in Hercynia ... and was a betrayer of his fatherland and a satellite of the Roman emperor' (*A*. 2.45.3):

> fugacem Maroboduum appellans, proeliorum expertem, Hercyniae latebris defensum, ... proditorem patriae, satellitem Caesaris.

Although Tacitus has told us earlier that Arminius had formerly been a soldier in the Roman army and could speak Latin (2.10.3), it seems unlikely that a German warrior would be so familiar with Virgil's *Georgics* that he was able to describe Maroboduus in the same terms as Virgil had used to describe a skulking snake (3.544–5 'frustra *defensa latebris* | uipera', 'the viper vainly protected by its lair'). Of course verisimilitude is not to be expected from the speeches of barbarians portrayed in Latin historical texts: when a chief of the Britons says 'where they make a desert, they call it peace' (*Agr*. 30.5 'ubi solitudinem faciunt, pacem appellant'), he alludes to a speech in Book 8 of Livy, an allusion no doubt undetected by the majority of the modern politicians whose repetition of Tacitus' statement has turned it into one of the most high-profile quotations of the age.[2] But Arminius'

For their comments on an earlier draft of this Introduction I am most grateful to A. Chahoud, C.S. Kraus, D.S. Levene, R.H. Martin and S.P. Oakley. All dates are AD unless stated otherwise.

[1] See Schama (1995) 100–20, Ash (2006a) 117–47.
[2] Cf. Liv. 8.13.14–15 'As far as the Latins are concerned, you can procure peace for yourselves in perpetuity either by savagery or by forgiveness ... You may destroy the whole of Latium and make of it vast deserts [*solitudines facere*] ...' (the speaker is L. Furius Camillus, cos. 338 BC). An internet search will reveal the popularity of the quotation

allusion to Virgil constitutes an interesting challenge to Tacitus' readers: on the assumption that readers recognise – and are intended to recognise – the allusion, which comes from the memorable description of the plague at the end of *Georgics* 3, they are invited to supply for themselves the information which Tacitus has omitted, namely, that the description is that of a viper. Now it is noteworthy that Velleius Paterculus, a historian contemporary with Arminius and Maroboduus, explicitly likens Maroboduus to a snake (129.3): 'Maroboduum inhaerentem occupati regni finibus ... uelut serpentem abstrusam terra' ('Maroboduus, clinging to the borders of his occupied kingdom ... like a snake concealed in the ground'). Since snakes are reasonably common as terms of abuse,[3] this may be simply coincidence; but it is worth asking whether the three texts illustrate some more complicated historiographical phenomenon.

It has often been stated that Tacitus, given his disaffected attitude towards the emperor Tiberius, will have taken no notice of a historian such as Velleius,[4] who had served as a soldier under Tiberius and whose admiration for his former general is considerable. A few chapters earlier in Book 2, however, Tacitus tells the story of a slave who in 16 tried to rescue his master – Agrippa Postumus, Augustus' grandson – from exile (2.39.1). The attempt was thwarted because Agrippa had already been killed two years before, so the slave 'turned to greater and more headlong schemes' (2.39.2 'ad maiora et magis praecipitia conuersus'): travelling to Etruria, he decided to impersonate his dead master. The expression with which Tacitus describes the false Agrippa Postumus is almost identical to that with which Velleius had described the *real* Agrippa Postumus at the time of his exile in 7 (112.7 'in *praecipitia conuersus*'). Since the expression is otherwise unparalleled, the almost inevitable conclusion seems to be that Tacitus, in describing the antics of the slave, has alluded to Velleius' description of the man whom the slave was impersonating.

---

with politicians, one of the most recent examples being Fouad Siniora, the prime minister of Lebanon (July 2006); for some others from the past forty years see Benario (2007) 66. After the Germans invaded Poland in 1939, the British dropped nearly 850,000 leaflets over Germany in the following spring that read, 'Sie verwüsten ganze Länder und nennen es Frieden' ('You lay waste whole countries and call it peace'). (Ironically, Tacitus' words are part of a longer and more complicated sentence and they become quotable only at the cost of being wrenched from their original context: see e.g. Ogilvie and Richmond (1967) on 30.5 *falsis nominibus*.)

[3] See e.g. *OLD uipera* b.
[4] Velleius was 'ignored by all subsequent historians' (Martin (1981) 202). His very existence was denied by Syme (1958a) 358 ('The Roman historians subsequent to Livy have perished utterly'), who omitted him from his survey of 'history at Rome' (140–1). Twenty years later Syme (1978b) attacked 'mendacity in Velleius' (= (1984) 1090–1104). See also below, pp. 24–6.

Introduction

If modern historians were to set about writing the history of (say) the Tudor age, they would be expected to include surviving contemporary accounts amongst their source material. But it is clear that Tacitus, though having read Velleius, has not used his work straightforwardly as a source: by alluding to Velleius' description of the real Agrippa he has either underlined the falsity of the fake Agrippa or he has 'colluded' in the construction of the man's false identity. However we interpret the allusion, Tacitus is involved in a literary procedure rather than one that we would categorise as 'historical'. Such involvement is endemic in the tradition of Latin historical writing. In the preface to his history of the Second Punic War, for example, L. Coelius Antipater (fl. 120–110 BC) evidently discussed the rhythm of his sentences (Cic. *Orat.* 229–30). It is inconceivable that such a discussion should be found in the preface to a modern work of history, but it gives some indication of the intellectual world in which Latin historians operated.[5]

When Tacitus returns to Maroboduus later in Book 2 of the *Annals*, the now worsted chief has been begging for aid from Tiberius himself (2.63.2–3):

> responsum a Caesare tutam ei honoratamque sedem in Italia fore, si maneret; sin rebus eius aliud conduceret, abiturum fide qua uenisset. ceterum apud senatum disseruit non Philippum Atheniensibus, non Pyrrhum aut Antiochum populo Romano perinde metuendos fuisse. extat oratio qua magnitudinem uiri, uiolentiam subiectarum ei gentium et quam propinquus Italiae hostis, suaque in destruendo eo consilia extulit.
>
> The reply from Caesar was that there would be a safe and honourable abode for him in Italy if he were to remain there; but, if something else suited his affairs, he could depart with the same trust as he had come. Yet before the senate he said that Philip had not been a source of such dread to the Athenians, nor Pyrrhus or Antiochus to the Roman people. There survives the speech in which he emphasised the greatness of the man, the violence of the races subject to him, how close to Italy he had been as an enemy, and his own plans in his destruction.

Maroboduus went into exile at Ravenna in accordance with the terms of Tiberius' offer, about which Velleius exclaims as follows (129.3): 'how he confines him, honourably yet securely!' ('quam illum ut *honorate* ita *secure* continet!'). *continet* continues the metaphor of Maroboduus as a snake,[6] but *honorate* and *secure* comprise exactly the same combination of ideas (in one case expressed by the very same word) as Tacitus' *tutam ... honoratamque*.

---

[5] Similar issues arise with the *Germania*: see below, Chapter 4.
[6] For *continere* used of animals and the like cf. Cic. *Phil.* 13.5; Columella, *Rust.* 7.3.25; Sen. *Dial.* 5.40.2; Plin. *Ep.* 9.25.3; Amm. Marc. 24.5.2.

How is this similarity to be explained? It is possible that Tacitus is again alluding to Velleius, as in the earlier episode concerning Agrippa Postumus. Yet the two Tacitean passages are not quite of the same order, since at 2.63.2–3 Tacitus is representing a speech of Tiberius. An alternative possibility is therefore that Tacitus read in the senatorial archives (*acta senatus*) a speech that the contemporary Velleius, as a senator and former praetor, heard in the senate from Tiberius' own lips. The difficulty with this hypothesis is that, as is well known, there is only one reference in the whole of the *Annals* to Tacitus' consultation of the *acta*, and that in a very late book (15.74.3): he gives us no hint that he is using the *acta* here in Book 2. It will be noticed, however, that Tacitus discloses that Tiberius' speech on Maroboduus was extant. The natural inference from this disclosure is that the extant copy of the speech was different from the one in the senatorial archives: on the one hand, it would be superfluous to remark on the survival of an archival speech, since the preservation of the *acta senatus* was taken for granted; on the other hand, given that Tacitus evidently wanted to allude to his source at this point, it would be perverse of him not to refer to the *acta* explicitly if that were the basis of his information.[7] It thus seems that Tiberius' speech on Maroboduus had been published, and the strong implication is that Tacitus had read the speech.

The most likely conclusion is, therefore, that Velleius and Tacitus are alluding to the same imperial speech on Maroboduus: Velleius as a senator perhaps heard it being delivered in the senate, while Tacitus read the published version of it roughly a century later. And – to return to the question with which we began – it is clearly possible that the same Tiberian speech lies behind Maroboduus' metaphorical description as a snake by both Velleius and Tacitus; the difference between the two authors is that in Tacitus the metaphor has been transferred to the mouth of Maroboduus' rival, Arminius, and requires to be elicited from an allusion to Virgil's *Georgics*.[8] These three passages from Book 2 of the *Annals* give some idea of the textual complexity which lies behind the work but which is often irrecoverable for lack of evidence.

A further passage relating to Arminius raises a rather different issue. In a famous and evocative passage from *Annals* 1 Germanicus, nephew and adopted son of the emperor Tiberius, visits the site where Arminius had ambushed and destroyed three Roman legions six years earlier in AD 9 (1.61.2): 'medio

---

[7] Suetonius has a very similar statement (*Tib.* 28 extat ... sermo eius) which, as remarked by Goodyear (1981) 185, 'seems a rather odd way of referring to the *acta*'.

[8] The examples of Tiberian vocabulary in the *Annals* proposed by Miller (1968) have been countered on largely methodological grounds by Wharton (1997), who nevertheless acknowledges that Tiberian vocabulary may exist.

campi albentia ossa' ('in the middle of the plain there were whitening bones'). Here Tacitus has combined an allusion to Book 9 of the *Aeneid* (230 'castrorum et *campi medio*', 'in the middle of the camp and plain') with another to Book 12 (36 '*campi*que ... *ossibus albent*', 'and the plains ... were white with bones').[9] Now it is highly unlikely that Tacitus had any evidence for whitening bones discovered in the middle of a German field a century before he was writing; to give substance to his narrative, he has simply incorporated an apparently factual detail that in reality is taken from Virgil.[10] If we compare this example with that of the fake Agrippa Postumus in Book 2, we see that we are presented with a paradox. Velleius, whom Tacitus might have been expected to use as a historical source, is alluded to for seemingly literary purposes, whereas Virgil, to whom Tacitus might have been expected to allude for literary purposes, is instead used as a 'source' to provide factual detail. This is perhaps surprising if one has been accustomed to drawing a clear distinction between 'using *x* as a source' and 'making an allusion to *y*', the former being the kind of language traditionally associated with the scholarly approach to historical texts (*Quellenforschung* or source-research), the latter being usually reserved for the literary discussion of poetry.[11]

The subject of literary allusion is variously contentious. Regardless of the terminology used to refer to the phenomenon,[12] the scholarly reader's first task is to decide what constitutes an intertextual relationship. Though it may sometimes be possible to argue on the basis of a general similarity of thought that a relationship exists between given passages, the argument is considerably strengthened if one can point to similarities of language or expression. When Germanicus sets sail upon the Ocean in 16, he first encounters a calm sea, 'placidum aequor' (*A*. 2.23.2). This same phrase occurs twice in the *Aeneid* (8.96; 10.103) and, when hail starts to pour down a few moments later, 'effusa grando', we might begin to suspect a patterning of Virgilian allusion (cf. *Aen.* 10.803 'uelut *effusa* ... *grandine* nimbi'); but, since the former phrase appears also in Propertius (1.8a.20) and Manilius (4.285), perhaps the most one can say is that it is 'poetic'.[13] Before setting off on his

---

[9] The former phrase was also reproduced by Sil. 9.271 'campi medio'; the latter was imitated also by Ovid, *Fast*. 1.558, 3.708 and Sen. *Oed*. 94, but none of the passages has *campi*.

[10] For such 'substantive imitation' see Woodman (1979) 148 (= (1998) 76–7). For another possible example, also German, see below (p. 60) on *G*. 17.1 ~ *Aen*. 3.594, with the note of Horsfall (2006) on the latter passage.

[11] Thus the subject of Hinds (1998) is exclusively poetry.

[12] Among the various related terms are echo, imitation, influence, intertextuality, parallel, reception, reference and reminiscence: for some of these see e.g. Russell (1979), Wills (1996) and Hinds (1998).

[13] *placidus* had been used of water since Ennius (*Ann*. 377 'placidum mare') but seems more common in verse than prose (*TLL* 10.1.2281.9–28).

journey, Germanicus had set up a victory trophy with an inscription which, says Tacitus, began as follows (2.22.1): 'debellatis inter Rhenum Albimque nationibus' ('the nations between Rhine and Elbe having been defeated'). The ablative absolute looks innocent enough at first glance, but Tacitus has described the inscription itself as 'haughty' ('superbo cum titulo'). The conjunction of terms will remind some readers of the famous mission urged upon Aeneas by his father Anchises (*Aen.* 6.853): 'parcere subiectis et *debellare superbos*' ('spare your subjects and defeat the haughty'). It would be typical of Tacitus to suggest that, while Germanicus is indeed inflicting defeats, the values incorporated in the Romans' destiny are being perverted; but is the conjunction of terms – which seem not to be conjoined by any other Latin author – sufficient to constitute an allusion?[14] When Germanicus is in the middle of his maritime journey, his encounter with the hailstorm takes place in what 'is believed to be the ultimate sea' (2.24.1). The Latin phrase is *nouissimum ... mare*, the very same as that which, in its Greek equivalent (καινὴν θάλασσαν), Germanicus himself used in a speech in Egypt a couple of years later.[15] It would be remarkable (and extremely ironic) if Tacitus were here using Germanicus' own words, rather in the way that he alludes to Tiberius' speech on Maroboduus later in this same book, but he uses the expression *nou(issim)um mare* elsewhere (*Agr.* 10.4) and it had appeared earlier also in Catullus (4.23-4; 66.45) and Seneca (*Q Nat.* 3.29.7). In this short passage from Book 2 of the *Annals*, therefore, chosen more or less at random, we have considered four examples of verbal similarity: comparative evidence denies the status of allusion to two of them, and we are left with one probable and one possible allusion to the *Aeneid* (respectively 10.803 and 6.853).

The relationship between Tacitus and Virgil, which many scholars have explored, has proved controversial. To continue with Book 2 of the *Annals*, Tiberius at the start of the narrative is trying to extract Germanicus from his campaigns on the German frontier and to bring him back to Rome; but, 'the keener his soldiers' enthusiasm towards him, and his uncle's will opposed' ('et auersa patrui uoluntas'), the more determined was Germanicus to conclude a speedy victory (2.5.2). Goodyear in his commentary first acknowledges reluctantly that 'perhaps the closest precedent' is *Aen.* 12.647 'quoniam superis *auersa uoluntas*', but he then adds that 'obligation to Vergil is not certain'.[16] However, given that the expression occurs in no other text

---

[14] An allusion is implied by Baxter (1972) 263, though he makes no comment on the uniqueness of the terms.
[15] *P Oxy.* 2345 recto, line 16 (text conveniently available in Goodyear (1981) 458). Of course καινή is here equivalent to *nouus* in its sense of 'new'.
[16] Goodyear (1981) 200.

and that Tacitus undeniably imitates Virgilian phraseology on numerous other occasions, perhaps Goodyear was being too sceptical. Nevertheless, if we admit that the passages are related, what are we to make of the parallel? Perhaps this is simply a case of linguistic enhancement, in the same way as Agricola's early life, as described by his son-in-law, is embellished by a succession of Ciceronian phrases (*Agr.* 4.2–3): *bonam integramque* (*Mur.* 14, 79; *Clu.* 124; *Planc.* 15); *magnae excelsaeque* (*Mur.* 60; *Inv. rhet.* 2.163; *Off.* 1.81; 2.37; 3.24; *Fam.* 1.9.22; 12.25.5); *speciem gloriae* (*Fam.* 10.12.5);[17] *uehementius ... caute* (*Orat.* 228); *mitigauit ... aetas* (*Mur.* 65; *Cael.* 77); *retinuit ... modum* (*Off.* 1.104). This would certainly be the position of Goodyear, who elsewhere states it as a general rule that, 'when Tacitus quite clearly uses phrases from Vergil, he does so primarily to enhance his expression, not to suggest the circumstances in which these phrases originally occurred'.[18] In the present case Goodyear does indeed declare an allusion to be 'highly improbable'; but other modern scholars have been tempted to see more behind Tacitus' Virgilian phraseology than a simple parallelism of language, and it would be in keeping with Tacitean cynicism if by means of this parallel the *princeps*, famous for his rejection of divine honours, were being equated with the gods (*superis*). If Tiberius is equivalent to the gods, however, it would follow that Germanicus is being equated with Turnus, and this conclusion, though embraced by some, is difficult: for, if Germanicus is to be identified with any Virgilian figure, that figure is usually said to be Aeneas.[19]

Tacitus' historical narratives can be as intertextually dense as the verses of many a Latin poet and, no matter what side we take in the debate over his deployment of Virgilian language, the very existence of that debate indicates that 'literariness' is fundamental to the nature of his narrative. But, just as Virgil derived narrative material from the texts to which he alluded, so we have seen that the same is true of Tacitus; the problem in the latter case is that we usually have difficulty in identifying the texts in question. In the *Histories* Tacitus refers once to Sisenna (3.51.2), but a first-century BC historian does not constitute authentic information for the events of 69: no doubt Tacitus – on the assumption that he has not simply taken over a reference from his immediate source – was inquisitive for analogies with the civil war about which he himself was writing; perhaps too he was attracted to Sisenna's mannered word-order and unusual diction.[20] Elsewhere in the *Histories* he refers to Vipstanus Messalla and the elder Pliny (3.25.2, 28),

---

[17] This example is mentioned by Heubner (1984) ad loc.
[18] Goodyear (1972) 325.
[19] Savage (1938–9) and (1942–3).
[20] His diction is usefully summarised by Briscoe (2005) 70–1.

but, apart from the conventional allusions to nameless *auctores* and the like, these are the only references in a narrative of roughly two hundred pages. He frequently shares similarities of expression with his contemporaries, Suetonius and Plutarch, when they are describing the same points of the same stories; these similarities have been used to support the argument that all three writers depended on a common source.[21] More sources are named in the *Annals*, as one might expect of a much longer work, and there is a flurry of names at 13.20.2: Fabius Rusticus, the elder Pliny and Cluvius Rufus.[22] Tacitus then continues: 'for myself, with my intention of following an authorial consensus, I shall transmit under their own names any diverging accounts they have handed on' ('nos consensum auctorum secuturi, quae diuersa prodiderint, sub nominibus ipsorum trademus'). Since Tacitus' reference to 'following an authorial consensus' constitutes a statement of intent (*secuturi*), it has been taken by scholars to apply to the *Annals* as a whole; but, if that is correct, his statement is at odds with the priority that scholars often assign to his use of the *acta senatus*.[23]

At the end of Book 2 of the *Annals* there is a tantalising passage in which Tacitus refers explicitly to his consultation of sources (2.88.1):

> reperio apud scriptores senatoresque eorundem temporum Adgandestrii principis Chattorum lectas in senatu litteras quibus mortem Arminii promittebat, si patrandae neci uenenum mitteretur ...

> I discover among writers and senators of those same times that a letter of Adgandestrius, princeps of the Chatti, was read out in the senate, in which he promised Arminius' death if poison for accomplishing the execution were sent to him.

Unfortunately the text and interpretation of this passage are uncertain.[24] Some readers think that *scriptores senatoresque* is a hendiadys, 'senatorial writers', but nowhere else in Latin literature are historians identified as senators. Others think that Tacitus is referring to two separate groups, but, if that is the case, *apud* combines oddly with *senatores*, since *apud senatores* should mean 'in the presence of the senators' (as Cic. *Verr.* 5.150, 171). Since an additional difficulty is that 'Adgandestrius' is said to be an implausible German name, various scholars have attempted to emend the text. Thus Goodyear in his commentary proposes: 'apud scriptores senatoriaque

[21] In the case of *H*. 1 the parallels are clearly set out by Damon (2003) 291–302.
[22] These three authors, along with the other first-century AD historians whose works have survived only in fragments, will be discussed fully in Cornell *et al.* (forthcoming). See also below, pp. 26–8.
[23] In support of the *acta senatus* see esp. Syme (1984) 1014–42; (1988) 199–222; Talbert (1984) 326–34. See also below, pp. 177–81.
[24] See Goodyear (1981) 445–6.

eorundem temporum acta Gandestrii ...' ('among the writers and senatorial records of those same times ...'). This emendation, modifying an earlier suggestion by Mommsen, would, if correct, have the striking consequence of introducing into the text a second acknowledgement by Tacitus that he had consulted the senatorial archives. For that very reason the emendation deserves careful consideration;[25] but how likely is it to be correct? There are three main problems. Although *apud* regularly governs a personal noun to mean 'in the work of', it is not until later Latin that it is found governing a noun referring to the work itself as opposed to its author:[26] hence *apud senatoria acta* is unlikely Latinity. Second, although Tacitus characteristically varies or avoids technical or official expressions (including those for official publications), the phrase *senatoria acta* is itself unparalleled anywhere. Third, although Roman historians will draw attention to the fact that they are relying on a contemporary author,[27] the senatorial archives were by definition contemporary documents: hence *eorundem temporum* makes good sense with *scriptores* but is quite redundant with *senatoria ... acta*. For these reasons it seems unlikely that Goodyear's proposal is correct: thus it remains the case that Tacitus' only reference to his consultation of the *acta senatus* is at 15.74.3.

The relationship between Tacitus and his sources has been much discussed in the wake of the discovery and publication of the *Senatus Consultum de Cn. Pisone Patre*.[28] Most scholars believe that Tacitus' account of Germanicus' last days and Piso's subsequent trial reveals a knowledge of the contents of the inscription, but how did he come by that knowledge? Despite the fact that the inscription gives an utterly different date for the trial (10 December 20) from that which scholars had inferred from Tacitus (before 28 May 20), the general belief is that Tacitus consulted the copy of the *senatus consultum* deposited with the *acta senatus* and that the *acta* provided him with some of the information which appears in his narrative but which is not to be found in the inscription itself.[29] Yet whether this is the case is uncertain. The sources he actually mentions in the course of his narrative of Germanicus and Piso are earlier historians, the *acta diurna*[30] and oral testimony: A. 3.3.2 'non apud auctores rerum,

---

[25] It has been supported recently by DeRousse (2007); interestingly, Syme (1988) 212–13 argued against it.
[26] See *TLL* 2.338.20–6 (first in Apuleius). Goodyear acknowledged 'the strain on *apud*'.
[27] So again at A. 5.9.2 'temporis eius auctores'; 12.67.1 'temporum illorum scriptores'; 13.17.2 'plerique eorum temporum scriptores'; see Marincola (1997) 281–2.
[28] Eck *et al.* (1996).
[29] See e.g. Griffin below (pp. 177–80).
[30] The *acta diurna* seems to have been a gazette that included stories of charioteers, dogs, miraculous events and the like (Baldwin (1979) 198).

non diurna actorum scriptura reperio' ('I do not find in the authors of affairs or in the daily account of events'); 3.16.1 'audire me memini ex senioribus' ('I remember hearing from my elders'). Why not mention the *acta senatus* if it was a crucial source of information? Again, when Tacitus was engaged in writing the *Histories* around 106 or 107, his friend Pliny wrote him a letter providing more information about a senatorial trial of 93 in which Pliny had been one of the prosecuting team. Pliny prefaces his account by acknowledging that Tacitus will already know something of the trial 'since it is in the public records' (*Ep.* 7.33.3 'cum sit in publicis actis'): it is surely significant that Tacitus' knowledge is assumed by Pliny to derive, not from the *acta senatus* (commonly supposed by scholars to be the source of his information for 'senatorial' matters in the *Histories*) but from the more mundane and widely disseminated *acta diurna*.[31] Pliny's letter tends to support the impression that any consultation of the *acta senatus* by Tacitus was exceptional rather than regular.

However that may be, Tacitus' account of Piso's trial (*A.* 3.7–19) has the dissenting character that typifies his narrative as a whole and makes his work so congenial to modern readers. We are instinctively attracted to a writer who appears determined to expose the crimes of autocrats and the corruption of a debased society. Those living comfortably in western democracies, where dissent has been cultivated as a way of life for at least the past half-century, find in the author of the *Histories* and *Annals* a fellow spirit; those crushed by one of the terrible tyrannies of our time can see in Tacitus' text, if they are permitted to read it,[32] a pale reflection of their own far worse and more desperate circumstances.

In an age which has seen ruthless totalitarian regimes annihilate countless millions of their own citizens, there is a natural urge amongst some of the survivors to recapture the identities, and to preserve the memory, of as many of the massacred as possible. One's identity is inseparable from one's name, and, just as our war memorials list movingly the names of the many thousands who have died in battle for their country, in the same way much effort is devoted to recording the names of those whose lives were taken away from them for reasons of politics or ideology or to secure the power of a few (there is usually not much difference).[33] Tacitus, while describing

---

[31] It is rightly inferred from Pliny's letter that Tacitus was away from Rome at the time of the trial (see Sherwin-White (1966) 444): compare the parallel circumstance of Julius Valerianus, who, when Pliny sent him news of a case, was out of Rome (*Ep.* 5.4.4) and is told that he will be able to read a relevant document of Trajan's because 'it is in the public records' (*Ep.* 5.13.8 'leges ipsum: est in publicis actis').

[32] Tacitus was banned in communist eastern Europe (Mellor (1995) liii).

[33] Thus e.g. S. Klarsfeld, *French Children of the Holocaust: A Memorial* (New York 1996). The victims of communism are beyond counting and, in most cases, beyond identifying.

Introduction

the successive fates of six individuals who had been forced by the regime to commit suicide in 66 (A. 16.14-15, 17-19), interrupts his narrative to issue this extraordinary apologia (16.16):

> Etiam si bella externa et obitas pro re publica mortis tanta casuum similitudine memorarem, meque ipsum satias cepisset aliorumque taedium exspectarem, quamuis honestos ciuium exitus, tristis tamen et continuos aspernantium; at nunc patientia seruilis tantumque sanguinis domi perditum fatigant animum et maestitia restringunt. neque aliam defensionem ab iis quibus ista noscentur exegerim quam ne oderim tam segniter pereuntis. ira illa numinum in res Romanas fuit, quam non, ut in cladibus exercituum aut captiuitate urbium, semel edito transire licet. detur hoc inlustrium uirorum posteritati ut, quo modo exequiis a promisca sepultura separantur, ita in traditione supremorum accipiant habeantque propriam memoriam.

> Even if it were foreign wars, and deaths met on behalf of the state, that I were commemorating with such similarity of circumstance, not only would I have been afflicted by satiety myself but I would be expecting aversion from others who feel repugnance at the departures of citizens which, however honourable, are nevertheless grim and constant; but, as it is, servile passivity and so much blood wasted at home weary the spirit and numb it with sorrowfulness. And yet, from those to whom such matters will become known, I would be inclined to demand no other justification than that I do not reject those perishing so sluggishly. This was the anger of the divinities against Roman affairs, and one cannot, as in the case of disasters to armies or the capture of cities, pass over it after but a single reference. Let this concession be granted to the posthumous repute of illustrious men: just as it is by their exequies that they are excepted from indiscriminate burial, so in the transmission of their final moments may they receive and retain their individual memorial.

Whether or not he actually believed in the gods and their anger,[34] Tacitus in this remarkable and characteristically elusive statement counters the potential charges of morbidity and monotony by declaring that his narrative preserves the memory of Nero's individual victims. This has been a consistent theme throughout his writing.

At the start of his very first work Tacitus begins by naming biographers who had been murdered for memorialising the names of others who had been murdered in their turn and whom he himself is careful to name (*Agr.* 2.1). This relay of violence climaxes in the public burning of the biographies themselves: 'Evidently they thought that in that fire the voice of the Roman people, the freedom of the senate and the conscience of the human race would be destroyed' (*Agr.* 2.2). In the *Annals* an attempt to suppress

---

[34] For a recent discussion of Tacitus and religion see Davies (2004) 143–225. See also below, pp. 168–72.

memory by the burning of historical books provokes him to open scorn (*A*. 4.35.5):

> quo magis socordiam eorum inridere libet qui praesenti potentia credunt exstingui posse etiam sequentis aeui memoriam. nam contra punitis ingeniis gliscit auctoritas, neque aliud externi reges aut qui eadem saeuitia usi sunt nisi dedecus sibi atque illis gloriam peperere.
>
> It is pleasant to deride all the more the insensibility of those who, by virtue of their present powerfulness, believe that the memory even of a subsequent age too can be extinguished. On the contrary, the influence of punished talents swells, nor have foreign kings, or those who have resorted to the same savagery, accomplished anything except disrepute for themselves and for their victims glory.

Earlier Tacitus had explained his own role in the perpetuation of disrepute and glory, telling us why he has named names: 'to prevent virtues from being silenced and so that crooked words and deeds should be attended by the dread of posterity and infamy' (*A*. 3.65.1 'ne uirtutes sileantur utque prauis dictis factisque ex posteritate et infamia metus sit').[35] Virtue has the reward of commemoration in his pages; the dread of posterity and infamy is a reminder to his readers that their own crooked words and deeds are liable to be attributed to them by name and recorded in the annals of some future Tacitus.[36]

If it is self-evident that Tacitus' own works have survived, it is sobering to reflect on the reason. For more than fifty years Sir Ronald Syme, generally and rightly regarded as the pre-eminent Tacitean scholar of the modern age, drew repeated attention to Tacitus' merits as a perspicacious and painstaking historian; yet in the final sentence of his *Tacitus* he famously proclaimed, 'Men and dynasties pass, but style abides'.[37] In the great man's opinion it was style that counted in the end.

It is difficult even to describe the combination of elements that make up Tacitus' unique and compelling manner of expression.[38] One can only read, ponder and marvel. But in the modern age there are very few lovers of literature – very few lovers even of classical literature – who can read his work in the original Latin. It is a bitter irony that, though numerous scholars are currently obsessed with so-called 'reception studies', almost none of their cultural dirigisme is devoted to anything so fundamental as the teaching of a classical language. Most potential readers of Tacitus are today deprived

---

[35] For the interpretation of this passage see Woodman (1995) (= (1998) 86–103).
[36] See Luce (1991).
[37] Syme (1958a) 624. For Syme and Tacitus see below, Chapter 21.
[38] For a discussion of his sentence structure in particular see below, Chapter 13.

Introduction

of 'receiving' his text in any meaningful sense whatsoever. The consequence is that such readers are precluded from experiencing the very element of Tacitus that, in Syme's opinion, above all ensures his survival from one generation to the next. Writing in the 1950s, Syme could not have foreseen that within little more than ten years the common link that bound western civilisation to the Renaissance, and the Renaissance to antiquity,[39] would be broken – and for ever.[40] Interest in ancient Rome may never have been greater than it is today, but those who require the key to its understanding are increasingly dependent on a small number of professionals who are fortunate enough to know Latin and Greek. Of course anyone can flick through a vernacular translation in an attempt at finding out 'what Tacitus says' about a particular episode, but this procedure renders Tacitus indistinguishable from any other translated source, destroys the individuality of his voice, fails to capture the manifold nuances of his speech and cannot begin to communicate the overpowering effect of the original Latin.

The infinite complex of events that we call 'history', of which our own lives are an infinitesimal part, is an abstraction, insubstantial and intangible, but nevertheless as real as we are ourselves. It is historians who by their various narrative constructions make a very small proportion of those events come alive for us, who transform that abstraction into a readable reality. No one disputes that, in the case of ancient Rome, Tacitus is the supreme master of this genre and that his supremacy results from a uniquely felicitous

[39] For this link as it relates to Tacitus see Mellor (1995). There is more detail in Chapters 16–19 below.
[40] I am referring here principally to England, where Syme was writing, and to my own experience as a student and tironic university lecturer in the decade 1965–75. After the abolition in 1960 of the Latin requirement for those seeking entry to Oxford and Cambridge, C.A.R. Crosland, whose first subject at Oxford had been Classics, was appointed Secretary of State for Education in the Labour Government in 1965 and his memorable ambition 'to destroy every fucking grammar school in England' was complemented by his determination to introduce so-called comprehensive education (Circular 10/65). Since the new comprehensive schools were very large by design and needed complicated timetables, and since their educational ethos was an evangelical egalitarianism, subjects perceived as elitist and of minority interest, such as Latin, were rapidly eliminated. In a classic case of a self-fulfilling prophecy, the teaching of Latin became mostly restricted to independent schools, and by the mid-1970s the supply of qualified Latin students applying to provincial universities was very severely reduced and in some cases non-existent. Labour politicians later sought to score political points off the subsequent Conservative government by drawing attention to the lamentable fact that Latin was no longer being offered in the schools that most children attended – thereby conveniently forgetting (or pretending to forget) that they had been only too happy to support their own government in engineering this state of affairs. My impression (which may not be correct) is that the rest of Europe experienced a similar decline in Latin teaching over the same period; certainly, at the start of the following decade, Sir Kenneth Dover announced that the future of Classics 'may perhaps be brighter in the United States than in Europe' (*Aristophanes: Frogs* (Oxford 1993) vi).

union of medium and message. Anyone who cares about the past and about literature will regret deeply the danger that within a relatively short time, perhaps within the foreseeable future, no one will any longer be able to read the texts of this transcendent writer in the language in which he wrote them. It is greatly to be hoped that this *Companion*, by stimulating or sustaining an interest in Tacitus, will do something to help delay this process – or will even encourage some Latinless readers to believe that learning Latin is worthwhile, if the prize is to be able to read Tacitus.

FURTHER READING

The bibliography of Tacitean scholarship is considerable. Reference to works published in the half-century 1954–2004 is most easily accessed via the six invaluable surveys produced by Benario between 1964–5 and 2004–5 (see the Bibliography). Mention should also be made of *ANRW* 2.33, parts 2–5 of which deal with Tacitus: note especially the bibliographical essay on his historical works by Sage (1990) and the extremely detailed and systematic bibliography of the *Annals* for the years 1939–80 by Suerbaum (1990). The most recent study of Tacitus is Sailor (2008).

Verbal parallels between Tacitus and other authors were assembled above all by Fletcher (1964), incorporating his earlier contributions, and in later papers from 1969 to 1986 (see the Bibliography). For the case of Virgil in particular see Miller (1961–2) and (1987), Baxter (1971) and (1972), Bews (1972–3) and Foucher (2000) 305–20. One of the earliest studies was Schmaus (1887); for similar studies of Seneca and Lucan see respectively Zimmermann (1889) and Robbert (1917). For a general study of Tacitean allusion see Lauletta (1998). Tacitus' sources are discussed by Syme (1958a) 176–90 and 271–303 and Sage (1990) 893–900 and 997–1017; on the *Annals* in particular note Questa (1967) and Devillers (2003). For the *Senatus Consultum de Cn. Pisone Patre* see the Further Reading at the end of Chapter 11. As for Tacitus' style, there are treatments of *uariatio* by Sörbom (1935), of sentence structure and the like by Kohl (1959) and Voss (1963), of vocabulary by Kuntz (1962) and Adams (1972) and (1973) and of sustained metaphors by Woodman (1998) 190–217, (2006a) and (2006b). Goodyear (1968) (= (1992) 125–37) was particularly concerned with the question of whether or in what ways Tacitus' style changes during the course of the *Annals* (note also (1970) 35–42). As always, there is much stimulating material in Syme (1958a), especially Appendixes 42–60. See also the Further Reading section of Chapter 13.

PART I
Contexts

I

A. M. GOWING

From the annalists to the *Annales*: Latin historiography before Tacitus

What, one wonders, was in the history section of Tacitus' library? At the core of the Greek section, we may safely assume, would reside Herodotus, Thucydides and Xenophon, with Polybius close by. Interestingly enough, however, in his extant writings Tacitus finds no occasion to mention any of these authors (Xenophon is mentioned once, as a philosopher, at *D.* 31.6); and his debt to the Greek historiographical tradition has never been fully explored – largely because it is not at all clear how great that debt is (in distinct contrast to his predecessors Sallust and Livy, whose respective debt to Thucydides and Herodotus is mentioned explicitly by Quintilian, *Inst.* 10.1.101).[1] Rather, the influences at work on Tacitus seem to lie more substantially and understandably on the Latin side.

Yet even here the list of Roman historians actually named by Tacitus is markedly circumscribed: no early annalist receives mention. In fact, with the exception of Julius Caesar (and two references to the Sullan historian Cornelius Sisenna), he names no historian prior to Sallust and Livy. The historical work of Asinius Pollio receives cursory notice, most significantly in the great speech of the historian Cremutius Cordus at *A.* 4.34.4. With respect to those writing after Livy, in the *Annals* Tacitus identifies as sources for various pieces of information Pliny the Elder, Cluvius Rufus and Fabius Rusticus, as well as the memoirs of Agrippina the Younger and the Neronian general Domitius Corbulo.[2]

---

[1] See, however, Flach (1973) 40–52, who usefully discusses the influence of Greek (Hellenistic) historiography on Roman historiography after Sallust, with special emphasis on Thucydides and Tacitus. Keitel (1984), esp. 322–5, detects the influence of Thucydides in the connections Tacitus makes between the civil wars and the Augustan principate.

[2] Historians or sources named by Tacitus: Julius Caesar (as a source, only at *G.* 28.1; cf. *Agr.* 13.1); Cornelius Sisenna (*H.* 3.51.2; cf. *D.* 23.2, in the mouth of Aper); Sallust (*A.* 3.30.2); Asinius Pollio (*A.* 4.34.4; cf. *D.* 12.6, in the mouth of Maternus); Livy (*A.* 4.34.3; *Agr.* 10.3); Pliny the Elder (*A.* 1.69.3; 13.20.2; 15.53.3; *H.* 3.28); Agrippina the Younger (*A.* 4.53.2);

What one observes, in short, is that on those very rare occasions when Tacitus offers the name of a historian, he does so usually in order to identify a source of information, not a source of influence, guided by the notion that identification of the source is necessary only in the case of significant discrepancies (cf. *A.* 13.20.2). Thus assembling a list of historians named or identified as such by Tacitus does very little to help us appreciate those historians who most influenced him. And it is chiefly influence that interests me in this chapter. That is: what – and what sort of – historians were available to him to read? What were the chief characteristics of the tradition in which Tacitus worked? And, of his predecessors, to whom did he look for inspiration and guidance?

The annalists

Naturally, it should not be inferred from Tacitus' failure to name specific individuals that he was unfamiliar with the annalists and early Roman historiography. That tradition, however, was nearly three centuries old by the time he took up the challenge of writing history at the close of the first century AD. Although we should not overlook the fact that early on poetry was an accepted medium for narrating historical events (or underestimate poetry's influence on Tacitus, who may well have read Ennius' *Annales* with as much approval as he read Cato[3]), by the late third and early second centuries BC a prose tradition had begun to take shape, beginning with Fabius Pictor. Drawing information chiefly from pontifical *annales*, an annual record of events occurring in or involving Rome that had been recorded on *tabulae*, from perhaps the very founding of the city (so Cic. *De or.* 2.52),[4] Fabius composed his own *Annales*, an account of Roman history, in Greek, ranging from the founding of the city down to the end of the Second Punic War in 210 BC. Amongst subsequent 'annalists' Greek rapidly gave way to Latin, though the *annales* continued to serve as an important source of information. While the term 'annalist' is applied somewhat indiscriminately (not all of those counted as 'annalists'

Cluvius Rufus (*A.* 13.20.2; 14.2.1; cf. *H.* 4.43.1); Fabius Rusticus (*A.* 13.20.2; 14.2.2; 15.61.3; *Agr.* 10.3), Corbulo (*A.* 15.16.1). On many occasions Tacitus refers to unnamed sources (see Furneaux (1896) 13 n. 7); and occasionally he will identify someone as a historian but not explicitly as a source (e.g. Servilius Nonianus at *A.* 14.19, on whom see further below). On Tacitus' avoidance of names and his general practice, see Marincola (1999) 401 with refs.

[3] It could be argued, moreover, that a list of the imperial 'historians' who exercised an influence on Tacitus should in fact include the poet Lucan: see Klingner (1958) 202–3; for parallels between the two authors see Robbert (1917).

[4] The precise nature of the *annales* is much disputed, but see in general Frier (1999).

unquestioningly trusted the information to be found in the *annales*: see, for example, the caution of Cato the Elder, fr. 77P = 81C), we have the names and fragments (some substantial) of roughly twenty individuals, spanning the period of about a century.[5]

Naturally enough, the annalists focus much of their attention on Rome's wars of expansion and on domestic politics. While it is impossible to point to any one historian as exercising special influence on Tacitus, we can surmise what he might have admired. Fabius Pictor, for instance, favoured a history that was, as Badian has put it, 'morally and politically committed', a phrase that describes well Tacitus' own work; like Tacitus and indeed like many Roman historians, Fabius was a senator, a circumstance that inevitably shaped the interests and perspective evident in his work. He also earned the respect of many subsequent historians (e.g. Polyb. 1.14; Dion. Hal. *Ant. Rom.* 7.71.1; Liv. 22.7.1).[6] The direct influence of Cato the Elder has been observed in the opening words of the *Agricola*,[7] but more broadly one could easily imagine that Tacitus would have found much in the *Origines* to admire and perhaps even to imitate. (One might detect, for instance, a nod to Cato in the brief, *Origines*-like digression on the history of Smyrna at *A.* 4.56, a nod marked by the rare reference to Cato in that chapter. The only other occasion on which he is named in the *Annals* occurs at 3.66.) Coelius Antipater, for all intents and purposes, inaugurated the tradition of the historical monograph with a seven-book study of the Second Punic War, a form later adopted by Sallust and then of course by Tacitus. Tacitus surely would have approved of Sempronius Asellio's distinction between *annales* that amounted to little other than a chronological record and a more sophisticated approach to history that explicated the *consilium* and *ratio* behind events (fr. 1P = 1C *etiam quo consilio quaque ratione gesta essent demonstrare*; cf. Tac. *H.* 1.4.1 *ut ... ratio etiam causaeque noscantur*).[8] And he perhaps shared with Sallust (*Iug.* 95.2) an admiration for the Sullan historian Cornelius Sisenna, who, as noted above, is identified at *H.* 3.51.2 as a source for an anecdote drawn from 87 BC. Sisenna's *Historiae*, continued by Sallust's, focused on the momentous first two decades of the first century BC and represented for Cicero the most substantial advance in the genre to date (Cic. *Leg.* 1.7). Indeed, the move away from the sweeping sort of *ab urbe condita* historiography practised by the majority of the annalists to more circumscribed periods and topics (such as we observe in Sisenna, who

---

[5] For difficulties with the term 'annalist', see Verbrugghe (1989) 199–21.
[6] Badian (1966) 6.
[7] See Ogilvie and Richmond (1967) on *Agr.* 1.1 (where their reference should be corrected to Cato fr. 2P = 2C); Syme (1958a) 121.
[8] See also below, pp. 175–6.

should not be classed among the annalists[9]) anticipated the approach to history that Tacitus would prefer.[10]

Tacitus' familiarity with the annalists may be detected in other ways as well. Even though he names no annalist, Tacitus provides as succinct a summary of annalistic historiography as one will find, in the passage most relevant to the question of influence, *Annals* 4.32. Here he draws a distinction between the sort of 'battlefield and forum' historiography characteristic of most pre-Augustan Latin historical writing and that which centered on the '*princeps* and imperial court', which he would himself practise. He explicitly asserts that his writing, his *annales*, has nothing in common with those who wrote of the 'ancient history of the Romans'. His characterisation of the interests of the annalists is precise and accurate (4.32.1):

> ingentia illi bella, expugnationes urbium, fusos captosque reges aut, si quando ad interna praeuerterent, discordias consulum aduersum tribunos, agrarias frumentariasque leges, plebis et optimatium certamina libero egressu memorabant.

> They [i.e. Republican historians] wrote with free rein about great wars, city sieges, kings routed and caught, or, whenever they turned their attention to domestic affairs, about the agitations of consuls against tribunes, agrarian and grain legislation, or disputes between plebs and optimates.

He contrasts this – sharply – with his own subject matter (4.32.2):

> nobis in arto et inglorius labor: immota quippe aut modice lacessita pax, maestae urbis res et princeps proferendi imperi incuriosus erat. non tamen sine usu fuerit introspicere illa primo aspectu leuia ex quis magnarum saepe rerum motus oriuntur.

> My task, on the other hand, is constricted and inglorious: a peace undisturbed or only slightly ruffled, the gloomy affairs of the city, an emperor indifferent to extending the empire. Despite this, it will be of some benefit to inquire into those matters which at first glance seem trivial but from which the stir of great events often arises.

The annalists, in terms of subject matter, particular and general, would therefore *appear* to have nothing to offer Tacitus. There is instead a studied contrariness about this passage, which, while seeming to denigrate his task, actually has the effect of detaching it from, and elevating it above, the work of his predecessors.[11]

---

[9] Rawson (1979) 335.
[10] See below, n. 22.
[11] On the passage see Martin and Woodman (1989) ad loc.; also below, pp. 226–7.

Yet Tacitus is being a little coy. As he describes it, the annalists' subject matter is after all not so very different from his own: war and military conflict, the adventures of client and renegade kings, senatorial disputes and legal matters all come under his purview. He is quite right that the principate – and the presence of the *princeps* – adds a dimension to his task (and that of every imperial historian) entirely missing from that of the annalists (see especially the remarks at *H*. 1.1 and *A*. 1.1, discussed below),[12] but it is hard to accept that he believed he had nothing in common with them. Indeed, the very fact that he refers to his *own* work as *annales* – and the fact that he uses the annalistic framework – implies a desire to connect his efforts with the tradition at large.[13] On the whole, however, and despite his sweeping categorisation of all Republican historians as 'distinguished writers', *clari scriptores* (*A*. 1.1.2) – an exaggeration perhaps intended to underscore the accompanying excoriation of post-Augustan historians – Tacitus would doubtless have lamented with Cicero the poverty (and the more colourful qualities) of the Latin historiographical tradition before the end of the Republic (*Leg*. 1.5, written probably in the mid-40s BC). In terms of style and substance, Tacitus reserved his admiration for later practitioners of his craft, the 'literary historians' Sallust and Livy.[14]

Late Republican and early imperial historiography: Sallust and Livy

It is no accident that immediately following the remark at *A*. 4.32 comes the great speech of the Tiberian historian Cremutius Cordus, in some sense a review of the key historical sources for the transition from Republic to Principate: Livy, Asinius Pollio, Messalla Corvinus, Cicero, Caesar, the letters of Antony, poetry. Cordus' speech is of course in large part a paean to the power of historical writing – just as his whole trial and subsequent suicide bear witness both to the anxiety a historian could provoke in a paranoid emperor and to the authority of the emperor to silence him ... or, as Tacitus smugly alleges, vainly attempt to silence him (*A*. 4.35.5). No annalist ever created a stir such as this, and thus the episode underscores the

---

[12] See Noè (1984) 140–7.
[13] While not securely attested as the *title* of the work, Tacitus does apply the *term* to it at *A*. 4.32.1 (cf. 3.65.1; so too Livy in describing his work at 43.13.2). See discussion by Goodyear (1972) 85–7. On the allusive properties of the word *annales*, see Sage (1990) 974; and esp. Ginsburg (1981) 96–100 (the concluding remarks of this important study that examines Tacitus' use of and deviations from an annalistic framework). For the distinction between *annales* and *historiae* (which seems not to have existed in Tacitus' mind), see Frier (1999) 216–19 and *passim*; see also Verbrugghe (1989), esp. 195–9.
[14] The distinction ('literary historians') is that of Badian (1966) 2.

difference between the historians of the Republic (who, as Tacitus observes at *H.* 1.1.1, enjoyed *libertas* to write what they wished) and those writing under the Principate (whose *libertas* was merely illusory, *H.* 1.1.2).

Sallust (c. 86–35 BC) writes on the cusp of the transition from Republican to imperial historical writing; Livy (c. 59 BC – AD 17), on the other hand, is arguably the first imperial historian, at least in the sense that he writes in the shadow of the first emperor.[15] In Sallust Tacitus found an entirely congenial personality, and really the first Roman historian who may be said to have exercised considerable and readily observable influence on him. We should not underrate the importance to Tacitus of Caesar the author, clearly a valued source for the *Germania*: 'summus auctorum diuus Iulius' (28.1 'the divine Julius, the greatest of authors'); but, if Tacitus admired Caesar's authority (and he does so, in my opinion, because among other things Caesar was an authoritative first-hand witness to the events he describes), the author whom he most revered for his skill as a writer was Sallust, identified in the *Annals* as 'the most brilliant author of Roman history', 'rerum Romanarum florentissimus auctor' (*A.* 3.30.2).[16]

The reason for Tacitus' affection must lie partly in the fact that Sallust anticipates the sort of historiography Tacitus found most congenial to his own tastes and interests; both the *Bellum Catilinae* and the *Bellum Iugurthinum* contain much that will be familiar to any reader of Tacitus, especially the manner in which Sallust draws his characters (consider, for example, the Sallustian borrowings in Tacitus' introduction of Sejanus at *A.* 4.1[17]), his attention to their psychology (compare, for example, Tacitus on Nero's agitation following the murder of Agrippina at *A.* 14.10 with Sallust on Bocchus on the point of betraying Jugurtha at *Iug.* 113.1–3), the style of writing and a fascination with the corrupting influences of power and money. Imitation being the most sincere form of flattery, Tacitus' prose style has more in common with that of Sallust than of any other extant Latin author.[18] This imitation may extend as well to how Tacitus schooled himself in his craft: like Sallust, he began with a series of minor works, warming up gradually, again like Sallust, to more ambitious projects. Is it mere

---

[15] It does not, that is, tell the whole story to describe Livy as 'the last of the Republican prose writers' (so Syme (1958a) 138), though it is important to stress that Livy is more representative of the culmination of Republican historiography than of the dawn of its imperial version. Woodman (1988) 136–40 offers a balanced view.

[16] The adjective *florentissimus* is difficult to render with a single word in English, but inherent in it are the notions of 'thriving' and 'most vivid' – a sense, that is, that Sallust's influence as a historian was and still is potent. See Woodman and Martin (1996) ad loc.

[17] See Martin and Woodman (1989) ad loc.

[18] For Sallust's influence on Tacitus, see in general Syme (1958a) 728–32; (1964a) 292–6, 305–7; Martin (1981) 20–2; also below, pp. 197–9.

coincidence that the first of these may well have been called the *Historiae*, the title of Sallust's own *magnum opus*?[19]

Tacitus obviously admired the Augustan historian Livy, but in what sense? He is not technically a continuator of Livy – Livy's history terminated at 9 BC, whereas Tacitus picks up not long after, with the accession of Tiberius in 14[20] – and in any case he alleged that the Augustan period had not lacked for capable chroniclers, the *decora ingenia* or 'distinguished talents' of *A*. 1.1.2. He has, the phrase implies, more than one person in mind, and among them is certainly Livy, a historian deemed 'among the best known for his eloquence and reliability', 'eloquentiae ac fidei praeclarus in primis …' – or so he has the historian Cremutius Cordus remark in the *Annals* (4.34.3), echoing the assessment of *Agr*. 10.3, where Livy and Fabius Rusticus are termed *eloquentissimi auctores*. Like many of the annalists and other Republican predecessors, Livy composed a history of Rome from its beginnings, *ab urbe condita*, down to his own day. Yet there is a crucial difference between the circumstances of Livy and those of his forerunners. While the date at which Livy began writing is disputed (before Actium or afterwards?), the bulk of the writing was clearly done over the course of Augustus' lengthy reign. The influence of the changed political situation at Rome and of the new *princeps* is apparent in Livy's work – Augustus, the first emperor, furnishes the (usually unspoken) standard against which so many characters and events in Livy's history are to be measured. This, rather than a particular approach to writing and composing history, is in fact something he may share with Tacitus, whose experience of the emperor Trajan invariably influenced his historical perspective and practice.[21] In some respects, it could be argued, Tacitus does for early imperial history what Livy had done for the history of the Republic – he interprets the past in terms of the present.[22]

---

[19] As with the title of the *Annals*, that of the *Histories* is equally uncertain, though *historiae* is the term that Pliny the Younger uses to describe Tacitus' first major historical work (*Ep*. 7.33.1). See again Goodyear (1972) 85–7.

[20] For the notion that Tacitus came to regard 14 as an historically problematic starting point and determined to compensate by composing a work stretching back still further in time (thus overlapping with Livy), see *A*. 3.24.3 with Woodman and Martin (1996) ad loc.; cf. Syme (1958a) 372–5.

[21] See e.g. Syme (1958a) 473–6, 495–6, who attributes, for instance, Tacitus' emphasis on the dealings of both Tiberius and Claudius with Parthia to the influence of Trajan (there are admittedly chronological difficulties with this view, but see Rutledge (1998)). Trajan's overall influence is not doubted; its nature, much debated (see Sage (1990) 948–52 with notes; also below, pp. 39–43).

[22] See, however, the cautions of Kraus and Woodman (1997) 92–3. Tacitus abandons, moreover, as did most imperial historians after Livy, the *ab urbe condita* approach: see Klingner (1958) 195.

Perhaps the most valuable point to stress in thinking about the impact of Livy and Sallust on Tacitus is this: Livy is often said to represent the Ciceronian ideal in historical writing, whereas Sallust, especially in terms of style, chose a different course.[23] Yet while it is common practice to stress the differences between Sallust and Livy (and Tacitus' overall preference for the former[24]), Tacitean historiography successfully marries the two ideals, combining the trenchant, incisive analysis and punchy prose style favoured by Sallust with Livy's somewhat keener sense of the historical moment and broader view of history.

The post-Augustan historians

Little remains of the post-Augustan historians, and, while that would seem to render problematic our ability to gauge their influence on Tacitus, he famously castigates the whole lot of them, and more than once. He would seem, in short, to distance himself from all practitioners of the genre after Livy. At *Histories* 1.1.1 he indicts all historians writing after the battle of Actium in 31 BC – the point at which the *magna ingenia* of the earlier period ceased to exist, the disastrous consequence of the emergence of the Principate and its concomitant vices, namely, disregard for truth born of a desire to flatter or to damage. The point is reiterated in the opening chapter of the later *Annals*, as Tacitus dissociates himself from the flatterers and hate-mongers among his fellow historians, claiming instead that *he* writes *sine ira et studio* (*A*. 1.1.2–3).[25] Yet whom exactly does he mean?

Velleius Paterculus

The one historian – other than Curtius Rufus[26] – to survive in substantial measure from the post-Augustan period would appear to have been on his list. Modern scholars have been generally ill-disposed to Velleius Paterculus

---

[23] See esp. Woodman (1988) 117–59 for a comparative study of Sallust and Livy and the nature of their respective debts to Cicero. Simply in terms of language and style, Tacitus' debt to both may be readily appreciated via Syme (1958a) 728–34.

[24] E.g. Syme (1959) 75: 'The direction which the Principate had taken justified a return to the sombre and pessimistic conception of politics and of human nature that Sallust had made classical. In sentiment as in style, Livy does not fit into the development of Roman historiography that links Sallust to Tacitus.' It should be noted, however, that Tacitus is as capable of adapting Livian material as he is Sallustian: for fine examples of both practices, see Ginsburg (1993); see also, as a further example of Tacitus' multiple borrowings from Sallust, Livy and Caesar in a single if extended passage, the commentary of Martin and Woodman (1989) on *A*. 4.46–51.

[25] For discussion of these passages see Marincola (1999).

[26] On Curtius see below, n. 33.

(for perhaps precisely the same reasons Tacitus may have disliked him), but his slender Roman history is of tremendous interest in many respects.[27] While we might reasonably surmise from what he has said about his imperial predecessors that he would not have much liked what he read, Tacitus clearly *had* read Velleius, traces of whom Woodman in particular has plausibly located in Tacitus.[28] Echoes such as those at *A*. 2.39.2, where Tacitus describes the false Agrippa Postumus with a phrase similar to that used by Velleius of the real Agrippa Postumus, further suggest that he is engaging with Velleius in ways that go beyond mere verbal borrowings.[29] But there are no signs that Velleius was an important source for Tacitus' account of Tiberius in the *Annals*.

The brief Roman history, published in 30, covers more in a mere two books than Livy covered in 142.[30] A standard modern Latin edition of Velleius, W.S. Watt's 1998 Teubner, runs to less than 100 pages; what survives of Livy fills several volumes and hundreds of pages, despite being a fraction of the original whole. Velleius' Book 1, much of which is lost, covers the founding of Rome, its expansion and emergence as an international power, and concludes with the destruction of Carthage in 146 BC. This represents about 600 years of Roman history and telescopes events much more severely than Book 2, which survives largely intact. Book 2, by contrast, handles about 170 years in 131 chapters. Specifically, beginning roughly with the Gracchan period and the latter third of the second century BC, Book 2 focuses on the civil discord that preceded the war between Caesar and Pompey and, ultimately, the principate of Augustus and then Tiberius. The final quarter of Book 2 is devoted to Tiberius' career, with greatest attention paid to his military activities under Augustus, from c. 23 BC to AD 14 (2.94–125), and a relatively small portion – a mere five chapters – dedicated to the first sixteen years of his reign proper, 14–29 (2.126–30), overlapping with what Tacitus covers much more expansively in *Annals* 1–5.

Clearly, it is not Velleius' purpose to replace Livy. But he does want to bring *his* emperor – to a far greater and more explicit degree than Livy apparently did with Augustus (though this is hard to ascertain, given the loss of Livy's Augustan books) – within the compass of his project, to show that Roman history culminates now with Tiberius ... and that Tiberius is as

---

[27] For summary and recent bibliography, see Gowing (2007).
[28] Woodman (1975) 17 with n. 69; see also Woodman (1983b) 171 on Vell. 2.71.1.
[29] For this see above, p. 2.
[30] A longer, more ambitious work was planned, the precise nature of which is unknown, though it was clearly meant to expand on much of the material covered in the present history (see e.g. 2.96.3 with Woodman (1977) ad loc.). On the publication date see Woodman (1977) 40 n. 5 with refs.

capable as his predecessor, if not more so. Thus Tiberius supplants Augustus as the paradigm of the good emperor: the work concludes with a prayer entreating the gods to make Tiberius, not Augustus, the model for all future emperors (2.131.1–2).

This information is relevant insofar as it helps us better understand what Tacitus was *not* trying to do: to promote Trajan (and perhaps Hadrian as well) in the same way. Livy ends the *Ab urbe condita* with Augustus; Velleius ends his history with Tiberius. In neither case, however, did they end with the death of the emperor, in contrast to Tacitus, who ends the *Histories* with the death of Domitian, the *Annals* with the death of Nero. This fact alone reveals something about how differently Tacitus viewed his material and his task. He would in any case have disliked the superficiality of Velleius' work, especially in comparison with the monumentality of Livy's. More significantly, however highly he may have thought of Trajan, Tacitus refrained from giving the appearance of writing a history that could be construed as imperial panegyric or propaganda (both aims that have been attributed to Livy and Velleius). And, if Velleius sees Tiberius as an end, Tacitus sees him as a beginning, leaving in abeyance the question of where Rome's future lies. *His* history was not written to promote an emperor. Rather, it would provide anyone who aimed at such power with the lessons of recent imperial history. By contrast, schooling Tiberius in the nuances of power was quite far from the mind of Velleius.

The fragmentary imperial historians

Of Velleius – and of the other first-century imperial historians nearly contemporary with Tacitus himself, all of whom survive either in a few fragments or are simply names to us (see the Further Reading section below) – one thing is certain: none of them wrote anything transformative of the genre. It is perhaps no accident that we know little about these other historians, practically all of whom, it should be emphasised, were senatorial; their works simply did not attain the status of Sallust's or Livy's. It is to these two that Tacitus' coeval Quintilian gives pride of place when he comes to assess the Roman contribution to historiography; of more recent writers, he names Servilius Nonianus, Aufidius Bassus and Cremutius Cordus (*Inst.* 10.1.101–4). There are other 'competent writers', *scriptores boni*, among the historians, he notes, but these three are the highlights.

His remarks are revealing, however, and may well hint at Tacitus' own views of these writers. Cremutius' *libertas* is the quality Quintilian singles out for comment, and, given the historian's role in the *Annals* as a mouthpiece for the power of historiography and the ultimate inability of emperors to control it, Tacitus must be counted among his *amatores* (Quint. *Inst.* 10.1.104). Indeed, Tacitus clearly admires Cremutius Cordus a good deal – if not for his writing, then for his example (cf. Sen. *Cons. Marc.* 1.2–4, confirming general respect for Cremutius and his association with *libertas*). It should also be borne in mind that Cremutius was a contemporary of Velleius Paterculus as well as of Seneca the Elder (c. 50 BC – AD 40), who had written a history spanning the civil wars of the late Republic down through the reign of Tiberius (fr. 1P = 2C); and, while Cremutius' history (which covered the civil war between Caesar and Pompey and went down to c. 18 BC) was not a possible source for Tacitus, his life and example made a far greater impression on Tacitus than did Velleius'. This reveals something of what Tacitus values in other historians; it is not merely a question of how well they write history, but of the authority conferred on their work by their character and personality.[31]

This perhaps accounts for his disparagement of sources for the Flavian period, which included the history of Pliny the Elder: he would be among those alleged to have been unduly influenced by *adulatio* (*H.* 2.101.1). Pliny's *A fine Aufidii Bassi*, a work in thirty-one books published in 79 and evidently spanning the period from around 31 (continuing the history of Aufidius Bassus) to the early years of Vespasian, must have been a valuable source of information for Tacitus.[32] It was not, however, an achievement he particularly admired in the same way he admired Sallust or Livy.

Although he chronicled the German campaigns of Tiberius in a monograph and in his broader history the first part of that emperor's reign, Aufidius Bassus is not mentioned by Tacitus as a source. Indeed, he is referred to only once, briefly but enthusiastically in the *Dialogus*, where he is paired (as by Quintilian) with Servilius Nonianus (*D.* 23.2). Servilius, too, receives scant notice in Tacitus, though he was important enough to receive a curt but favourable obituary – and was a sufficiently well-known historian to be identified as such (*A.* 14.19).[33] We know nothing, however, of his work (his career encompassed the reigns of Tiberius and Nero), and the mere fact of his being mentioned in favourable terms by Tacitus does not say much about its impact.

---

[31] See Marincola (1997) 251–2; Klingner (1958) 198 (Cordus), 199–201 (Seneca).
[32] For Tacitus' references to Pliny see above, n. 2.
[33] In contrast, for instance, to Curtius Rufus, who had written a (mostly extant) history of Alexander the Great and whose career spanned the reigns of Tiberius, Gaius and Claudius. Tacitus finds him interesting enough to include a comparatively long digression about him and his career, but neglects to identify him as a fellow historian (*A.* 11.20.3–21), leading some to conclude (probably wrongly) that he must have been the father of the historian rather than the historian himself. See Koestermann (1967) on 11.20.3. For Nonianus, see the classic study by Syme (1964b).

Perhaps the most discussed historian utilised by Tacitus is Cluvius Rufus.[34] Here, too, the parameters of his history are not fully known, but Tacitus uses him as a source for the reign of Nero and for events of 68–9. Something of Cluvius' influence may be gauged by the fact that he appears to have been highly regarded as a historian, consulted extensively by Plutarch, Suetonius, Cassius Dio and probably Josephus. While Tacitus' considerable dependence on Cluvius is well established, the fact that he offers no comment on the quality of his work – as he does in the case of other cited sources or historians, such as Fabius Rusticus (cf. *Agr.* 10.3), a parallel source for the reign of Nero (*A.* 13.20.2; 14.2.2; 15.61.3) – suggests that he found him generally trustworthy and useful but not particularly distinctive as a writer. He does, however, praise him by an interesting indirection: he reports a speech against Eprius Marcellus by Helvidius Priscus, one of the few characters Tacitus openly admires (cf. *H.* 4.5), in which he invokes the example of Cluvius Rufus as a wealthy and eloquent man who had managed to maintain high standards while serving in the court of Nero, in contrast to Marcellus' conduct under Vespasian (*H.* 4.43.1).[35] This puts Cluvius in the camp of Cremutius Cordus, as a writer to be admired as much for the conduct of his life as for his literary endeavours.

Conclusion

However little may survive of early imperial historiography, it should nonetheless be stressed that, in comparison with the late Republic, historical writing was very much in vogue and in full vigour. I have mentioned here the chief practitioners, but, apart from these, we know that many other individuals turned to writing history. Perhaps most intriguing among these were the emperors themselves. Augustus had penned his *Res Gestae* (its influence has been detected in Tacitus[36]); Tiberius wrote an autobiography that was consulted by Tacitus' coeval Suetonius (*Tib.* 61.1); Claudius composed a substantial history, the nature of which is, however, not clear (Suet. *Claud.* 21.2);[37] the emperor Nero planned to compose an epic, at one point

---

[34] See in general B.M. Levick's remarks on Cluvius in Cornell *et al.* (forthcoming); and Syme (1958a) 178–9, 293–4, 675–6. G.B. Townend published a series of important articles between 1960 and 1964, tracing the influence of Cluvius in Cassius Dio and Tacitus in particular: see esp. Townend (1964).

[35] Some confirmation of Cluvius' integrity may be found in the letter by Tacitus' friend Pliny the Younger, reporting a conversation Pliny overheard between Verginius Rufus and Cluvius in which the latter seems to assert and defend the truthfulness (*fides*) of his history (*Ep.* 9.19.5).

[36] See in general Urban (1979).

[37] Fragments in Peter (1967) and Cornell *et al.* (forthcoming).

From the annalists to the *Annales*

envisioned to be 400 books long, on the history of Rome (Cass. Dio 62.29). These were not necessarily works intended merely (or even) to secure the emperors' reputation as intellectuals and accomplished writers. Rather, they set forth a very particular view of history that ensured that the past would be seen through the eyes of the man in power. Earlier Romans, to be sure, had used *commentarii* for precisely the same end – think of Sulla or Caesar – but none of them had wielded the absolute power of an emperor. Whether or not Tacitus paid any attention to what emperors wrote (he did, at least, evidently read Augustus) or, if he did, whether he found anything useful in them, we simply cannot know.

To return to Tacitus' bookshelf, we might find there cherished and well-thumbed copies of Cato, Sallust and Livy, with the later historians occupying a dingy corner of the bottom shelf – texts his craft required him to own but which he rarely read for pleasure.[38] It was nonetheless, we may be sure, a well-stocked library. While it is clear that Tacitus does indeed have his debts to various practitioners of his chosen genre, it is very difficult to point to any one text or author who exclusively served as model. But this only underscores the profound originality of Tacitus himself. Like other great Roman writers before him, his genius lay in his ability not to copy and imitate, but to innovate and transform.

FURTHER READING

Surveys of Roman historiography prior to Tacitus are plentiful. Good overviews in English and useful in both general and particular ways may be found in Kraus and Woodman (1997) and Mellor (1999). With specific reference to Tacitus and his place in the tradition, Laistner (1947) 103–22, Syme (1958a) 132–56, Klingner (1958), Martin (1981) 13–25, Noè (1984), and Martin and Woodman (1989) 1–10 are representative; Flach (1973) attempts to trace the influence of the tradition on Tacitus in some detail. The best general discussion of the annalists and the annalistic tradition is to be found in Oakley (1997) 21–108; Badian (1966) remains useful; see also Frier (1999) 201–24; Kraus and Woodman (1997) 119 offer a succinct bibliography. For the Julio-Claudian historians in general, Wilkes (1972) is valuable. There is also a good deal of recent and forthcoming work in the field of Roman historiography. Marincola (2007) contains articles by leading scholars on all aspects of Roman historiography and historians; Feldherr (2009) is almost as comprehensive. Much work has been done as well on the fragmentary historians. Peter (1967) is gradually

---

[38] As Marincola (1999) 403 has aptly observed, '[Tacitus'] eyes are not on Cluvius Rufus or Servilius Nonianus or Fabius Rusticus: they are on Livy and Pollio and beyond them on Sallust and so on back to Cato.' In contrast to Marincola, however, I am less inclined to regard Tacitus' expressed distaste for early imperial historians as merely a rhetorical pose: I imagine he really believed Livy and Sallust to be great writers, and the rest quite mediocre.

being superseded: Chassignet (1996–2004) and Beck and Walter (2001–4) have now re-edited the fragments of the annalists (essentially Vol. I of Peter); in addition, a team of scholars under the general editorship of T.J. Cornell is preparing *The Fragments of the Roman Historians,* an edition and translation of the fragments that will replace Peter and is to be published by Oxford University Press. All three works feature a re-editing of the fragments as well as updated discussions and bibliographies.

2

A. J. WOODMAN

Tacitus and the contemporary scene

I

Tacitus' first historical work can be dated with unusual precision. Internal evidence indicates that he was writing the preface to the *Agricola* between October 97 and late January 98 and that he was finishing the work after Trajan had become emperor (3.1, 44.5).[1] Since we know from Pliny (*Ep.* 2.1.6) that Tacitus was suffect consul in 97, he may even have started writing the *Agricola* while still in office. Tacitus described the *Agricola* (3.3) as an 'interim book' and said that in due course he would write a larger work covering both the reign of Domitian (81–96) and the present time. This larger work, which we know as the *Histories* and which in the event covered the years 69–96 but excluded the present time, was in progress around 107, since that is the approximate date of the letter in which Pliny refers to it (*Ep.* 7.33.1). In the *Histories* (1.1.4) Tacitus repeated his promise of writing about the present time, but in his last and most celebrated work, the *Annals*, he went further back still to the years 14–68. The composition of the *Annals* seems to belong to the period after 113, when he returned from his proconsulship of Asia, but the precise dates are unknown.[2] Of his two other shorter works, the *Germania* is assumed to have been written in 98; the date of the *Dialogus* remains unclear: the most likely year is perhaps 102, when Fabius Iustus (to whom the work is dedicated) was consul;[3] but this is not certain and the evidence is disputed.

For their comments on earlier drafts of this chapter I am most grateful to R. Ash, A.R. Birley, C.S. Kraus, D.S. Levene, R.H. Martin and C.B.R. Pelling.

[1] At *Agr.* 3.1 Nerva is referred to as 'Nerua Caesar' and Trajan as 'Nerua Traianus': this suggests that the passage was written after Trajan was adopted by Nerva (Oct. 97) and before Nerva died and was deified (Jan. 98). At 44.5 Trajan is referred to as *princeps*. For the notion that the *Agricola* was not Tacitus' first work see Beck (1998).
[2] He may have been writing Book 4 in 115 (see Martin and Woodman (1989) 102–3).
[3] See Mayer (2001) 22–7.

II

In the published correspondence of the younger Pliny, Tacitus receives more letters than anyone else. Since no letter from Tacitus to Pliny has survived, it is easy to think of the correspondence as a one-way conversation in which the enthusiastic but second-rate younger man repeatedly importunes his brilliant but unforthcoming elder.[4] The first letter (1.6) is on the subject of hunting wild boar, and in the course of it Pliny – surely not without a certain humour – recommends silence (2 *silentium*) to Tacitus on the grounds that literary reflection will be aided thereby:

> Ridebis, et licet rideas. ego, ille quem nosti, apros tres et quidem pulcherrimos cepi. 'Ipse?', inquis. Ipse; non tamen ut omnino ab inertia mea et quiete discederem. ad retia sedebam; erat in proximo non uenabulum aut lancea, sed stilus et pugillares; meditabar aliquid enotabamque, ut, si manus uacuas, plenas tamen ceras reportarem. [2] non est quod contemnas hoc studendi genus; mirum est ut animus agitatione motuque corporis excitetur; iam undique siluae et solitudo ipsumque illud silentium quod uenationi datur magna cogitationis incitamenta sunt. [3] proinde, cum uenabere, licebit auctore me ut panarium et lagunculam sic etiam pugillares feras: experieris non Dianam magis montibus quam Mineruam inerrare. uale.

> You will laugh, and you may well laugh. I, the man you know, caught three boars – and in fact very fine ones. 'Personally?', you ask. Personally, though not so that I abandoned entirely my usual idleness and calm. I sat by the nets; nearby there were, not a hunting spear or lance, but pen and writing tablets; I pondered and took notes, so that, if I returned empty-handed, at least my wax tablets would be full. There is no reason for you to look down on this form of studying. Although it is wonderful how the mind is stimulated by the exercise and movement of the body, nevertheless woodland surroundings and solitude and the very silence which is needed for hunting are great encouragements to thought. Accordingly, when you go hunting, you have my authority to take with you your writing tablets as well as your hamper and flask. You will find Minerva, no less than Diana, roaming in the hills.

Pliny's reference to physical and mental activity (2 *animus ... motu ... corporis excitetur*) shares phraseology with Tacitus' *Dialogus* (36.1 'great eloquence, like a flame, is nourished by fuel and stimulated by movement [*motibus excitatur*] and gleams when burning'). It has often been assumed that Pliny is making a complimentary allusion to the work of his addressee and that this allusion in turn may help in determining the date of his friend's oratorical work.[5] But these assumptions are by no means secure.

---

[4] For a discussion of the two men see Griffin (1999), Giua (2003). For Pliny's career see Birley (2000b) 5–17.

[5] See Murgia (1985) 171–81; discussion of the dating in Brink (1994a) 256–64.

In a later letter to Tacitus, dated to the years 107–8, Pliny attributes to his correspondent an awareness that the countryside is conducive to writing poetry (9.10.2): 'the poems which you think can be executed very nicely amidst copses and groves [*inter nemora et lucos*]'. Though the combination of these two nouns is found elsewhere, it is generally accepted that here Pliny is indeed referring to the *Dialogus*, in which the expression occurs twice in contexts of study and literary composition (9.6 *in nemora et lucos*; 12.1 *nemora ... et luci*). Now the whole point of the humour in *Epistle* 1.6 is that Pliny is recommending to Tacitus a way of studying and writing with which Tacitus, despite his name, is *not* familiar: hence the words 'There is no reason for you to reject this type of studying'. It would be very strange indeed if Pliny made this recommendation to a correspondent who was already believed by him to have expressed, in a work of his own, the view that the countryside was conducive to literary composition. The inference must be that, when Pliny wrote his first letter to Tacitus, his friend's *Dialogus* had not yet appeared and hence Pliny in that letter cannot be alluding to it. This conclusion may be supported by some further evidence.

It has not been realised that the collocation of the ablative *motu* and the participle *excitatus* as found in *Epistle* 1.6 occurs earlier in Cicero's translation of Plato's *Timaeus* (*Tim.* 44 'And when because of necessity he had sown bodies [*corpora*] with the minds [*animis*], and when there was both influx to the bodies and efflux, it was first necessary that there should exist one sensation, common to all, stimulated by quite violent emotion [*motu excitatum*] and linked to nature'). And, since Pliny not only has the singular *motu* but also has references to *animus* and *corporis* which seem to pick up Cicero's *animis* and *corpora*, it appears quite likely that he is alluding to Cicero, his revered literary model. An alternative possibility[6] is that Pliny is echoing Quintilian, his teacher (cf. *Ep.* 2.14.9; 6.6.3), who, after recommending that an orator should practise daily either before a live audience or privately in silence, says that among the advantages of the former course is 'movement of the body, which itself ... stimulates the orator' (10.7.26 '*motum corporis, qui et ipse ... excitat oratorem*'). As for Tacitus, although it is obviously possible that he too was alluding to either Cicero or Quintilian, a more immediate source is provided by his friend's letter.[7]

Pliny's other letter to Tacitus in Book 1 is a lengthy discussion of the virtues of brevity and fullness in oratorical style (20): halfway through, Pliny expresses the idea of 'different emotions' in a phrase (12 *diuersis animi*

---

[6] Suggested by R. Ash.
[7] It should of course be recognised that Tacitus in the *Dialogus* shows a knowledge of Quintilian (Mayer (2001) 22).

motibus) that recurs in no other classical author apart from Pliny's present addressee, who uses it thrice (*H.* 4.31.4; 5.15.2; *A.* 1.25.2). Since Pliny's letter was written long before Tacitus had started on the *Histories*, we are perhaps to assume that the phrase was originally Pliny's and that it appealed to his addressee and remained in his mind. This 'one-way conversation' is beginning to look less one-way.

Since *Epistles* 1.6 and 1.20 are both addressed to Tacitus, the date of their publication is less relevant than the date of their composition: even if the publication of Book 1 was withheld until around 105, as Syme believed,[8] Tacitus as recipient of the letters would obviously have had access to their language as soon as he received them in the late 90s. Hence another letter in Book 1, but not addressed to Tacitus, becomes particularly significant. In 1.9 Pliny, on the basis of withdrawing to his country villa near Ostia, recommends farm life to Minicius Fundanus (7): 'accordingly, at the very first opportunity, you too should leave that noise and the pointless turmoil [*strepitum istum inanemque discursum*] and the very silly tasks'. The only other author to combine *strepitus* and *discursus* in extant Latin is Tacitus in a battle scene in the *Agricola* (35.3): 'the charioteered cavalry filled the middle of the plain with noise and turmoil [*strepitu ac discursu*]'. Earlier in the letter Pliny says that, after retiring to the country, 'the recollection comes over' one that one has wasted one's time in the town (3 *subit recordatio*). The only other author to use this phrase again, apart from Pliny himself (*Ep.* 4.24.1), is Tacitus in the *Histories* (3.31.3 *subit recordatio*). Once one is in the countryside, says Pliny, there is no malicious conversation (5): 'no one in my house criticises anyone in malicious conversations [*sinistris sermonibus*]'. The only other author to use this phrase is Tacitus in a reference to Romanius Hispo and Granius Marcellus in the *Annals* (1.74.3): 'he incriminated Marcellus for having held malicious conversations [*sinistros ... sermones*] about Tiberius'.

The number, exclusivity and clustering of these parallels clearly suggest that there is an intertextual relationship between *Epistle* 1.9 and the works of Tacitus. Since the letter, on any of the proposed dates, was published well before Tacitus started to write the *Annals*, it must be Tacitus who is alluding to Pliny. If that is the case, it seems to follow that, when Tacitus was writing the *Agricola*, he already had access to Pliny's letter; and, since the *Agricola* belongs to the years 97–8, it means that Book 1 of Pliny's letters was published shortly after the composition of its letters in the late 90s and was not withheld until around 105. If this seems too implausible a conclusion, one would be obliged to envisage a more complicated scenario in which Pliny in

---

[8] Syme (1958a) 663.

one part of his letter (7) echoed Tacitus' *Agricola*, while Tacitus many years later in the *Annals*, perhaps responding to Pliny's echo, alluded to another part (5) of the same letter.

That Tacitus in the *Annals* alluded to this letter is not in doubt. In the remains of another of Pliny's villas, at Tifernum in the upper Tiber valley, roof tiles have been discovered, some of which are inscribed with his own initials (C P C S),[9] while others are dated to 7 and 15 and are inscribed with the name of M. Granius Marcellus (*CIL* 11.8107 *M. Grani Marcelli*, cf. 6689.118–19). Scholars infer from the tiles that Pliny inherited the estate from the family of Granius Marcellus.[10] Now Tacitus tells us that in 15 Granius Marcellus was accused not only of criticising the *princeps* in malicious conversations, as we have just seen, but also of two religious crimes: placing a statue of himself in a more elevated position than his imperial statuary, and slicing Augustus' head off another statue and replacing it with the head of Tiberius (1.74.3). Marcellus' case is the third in a triptych of religious cases which Tacitus describes and of which the first is that of one Faianius, who, when selling his gardens, had included in the sale a statue of Augustus that was situated in the gardens (1.73.2). Such sales are precisely the subject of a letter of Pliny to Trajan (10.8), referring to permission he had earlier sought from Nerva to transfer to the local town the imperial statues which *he* had inherited as part of his Tifernum estate – presumably from Granius Marcellus! Evidently Tacitus, when describing cases which in terms of the defendant and the charge have a doubly direct relevance to his friend Pliny, has used Pliny's own phraseology.[11]

III

Pliny was only one of a remarkable number of well-known writers whose lives and careers overlapped with those of Tacitus.[12] The correspondence and other evidence reveal an intensely literary and 'bookish' society in which members of the upper class would exchange work in progress and read or listen to one another's compositions with perhaps a view to making

---

[9] I.e. Gaius Plinius Caecilius Secundus.
[10] See Champlin (2001) 122–3.
[11] *Ep.* 10.8 was written in 99 (Sherwin-White (1966) 64, though he nowhere seems to mention the date of *publication*).
[12] For some of these lives and careers see also the Chronological Table, pp. 330–1. Tacitus' birth is usually dated within the years 56–8 and his family background ascribed to Gallia Narbonensis (see below, p. 327), though Trier has been suggested as his actual birthplace on the grounds that the presumed father of the historian was procurator of Gallia Belgica (cf. Plin. *HN* 7.76): so Birley (1999) xlvii, following Syme (1958a) 614.

comments and improvements. Our uncertainty about the exact publication dates of many of the relevant works makes it difficult to know who is reading whom, and when. Tacitus refers to the fact that the doctor Charicles was not allowed to take charge of Tiberius' health (*A*. 6.50.2 *regere ualetudines*): the reason was that Tiberius had earlier made a decision to take charge of his own health, as the biographer Suetonius mentions in his *Life* of Tiberius (68.4 *ualetudinem ... rexerit*). One explanation for this coincidence of language and subject may be that both authors were reading the same source. But, when Tacitus in the *Histories* says that it was uncertain whether Valerius Festus 'tempted Piso to revolution' (4.49.1 *temptauerit ... Pisonem ad res nouas*), he was writing well before Suetonius used the same expression in the same *Life* of Tiberius (12.3 *temptare ... animos ad nouas res*). The likelihood here is that Suetonius has been reading Tacitus. Similarly, when Tacitus had said memorably of Germany that 'no one there smiles at vice' (*G*. 19.1 *nemo illic uitia ridet*), the expression stuck in the mind of the satirist Juvenal, since he reproduced it many years later in an ethnographical context (13.171–3 *illic | ... ridet | nemo*). When Juvenal describes the Pontifex Maximus by the phrase *pontifici summo* (4.46), the explanation is said to be metrical; the only other author to substitute *summus* for *maximus* is Tacitus (*A*. 3.58.3), but the relevant dates are so tight that we cannot assign priority. However, when both Tacitus (*A*. 15.41.1) and Juvenal (8.13) substitute 'Great Altar' (*magna ara*) for 'Greatest Altar' (*ara maxima*), the later dating of Juvenal's eighth satire makes it likely that, in addition to preserving his hexameter rhythm, he is imitating a characteristic bizarrerie of the historian.[13]

On other occasions, however, we can know that Tacitus is the imitator. Since Statius died in or before 96, the various striking parallels of phraseology between his *Thebaid* and Tacitus' *Histories* and *Annals* must be a result of the historian's reading: for example, *maestam ... noctem* ('mournful night', *H*. 3.38.4 ~ *Theb*. 8.665) or *orbas ... domos* ('orphaned homes', *A*. 14.27.2 ~ *Theb*. 3.74). Tacitus describes the start of Agricola's career (*Agr*. 5.1 'Prima castrorum rudimenta') in similar terms to those used by Statius in the *Silvae* to praise the son of an earlier governor of Britain, Vettius Bolanus, at the start of his career (*Silv*. 5.2.8–10 'quid si militiae iam te, puer inclite, *primae | clara rudimenta* et *castrorum* dulce uocaret | auspicium?'). Though the parallel is not absolutely exact, the strong similarity suggests that Tacitus was engaging with Statius' text and that his cool appraisal of Bolanus' governorship later in the work (*Agr*. 8.1, 16.5) may have been intended as a response

---

[13] On Tacitus and Juvenal see Courtney (1980) on Juv. 2.102–3; Syme (1984) 1142–57.

to the encomium of Bolanus that Statius included in his poem to the man's son (lines 54–6, 140–51).[14] After Statius' death, Tacitus' reference to 'breaking courage' (*H.* 2.99.2 *infringere ... uirtutem*) implies that he was reading his posthumous and unfinished *Achilleid* (~ 1.888).

Another epic poet, Silius Italicus, is mentioned by Tacitus in the *Histories* (3.65.2): Silius had a military and political career in addition to being the author of the *Punica*, the story of Rome's war with Hannibal. When Tacitus in the *Annals* says 'nor does it make a difference to anyone whether you delight more in exalting the Punic or Roman lines' of battle (4.33.4), he perhaps had Silius' poem in mind, even though it had been published many years before.[15] Certainly he had read Silius with care: *iacuit immensa strages*, his memorable description of the aftermath of Sejanus' fall (*A.* 6.19.2 'the wreckage stretched indefinitely'), is straight from Silius (9.137–8), as is the senators' 'penetration by panic' a few chapters later (*A.* 6.24.3 *penetrabat pauor* ~ 16.514). Tacitus likes such periphrases as 'the coverings of helmets' (*A.* 12.35.3 *galearum ... tegmina*), but the expression is Silian (1.475–6; 5.197).

Since Valerius Flaccus had died before 95 (cf. Quint. *Inst.* 10.1.90), any exclusive parallels with his *Argonautica* must be due to Tacitus' reading: his remarkable use of the Greek accusative at *H.* 3.74.1 'aramque posuit casus suos in marmore expressam' ('and he established an altar depicting in marble his own fortunes') is an exact replication of the same usage in Valerius (1.398 *casus ... expressa*, 2.654 *casus expressa*). 'We would have thought Valerius an unlikely source for Tacitean imitation', remarks E. Courtney, 'but it all goes to show the attention which Tacitus paid to searching out syntactical oddities.'[16]

IV

Valerius Flaccus is generally believed to have been one of the quindecimvirs, a priesthood held also by Tacitus, as he tells us himself in the *Annals* (11.11.1):

> Isdem consulibus ludi saeculares octingentesimo post Romam conditam <anno>, quarto et sexagesimo quam Augustus ediderat, spectati sunt. (utriusque principis rationes praetermitto, satis narratas libris quibus res imperatoris Domitiani composui. nam is quoque edidit ludos saeculares iisque intentius

---

[14] For similar coolness towards Bolanus see *H.* 2.97.1; see also below, pp. 55–6.

[15] Tacitus' argument at this point is very similar indeed to Juv. 1.162–7 (perhaps contemporary).

[16] Courtney (2004) 428. As far as can be ascertained, all the parallels quoted in Section III are exclusive to Tacitus and the authors concerned, although one should always bear in mind the theoretical possibility of a lost common source in each case.

adfui, sacerdotio quindecimuirali praeditus ac tunc praetor; quod non iactantia refero sed quia collegio quindecimuirum antiquitus ea cura et <ii> magistratus potissimum exsequebantur officia caerimoniarum.)

With the same men as consuls [47], the Secular Games were witnessed in the 800th year after Rome's founding, the 64th from when Augustus produced them. (I am passing over the calculations of each princeps, sufficiently described as they are in the books in which I compiled the affairs of the Commander Domitian [i.e. the *Histories*]. For he too produced Secular Games [in 88], and I was present at them with particular attentiveness – endowed as I was with the quindecimviral priesthood and praetor at the time, which I do not record from boasting but because the college of quindecimvirs has been concerned with them since antiquity, and it was those magistrates in particular who carried out the duties of the ceremonies.)

This passage is usually taken as evidence of Tacitus' 'almost morbid fear of self-glorification',[17] but another interpretation is possible. The passage develops into a parenthetical digression, and the explanatory reference with which Tacitus concludes his digression (*quod* ..., 'which ...') answers the implied question of why his priestly and magisterial positions were relevant to his presence at the Games; but this is only the last in a series of implied questions and answers that starts at the very beginning of the digression. Why is Tacitus silent here about the calculations on which Augustus and Claudius based their holding of the Games? Because he has already described them in the *Histories*. Why were they described in the *Histories*? Because Domitian, with whom he dealt in the *Histories*, also celebrated Secular Games. In fact the only gratuitous statement in the digression – the only statement not generated by an implicit question – is that which informs us that Tacitus himself attended Domitian's Games. Moreover, there would be no need for a digression at all if Tacitus had kept silent about the interval of sixty-three years separating Claudius' Games from those of Augustus. It is because the interval of sixty-three years raises an initial question (namely, whether Claudius was justified in holding the Games when he did) that Tacitus is obliged to answer it by reference to the imperial calculations. In other words, both the digression itself and the allusion to Augustus' Games by which it is triggered have been exploited by Tacitus for the purposes of introducing the reference to his own attendance at Domitian's Games. This reference is the focus and climax of the digression, and to say that Tacitus' words 'grudgingly concede' a brief note about the author's career seems misguided.[18] Moreover, if Tacitus in the *Histories* had written at such a level of detail as the imperial calculations by which the Games of 17 BC and AD 47 were defended, as he says he did, it

---

[17] Syme (1958a) 113.
[18] Syme (1958a) 534.

seems inconceivable that he remained silent about his own involvement in Domitian's Games. Thus, on this hypothesis, his self-reference here in the *Annals* repeats information which he had already supplied elsewhere, even though repetition is the reason he gives for *declining* to mention the calculations of Augustus and Claudius in the first place. The historian seems at least as interested in alluding to his own privileged attendance at the Games as he is in the holding of the Games themselves.

Such forthrightness about his prominence during Domitian's reign contrasts strikingly with his total silence on the subject in the preface to the *Agricola*, where, as in the rest of that work, Domitian is mentioned only to be condemned. Of course it can be argued that, as consul in 97 and almost certainly recommended for that magistracy by Domitian before his death, he was placed in an impossible position: since so recent and so high a pinnacle could be neither denied nor convincingly explained away, silence was the wisest course. When he came to write the preface to the *Histories*, however, a decade or so had intervened (1.1.3):

> dignitatem nostram a Vespasiano inchoatam, a Tito auctam, a Domitiano longius prouectam non abnuerim, sed incorruptam fidem professis neque amore quisquam et sine odio dicendus est.
>
> That my political standing was begun by Vespasian, enhanced by Titus and advanced still further by Domitian I would not deny, but those who profess incorruptible reliability must not speak of anyone with affection, and without hatred.

Here Tacitus, though anxious to claim the authority that derived from a political career,[19] is also on the defensive (*non abnuerim*, 'I would not deny'), since his indebtedness to successive emperors places his impartiality at risk. The logic of his statement dictates that the risk was of repaying the benefits with an affectionate treatment (*amore*); but there is a paradox here, since the emperor to whom Tacitus owed most was Domitian, whom Tacitus, as readers of the *Agricola* would remember, regarded as fit only for hatred (*odio*). Tacitus in his works becomes increasingly candid about his involvement in Domitian's reign, while declining to act upon his promises to write about Trajan.

V

The year 112 was important for both Trajan and Tacitus. On 1 January the complex of buildings known as Trajan's Forum was dedicated.[20] This was

---

[19] For such authority see Marincola (1997) 133–48, esp. 143–4. It is not possible to identify exactly the stages of Tacitus' career to which reference is made at *H.* 1.1.3 (Birley (2000a) 234, 237–8).

[20] For the date see Smallwood (1966) 32 (no. 22); Blake and Bishop (1973) 12.

one of the wonders of the ancient world:[21] when the emperor Constantius II visited Rome almost two and half centuries later, 'he stood stock still in amazement' at the sight of Trajan's masterpiece (Amm. 16.10.15 'haerebat attonitus'). As for Tacitus, in the spring of the same year he departed for Asia as proconsul of the province for the next twelve months.[22] Just as in his earlier years he had been selected for one of the two imperial quaestorships (*quaestor Augusti*),[23] so he ended his career with the position which, along with the proconsulship of Africa, was the climax of any political life. This crowning achievement confirmed his status as a privileged politician who had been in receipt of continuous imperial favour for almost four decades.

Tacitus was setting off for Asia at a particularly sensitive moment. In the following year Trajan was to embark on a war with Parthia, and it is inconceivable that such a venture was not already being planned a year in advance. Tacitus' province lay directly on the route between the western empire and Parthia: legions and other persons and items to be transported would almost certainly be obliged to pass through Asia on their way further east. The governor of the province during these months of preparation was therefore in a key position and could scarcely have avoided involvement in the emperor's strategic thinking.[24]

When Tacitus returned to Rome in the spring of 113, he may have been in time to witness the dedication of Trajan's Column on 12 May.[25] This edifice, together with the pedestal on which it stands, is 115 ft (35 m) high and displays a spiral series of 155 engraved pictures illustrating scenes from Trajan's two wars in Dacia (101–2 and 105–6). The arrangement of these scenes is such that Trajan appears in them 'as the awesome protagonist whose effect on events is decisive, almost as if it were he alone against the Dacians', while the designer of the pictures is to be seen 'as a historian in stone'.[26] Most remarkably of all, the Column was sited between the two buildings that housed Trajan's Greek and Latin libraries, as if the military victories that it commemorates demanded not only literary celebration by historians and poets, as was to be expected, but a physical setting in which their works could be enshrined, preserved for posterity and, of course, read. The Column dominated the libraries and dictated by example how they

---

[21] Packer (1997) and (2001); Gowing (2005) 146–51.
[22] Birley (2000a) 235–6.
[23] See Birley (2000a) 230 n. 2, 237–8.
[24] Noted by Rutledge (1998) 142.
[25] For the date see Smallwood (1966) 32 (no. 22); Blake and Bishop (1973) 16.
[26] The quotations are from Brilliant (1984) 97–9 and 100. It has, however, been argued by Claridge (1993) that the reliefs were put on the Column only after Trajan's death.

should be filled. The lesson could scarcely fail to be drawn by a writer such as Tacitus, whose privileged political career was now at an end.

It might have been expected that Trajan's war against Parthia, especially if Tacitus had had personal involvement in the planning of it, would provide the historian with the stimulus to carry out his original and twice-stated intention of writing an account of the present age. If we may judge from the evidence of a later time, the confrontation between Rome and Parthia was a topic that historians found extremely attractive. When the two powers went to war fifty years later in 162, historians immediately rushed to write accounts of it, or so we are told by their contemporary Lucian in his essay on how to write history (*Hist. conscr.* 2, 14ff.). One writer whom Lucian happens not to mention is Fronto, who was actually given instructions by the emperor of the day, Lucius Verus, as to how he should narrate the war and portray Verus himself in the best possible light.[27]

Yet Tacitus did not simply decline the topical subject of Trajan's Parthian War in favour of describing the Julio-Claudian emperors in the *Annals*. One conspicuous feature of the *Annals* is 'the regularity with which the narrative of events in Rome is punctuated by extensive sections on Parthia'.[28] In the extant books there are in fact thirteen occasions on which Tacitus turns to Parthian affairs: some of these occasions consist of fairly extensive episodes, yet in none of them does he reveal the slightest hint that Parthia was the scene of contemporary military operations; there is never a parallel drawn between 'then' and 'now'; no reference to the fact that in 116 Parthia will provide Trajan with the title 'Parthicus' and the coin legend 'Parthia capta'.[29] Since Pliny makes it clear 'how much is owed to the *princeps*' from a recipient of such imperial favour as Tacitus (*Pan.* 90.3 'quantum debeant principi'), the latter's silence seems remarkable. What, if anything, had happened?

It was perhaps in the same crucial year 112 that Trajan issued his so-called 'restored coinage'.[30] On these coins were depicted those earlier *principes* whose reigns now entitled them to be declared officially worthy of admiration, namely, Julius Caesar, Augustus, Tiberius, Claudius, Galba, Vespasian, Titus and Nerva.[31] This sequence of coins constitutes a selective history of the early Empire in numismatic form. Not only is the list

---

[27] Fronto, p. 108 VDH² (= Loeb ed., vol. 2, pp. 196–7).
[28] Ash (1999b) 114, quoting 2.1–4, 56–60; 6.14, 31–7, 41–4; 11.8–10; 12.10–14, 44–51; 13.6–9, 34–41; 14.23–6; 15.1–18, 24–31.
[29] Dio 68.28.2; Smallwood (1966) 33, 39–40 (nos. 23, 49, 54); Syme (1958a) 239 and n. 4; Lightfoot (1990) 120; Bennett (2001) 199. For comparable reticence in the case of Plutarch see Pelling (2002a) 253–65.
[30] Seelentag (2004) 413–19.
[31] See Mattingly (1926); Komnick (2001).

interesting in itself, but each of these leaders was associated with some special quality on the reverse of his coins: thus Augustus is *pater patriae* ('Father of the Fatherland') and Galba is matched with *libertas* ('freedom'). Particularly striking is the presence on the coinage of Tiberius, the most memorable of Tacitus' presentations in the *Annals*. On the reverse of his coins is a seated female figure who has been variously identified as Iustitia (Justice), Pax (Peace) or simply Livia.[32] If the first of these three identifications seems hard to believe, it is worth recalling that roughly thirty years earlier Titus had issued Tiberian coins depicting Livia, and on them the legend *Iustitia* is prominently displayed.[33] It is tempting to speculate that the appearance of the restored coinage acted as a provocation for a historian who had already dealt with the period from Galba to Domitian in the *Histories*; at the very least, his iconoclastic treatment of the earlier *principes* in the *Annals* stands retrospectively in eloquent contrast to their serial canonisation by Trajan.

In Book 3 of the *Annals* Tacitus expressed the hope that his work would compare favourably with those of earlier historians and, perhaps providing a source of inspiration for posterity, would enjoy an honourable survival in the future (55.5). In his consciousness of the literary tradition, and of his own hoped-for place in it, Tacitus was no different either from his friend Pliny, who wrote to him on the subject (*Ep.* 9.14),[34] or from other classical writers. Trajan's Greek and Latin libraries at once symbolised that tradition and preserved the volumes that were its physical manifestation; in these two buildings there reposed the texts that constituted the challenge for those contemporary historians whose own ambition was to see their works likewise preserved for posterity. Yet it is said that, when in the third century AD the emperor Tacitus wished to pay tribute to the historian and namesake whom he claimed as an ancestor, he ordered the works of Tacitus to be placed in libraries (*SHA Tac.* 10.3). Perhaps one is to make the melancholy inference that they were not there already. Perhaps towards the end of his life the historian had developed a different perspective on the present time from that of Trajan – and from

---

[32] See Komnick (2001) 127 (and pl. 26, Trajan type 58.0), who notes 'Livia (?)'.

[33] 'The inclusion of Tiberius, to us who have read our Tacitus, is more surprising. But the favourable judgement passed on him by … Titus and Trajan forces us to recognise that his reputation had recovered from its contemporary slanderers and that his public services were at least held to atone for any possible private vices' (Mattingly (1966) xc). See Lichocka (1974) 24–31.

[34] Cf. *A.* 4.61, where Tacitus contrasts the ephemeral eloquence of one Q. Haterius with that of those whose 'meditatio et labor in posterum ualescit' – words which are 'Clearly Tacitus' testimony to his own quality' (Syme (1958a) 624 n. 3). For Pliny see further Mayer (2003).

that which he himself had expressed two decades earlier in the preface to the *Agricola*.

FURTHER READING

Syme (1958a) remains the classic contextualisation of Tacitus and his works; standard introductions are Martin (1981) and Mellor (1993). The younger Pliny is currently a fashionable scholarly subject: see Hoffer (1999), Morello and Gibson (2003) and (forthcoming), and Marchesi (2008). For recent discussion of the shared literary milieu of Tacitus and Pliny see e.g. Boyle and Dominik (2003) with further references. For allusion in Tacitus see the references in the Further Reading section appended to the Introduction above. For the latest discussion of Tacitus' life and career consult Birley (2000a). For libraries see Boyd (1916), Casson (2001) and especially Horsfall (1993).

PART II
Texts

3

A. R. BIRLEY

The *Agricola*

The *Agricola*'s first words, echoing the opening of Cato the Elder's *Origines* (fr. 2P = 2C), are as follows: 'to record for posterity famous men's deeds and characters is an ancient practice not abandoned even in our times' (1.1). There used to be no criticism, even of those who wrote their own *Life*; 'but now, about to relate a dead man's life, I have needed indulgence, which I should not have sought if planning an invective, so savage and hostile to excellence are the times [*infesta uirtutibus tempora*]' (1.4). The end of this sentence echoes Cicero's complaint in 46 BC (*Orat.* 35 *tempora ... inimica uirtuti*). Tacitus then recalls how Arulenus Rusticus' *Life* of Thrasea Paetus, and that of Helvidius Priscus by Herennius Senecio, had resulted in the death penalty for their authors and in their books being burned (2.1).[1] Tacitus did not need to specify that Thrasea and Priscus were senators and Stoics, who had met their deaths for 'opposition'. The fate of Rusticus, Senecio and others, condemned in 93, would be taken up again just before the end of the work (45.1), but for the moment Tacitus continues: 'No doubt they thought that in that fire the voice of the Roman people, the liberty of the senate and the conscience of mankind had been wiped out, since in addition the teachers of philosophy [*sapientiae professoribus*] had been expelled and all noble accomplishments driven into exile, so that nothing honourable might anywhere confront them' (2.2). Whereas 'the former age [*uetus aetas*] witnessed an extreme of freedom, we have experienced the depth of servitude' (2.3).

Domitian is not here named. Indeed, apart from ten hostile words about his conduct as an 18-year-old (7.2), he is not mentioned until near the end of the work, where hero and tyrant are continuously contrasted (39.1–45.2). In the last section of the preface, Tacitus cautiously hails the dawning of the new era inaugurated by Nerva Caesar and the further increase in

---

[1] This sentence is introduced with *legimus*, 'we have read' or 'we read'. Quite what is meant by this (if the text is correct) is not clear: see e.g. Turner (1997).

happiness under Nerva Traianus (3.1). Thus the time of writing was *prima facie* after Trajan's adoption, in October 97, but before Nerva's death three months later. The single further reference to Trajan, however, where Tacitus regrets that Agricola did not live on 'into the dawn of this most blessed age and to see Trajan as *princeps*' (44.5), belongs after Trajan had become emperor. Perhaps Tacitus was writing after Nerva's death, but in the preface refrained from writing *diuus Nerua* in the same breath as praising him for having 'combined what were formerly incompatible, Principate and liberty [*res olim dissociabiles ..., principatum ac libertatem*]'. He introduces this famous tribute and what follows, Trajan's 'daily enhancement of the happiness of the times', with *quamquam*, 'although', to which *tamen*, 'nevertheless', responds: 'nevertheless by the nature of human frailty, remedies take longer to act than diseases' (3.1). This thought echoes, in milder form, Livy's anxiety in his preface about 'these times, in which we cannot endure either our ills or the remedies' (*praef.* 9).[2]

A reminiscence of Livy is easy to reconcile with what follows: after fifteen years of enforced silence, Tacitus too was determined to write history and to overcome 'the charm of indolence itself' (3.1), to which it was difficult not to succumb in those years. 'It will not be an unpleasant task to put together, even in a rough and uncouth style, a record of our former servitude and a testimony to our present blessings. This book, in the meantime, intended to honour Agricola, my father-in-law, as a tribute of dutiful affection, will either be commended – or condoned' (3.3). The reference to lack of literary ability is conventional self-deprecation. His readers will have known otherwise; not long before, a close friend had described him as *eloquentissimus*, referring to the funerary *laudatio* that Tacitus, then consul, had delivered for Verginius Rufus (Plin. *Ep.* 2.1.6).[3] When praising Verginius, 'Tacitus cannot have failed to see that another great and good man might be honoured in like fashion. Verginius survived the emperors whose suspicion and hatred he incurred: Julius Agricola died before the truth could be told.'[4] Tacitus deeply regretted that he had been absent from Rome when Agricola died (45.5). But, even if he had been there, he could hardly have praised Agricola as he deserved: 'what [Domitian] dreaded most of all was for the name of a

---

[2] The *Agricola* is mostly accepted as Tacitus' first work, although some believe that the *Dialogus* was slightly earlier, e.g. Murgia (1980). Beck (1998) has argued that the *Germania* came before *Agricola*, in early 98, with the latter composed near the end of that year. His arguments, depending to some extent on his interpretation of *G.* 33.2, *urgentibus imperii fatis*, are not conclusive, but worth considering.

[3] A little later Pliny repeated this description, adding that a particular excellence in Tacitus' oratory was his majestic delivery (Plin. *Ep.* 2.11.17 σεμνῶς).

[4] Syme (1958a) 121.

subject to be exalted above that of the emperor' (39.2). So this book was, in a sense, a belated funerary encomium.

It was also an apologia for those who had continued to serve Rome under a tyrant: not merely Agricola, but Tacitus himself as well and many others, not least Trajan. Immediately before describing Agricola's death, Tacitus produces what seems like an outburst: 'Those whose habit it is to admire what is forbidden ought to know that there can be great men even under bad emperors, and that obedience and restraint [*obsequium ... ac modestiam*], if coupled with hard work and energy [*industria ac uigor*], attain to the same height of praise as reached by many who, taking perilous paths, have become famous by an ostentatious death, with no benefit to the Commonwealth' (42.4). As Syme stressed, '[a]ttacking those who admired the martyrs unduly, Tacitus defends his father-in-law – and shields his own conduct under the tyranny of Domitian'. More than just a laudatory *Life*, the work 'is a document of Roman political literature, a manifesto for the Emperor Trajan and the new imperial aristocracy'.[5]

Agricola's family needed no lessons in resistance to tyranny. His father Graecinus, 'noted for his study of eloquence and philosophy', was a martyr to principle, who lost his life for declining to obey Caligula, as emphatically stated in the second sentence of the biography proper (4.1). As for Agricola himself, he 'used to tell, I recall, that in his early youth [as a student at Massilia], he would have drunk in the study of *philosophia* more deeply than permitted to a Roman and a senator, had not his prudent mother restrained' him. As he grew up, discretion prevailed, 'and he did retain from philosophy, what is very difficult, moderation' (4.3).

It is pointless to complain that the *Agricola* does not fit any one literary genre. Although the work is a *uita*, as stated at the outset (1.4), no previous Latin biographies survive for comparison, except those by Cornelius Nepos. Tacitus perhaps wanted to show off his talents: 'within its brief compass [the *Agricola*] contains, and integrates in a unique manner, five or six different elements. To each is given an appropriate style and tone.'[6] Preface and epilogue are Ciceronian, while the biography proper is reminiscent of Sallust and Livy. The work is a tribute to Agricola's 'merits' or 'excellence', *uirtutes*: the word occurs four times in the first chapter alone (1.1–4). Various *uirtutes* are specified throughout the work. Near its end, referring to the time, some five years after Agricola had retired, when there was a series of military disasters, Tacitus writes that 'everyone was comparing his energy,

---

[5] Syme (1958a) 25, 125; also Syme (1970) 2–3, 13–15, 131–2. He is followed by (among many others) Birley (1975) and (1999). Cf. Petersmann (1991) 1803–5; Beck (1998) 94, with n. 165.
[6] Martin (1981) 39; see also Martin (1969) 124–6.

steadfastness and spirit schooled in warfare [*uigorem, constantiam et expertum bellis animum*] with the inaction and timidity of others' (41.3). Then very different qualities are emphasised: 'moderation', *moderatio*, and 'good sense', *prudentia* (42.3; the former also mentioned at 7.3), and, in the 'outburst' already quoted, *obsequium* and *modestia* are praised – provided that they are combined with *industria* and *uigor* (42.4).

Because it was principally in Britain that Agricola displayed his virtues, almost half the work is devoted to the governorship (18–38), divided into two equal halves by a dramatic digression, the mutiny of the Usipi (28). If one adds the passages covering Agricola's service in the same province as military tribune (5.1–3) and legionary legate (7.3–8.3), the geographic and ethnographic excursus (10.1–13.3) and the section on Agricola's ten predecessors (14.1–17.2), a good two thirds of the work is about Britain. The name *Britannia* occurs forty-one times, the *Britanni* another twenty-two. It may be added that Tacitus repeats the name *Agricola* forty-five times.

Apart from the explicit details about Agricola's *uirtus*, there are allusions, which contemporaries must have recognised. Caesar (*diuus Iulius*) is mentioned a single time, as 'the first of all the Romans to enter Britain with an army'. What follows is hardly flattering: 'although he terrified the inhabitants in a successful battle and took possession of the coast, he can be seen to have pointed it out to posterity rather than to have handed it over' (13.1). Yet there is a latent comparison between Agricola and Caesar in much of the work. Just as Caesar had conquered Gaul, so 'Britain was first completely conquered then' – at the time when Agricola was governor (10.1). Agricola is made to spell out the proud claim, addressing his army before Mons Graupius: 'I have gone beyond the limits reached by former legates and you have exceeded those reached by previous armies. The furthest point of Britain is no longer a matter of report or rumour: we hold it, with camps and with arms. Britain has been discovered and subjugated' (33.3). The Britons against whom Agricola was to fight are like the Gauls used to be, before they lost their *uirtus* together with their freedom (11.4) – to Caesar, such is the unspoken thought. In two chapters, 18 (on Agricola's first campaign as governor) and 35 (on his final battle), the sentence construction is surprisingly similar to that of Caesar.[7]

The statement at 18.5, *clarus ac magnus haberi Agricola*, 'Agricola was held to be famous and great' (after his first campaign), directly echoes Sallust on Cato the Younger (*Cat.* 53.1 *Cato clarus atque magnus habetur*). Like Cato, of whom Sallust says that 'the less he sought glory,

---

[7] See Lausberg (1980) 414–16.

the more it reached him' (*Cat.* 54.6), Agricola did not seek it, but *ipsa dissimulatione famae famam auxit*, 'his very disregard of fame made him more famous' (18.6).[8] The context of Sallust's remarks is his famous comparison between Cato and Caesar, outstanding representatives of two different kinds of *uirtus*. Agricola combines the qualities that Caesar and Cato had separately possessed: he was 'strict', *seuerus*, and 'compassionate', *misericors* (9.3), the chief characteristics of Sallust's Cato and Caesar (*Cat.* 54.2). Further, he had Caesar's 'accessibility', *facilitas* (*Cat.* 54.3; *Agr.* 9.3), and Cato's 'incorruptibility', *integritas*, and 'temperance', *abstinentia* (*Cat.* 54.2, 6; *Agr.* 9.4); his *modestia* (42.4) was also a characteristic of Cato (*Cat.* 54.6).[9] Tacitus was claiming for Agricola the qualities of the Stoic senators' great exemplar.

More remarkable still, some phrasing hints at Alexander the Great. During Agricola's first service with the army, *militaris gloriae cupido*, 'a passion for military glory entered his soul' (5.3). This echoes the 'yearning', *pothos* (πόθος), for which Alexander was famous.[10] Agricola's army responded to its victory in the sixth season by 'roaring out that nothing was impassable to their *uirtus*, Caledonia must be penetrated and the furthest limit of Britain found at last' (27.1). This was exactly how Alexander was portrayed by Curtius Rufus: 'nature has made nothing so deep that it cannot be overcome by *uirtus*' (Curt. 7.11.4). The great conqueror 'was seized by a desire to look at the Ocean and to reach the ends of the world' – in the east (Curt. 9.9.1); Agricola tells his men that 'it would not be inglorious to die at the very place where the world and nature end' – in the far west (33.6).[11] Other evidence for Agricola at the world's end is found by combining a story in Plutarch and a Greek inscription. The grammarian Demetrius of Tarsus, featured in a dialogue whose dramatic date is just before the Pythian festival of 83–4, had recently returned from Britain, where he had sailed around the islands (Plut. *Mor.* 410A; 419E). Two silvered bronze plates found at York were surely dedicated by this man: 'To the gods of the governor's residence

---

[8] This is an example of an epigram adapted from Sallust, but outdoing him for brevity. See on this Šašel Kos (1990) 100, and, on adaptation, 90–1, citing Sen. *Controv.* 9.1.13–14. She identifies thirty-one *sententiae* in the *Agricola*, while noting (108–9) that more can be found.

[9] The foregoing remarks, indebted to Lausberg (1980), can only sketch some of the arguments which she sets out in detail.

[10] See e.g. Arr. *Anab.* 5.27.6, where, to be sure, Alexander's yearning is treated as irrational, as by Curt. 9.2.12, 'yearning overcame reason' (*uicit cupido rationem*). This criticism could not apply to Agricola, whose early quest for glory, first apparent in connection with philosophy at Massilia, was 'soon moderated by reason and age' (4.3 *mox mitigauit ratio et aetas*).

[11] Borzsák (1982) 37–46; see also Borzsák (1994) 126–32.

Scrib(onius) Demetrius' and 'To Ocean and Tethys Demetrius' – the latter deities are those to whom Alexander set up altars at the Indus in 325 BC (Diod. Sic. 17.104).[12]

The account of Agricola's activity in Britain has been examined with especial care by archaeologists, with varying conclusions. For one thing, there has been disagreement about the chronology of the governorship. The earlier dating is now favoured: the first year was 77; the great battle of the seventh season was in 83; Agricola's return to Rome was in spring 84.[13] Tacitus' reluctance to provide British geographical names also creates difficulties. There are only thirteen in the text printed by modern editors: a region, Caledonia (10.3; 11.2; 25.3; 27.1; 31.4), clearly the land beyond the Firths of Forth and Clyde; four states (or 'tribes'), the Silures (11.2; 17.2), Brigantes (17.1; 31.4), Ordovices (18.1, 2) and Boresti (38.2); three islands or groups of islands, Orcades, Thule (10.4) and Mona (14.3; 18.3); three estuaries, Taus (22.1), Bodotria (23; 25.1, 3) and Clota (23); the site of the battle, Mons Graupius (29.2); and a harbour, *Trucculensis portus* (38.4). Numerous attempts have been made to locate Mons Graupius. A favoured location is the Mither Tap of Bennachie in Aberdeenshire,[14] but this hardly suits passages in Calgacus' and Agricola's speeches: that their armies were at the end of the island, with nothing beyond except sea and rocks. As Henderson points out, '[t]he very lateness of the season when the battle was fought constitutes a strong argument for its very high latitude'. It is true that no Roman camps have yet been located beyond the Great Glen; future exploration may reveal them. An ideal site might be in Sutherland, between Ben Loyal, 'Queen of Highland peaks', 2,500 ft (764 m) high, and the sea.[15]

The account of the battle's aftermath, how Agricola led his army 'into the territories of the Boresti' (38.2), and the fleet 'held the Trucculensian harbour' (38.4), has caused further perplexity. Minor adjustments to the text by Wolfson produce far better sense. The *Boresti*, not attested by any other source, can be dispensed with: *in finis Borestorum exercitum deducit* can be emended to *in finis bore<o>s totum exercitum deducit*. For the equally

---

[12] *RIB* 662–3. The identification is accepted by Wright in *RIB*, ad loc.
[13] For the early dating see Raepsaet-Charlier (1991) 1843–4; Birley (2005) 77–8, accepting the dating of Agricola's consulship to 76, as argued by Campbell (1986).
[14] Cf. Birley (2005) 89, with further refs.
[15] Henderson (1985) 330; see also Henderson (1984). Rivet and Smith (1979) 370–1 summarise theories about the name *Graupius*, comparing the supposed true form *Craupius* with Old Welsh *crup* and modern Welsh *crwb*, 'hump'. They postulate a Pictish **crub*. One may note the hill (1,017 ft = 310 m) now called in Gaelic *Meall Leathad na Craoibhe*, 'sloping hump of the trees', overlooking the sea at the Kyle of Tongue, on the north side of Ben Loyal. *Craoibhe* closely resembles **crub*.

unattested *Trucculensem,* read as *trutulensem* by E²ᵐ (the contemporary corrector of the *codex Aesinas*[16]) and frequently emended, Wolfson offers *tru<x> Tulensem*: the first adjective refers to the demeanour of the fleet, *trux*, the second to the harbour of *T(h)ule*, Shetland (Mainland). For the final words of 38.4, where the transmitted text reads *unde proximo Britanniae latere praelecto omni redierat*, he offers *[un]de proximo Britanniae latere praeuecta omnis re<s a>dierat*. The passage may now be translated as follows (38.2–4):

> And as the summer was already over and the war could not be extended further, he led the entire army down into the northern extremities. [3] There he took hostages and instructed the prefect of the fleet to sail round Britain: forces were allocated for the purpose and panic had gone before. He himself, marching slowly, to intimidate new peoples by the very delay with which he traversed their territory, settled the infantry and cavalry in winter quarters. [4] And at the same time the fleet, its ruthlessness enhanced by rumour and by favourable weather, held the Thule harbour; having sailed on from the nearest side of Britain, it had tackled all eventualities.[17]

As Wolfson also shows, where Tacitus at 10.4 refers in advance to the circumnavigation of Britain, *dispecta est Thule* should mean 'thoroughly inspected' (not 'seen from far off', 'glimpsed' or the like):

> It was then that a Roman fleet for the first time circumnavigated this coast of the remotest sea and confirmed that Britain is an island; and at the same time it discovered the islands, hitherto unknown, which they call Orcades, and subjugated them. A close examination of Thule was also made, because the order had been to go this far.[18]

It is worth citing here Xiphilinus' epitome of Cassius Dio (66.20.2–3):

> Meanwhile, war having broken out again in Britain, Gnaeus Julius Agricola overran the whole of the enemy's territory there; and he was the first of the Romans whom we know to have discovered that Britain is surrounded by water. For certain soldiers, having mutinied and murdered centurions and a tribune, fled into ships and putting out to sea sailed round the western part of Britain, just as the wind and the waves happened to carry them; and without realising it, as they approached from the opposite direction, they put in at the camps on the first side again. Thereupon Agricola sent others to try the voyage around Britain and learned from them that it is an island. These things, then,

---

[16] For the *codex Aesinas* see below, pp. 246–8.
[17] Wolfson (2008) 35–46.
[18] Wolfson (2008) 29–34. He produces better sense by punctuating with a full stop after *quia hactenus iussum*, then reading *sed hiems appetebat et mare pigrum* ... (following the B manuscript), rather than the editors' *iussum, et hiems appetebat. sed mare pigrum* ...

happened in Britain, on account of which Titus was acclaimed as *imperator* for the fifteenth time. But Agricola lived in disgrace for the rest of his life, and in hardship, because he had done deeds too great for a general; and finally he was murdered by Domitian for no other reason than this, even though he had received triumphal honours from him [Domitian].[19]

Titus' fifteenth imperatorial acclamation is datable to autumn 79.[20] Either Dio or Xiphilinus has condensed and garbled the story: Tacitus (*Agr.* 28) is clear that the mutiny took place in Agricola's sixth season, 82, not in 79; and the acclamation was obviously not taken for 'the overrunning of all enemy territory', which means the complete conquest of Britain, Tacitus' *perdomita Britannia*. All the same, Dio's version suggests that Agricola's naval operations were regarded as hardly inferior to his victory on land. This is underlined by Dio's reference in an earlier book: 'But in the course of time, to be sure, [Britain] has been clearly proved to be an island, first under the propraetor Agricola and now under the emperor Severus' (39.50.4).[21]

It was Pytheas of Massilia who first saw Thule. Wolfson suggests that Agricola 'as a young student at ... Massilia (*Agr.* 4.2), the home town of Pytheas, ... would have imbibed not only traditional philosophy, but also the seafaring aura of the town, the four hundred years of Pytheas' legacy and the works of Pytheas, the "Massaliot philosopher"'.[22] It is immaterial in the present context where Pytheas' Thule actually was. Agricola and his contemporaries (as later Ptolemy) took Thule to be Shetland.[23] One may legitimately speculate that this connection helped to form Agricola's ambitions. It may be added that his home town, Forum Iulii (4.1), had been an Augustan naval base (*A.* 4.5.1).

---

[19] The MSS' παρὰ τοῦ Τίτου, 'from Titus', is surely a corruption of παρὰ τούτου, 'from him'.

[20] In *CIL* 16.24, of 8 September 79, Titus is still *imp. XIIII*; he is *imp. XV* in *ILS* 98 and 262, both datable to 79.

[21] Dio's source is unknown: was it the *Agricola* or perhaps a later version in the *Histories*? For his assertion that Agricola 'was murdered by Domitian', he might have simply read between the lines of Tacitus' elaborate version (43.2–3 'the persistent rumour that he had been poisoned ... I would not venture to assert that we have any evidence'), followed by further items of supposedly suspect behaviour by the emperor, and concluded that it was murder.

[22] Wolfson (2008) 31–2, quoting Cleomedes, *De motu circ.* 1.7. His dating of Agricola's studies at Massilia to 'c. AD 56' may be a little late. To judge from *Agr.* 4.2 (*paruulus*) and 4.3 (*prima in iuuenta*), Agricola must have gone there in about 53, aged about 13, and may have stayed for up to four years. On Agricola and Massilia (but not mentioning Pytheas) cf. also Gärtner (1983).

[23] But it can be argued that for Pytheas too Shetland was Thule: thus Wolfson (2008) 15–24.

There is no question but that Tacitus deliberately plays down the achievements of Agricola's predecessors. Pliny the Elder writes that 'Roman forces, in almost thirty years,[24] have carried our knowledge of Britain no further than the neighbourhood of the Caledonian forest' (*HN* 4.102). In other words, either Petillius Cerialis, governor from 71 to 73 or 74, or even Vettius Bolanus, in office from 69 to 71, had already gone beyond the Forth–Clyde isthmus. Not long before Tacitus wrote, Statius addressed a poem to the son of Bolanus, and recalled the latter's career:

> What glory will excite the Caledonian plains, when some aged inhabitant of the savage country relates, 'Here your parent used to give judgement, on this turf address the squadrons; he placed watchtowers across wide tracts, and forts a long way off – do you see them? – and surrounded these walls with a ditch; these gifts, these weapons he dedicated to the gods of war – you can still make out the inscriptions; this cuirass he himself put on at the call to arms, this one he seized from a British king'. (*Silv.* 5.2.142–9)

Tacitus portrays Bolanus as thoroughly inactive (8.1; 16.5). However, it can be argued that Bolanus had not only had some success against Venutius, the ex-husband of the Brigantian ruler Cartimandua (rescued in 69, cf. *H*. 3.45.2, not naming Bolanus), but that he had created the initial phase of the 'Gask Ridge frontier', a line of watchtowers and forts that ran from near Falkirk to the Tay, precisely in the 'Caledonian plains'.

As for Cerialis, Tacitus credits him with the resumption of an aggressive policy and the partial conquest of the Brigantes, Britain's largest people (8.2–3; 17.1–2). Archaeology shows that he penetrated the northern Pennines and built the first fort at Carlisle, datable by dendrochronology to winter 72–3.[25] Hence one must abandon the old view that Agricola's second season (20.2–3) was confined to northern England. Tacitus' account of that season, and indeed of the next one, simply shows that he was operating in territory where his predecessors had campaigned: 'many states which up to that moment had operated on equal terms abandoned violence and gave hostages' (20.3); 'the enemy were baffled and in despair, because they had been used to making good the summer's losses by successes in winter and now they were under pressure in summer and winter alike' (22.3). But the 'many states' cannot be the Brigantes of northern England, who were a single *ciuitas* (17.1): they were surely in southern Scotland.[26]

---

[24] That is, by about the year 72.
[25] For references see Birley (2005) 67.
[26] See Birley (1953) 13–14; Shotter (2000) and (2002); Birley (2005) 56–84; on the Gask Ridge, Woolliscroft and Hoffmann (2006).

The repeated mentions of Thule by contemporary poets need consideration.[27] Statius portrays the duties of Domitian's *ab epistulis*, Abascantus, as:

> to learn what laurelled message comes from the North, what news from wandering Euphrates, or from the banks of Ister with two names, or from the standards of the Rhine, how much the end of the world has yielded, and Thule round which the ebbing floodtide roars – for every spear raises joyful leaves and no lance is marked with the ill-famed feather. (*Silv.* 5.1.88–93)

The 'end of the world' and 'Thule' must refer to Agricola's conquests. Silius Italicus, praising the Flavians, affirms that 'the father [Vespasian] shall present to this [family] unknown Thule for conquest', *huic pater ignotam donabit uincere Thulen* (3.597) – in other words, to his son, Domitian.[28] In a later passage (17.416–17) Silius describes how the 'blue-painted inhabitant of Thule, when he fights, drives round the close-packed ranks in his scythe-bearing chariot', recalling Tacitus' account of British charioteers at Mons Graupius (*Agr.* 36.3). Juvenal, without naming Thule, clearly alludes to it: 'our arms we have indeed pushed beyond the shores of Ireland and the recently captured Orkneys and the Britons satisfied with the shortest night' (2.159–61). In a later satire he jokes that 'Thule is talking about hiring a rhetoric teacher' (15.112).

Tacitus would hardly have been surprised if Silius gave the credit for conquering Thule to an emperor rather than to Agricola. It was another matter that Statius, in the poem already quoted, made it seem as if Bolanus had got there first: 'You should learn from your father, how great he was, as, bearing his orders, he entered Thule that bars the western waves' (*Silv.* 5.2.54–6). Bolanus may, perhaps, have reached the southern edge of 'Caledonia' – far more than Tacitus allows him – but he certainly did not 'enter Thule'. That claim may have caused Tacitus to play down Bolanus' governorship. As for the emperor, in the description of Agricola's campaigns none is mentioned. 'If the spirit of the army and the glory of the Roman name had permitted it, a frontier had been found within Britain itself' (23), Tacitus writes of the fourth season, with no reference to Titus, then emperor, or a little later, to Domitian, who must have ordered the renewed advance in the sixth season (25.1). Likewise, in Agricola's speech, it is 'under the auspices of the Roman Empire' (33.2), not of the emperor, that he tells his men that they have been fighting. All the same, despite the undoubted weighting in the account, with

---

[27] See Wolfson (2008) 47–62.
[28] Wolfson (2008) 54–5 convincingly reads *huic*, found in three MSS, rather than *hinc*, as in modern editions.

predecessors' roles played down[29] and Agricola's enhanced, there is no need to dismiss the details of the campaigns as largely invented (as some have done). Tacitus could have consulted his father-in-law's memoranda and talked to men who had served under him; and, indeed, he may have served in Britain himself, as military tribune, in the early stages of the governorship.[30]

Agricola's encouragement of civilian development, described in a famous passage (21.1–2), needs discussion:

> The following winter was taken up by most beneficial measures. His intention was, in fact, that people living in widely dispersed and primitive settlements, hence naturally inclined to war, should become accustomed to peace and quiet by the provision of amenities. Hence he gave encouragement to individuals and assistance to communities to build temples, marketplaces and town houses. He praised those that responded promptly and censured the dilatory: hence there was competition for esteem instead of compulsion. Further, he educated the sons of the leading men in the liberal arts and rated the Britons' natural talents above the trained skills of the Gauls. So those who just lately had been rejecting the Roman tongue now conceived a desire for eloquence. Hence our style of dress, too, came into favour and the toga was everywhere to be seen. And gradually they went astray into the allurements of evil ways, colonnades and warm baths and elegant banquets. Those who had no experience of this called it 'civilisation', although it was part of their enslavement.

The final, apparently cynical comment may have been meant as favourable to Agricola – compare the remark about the advantage that the conquest of Ireland would have brought: 'freedom as it were removed from sight' (24.3). Still, Braund argues that 'the target of Tacitus' closing remarks is not Agricola, but the Britons: his salutary planning is contrasted with their misidentification of the nature of civilisation'.[31] At all events, this is the classic passage in the surviving literature for 'state-sponsored Romanisation'.[32]

Comment is also required on Calgacus' passionate verbal onslaught on Roman imperialism, of which the epigram, 'They make a desert and call it

---

[29] As well as criticism, direct (of Bolanus) or implicit (of Cerialis), one must note the brief but entirely positive verdict on Frontinus, 'a great man, in so far as was permitted' (17.2). Frontinus was a key supporter of Trajan, consul with him in 98 and 100.
[30] Suggested by Birley (2000a) 237.
[31] Braund (1996) 161–5. Of course, 'the allurements of evil ways' (21.2) recalls the effects of Trebellius' inactive government: 'now the barbarians, as well, learned to condone seductive vices' (16.3).
[32] Compare Pliny the Elder: Rome's mission was 'to soften people's ways, to bring the clashing wild speech of infinite different peoples to a common conversation through a common tongue and to supply civilisation [*humanitas*] to men, so that all races might, in a word, belong to one single fatherland' (*HN* 3.39).

peace' (30.5), is the best-known item.[33] Of course, Tacitus gave Agricola's opponent a set of standard criticisms, similar to those put in the mouth of Critognatus (Caes. *B Gall.* 7.77) or in Mithridates' letter (Sall. *Hist.* 4.69). It has been suggested that Tacitus was expressing his own criticism of the Principate.[34] But for Braund 'Calgacus' denunciation of Roman maladministration is completely out of place when deployed against Agricola ... It might have been appropriate against another Roman governor or against the emperor himself.'[35]

We cannot be certain about Tacitus' motives with this speech or with the work as a whole. But he surely felt compelled to remind his contemporaries of Agricola's achievement: he had conquered the furthest limit of the world. At the beginning of the *Histories* he repeated the claim: *perdomita Britannia*, but with the – clearly indignant – addition *et statim missa*: 'Britain completely conquered – and at once let go' (*H.* 1.2.1), meaning the abandonment of Agricola's conquests by Domitian.

FURTHER READING

Because of its focus on Britain, the *Agricola* has understandably attracted most interest among British scholars. The standard English commentary by Ogilvie and Richmond (1967) now requires revision; the latest is Soverini (2004); a new commentary by C.S. Kraus and A.J. Woodman is in preparation for the series Cambridge Greek and Latin Classics. Among translations into English may be mentioned Mattingly (1948) and Birley (1999), the latter with fairly detailed historical notes. The studies by Syme (1958a) and (1970) are still important, particularly on the political background. Braund (1996) 147–96 has many valuable insights. Contributions by philologists include those by Borzsák (1968) 399–416, Dorey (1969b), Martin (1981) 39–49, Petersmann (1991), Beck (1998) and Wolfson (2008).[36] The textual emendations of the last named are particularly important for reassessing the nature of Agricola's achievement in Britain. This has been the subject of repeated debate among historians and archaeologists. Re-emphasis on the role of Agricola's predecessors, Bolanus and Cerialis, was first urged by E. Birley (1953) 10–19 (originally published in 1946) and has been taken further by Hanson (1987) and (1991), Shotter (2000) and (2002) and Woolliscroft and Hoffmann (2006).[37] All the governors of Britain are treated in detail by Birley (2005).

---

[33] See above, p. 1 and n. 2.
[34] Borzsák (1968) 409–11.
[35] Braund (1996) 167–70.
[36] Is it pedantic to complain that some philologists refer to Agricola as 'proconsul' of Britain? Thus Dorey (1969b) 10; repeatedly, Petersmann (1991) 1798–801; Beck (1998) 63.
[37] The presentation by these authors of their important work on the Gask Ridge is marred by their treatment of Tacitus, e.g. at 191: Tertullian, *Apol.* 16, 'straightforwardly calls [Tacitus] a liar', without indicating who Tertullian was or the context.

4

RICHARD F. THOMAS

The *Germania* as literary text

Scholars in the early decades of the twentieth century were responsible for ethnographically oriented studies that invalidated much of the preceding, mostly nineteenth-century, scholarship.¹ Tacitus, particularly in the first half of the *Germania*, is guided as much by ethnographical commonplaces and generalisations as by any individual or empirically derived autopsy. As Syme succinctly put it, 'If Cornelius Tacitus was ever on the Rhine, he discloses no sign of it in the *Germania*'.² Sources were available, from Posidonius to Caesar, to Pliny's *Bella Germaniae* (and the *Naturalis Historia* as well), to Aufidius Bassus' *Bellum Germanicum*. Information could have been had from returning merchants and soldiers, as was the case with Pliny. But Tacitus does not tell us much on any of this. Rives, following Lund, is surely right: 'although the work does contain a few verifiable observations, it is so shaped by ethnographic preconceptions as to be virtually unusable as a historical source'.³ Hence the somewhat hostile reaction of Syme.⁴ Rives himself mitigates Lund's historiographically bleak assessment, looking in particular to archaeological and other records, and suggesting that use of Tacitus involves 'careful evaluation and a willingness to acknowledge uncertainty'.⁵ But the fact remains that the *Germania* is far from reliable as a historical, anthropological or sociological work, however important it has been in the realm of reception. So the question remains as to what precisely the *Germania* is trying to be or do. There is also the question of how we are to read it.

Dorey was generally correct in noting that the *Germania* is 'written in the style of oratory rather than the style of narrative, because that type of style was by tradition considered most suitable for disquisitions on ethnography'.⁶ He

---

¹ Trüdinger (1918); Norden (1923). See also below, pp. 294–5.
² Syme (1958a) 126–7.
³ Rives (1999) 57; cf. Lund (1991a) 1951–4.
⁴ Syme (1958a) 126–9.
⁵ Rives (1999) 56–66 (quotation from 66).
⁶ Dorey (1969b) 14. Gudeman (1928) 368–74 collected most of the stylistic and rhetorical peculiarities of the *Germania*, under four categories: 'Collocatio verborum'

59

also collects some of the 'many fine passages in the *Germania*', but ultimately concludes, with apparent reluctance, that, 'in spite of the interesting nature of the work, there is something that the *Germania* lacks to make it a great work of literature', finding that 'the whole subject matter of the *Germania* is too remote from his personal experience; he is too detached from it to give of his best'.[7] This may be right, but there should be more to the work of Rome's great literary historian. Ethnographical writing was indebted not only to oratory, but had also passed into the realm of poetry,[8] and there is material in the *Germania* that looks as much to Roman epic, Virgil and Lucan in particular, as to anything else. One instance will suffice here, but we will return to Tacitus' poetic and creative (as opposed to historical) processes later. At 17.1 the subject of clothing comes up: *tegumen omnibus sagum fibula aut, si desit, spina consertum: cetera intecti* ... ('They are all clothed with a cloak, fastened with a clasp or, should that be lacking, with a thorn: otherwise unclothed ...'). This thorn looks suspicious, and Gudeman in his commentary notes of *spina consertum* that 'the phrase is poetic', citing Virg. *Aen*. 3.594 *consertum tegumen spinis* ('clothing fastened with thorns') and Ov. *Met*. 14.166 *spinis conserto tegmine nullis* ('his clothing fastened with no thorns'). He does not mention that both poetic texts describe Achaemenides, the bedraggled and pathetic Greek whom Odysseus left behind in the land of the Cyclopes and who in Virgil will narrate the Odyssean story to which Aeneas can otherwise not have access. Virgil's text continues: *ac cetera Graius*, 'but otherwise Greek', and the (Greek) accusative of respect, brilliantly glossed by Virgil's *Graius*, is surely also the model for Tacitus as he continues with the same word and construction: *cetera intecti*. Why this intertext is there is hard to say – of course Tacitus mentions Ulysses' going to Germany in his long wandering (3.2) – but it is clearly there. In Virgil Achaemenides has reverted to a state of primitivism, his Greekness erased as he seems physically at home in the land of the primitive Cyclopes. And in this connection Tacitus too has reason to suggest German primitivism, as we shall see.

Structure and content

As has long been noted, the *Germania* falls into two roughly equal parts: the first (1–27.1) constitutes an ethnographical essay on the Germans and Germany as a more or less single entity; the second (27.2–46) is a catalogue of the constituent elements, treating the land and its people tribe by

(anastrophe, asyndeton, chiasmus, alliteration, etc.), 'Brachylogy' (chiefly ellipsis and zeugma), 'Inconcinnity', and 'Poetical and figurative features'.
[7] Dorey (1969b) 16–17.
[8] See Thomas (1982) *passim*.

tribe and region by region. This gives rise to a certain amount of tension, as the very real individualities and differences that emerge in the second half somewhat belie the implication of the first half that there is such a thing as 'Germania'. One way to look at the work is through the lens of genre. Both parts look as much to oratory and rhetoric as they do to any strictly historiographical works we could come up with, but they do so in different ways, and my own sense is that the first half is more conventional, the second the vehicle for a more lively narrative, characterised by high levels of *enargeia* ('vividness') and more poetic in nature.

The monograph (1–27.1)

This is the true ethnography, and it follows the conventions of the genre: 1 *situs* and boundaries; 2–4 origin, name and physical characteristics of the Germans; 5 produce and minerals; 6–8 arms and military characteristics; 9–10 religion; 11–15 political systems; 16 housing; 17 clothing; 18–21 marriage and relationships; 22–4 drinking and other entertainment; 25 use of slaves; 26 agricultural habits; 27.1 funerals. The ethnographical tradition normally treats the various categories (*situs*, climate, produce, peoples) separately, but Tacitus has skilfully created transitional bridges. So at 4 (transition to produce) the Germans have become used to cold and hunger on account of the (bad) climate and soil (*frigora atque inediam caelo soloue assueuerunt*); at 6.1 (transition from mineral to arms) iron is not abundant, as one can tell from their weapons (*ne ferrum quidem superest, sicut ex genere telorum colligitur*); at 8.1 (transition from warfare to religion) prophetically inspired women have bolstered wavering armies; at 10.3 (transition from religion to politics) duelling individuals decide the outcome for the state; at 17.2 (transition from clothing to marriage) the focus is on women's clothing; at 21.2 (transition from relationships to food and drink) food is shared between guest and host (assuming the phrase *uictus inter hospites communis* belongs here); at 26.4 (transition from agricultural practice to funerals) talk of the seasons leads to death – as is common in Roman poetry. The result of all of this is the production of a seamless essay, a monograph whose coherence and unity are communicated by the connectedness of the narrative in a very appealing way. While *Agr.* 10–12 (the ethnography of Britain) is a more traditional sketch, subordinate to the historical concerns of that work and with separate ethnographical categories enumerated, in the first half of the *Germania* Tacitus has produced a self-standing genre, truly an essay whose generic justification is that it is interested in the Germans for reasons other than the purely historical. The list style will return in the second half, which will have its own, distinct, generic affiliations.

The catalogue (27.2–46)

The catalogue of German tribes opens with a strong didactic flavour (27.2):

> nunc singularum gentium instituta ritusque, quatenus differant, quae<que> nationes e Germania in Gallias commigrauerint, expediam.

> Now I shall set forth the customs and rites of individual races, the extent of their differences, and what tribes have migrated from Germany into the Gallic provinces.

This was a compositional technique Tacitus would employ again in the *Annals* (4.1.1 *nunc originem, mores et quo facinore dominationem raptum ierit, expediam*, 'now I shall set forth his [sc. Sejanus'] background, his character and the crime with which he proceeded to grab power') and the *Histories* (1.51.1 *nunc initia causasque motus Vitelliani expediam*, 'now I shall set forth the beginnings and causes of the Vitellian uprising'). The technique is appropriate for didactic beginnings, and Tacitus has prose precedents – for instance Varro, embarking on individual etymologies at *Ling.* 5.7.1 (*nunc singulorum uerborum origines expediam*, 'now I shall set forth the origins of individual words'; also 5.57.1) – but, as has been noted,[9] the device (*nunc ... expediam* + direct object or object noun clauses) takes us in the direction of poetry, first Lucretian (2.62–6; 4.633–4; 6.239–45, 495–7, 639–41, 680–2, 738–9, 1090–3) and then, more significantly for Tacitus, Virgilian (*G.* 4.149–50; *Aen.* 6.756–9; 7.37–40; 11.314–15). The *Aeneid* passages are activated in Tacitus' instance: *Aen.* 6.756–9 introduces the parade of Italian and Roman leaders (757 *qui maneant Itala de gente nepotes*); *Aen.* 7.37–40 comes at the introduction to a book that will conclude with a catalogue of the tribes of Italy: *nunc age, qui reges, Erato, quae tempora, rerum | quis Latio antiquo fuerit status, aduena classem | cum primum Ausoniis exercitus appulit oris, | expediam* ('Come now, Erato, who the kings were, what the times were like, how things were in ancient Latium, when first the foreign army drove its fleet to Ausonian shores, these shall I set forth'); the catalogue itself, which the Muses are to sing (following the Homeric catalogue of ships introduction at *Il.* 2.484–92) will be introduced in parallel style, not with *expediam* (no longer possible), but with the same object noun clauses: 7.641–4 *cantus mouete, | qui bello exciti reges*, etc., 'sing what kings were stirred up in war', etc.; *Aen.* 11.316–23 has Latinus setting forth the *situs* (324 *est antiquus ager*) in which he plans to allow the Trojans to have their Italian *origo*. And closer to hand Tacitus also had Sil. 11.1–3, a different catalogue of the Italians, namely of those who

[9] Miller (1987) 97.

defected to Hannibal. Tacitus' manner of opening the second half, therefore, well prepares us for the catalogue of German tribes, and well prepares us for the poeticism that will pervade the work.

Two rivers

Rivers are a fundamental part of the ethnographic tradition,[10] and they, particularly two of them, are the immediate definers of Tacitus' Germany (1.1): *Germania omnis a Gallis Raetisque et Pannoniis Rheno et Danuuio fluminibus ... separatur* ('All of Germany is separated from the Gauls, Raetians and Pannonians by the Rivers Rhine and Danube'). The two rivers, which Tacitus will use to orient his discussion, appear in a colourful description, the Danube in personification: it 'approaches more peoples' (*plures populos adit*) than the Rhine and six of its mouths break out into the Pontic sea, while the seventh is 'swallowed by marshes' (*paludibus hauritur*). As Gudeman noted in his commentary, the two rivers are presented by means of a precise stylistic parallelism (1.2):

inaccesso ac praecipiti — vertice — ortus — miscetur
molli et clementer edito — iugo — effusus — erumpat

The emphasis on the rivers of course reflects an important reality for the Romans, for whom the two rivers formed the boundaries of Lower Germany and Pannonia respectively. Accordingly, Tacitus' treatment defines Germans as Transrhenane and Transdanubian, as he more or less moves down the Rhine at 30–4. He claims to do the same for the Danube at 41.1 (*quo modo paulo ante Rhenum, sic nunc Danuuium sequar*, 'as I did a little earlier with the Rhine, I shall now follow the Danube'), although, as Rives notes,[11] this is only partially true in both cases. Cultural status and degree of civilisation in part depend on distance from these rivers – and from Rome – and have a direct impact on the cultural images and evaluations that emerge. One 'river' in particular, namely Ocean, will concern us later.

History as digression (33 and 37)

Where ethnographical description normally functions as a digression within historical writing, in the *Germania* it is the other way around – the historical is a digression from the ethnographical. Tacitus leaves it till chapter 37 to situate Germany and the Germans within Rome's own historical context. He

---

[10] Thomas (1982) 15–16; Jones (2005) 37–47.
[11] Rives (1999) on 30–4 (p. 245) and 41.1.

does so almost casually, via treatment of the Cimbri, now in Jutland but once a terror to Rome. The wording recalls Livy's preface both in its affinities and by way of difference (37.2): *sescentesimum et quadragesimum annum urbs nostra agebat cum primum Cimbrorum audita sunt arma Caecilio Metello ac Papirio Carbone consulibus* ('our city was in its 640th year when we first heard (from) the arms of the Cimbrians, during the consulships of Caecilius Metellus and Papirius Carbo'). The sentence looks to Livy's attempt to trace his city's history back 'beyond its 700th year' (Livy, *praef.* 4 *supra septingentesimum annum*). But the sentence as it continues also displays its resistance to the prosaic: consular year markers at the wrong end of the sentence, an inverted *cum*-clause, and language that again takes us back to Virgil: *cum primum Cimbrorum* **audita sunt arma**. Indeed we are suddenly back in the tenuous world before Actium, when the Germans stood to profit from Rome's civil discord: Virg. *G.* 1.509 *hinc mouet Euphrates, illinc Germania bellum* ('on one side the Euphrates stirs up war, on another, Germany'). Back then, when Octavian was still just a man, it was the Germans who heard ominous and strange arms, in lines that the inverted *cum*-clause of Tacitus neatly inverts: *G.* 1.474–5 **armorum** toto **sonitum** Germania caelo | audiit ('Germany heard arms sounding across the whole sky'). At one time we heard the arms of the Germans – and responded; in times of our civil war they hear our arms.

In *Germania* 37.3 this historical digression situates German superiority to other foes of Rome in their possession of a quality once held dear by the Romans (37.3): *non Samnis, non Poeni, non Hispaniae Galliaeue, ne Parthi quidem saepius admonuere: quippe regno Arsacis acrior est Germanorum* **libertas** ('neither Samnite nor Carthaginians, neither Spains nor Gauls, not even Parthians have more often taught us a lesson: the freedom of the Germans makes for more ferocity than the monarchical system of Arsaces'). *Libertas*, once the Roman ideal, becomes the greatest threat when possessed by others, and that is why the Germans matter. This final sentiment is conveyed by way of an appealing chiastic arrangement (*regno Arsacis ~ Germanorum libertas*). The historical digression continues: the East could only boast one victory, over Crassus (37.3); Germans, on the other hand, on five occasions from 113 BC on, 'routed or captured' (37.4 *fusis uel captis*) some six Roman generals, most notably and recently Quintilius Varus in AD 9. Even Roman successes over the years, under the commands of Marius, Julius Caesar, Drusus and Nero, Germanicus – these all came at a cost (37.4 *nec impune*). Whatever Caligula did in 39 belongs in neither group: 37.4 *ingentes Gai Caesaris minae in ludibrium uersae* ('Gaius Caesar's big threats ended up as a farce'). This 167-word digression, encapsulating all Rome's complex contact with the Germans, ends (37.5) with allusion to the uprising of Julius Civilis (69–70), 'occasioned by our discord and civil wars' (*occasione discordiae nostrae et ciuilium armorum*), and with a final epigram capturing the ineffectiveness and posturing of Domitian in 83, 'with the celebration of triumphs rather than actual victories' (37.5 *triumphati magis quam uicti*).

Historical digression occurs earlier in the *Germania*, at 33, where, in a much vaguer but potent way, history and the consequences of German contact for Rome's future also intrude into the ethnographical material. Tacitus alludes, with no apparent desire to inform readers about the event itself, to an event otherwise unknown to the record, and he does so to make a point, not about Germany, but about Rome and the limits of Empire. In a brief discussion of the Tencteri and Bructeri and the displacement of the latter by neighbouring tribes, Tacitus reflects on causality: did the other tribes go after the Bructeri through disgust at their arrogance or desire for plunder, or because 'the gods were on the side of Rome' (33.1 *seu fauore quodam erga nos deorum*)? Of the actual extermination, as it is presented (the claim is made of 60,000 dead), we know little. Candidates are events in 83 and 97,[12] but historical specificity does not matter, since Tacitus has a larger point. 'Long live intertribal hatred!', almost as good as sure alliance (33.2 *maneat, quaeso, duretque gentibus, si non amor nostri, at certe odium sui*), since the discord of our enemies is a great gift of fortune 'inasmuch as the destiny of our Empire presses hard' (33.2 *urgentibus imperii fatis*).

This last phrase is as controversial as any in Tacitus, not because *urgentibus*, surely correct, is only partially evidenced by the MSS (a few, including the *codex Aesinas*,[13] present *urgentibus iam*) but because some scholars need their historians to be optimists – this against the universal tendency of the Roman literary mentality to see decline and deterioration as natural forces. An enormous scholarly literature on this passage is still being produced,[14] but nothing can remove a sense of the Empire's necessary doom, communicated through the Latin language and through prominent intertexts such as Livy 5.22.8 on the fall of Veii and the passing of the Etruscan world after all their years of greatness and wealth, since 'in the final end destiny pressed hard' (*postremo iam fato quoque urgente*). Similarly Virgil on the dying Camilla at *Aen.* 11.587 *quandoquidem fatis urgetur acerbis* ('since she is oppressed by a harsh destiny'). Tacitus knew as well as Virgil that (*pace* Jupiter to the contrary) no Empire is *sine fine*. Here in 33 the digression ends with Rome helped, at least for the time being, by German discord, a neat anticipation and inversion of the Batavian revolt of 69,

---

[12] See Rives (1999) 257–8 on 33.1.
[13] For the *codex Aesinas* see below, pp. 246–8.
[14] See e.g. Lund (1991b) 2127–47 for a good summary of some of it; also above, p. 48 and n. 2.

where, as we saw, Roman discord becomes the cause: *occasione discordiae nostrae et ciuilium armorum* ('on the opportunity provided by our discord and civil war').

Ethnography and cultural poetics: Chauci to Cherusci (34–6)

The catalogue at 27.2–46 groups various tribes together, contrasts them, has them at odds with one another or with Rome, as Tacitus moves generally (but not always) from west to north and east. The result is a set of clusters, each with miniature narratives and colours, together creating an appealing ethnographical pastiche through vivid detail that the author has developed from his sources or – more frequently, I believe – from his own literary imagination. I turn to some of these.

In the historical digressions of *G.* 33 and 37 Tacitus focused on German *libertas*, intimations of Roman civil war and further intimations of Roman *imperium cum fine*. The material between these two digressions is on one level simply part of the catalogue of tribes that began at 27.2 and continues to the end of the work, as Tacitus moves north-east from the lower Rhine, with 34 devoted chiefly to the Angrivarii, Chamavi and getting us to the Frisii and the North Sea, 35 moving east to treat the Chauci, and 36 looping back south and focusing on the Cherusci, while 37 takes us north to the Cimbri. It is also the case that all the tribes treated from 38 will be generally classified as 'Suebi', so the tribes of 34–6 invite study as a unified section.

Well before Tacitus' time poets had subsumed the ethnographical tradition into treatments of cultural change. Virgil in particular in all three works (e.g. *Ecl.* 4; *G. passim*; *Aen.* 7.475–539; 8.314–46) had portrayed Italy throughout historical time in relationship to the Saturnian (golden) and Jovian (iron) ages. The result is a complex set of oppositions between the primitive and the civilised, spontaneous productivity and agriculture, peace and war, natural justice and the need for laws, and so on.[15] He did so moreover within the generic framework of ethnography, the form Tacitus elevated to the status of a genre in writing the *Germania*.[16] In the process Virgil created a way of talking about civilisation and culture that belongs as much to literature and the fantastic as it does to the world of history and science, and Tacitus cheerfully puts himself into that literary tradition. Virgil in particular complicates the ability to make clear-cut value judgements, and also presents us with versions of the primitive that are not always pleasant or immune to fault (*Aen.* 9.598–620).

---

[15] Thomas (2004); Feeney (2007) 108–37.
[16] See Thomas (1982) *passim*.

The *Germania* as literary text

Germania 34–6 fit into this tradition and conspire to define two German tribes as representing contrasting poles within the system of ethnographic cultural history. The Saturnian/primitive/golden age is often situated at the end of the world (Hyperboreans, Isles of the Blessed).[17] According to convention, the civiliser approaches the ends of the world; in mythology, but also in the *Germania*, this is Hercules and particularly Odysseus. Early in the work Tacitus reflects a centuries-old debate going back to Eratosthenes about how far Odysseus went and whether the Homeric wanderings were in fact in the Ocean.[18] The scholarly move was even given a name: *exōkeanismos*, 'setting out in the Ocean' (Strabo 1.2.37). So Odysseus, like Hercules, may even have reached the northern, Germanic, Ocean (3.2): *ceterum et Ulixen quidam opinantur longo illo et fabuloso errore in hunc Oceanum delatum adisse Germaniae terras* ('but some also think that Ulysses was transported in his long and storied wandering into this Ocean and got close to the territory of Germany'). Back in the real world of *G.* 34 the Romans are the new civilisers, and they look a lot like Odysseus (2): *ipsum quin etiam Oceanum illa temptauimus* ('in fact we have also made an assault on Ocean in that area'). The expedition of Drusus against the Chauci in 12 BC, which may have reached the Cimbrian peninsula and allowed Augustus to trumpet his claims to have boldly gone where no Roman had gone before (*Res Gestae* 26.4),[19] is presented in terms of cultural *audacia* ('boldness' or 'daring'), with Oceanus personified and resistant to the explorer: *nec defuit audentia Druso Germanico, sed obstitit Oceanus in se simul atque in Herculem inquiri* ('Drusus Germanicus had plenty of daring, but Ocean resisted inquiry on the subject of himself and of (the pillars of) Hercules').

The wording brings up some relevant intertexts. Most famously *audacia* in seafaring looks to Horace, *Carm.* 1.3, the poet's propemptikon to Virgil that quickly turns to criticism of man's seafaring: 21–4 *nequiquam deus abscidit | prudens Oceano dissociabili | terras, si tamen impiae | non tangenda rates transiliunt uada* ('in vain did the god in his foresight cut off the lands with separating Ocean, if in spite of that impious ships go racing across waters not meant to be touched'). Horace will go on to mention the canonical figures who did such things – Prometheus, Daedalus and, again, Hercules. Horace's poem is but the best-known instance of this theme,[20] and there is another that gets us close to Tacitus. Rives follows Labuske in taking the 23-line sole remnant of the writings of Albinovanus Pedo, quoted

---

[17] See Thomas (1982) 21–7.
[18] See Rives (1999) on 3.2.
[19] See Rives (1999) on 34.2.
[20] See Nisbet and Hubbard (1970) 44.

by Seneca the Elder at *Suas.* 1.15, as treating the expedition of Drusus.²¹ The subject of *Suas.* 1 is Ocean, with various disquisitions on whether it is, for Alexander as for others, the ultimate boundary of the world – not irrelevant to the treatment of Drusus at G. 34. But Courtney and Hollis are surely right to see the poem rather as treating a storm encountered by Drusus' son Germanicus – some years later in 16, but also taking place in the North Sea.²² Pedo was probably present (cf. Tac. *A.* 1.60.2) and Tacitus himself treats the incident at *A.* 2.23–4, in highly poetical mode.²³ Indeed Tacitus there engages in a demonstration of his own poetic powers, showing he can match the poets, Virgil and others, in storm-scene vividness (*enargeia*). '*Quo ferimur?*' ('Where are we being taken?'), asks a distraught bowman in Pedo's fragment, at the beginning of a speech posing in high rhetorical fashion a series of questions concerning their fate (16–23) and speculating on the world beyond Ocean to which they are being driven (18–19): *anne alio positas ultra sub cardine gentes | atque alium bellis intactum quaerimus orbem?* ('Are we seeking races set far off beneath a different pole, and a world untouched by war?').

Of Pedo's fragment Hollis notes that 'there may be hints of the Hyperboreans', citing Mela 3.5.36–7 *sub ipso siderum cardine … non bella nouere* ('under the very pole of the stars … they know no wars'), which makes certain the conjecture of *bellis* for meaningless *liberis* in Pedo.²⁴ This is the context into which I place G. 35–7 (on the Chauci, Cherusci and Cimbri). The Chauci are the more northern, bordering on Ocean, and there are cultural consequences to this removal. At the outset Tacitus makes it clear that he is shifting his gaze northward, beginning with the Chauci, whom he seems to situate on the North Sea as it curves up the Jutland peninsula, and ending with the Cimbri, situated on the northern tip of the peninsula. In the middle come the Cherusci (36), who have nothing to do with the north, but whose positioning supplies a cultural contrast. Once noble and just, they are now called lazy and stupid (36.1 *qui olim boni aequique Cherusci, nunc inertes ac stulti uocantur*), since they had nurtured a state of excessive and languid peace (*nimiam ac marcentem … pacem*), a deluded policy when one is surrounded by the violent and the strong (*quia inter impotentis et ualidos falso quiescas*).

The contrast with the Chauci (35) is marked. They too prefer peace, but a peace that is backed up by readiness of mind for battle and the equipment to sustain it. In chief they depend on justice, the source of their nobility:

---

[21] Rives (1999) 264–5 on 34.2; Labuske (1989).
[22] See Courtney (2003) 315–19 and 522; Hollis (2007) 373–81.
[23] See also above, pp. 5–6.
[24] Hollis (2007) 379 on 18–23.

The *Germania* as literary text

> tam immensum terrarum spatium non tenent tantum Chauci sed et implent, populus inter Germanos nobilissimus quique magnitudinem suam malit iustitia tueri. sine cupiditate, sine impotentia, quieti secretique nulla prouocant bella, nullis raptibus aut latrociniis populantur. id praecipuum uirtutis ac uirium argumentum est quod, ut superiores agant, non per iniurias assequuntur; prompta tamen omnibus arma ac, si res poscat, exercitus, plurimum uirorum equorumque; et quiescentibus eadem fama.

> Such a measureless area of territory is not merely occupied but actually filled up by the Chauci, the most noble people of all the Germans and one that prefers to preserve their greatness by the exercise of justice. They are free from greed and lack of self-control, tranquil and secluded they provoke no wars, and do not pillage by means of plundering or banditry. The chief proof of their excellence and strength is that their superior position is not achieved through injustice; nevertheless they are all ready for combat, with an abundance of armies, men and horses, should the situation require it. And their reputation is just as good when they are keeping the peace.

Not exactly the Hesiodic golden age, but a version of it, such as would be acceptable and plausible against the realities of a German tribe. Though ready for war, they keep the peace, lack avarice, are self-controlled and live by a voluntary code of justice.

Ethnographical *thaumata*: Fenni to Chatti (46)

Other tribes in the second half of the work are for the most part not viewed through the lens of cultural poetics, but, as we shall see, are notable mostly for the ethnographical *thaumata* (wonders) that Tacitus ties to them. There is one notable exception, those tribes with whom the work ends, truly inhabitants of the ends of the earth, the Fenni, Hellusii and Oxiones (46.3–4). The latter two are utterly beyond the pale (though Tacitus expresses scepticism: 46.4 *cetera iam fabulosa*, 'the rest is fairy tale'), with human faces but with the limbs and bodies of wild beasts (*ora hominum uultusque, corpora atque artus ferarum gerere*), ending his work in the world of the *Odyssey* and Herodotus 4.22–5. The same is doubtless true of the Fenni, but in Tacitus' description they are at least human, though a regression from the Chauci into a state of pure and complete primitiveness, 'the absolute antithesis of civilisation',[25] as far from Rome as one could get. They most closely resemble Lucretius' cavemen (5.925–87), the Scythians of *G.* 3.349–83, or the Fauns and Nymphs who inhabited Virgil's Latium before the exile Saturn arrived and brought on the Golden Age (*G.* 46.3): 'no arms, no horses, no homes;

---

[25] Rives (1999) 327.

their food grass, their clothing skins, their bed the ground' (*non arma, non equi, non penates; uictui herba, uestitui pelles, cubile humus*). The life they lead they consider more blessed (*beatius*) than that obtained by tilling fields, building houses or implicating their own and their neighbours' affairs in hope and fear. So, free from warfare, without care (*securi*) of human and divine they have attained a perfection based on utter lack of everything, reaching the most difficult state of having nothing for which they even need to pray. This ending has nothing to do with real Germans, everything to do with real Romans.

The catalogue of tribes that ends with the Fenni and fable begins with the Chatti (30–1), recently engaged by Domitian (pointedly unnoted by Tacitus), so we may assume there is truth to the details assigned to them. In the first of these chapters the Chatti receive their own ethnographical sketch: *situs* is vividly conveyed by poetic use of *raresco* (30.1 *durant siquidem montes, paulatim rarescunt*, 'even though the mountains last a long way, they gradually get lower'), and with personification of the Hercynian forest (*et Chattos suos saltus Hercynius prosequitur simul atque deponit*, 'the Hyrcanian glade escorts its Chatti all the way and puts them down (in the plain)'); their hardiness, a feature of Germans in general, is particularly marked (30.2 *duriora genti corpora*). This is matched by a greater intellectual power (*maior animi uigor*), and a quasi-Roman quality of discipline and trust in their leaders. The strength of their infantry (30.3 *omne robur in pedite*) aligns them with the Britons in the *Agricola* (12.1 *in pedite robur*). These warriors carry iron tools (*ferramentis*) with them, and, where others would go out to battle, you would see (*uideas*) the Chatti go out to war.[26] The passage as a whole is stylistically spare, a string of infinitives with direct objects. The effect is grim, as in the next chapter (31), which Tacitus devotes to odd ethnographical *thaumata* for which he may or may not have had evidence – there is none independent of the passage. The Chatti leave beard and hair uncut until they have had their first kill. Cowards and the unwarlike remain unkempt (*ignauis et imbellibus manet squalor*) and are put in the front rank in fighting, pointed at by the enemy and their own alike. The entire passage is haunted by a sense of strangeness.

Ending: amphiboly and sententious clausulae

The *Germania* remains an opaque work, holding different purposes for different readers: to some it delights, to others it instructs, others find a prelude

---

[26] *uideas*, the only example of this verb in the second-person present subjunctive in Tacitus, is intended to communicate vividness: see Gilmartin (1975) 103; and also below, p. 154.

to invasion, while yet others see it as extolling primitivism and holding up the German as a model of what Rome has ceased to be, the Empire headed towards its inevitable demise. The work's resistance to ultimate and universally accepted conclusions is in part due to the difficulty of voice. Narration and focalisation blur into each other and this occurs frequently in the epigrammatic utterances, where sententious and frequently ambiguous clausulae leave the reader wondering about the work's larger purposes. This is of course true of Tacitus' later works, where the *sententiae* often carry much of the explosive force this author holds in check with the idiosyncracy of his writing.[27] It is therefore instructive to see the epigrams of the *Germania* as propaedeutic to those that were to come. A few examples: 5.2 *argentum et aurum propitiine an irati di negauerint dubito* ('whether it is out of kindness or anger that the gods have denied them silver and gold I do not know'). This serves as an arch comment on Rome as much as on Germany, with the non-committal *aporia* deepening the sense of irony. At 6.4, concluding a section on the manner of warfare and the disgrace involved with abandoning the shield, Tacitus concludes on a grim note: *multique superstites bellorum infamiam laqueo finierunt* ('and many such survivors of wars have ended their ill repute with a noose'). Elsewhere we find a pair of *sententiae*, the first capturing the paradox that the best warriors in peacetime hand operations over to women and the elderly: 15.1 *iidem homines sic ament inertiam et oderint quietem* ('the same men both love idleness and hate peacefulness'); then on gift-giving among tribes (horses, weapons, etc.), involving money only after contact with Rome: 15.2 *iam et pecuniam accipere docuimus* ('we have taught them to take money as well').

This manner predominates where Rome is explicitly or implicitly present. So at 19.2, on the absence of divorce and on the killing of children born after the drawing up of the will (*agnati*): *plusque ibi boni mores ualent quam alibi bonae leges* ('good character has more power there than good laws elsewhere'); at 25.2 the 'lack of status of freedmen is evidence of freedom' (*impares libertini libertatis argumentum sunt*), developed at *A.* 14.39.2 where it is explicitly aimed at the Roman elevation of freedmen in the Empire: Nero's freedman Polyclitus, so far from being able to negotiate with rebellious Britons, is mocked by them because 'the power of freedmen was as yet unknown, since freedom still flourished among them'. At 34.2 Tacitus implicitly criticises the failure of Romans after Drusus to explore the northern reaches of Ocean: *sanctius ac reuerentius uisum de actis deorum credere quam scire* ('it has seemed more religious and reverent to believe in the works of the gods than to find out about them'). Similarly the epigram

---

[27] See below, pp. 202–3.

at 37.5 fairly or otherwise belittles Domitian's campaign against the Chatti: *proximis temporibus triumphati magis quam uicti sunt* ('in recent years they have been triumphed over more than actually defeated'), and there is the insinuation – 'a cynical epigram', in the words of Birley[28] – at 42.2 about the financial (rather than military) support of German kings: *raro armis nostris, saepius pecunia iuuantur, nec minus ualent* ('occasionally we help them with our armies, more often, with money, just as effective').

Instruction, delectation, exhortation to conquest or muted diatribe against Rome? We will never know for sure, but the *Germania* is clearly rehearsing much that will reach maturity in the larger historical works to come. It may not be the literary masterpiece that those works clearly constitute, and its reception and infamy in the twentieth century are out of proportion to its actual merits,[29] but it is in its very strangeness an attractive study, a senatorial view of an alien culture, with Rome, equally alien at times, always part of the mix.

FURTHER READING

Most work on the *Germania* is in German. Lund (1991b) is an invaluable and comprehensive collection of the bibliography, with summaries and assessments provided. Among scholarship since Lund, O'Gorman (1993) is of some interest, while Birley (1999) has a good general introduction. Krebs (2005) chapter 2 ('Tacitus' *imago Germaniae* aus der Perspektive ihrer Wirkungsgeschichte') sees the work as educating Romans with an eye to Roman conquest; Rives (1999) is valuable for historical commentary, but also for much on literary and rhetorical aspects of Tacitus.

---

[28] Birley (1999) 129.
[29] For this see below, pp. 295–9.

5

SANDER M. GOLDBERG

The faces of eloquence: the *Dialogus de oratoribus*

Few live in a Golden Age. Fewer still ever know that they do. Even Cicero thought eloquence in short supply among his contemporaries, and complaints and regrets over oratory's diminishing quality mounted among his successors. The laments usually came embedded in a wider discourse of decline that tied oratory's downward trajectory to the indolence, greed and intellectual laxity of a grasping and complacent world: Romans were not inclined to fault their political system for the problem. Seneca the Elder, the first imperial author to address the question of decline, shrugs off a political explanation, and a century later the Greek author of the famous treatise *On the Sublime* flatly rejects what he calls 'that old cliché' that oratory flourishes with freedom and withers under tyranny. The cliché as he knew it derived from the Attic canon of orators, which implicitly identified great oratory with the death struggles of the independent polis, but the treatise reveals its Roman orientation by preferring a familiar Roman reason for oratory's plight, namely, undue love of wealth and pleasure.[1]

Romans of the first century AD may well have hesitated to follow the political thread of the argument to their emperor's door, but intimidation was not the only reason to hesitate. Those of a historical bent might conclude from the Republic's demise that not liberty but licence had nourished the eloquence of its oratorical Golden Age, and they might well prefer other measures of oratorical success. What might these be, and at what cost do they come? Did modern oratory remain worthy of its illustrious past? The fraught complexity of such questions finds its frankest exploration in that great anomaly of the Tacitean corpus, the *Dialogus de oratoribus*.

---

[1] [Longinus], *Subl.* 44. Petron. *Sat.* 88 makes a similar point with more irony than earnestness. Serious Roman discussions include Sen. *Controv.* 1 praef. 6–7; Vell. Pat. 1.16–17; Plin. *HN* 14.2–6; Sen. *Ep.* 114; Pers. 1. Williams (1978) 6–25 provides a convenient survey. Cf. Cic. *Off.* 2.67; *De or.* 1.19–20 on the contemporary *eloquentium paucitas*. He attributes the problem to the rigours of proper oratorical training, but Caesar's dictatorship was no doubt an inhibiting factor. See Heldmann (1982) 207–13; Dugan (2005) 177–89.

The work is not a treatise, not a history and not written in 'Tacitean' style. Created at an uncertain date and for an uncertain readership, it ranks among the most fascinating and problematic literary documents of the late Principate.[2] Not even its subject is entirely clear, although a central theme is established at once (1.1):

> Saepe ex me requiris, Iuste Fabi, cur, cum priora saecula tot eminentium oratorum ingeniis gloriaque floruerint, nostra potissimum aetas deserta et laude eloquentiae orbata uix nomen ipsum oratoris retineat; neque enim ita appellamus nisi antiquos, horum autem temporum diserti causidici et aduocati et patroni et quiduis potius quam oratores uocantur.

> You often ask me, Justus Fabius, why, although earlier epochs teemed with the talents and fame of so many distinguished orators, it is especially our own age which, barren and bereft of praise for eloquence, barely retains even the name 'orator'. Indeed, our age calls only the ancients by that title, while the skilful speakers of these days are called pleaders and advocates and attorneys and anything rather than orators.

The question never receives an unequivocal answer in an authorial voice. Tacitus instead reports a conversation on this topic that he claims to have witnessed in his youth (1.2 *iuuenis admodum audiui*). Like Cicero in *De oratore*, he projects a discussion of present concerns into the past, though what he intends by his Ciceronian allusions, what he himself thinks of his characters' arguments and even what he means by 'laus eloquentiae' never become explicit.[3]

The dramatic date of the conversation is 75, six years into Vespasian's reign. Recitation of a *Cato* by the senator Curiatius Maternus, who has abandoned his oratorical career to write plays, caused offence in high places. The next day, his friends Marcus Aper and Julius Secundus pay a visit and urge him to forgo such risky ventures. Aper speaks passionately of oratory's traditional role in Roman life and of Maternus' obligation to resume his forensic pursuits. In doing so, Aper shows little tolerance for the poets' effete and affected world, nor does he concede any decline in the orator's social standing, power or eloquence. His very language rejects Fabius Justus' initial premise (e.g. 6.1 *oratoria eloquentia*; 7.3 *oratorum gloria*). Maternus' spirited rejoinder on poetry's behalf (11–13) is then quickly followed by

---

[2] Its dedicatee, Fabius Justus, became suffect consul in 102, which may have provided the occasion for publication, but dates ranging from 96 to c. 105 have been advanced. See Murgia (1980), (1985); Brink (1994a); Mayer (2001) 22–7.

[3] See Haß-von Reitzenstein (1970) for the structural affinities of Tacitus and Cicero; Mayer (2001) 27–31 for the linguistic ones. Tacitus' self-effacement, however, is distinctly un-Ciceronian, withholding historical context even as it establishes literary context. See Levene (2004) 191–5.

the arrival of another visitor, Vipstanus Messalla (14.1), who vehemently champions 'ancient' over contemporary oratory (25–6) and, when asked to identify the causes of oratory's apparent decline, faults the modern system of education (28–35).[4] To this Maternus replies that each age gets the oratory it requires. A return to Ciceronian eloquence might seem a fine thing, but not if it meant reverting to the social discord that motivated it. Who would prefer the cacophony of the late Republic to the tranquillity of the present, when affairs of state rest not with an ignorant mob but with the one wisest and most capable citizen (41.4 *sapientissimus et unus*)? Messalla is prepared to disagree, but the hour is late, so the conversation quickly ends with good-natured laughter and an affectionate departure. They have all debated these issues before (4.1, 15.1) and will certainly do so again.

The conversation is of course a fiction, but the speakers are real. Tacitus calls Aper and Secundus his teachers (2.1), and Secundus is also recalled with affection by Quintilian. Vipstanus Messalla appears in Tacitus' *Histories*: he commanded a legion in 69, and then in 70, while still in his early 20s, secured his reputation as an orator when he came to the defence of his half-brother M. Aquilius Regulus, a notorious Neronian prosecutor.[5] Tacitus thus endows him with a young man's talent for seeing complex issues simply. Only Curiatius Maternus remains unidentified, though he is not for that reason likely to be fictional: his allusion to 'breaking the power of Vatinius' probably conceals a contemporary reference (11.2). All three speakers remain in character, and their dialogue moves easily from the relative merits of poetry and oratory (Aper and Maternus) to the current state of oratory (Aper and Messalla) to the role of oratory in the contemporary world (Maternus, responding to Aper's initial claim). Their arguments are so adroitly interwoven that no one 'winner' emerges and no one view is clearly Tacitus' own, but the *Dialogus* is widely understood as a study in oratorical decline and its causes.

There are good reasons for this view. Individual characters attract or repel us, and the resulting personal engagement inevitably colours the response to their arguments. Not only does Aper, a self-made man from Gaul, defend contemporary oratory with a shameless, brash self-confidence that puts

---

[4] Messalla's late arrival may recall that of Alcibiades in Plato's *Symposium*. See Allison (1999); Rutledge (2000). Secundus alone has no formal speech in the *Dialogus*: the lacuna in our text before 38 is not long enough to have contained one, nor does Ciceronian precedent suggest a fourth speaker. See Murgia (1981); Häussler (1986) 73–7; Haß-von Reitzenstein (1970) 106–11.

[5] Cf. *H.* 3.9.3; 4.42.1. He also wrote a military memoir, which Tacitus consulted (*H.* 3.25.2, 28.1). Secundus appears at Quint. *Inst.* 10.1.120–2, 3.12–15; 12.10.11. Aper is otherwise unknown. For these figures in their contemporary context, see Brink (1993) 338–46.

many modern critics on edge, but other speakers repeatedly question his sincerity.[6] Forceful and passionate – Tacitus may play on his name at 11.1 (*aper* = 'boar') – he invariably strikes wrong notes along with right ones. His truthful and frank explication of oratory's role in Roman society and of a senator's responsibilities towards his clients may be undermined by his avowed models, Eprius Marcellus, Vibius Crispus and Cassius Severus (8.1–4; 19). Marcellus and Crispus grew immensely rich by pursuing accusations against their fellow senators: their very names recall the vicious oratory of the imperial prosecutors (*delatores*) that is often taken as a symptom, if not a cause, of oratory's debasement in the first century.[7] Theirs is the eloquence Maternus soon condemns as mercenary and bloodstained (12.2 *lucrosa et sanguinans eloquentia*). Cassius Severus, whom Aper takes as the pioneer of the new, practical oratory he champions, was not himself a *delator*, but was famously acerbic and aggressive, and overly fond of prosecution.[8] How, we might wonder, could oratory take a turn for the better under his influence?

The figures arguing for oratory's decline are far more sympathetic. Though Messalla, the one speaker to embrace the thesis explicitly (15.1), is somewhat prissy in his dedication to tradition, his excess is easily excused as the over-exuberance of youth and he has admirable predecessors. His argument for broad and rigorous education recalls Crassus' position in *De oratore*; behind his condemnation of affected speech lie the arguments of Quintilian's (lost) treatise on the corruption of diction (*De causis corruptae eloquentiae*) and the reformist agenda of the *Institutio oratoria*. His distaste for declamation as an educational tool sits well with modern critics who trace the decline of much imperial literature to the artificialities and absurdities that declamation encouraged.[9] Maternus, the one person in the group to make sacrifices and to take risks in defence of his convictions, evokes even greater sympathy. His concluding speech is often taken to be ironic in its praise of the Principate, but, even if we resist that reading, its abject surrender to the times produces a strikingly deflating view of oratory. Modern readers moved by Tacitus' historical narratives to take a dark view of political life in first-century Rome readily find in these speeches not just

---

[6] Maternus at 16.3 and 24.1–2; Messalla at 15.2 and 28.1. Their language recalls the similar comment made about Antonius at Cic. *De or.* 1.263, with some accommodation by Antonius himself at 2.40, but Aper never suggests he is merely the devil's advocate.

[7] So Syme (1958a) 331–3 and especially Winterbottom (1964) 90–4.

[8] Sen. *Controv.* 3 praef. 1–7; Quint. *Inst.* 10.1.116–17; 11.1.57; Macrob. *Sat.* 2.4.9. See Rutledge (2001) 209–12; Heldmann (1982) 163–98.

[9] On Messalla's echoes of Cicero and Quintilian, see Brink (1989) 484–94. Scholarly appreciation of declamation has revived, though traces of the old prejudice remain. See Kaster (2001).

the proof of Fabius Justus' initial premise, but the conviction that Tacitus shared it.

Yet there are reasons to hesitate. Tacitus says in the preface that Fabius' presumption of oratorical decline is widely held, but that is not the same as saying it is true. His only first-person singular statement is a refusal to venture an opinion (1.2): 'cui percontationi tuae respondere, et tam magnae quaestionis pondus excipere … uix hercle auderem si mihi mea sententia proferenda' ('I would scarcely dare to reply to your earnest inquiry and to assume the burden of so great a question if I had to offer my own opinion'). The false modesty of this hesitation is common in dedicatory prefaces – Cicero's *Orator* provides a close verbal parallel – but authors do not commonly advance a substantive thesis in such a preface only to back away from it in this way. Tacitus' traditional pose produces a unique effect. Nor is Aper, his champion of modernity, as easy to dismiss as some have wished. There had always been resistance to the palpable snobbishness behind modern distaste for the *arriviste* Aper. Now there is reason to doubt its substance. The Ciceronian model suggests balance in dialogues of this sort, a genuine dialectic in the Academic style of arguing both sides of a question, and Aper's position actually has much to commend it.[10]

First, Eprius Marcellus and Vibius Crispus cannot simply be dismissed as models of villainy. They did indeed grow rich prosecuting under Nero, and they are memorably paired in Tacitus' *Histories*, scurrying for shelter in 70 when the senate tried to rise against the Neronian *delatores* (H. 4.43.2). Aper's acknowledgement that they were morally compromised (8.3 'neuter moribus egregius') finds ample confirmation in the pages of the *Histories* and *Annals*. Yet the full story is more complex. Prosecution was not in itself an evil. Though it could be abused, as it certainly was under Tiberius, civil order is impossible without it (cf. Cic. *Off*. 2.49–51), and even Tacitus' Messalla acknowledges without complaint that the prosecution of distinguished elders was a traditional route to advancement for ambitious young men (37.7). He himself defended a *delator*, his half-brother Regulus, and Maternus' allusion to 'shattering the power of Vatinius' sounds very like a past prosecution. The great fault was to be *only* a prosecutor, which was not the case for either Marcellus or Crispus.[11] Both men were in other respects neither unrefined nor unaccomplished. Marcellus was already in middle age, a distinguished orator with a long string of magistracies behind him, when

---

[10] Champion (1994) and Goldberg (1999) argue for the rehabilitation of Aper, but see now Dammer (2005).

[11] For prosecution as governmental necessity, see Crook (1995) 138–9; Rutledge (2001) 9–16, 175–81, and for the careers of Marcellus and Crispus, Rutledge (2001) 225–8 and 278–82 respectively.

catapulted to wealth by the condemnation of Thrasea Paetus in 66. Other prosecutions followed, but after the upheavals of 69 Marcellus went on to serve Vespasian as proconsul of Asia for an extraordinary three-year term and held a final consulship in 74. Crispus, too, was a distinguished orator before becoming notorious as a prosecutor, and though nearly 60 by the end of Nero's reign, he held important consular appointments under Vespasian, including the proconsulship of Africa, and then a third consulship under Domitian.

The two men cultivated very different styles of speaking. Marcellus could be savage and belligerent (*A.* 16.29.1 'toruus ac minax'), but 'agreeable' and 'elegant' are Quintilian's words for Crispus (*Inst.* 5.13.48 'uir ingenii iucundi et elegantis'; cf. 10.1.119; Juv. 4.81–3), and he recommends the reading of Crispus' speeches. There was clearly no uniform manner associated with *delatores*, which is why Aper can in the same breath praise the eloquence of both Messalla and Regulus (15.1). The blunt and brutal style often imputed to the *delatores* is largely a modern construct owing more to the personal prejudices of Tacitus and Pliny than to the historical record.[12] Marcellus and Crispus were not paragons, but they were nonetheless distinguished magistrates and successful orators. Their careers illustrate less the corruption of eloquence than the problematic relationship between rhetoric and morality. That is a dilemma hardly unique to the Principate: Quintilian's insistence that a good orator had to be a good man looked back to Cato over two centuries before and is pursued at such length precisely because the question is so complex (*Inst.* 12.1). Men like Marcellus and Crispus are not easily characterised.

This more nuanced view of *delatores* and their oratory invites a broader challenge to the thesis of oratorical decline. Oratory certainly changed in the course of the first century. Important orators such as Cassius Severus and Galerius Trachalus were said to be better heard than read. Their speeches must have contained fewer of the stylistic flourishes that text-based criticism delights in revealing, but that does not mean such texts were unworthy of study.[13] Quintilian traces a history without break from Cicero to Asinius Pollio, Domitius Afer, Julius Africanus and beyond without a hint of regret for a lost standard. 'Those who write about oratory after us', he concludes, 'will have abundant material for genuine praise among those active today ... Those in their prime rival the ancients, and the diligence of the aspiring young imitates and follows them' (*Inst.* 10.1.122). Tacitus wrote an example

---

[12] Rutledge (1999) 566–72. Pliny's personal dislike of Aquilius Regulus has done much to feed the stereotype. For Regulus' career, see Rutledge (2001) 192–8.

[13] Sen. *Controv.* 3 *praef.* 3; Quint. *Inst.* 10.1.119. Yet Demades kept his place in the Attic canon without any speeches extant (Cic. *Brut.* 36, Quint. *Inst.* 12.10.49).

of such diligence into the *Dialogus* in the form of his own youthful self in silent attendance on his elders. Messalla's complaint that aspiring orators no longer apprentice themselves to successful practitioners in the traditional way is thus refuted by the work's very *mise-en-scène*, and we know that by 104 or so Tacitus had himself assumed the master's role formerly played by Aper and Secundus: Pliny asked him to recommend potential tutors from among the youth of his entourage (*Ep.* 4.13.10 'copia studiosorum'). The earnest, honest discourse of the *Dialogus* is not itself an advertisement for decline.

We also know, though sometimes forget, that Roman book culture continued to ensure the celebrity of successful orators, much as Aper claimed. Tacitus himself told his friend Pliny of a chance encounter in the Circus, where an impromptu literary conversation with a stranger led the man to ask who he was. When Tacitus said (with evident pride), 'You know me from your reading', the man immediately asked, 'Are you Tacitus or Pliny?' Since Pliny published no monographs and Tacitus published neither letters nor epigrams, what linked the two authors in the stranger's mind must have been their published speeches.[14] The letter is dated c. 106–7, i.e. after the *Dialogus* and well after the excitement of 99/100, when Tacitus and Pliny together successfully prosecuted the corrupt provincial governor Marius Priscus. Pliny took great pride in the result, 'renowned for the celebrity of the defendant, beneficial for the severity of the example, lasting for the significance of the issue' (*Ep.* 2.11.1). If Tacitus had a different view, it has left no trace. His encounter in the Circus only confirms what Quintilian implies and Pliny's correspondence often illustrates: speeches still circulated, still made reputations and were still sources of pride to their authors. The decline that modern eyes read into the history of imperial oratory is not what Quintilian saw in it, nor is it reflected in the careers of men like Tacitus and Pliny.[15]

Context is key. Debate over the *Dialogus* often turns less on what the text says than on the choice of background against which it is read. Biography is an important part of that context. The author of the *Dialogus* is not necessarily the gloomy ironist of the historical writings. Tacitus, like Pliny,

---

[14] Tacitus in Plin. *Ep.* 9.23.2–3: '"Nosti me, et quidem ex studiis." Ad hoc illum: "Tacitus es an Plinius?"' *studia* (lit. 'studies') clearly means 'forensic speeches' at Plin. *Ep.* 4.16.1; 6.2.2, 11.3; *D.* 15.1 might be added. Pliny and Tacitus are also paired as orators in *Ep.* 7.20.5–6. Sherwin-White (1966) 506–7 notes this anecdote's similarity to Aper's claim at *D.* 7.4. Cf. his sneer at 10.2 that tourists rarely ask to see a poet. Mayer (2001) 6 ignores this evidence in claiming that Tacitus published no speeches.

[15] Crook (1995) 180–7 draws the appropriate conclusion. No contemporary evidence supports Syme (1958a) 465 and Mayer (2001) 7–8 in their belief that the *Dialogus* reflects Tacitus' disillusion with oratory after the trial of Priscus.

actually lived the kind of life Aper extols, and he prospered no less under Domitian than under Trajan. In assessing his attitude toward oratory, we need to remember that other 'Tacitus', the prominent orator and distinguished public servant whose long list of honours once made an impressive display on the Via Nomentana.[16]

A second ingredient of context, easier to acknowledge than to add to the reckoning, is the effect of time on the substance of argument. Maternus' notorious dismissal of liberty as licence, for example, has long been recognised as an explicit contradiction, even parody, of a claim Cicero made in his own history of oratory, the *Brutus*:[17]

> nec enim in constituentibus rem publicam nec in bella gerentibus nec in impeditis ac regum dominatione deuinctis nasci cupiditas dicendi solet. pacis est comes otique socia et iam bene constitutae ciuitatis quasi alumna quaedam eloquentia. (Cic. *Brut.* 45)

Not among those ordering a government or waging wars or hampered and bound by the domination of kings is the desire for speaking accustomed to be born. Eloquence is the companion of peace and the ally of leisure and, as it were, a kind of nursling of a well-ordered state.

> Non de otiosa et quieta re loquimur et quae probitate et modestia gaudeat, sed est magna illa et notabilis eloquentia alumna licentiae, quam stulti libertatem uocant, comes seditionum, effrenati populi incitamentum, sine obsequio sine seueritate, contumax temeraria adrogans, quae in bene constitutis ciuitatibus non oritur. (*D.* 40.2)

We are not speaking about a leisured and calm thing that delights in respectability and modesty, but that great and notable eloquence that is the nursling of a licence fools call liberty, a companion of sedition, an inducement for an unbridled people, without deference, without dignity, a stubborn, rash, arrogant thing that does not arise in well-ordered states.

Tacitus boldly eliminates all apology for the metaphor and extends the personification of *eloquentia*. His sentiment is even bolder. Behind Maternus' repudiation of eloquence lies a redefinition of the well-ordered state and its requirements: Vespasian's Rome, not Cicero's, is now the ideal. This

---

[16] For Tacitus' public career, see Birley (2000a), esp. 238–47 on his later years. The funerary inscription found along the Via Nomentana is *CIL* 6.41106. For the relationship of Pliny and Tacitus, see Griffin (1999) and, with special attention to the *Dialogus*, Dominik (2007); also above, pp. 32–5.

[17] There are additional echoes, most notably Cic. *De or.* 2.35 ('et languentis populi incitatio et effrenati moderatio') and *Rep.* 1.68 ('ex hac nimia licentia, quam illi solam libertatem putant'), but the intellectual engagement is clearly with *Brut.* 45. For the rest see Gudeman (1914) 497–9.

preference for order over eloquence, so inconsistent with Maternus' earlier commitment to outspoken tragedy, is fundamental to the argument that his praise of the Principate is not what it seems: 'Maternus' critique of freedom is a statement whose foundation rests on a view that radically denies the disjunction between liberty and order. Is Cicero then to be numbered, we ask, among the *stulti*? – a question that serves to render our acceptance of the surface meaning somewhat vulnerable to doubt.'[18] That doubt lies, in one form or another, behind most interpretations of the *Dialogus* as oratory's obituary and post-mortem, but it reckons without one historical reality.

A century and more separate Tacitean text and Ciceronian intertext, years that brought not just the destruction of the Republic and emergence of a new imperial system, but a fundamental change in the memory, and thus the very meaning, of the defunct Republic.[19] Readers of Tacitus' generation were well schooled in the conflicts and corruptions of that dying state, which they often saw through Cicero's eyes: the Catilinarians, Verrines, Philippics and *Pro Milone* were mainstays of the curriculum. What would an experienced, dedicated public administrator like Tacitus think of a political system that spawned Catiline's plots and Verres' excesses, which dwarfed those of a Marius Priscus? Tacitus' very belatedness enabled him to see beyond the arguments of the *Brutus* to the governmental failures of the late Republic, and he knew the price Cicero soon paid for the hollow eloquence of the Philippics. We need not number Cicero among the *stulti* to believe that the ensuing years taught his successors new ways to think about *libertas* and its alternatives. What matters for understanding the *Dialogus* is less *our* Cicero than the Cicero of Tacitus and his contemporaries.

Historicising the text, however, does not solve all its problems. Contradictions remain, and some readers therefore seek new strategies for reading that need not presume more coherence than the text actually offers. A rhetorical approach, for example, one that values well-crafted argument and immediate effects over the consistency and coherence prized by modern readers, could provide a more fruitful way to understand the complexities and apparent contradictions we inevitably encounter. Romans did not necessarily read as we do or expect what we expect in a text.[20] Tacitus' calculated juxtapositions and inconcinnities still draw readers into the discussion: much of the current scholarly debate is in fact a continuation

---

[18] Bartsch (1994) 111. For other explanations of the contradiction, see Luce (1993) 22–5; Winterbottom (2001) 150–4.
[19] See especially Gowing (2005) 109–20 and, for the evolution of Cicero's reputation in the first century, Winterbottom (1982) 238–44.
[20] So Luce (1993) 33–8 and, from a different perspective, Levene (2004) 195–7.

of positions advanced by Maternus, Aper, and Messalla. But what is the argument really about? Where does the *Dialogus* fit in the larger scheme of Roman literary discourse?

The fact that some truth lies in each speech and some of Tacitus in each speaker means that no part of the work is dispensable. The initial discussion of poetry is therefore not simply a frame for the rhetorical discussion that follows but a demand that we understand *eloquentia* as a quality common to poetry and oratory. The *Dialogus* thus places itself in the larger literary history that Romans worked hard, though somewhat idiosyncratically, to create for themselves.[21] Yet it makes rather odd use of literary history. Aper, for example, evokes the dreary milieu of the recitation hall in terms that Juvenal later made notorious (Juv. 1.1–21; 7.36–59), but his claim that poetry suits only those unfit for public life is untrue as well as unfair. Ovid is the obvious exception to Aper's rule, but others run the gamut from Lucilius, who chose poetry over a senatorial career, to Pomponius Secundus, who pursued both. Tacitus never grounds literary claims in the facts or the arguments of literary history, a refusal that leads to striking distortions and some peculiar appeals.

Maternus' first speech on the allure of poetry is replete with historical inconsistencies. His desire to retreat to 'woods and groves' for writing his verses is of course a commonplace: Horace and Virgil had long since rung the changes on that idea.[22] Maternus then praises such rustic haunts for producing the very language of poetry (12.2):

> haec eloquentiae primordia, haec penetralia; hoc primum habitu cultuque commoda mortalibus in illa casta et nullis contacta uitiis pectora influxit: sic oracula loquebantur.
>
> These places are the origins of eloquence, these are its sanctuaries. In this guise and manner eloquence first made itself agreeable to mortals and flowed into breasts still pure and touched by no vices. Thus did oracles speak.

With this claim, however, the argument moves from commonplace to absurdity. Roman poets had spent the last three centuries striving to escape the speech of rustics and oracles. Ennius, Rome's first great epic poet, proudly left behind the kind of verses that 'fauns and seers used to sing' (*Ann.* 206–7) and, when it came to matters of diction and metre, Horace expected poetry to shake off all traces of the country (*Epist.* 2.1.160). The pastoral

---

[21] Schwindt (2000) 22–46 examines the Roman way of doing literary history. For the *Dialogus* in this context, see Schwindt (2000) 196–206 and esp. Levene (2004).

[22] E.g. Hor. *Epist.* 2.2.65–86; Virg. G. 2.475–540. (Maternus quotes G. 2.475 at D. 13.5.) Aper's words at 9.6 ('utque ipsi dicunt in nemora et lucos') declare the commonplace, confirmed by Quint. *Inst.* 10.3.22. Whether Plin. *Ep.* 1.6.2 and 9.10.2 echo Tacitus or vice versa, the cliché remains a cliché. See also above, pp. 32–3.

world that Maternus extols is a fiction. The country was always important to Roman poets, but primarily as a foil to the city. Elegy, satire and epigram are urban at their core. In tragedy, Maternus' chosen field of endeavour, woods and groves are fonts of evil (e.g. Sen. *Thy.* 650–6; *Oed.* 530–47), and Maternus conveniently forgets that the contemporary tragedian he professes to admire, Pomponius Secundus, was a consul and provincial governor and won triumphal honours for military success in Germany. Maternus' idea of poetic calm is thus every bit as affected as Aper asserts.

The defence of modernity in Aper's second speech strikes other familiar notes. Its assault on 'antiquity' as a critical term recalls the argument Horace reduced to absurdity in his letter to Augustus: if poems, like wine, improve with age, how many years does it take to turn a bad poem into a good one? So Aper asks how many years it would take to turn Cicero and Pollio, whose speeches their own grandfathers could have heard, into 'ancients'.[23] Messalla will dismiss this line of argument as a quibble (25.1–2), but the Horatian recollection signals Aper's serious intent. Behind this challenge to the authority of the past lie, for him no less than for Horace, two great bugbears of literary history, periodisation and canonicity, and Aper promptly adds a third when he remarks that eloquence has no single face (18.3). This too is neither a new nor unexpected observation, but its context is both. Cicero and Quintilian made this point in introducing the wide range of styles an accomplished speaker must master.[24] Aper's observation is not technical but historical, embedded in a survey of past orators that challenges the authority of the defunct and the superseded.

This is significant because Romans generally tied the history of oratory to the education of orators: the past is a model for the future. Yet conditions change, as does language itself. When does the old simply become the old-fashioned? Cicero touched on this problem in the *Brutus* when he cast Cato as the Lysias of his evolutionary scheme, only to concede, in response to Atticus' amused objection, that, for all his virtues, the antique Cato was hardly a Lysias.[25] Aper recalls Atticus' laughter (21.1), and with it the underlying problem of putting an appropriate value on the past. All three of Tacitus' speakers struggle with this problem, and Quintilian, too, felt it keenly as he sought to balance the benefit of studying earlier works with

---

[23] Aper's argument at *D.* 16.4 recalls Hor. *Epist.* 2.1.34–49; at 18.3 (valuing the old over the new) the echo is of *Epist.* 2.1.76–8.
[24] So Quint. *Inst.* 12.10.69, introducing the three styles, and Cic. *De or.* 3.34, introducing the four qualities of good style.
[25] *Brut.* 293, responding to Cicero's claim at 68. See Schwindt (2000) 106–12. Dugan (2005) 189–204 phrases the problem of 'placing' Lysias in terms of synchronic and diachronic narrative. For the importance of placement in literary history, see Levene (2000) 159–61.

the danger of being inhibited by them (e.g. *Inst.* 2.5.21; 8.5.32; 10.1.43) or, as he was beginning to fear, of reducing them to reservoirs of the odd and archaic.

That third possibility, along with the stylistic affectations it would introduce, still lay over the horizon, where it had best remain. An essay on Tacitus and the oratory he knew needs to stop before Fronto and Gellius come into sight, but it is typical of the *Dialogus* to suggest more than it says and to point ahead as well as behind. Its own placement in a master discourse – intellectual biography? political commentary? rhetorical theory? literary history? – will likely remain unresolved, and that very ambivalence is central to its appeal. The dialogue continues.

FURTHER READING

The landmark commentary of Gudeman (1914) remains valuable for its wealth of comparanda, but readers will naturally look first to more modern editions. Anglophone readers are especially well served by Mayer (2001), very strong on matters of style and structure though conservative, on occasion even reactionary, in its literary judgements. Costa (1969) provides a good general introduction, Luce (1993) a rich and keenly reasoned analysis of the main interpretative problems. Helpful bibliographic review is provided by Bo (1993).

The *Dialogus* has begun attracting attention as a cultural, not just a narrowly rhetorical, document. The trend began with Williams (1978) 26–51. Especially important are Bartsch (1994) 98–125, Levene (2004), and Van den Berg (2006).

6

RHIANNON ASH

Fission and fusion: shifting Roman identities in the *Histories*

Introduction

When Pliny the Younger wrote to his friend Titinius Capito explaining his current reluctance to follow in the footsteps of his formidable uncle Pliny the Elder and write a historical work, one reason for his hesitation stands out sharply (*Ep.* 5.8.12):

> tu tamen iam nunc cogita quae potissimum tempora aggrediamur. uetera et scripta aliis? parata inquisitio, sed onerosa collatio. intacta et noua? graues offensae, leuis gratia.

> However, be considering already now what time period in particular I should tackle. Olden times which others have written about? The material is at hand, but collating it will be hard work. Recent times untouched [by others]? There is huge potential to offend, but little chance to please.

Pliny eloquently encapsulates here the Scylla and Charybdis confronting any historian considering appropriate subject matter for his projected work.[1]

When Tacitus contemplated his first foray into the genre of history after publishing his so-called minor works,[2] he too faced difficult choices about the chronological boundaries of his historical narrative. As it happens, his audience probably already had expectations about the likely subject matter, expectations raised by Tacitus himself. In the *Agricola* (3.3) Tacitus implies that he is planning a future historical narrative covering the principates of Domitian (81–96), Nerva (96–8) and Trajan (98–117):[3] 'non tamen pigebit uel incondita ac rudi uoce memoriam prioris seruitutis ac testimonium

---

[1] Ash (2003) discusses this letter.
[2] For the publication dates of the minor works see above, p. 31.
[3] The fact that Trajan was in power when Tacitus planned his historiographical debut potentially made him a less attractive focal point for a historical narrative, since anyone writing about the current Empire and publishing the work during that emperor's lifetime risked charges of positive bias (cf. Plin. *HN praef.* 20).

praesentium bonorum composuisse' ('However, it will not cause regret to have written a narrative commemorating our previous servitude and giving evidence of our current good fortunes, even in an unformed and rough voice'). The formulation here suggests a polarised account, documenting the dark years of Domitian and, after the pivotal year 96, turning to better times under Nerva and Trajan.[4] Yet notoriously Tacitus never fully delivers this promise (perhaps never made seriously in the first place). In his first historical work, the *Histories*, he chose to cover the years 69–96 (the civil wars of 69, then the Flavian dynasty), while in his second, the *Annals*, he went even further back in time to narrate events from 14 to 68 (the Julio-Claudian emperors from Tiberius to Nero). There is a certain logic to this trajectory. In teleological terms, the dynastic and political problems depicted in the *Annals* generated the conditions necessary to trigger the destructive civil wars that open the *Histories*, so the pair of historical works forms a natural diptych.[5] We would doubtless have a much clearer sense of the intricate relationship between the *Histories* and the *Annals* if the missing books of each had survived.[6] Just as in the case of Livy, when we analyse Tacitus' historical narratives, we face large historical fragments of whole works.

Yet, although Tacitus' selection of a relatively recent period of history brought with it tough challenges, there were also advantages. For one thing, he could consult eyewitnesses to events, the next best thing to writing about affairs the historian had witnessed himself.[7] For instance, Tacitus' own father-in-law Agricola was directly affected by the civil wars when marauding Othonian troops killed his mother in an early campaign of 69, which

---

[4] Tacitus reinforces this message at *H.* 1.1.4: 'quod si uita suppeditet, principatum diui Neruae et imperium Traiani, uberiorem securioremque materiam, senectuti seposui, rara temporum felicitate, ubi sentire quae uelis et quae sentias dicere licet' ('If life is supplied to me, I have reserved the principate of the divine Nerva and the rule of Trajan, material which is more fruitful and safe, for my old age, because of the rare felicity of times when you can think what you want and say what you think'). Alternatively, at *A.* 3.24.3 he implies that he will instead cover the period before Tiberius' principate.

[5] So much so that Jerome (c. 347–420) in his commentary on *Zachariah* 3.14.1–2 refers to thirty books of (what he calls) Tacitus' *Lives of the Caesars*, showing that he was reading a consolidated edition of the *Annals* (placed first) and the *Histories* (placed second). See also below, pp. 241–2.

[6] We lack most of *A.* 5, part of *A.* 6, all of *A.* 7–10, part of *A.* 11, part of *A.* 16, all of *A.* 17–18, part of *H.* 5 and all of *H.* 6–12. The total of thirty books comes from Jerome: positing 18 books of the *Annals* and 12 books of the *Histories* is attractive (rather than, as is sometimes suggested, 16 and 14 respectively), given the chronological extent of the material to be covered in the missing books and the importance of the hexad (grouping of six books) as an organisational unit in the *Annals*. On one aspect of this whole problem, see Ando (1997) 285–303.

[7] See Marincola (1997) 63–86 on autopsy.

prompted him to join Vespasian's party (*Agr.* 7.1–2).⁸ We know too that Tacitus received from Pliny the Younger detailed accounts of various events, including the spectacular eruption of Vesuvius in 79.⁹ Modern critics refer to this phenomenon as 'vicarious autopsy', a useful way to enhance the credibility and value of a historical work.¹⁰ Moreover, when Tacitus admits in the *Histories* (1.1.3) that his career was launched by Vespasian, advanced by Titus and further promoted by Domitian, he makes a clear point about authorial *auctoritas* (and also confronts a possible charge of bias): his own career unfolded during the period about which he proposes to write, adding special conviction to his narrative.

Another advantage of writing about relatively recent history is directly related to one of the main challenges identified by Pliny, namely the fact that the audience will potentially have a personal stake in reading about events in which either they themselves or members of their family had participated. So Pliny tells his friend Paternus about a recent incident when a historian reciting his work is confronted by the 'friends of a certain person' (*amici cuiusdam*), who beg him not to read out the rest of the narrative, which clearly contained something detrimental to the man's reputation (*Ep.* 9.27). Historiography's memorialising function and its concern with exemplarity guaranteed that prominent public figures and their families would make special efforts to read works addressing recent events, anxious to know how posterity would view their actions.¹¹ Pliny uses this incident about the unnamed historian to illustrate the *potestas* ('power') of historiography as a genre (*Ep.* 9.27.1): Tacitus' decision to write about recent history in his first historical work certainly gave him access to that power in its sharpest and most searing form. Of course, there was always the possibility of censorship (or worse), as the account of the trial of the historian Cremutius Cordus reminds us (*A.* 4.34–5), but Tacitus cleverly sets up in advance his own 'insurance policy' by characterising the year 96 as a watershed and by polarising Domitian's *saeuitia* and the enlightened attitudes of Nerva and

---

⁸ Tacitus describes the Othonian raid at *H.* 2.12–15, but conspicuously avoids naming Agricola's mother, focusing instead on the brave defiance of an unnamed Ligurian woman (2.13): see further below, pp. 93–5.
⁹ Plin. *Ep.* 6.16 and 6.20 on Vesuvius, with Berry (2008). Another letter with chunks of 'raw material' for Tacitus' *Histories* is *Ep.* 7.33.
¹⁰ Woodman and Martin (1996) 168–9 have a helpful note.
¹¹ This moralising function of historiography is often associated with Tacitus' famous assertion about the main purpose of annalistic history at *A.* 3.65.1: '... ne uirtutes sileantur utque prauis dictis factisque ex posteritate et infamia metus sit' ('so that admirable qualities are not silenced and wicked words and deeds are accompanied by fear from earning a bad reputation in posterity'). Woodman (1995) argues that Tacitus is not expressing a general rule here (= (1998) 86–103).

Trajan (*Agr.* 3).[12] Any attempt to suppress or interfere with Tacitus' debut as a historian would quickly align Trajan with his dubious predecessor Domitian, effectively effacing the palatable polarity of the *optimus princeps* ('the best emperor') Trajan and the tyrannical Domitian.

A top-heavy narrative

One intriguing aspect of the *Histories* is its extraordinarily 'top-heavy' structure. The first three books narrate the events of a single year, 69, in remarkable detail, leaving the remaining nine to incorporate material from twenty-seven years over the principates of Vespasian, Titus and Domitian. In theory, after *Histories* 1–3, this means roughly three years per book, although in practice even this model is not quite right: the surviving *Histories* 4 and 5 do not even announce the consuls for the year 71, and indeed the central panels of these books (4.12–37, 54–79; 5.14–26) narrate the Batavian revolt in Germany and then Gaul led by the former Roman auxiliary Julius Civilis between 69 and 70. In order not to confuse his readers, Tacitus postpones his account of these events until *Histories* 4 and 5, although the revolt was already being prepared between August and November 69, with trouble openly breaking out in December 69. He could therefore have legitimately treated this war in *Histories* 3, but resists such an arrangement.[13]

There are certainly advance notices of the trouble (3.46.1):

> turbata per eos dies Germania, et socordia ducum, seditione legionum, externa ui, perfidia sociali prope afflicta Romana res. id bellum cum causis et euentibus (etenim longius prouectum est) mox memorabimus.

> Over that period trouble was brewing in Germany. Thanks to the inefficiency of the generals, mutiny amongst the legions, the violent nature of the enemy and the treachery of our allies, the Roman state was nearly brought to ruin. This war, along with its causes and outcomes, we will relate in due course (for it extended over rather a long time).

Yet, by postponing the account of the Batavian revolt until *Histories* 4 and 5, Tacitus follows the top-heavy distribution of material in *Histories* 1–3 with a narrative that unfolds almost as slowly over *Histories* 4 and 5. It is also possible that Tacitus reserved the Flavians' famous triumph (June 71) for victory in the Jewish war as the climax of *Histories* 6, particularly if

---

[12] Pliny's *Panegyricus*, the written version of his speech of thanks to Trajan for a suffect consulship and originally delivered in 100, develops similar antithetical contrasts between Domitian and Trajan (Nerva, named only ten times in the speech, is allocated a relatively low profile). See further Bartsch (1994) 148–87; and Hoffer (2006) 73–87, esp. 74–5 on the 'problem' of how to present the dead Nerva when Trajan's accession is being celebrated.

[13] Wellesley (1972) 141–2 discusses the chronology.

we acknowledge that he liked the hexad as a meaningful narrative unit.[14] This triumph was celebrated even though the fortress at Masada was still holding out (and did so until April 73), but Roman historians saw it as a pivotal moment: Pliny the Elder, for one, apparently chose it as an uplifting ending for his history.[15] Although separate triumphs had been decreed to Vespasian and Titus individually, it was the first time that a father and son had held a joint triumph.[16] If Tacitus did indeed arrange his material in this way, leaving the events of twenty-five years to cover in *Histories* 7–12, he would have created a memorable experience for his readers, travelling with painful slowness in the first hexad through the self-destructive events of the civil war and the delicate process of reconstruction immediately afterwards (the years 69–71), then proceeding briskly (the years 72–96) through the principates of the three Flavian emperors in the second hexad. We can compare this narrative deceleration for the events of the civil war with Lucan's strategy in his *Pharsalia*, where expansive narration of the civil war between Pompey and Caesar, harrowing though it is, at least postpones enforced happiness when the victor emerges, or, as Lucan's distraught Roman *matrona* expresses it (2.40–2): 'nunc flere potestas, | dum pendet fortuna ducum; cum uicerit alter, | gaudendum est' ('Now we have the capacity to weep, as long as the destiny of the two generals hangs in the balance. Once one of them has won, we will have to rejoice').[17] Lucan's typically paradoxical reading of civil war resonates provocatively with Tacitus' top-heavy narrative, in which civil strife wins the lion's share of the text.

The remarkable attention that Tacitus lavishes on the civil war demands explanation, particularly if we consider Seneca the Elder's powerful aphorism, *optima ciuilis belli defensio obliuio est*, 'the best defence in the case of civil war is forgetfulness' (*Controv.* 10.3.5). When the *Histories* was published in about 109, this particular civil war was already forty years in the past, but the broad scheme of events would still have echoed loudly with contemporaries, because the civil wars of 69 had clear links with more recent history. After Domitian's assassination in 96, there was a narrowly

---

[14] For the triumph, see Joseph. *BJ* 7.119–57; Suet. *Vesp.* 8.1, *Tit.* 6.1, *Dom.* 2.1; Dio 65.12.1ª; Beard (2003) 453–8. For the hexad see above, n. 6.

[15] Levick (1999a) 93. Our only verbatim quotation from Tacitus in the fragments (Oros. *Hist. Adv. Pag.* 7.19.4 = fragment 4) relates to Vespasian's closure of the temple of Janus in 71 after the triumph. See Barnes (1977) 229–30.

[16] Jones (2000) 57 (Oros. *Hist. Adv. Pag.* 7.9.8–9, drawing on a missing section of Tacitus' *Histories*).

[17] Masters (1992) 183 analyses the dynamics of Lucan's narrative *mora* ('delay') in the poem surrounding Sextus' consultation of Erictho before the final battle: 'So the (Caesarian) impatience of delay becomes a means by which to introduce a (Pompeian) delay into the sequence of the narrative, and, as so often in this paradoxical poem, the narrative's declared sense of urgency is undercut by the reality of its failure to progress anywhere'.

averted crisis under the elderly Nerva (a figure highly evocative of the *senex*, 'old man', Galba), when a complete lack of clarity about the succession raised the ugly possibility of civil war, particularly after a praetorian mutiny in the summer of 97.[18] Trajan's adoption luckily forestalled trouble, but, in reading Tacitus' extensive account of 69, his audience could have visualised an alternative version of their own recent history. Indeed Tacitus actively encourages this, through, for example, Galba's speech on the reasons for adopting Piso (*H.* 1.15–16), which raises questions highly relevant for Nerva's much more successful adoption of Trajan;[19] and the narrative even has its own explosive praetorian mutiny in Rome under Otho, which Tacitus covers extensively in comparison with the parallel tradition (1.80–5).[20] Of course, Books 1–3 of Tacitus' *Histories* narrate real events, but embedded in the account is a hint of counterfactual history, raising the possibility that the civil war could have been replayed in 97.[21] Tacitus activates this possibility again in *Annals* 1 when narrating the aborted mutinies of the legionaries in 14 in Pannonia and Germany after Augustus' death: neither mutiny triggered civil war, but Tacitus' unusually extensive coverage (Dio 57.4–5 offers only two chapters) constantly raises the spectre of civil war by pointed formulation.[22]

Fission: disintegration and collapse

While addressing his newly adopted son, Piso, Tacitus' Galba depicts the Roman state as a 'vast imperial body' (*H.* 1.16.1 *immensum imperii corpus*), unable 'to stand and keep its balance without a controller' (*stare ac librari sine rectore*). It is Vespasian who will eventually emerge from the chaos as the 'greatest controller of any age' (Plin. *HN* 2.18 *maximus omnis aeui rector*), but not before Tacitus' audience witnesses two devastating civil war battles near Bedriacum in northern Italy, bizarrely played out on the same site (Othonians vs Vitellians, 2.39–45; Vitellians vs Flavians, 3.16–35), and culminating in the metaphorical 'decapitation' of the Roman state

---

[18] Eck (2002b); Alföldy (2004). On Nerva's career before 96, see Murison (2003) 147–57.
[19] See Sage (1990) 851–1030, esp. 861–2 on the links between Galba's speech and the treatment of Nerva's adoption of Trajan in Pliny's *Panegyricus*.
[20] Plut. *Otho* 3.2–8, Suet. *Otho* 8.2 and Dio 64.9.2–3 narrate the praetorian mutiny relatively briefly. See Damon (2003) 261–73 for analysis of Tacitus' version.
[21] On counterfactual history, see Morello (2002) and O'Gorman (2006).
[22] Tacitus repeatedly introduces civil war as a reference point for the mutiny narratives at key points in *Annals* 1: *ciuilium ... bellorum uictores* (1.19.3); *ciuile bellum* (1.36.2); *iras ... ciuiles* (1.43.3); *ciuilium armorum* (1.49.1). On the unifying metaphor of madness (especially evocative of civil war) running through Tacitus' version of these mutinies, see Woodman (2006a).

when the Capitoline temple in Rome burns down. Not even the infamous Gaulish invaders of the city early in the fourth century BC managed this dubious achievement, as Tacitus points out (*H*. 3.72.1), but the burning of the Capitol will explicitly convince contemporary Gauls that the end of the Roman Empire is imminent (4.54.2). Both Tacitus (3.83.2) and Suetonius (*Vesp*. 8.5) call the city *deformis*, 'disfigured', after the Capitoline temple burns down; and Tacitus poignantly gives the temple its own 'obituary' (3.72) to mark the cataclysmic moment.[23]

Yet the Empire's metaphorical decapitation has already been preceded by the shocking and brutal decapitation of an individual emperor, Galba, and his adopted son Piso, by Roman soldiers in the forum. Tacitus recreates the aftermath vividly (1.44.2):

> praefixa contis capita gestabantur inter signa cohortium iuxta aquilam legionis, certatim ostentantibus cruentas manus qui occiderant, qui interfuerant, qui uere, qui falso ut pulchrum et memorabile facinus iactabant.
>
> Their severed heads were being carried along fixed on poles amidst the standards of the cohorts and alongside the legion's eagle, as men vied with one another and showed off their bloody hands – those who had done the killing, those who had been present, some legitimately, some falsely, they were all boasting as if it were a fine and memorable deed.

This extraordinary incorporation of severed heads into the archetypal symbols of order and discipline within the Roman army, the standards and the legionary eagle, eloquently expresses the disastrous fragmentation of normal Roman identity in civil war. After all, Roman soldiers swore an oath to protect their emperor's life at all costs, and their standards, the most important of which bore the image of an eagle, were highly emotive objects, whose loss was the ultimate disgrace for a legion (Livy 7.13.4; 9.15.7).[24] These standards were normally kept in a special shrine (*sacellum*), anointed with expensive oils and garlands (Plin. *HN* 13.23; Suet. *Claud*. 13.2) and serving as a focal point for military oaths (Tac. *A*. 15.16.2). Indeed Augustus' efforts to retrieve the standards lost with Crassus in 53 BC, finally recovered in 20 BC and celebrated on his coinage, eloquently express their value.[25]

It is particularly striking that Tacitus explicitly links the severed heads' desecration to Roman soldiers. The parallel tradition, as so often, is revealing.

---

[23] Ash (2007a) discusses the symbolism of destroying the Capitoline temple.

[24] See Oakley (1998) 161–2 for the emotive power of the standards. On the military oath in the imperial period, see *OCD* s.v. '*sacramentum* (military)'. It was normally the most strictly observed of all Roman oaths (Dion. Hal. *Ant. Rom.* 10.18); and the Roman army was usually 'a highly sacralised community' (Lendon (1997) 253).

[25] Augustus, *RG* 29.1–2; Prop. 3.5.48; Ov. *Fast*. 5.584–90; Vell. Pat. 2.91 with Woodman (1983b) 268; Luc. 8.358; Suet. *Aug*. 21.3; *Tib*. 9.1.

In Plutarch (*Galb.* 27.4), a single soldier displays Galba's severed head on a spear, whirling it around in the manner of Bacchants and thereby evoking Pentheus' severed head in Euripides' *Bacchae*. This is part of a wider strategy whereby Plutarch associates the events of 69 with the tragic stage.[26] Yet, by associating the desecration with one specific soldier, Plutarch focuses the blame on an individual: it is still undeniably horrifying, but in a different way from Tacitus' accentuation of collective responsibility amongst the legionaries as a group. In Suetonius, Otho hands the gruesome trophy (only Galba's head is mentioned) 'to camp-followers and soldier's attendants, who carried it fixed on a spear around the camp with considerable mockery' (*Galb.* 20.2 'lixis calonibusque ... qui hasta suffixum non sine ludibrio circum castra portarunt'). These declassé hangers-on engage in the tasteless display, rather than the legionaries, as in Tacitus, but the difference is expressive. What sort of terrible metamorphosis have these soldiers undergone to be capable of sullying their eagle and standards so grotesquely with the severed heads of Galba and Piso? A corrosive moral decay must have eaten into their souls to make this possible.

Tacitus deftly encapsulates the soldiers' moral bankruptcy during this civil war, not just by such suggestive details, but by scenes formally set off from the main narrative. One memorable instance follows the Flavians' victory over Vitellius' dilapidated forces at the second battle of Bedriacum. He tells the story to illustrate 'how greatly the victors lacked respect with regard to what was right and wrong' (3.51.1 'tantam uictoribus aduersus fas nefasque irreuerentiam') and appealing to 'most celebrated authors' (3.51.1 'celeberrimi auctores') as his authority. The episode involves an unnamed common soldier, who proudly declares to his superiors that, after killing his brother in battle, he deserves a reward (3.51.1): 'nec illis aut honorare eam caedem ius hominum aut ulcisci ratio belli permittebat' ('the law of mankind did not allow them to honour that murder, but nor did practical considerations of this war allow them to take vengeance for it'). Tacitus then compares this story with an incident from 87 BC (recorded by Sisenna, cited by Tacitus as his source, but also featuring at Livy, *Per.* 79), when a soldier inadvertently kills his brother and then commits suicide after realising what he has done.[27] A simple syncrisis of the two events allows Tacitus to comment pointedly on the moral deterioration between then and now.[28] Even civil wars under the republic were of a higher calibre, it seems.

[26] See Keitel (1995).

[27] 'Brothers in Roman literature more often symbolise conflict than mutual support' (Wiedemann (1993) 55; also Woodman and Martin (1996) on *A.* 3.8.1).

[28] Hardie (1992) 51–71 discusses the incident and similar instances from epic.

Fission and fusion

It is conspicuous that this moralising tale is attached to the victorious Flavians, rather than the defeated Vitellians (the easy target), thus demonstrating Tacitus' independence as a historian from pro-Flavian accounts of the civil war.[29] Even so, the episode is balanced by a related story earlier in the narrative (*H*. 3.25.2–3) about a Vitellian soldier, Julius Mansuetus, who attacks an enemy soldier, only to discover belatedly that the man is his father. The son then buries his father, evoking pity and cursing of the civil war, but there is a twist: those denouncing the war continue killing their relatives just as enthusiastically as before. In moral terms, the Vitellian soldier who ignorantly kills his father and then buries him is a better man than the Flavian soldier who kills his brother and then seeks a reward. Yet neither episode is morally uplifting, and together the two dovetailed incidents demonstrate and explore the collapse of ethical standards and the erosion of Roman identity brought about by civil war, regardless of partisan loyalty. There is also a historiographical issue at stake here. Woodman has argued that neither story is genuine, since two poems attributed to Seneca the Younger describe a very similar incident in the civil war between Octavian and Antony about soldiers unwittingly killing their brothers ([Seneca], *Epig.* 69 and 70). Thus Tacitus, inspired by this source, apparently created his own modified versions in the pair of episodes from the *Histories*.[30] If Tacitus is using his imagination here rather than relaying genuine incidents, then this underscores what a fundamental and urgent role he regarded his moralising voice as playing in the historical narrative. Sometimes the 'truth' is less important than the emotional impact of particular episodes on his contemporary audience, especially since fratricide is so central to Roman identity via the foundation myth of Romulus and Remus. Tacitus' readers would have responded to the trope of this fratricidal Flavian soldier as a warped latter-day Romulus, whose individual story is a curious synecdoche for the whole civil war.

We began this section with the metaphor of the Roman Empire as a vast body unable to stand on its own and being 'decapitated' when the Capitoline temple in Rome burns down. Tacitus also uses the concept of the body expressively in a memorable *exemplum* about a Ligurian woman, captured by marauding Othonian soldiers in the town of Albintimilium (*H*. 2.13.2):[31]

> auxit inuidiam praeclaro exemplo femina Ligus, quae filio abdito, cum simul pecuniam occultari milites credidissent eoque per cruciatus interrogarent, ubi

---

[29] A similar instance occurs at *H*. 3.71.4, where Tacitus expresses doubts about whether the Vitellians or Flavians were responsible for setting fire to the Capitoline temple. Other sources (Joseph. *BJ* 4.649; Suet. *Vit.* 15.3; Dio 64.17) suggest that the Vitellians were to blame. See further Wellesley (1972) 16–18.
[30] Woodman (1983a) 116–19 (= (1998) 13–16).
[31] On this episode see Ash (2007b) 113–14.

filium occuleret, uterum ostendens latere respondit, nec ullis deinde terroribus aut morte constantiam uocis egregiae mutauit.

A Ligurian woman increased the odium [for the Othonian soldiers] by her pre-eminently fine exemplary conduct. She had hidden her son, but, since the soldiers believed that money had been concealed together with him and therefore were interrogating her by torture about where she was hiding her son, she pointed to her womb and replied that he was hiding there; and from then on, not by means of any terrors nor even fear of death did she change the consistency of her excellent utterance.

This chilling scene, recounted by Tacitus in a single complex sentence where an elaborate set of subordinate clauses dwarfs the simple main clause, is unusually expressive about disintegrating Roman identity during civil war.[32] Firstly, these soldiers target this woman not because she holds any crucial information, but because they regard her as an easy means to track down some money (a highly degrading motive). Not only that, but she is explicitly identified as Ligurian. Since Liguria in north-west Italy formed one of the eleven Augustan *regiones* of Italy (Plin. *HN* 3.46–9), this woman was probably a Roman citizen, but this status offers her no protection. The Roman soldiers behave like predatory barbarians, whereas the Ligurian woman shows exemplary bravery of a type that should ideally be celebrated as a Roman trait. This sort of moralising through polarised identities involves a rather different narrative technique from the fratricidal motif activated at *Histories* 3.51, but it coheres with a broad pattern in the *Histories*: impressive qualities can be manifested by women and low-class individuals, even slaves, such as the *egregium mendacium* ('excellent lie') of Piso's slave who falsely claims to be his master when confronted with assassins (4.50.2), whereas Roman soldiers often behave like foreign invaders (1.45.1; 2.12.2, 87.2, 89.1, 90.1; 3.72.1). The fact that this story involves a woman only makes it more memorable and shocking. For, although Tacitus signals his plan to include appropriate *exempla* (1.3.1; 3.51.2), we have only two other references in the surviving books of the *Histories* to *exempla* about women (Galeria 2.64.2, Epponina 4.67.2).[33] In addition, the scene would doubtless stick in the minds of Tacitus' audience because torture was normally reserved for slaves; and, because scenes of torture were a staple of the declamation schools (e.g. Sen. *Controv.* 2.5; 8.3; 10.5), they would have been quite capable of supplying the grisly details for themselves, although Tacitus himself refrains from expanding the scene, perhaps to avoid compromising

---

[32] Damon (2003) 16–19 discusses such 'appendix sentences'; see also below, pp. 205–6.
[33] In the *Annals* Tacitus is similarly selective about providing *exempla* featuring women: Epicharis (15.57.2) and Arria (16.34.2) are memorable instances.

the dignity of his genre. Finally, the memorable finale, where the woman defiantly points to her womb as the 'hiding place' of her son, offers an unusual example of family loyalty in a narrative where such bonds are more usually betrayed. Her one word answer to the soldiers (presumably '*latet*', 'he is hiding', in direct speech) is reinforced by the expressive non-verbal gesture of pointing to her womb, demonstrating that no amount of pain will force her to break the maternal bond with her son.

This unnamed woman stands out in fine relief from the surrounding narrative about military campaigns and battles, and the tableau undoubtedly satisfies the moralising agenda of ancient historiography. Yet it is also disturbing, since the occasion for the Ligurian woman's impressive bravery (itself a positive *exemplum*) has been created by Roman soldiers in a self-destructive context that is unsettling for Roman readers, forced to witness such deeply aberrant conduct. Nonetheless, the Romans clearly saw some moral value in memorialising their own misdeeds for posterity. We can compare here the rationale of Valerius Maximus, whose work, *Facta et dicta memorabilia* (*Memorable Deeds and Sayings*), was composed under Tiberius. Valerius says (4.1.12): 'propositi … nostri ratio non laudanda sibi omnia, sed recordanda sumpsit' ('The rationale for my work has not been that everything should be praised, but remembered').[34] Historians had more scope than Valerius for selecting and elaborating particular *exempla* in their own narratives. That Tacitus has chosen this particular instance is revealing. For although the Ligurian woman's behaviour is certainly praiseworthy, the civil war context is so damning. Tacitus, however, relishes such moral complexities. The story of the Ligurian woman vividly encapsulates the widespread disintegration and collapse of Roman identity in the power vacuum after Nero's suicide.

Fusion: restoration and survival

We have seen how the painfully leisurely pace and detailed narrative offered by *Histories* 1–3 relentlessly unmasks and commemorates for posterity the collective shame of these civil wars. In this conflict, Roman soldiers are regularly seen to behave like foreign invaders, and the traditional agents of control, such as the senate and even the emperor, remain utterly powerless to influence events unfolding in their name. Even Vespasian's civil war campaign is hijacked by the rogue Flavian general Antonius Primus, who steamrollers the official plan to invade Italy via Anatolia with forces led by Mucianus while Vespasian conducts a grain blockade of Egypt (2.82.3).

---

[34] On Valerius Maximus and memory, see Gowing (2005) 49–62.

So far, normal hierarchies of power have been repeatedly inverted or side-stepped and any respect for the Roman state has slowly drained away in a welter of self-destruction and violence culminating in the burning of the Capitoline temple in Rome. By the end of *Histories* 3, Tacitus' audience is left bruised and battered. How can the process of reconstruction be set in motion? And what does it now mean to be Roman in such a morally debased world? No wonder Tacitus opens the fourth book on such a cautious note (4.1.1): 'Interfecto Vitellio bellum magis desierat quam pax coeperat' ('After Vitellius had been killed, it was more the case that war had stopped than that peace had begun'). Beginnings and endings of books are always significant moments in Tacitus: if anything, the bloody scenes at the opening of *Histories* 4, where the victorious Flavian soldiers hunt down defeated Vitellians so that 'the streets were full of corpses, the forums and temples bloodsoaked' (4.1.1 'plenae caedibus uiae, cruenta fora templaque') suggests brutal continuity, not a fresh start.

In Roman historiography, the well-established mechanism for bolstering the physical and moral calibre of the Roman (or any other) state was the Sallustian notion of *metus hostilis*, 'fear of the enemy'.[35] An intimidating external threat could reconcile internal differences and persuade individuals that their own selfish concerns were less important than the greater collective good of the state. For Sallust, Carthage's defeat meant the removal of *metus hostilis*, leading to inevitable Roman decline. In Tacitus' narrative, such external threats certainly exist – the short-lived invasion of the Sarmatian Rhoxolani (1.79) is a timely reminder – but the centripetal momentum of the civil war is so acute that the danger of foreign invasion is temporarily ignored. What we see in *Histories* 4 and 5 is a staggered and stalling reactivation of *metus hostilis* as a beneficial force: it does kick in, but only in a gradual and halting way.

A crucial sequence in plotting the Roman recovery is the elaborate tripartite narrative of Julius Civilis' Batavian revolt (4.12–37, 54–79; 5.14–26), a war Tacitus finds hard to categorise straightforwardly as civil or foreign, since it contains both elements (1.2.1; 2.69.1; 4.22.2).[36] The suggestively named leader, Civilis, is a murky figure, at once an enemy from within, a former auxiliary leader trained in Roman fighting techniques, and an outsider, a Batavian noble, who plays on his heritage to win supporters for his cause. Tacitus encapsulates his slippery nature in his opening sketch (4.13.2):

---

[35] Sallust uses the phrase *metus hostilis* at *Iug.* 41.2. See further Earl (1961) 13 and 41; Lintott (1972) 626–38; Levick (1982) 53–62; Levene (2000) 178–80.
[36] On Civilis, see Haynes (2003) 148–77.

sed Ciuilis ultra quam barbaris solitum ingenio sollers et Sertorium se aut Annibalem ferens simili oris dehonestamento, ne ut hosti obuiam iret, si a populo Romano palam desciuisset, Vespasiani amicitiam studiumque partium praetendit.

Yet Civilis had a more versatile mind than barbarians usually do, and declared himself to be another Sertorius or Hannibal because of a similar facial disfigurement, although he made a pretence of friendship with Vespasian and enthusiasm for the cause, fearing that if he openly rebelled against the Roman people, an attack might be made on him as an enemy.[37]

Here, the one-eyed Civilis simultaneously evokes both a foreign enemy, Hannibal, and a Roman who turned his back on the state, Sertorius. These dual foreign and domestic identities aptly reflect the fluctuating role of Civilis (and his war) in the narrative.

Civilis' Batavian revolt finally implodes when the Gallic states participate and the arrival of multiple leaders with different aims causes the whole campaign to fragment (a pattern that echoes some aspects of the Roman civil wars of *Histories* 1–3, particularly Otho's campaign). The final Roman battle with Civilis' forces (5.14–18), fought near the legionary camp at Vetera, is perhaps the closest Tacitus comes (in what survives of the *Histories*) to elaborating a more reassuring 'Roman versus foreign' military clash, but his audience's enjoyment is muted because it happens on the same site as an ignominious massacre by Civilis' men of Roman legionaries who have surrendered (4.60); and the fact that the Roman general Petilius Cerialis manages to win only because of a Batavian deserter, who shows him how to outflank the Germans by identifying solid ground bordering the marshy terrain of the battlefield (5.18.2), hardly allows much room for patriotic fervour. This battle is almost a false start along the road to recovery and the restoration of Roman pride.[38]

Where we can really detect a shift in gears and a sense of recovery in Roman national identity is in Tacitus' famous (or infamous) ethnographical excursus on the Jews, outlining their history, customs and religious practices in terms of the 'other' (*H.* 5.2–13).[39] Tacitus presents Jewish culture as an inversion of everything that a Roman reader would regard as normal and the tone is, at best, perplexed and, at worst, hostile. Jewish exclusivity, monotheism, burial practices and so forth are described by Tacitus for

---

[37] In describing Civilis' facial disfigurement (*simili oris dehonestamento*), Tacitus famously alludes to the description of Sertorius (*dehonestamentum corporis*) in Sallust's fragmentary *Histories* (1.88).
[38] On this battle as source material for Tacitus' self-imitation at *A.* 1.61–5, see Woodman (1979) 143–55, 231–5 (= (1998) 70–85).
[39] The classic study of the 'other' is Hartog (1988).

Roman consumption in starkly polarising and often pejorative language. This section of the *Histories* above all tends to make modern readers uneasy. Yet the context is important. Tacitus here constructs his narrative against the established ancient literary backdrop of ethnography, a way of writing that often exaggerates and simplifies the collective characteristics of a group, partly to entertain and partly to reinforce what was distinctive about the writer's own culture. Ethnography could be formulated as an independent monograph (e.g. Tacitus' *Germania*) or as an ethnographical excursus included as a distinct section within a continuous narrative (e.g. Sallust on Africa, *Iug.* 17–19, or Tacitus on Britain, *Agr.* 10–12).[40] Ancient readers, familiar with the device, would recognise certain set introductory formulae signalling their entry into an ethnographical segment and whetting their appetites for entertaining or shocking ethnographical details to come. The distinctive ethnographical format of the excursus on the Jews can be contrasted sharply with the tripartite account of the Batavian revolt, which is embedded in the main narrative and where the differences between the two sides are frequently elided.

For Tacitus' readers, the upcoming narrative of the Jewish war, to which this excursus forms an introduction, arguably plays a crucial transitional role within the *Histories*. Only now will the Roman state make the leap from self-destructive civil wars to a foreign campaign: domestic and external national identities are once again polarised and the differences between opposing sides are (finally) more prominent than the blurring of differences typical in those successive conflicts where Roman fought Roman. This 'restorative' function of the excursus is, however, masked because the *Histories* breaks off at 5.26, leaving so much of the Jewish war still to be narrated. In fact, the striking point about *Histories* 4–5 is not that Tacitus devotes so much attention to the Jews, but that he treats the Batavian revolt (almost ignored by other sources) so extensively.[41] The more reassuring character of the Jewish war (signalled by the formal ethnographical excursus) contrasts sharply with the twilight world of the chameleon-like Julius Civilis and his Batavians. After the fragmentation apparent in *Histories* 1–3, we can see some initial signs of (physical and moral) reconstruction in *Histories* 4–5, but the incomplete nature of the text makes reading and interpreting Tacitus' depiction of the Roman state after the civil wars highly challenging. Fission is followed by early signs of fusion: it would indeed

---

[40] On ethnography in general see Thomas (1982) and the specific studies of Green (1993) and Oniga (1995) on Sallust; also above, Chapter 4.

[41] Tacitus' account, 'almost completely unsupported by other evidence' (Murison (1991) 1707), is the most elaborate one we have.

have been fascinating to see how that pattern developed in the missing books about the Flavian dynasty.[42]

FURTHER READING

Tacitus' *Histories* has generally been less well served by dedicated book-length studies than the *Annals*, but a number of books discuss the *Histories* under the auspices of general studies of our author. The best place to start is with Martin (1981) and Mellor (1993). These both offer clear and helpful introductions to the author and his works. Ash (2006a) is designed to be a non-specialist's introduction to Tacitus: it includes a dedicated discussion of the *Histories*, as well as a chapter about the reception of Julius Civilis. For those wanting to set Tacitus in a broader historiographical context, Kraus and Woodman (1997) is an illuminating read, as is Marincola (1997), a wide-ranging study that also incorporates the Greek tradition.

More specialised treatments of the *Histories* are also available, including Ash (1999a), which offers studies of Galba, Otho, Vitellius, Vespasian and the general Antonius Primus, as well as an analysis of Tacitus' characterisation of the various armies. Haynes (2003) offers a reading of the text based on critical theory. Woodman (1998) assembled and revised some of his most important articles on Tacitus, which will hold special interest for those interested in Tacitus' Latin, as will his book on rhetoric in classical historiography (Woodman (1988)). Two recent commentaries in the Cambridge Greek and Latin Classics series should also help students who want to read the *Histories* in Latin: Damon (2003) and Ash (2007b), both of which have helpful introductions.

There is a wide range of articles about the *Histories* available in scholarly journals (too many to list here), but special attention should be drawn to the scholarship of Keitel (e.g. (1987) and (1992)) and Morgan (e.g. (1992) and (1994)). One particularly interesting essay is Levene (1997). There is also a special volume of *Arethusa* 39 (2006) on Tacitus, which contains several articles on the *Histories*.

The historical background to the *Histories* is complex and kaleidoscopic, but readers can consult Morgan (2006) and Wellesley (2000), which also has a helpful introduction and bibliographical overview by Levick, whose biography of Vespasian (1999a) is a comprehensive study of one of the main protagonists of the *Histories*. The emperor Nero also casts a long shadow over the text and those looking for a good study should consult Griffin (1984). It is also invaluable to compare Tacitus with the 'parallel tradition', which includes the biographies by Plutarch (*Galba* and *Otho*) and Suetonius (*Galba, Otho, Vitellius* and *Vespasian*), as well as Cassius Dio's epitomised *Roman History*. Josephus' *Bellum Judaicum* is partisan, but interesting.

---

[42] I should like to thank David Levene for helpful comments on this piece.

7

CHRISTINA SHUTTLEWORTH KRAUS

The Tiberian hexad

Tacitus had provocatively opened the
Annals with Augustus' death.[1]

Succession

In undertaking his history *Ab excessu Diui Augusti* – now commonly known as *Annals* – Tacitus faced the problem of where and how to begin. The earlier *Histories* open with the consuls of 69, and much has been written on the importance of this timing for Tacitus' historiographical aims. In particular, electing to start not with the death of Nero but with the magistrate year establishes a thematic dissonance between the forthcoming narrative of the principates of Galba through Domitian and the traditional means of recording Roman history, which was structured by annual consular dating.[2] But the choice of annalistic format did not oblige Tacitus to begin with 1 January: previous annalistic history had accommodated the different calendars of the Republican year, and events could easily take precedence over the calendar. So Livy elects to use the sack of Rome by the Gauls as the dividing point between his Books 5 and 6; and, though the move from monarchy to Republic is marked by the establishment of consular elections (1.60.3; 2.1.7), he is interested more in the process of change than in the time of year, more in the annual nature of the offices than in any particular *annus* or part thereof.

Tacitus, too, focuses from the start on the process of change from one form of government to another. As he surveys the shift from monarchy to Republic to civil strife to Principate, key words (given in *italic* below) denote types of 'regime' (*A.* 1.1.1):

> Vrbem Romam a <u>principio</u> *reges* habuere; libertatem et *consulatum* L. Brutus instituit. *dictaturae* ad tempus sumebantur; neque *decemuiralis potestas* ultra biennium neque tribunorum militum *consulare ius* diu ualuit. non **Cinnae**, non

[1] Wallace-Hadrill (1983) 2.
[2] The classic treatment is that of Ginsburg (1981).

The Tiberian hexad

> Sullae longa *dominatio*; et **Pompei Crassique** *potentia* cito in **Caesarem, Lepidi** atque **Antonii** *arma* in **Augustum** cessere, qui cuncta discordiis ciuilibus fessa nomine *principis* sub *imperium* accepit.

> The city of Rome from its inception was held by kings; freedom and the consulship were established by L. Brutus. Dictatorships were taken up only on occasion, and neither did decemviral power remain in effect beyond two years, nor the military tribunes' consular prerogative for long. Not for Cinna nor for Sulla was there lengthy domination, and the powerfulness of Pompeius and Crassus passed quickly to Caesar, the armies of Lepidus and Antonius to Augustus, who with the name of princeps took everything, exhausted as it now was by civil dissensions, under his command.[3]

The proper names (in **bold** above and below) that pile up in the third sentence mark the emergence of the dynasts – a proliferation of *nomina* that will rapidly yield to *Augustum*, the *nomen principis*. With the next paragraph, at the start of the narrative proper, Tacitus moves back from the battle of Actium (*Antonii arma*) and allows even more names in, magnifying the period between Philippi and Actium (42–31 BC) and stressing the contested plurality of power in those years (1.2.1):

> Postquam **Bruto** et **Cassio** caesis nulla iam publica arma, **Pompeius** apud Siciliam oppressus exutoque **Lepido** interfecto **Antonio** ne **Iulianis** quidem partibus nisi **Caesar** dux reliquus ...

> When after the slaughter of Brutus and Cassius there were no more republican armies and Pompeius had been overwhelmed off Sicily and, with Lepidus cast aside and Antonius killed, not even the Julian party had any leader left but Caesar ...

This Pompeius and this Caesar are the sons of the homonymous men at 1.1.1 – and this Brutus the imitator of the Brutus who instituted *libertas* and the consulate. The repeating names suggest that this is yet another example of history repeating.[4]

Yet Augustus, despite being the end point of these two briefly sketched chronologies, is not Tacitus' goal. Instead, the historian is working toward yet another movement, not from one form of government to another but to a string of proper names that, despite their apparent uniqueness, can, in fact, be bundled together into *et cetera*, 'and so on'. Following the opening survey, in his preface Tacitus twice gives us the chain of rulers specifically relevant to this work, first as the topic of other men's histories, then of his own (1.1.2–3):

> sed ueteris populi Romani prospera uel aduersa claris scriptoribus memorata sunt, temporibusque **Augusti** dicendis non defuere decora ingenia ... **Tiberii**

---

[3] All translations of the *Annals* are taken from Woodman (2004).
[4] See e.g. Kraus (1998); for naming in the preface see O'Gorman (1995) 97 and (2000) 127–8.

Gaique et Claudii ac Neronis res florentibus ipsis ob metum falsae, postquam occiderant recentibus odiis compositae sunt. inde consilium mihi pauca de **Augusto** et extrema tradere, mox **Tiberii** <u>principatum</u> et cetera.

The Roman people of old, however, had their successes and adversities recalled by brilliant writers; and to tell of Augustus' times there was no dearth of deserving talents ... The affairs of Tiberius and Gaius, as of Claudius and Nero, were falsified through dread while the men themselves flourished, and composed with hatred fresh after their fall. Hence my plan is the transmission of a mere few things about Augustus and of his final period, then of Tiberius' principate and the remainder.

His primary subject is the succession of the Empire from Augustus, its inventor and first holder, to the second *princeps*, and the third, and so on. The polysyndetic *Tiberii Gaique et Claudii ac Neronis* sums up the Julian and Claudian dynasties with an economical inevitability. As he will do at 1.2.1, however, Tacitus then steps back and expands, refocusing our attention on the movement from Augustus to Tiberius (*inde ... cetera*). For that, it turns out, will be the point of greatest interest – not just in measuring Tiberius against his precursor (below), but even in starting the Principate and its master narrative.

Tacitus returns repeatedly to the issue of this first succession. Though it seems that there remained at least the theoretical possibility that Augustus' was not necessarily a hereditary monarchy (1.13.2–3), with the perfect vision of hindsight the historian elevates those potential successors who were, in fact, related by marriage, adoption, or birth to the first *princeps* (1.3.1–5). The list of *subsidia dominationi* (1.3.1), beginning with Claudius Marcellus, Augustus' nephew, progresses through Marcus Agrippa, Tiberius Nero and Claudius Drusus to the sons of Agrippa, Gaius and Lucius (1.3.1–2).[5] Even more briefly than they are introduced, Tacitus strips them away: 'But, when Agrippa had departed from life, both L. Caesar, while travelling to the Spanish armies, and Gaius, while retiring from Armenia and weakened by a wound, were carried off by fatefully early deaths or by the guile of their stepmother Livia; and, with Drusus' life extinguished previously, [Tiberius] Nero alone of all the stepsons was left. Everything inclined in his direction' (1.3.3 *Nero solus e priuignis erat, illuc cuncta uergere*). Though now the universal focal point, Tiberius is immediately himself given a support (1.3.5 *munimentis*), Germanicus the son of Drusus. The artificiality of this arrangement is brought home with the information, 'notwithstanding that there was a young son in Tiberius' house' (1.3.5). By the time we reach the

---

[5] A third son, Agrippa Postumus, is relegated to an explanatory background clause (1.3.4 *nam*); he will not survive his banishment.

end of the third paragraph of the *Annals*, then, we have seen the world contract – twice – to Augustus (1.1.1 *qui cuncta ... accepit*; 1.2.1 *ne ... quidem nisi Caesar dux reliquus*), expand again to encompass all the imperial hopefuls, then contract to Tiberius (*solus ... cuncta*) – only to expand again, to include both his natural and adopted sons.

In his statement of purpose (1.1.3), Tacitus repeats the word *princeps* in its abstract, substantive form, *principatum*. That echo of *principis* (1.1.1) closes a double ring that opens in the history's first phrase, *Vrbem Romam a principio*. The record of the Principate begins with these *Annals* – but, equally, these *Annals* reverse the trajectory of Livy's history, which began *a primordio urbis* (*praef.* 1) with the regal period and progressed through the Republic. Tacitus' connection of *principium* to *princeps* points at the similarity between Augustus' sly designation for monarchic power and the regal period, while simultaneously alerting us to his own role as successor to the writer of the *Ab urbe condita*.[6] When he moves to the content of his form (1.1.3), he reaffirms and closes that ring, now envisioning the new government not as a specific person (*rex*) or even a title (*nomen principis*), but as an abstract, generalisable thing, *principatus*.[7]

In a complementary move, there is a shift from history (1.1.1) to literary history (1.1.2–3 *scriptoribus ... memorata sunt ... ingenia ... compositae sunt ... tradere*), moving back to the Republican past – now simply designated as *ueteris populi Romani prospera uel aduersa* – and continuing the sequence to Augustus and beyond, in what will eventually be proved a table of contents for the *Annals*.[8] The similarity in structures, in which both sequences culminate in Augustus, suggests that the history one writes about and the history one writes are commensurate, that the text both reflects and constructs the world.[9]

A significant consequence of this is that we see already from the beginning of the *Annals* the tendency of Empire – and of narrative about Empire – to replicate itself, by voraciously multiplying and consuming its parts.[10] The combination of growth and consumption is clear in Tacitus' description of how Augustus the Augmenter/Augmented behaved (1.2.1): *insurgere paulatim, munia senatus magistratuum legum in se trahere* ('he rose up gradually and drew to himself the responsibilities of senate, magistrates and laws'). The problem of how to represent the continuation of the Principate from

---

[6] Woodman (1997) 94; O'Gorman (1995) 93–4.
[7] On the term see Gowing (2005) 40 n. 27.
[8] Woodman (1998) 23.
[9] This is an idea and a technique that Tacitus owes primarily to Livy among his Latin precursors, and Herodotus among his Greek.
[10] Above all, see Henderson (1989) and Quint (1993).

its first to its second (etc.) holder overlaps with Tacitus' problem of how to write history that successfully continues the historiography that precedes him. From the first, just as the 'one and only' ruler of Rome (e.g. 1.6.3, 9.4; H.1.1.1) was threatened, augmented and buttressed by potential successions, partners and doubles, so Tacitus' text challenges, emulates and doubles his historiographical precursors.[11]

Livy's role in the opening paragraphs we have already seen. He is strongly evoked as well at the death of Augustus (1.5.4), where Livia controls access to information in the same way that Tanaquil does while arranging the successor to Tarquinius Priscus (Livy 1.41).[12] Sallust, too, is prominent. The allusion in 1.1.1 *Vrbem Romam a principio reges habuere* to *Cat.* 6.1 *Vrbem Romam, sicuti ego accepi, condidere atque habuere initio Troiani* ('Trojans, as I understand it, founded and held the city of Rome from the beginning') has been well recognised.[13] As with the beginning of *Annals* 4, where a strong allusion to the *Bellum Catilinae* helps bring out the potentially monographic quality of this Sejanus book, so here quotation of the opening words of Sallust's archaeology suggests that the *Annals* will participate in the Sallustian analysis of socio-political debasement reflected by and concentrated in a single, poisonous citizen whose own corruption exploits that of his state.[14] Tacitus' positioning of himself as successor to his historiographical precursors advertises that this text will be both Livian and Sallustian, both annalistic and monographic – a combination of the deeds of the Romans and the deeds of the individual emperors.

illuc cuncta uergere

Tacitus' Tiberius bodies forth the preface's flirtation with rivalrous plurality. He is, famously, hooded, withdrawn, secretive, *simulator* and *dissimulator* at once. He is also a man for whom Tacitus has considerable respect (all appearances to the contrary).[15] He comes gradually in to the narrative, always in a context of pairing or syncrisis. First, as one of two stepsons

---

[11] For Tacitus' intertextual games see above, pp. 1–7; on the *aemulatio* in Tacitus' prefaces see Marincola (1999).

[12] Charlesworth (1927). There is much historiographically significant Livy in Tacitus: see Kraus (1994b) for one point of overlap.

[13] Goodyear (1972) ad loc.; for Tacitus' use of his precursors see Woodman (1979) (= (1998) 70–85); also above, pp. 2–4, and Chapter 1.

[14] For Tacitus' biographical mode, especially in the case of Tiberius, see Syme (1974) (= (1984) 937–52) and Kraus (2005), with refs. there cited.

[15] Tacitus' 'portrait of Tiberius consists of a whole series of modifications or adjustments, as if he were photographing his subject from a series of different angles and in different lights: none of the frames, whether in close-up or not, is contradicted by another, but each produces a different effect' (Martin and Woodman (1989) 31).

(1.3.1); when all the other successors have died away, he is still *priuignus* (1.3.3) – and his mother, the archetypal stepmother (1.10.5), pulls his and the Republic's strings (1.3.3 *matris artibus*; 1.4.5 *matrem muliebri inpotentia … seruiendum feminae*). Stressing Tiberius' adoptive status, and stressing too the series of adoptions in the melee of would-be *principes*, Tacitus keeps us focused on the obliquity with which power is approached and secured.[16] Even after *illuc cuncta uergere*, a blood-related potential successor, Agrippa Postumus, is still in play, though already in exile (1.3.4). Tacitus brings him back into the narrative for Tiberius' first character sketch. Foreshadowing the famous paired assessments of Augustus (1.9–10), this is couched as a syncrisis embedded in a rumour (1.4.2–3):

> by far the greatest number [of people] spread various rumours of the masters looming over them: Agrippa was callous and blazing from ignominy, unequal to so great a task in both age and experience of affairs; Tiberius Nero was mature in years and proved in war, but with the old and endemic haughtiness of the Claudian family; and many indications of his savagery, despite attempts at their suppression, kept breaking out.

Though Livia and Sallustius Crispus, her *particeps secretorum* (1.6.3), dispatch Agrippa as the first deed (*facinus*) of the new principate, hardly a page goes by before Tacitus confronts Tiberius with another potential rival, Germanicus (1.7.6; p. 107 below). Whether based in fact or paranoia (not always his own!), Tiberius is constantly throughout the hexad in counterpoint with men who may – or could – or might – replace him.[17] Tacitus finishes the first major unit of his *Annals* with the man's obituary, in which we see Tiberius' whole life as moving through a series of stages, confronted always either with rivals or with partners (including even Augustus, with whom he shared *tribunicia potestas*), never alone until the very end (6.51).[18] His alarming declaration that he would undertake the oversight of a part, rather than the whole, of the *res publica* (1.12.2) coheres with both his introduction and his obituary. The Tacitean Tiberius will be, must be, judged in his relationships with others.

Comparatio is a rhetorical and conceptual tool. Comparing types of government allowed historians and philosophers to evaluate the strengths and weaknesses of each – and, in particular, to see where one might (or must) tip, blurrily, into another. Tacitus' beginning puts various constitutional forms

---

[16] Adoption continued to be a cornerstone of imperial ideology: see below, pp. 215–18.
[17] Tiberius discusses his own potential successor at 6.46.1.
[18] Woodman (1989) 198–9 (= (1998) 157–9), on the obituary, argues convincingly that Tiberius wanted helpers and associates. For Sejanus, his most notorious 'partner', see Bird (1969); Martin and Woodman (1989) Index 1, s.v. 'Sejanus'.

side by side: on Augustus' death, the debate about whether the Republic should be restored begins (1.4.2), a debate that will be repeated historiographically at least until the accession of Trajan.[19] Throughout the *Annals*, both through familial allusion and the ceaseless play of the 'republican' annalistic form against the imperial content, Tacitus keeps alive the comparison of types of regime.

Ancient historiography is strongly rooted in the tradition of epideixis – that is, the rhetorical categories of praise and blame. *Comparatio* is a crucial element here, as well, especially when the movement is from one ruler to another.[20] In choosing his successor, Tacitus insinuates, Augustus was proleptically playing a particularly unpleasant game. In his final imperial act, rumour has it, 'by the basest of comparisons he had sought glory for himself' (1.10.7). This comparison of successor to precursor, of course, is also the central act in the exemplary habit that structured Roman elite culture and its historiography. The past – especially the familial past – is there for men to imitate or avoid;[21] the imitation, in particular, can be successful only when so evaluated by a judging community.[22] This holds not only for historical actors, but for their chroniclers as well. By introducing Tiberius as he does, Tacitus confronts us with the omnipresent weight of the past, both lived and written, and with the insistent pressure in the present to judge and be judged.

Whether true or not, the rumour about Augustus' cutting *comparatio deterrima* was not idle. The figure against whom Tiberius is most consistently judged is, in fact, his adoptive father.[23] This is an emulous relationship that Tiberius embraces.[24] From the beginning, he is keen to remain within the boundaries set by Mr Big (*aug-*) (1.14.4): 'candidatos praeturae duodecim nominauit, numerum ab Augusto traditum; et hortante senatu ut *augeret*, iure iurando obstrinxit se non *excessurum*' ('He nominated twelve candidates for the praetorship, the number transmitted by Augustus; and when

---

[19] Syme (1958a) 28 and Index s.v. 'republicanism'; Wiseman (1991) 73–4; for an acute discussion of the historiography of republicanism see Gowing (2005). On earlier constitutional debates see Pelling (2002b).
[20] E.g. Plin. *Pan.* 53.1, 6; see Vell. Pat. 2.126.2 with Woodman (1977) ad loc. and Lausberg (1998) 625–6 s.v. 'comparatio'.
[21] On *imitatio* and the family see Flower (1996); on exemplarity and historiography, Chaplin (2000); Roller (2004); Kraus (forthcoming).
[22] Roller (2004) 4–5.
[23] Cf. Woodman and Martin (1996) 11, 'By means of reference, contrast and comparison the precedent of the Augustan principate is placed constantly before the reader of *Annals* 3'; on the implicit comparison of Tacitus' emperors with Domitian see Walker (1952) 204–34.
[24] Levick (1999b) 82–3; specific examples at Woodman and Martin (1996) on *A.* 3.56.3 *quo tunc exemplo*.

the senate urged him to augment it, he pledged on oath that he would not exceed it').[25] As his rule develops, he returns to this as a principle: 'Tiberius did not allow himself to infringe [Divine Augustus'] words' (1.77.3); 'I observe all [Divine Augustus'] actions and words as if law' (4.37.3). Yet the possibility of a *comparatio deterrima* gnaws at him: his observance of Augustus' precedent is not without (personal) cost.[26]

Germanicus and the women

Women have their uses for historians.[27]

After his first ardent rush back from Illyricum to Augustus' bedside (1.5.3), the Tacitean Tiberius tends to remain still. If not in Campania or on Capri (3.21.2–64.1; 4.57–6), he can generally be found at Rome. Yet the geographical reach of the Tiberian hexad spans the empire, from Britain to Egypt, north to the Rhine forests and east to Antioch. Hence, despite Tacitus' claims to write *in arto* (4.32.2),[28] his text enjoys that 'room to move' that he attributes to the expansive historians of the republic (4.32.2 *libero egressu*). By returning us periodically to Rome, the heavy-handed punctuation of the text by *At Romae* (e.g. 1.7.1; 2.82.1; 3.22.1; 6.2.1) introduces a structural responsion between the centre and periphery that reinforces Tacitus' implicit demand that we compare the imperial centre with the other important players. In particular, Tacitus plays Tiberius against Germanicus, on the one hand, and two imperial women, on the other – characters who are as consistently to be found outside Rome (Germanicus and Agrippina) as in it (Livia).

The process of *comparatio* begins after Tiberius' reluctant entry into power (1.6–15), when the narrative shoots north for two simultaneous mutinies, in Pannonia (1.16–30) and Germania (1.31–49). With these paired narratives, which are put in explicit counterpoise (1.31.1 *isdem ferme diebus isdem causis*),[29] Tacitus opens up the implications of his first chapters, in which he began tracing a net of relationships among the members of the imperial family. Tiberius' sons, who were introduced at 1.3.5 *Germanicum Druso ortum ... in domo Tiberii filius iuuenis*, are picked up chiastically.

---

[25] For a complex discussion of this play between increase (*aug-, exc-*) and limit see O'Gorman (2000) 24–5.
[26] E.g. at 1.76.4 'As to why Tiberius himself kept away from the spectacle, there were various interpretations, some saying it was because of his aversion to gatherings, some his grimness of temperament and dread of comparison [*metu comparationis*], because Augustus had attended affably [*comiter*].'
[27] Syme (1986) 168.
[28] For this interpretation see below, pp. 226–7.
[29] See Woodman (2006a).

Tacitus first brings his natural son Drusus from Rome to put down the Pannonian mutiny (which he does with a certain violent efficiency), then moves west to the adopted Germanicus, who is already in Gaul (1.31.2, 33.1) and about to be embroiled with similar problems – which he handles ineptly and histrionically. The narrative of foreign affairs will remain primarily with Germanicus until his death in Syria at 2.73 (a story continued until his ashes return to Rome, 3.1–6). Thus, though Drusus is consul in 15, the campaign year is all Germanicus' (spring and summer against the Chatti and Cherusci, 1.55–8, 59–71). Tacitus uses Germanicus to continue the succession debate: before his official introduction at 1.33.1, he is mentioned thrice, each time in the context of imperial prerogatives (at 1.3.5 he is a *munimentum* in addition to Tiberius' own son; at 1.7.6 he causes Tiberius to fear 'lest [he] ... prefer to hold rather than to wait for command'; at 1.14.3, together with Livia and Drusus, Germanicus receives princely honours). Finally, just before he comes on the scene in Germany, we are told that 'Cassius Chaerea, who later achieved his memorial among posterity for the slaughter of C. Caesar, ... opened up with his sword a passage through the armed [mutineers]' (1.32.2). We have already met a Cassius who helped kill a Caesar (only to be killed himself: 1.2.1 *Bruto et Cassio caesis*). With the assassin of 'Caligula' we are pulled forward to the year 41, the convenient habit of Roman names repeated from one generation to the next underscoring, as so often, the tendency of Empire to duplicate itself, and of history to move through cycles both exemplary and traumatic. Germanicus is thus brought into the narrative in contexts that consistently remind us that, even with Augustus safely cremated and Tiberius in charge, there is always the next emperor to reckon with.[30]

Tiberius is brought into the narrative proper as Augustus' stepson (1.3.1 *priuignos*; 1.3.3 *solus e priuignis*), a precise designation that puts him as much in point with his mother as with his 'father'. And indeed Livia Augusta takes her own oblique position with regard to the Empire, being first designated as Gaius' and Lucius' 'stepmother' (1.3.3 *nouercae Liuiae*). Tiberius' move to the centre of power pulls the relationships straight, however – he is suddenly *filius* ('son') and Livia now seen not in relation to other potential successors but to her own child (1.3.3 *matris*, 'his mother'). Tiberius, then, arrives on the scene as a stepson and a son, accompanied by a stepmother who is also a mother.[31] This tangle of designations appropriately alerts us

---

[30] Gaius is, of course, Germanicus' child – and himself appears at 1.40.4 as the *paruulus filius* ('tiny little son') whom Agrippina cradles as she is escorted from the mutinous camp.
[31] See especially 1.10.5 *grauis in rem publicam mater, grauis domui Caesarum nouerca* ('her burden on the state as a mother being matched by that on the Caesars' family as a stepmother'). On representations of ancient stepmothers see Watson (1995).

to how an imperial character's label will determine what his or her place is – and to how filiation can both make and break a life.

When Germanicus enters the narrative proper, it is also with women at his side, women who are themselves locked in a heated rivalry, which Tacitus represents – again – with a comparative expression, the adjective *commotior* (1.33.1–34.1):

> Meanwhile Germanicus ... received the news that Augustus had passed away. He had the latter's granddaughter Agrippina in marriage and several children by her, being himself the offspring of Drusus (Tiberius' brother) and the grandson of Augusta, but tense [*anxius*] from his uncle's and grandmother's concealed hatred of him, the reasons for which were all the more bitter because unjust. (The memory of Drusus among the Roman people was considerable, and it was believed that, if he had been in charge of affairs, he would have given them back their freedom. Hence goodwill [*fauor*] toward Germanicus, and the same hope [*spes*]. For [*nam*] the young man had the instinct of an ordinary citizen and a remarkable affability [*mira comitas*] quite different from Tiberius' conversation and look, arrogant and dark as they were.) In addition there were womanly affronts, with Livia's stepmotherly goadings of Agrippina [*nouercalibus Liuiae in Agrippinam stimulis*], and Agrippina herself a little too volatile [*commotior*], except that, with her chastity and her love for her husband, she turned her (albeit untamed) spirit to good effect.

The two couples – Tiberius and his mother Livia, Germanicus and his wife Agrippina – are not, of course, precisely comparable; but that is partly the point. Descent (Germanicus from Drusus the potential republican, Agrippina from Augustus ~ Tiberius from not-Augustus), appearance and manner (accessibility ~ arrogance; [implied] beauty, cf. 2.73.1 'his good looks' ~ severe countenance), popularity (favour ~ [implied] lack of favour), affection (marital love ~ familial hate) are all measured one against the other. Tacitus' closing statement (1.34.1 'the closer Germanicus now was to that highest of all hopes, the more emphatically did he strive on Tiberius' behalf') imagines an equilibrium (*quanto ... tanto*) that has already been challenged by this introduction. It is also the only statement in this paragraph – apart from the prosopographical details, themselves hardly innocent (see below) – that specifies something about *Germanicus* himself, rather than reflecting a perception of him. The detail about his affability, in particular, seems at first to be a flat statement of fact: but *nam* makes it explanatory of the crowd's *fauor et spes*, while *mira* not only indicates a kind of admiring judgement, but echoes Tiberius' own perception of Germanicus' popularity at 1.7.6: *mirus apud populum fauor* ('remarkable goodwill among the people').

Strong links anchor this brief introduction to the rest of Germanicus' portrait in the *Annals*. Aside from *mira* and *fauor*, which take us back to

Tiberius' first days as *princeps*, *anxius* – here used of the effect Tiberius and Livia have on their relatives – picks up the adjective used to characterise the emperor himself in dealing with the honours proposed for his mother (1.14.2). The next honours to be decided? Those of Germanicus Caesar (1.14.3). Germanicus' identification as the son of a father who might have returned Rome to a republic is echoed later, during his last illness (e.g. 1.33.2 *libertatem redditurus ... ciuile ingenium* ~ 2.82.2 *ciuilia ingenia ... reddita libertate*), while his own self-modelling as the son equal to a famous father surfaces, for example, at 2.7–8, where he summons up Drusus as a model to guide him militarily. Germanicus' wife and numerous children, highlighted here, as elsewhere in the *Annals*, remind us of his family's role in the Principate (brother Claudius, son Gaius, grandson Nero) – and would remind Tiberius of his own unhappy and childless marriage to Julia Augusti,[32] who, though providing Tiberius with a closer agnate relationship to Augustus than Germanicus enjoyed, exhibited anything but *amor mariti*. It was his own marriage to another daughter of Agrippa that Tiberius cherished, but that was ruined by imperial ambition (Suet. *Tib.* 7; Dio 54.6).

The Tacitean portrait of Germanicus is famously ambivalent. The germs of that ambivalence are clear at 1.33: he is the target of Tiberius' jealousy, yet he works hard for Tiberius; he is paired with a woman who, it is implied, will push as hard for him as Livia does for Tiberius; he is popular, where Tiberius is not, and open, where Tiberius is obscure. As his portrait develops, however, it becomes obvious that that popularity and openness are increasingly problematic in a world of increasingly cloaked behaviour: whether right or wrong, Germanicus' is the kind of personality that cannot succeed in a Principate.[33]

There are suggestions earlier on as well that, however much Germanicus strives for Tiberius (*pro Tiberio niti*), he is doomed to disaster. His first mention in the text is 1.3.5–7:

> [Augustus] installed Germanicus ... over the eight legions on the Rhine ... As for war, none survived at that time except against the Germans, more to erase the infamy of the army lost with Quintilius Varus than through any desire of extending the empire .... At home things were calm, magistrates had the same designations. But the younger men had been born after the Actian victory, and the majority even of the elderly in the course of the citizens' wars: what size was the remaining proportion, who had seen the republic?

The defeat of Varus and the battle of Actium are parts of Germanicus' world both physically and thematically. It is the attention he pays to the bodies of

---

[32] The couple had one son who died in infancy.
[33] See Pelling (1993).

the legions killed in the Teutoburger Wald that jeopardises his command in Germany, nearly results in a second massacre and brings him Tiberius' (justified) disapproval (1.62.2). That unfolding debacle in the German forests also establishes Germanicus as a man overly emotional (1.61.1), dependent on his wife (1.69.2) and as a potential hero of epic[34] – but definitely not as an imperial general.

Actium, his much celebrated victory over Cleopatra and Antonius in 31 BC, was the battle that confirmed Augustus' sole power at Rome. Tacitus' several introductions of Germanicus nowhere identify his mother. She was Antonia, daughter of Antonius and Augustus' sister Octavia. Germanicus is, therefore, related on both sides to civil war.[35] His slow progress through the East (where he will die, either of a disease or of poison, in Syria) takes in the sights, especially the Dalmatian coast, Troy and Egypt (2.53–4, 59–61 [excerpts]):

> But Germanicus ... after visiting his brother Drusus .... went to the bays renowned for their Actian victory and, enshrined by Augustus, the trophies, and the encampment of Antonius, everywhere accompanied by the recollection of his own ancestors. For, as I have recalled [at 2.43.5], Augustus had been his great-uncle and Antonius his grandfather; and vivid was the vision there of sadness and delight.

He goes on to Athens, which he enters modestly; then to Troy (via Lesbos, where Agrippina has another child), 'in his desire to become acquainted with old places celebrated by fame' (*cupidine ueteres locos et fama celebratos noscendi*). In the following year he travels to Egypt 'to become acquainted with antiquity' (*cognoscendae antiquitatis*):

> But his pretence was concern for the province, and he alleviated the prices of crops ... and he adopted many habits welcome to the public – walking around without soldiery, his feet uncovered, and in an attire identical with that of the Greeks, in emulation of P. Scipio ... Tiberius, after a mildly scathing reference to his style and clothing, berated him very sharply because, contrary to the established usage of Augustus, he had gone into Alexandria without the princeps' consent. ... But Germanicus ... travelled up the Nile ... Then he visited the vast vestiges of old Thebes. And on the massive structures there remained Egyptian letters, summarising its former wealthiness ... Germanicus directed his attention to other marvels, too [*aliis quoque miraculis*].

The extended narrative begins with memorials to Germanicus' family, in which he visits not only his own living brother, but also the Augustan

---

[34] O'Gorman (1995) 108.
[35] For the importance of prosopography, even when implicit, in understanding Roman history see Damon (1994).

trophy at Nicopolis, together with the *castra Antonii*.³⁶ The scene, delicately sketched, conjures up memories (cf. *recordatione, memorauimus, imago*) of Odysseus tracing Trojan topography in the sand (Ov. *Ars Am.* 2.123–40) or of the Trojans visiting the abandoned Greek compound (Virg. *Aen.* 2.27–30). Germanicus' progress takes in famous sites associated with both sides of his family: Troy and especially Egypt.³⁷ In every case, he is eager to learn about the past – a tendency to turn backward that metaphorically continues his association with the Roman past, i.e. the Republic; but one which also contrasts with Agrippina's fecundity. Germanicus does consult an oracle at Colophon, but his interest is otherwise firmly in measuring antiquity, as he admires the uncountable depths of the Nile (2.61.1) and invites Tacitean comparison of the extent of empires past and present (2.60.4, 61.2).

Germanicus himself is unaware of the havoc he is causing. Though he has civil war in his genes, he yet unthinkingly manipulates grain prices in Alexandria, a potentially revolutionary action that serves as a pretext (!) for his sightseeing; he imitates the *popularis* behaviour of Scipio Aemilianus in Egypt and of Antonius in Athens;³⁸ and, most of all, he follows the urging of his *cupido*, which repeatedly sends him back, prompting him to pay homage to the Roman dead in the forest of Teutoburg (1.61.1) and to visit the site of ruined Troy (2.54.1). With his fecund wife beside him, he measures out the limits of Roman *imperium*, from the *fossa Drusi* to Parthia to Elephantine. His travels eerily combine the future of Empire, contained in Agrippina's womb, with the past of the Republic, just as they move Tacitus from his confection of annalistic, imperial historiography into a kind of paradoxographical (2.61.1 *miraculis*), ethnographic antiquarianism.³⁹ The latter suspends forward motion in favour of a kind of aimless wandering inappropriate for a Roman emperor.⁴⁰ Tiberius sees only the threat to himself from this foolish, charismatic young man who could blockade Rome's food supplies if he wanted to, or swoop down upon the capital with his German legions; but Germanicus has no eye for the future. It is ironically fitting, then, that when Agrippina returns to Rome with his ashes, she carries them before her in an urn, repeating the gesture that we have seen earlier, as she carries her children, either in her womb or outside it (3.1.4).

---

³⁶ Tacitus does not mention that Augustus' trophy was on the site of his own *castra*; his description of this Actian tourism thus distinguishes between the permanence of Augustan victory and the transient topography of encampment (*castra Antonii*).
³⁷ See respectively Sage (2000) 212–14 and Foertmeyer (1989) 104–58.
³⁸ See Goodyear (1981) on 2.53.3.
³⁹ Gabba (1981). On Germanicus' travels see O'Gorman (2000) 62–6; on Agrippina see below.
⁴⁰ Germanicus' travel to Egypt may assimilate him to (impractical, if not sybaritic) philosophers, on whose eastern travels see Parker (2008) 263.

The Tacitean Agrippina is a kind of hypostatised womb, a perpetual reminder of the power of genealogy in the development of the Principate.[41] After Germanicus' death, she returns throughout the pages of *A*. 3 and 4 as an irritant (4.52), as someone to be kept from marriage (4.53) and as a preserver of memory: her human fertility turns to literary fertility, as her eponymous daughter is revealed to be the author of one of Tacitus' written sources (4.53.2). After the break-off of Book 5, she reappears only to die (*A*. 6.25–6) – but Tacitus' obituary notice continues the sense of her importance as more than just a point of prosopographical interest (6.25):

> Their pain at this [the death of Drusus] had not yet abated, when they heard about Agrippina, who I deem lived on after the killing of Sejanus because she was nurtured by hope .... Certainly Tiberius flared up with the foulest charges, accusing her of immorality and Asinius Gallus as her adulterer, and that his death had driven her to an aversion for life. (But in fact Agrippina, impatient of equality and greedy for mastery [*aequi inpatiens, dominandi auida*], had cast off female flaws in a preference for men's concerns.) Caesar added that her decease had taken place on the same day as Sejanus had paid the penalty two years previously and that the fact should be handed down to memory.

This spiteful paragraph, in which Tiberius and Tacitus together assess Agrippina, immortalises her as a Clytemnestra figure, more man than woman, imperial in her inability to bear an equal (cf. Lucan 1.124–5). Tiberius, in particular, sees her not as a mother of princes, but as a lustful woman, who in her uncontrolled sexuality is the twin to Sejanus. Of her many children, who populated the earlier books, not a word.

By contrast, the role of mother is emphasised for Livia Augusta, whose obituary opens what little remains of Book 5:

> Her first marriage and children [*liberi*] were with Tiberius Nero .... Thereupon Caesar, in his desire for her good looks, removed her from her husband ... and so swiftly that he allowed not even an interval for childbirth [*ad enitendum*], installing her at his own hearth while she was still heavily pregnant [*grauidam*]. She produced no progeny thereafter [*nullam posthac subolem edidit*], but, being connected to the blood of Augustus through the union of Agrippina and Germanicus, had great-grandchildren [*pronepotes*] in common with him. In the purity of her house she conformed to old-time convention but was affable beyond what females of antiquity approved; an unruly mother [*mater inpotens*], a complaisant wife and a good match for the qualities of her husband and the hypocrisy of her son [*filii*] ... She was praised before the rostra by her great-grandson [*pronepote*], C. Caesar, who later took control of affairs.

---

[41] Associated 'inextricably with her uterus' (O'Gorman (2000) 73–4). Her daughter and namesake took on the same role with her last words, *uentrem feri* (14.8.5 'stab my womb [first]').

As in Agrippina's case, the obituary mentions the woman's manners and her sex life, but whereas Tacitus omits Agrippina's many children, despite their having figured so prominently in the preceding books, in Livia's send-off he adverts to all her descendants, even co-opting Agrippina's children. Though she (notoriously) bore no child to Augustus, Livia entered the *Annals* as mother and stepmother (above, p. 108). These roles are the natural inverse of each other: it is the stepmother who displaces the mother, often bringing in her own offspring to supplant the legitimate children. As discussed above, however, Livia's position in the dynasty, together with the Principate's reliance on an interweaving of adoptive and cognate relationships, problematises the position of 'mater' from the beginning, a problematic that Livia's obituary does little to solve.

Livia's final assessment is further marked by elements traditional in a woman's obituary: aside from children, we see her nobility of blood, maintenance of decent home life and attractive appearance.[42] In Tacitus' hands the last, in particular, borders on the pejorative, reminding us of the dangers posed by *comitas* and *forma*. These were Germanicus' traits. More worldly-wise than her step-grandson, Livia knew better how to use them, but a strong allusion to Livy points out just how close to the edge she skated. With *cupidine formae* Tacitus evokes Livy's Lucretia, the most famous wool-maker of them all, whose chastity was violated by Sextus Tarquinius (1.57.10 *cum forma tum spectata castitas incitat*: 'both her beauty and her demonstrated fidelity inflamed him').

Lucretia's end was not for Livia. And, as Purcell points out,[43] the (perceived) problem with Livia is that she had far too much real *potentia*, including being legally free of male control (*tutela*) and enjoying tribunician *sacrosanctitas*. Her maternity extends beyond normal range: despite her (relative) lack of offspring, she enjoyed the *ius trium liberorum* and was proposed for the title *mater patriae* (1.14.6, refused by Tiberius), a female version of the emperor's role. If the *Annals* was originally called *Ab excessu diui Augusti*, then it is in fact Livia who determines the narrative's starting point: for it is she, at 1.5.4, who controls access and the flow of information in and out of the house at Nola in which Augustus lay dying – or dead.[44]

---

[42] Tacitus omits her famous wool-making and cooking/medicinal skills: Purcell (1986) 94–5 and especially n. 94 for the ancient sources.
[43] Purcell (1986) 96.
[44] On Tacitean women controlling borders and on display see O'Gorman (2000) 69–77 and 128–30 (especially 130, on 1.5.4: 'the narrator's voice, therefore, competes with that of the empress'); Santoro L'Hoir (2006), esp. 111–57; for Livy's role in this episode see above, p. 104.

FURTHER READING

For Tiberius the man, see the biographies by Levick (1999b) and Seager (2005), both second editions; there is much valuable information in the first six volumes of Syme's *Roman Papers* (Oxford 1979–91). The relationship between contemporary culture and Tiberius' intellectual interests is explored by Champlin (2006–7). Woodman (1998) contains seven of the author's classic papers on the Tiberian hexad; see also his commentaries, co-authored with Ronald Martin, on *A.* 3 (1996) and 4 (1989 and often reprinted). On the form of 'annals' there are useful discussions by Ginsburg (1981) and Rich (2009), and detailed analysis of selected connective and contrastive narrative phrases, which often leads to important historiographical conclusions, in Chausserie-Laprée (1969) and Mendell (1911). Finally, for the effect of rhetorical form on the content of historiography, in addition to the works cited in the essay, see Sinclair (1995). There is useful material on Tacitean obituaries in Gingras (1992) and Pomeroy (1991); on women in Tacitus see especially Ginsburg (2006); on the battle of the Teutoburg Forest see Pagán (2002); for an extensive discussion of the historiographical comparison of empires in the Republican and imperial periods see Yarrow (2006).

8

S. J. V. MALLOCH

Hamlet without the prince? The Claudian *Annals*

Claudius' story?

With the benefit of hindsight Tacitus can single out a moment for emphasis that may seem trivial when viewed from a contemporary perspective. Claudius is the subject of one such moment in 20. Thanks are proposed in the senate to individual members of the imperial family for avenging the death of Germanicus. L. Asprenas draws attention to the omission of Claudius' name, and it is added at the end.[1] Pondering the moment, insignificant in itself, Tacitus is struck by 'the mockeries made of mortal affairs in every business: in fame, in hope, and in veneration everyone was destined for imperial power rather than the future *princeps* whom fortune was keeping in hiding' (3.18.4). Tacitus clearly relished the irony of the situation, and it gave him the opportunity to glance forward in his work.[2] In 20 Claudius had been forgotten, as he would later be in 41 before the discovery that resulted in his elevation to Empire;[3] and his liminal presence under Tiberius prefigures his marginality in his own reign. Claudius' passivity will become the central feature of Tacitus' portrait of an emperor dominated by his wives and freedmen.[4] Tacitus is explicit: Claudius was 'submissive to spouses' commands'

---

[1] Note that at *SCPP* 148 Claudius is the last member of the imperial family to be thanked.
[2] Cf. proleptic notices at *A*. 1.13.3, 32.2 (with Pelling (1993) 82 n. 59; Malloch (2004) 205 n. 29); 4.31.3; 6.32.4; 11.25.5 (two in the final sentence).
[3] Cf. Suet. *Claud.* 10.2; Dio 60.1.2. As Woodman and Martin (1996) on *A*. 3.18.4 well point out, Tacitus' reference to fortune's (*fortuna*) keeping Claudius in hiding (*in occulto*) is 'presumably a sardonic allusion' to Claudius' hiding behind a curtain on Gaius' death and his later chance discovery and elevation to Empire.
[4] It is, in fact, the dominant tradition on Claudius: cf. Sen. *Apoc.* 6.2; 8.1; 13.5; Juv. 14.329–31; Suet. *Claud.* 25.5; 29.1; *Vit.* 2.5; Dio 60.1.3, 2.4–7, 8.6, 14, 15.5, 18.3, 28.2, 28.4, 31.5, 31.8, 32.1–2, 33.3a, 33.6, 33.10; Aur. Vict. *Caes.* 4.5, 12; *Epit.* 4.3. Tacitus can present Claudius positively (see below), but these odd occasions do not fundamentally adjust the negative portrait; rather, they throw it into sharper relief. For Claudius' depiction in the ancient sources, see Syme (1958a) 259–60, 436–7; Momigliano (1961c) 77–9; Vessey (1971); Martin (1981) 144 and (1990) 1579; Griffin (1982a) 418, (1990) 483–4 and (1994); Huzar (1984) 612–18; Hurley (2001) 14–17.

(12.1.1); and later he remarks on the 'mentality of a *princeps* who showed neither approval nor hatred unless each had been implanted and ordered' (12.3.2).[5] Tacitus pushes Claudius' passivity so far that he is displaced as the focus of his own history: Claudius ends up a character in other people's stories. In the extant text these dramatic stories revolve around the fall of Messalina, the power of the freedmen, the domination of Agrippina and the rise of Nero. The portraits of Messalina as the sexual fiend and Agrippina as the scheming, power-hungry *dominatrix* become delineated as the women take the stage. The freedmen's ability to manipulate and control Claudius with devastating effect is shown in their destruction of Messalina. These characterisations in turn reflect back on Claudius as a husband and ruler, and more generally criticise a system that allowed women and subordinates excessive political power.[6]

Annals 11 culminates in thirteen vivid chapters describing the doom of Messalina. The episode is preceded by the simultaneous termination of Claudius' censorship and his ignorance of palace affairs (11.25.5 'condiditque lustrum ... isque illi finis inscitiae erga domum suam fuit'),[7] which closes, 'ring style', an account of Claudius' censorship that started at 11.13.1 with a statement of his ignorance of his marital situation and his assumption of censorial duties ('at Claudius, matrimonii sui ignarus et munia censoria usurpans').[8] Claudius' passivity has already been demonstrated during the downfall of D. Valerius Asiaticus and Poppaea Sabina (11.1–4)[9] and is ironically heightened by his newly gained knowledge: Tacitus switches focus

---

[5] Tacitus also focalises commentary on Claudius through Silius (11.26.2) and the imperial freedmen (11.28.2).

[6] For Messalina and Agrippina, see Ginsburg (2006); Santoro L'Hoir (2006) ch. 3. For the imperial freedmen, see Duff (1958); Weaver (1972). Modern historians generally reject the image of a Claudius dominated by his freedmen and argue that he permitted them power: see e.g. Wiedemann (1996) 237–8; Levick (1990) 83; Millar (1967) 15, (1992) 74–7; cf. Scramuzza (1940) 85–9.

[7] Claudius' final acts as censor elicit from Tacitus his most positive comments about the *princeps* in the extant text (11.25.2–4). Claudius' competency and dignity pave the way for the highly artificial intersection of the closure of his censorship and the proleptic notice of his subsequent knowledge of Messalina's *flagitia*. Claudius' salutary acquisition of knowledge could hardly have been foregrounded by a hostile characterisation; but Tacitus denies him a change for the better first by stating that he was forced to take notice of and punish Messalina's outrages ('noscere ac punire adactus') and then by looking forward to his incestuous marriage to Agrippina (11.25.5).

[8] Cf. Martin (1990) 1580 n. 223. Tacitus is partial to 'ring composition': see Martin and Woodman (1989) index s.v. 'ring structure'; Woodman (1998) 145–9, 229–30.

[9] Claudius' marginality is particularly emphasised by his not being the subject of the ironic sentence (11.3.1) in which he hands down a judgement of death on Asiaticus that apes the opinion of L. Vitellius: 'and the words of Claudius followed in favour of the same clemency' ('et secuta sunt Claudii uerba in eandem clementiam'). For this episode, see Mehl (1974) 13–39.

from his censorship to Messalina and Silius (11.26.1) – and practically omits Claudius from the story until 11.31.[10] Tacitus works hard to emphasise Claudius' marginality. The reaction to the wedding of Messalina and Silius is not led by Claudius (cf. 11.25.5) but by Narcissus, an influential freedman at the centre of power in the imperial *domus* (cf. 11.28.1).[11] Narcissus distinguishes himself by bringing Messalina's affair to Claudius' attention, and Claudius ultimately gives him complete control over the response (11.29.2–3, 33). He dominates the events – 'there was universal obedience to the freedman' (11.35.1 *omnia liberto oboediebant*) – and even marginalises Messalina as part of his strategy of destroying her (cf. 11.34.2–3, 37.2). His energy in pursuing his goal contrasts with the fear (11.31.1), agitation (11.33.1), confusion (11.34.1) and silence (11.35.1) that define Claudius' reaction to the situation. Finally, the dining scene that rather perversely follows the slaughter of Silius and his associates brings out the worst in Claudius: only food and wine put him in the mood to summon Messalina to plead her case (11.37.2), and later, unmoved at the news of her death, 'he requested a cup and celebrated the party as usual' (11.38.2; cf. Suet. *Claud.* 39.1). The convivial context adds more negative connotations to his passivity, and, by evoking the incompatibility between dining and death already exploited in the case of Poppaea Sabina (11.2.2), Tacitus emphasises the inappropriateness of Claudius' handling of the situation.[12]

Claudius has reached a low point from which he will not recover. His marriage to Agrippina is decided by his freedmen (12.1.1–3.1), who are at the zenith of their domination, and L. Vitellius, ever sensitive to shifts in power (12.4.1, cf. 11.34.1), assists by pursuing Agrippina's enemies and winning over the senate (12.4, 5.2–6.3). Behind the freedmen and Vitellius looms the figure of Agrippina, who Tacitus says had long been insinuating herself into Claudius' confidence and affections (12.3.1).[13] The wedding brings to Claudius' principate a new phase, which Tacitus associates with Agrippina, who now propels the narrative.[14] She begins to assert a

---

[10] Claudius' removal to Ostia at 11.26.3 is focalised through Messalina's planning and is primarily a plot device. At 11.30 Tacitus is concerned with Messalina's denouncers, and he brings Claudius into full view only when he summons his advisory council at 11.31.1.

[11] For Messalina and Silius, see Fagan (2002); for Messalina in Tacitus, see Joshel (1997); Questa (1998) ch. 2.

[12] Cf. 3.9.3; at *SCPP* 66–8 Cn. Calpurnius Piso's banquets in the aftermath of Germanicus' death count against him. For the incompatibility of mourning and dining, see Roller (2001) 164 n. 55; for death and banquets, see Paul (1991) 164–6; Gowers (1993) 38; for Claudius and banquets, cf. 12.64.2; *H.* 1.48.3; Sen. *Apoc.* 8.2; Suet. *Claud.* 33.1; Dio 60.2.5–7, 7.4; Aur. Vict. *Caes.* 4.1; *Epit.* 4.3.

[13] For Tacitus' portrayal of Agrippina, see Ginsburg (2006).

[14] The shift in power from the freedmen to Agrippina is marked by an echo: compare 11.35.1 'omnia liberto oboediebant' ('there was universal obedience to the freedman') with 12.7.3

Hamlet without the prince? The Claudian *Annals*

masculine domination; austere and more often arrogant in public, she was not unchaste in private except to advance her power (12.7.3), a sinister foreshadowing of allegations of her incest with Nero.[15] Agrippina reduces Claudius' authority by her presence at the reception of Caratacus (12.37.4; see below) and at the spectacle on Lake Fucine (12.56.3), and she exerts a destructive influence over him in politics (12.59.1). Indeed, Tacitus further blackens Claudius' performances in the senate in *Annals* 12 by indicting his complaisance (12.61.2, cf. 11.28.2) and the political power of the freedmen (12.53.2–3, 60.4).

Once Tacitus has Agrippina establish her influence over Claudius, he has her scheme to place Nero in the line of succession. *Annals* 12 charts his rise to power: from his marriage to Claudius' daughter Octavia (12.3.2, 9, 58.1) and his adoption by Claudius (12.25–6), to his assumption of power on Claudius' death (12.68–69.2). Nero's accession closes an account of one principate that has become increasingly preoccupied with the next. The ultimate demonstration of this tendency is Tacitus' refusal to commemorate Claudius' life with an obituary. That would have interrupted the forward thrust of the narrative by awkwardly shifting the focus back to Claudius, and it would have accorded him an importance that the preceding narrative had deliberately denied him. Appropriately, Tacitus focalises a brief summary through the funeral eulogy given by Nero (13.3.1) and parts of Nero's subsequent speech to the senate can also be read as a commentary on Claudius' principate (13.4).

Structure and narrative

Tacitus' use of Republican historiographical forms in the Tiberian *Annals* to narrate imperial history created a structural tension that emphasised how the history of the Principate was very different from the history of the Republic, despite the façade of the 'republic restored'.[16] This tension is less evident in the Claudian *Annals* as Tacitus often adopts a narrative structure that privileges thematic coherence and artistic effect over a chronological arrangement. Tacitus was entering a new phase of his work – it had perhaps

---

'uersa ex eo ciuitas, et cuncta feminae oboediebant' ('as a result of this [Agrippina's marriage to Claudius], the state was changed and there was total obedience to a woman').

[15] Cf. 14.2; Suet. *Nero* 28.2. Agrippina had supposedly committed incest earlier with her brother, the *princeps* Gaius: cf. Suet. *Calig.* 24.1; 36.1; Dio 59.3.6, 22.6, 26.5; Ginsburg (2006) 116.

[16] Ginsburg (1981). Rich (2009) has demonstrated that Republican historiography was not structured as uniformly as Ginsburg claimed: various Republican (and probably early imperial) writers offered Tacitus different models for arranging the narrative year. See also Feeney (2007) 190–1; and above, p. 100.

already begun with the Gaian *Annals* – and he adjusted his technique accordingly.[17] Yet this was not a radical break with the past: departures from a rigid annalistic structure are already evident in the Tiberian *Annals*,[18] and for narratives that elevated theme over chronology Tacitus could look to Livy, Sallust's *Histories* and earlier Roman historians such as Cato the Elder.[19] In the Claudian *Annals*, therefore, Tacitus remains very much in the tradition of his Republican predecessors. Accordingly, some narrative years, for example 47 and 52, take on a 'traditional' appearance in their interweaving of domestic (palace and senatorial) and foreign events, and in their use of digressions or antiquarian material.[20] An old-fashioned item will also appear in a narrative year that has an 'unconventional' structure: the year 51, which opens with events at Rome (12.41–3) but is otherwise devoted to external affairs (12.44–51), contains the first notice of prodigies – a common feature of Republican historiography – in the extant text of the *Annals* (12.43).[21] It is in his treatment of palace politics and foreign affairs that Tacitus displays considerable structural flexibility. The year 48 is dominated by the fall of Messalina and the rise of Agrippina (11.25.5–38.4; 12.1–4.3). The years 53 and 54 focus exclusively on internal affairs, whereas 50 and 51 are preoccupied with events external to Rome. Some of Tacitus' techniques in these larger narrative units can be illustrated through his treatment of British affairs at 12.31–40.

The year 50 (12.25.1–40.5) is largely devoted to the first treatment of British affairs in the extant text of the *Annals* (12.31.1–40.5). Tacitus reports small-scale conflicts with the Iceni, Decangi and Brigantes (12.31.1–32.2), before concentrating on a larger war against the Silures, who are led by Caratacus (12.33.1–40.4). The action ranges between Britain and Rome: the Silures are dramatically defeated and Caratacus is seized, taken to Rome and there pardoned by Claudius; the senate reacts jubilantly to Caratacus' capture; back in Britain the Silures revolt again; the legate, P. Ostorius Scapula, dies and is replaced by A. Didius Gallus, who faces more trouble from the

---

[17] For explanations of changes in the narrative structure in the later *Annals*, see Syme (1958a) 269–70; Griffin (1982b) 216, and also below, pp. 182–3; cf. Martin (1990) 1580–1.
[18] See Ginsburg (1981); below on 6.38.1.
[19] See Rich (2009) sections 3, 4, 5; cf. Kraus (1994a) 10 n. 44.
[20] Digressions: 11.14, 22.3–6; 12.24, 63. For digressions in Tacitus, see Theissen (1912); Hahn (1933); Syme (1958a) 309–12. End-of-year notices of the traditional type (for which see Ginsburg (1981) 31–52; Martin (1990) 1581) do not occur in the Claudian books.
[21] After 12.43 notices appear intermittently (12.64.1; 13.58; 14.12.2, 32.1; 15.7, 22.2, 47; 16.13.1–2), but prodigies themselves are embedded in episodes throughout the narrative (e.g. 1.28.1, 76.1; 4.64.1; 11.4.2; 13.17.1, 24.2; 14.22.1). For prodigies in Tacitus and the Roman historians, see Damon (2003) on *H.* 1.86; also Krauss (1930); Walker (1952) ch. 12; Syme (1958a) 312, 523–4; Levene (1993); Davies (2004).

Hamlet without the prince? The Claudian Annals

Silures, now led by the Brigantian Venutius; Venutius invades the kingdom of Cartimandua, queen of the Brigantes, but is defeated by Cartimandua with Roman assistance. Tacitus concludes by remarking that he has treated events over several years (and under two governors) to aid the remembrance that they deserve, but that he now returns to the chronological sequence, a point he reinforces immediately by opening the new year with the consuls, a reference that functions primarily as a temporal indicator, now that under the Empire there is no real transfer of power year by year (12.40.5 'haec, quamquam a duobus pro praetoribus [viz. Ostorius and Didius] plures per annos gesta, coniunxi, ne diuisa haud perinde ad memoriam sui ualerent. ad temporum ordinem redeo. [41.1] Ti. Claudio quintum Servio Cornelio [Orfito] consulibus ...').[22]

The wars in Britain allowed Tacitus to write the type of history that he had claimed was not there for him to write in the grim years of Tiberius' later principate: 'the locations of peoples, the vagaries of battle, the deaths of illustrious commanders'. It was such narratives, Tacitus claimed, that excited readers and kept their interest (4.33.3).[23] In the British narrative Tacitus arrests the reader's attention early with small-scale conflicts (12.31.1–32.2). In an exciting opening that recalls Corbulo's arrival in lower Germany (11.18.1) Scapula lands in Britain to find tribes invading allied territory. He responds dynamically, 'aware that it is first outcomes by which fear or confidence is generated' ('gnarus primis euentibus metum aut fiduciam gigni'), sweeping his fast cohorts along, slaughtering the enemy and, as part of an attempt at pacification, pursuing those who had scattered (12.31.1–2). Scapula defeats the Iceni and other tribes that joined them in resistance, and Roman brilliance is underlined by his commanding only allied troops, by the 'many brilliant deeds' ('multa et clara facinora') of the Britons and by Scapula's son's winning the honour of saving a fellow citizen (12.31.4). This short sketch of tribal unrest and decisive Roman response, and those that follow in 12.32, establish confidence in Rome's assertion of power in Britain as an introduction to the war against Caratacus, a war that would be more variable in its course. It too would interest and excite: the terrain in which Caratacus takes up position (12.33), and which terrifies Scapula (12.35.1); Caratacus' flurry of activity before the battle and speech to the troops (12.34); Scapula's hard-earned victory and capture of Caratacus

---

[22] Consuls' names reduced to being a date: Ginsburg (1981) 10–17; Feeney (2007) 192 (discussing A. 13.9.3–11.1 but noting the parallel with 12.40.5–41.1).
[23] On this passage see Woodman (1988) 180–5 and Martin and Woodman (1989) ad loc., who rightly read 4.32–3 as referring to the latter part of Tiberius' principate; the future *quaeque referam* ('and what I shall record') takes in events down to 37. For a different interpretation, see below, pp. 226–7. Note also Kraus (1994a) 12.

(12.35–36.1); Caratacus' presentation at Rome (arguably more interesting than if he had died on the battlefield); the bloody reversal of Roman fortunes on the island (12.38.3)[24] and attendant deterioration both in the style of warfare (12.39.2) and in the quality of Roman leadership (12.40.1, 4); and the involvement of a British queen (12.40.3). Tacitus was clearly interested in this material: he could revisit terrain familiar from the *Agricola* and sketch an episode that was absent from his earlier work.

Tacitus self-consciously privileges artistry and thematic coherence over chronology (12.40.5). Chronological distortion for thematic reasons occurs elsewhere in the Claudian *Annals*. In the year 47 he narrates affairs in Parthia and Armenia that we know actually began in 41 (11.8–10). There Tacitus subordinates chronological accuracy to thematic unity, but remains silent about the fact that he is doing so.[25] A principal difference in the Caratacus episode is that Tacitus is candid about his chronological manipulation. He places the episode in the year 50 but internal evidence suggests that he has picked up the story from c. 47, Caratacus' capture is dated to 51 (12.36.1), and subsequent events continue into the 50s.[26] Tacitus' claim of a return to the chronological sequence is both a defence of his method against criticism and an acknowledgement that chronology was a useful and important structural device, especially for events at Rome, to which he returns at 12.41.1. Yet by explicitly laying aside the annalistic arrangement for a thematic treatment Tacitus reveals a liking for the freer mode of composition.

This is not the first time Tacitus has been so candid about chronological manipulation. At 6.38.1 he admits to combining two seasons of Parthian affairs into one account to relieve the reader from domestic evils (6.31.1–37.4):[27] commenting on structure is a comment on Tiberius' principate. In the Caratacus episode there is no comparable use of structure – it is not relief from the main narrative that Tacitus provides, but a story worth remembering (cf. 12.40.5). Affairs at Rome are addressed in ways that allow Tacitus to pursue the themes of the wider narrative. Claudius receives Caratacus at Rome (12.36.2–37.4) and he appoints Gallus to succeed Scapula, 'so that the province should not be without a governor' (12.40.1). Both acts attest to Claudius' involvement in foreign affairs, one

---

[24] The preceding sentences add point to the reversal: the senate's exaggerated praise of Caratacus' capture and Ostorius' award of the *insignia* of a triumph for successes up to that time (12.38.1).

[25] See Malloch (2005) 79–81.

[26] Scapula presumably arrived in Britain, a new leader with an unfamiliar army (12.31.1), in 47, the year in which his predecessor, A. Plautius, held his *ouatio* in Rome; he held the legateship until about 52, when he was replaced by Gallus, who remained in office until 57. For Scapula and Gallus, see Birley (2005) 25–37, 41.

[27] For this episode, see Ash (1999b).

aspect of his administration that is treated favourably in his funeral eulogy and popularly acclaimed (13.3.1).[28] But in the Claudian *Annals* Tacitus prefers to undermine or question Claudius' competency:[29] Claudius' boasting about the capture of Caratacus worked rather to glorify the British king (12.36.2), and does his pardon of Caratacus demonstrate statesmanship or show again his tendency to follow the lead of others?[30]

Agrippina's conspicuous presence at Caratacus' reception (12.37.4) is a black mark against Claudius. Here again is a sign that his wife exerts influence over him. But Agrippina's cameo serves mainly to build on her own role in the Claudian *Annals*: her presence is further evidence of her thirst for power, which is validated and reinforced by the attention she receives from Caratacus and his family. Ominously for her and for Claudius, Agrippina's self-description as 'imperii socia' ('partner in power') recalls the descriptions of Sejanus as 'socius laborum' ('partner in toil', 4.2.3) and 'adiutor imperii' ('assistant in power', 4.7.1) and shows how much further than Sejanus Agrippina had gone – and would go. Tacitus also throws Agrippina into sharp relief through the figure of Cartimandua. She smartly and ruthlessly secures Caratacus and hands him over to Rome (12.36.1). Later (12.40.3) she traps Venutius' brother and family connections by 'cunning means' ('callidis ... artibus') and Venutius and his army are prompted to invade her kingdom at the ignominious prospect of submitting to female power ('ne feminae imperio subderentur').[31] Cartimandua's strength and initiative evoke Agrippina, and her enemies' description reinforces the parallel: female power ('feminae imperio') calls to mind Agrippina's own claim to exercise power with Claudius and Tacitus' portrayal of her domination. Tacitus' use of Cartimandua to comment on the Roman political scene evokes the similar commentary offered by the dynastic intrigues in the eastern narratives of the Claudian *Annals*.[32]

---

[28] Elsewhere Tacitus has Claudius receive foreign embassies (11.10.4, cf. 16.1), install kings (11.8.1, 16.1; 12.11), instruct client kings (11.9.2; 12.20.2) and order and reward governors (11.19.3–20.2, 20.3; 12.29.2, 54.4, cf. 48.3).

[29] For example, Claudius comes out badly from the comparison with Corbulo at 11.18–20 (Malloch (2005) 81–2); at 12.20.1 Tacitus makes Claudius respond to Eunones' letter with a mixture of doubt, resentment and bloody-mindedness, and the sounder advice of others prevails.

[30] The statement *ad ea Caesar ueniam ipsique et coniugi et fratribus tribuit* ('at that Caesar granted pardon to him [Caratacus] and to his wife and brothers') follows Caratacus' speech extolling the virtues of a pardon (12.37.4). Cf. Claudius' aping L. Vitellius at 11.3.1 (quoted above, n. 9).

[31] At *Agr.* 16.1 the British tribes rebel under the leadership of Boudicca (cf. *A.* 14.35.1). But Tacitus is referring to Boudicca in her capacity as military leader, not as queen (so Ogilvie and Richmond (1967) ad loc.); it is the prospect of submitting to Cartimandua's rulership that the Silures loathe.

[32] See Keitel (1978); on 11.8–10, see Malloch (2005) 79–81.

The battle for history

In the year 48 indigenous nobles with Roman citizenship from Gallia Comata sought the right to hold office at Rome. The request provoked fierce debate. Tacitus first gives the arguments of the opponents of the Gauls in Claudius' advisory council and then Claudius' speech in support of the Gauls in the senate, which led to the privilege being extended to the Aedui, long-time allies of Rome (11.23–25.1). Part of Claudius' speech has survived on an inscription discovered at Lyon in 1528[33] and can be compared with the version Tacitus gives Claudius in the *Annals*. Scholars have been preoccupied with the relationship between these two texts, and the historical issues involved in the Gauls' request.[34] My focus here will be on the use of memory in the debate. Tacitus showcases a battle for control of the memory of Rome's past, how the past should be remembered and what lessons it has for the political present. The participants' weapons are the representations of Rome's regal and Republican history that permeate their arguments in the form of *exempla*.[35]

Claudius' opponents cut a poor figure through their manipulation and sensationalisation of the Republican *exempla* they use in re-reading the past to oppose change in the present. The enfranchisement of the Veneti and Insubres (i.e. Transpadane Gaul) is represented as an assault on the senate (11.23.3); the admission of the Gauls to the senate in 48 is made to evoke the Gallic sack of Rome in 390 BC (11.23.4), thereby exploiting one of the darkest events in Roman history and its great legacy, fear of the Gauls;[36] and the assertion that the Gauls besieged Julius Caesar at Alesia ignores the fact that he besieged *them* as part of what was one of his great victories. These distortions overshadow one successful argumentative strategy: characterising Gallic wealth as a threat was effective in light of the greater financial resources then needed to enter the senate (cf. 11.22.6) and the wider cultural awareness of Gallic opulence (cf. 11.18.1).

The opponents' dubious use of Republican memory contributes to and emphasises the weakness of their position. Stronger is the performance of

---

[33] *CIL* 13.1668 = *ILS* 212 = Smallwood (1984) 97–9 (no. 369). The standard modern edition is Fabia (1929); English translations are given by Braund (1985) 199–201 and Levick (2000) 178–80.

[34] It is generally agreed that Tacitus knew the original speech from an inscribed version, from the *acta senatus*, or from a published collection of Claudius' speeches. See further Griffin (1982a), with earlier bibliography, and also below, pp. 180–1; add Syme (1999); Riess (2003).

[35] For memory of regal and Republican Rome in early imperial literature and culture, see Fox (1996); Gowing (2005). For the culture of memory in the early principate, see Flower (2006). For *exempla* in Roman historical literature, see Chaplin (2000); Gowing (2005).

[36] On this legacy, see Oakley (1997) 345, (1998) 126.

Claudius, who figures both as a historical and (in Tacitus' account) literary participant. In the inscribed text of his speech Claudius seeks to demonstrate Rome's history of constitutional flexibility and innovation as a precedent for granting the Gauls the right to hold office at Rome. In support he sets out the idiosyncratic succession of Rome's kings (col. 1, lines 8–27) and sketches the development of powers and offices under the Republic (col. 1, lines 28–40). The *exempla* that Claudius uses in his extant speech are varied by Tacitus as part of a broader reconfiguration of the *princeps*' argument: Claudius subordinates Rome's history of constitutional development (11.24.7) to Rome's history of openness to foreigners (cf. 11.24.1). Under the Spanish *princeps* Trajan the latter theme was more relevant for Tacitus (himself probably of provincial origin),[37] and the admission of the Gauls to the senate in 48 was one stage in that theme's history.[38] Tacitus' re-casting of the extant speech has the literary Claudius engage not with the historical Claudius but with the arguments of his opponents. He illustrates his thesis of Roman openness to foreigners with Greek and Roman regal precedents, and he meets his opponents on their own ground by deploying Republican *exempla*. In two instances of hypophora at 11.24.5 Claudius uses one *exemplum* as an objection and another to rebut it:[39] '"But", it will be said, "we fought against the Senones." Of course, the Vulsci and Aequi never drew up a line of battle against us! "We were taken by the Gauls." But we gave hostages to the Etruscans and we submitted to the yoke of the Samnites!' ('at cum Senonibus pugnauimus. scilicet Vulsci et Aequi numquam aduersam nobis aciem instruxere! capti a Gallis sumus. sed et Tuscis obsides dedimus et Samnitium iugum subiimus!'). Both objection and rebuttal are historically true, but Claudius makes his argument rhetorically more effective by countering the opponents' citation of Gallic aggression with Italian aggression, and in the second part by using *exempla* humiliating to Rome. Thus he neutralises much of the patriotic force and sensationalism of the opponents' arguments.

Claudius displays greater sophistication and historical self-awareness than his opponents. In fact, he appears very post-modern in his demonstration at 11.24.5 that perspective can determine one's reading of the past. But the relativism goes only so far: not every reading of history is equally valid. *exempla* can strengthen an argument, but the reading of the past that they construct is convincing only if the argument to which they contribute is sound; in turn the interpretation of the past that they offer is reinforced by the argument's success. Claudius is ultimately successful in the debate

---

[37] For Tacitus' background, see Birley (2000a), (2005) 281.
[38] Griffin (1982a) 418, cf. (1990) 484.
[39] For discussion of hypophora (imagined objection followed by counter-objection) see e.g. *Rhet. Her.* 4.33–4.

because Tacitus makes him effectively deploy well-chosen *exempla* in a strong argument that engages with and rebuts his opponents.[40] The opponents are unsuccessful because they employ and manipulate their *exempla* within an argument that is easily rebutted. The vision of the past to which their precedents contribute accordingly suffers.

Tacitus demonstrates through the debate that memory crucially informs political decisions in the Principate and can offer a commentary on the Principate itself: the Republican past that the opponents construct by invoking old-fashioned Roman values and harking back to the happy time when a senate comprising only Italian- and Roman-born members ruled over kindred peoples (11.23.2) is unsuccessful because it strikes a discordant note with contemporary, imperial reality; the opponents are out of touch with 'modern' Rome and her empire. In using the past to illustrate how different the imperial present is, Tacitus again touches on a theme that has preoccupied him since the inception of the *Annals*.[41]

FURTHER READING

The Gaian and early Claudian books of the *Annals* are, to borrow a phrase from Macaulay (1854), 'as hopelessly lost as the second decade of Livy' (123). The narrative picks up in 47, that is, halfway through Claudius' principate, and continues without significant interruption to 54, the end of Claudius' life and reign at the close of *Annals* 12.

The best edition of the extant Latin text is Heubner (1994), though the bibliography and critical apparatus in Wellesley (1986) are indispensable. The English commentary of Furneaux (1907) is still valuable and can be supplemented by the German commentary of Koestermann (1967). Woodman (2004) is the best English translation available. A good introduction to the Claudian *Annals* is Martin (1981); a more detailed treatment, in German, is Seif (1973).[42]

---

[40] Tacitus may in part be glancing at Claudius' intellectual interests (for which see Suet. *Claud.* 41–2; cf. Sen. *Apoc.* 5.4; Dio 60.2.1; Levick (1978); Huzar (1984)), and Claudius' success has also been read as Tacitus' endorsing his position.

[41] At 11.18–20 Corbulo's Republican style of generalship reveals him to be out of step with the imperial reality to which Curtius Rufus, with whom Corbulo is implicitly contrasted, is better suited (Malloch (2005) 81–3; for Tacitus and Corbulo, see also Ash (2006b); Geiser (2007)). For the Tacitean Germanicus as out of touch with the realities of the Principate, see Pelling (1993).

[42] Work on this chapter was undertaken in 2007 during my Alexander von Humboldt Research Fellowship in the Abteilung für Alte Geschichte, Ludwig-Maximilians-Universität, Munich, and in 2008 during my stint as a Lecturer in Classics in the University of Cambridge. I should like to thank Stephen Oakley for criticising a draft, and John Rich for supplying me with a preview of his paper.

9

E. E. KEITEL

'Is dying so very terrible?' The Neronian *Annals*

Nero is portrayed by all the ancient literary sources as a dilettante with artistic pretensions, a ruler who disgraces himself by performing publicly as a chariot racer, lyre player and actor.[1] He is also a murderer who wreaks havoc on his own family and the upper classes at Rome, the ruinous conclusion to the Julio-Claudian dynasty. In terms of composition and structure, the Neronian books are significantly different from Books 1–6. Instead of one major contrasting character to the *princeps*, such as Germanicus in *Annals* 1–2, Tacitus presents many.[2] As Syme observed, Tacitus did not want the history of this period to be just the history of Nero.[3] Many of these characters are put to death at the order of the *princeps*. By focusing on Tacitus' accounts of these deaths, we can see clearly how the historian frequently uses them to bring out strong contrasts between the characters of the victims and that of Nero, or, on occasion, to show their similarities. Such an examination will also touch on some of the central themes of the Neronian narrative.

Murder all in the family

Nero's reign begins with a murder engineered by Agrippina without her son's knowledge (13.1.1): 'Prima nouo principatu mors Iunii Silani proconsulis Asiae ignaro Nerone per dolum Agrippinae paratur' ('The first death in the new principate, of Junius Silanus, proconsul of Asia, was engineered without

---

[1] Tacitus, Suetonius and Dio all portray Nero in harsh terms. Tacitus and Dio, and to some extent Suetonius, likely drew on a common source that they supplemented with others: see Martin (1981) 207–8 (Syme (1958a) 437 rejects the idea of a common source). Among the other sources were those known as 'the deaths of famous men' (*exitus illustrium uirorum*), a genre that grew out of the Neronian persecutions. See Marx (1937); Syme (1958a) 92, 297–8; Questa (1967) 246–9; Devillers (2003) 43–5.
[2] Syme (1958a) 269. See also Martin (1981) 163. On the different annalistic technique in Books 11–16, see Syme (1958a) 269–70; Sage (1990) 984–97.
[3] Syme (1958a) 579.

Nero's knowledge through a deception of Agrippina'). Indeed the whole chapter sets the tone for the new regime. For Agrippina drives Claudius' influential freedman Narcissus to suicide, though this was opposed by Nero (*inuito principe*), whose still hidden vices of greed and extravagance had meshed well with the freedman's (13.1.3). And there would have been more murder, had not Seneca and Burrus intervened (13.2.1). In the early stages of Nero's principate they are able to control him, in part by permitting him some indulgence. They are also able to curb Agrippina.[4]

Nero's first victim is not his overbearing mother but his adoptive brother Britannicus. When Nero, by a throw of the dice, becomes the king of a party during the Saturnalia, he forces Britannicus to sing, hoping to humiliate him. But, when the boy sings a song hinting at his expulsion from his father's house and throne, the audience, whose dissimulation has been weakened by drink, shows pity (13.15.2). The bystanders' sympathetic reaction is a momentary lapse from their usual role and is yet another inversion in a scene aptly set during a festive season, when traditional roles of master and slave were reversed. The true king at last asserts himself and faces down the impostor. The audience's sympathy for Britannicus intensifies Nero's hatred toward him, and he plots his death by poison (13.15.3).

When the poison suddenly kills Britannicus at a family dinner, Tacitus distinguishes the reactions of the horrified guests: those sitting nearby shudder; the incautious (*imprudentes*) scatter; but those with a deeper understanding (*quibus altior intellectus*), including Agrippina, fix their gaze on the *princeps*, who, apparently unaware (*nescio similis*), explains that the youth has merely had a seizure (13.16.3). Whereas Nero was ignorant of the murder of Silanus, now it is Agrippina who is caught off guard and is unable, despite her best attempts, to conceal her terror, for she realises that she will be next (13.16.4).[5]

The final confrontation between Agrippina and Nero (14.1–10) unfolds in a richly dramatic fashion designed to contrast strongly Agrippina's bold resourcefulness, self-awareness and foresight with the opposite qualities in her son. After the abortive assassination attempt on the collapsing boat, Agrippina, having swum to shore incognito, coolly assesses her situation and concludes, as many have in the *Annals*, 'that the only remedy for plots

---

[4] See Martin (1981) 162 on the parallels and contrast of 13.1.1 with 1.6.1 and the setting out of the major themes of the Neronian narrative. Note also Woodman (1998) 26, 35.

[5] See the excellent discussion of this passage by Bartsch (1994) 12–16. Shortly before this scene, we are told that Agrippina's power was gradually broken when Nero succumbed to the seductive charms of the freedwoman Acte and entrusted himself to Seneca, who helped him carry on the affair (13.12.1–13.2).

'Is dying so very terrible?' The Neronian *Annals*

was if they were not understood' (14.6.1 *solum insidiarum remedium esse <sensit>, si non intellegerentur*).⁶ We move in the next chapter to Nero's abject terror and helplessness when he learns that she has survived (14.7.2):

> tum pauore exanimis et iam iamque adfore obtestans uindictae properam, siue seruitia armaret uel militem accenderet, siue ad senatum et populum peruaderet, naufragium et uulnus et interfectos amicos obiciendo: quod contra subsidium sibi?

> Then, faint with panic, he swore that she would be there at any time now, quick for vengeance, whether she armed the slaves or incited the troops, or if she made her way to the senate and people, making charges of shipwreck and wounding and murdered friends; what defence would he have against her?⁷

Abandoned by all and after a last attempt to bluff her way out (14.8.4), Agrippina meets her death with courage and complete awareness of its meaning (14.8.5): 'iam <in> morte<m> centurioni ferrum distringenti protendens uterum "uentrem feri!" exclamauit multisque uulneribus confecta est' ('as the centurion was already drawing his sword for death, she proffered her womb, crying out "Stab my belly!"; and with many wounds she was dispatched'). Tacitus then recounts her interview, long before, with the astrologer who predicted that Nero would rule but kill his mother. Her reply (14.9.3), 'occidat dum imperet' ('let him kill provided that he rule'), placed after the death scene as it is, only underlines Agrippina's understanding of power and the price it exacts.⁸ Juxtaposed with this is the terrified reaction of Nero, who realises the full horror of his crime only when news of its execution is brought to him (14.10.1): 'sed a Caesare perfecto demum scelere magnitudo eius intellecta est. reliquo noctis modo per silentium defixus, saepius pauore exsurgens et mentis inops lucem opperiebatur tamquam exitium adlaturam' ('But only when the crime was finally completed was its magnitude understood by Caesar. For the rest of the night, sometimes

---

⁶ Bartsch (1994) 20–1 contrasts Agrippina's pretence of not understanding with Julius Montanus' mistake in acknowledging that Nero was his attacker during one of his nocturnal forays (13.25.2).

⁷ Morris (1969) 99 remarks that Nero's reactions here are those of 'an hysterical actor'. On Nero's penchant for off-stage performances, see also Frazer (1966) 18–19.

⁸ Agrippina's last words recall Atreus' in the Roman tragedian Accius (204R³, *ap*. Cic. *Off.* 1.28), *oderint dum metuant* ('let them hate provided that they fear'), thus further associating her with the tragic stage, in particular with a dread character and his doomed house. So Morris (1969) 109–10. Woodman (1993) 123 notes that at 15.58.2 Nero recalls the vengeful Atreus of Seneca's *Thyestes*. Santoro L'Hoir (2006) 33–47 argues that Tacitus applies the myth of Atreus, based on the Aeschylean paradigm, to the Julio-Claudian dynasty from the opening of the *Annals*. For the tragic recognition of Nero and Agrippina in 14.7–8, see Santoro L'Hoir (2006) 90–1.

dumbfounded by silence, but more often rising up in fear and devoid of reason, he was waiting for dawn as if it would bring his destruction').[9]

Through a series of dramatic scenes, Tacitus creates in this narrative a paradoxical picture of Nero as skilled orchestrator of appearances and dupe of his mistress Poppaea and dependent on his advisers. Once Nero puts off the elimination of Agrippina no longer (14.1.1), he does very little else. Poppaea sets the plot in motion by goading Nero, calling him a ward and obedient to another's orders. After the first attempt fails, Seneca and Burrus, his advisers, whose precise role in the plot is uncertain, tactfully prompt the paralysed *princeps* to action (14.7.3-4). But Nero's only contribution is to throw a sword at the feet of Agrippina's freedman, Agermus, entrapping him on a false charge of plotting against him (14.7.6): 'scaenam ultro criminis parat' ('he himself set the stage for the charge').[10]

Dio's and Suetonius' accounts of the murder of Agrippina show how Tacitus has chosen to emphasise Nero's improvidence and lack of insight. In the epitome of Dio, Nero is not terror-stricken when the messenger from Agrippina arrives, and he needs no propping up by his advisers; he alone sends Anicetus to kill his mother and there is no *scaena* staged by the *princeps* to frame Agermus (Dio 62.13.4). Again, Agrippina has no suspicion of the plot as she sets out for Bauli; she is not shown reflecting at length after the 'accident', though she comes to the same conclusion about her best response (Dio 62.13.4); and the anecdote about her visit to the astrologer, so effectively placed in the *Annals*, appears in the epitome at the beginning of Nero's reign (Dio 61.2.2). Suetonius' account (*Ner.* 34.1-4) is couched in much less dramatic terms and offers no contrast between Agrippina's awareness and her son's lack thereof. The scene at Baiae is brief and without dialogue, and there is no death scene, no last words and no mention of the prophecy about Nero's rule. Here, as elsewhere in Suetonius, Nero is not in the control of his advisers; Seneca and Burrus do not figure at all in the plots against Agrippina and Octavia.[11]

The last major crime of Book 14 is the murder of Octavia, since eventually it is only his wife who stands in the way of his wish to marry Poppaea. Tacitus links Poppaea's appearance in the narrative with the beginning of

---

[9] For Morris (1969) 111, this passage is 'one of the strongest representations of the emperor's inability to foresee consequences; he exists for the present moment, especially for the drama in which he, as actor or director, may participate'.

[10] Morris (1969) 101 notes the contrast between Anicetus' effective action and Nero's contrived dramatics. See also Shumate (1997) 386. For the roles Nero played on stage, including Orestes, see Bartsch (1994) 38-42.

[11] See also Bartsch (1994) 214 n. 39. For Suetonius' lack of interest in minor characters, see Townend (1964) 351; Baldwin (1983) 534.

'great calamities for the state' (13.45.1 *magnorum rei publicae malorum*).[12] The historian describes Poppaea and Tigellinus as the counsellors of Nero when he was in a savage mood (15.61.2) and claims that, while people mourned her publicly, in private everyone welcomed her demise 'on account of her immorality and cruelty' (16.7.1 *ob impudicitiam eius saeuitiamque*). Octavia is portrayed throughout the *Annals* as a pawn and victim – first used by her mother Messalina when trying to save herself (11.32.2, 34.3), then married to Nero by Agrippina to further her ambitions. Until her death scene she is silent, having long since learned to conceal every feeling (13.16.4). Since Nero recoils from her despite her noble rank and proved purity (13.12.2), Seneca and Burrus allow him to dally with the freedwoman, Acte, lest he burst out into debauchery with the well-born (13.12.2). Pushed out of the centre of power, Agrippina takes up the cause of Octavia (13.18.2, 19.3). Just how dangerous Octavia might have been is made clear by popular protests when Nero divorces her. Motivated by a false rumour that Nero had taken back his ex-wife, the *uulgus* replace Poppaea's statues with Octavia's and must be dispersed by force (14.60.5–61.1). Poppaea, her hatred fed by fear, raises the familiar spectre of civil war, with Octavia at its head, her arguments calculated to appeal to Nero's fear and anger (14.61.2–3).[13]

In her death scene, Tacitus presents Octavia as a victim with distinctly tragic overtones. He may be ironically evoking Sophocles' *Antigone* to enhance his picture of Octavia's victimisation. As Antigone is led to her death, the chorus tries to console her by listing previous heroines of her family similarly doomed, justly or unjustly (Soph. *Ant.* 944–87). In Tacitus, the bystanders contrast Octavia's exile to those of other imperial women, Agrippina the Elder and Julia Livilla; unlike them, Octavia was young and had known no happiness to mitigate the *saeuitia* that followed (14.63.2).[14] To the unnamed speakers, Octavia's wedding day was 'in place of a funeral' (14.63.3 *loco funeris*), thus evoking the 'bride of death' theme from Greek tragedy (cf. Soph. *Ant.* 801–5).[15] As if to underline this theme, Tacitus states

---

[12] Sallustian reminiscences at 13.45.2 link Poppaea to Sempronia, the only woman involved in the Catilinarian conspiracy of 63 BC. See Koestermann (1967) ad loc. Tacitus thus links Poppaea to Sejanus, who recalls Sallust's Catiline, and signals that Poppaea will play a role in Nero's reign like that of Sejanus in Tiberius' reign. See Walker (1952) 76; Syme (1958a) 353.

[13] Sejanus also foments civil strife, by accusing others of doing the same. See Keitel (1984) 322–3 and Martin and Woodman (1989) on *A.* 4.2.2 and 4.17.3.

[14] Ferri (1998) argues that Tacitus took tragic elements in 14.63–4 from the *Octavia*, which in turn drew on *Antigone*. Billot (2003) 138–9 reads the bystanders' description of previous female Julio-Claudian exiles as the inverse of an *elogium* at a Roman funeral.

[15] For the 'bride of death' theme in *Antigone*, see Segal (1981) 179–81; Rehm (1994) 59–71.

that Octavia on her wedding day was escorted to a home in which she would have nothing except mourning (14.63.3 *deductae in domum, in qua nihil nisi luctuosum haberet*). Of course, Octavia has not changed houses, like a typical bride, but merely returned to the palace of Claudius, her father. As her execution draws near, Tacitus presents Octavia in a liminal state, but not that of the virgin en route to becoming a wife. Octavia's liminality is that between life and death: she is deprived of life but not yet at peace in death (14.64.1; cf. Soph. *Ant.* 850–2). Moreover, although both women are the victims of a tyrannical relative, Antigone has chosen her death in a way that Octavia has not.

Surrounded by troops, Octavia is tied up and her veins opened. She has to be carried into the baths and suffocated, because her terror has stopped her blood flowing. To this was added a 'more shocking savagery' (14.64.2 *atrocior saeuitia*): Octavia's head was cut off and taken to Poppaea.[16] Octavia's murder is just another in a string of perversions perpetrated by Nero. Tacitus expostulates about the thanksgiving offered for this murder and others (14.64.3): 'dona ob haec templis decreta que<m> ad finem memorabimus?' ('To what end shall I recount the gifts decreed on account of these things to temples?'). What formerly signified prosperity was now a token of disaster for the state (*publicae cladis insignia*). We shall return to the disaster theme later.

Nero and his victims

Now let us examine how Tacitus characterises the relationship between Nero and those of his victims who do not belong to his family. We turn first to those whom the *princeps* or popular opinion viewed as capable of ruling. The last formal obituary that marks the end of a year in the extant *Annals* is that of Memmius Regulus. When Nero falls ill and his sycophants claim that Rome will die with him, he contradicts them: the state has a resource in Regulus (14.47.1). According to Tacitus, Regulus survived this endorsement because he lived a quiet life, had only a modest fortune and came from a newly ennobled family. What the historian admired in Regulus is clear in the first sentence of the chapter: his authority, steadfastness and reputation (14.47.1 *auctoritate constantia fama*), which earned him as much glory as was possible in the shadow of the emperor.[17]

---

[16] Tacitus adds pathos by stating that no other exile affected onlookers with greater *misericordia*, mis-stating, perhaps inadvertently, Octavia's age (she was at least 22, not 19) and giving her a final appeal, though whom she is addressing is unclear (Ferri (1998) 346–8).

[17] Martin (1981) 175–6 argues that Regulus' is the last obituary because such a notice implies an ordered state where men of distinction die in their beds. With the revival of the *maiestas*

Regulus' qualities are the antithesis of Nero's inconstant, fearful and immoderate behaviour.[18]

Nero feels threatened by those who have what Regulus did not – a noble lineage and great wealth. Rubellius Plautus, a descendant of Augustus in the same degree as Nero, has both, while P. Cornelius Faustus Sulla, a descendant of the fabled Republican Cornelii, was the son-in-law of Claudius (13.23.1). Nero fears these two most of all (14.57.1), and Tigellinus, seeking to gain his own advantage over the *princeps*, plays on such fear to destroy them (14.57.2–3). Unsubstantiated allegations had already linked both men with attempts at the throne (13.19.3 Rubellius; 13.23.1 Sulla).[19] Amusingly, though not for Sulla, Nero keeps mistaking his sluggish nature for skilled dissimulation (13.47.1, 3; 14.57.3). Nor is Nero able to evaluate the validity of charges against the two men. Tacitus' account suggests that the wealthy Plautus, or his backers, might have actually posed a threat (14.58), while Sulla in this narrative clearly did not. Earlier, popular gossip interpreted the appearance of a comet as portending a change of ruler. Everyone's favourite was Rubellius Plautus, a person of old-fashioned ways, a severe demeanour and a spotless and quiet domestic life (14.22.1). The reader is left to contrast Plautus with Nero.[20] Paradoxically, Plautus is brought only more fame by the retirement that fear had led him to seek (14.22.1).[21]

C. Calpurnius Piso, the man who would replace Nero in the ill-fated conspiracy of 65, resembles him all too well. He is an adroit manipulator of appearances but lacks any real substance; he also has an aristocratic lineage and enjoys popular favour 'through virtue or for the outward semblance of virtues' (15.48.2 *per uirtutem aut species uirtutibus similes*). Piso also resembles the *princeps* in his lack of seriousness and his prodigality (15.48.3): 'sed procul grauitas morum aut uoluptatum parsimonia: leuitati

---

law the next year (14.48.2), that was no longer possible. See also Pomeroy (1991) 201–3. Henceforth Tacitus writes death scenes that may or may not include an obituary. For this change and other contrasts implied by Regulus' obituary, see Morford (1990) 1590–2.

[18] During Regulus' consulship in 31 Tacitus had referred to his *modestia* or self-control (5.11.1).

[19] In this instance, Burrus succeeds in restraining Nero by calming his fears and dissuading him from killing Agrippina and Plautus (13.20.3).

[20] Nero's *domus* could hardly be called *casta* or *secreta*, given his alleged sexual abuse of Britannicus, rumoured incest with Agrippina, adultery with Acte and Poppaea, and the very public debauchery of 15.37.4. Santoro L'Hoir (2006) 221–2 notes the contrast between the concealment of wickedness within the imperial *domus* in the Tiberian books and the flagrant licence in the later books, 'where corruption is open for public view and comment'.

[21] At 14.22.2, Tacitus suggests that Plautus did not seek these followers, but that those people flocked to him who were eager to support the new and uncertain. Nero also feels threatened by the character and great wealth of Gaius Cassius Longinus and the noble lineage of Junius Silanus Torquatus (16.7.1). Compare also Agricola at *Agr.* 18.6.

ac magnificentiae et aliquando luxu indulgebat' ('but he was far from a serious character or restrained in his pleasures: he indulged in frivolity and luxury and sometimes extravagance'). These are the qualities most men approve of in a ruler (15.48.3).[22]

Like Nero too, Piso can dissimulate smoothly. He refuses to let the assassination take place at his villa at Baiae, because he fears the contamination incurred by the violation of hospitality; the deed they have undertaken for the state (*pro re publica*) should take place at Rome. But these words were for public consumption. His true motives become clear in the next sentence: fear either that Lucius Junius Silanus Torquatus, a direct descendant of Augustus, may seize the Principate himself, or that the consul Vestinus Atticus may restore the Republic (15.52.1–3). After the death of Seneca, Tacitus recounts a rumour that reiterates the similarity between Piso and Nero. Subrius Flavus and the other centurions intended to replace Piso with Seneca after they had murdered Nero. For the conspirators had wished to give the impression that innocent men were installing a man of outstanding virtue, in contrast to Nero and Piso (15.65): 'quin et uerba Flaui uulgabantur, non referre dedecori si citharoedus demoueretur et tragoedus succederet (quia, ut Nero cithara, ita Piso tragico ornatu canebat)' ('and even the words of Flavus got around, that it made no difference in terms of disgrace if a lyre-player was removed and a tragic actor succeeded him – because, just as Nero sang to the lyre, so Piso sang in tragic costume').[23] The implied similarity of plotters to *princeps* continues as the conspiracy unravels. Tacitus juxtaposes in the same sentence the terror of Nero with the cowardice of Lucan, Senecio and Quintianus, who under the mere threat of torture betray their friends and relations without compunction (15.58.1). All are contrasted with the brave freedwoman Epicharis, who kills herself after repeated torture rather than betray the conspiracy (15.57).[24] Nero had been certain that a woman's body would not be equal to the pain (15.57.1).

Other victims of Nero summon up a composure in their last moments that reflects badly on the *princeps'* fear and panic.[25] Nero orders Ostorius Scapula to be killed quickly on trumped-up charges, because he feared his

---

[22] Syme (1958a) 575 calls the Tacitean Piso 'an inoffensive Nero' and notes how Tacitus' narrative confirms Piso's 'nullity'.

[23] See Woodman (1993) 112–13.

[24] Woodman (1993) 119 observes that Epicharis dies in private, with none of her fellow conspirators' theatrics and without betraying anyone else. Martin (1981) 183 points out the moral paradox of the conspiracy – that those of the lowest rank show the greatest courage and loyalty.

[25] According to Suetonius (*Ner.* 37.2), Nero never gave more than a few hours to those ordered to die, and, to avoid any delay, he brought physicians to immediately 'attend to' those who lingered.

military reputation and physical strength. Tacitus describes Nero as 'always frightened and more so because of the recently discovered conspiracy' (16.15.1 *pauidum semper et reperta nuper coniuratione magis exterritum*). Ostorius, when the soldiers arrive, turns the same courage against himself that he had often showed against the enemy (16.15.2). When Thrasea Paetus writes to Nero asking to know the allegations against him and for an opportunity to rebut them, Nero eagerly opens the letter hoping that Paetus, terrified (*exterritum*), may have written something that would add to the emperor's glory and harm his own reputation (16.24.2). This is not the case, and Nero becomes frightened of the expression, spirit and frankness of an innocent man and orders the senators to be called (16.24.2 *quod ubi non <e>uenit uultumque et spiritus et libertatem insontis ultro extimuit, uocari patres iubet*). In this context, Nero's ironic words to Caesennius Paetus after his inept performance in Armenia have added resonance: Nero pardons the commander on the spot, lest one 'so liable to fear' grow sick from more protracted anxiety (15.25.4 *tam promptus in pauorem*).

Tacitus at times uses the dignified deaths of Nero's victims, no matter how hurried and frightening the circumstances, to underline the *princeps*' cruelty. Nero proceeds so quickly against Plautius Lateranus, the consul designate, that he does not allow him to embrace his children or to choose his own death. Instead he is dragged to the place where slaves are executed. Plautius is cut down by the tribune Statius, a fellow accomplice in the Pisonian conspiracy, but, 'full of a resolute silence' (15.60.1 *plenus constantis silentii*), he dies without giving him away.[26] Nero, having neither charge nor accuser but 'having turned to the force of despotism' (*ad uim dominationis conuersus*), acts against Atticus Vestinus and sends soldiers to the consul's house. Vestinus, either fearing nothing or anxious to conceal his fear, had led a normal day and was having a dinner party. When the soldiers arrive, Vestinus rises without delay, and everything is hurried through at the same time. Tacitus describes the death in a series of brief clauses in asyndeton, ending (15.69.2): *nulla edita uoce, qua semet miseraretur* ('with no expression of self-pity').[27]

---

[26] In contrast to Piso, patriotism (15.49.3 *amor rei publicae*) motivates Plautius to join the conspiracy. Morris (1969) 233–4 points out the thematic contrast between juxtaposed death scenes of Piso and Plautius: the first an indictment of failure; the second a tribute to nobility.

[27] At 13.17.2 Tacitus claims that Nero's alleged sexual abuse of Britannicus makes his death not seem cruel, despite his being killed 'amid the sanctities of the table' (*inter sacra mensae*) and without a chance to embrace his sister and in front of the eyes of his enemy. Nero also delights at the thought of the fear Vestinus' guests must have felt while surrounded by soldiers (15.69.3). On Tacitus' use of these death scenes to accentuate Nero's cruelty, see also Marx (1937) 94.

To the emperor's fear and haste, some victims replied with deliberation and care. Seneca first refutes the allegations made against him, showing 'no signs of fear' (15.61.2 *nulla pavoris signa*); then, when he receives word of his death sentence, without fear he asks for his will (15.62.1 *interritus*). Seneca bravely dies a lingering and excruciating death, his only concern the suffering of his wife. He finally persuades her to go into another bedroom lest one or both of them lose their composure (15.63.3).[28] Although Seneca may not have been expecting the death sentence at this moment (15.61.2), he has prepared himself well, unlike Nero, as we shall see. He had earlier had his physician obtain hemlock (15.64.3). His body was cremated without any ceremony, according to instructions he had given at the height of his riches and power, even then thinking of his end (15.64.4).

Petronius, the *arbiter elegantiae* at Nero's court, stages a death that, like his life, plays with the conventions. Once detained, he does not tolerate the delays associated with hope or fear, but neither does he die in haste. Instead, he has his slit arteries bound up and converses on light topics with friends in a scene that gently parodies the Socratic death scene of Seneca (16.19.2). Even his will reverses the convention whereby one would flatter the emperor and leave him a bequest in the hopes that one would thus be protecting one's family. Instead, Petronius details the debaucheries of the *princeps* (16.19.3 *flagitia principis*), complete with the names of his male and female sexual partners. Petronius then destroys his signet ring, so it cannot be used against others.[29]

Nero and disaster

At *Annals* 16.16 Tacitus pauses for a moment to lament the dreary monotony of his subject matter in a passage somewhat reminiscent of the digression at *Annals* 4.32–3. In Book 4 Tacitus states that he misses the drama

---

[28] For a sensitive analysis of Seneca's death scene, see Hutchinson (1993) 261–8. Scholars are unable to agree on Tacitus' attitude towards Seneca. According to Dyson (1970), the treatment is wholly negative, including the death scene. Walker (1952) 222–5, while arguing that almost every appearance of Seneca is the subject of unfavourable comment, allows that Tacitus does accord him a magnificent death. Garson (1974) 26 reads Seneca's noble death as a partial rehabilitation of him. Syme (1958a) 552 is more nuanced: Tacitus would not be troubled by the conflict between Seneca's philosophical credo and his role as adviser to the emperor. Some of the charges against Seneca, especially his hypocrisy in amassing a great fortune amidst professions of austerity, are laid out by the notorious *delator*, Publius Suillius (13.42). For a summary of the dispute, see Griffin (1976) 441–4.

[29] Morris (1969) 258. For Petronius' will as a parody of the conventions, see Rankin (1965) 235. Note also the refusal of Antistius Vetus to name Nero chief beneficiary of his will in order to save some of it for his grandchildren. He does not wish to defile a life 'led very close to freedom' (16.11.1 *uitam proxime libertatem actam*) by a last act of servitude.

'Is dying so very terrible?' The Neronian *Annals*

and scope of the events at home and abroad that writers of Republican history recounted – great wars, stormings of cities, vicissitudes of battles, the brilliant deaths of commanders, political discord at Rome. His work is by contrast 'restricted and inglorious' (4.32.2 *in arto et inglorius*). But Tacitus does affirm the usefulness of his work (4.32.2), while admitting the dreariness of his subject matter – savage orders, constant accusations, treacherous friendships and the destruction of the innocent (4.33.3).[30]

By 16.16 the tone has grown even darker. While admitting the monotony and satiety that relating too many deaths can cause for himself and the reader, he draws a contrast between lives given for the state in foreign wars (*bella externa et obitas pro re publica mortes*) and the deaths of citizens at home (*honestos ciuium exitus*). While honourable, these latter were tragic and continuous (16.16.1): 'patientia seruilis tantumque sanguinis domi perditum fatigant animum et maestitia restringunt' ('the slave-like passivity and so much blood wasted at home weary the mind and oppress it with sadness'). He would ask from future readers no justification other than that he not have to hate those who died 'so sluggishly' (16.16.2 *tam segniter*). Divine anger at the Roman state requires invocation by the historian not merely on a single occasion, as when describing military disasters or the capture of cities, but frequently. Finally, Tacitus states that, just as 'illustrious men' (*uiri illustres*) have funerals distinct from everyone else's, so should each also have his own memorial (16.16.2 *memoriam*) in the recounting of his death.

Woodman has argued that Tacitus does indeed provide the material he bemoans the lack of at 4.32–3 (stormings of cities and so forth), but in a metahistorical form: so he describes the collapse of the amphitheatre at Fidenae in terms of warfare and a captured city.[31] I have argued that Tacitus in the Neronian books applies the language of war and captured cities to the domestic narrative in order to demonstrate that Rome is involved in an ongoing civil war in which the *princeps* makes war on his own people and encourages them to fight one another. The captured cities and defeated armies of 16.16.2 are now Rome itself and the Pisonian conspirators.[32]

By its kinship to 4.32–3, Tacitus' discussion at 16.16 suggests that things in Rome continue in the same vein but have become worse. Nero is not only the stock tyrant like Tiberius, revelling in his cruelty, but is also a disaster for the state on a scale far beyond that of his predecessors. There is nothing in the Tiberian books to compare with the great fire at Rome or the Pisonian

---

[30] For detailed discussion of this passage, see Woodman (1988) 180–5. See also below, pp. 226–7.
[31] Woodman (1988) 190.
[32] Keitel (1984) 307–8.

conspiracy.³³ While Tacitus does not explicitly blame Nero for the fire of 64, the reader could be forgiven for concluding otherwise.³⁴ Just before the fire, Tacitus recounts Nero's fabulous public banquet in which he enjoyed the city as if it were his own house (15.37.1), encouraged public debauchery and 'married' one of his eunuchs, not even concealing the consummation from public view (15.37.2–4). Disaster follows immediately: *sequitur clades* (15.38.1). And of course Nero is rumoured to have sung the Fall of Troy against the background of the burning city (15.39.3). After the fire, Nero makes use of the ruins of the country to build his marvellous new house (15.42.1). He plunders Italy, the provinces, even the temples of the gods (15.45.1).

Terrified by the Pisonian conspiracy, Nero places the city under arrest of a sort (15.58.2 *uelut in custodiam dedit*), with troops occupying the walls, the sea and the river. Continuous columns (*continua ... agmina*) of shackled prisoners are led to Nero's villa for interrogation (15.58.3). Later he distributes rewards to the troops and, 'as if about to recount the deeds in a war' (*quasi gesta bello expositurus*), he summons the senate and gives *triumphale decus* to three associates, including Tigellinus (15.72.1). After all this, however, Nero was fearful of the gossip that attacked him for killing 'distinguished and innocent men because of jealousy or fear' (15.73.1 *uiros <claros> et insontes ob inuidiam aut metum*), and he issues a collection of the allegations made and the confessions of the conspirators.³⁵

Patientia seruilis? Plautus, Piso and Paetus

Tacitus' comment about the *patientia seruilis* of Nero's aristocratic victims (16.16.1) is puzzling in light of the death scenes he presents. Does he refer merely to those who died *tam segniter* or does he mean to indict a whole

---

[33] The reign of terror after the death of Sejanus may be an exception. Certainly Tacitus wants us to believe that an *immensa strages* resulted (6.19.2). For the divergence between fact and impression in this passage, see Walker (1952) 83–4. For the *topoi* of the stock tyrant in Roman historiography, see Dunkle (1971); Tabacco (1985). For these *topoi* in Plato, Herodotus and Xenophon, see Gray (2007) 214–16.

[34] According to Tacitus it is uncertain whether the fire occurred by chance or 'by the cunning of the *princeps*' (15.38.1 *dolo principis*). Some people were feeding the fire, possibly under orders (15.38.7), and it began again mysteriously from the Aemilian estates of Nero's crony, Tigellinus (15.40.2). Suetonius (*Ner.* 38.1) and Dio (62.16.1–2) state categorically that Nero started the fire.

[35] Tacitus describes two of Nero's victims dying as if against a foreign foe: Junius Silanus, who perished with wounds in front 'as if in battle' (16.9.2 *tamquam in pugna*), and Ostorius (16.15.2; see above, pp. 134–5). These deaths, placed before the digression at 16.16, make it seem a natural outgrowth of the narrative and underline the perversity of Nero's rule. So Morris (1969) 252.

society for not resisting the tyranny of Nero? In three major death scenes in Books 14–16, the victim is exhorted in vain to press on, not to withdraw and simply await death. Looking closely at these 'failed exhortations', one sees some common themes and persistent ambiguity. First, Rubellius Plautus, already in exile, receives a message from his father-in-law, Lucius Antistius Vetus. Tacitus opens the chapter by reporting rumours (untrue) that Plautus had made his way to Corbulo's army; that Asia had taken arms in support of Plautus and that those sent to execute him had instead gone over to revolution (14.58.2 *ad spes nouas*). Such talk may have inspired Antistius' message, delivered by a freedman who arrived before the soldiers, that Plautus should flee a 'sluggish death' (14.58.3 *segnem mortem*). But the freedman then sketches in possible support for an attempt to take power, though in vague terms: the good and the bold will be drawn to the cause for different reasons; Plautus should shun no resource, and if he can repel the sixty soldiers sent to kill him, a war could be set in motion. They conclude: either he would save his life by this course or he would endure no worse by dying bravely rather than as a coward (14.58.4 *audenti quam ignauo*). But none of this moves Plautus (14.59.1). Tacitus lists Plautus' reasons for rejecting such advice: as an unarmed exile, he foresaw no help; he was tired of hope and uncertainty; finally, there was his love for his wife and children, who might suffer if Nero were disturbed by any worry (14.59.1). A subsequent message from Antistius reported by some sources has no effect. His two teachers of philosophy also urge steadfastness (*constantiam*) in awaiting death as a preferable alternative to an uncertain and anxious life (14.59.1). Tacitus draws no conclusion, though Plautus obviously has made no attempt to flee and is cut down while exercising.

A similar pattern appears in the exhortation of unnamed supporters to Piso as the conspiracy is starting to unravel (15.59). They too offer vague and unrealistic advice about rallying people and troops to his cause even while conceding the disloyalty of the other conspirators. Nero, they said, had not made provision for such a conspiracy and, it is implied, *ille scaenicus* ('that actor'), the antithesis of a brave man to the Romans, would not raise arms against the plot, though the reader knows otherwise (15.58.1–2).[36] They urge Piso not to be one of the timid (15.59.2): 'multa experiendo confieri quae segnibus ardua uideantur' ('many things can be accomplished by trying which seem difficult to the timid'). The emperor's troops will subject him to an unworthy death (15.59.3). Much more praiseworthy is it to die embracing the *res publica* and invoking help for freedom (*libertati*). The reader already knows that the last statement bears little resemblance to

[36] Woodman (1993) 121–2.

Piso's real motives for undertaking the conspiracy.[37] Piso retires to his house and prepares to die. But here his similarity to Nero resurfaces. His will is marked by disgusting flatteries (*foedis ... adulationibus*) of the *princeps* to protect the wife he had stolen from a friend, just as Nero had taken Poppaea from Otho.[38] His friends had appealed to Piso to justify his death to his ancestors and descendants, but, instead of leaving behind *gloria*, Piso leaves behind *infamia*, kept alive by the behaviour of his wife and her ex-husband (15.59.5).[39]

Finally, Thrasea Paetus consults his closest friends about whether he should try a defence in the senate or reject it (16.25.1). Some argue that Thrasea should defend himself (16.25.2): only the timid and fearful conceal their deaths; the people should be able to see a man who can face his death; why, even Nero might be moved to change his mind by such a miracle (*ipso miraculo*). But, if the *princeps* persisted in his cruelty, posterity surely distinguished 'the memory of an honourable death from the cowardice of those dying in silence' (*memoriam honesti exitus ab ignauia per silentium pereuntium*). Other friends counter that Paetus risks physical harm by appearing in the senate (16.26.2). He should also leave uncertain what the senators would have done if he had stood trial. They reject as an empty hope (16.26.3 *inrita spe*) the possibility that Nero would feel shame for his crimes. Paetus should not put his wife and daughter and others at risk. Paetus tells his friends he will make up his own mind, but he urges Arulenus Rusticus not to veto any senate resolution and asks him to think carefully about what sort of public career he would undertake in such a time (16.26.5).[40]

Paetus shares with Plautus a commitment to the tenets of Stoic philosophy, whereby a chosen death could bring a man freedom. Unlike Plautus, however, Paetus and Seneca 'stage' their deaths in imitation of Socrates' in Plato's *Phaedo* and thereby make a powerful moral statement against the

---

[37] See above, p. 134, and Woodman (1993) 115.

[38] In the *Annals*, Tacitus states that Poppaea seduced Nero, thus stressing the latter's malleability, whereas in his earlier version (*H.* 1.13.3) Tacitus relates that Nero has already made Poppaea his mistress when he asks his friend Otho to marry her to provide cover for the affair. See Martin (1981) 169. On the problems raised by the two accounts, see Chilver (1979) and Damon (2003) ad loc.

[39] Neither Seneca nor Thrasea says that he is seeking *gloria* by his death, but Seneca accedes to his wife's desire to die with him, not averse to her *gloria* (15.63.2). Each group of Thrasea's friends assures him that he will gain it if he follows their advice (16.25.1, 26.3). As Petronius dies, he naturally does not speak to his friends about those things by which he could seek 'the glory of steadfastness' (16.19.2 *gloriam constantiae*).

[40] Arulenus Rusticus, a Stoic, served as praetor in 69 and suffect consul in 92 and was put to death by Domitian for writing a biography of Thrasea Paetus (*Agr.* 2.1). This biography may well have provided the detail and eulogistic tone of the depiction of Paetus in *Annals* 16. See Martin (1981) 210.

cruelty of the tyrant. Paetus, like Seneca, makes a dying libation to Jupiter Liberator, but he uses his own blood. They both thus allude to the liberation of the soul from the body and perhaps to liberation from having to compromise their beliefs and behaviour in the face of Nero's tyranny.[41] The scale, tone and content of these two scenes do not seem to bear out Tacitus' own complaint about *patientia seruilis*.

Piso, Paetus, Plautus and Seneca share a concern for the safety of their families.[42] And Tacitus nowhere criticises this motive. So why the deliberately threadbare and unconvincing appeals? At the very least, they remind us of the conflicting considerations each man faced – duty to country, family, friends and self – as he tried to determine what was the right thing to do. Perhaps Tacitus intends us to see that the victims actually had no choice or that by choosing death they have made the only realistic one. Perhaps the weak arguments suggest the desperate straits of friends and supporters. Finally, each man dies with composure; the deaths themselves are hardly *segnes*. The text, then, presents a more nuanced picture of the aristocratic suicides than 16.16.2 might suggest. Tacitus' compassion is evident. The historian may judge a whole period harshly, but his judgement is much more discerning when it comes to individuals.

The death of Nero

By Book 16, the ancient reader might well have been wondering how Tacitus would portray the death of Nero. At this point we cannot know. Suetonius and the epitome of Dio both describe Nero's fearful and inconsistent behaviour caused by his inability to grasp his true situation (Suet. *Ner*. 40–7; Dio 63.27–9). While Nero may have exclaimed 'What a performer dies with me!' (Suet. *Ner*. 49.1 *Qualis artifex pereo!*), his is a squalid and inglorious end.

According to Suetonius, Nero first tries denial. After learning of Vindex's revolt, for eight days he does nothing: he blots out the whole affair with silence (40.4). When any good news arrives, he gives himself over to lavish

---

[41] On the libation to Jupiter Liberator, see Griffin (1976) 370–1. Cato the Younger's suicide, which consciously recalled the death of Socrates, was another model for the Stoics in the early Principate. See Griffin (1986) 195–6; Duff (1999) 144. For his life of Cato, Plutarch used the biography by Thrasea Paetus (Plut. *Cat. Min.* 25, 37). Tacitus' criticisms of Paetus' vanity and efforts to assert senatorial *libertas* against Nero have led some to conclude that his portrait of him is uniformly negative. So Walker (1952) 229–30. For a more nuanced view, see Martin (1981) 176–7, 186–7. Syme (1958a) 558 thought Paetus' efforts showed 'sagacity and restraint'.

[42] In the early Principate, the defendant's suicide terminated criminal proceedings and so prevented a sentence being passed that would have involved confiscation of his property and denial of burial (6.29.1).

feasting (42.2).[43] When he learns that other armies have revolted, he tears up the dispatches (47.1). When he tries to rally some troops to himself, they give evasive answers and one shouts out Turnus' words to his sister (*Aen.* 12.646): 'usque adeone mori miserum est?' ('Is dying so very terrible?'). Nero's death scene in Suetonius is almost a parody of those of his victims in the *Annals*. Abandoned by his friends (47.3), he flees the palace disguised in shabby clothes and heads to the villa of a freedman. His companions, instead of exhorting him to live, urge him to save himself from indignities by killing himself (49.1). While he does order a grave to be dug and water and wood to be brought, he still hesitates to die (49.2), thus allowing himself rather more time than he gave his victims. Nero weeps and laments his own death, as his Tacitean victims never do. He begs someone else to help him take his life by setting an example, whereas his victims in the *Annals* calmly set an *exemplum* for others (49.3).[44] Only when he learns that the senate has declared him a *hostis* (an enemy of the state) and hears how he would be put to death, does he, terrified (*conterritus*), pick up two daggers only to put them down again. At last, he stabs himself, but must be finished off by his freedman Epaphroditus (49.3; cf. Dio. 63.29.2).

Finale

Having seen off Nero, at least in Suetonius, we must ask in conclusion why Tacitus devoted so much space to the death scenes of the *princeps*' victims. First, he had a wealth of detailed material in the *exitus* literature written about this period. Secondly, the composure of many of Nero's victims and the care with which they took their own lives allowed Tacitus to present 'scenes' that rivalled those degrading performances enacted on stage by the *princeps*. In a heavily theatricalised world, some victims departed from Nero's script and claimed their own freedom with the courage, foresight and self-restraint he so lacked. And of course so many deaths set Nero's fear and cruelty in the harshest possible light. Finally, such scenes are an

---

[43] Goddard (1994) 72–3 argues that Suetonius uses Nero's feasting to exemplify his inability to act, his incompetence and his irresponsibility. On the theme of Nero's irresponsibility in these chapters, see also Bradley (1978) 242–3.

[44] So Seneca will not begrudge his wife's *exemplum* in choosing to die with him (15.63.2), while Paetus urges his wife not to follow the example of her mother by dying with him (16.34.2). As he makes his libation to Jupiter the Liberator, Paetus tells the young quaestor to watch, since he has been born into times 'in which it is useful to strengthen the spirit with steadfast examples' (16.35.1 *quibus firmare animum expediat constantibus exemplis*). After describing Subrius Flavus' defiant words to Nero and brave death (15.67), Tacitus remarks that Sulpicius Asper offered 'the next example of steadfastness' (15.68.1 *proximum constantiae exemplum*).

'Is dying so very terrible?' The Neronian *Annals*

element in Tacitus' central preoccupation as a historian: can there be good men under bad emperors, and what constitutes good behaviour under such a regime? In the *Agricola* he had disparaged those who gained fame by a showy death (*Agr.* 42.4 *ambitiosa morte*), which achieved nothing for the state, as opposed to moderates such as Agricola who worked within the system. Nearly two decades later, Tacitus seems to have reconsidered that judgement.[45]

FURTHER READING

Two studies of Nero by Griffin (1984) and Champlin (2003) can help the reader to a more balanced assessment of the emperor. For more on role-playing and theatricality in the early Principate, see Dupont (1985), Boesche (1987), Coleman (1990) and Bergmann and Kondoleon (1999). Ginsburg (2006) perceptively deconstructs the various ancient representations of Agrippina the Younger in the literary and visual traditions. On Domitius Corbulo, the third major figure whom Tacitus opposes to Nero, see Gilmartin (1973) and Ash (2006b). For the revolt of Boudicca, see Roberts (1988).

---

[45] For lack of self-control as the basic flaw in Nero's character, see Tresch (1965) 128–9. For Tacitus' apparent change of mind about senatorial suicides, see Martin (1981) 187. But Walker (1952) 230 argues that Tacitus' treatment of Thrasea Paetus accords with the sentiments of *Agr.* 42.4.

Many thanks to Cecil Wooten and Ada Boni for much Roman refreshment.

PART III
Topics

10

CHRISTOPHER PELLING

Tacitus' personal voice

As for myself, Galba, Otho, and Vitellius were not known to me through doing me either good or harm. I would not deny that my career owed its beginnings to Vespasian, its advance to Titus and its further progress to Domitian; but those who have promised to be unbiased must describe everyone without either affection or hatred. If I live long enough, I have reserved for my old age the richer and less troublesome material of the principate of the deified Nerva and the rule of Trajan, in this rare delight of the times when you can think what you like and say what you think. (H. 1.1.3–4)

Soon it was our hands that led Helvidius to prison; it was we who were shamed by the looks and the sight of Mauricus and Rusticus; it was we who were drenched by Senecio's innocent blood. Nero would at least remove his own eyes from such sights, and he ordered rather than viewed his crimes; it was a special part of the suffering under Domitian to see and be seen, when our sighs were noted down, when that savage, red face with which he fortified himself against shame was sufficient to mark out the pallor of so many men. (Agr. 45.1–2)

There was also the death of Junia, in the sixty-fourth year after the fighting at Philippi. She was the niece of Cato, the wife of C. Cassius and the sister of M. Brutus. Her will produced much talk among the people, because she was a wealthy woman and she mentioned in complimentary terms virtually all the leading men of the state, but made no mention of the emperor. That was taken in a way appropriate to a fellow-citizen, and Tiberius did not forbid the funeral to be celebrated with the eulogy from the front of the rostra and the other customary honours. Twenty funeral-masks of the most distinguished families were carried before the bier, and the names of Manlii and Quinctii and other similar nobility were to be seen. But the most glittering of all were Cassius and Brutus, for the very reason that their likenesses were not on view. (A. 3.76)

A personal voice can speak in several tones. The first of the passages quoted above is the one that gives most information about Tacitus himself; the second would seem the loudest cry from the author's heart; the third, on the face of it, is not about Tacitus himself at all. Yet all convey what Robert

Fowler, talking about Herodotus, called the author's 'voiceprint',[1] the distinctive slant that Tacitus gives on his imperial world. All, too, raise questions of the dynamic of text and reader. If every author is a mouth in search of an ear, the sound of this particular mouth attunes the reader to hear, and to listen, in a very particular way.

Take the third passage first, the one that has no grammatical personal markers – no first-person verbs, no 'ego' or 'nos', no reference to personal experience. But it is the last chapter of a book, and authors do not choose – and readers know they do not choose – such concluding material lightly.[2] It comes after a treatment of the deaths of two other Augustan luminaries, Asinius Saloninus and Ateius Capito (3.75). The second of these is contrasted with a further figure, Antistius Labeo – Capito the time-server and Labeo a man who had 'kept his *libertas* untainted'. The one style of behaviour looks forward to the Principate and the other back to the Republic, and Labeo was the more respected and Capito, unsurprisingly, the more successful. Still, Junia looks back even more clearly, and much more resonantly – Cato, Cassius and Brutus, all those great names of *libertas*, and Philippi, the battle where the free state died. This focuses the theme that so often recurs in the middle books of Tiberius' reign, the question of how much had changed since the Republic. The answer is a good deal, as the procession shows; but still not everything. Junia herself has survived so long, a relic of a distant age, and she can still be allowed her own display of *libertas*, the ostentatious omission of the emperor from her will. But the way Tacitus describes it shows the way things are going. 'That was taken *ciuiliter*' by the emperor, that is, in the way one citizen ought to treat another; but Tacitus' earlier narrative has shown that by now the *princeps* is anything but an ordinary citizen, and such civility is a topic for comment. Tiberius 'did not forbid' the customary ceremonial, again marking what might be expected as well as what happened. The next chapter will open Book 4 with the introduction of Sejanus, and an indication that the reign is about to take its decisive change for the worse. The next book closure will be the marriage of Agrippina and Cn. Domitius (4.75), a passage that looks forward as arrestingly as this one looks back. For that is the marriage that will produce the emperor Nero.

'Marking what might be expected ...'; but expected *by whom*? Partly, by the author: that is what makes it a voiceprint, the projection of the mind that has given this its prominent position and chosen the emphases to give. But the effect is to draw in the reader too, to imply the questions that would

---

[1] Fowler (1996).
[2] The more so for the intricate way in which the closural technique echoes the beginnings both of Book 1 and of Book 3: Woodman and Martin (1996) 489–90.

be in our minds – how *did* the emperor take that, then? Surely not lying down? The strong visuality at the end helps too, and the more so for its paradoxicality, if the most visually striking element of all was the 'glittering' pair who were there only in spirit.³ We form a picture of that procession, and are told how onlookers reacted at the time – and if we ask how Tacitus could possibly have known, the answer is probably not to be found in his source material but in the power of his intelligent imagination to re-create how people *must have* reacted, just as he reacts himself and we are led to react too. A circle of author, reader and historical onlooker is constructed, all assumed to be reflecting on the scene and all speaking with the same 'voice'.

But the circle is not always such a cosy one, and author and reader may not always be so straightforwardly at one. Take the first passage. Its subject is bias and partisanship, the sort of thing that he has just said has come to plague imperial historiography because of 'the delight in toadyism or, again, the hatred against those who rule' (*H.* 1.1.1). It makes a point about Roman history that here, as later in the proem of the *Annals*,⁴ this bias is part of an audience's expectation, one that the author needs to confront before he begins. It makes a point about Tacitus too that there is a case to answer, because of the successful career he has enjoyed under the Flavians: a point is insinuated here about his political experience and the insight he will have gained, and this builds his authority with his readers even as it may arouse their suspicions.⁵ So clearly here author and reader are *not* so at one with each other, when issues like this are at stake. For the moment, all Tacitus can do is to 'promise to be unbiased', and accept the consequential obligation – 'must describe …'. With subject matter that is so fraught, no one could be expected to accept the claim of impartiality without further ado: the proof of the programme will be in the reading, but it does constitute an acknowledgement that the audience will be on their guard, and indeed should be.

---

³ I agree with Woodman that the language 'compels us to infer that Cassius and Brutus were somehow "really" present' themselves (cf. Woodman and Martin (1996) 497–8; Martin disagrees). If so this circle of author, reader and onlooker is eerily expanded even further.
⁴ But there are subtle differences of emphasis between the two proems: Marincola (1999).
⁵ Cf. Marincola (1997) 143–4, rightly comparing the mention of Tacitus' praetorship and priesthood at *A.* 11.11.1; also above, pp. 37–9. This suggests one reason why modern distinctions between 'author', the flesh-and-blood character who married Agricola's daughter and was consul, and 'narrator', a figure constructed by the text, are misleading for Roman historiography. It fits generic expectations that, more often than not, the narrator speaks with the 'authority' of real-life political experience, and the reader knows it. The distinction would be particularly misleading for Tacitus, for it is a crucial point that flesh and blood may have to pay the penalty for the tones a 'narrator' strikes: witness Cremutius Cordus (*A.* 4.34–5). Nor is Tacitus alone in mentioning dangers: cf. esp. Hor. *Carm.* 2.1.6; Marincola (1997) 157–8.

He has just warned them too of the dangers of over-facile reading: 'you will find you have easily rejected [*facile auerseris*: note the grammatical marker to involve the reader] the self-seeking of an author, whereas detraction and anger find a ready reception: for adulation carries the foul charge of servility, whereas malice carries the false impression of a free spirit' (*H.* 1.1.2). So this sets out an agenda, and guides the reader into the questions to put to the text.

The final sentence will start the reader thinking too. Have the times indeed got better, as Tacitus says? Or, given that the Principate has always made it so difficult to 'say what one thinks', is this yet another adulatory gesture of the sort that so many writers had earlier found compulsory? Is that 'rare delight of the times, when you can think what you like and say what you think', simply a feature of Nerva's and Trajan's reigns, or also of old age when a writer has less to lose? A personal voice is sounding there, but it takes a fine ear to be sure what it is saying. And that too conveys something about the Principate, where it is so difficult to be sure that anything said, especially if it is said about an emperor, can be taken straight.

There is a further twist too, one that relates the experience of reading more closely to the experience of imperial life. Once we reach the narrative of the *Histories* we are plunged into a morass of rumours. Galba's heir Piso was thought to be an enemy of T. Vinius 'either because it was true or because that was the way that angry people wanted to think; and more credence is given when hate is alleged' (*H.* 1.34.1 *facilius de odio creditur*). It is put as a general truth,[6] and it echoes the sentiments of the proem ('detraction and anger find a ready reception ... malice carries the false impression of a free spirit'). Nor, with anything involving T. Vinius, is it difficult to believe in the hate he might excite ('the worst man alive ... weighed down by the hatred his crimes aroused', 1.6.1, cf. 12, 42, 48): a little later the narrator himself gives credence to such a feeling about Vinius, this time in the mind of Cornelius Laco (39.2).

By now, though, such malignity towards the powerful is not simply part of the fog that hides the truth, as it was in the proem. False, malicious beliefs have themselves become an important factor in the events. When Otho speaks to the soldiers, he himself talks about false descriptions: 'Others call these things crimes, Galba calls them cures; he applies the false name of strictness [*seueritas*] to savagery, thrift to greed, discipline to your punishments

---

[6] As Damon (2003) 170 notes, this leaves open the question of whose beliefs are in point: are they Tacitus' own, or is this a 'generalisation'? If the second, it is important that the reader too may be implicated.

and humiliations' (37.4). Yet Otho's language is itself false:[7] the previous narrative spoke only of Galba's 'old-fashioned unbendingness and excessive strictness' (18.3 *antiquus rigor et nimia seueritas*). As for Piso, Otho now reviles him for his 'moroseness and avarice' (38.1 *tristitia et auaritia*). Again, the narrative was more circumspect: 'on a correct estimation Piso was strict, but for those who took a more jaundiced view he was considered over-morose' (14.2 *deterius interpretantibus tristior habebatur*). Yet what matters now is not 'correct estimation': it is image that counts, not reality, or rather image comes to drive reality. The audience's own readiness to believe the worst of people (not, indeed, a tendency that the intervening narrative has generally countered, even if it does so here) can help them to understand why contemporary onlookers could have been so susceptible to a similar cynicism. So the reader is thrust into events, and helped to understand those responses of people at the time through a type of personal reaction that the text has both generated and warned against; but once again the circle of writer, reader and observer is not so cosy, and this time the reader is guided to a critique, but an engaged and understanding critique, of the observers rather than of the writer.

Lest affairs seem too distant for such involvement to be appropriate, another sounding of a 'personal voice' has indicated that the themes are not as remote as all that. The passage where Tacitus indicated the right way of looking at Galba's non-indulgence added some telling words: '... his old-fashioned unbendingness and excessive strictness, a quality which is too much for us now' (18.3). Those who caught a contemporary resonance in Piso's adoption[8] might well think that the story of January 69, and their complicated response to it, was coming very close to home.

What of the *cri-de-coeur* of the *Agricola*? This final humiliation of Domitian's reign is that 'we', the political elite, have been reduced to this. One can understand those who have sensed here 'a personal sense of guilt', indeed 'a passionate confession of collective guilt':[9] that is especially so in a work that has been so concerned with *libertas* and the threats to it both at home and on the frontier.[10] When we have seen that Calgacus and his Britons feel that death is better than servitude, what are we to make

---

[7] Thus Keitel (1991) 2779: 'Otho, while indicting Galba falsely on the charge of misusing language, succeeds brilliantly by doing exactly the same thing.'
[8] See esp. Syme (1958a) 150–6, 206–7, exploring the relevance of Nerva's adoption of Trajan in 97; also above, pp. 89–90. Broader parallels between 69 and 96–8 are seen by Cole (1992) 241–4.
[9] Respectively Ogilvie and Richmond (1967) 308 and Syme (1958a) 25.
[10] Liebeschuetz (1966).

of servility like this? And yet we have also just seen a strong defence of Agricola's own political path, for it produced more good for the state than the ostentatiously suicidal opposition of those who sought martyrdom (42.4):

> Let those know, who are accustomed to feel admiration for forbidden actions, that there can be great men even under bad emperors, and obedience and forbearance, if accompanied by hard work and energy, can attain that level of acclaim that many have achieved through a glory-seeking death, treading a precipitous path but doing the state no good.

Agricola himself was spared by his death the choice of whether or not to acquiesce in that final humiliation, but his own life shows that there was no easy answer.

The personal voice here projects 'our' misery, and invites a reader to share it imaginatively. It also acknowledges that there is an issue here, and perhaps a case to answer. The reader is invited to judge, without over-romanticised prejudice in favour of the suicidal show-offs. And if that reader finds such judgement agonisingly difficult, that too re-creates and draws us in to what living under a Domitian, and having to make those choices, was really like.

From 'I' to 'we'

We have seen that one does not need an 'I' – 'the odious pronoun'[11] – to hear a voiceprint. Still, Tacitus' 'I'-language is interesting, often lending emphasis to passages where a strong response is expressed.[12] That response is most often one of indignation, but need not be: there are also cases such as *A.* 2.88.1–3 ('I find in some authors ... we praise the old and neglect the modern'), where Tacitus marks his admiration for Arminius, or *A.* 4.67.2 ('I should imagine that it was the island's isolation that Tiberius found particularly attractive ...'), introducing a description of Capri that makes the reader understand its appeal. But, Tacitus being Tacitus, the darker tones predominate. Thus *A.* 4.1.1, introducing Sejanus, 'whose power I have mentioned before; now I will set out ...'. We should also note, however, that the emotional weight is carried not by those clauses but by the rest of the chapter: there is no 'I' in 'the anger of the gods against the Roman state, to which his fall was as catastrophic as his success' (4.1.2).

---

[11] Syme (1958a) 304.
[12] It is analysed well by Sinclair (1995) 50–77, who rightly brings it into connection with Tacitus' various uses of 'you' and 'we' language.

Tacitus' personal voice

Elsewhere too 'I'-passages, often in gentle ways such as 'as I have mentioned before', tend to cluster close, *but not necessarily in the identical context*, to strongly written and emotionally laden passages. That is true even in the apparently impersonal *Germania*. That too has what we may call 'authorial' 'I's, referring to the process of weighing the information and presenting it: 'I would believe ... if I may put it this way' (2.1 *crediderim ... utque sic dixerim*); 'I would not claim' (5.2 *nec ... adfirmauerim*); and the last word of the work is *relinquam*, 'I shall leave aside' a claim about monstrous beings at the edge of the world (46.4). Not much given away about the writer there, one might think – but those at 2.1 are followed by a rhetorical question: 'For who – quite apart from the dangers of a threatening and strange sea – would leave Asia, Africa or Italy and move to Germany, with its unlovely landscape, its foul climate and its dispiriting manners and prospect, unless this was their native land?' 5.2 is preceded by 'the gods have not given them silver and gold: I am uncertain whether this was an act of kindness or of wrath'. And 46.4 is preceded by a remark on the Fenni, who live particularly rough:

> But they regard this as a happier existence than to groan over fields and toil over houses, and to weigh their own and others' fortunes in hope and in fear: they need take no thought of humans or of gods, and have achieved the most difficult thing of all – *they* have no need even of prayers. (G. 46.3)

The voiceprint is unmistakable – but are such people a target for Rome, and, if so, does such hardiness make them more or less formidable? Or are they a model, with that idealised primitiveness to which Roman moral thinking could always lean, and, if so, given that 'groaning over fields' may be able to embrace not merely back-breaking labour over one's own fields but also sighing in anguish as one eyes another's, does it suggest that all such expansionist targeting is mistaken?

These, then, seem to be 'buttonholing' 'I's, drawing attention to the communicative process at times when it is important that a voiceprint should be heard. The later works use the same technique. Thus we find at *A.* 6.20.2 'I would not omit' (*non omiserim*) Tiberius' prophecy about the young Galba's future, then two chapters later Tacitus' own reflections on astrology, just after a heightened description of the 'immeasurable slaughter' of the end of his reign and some gloomy remarks about Gaius' coming reign (6.19.2–20.1), and just before the dreadful story of Tiberius' relishing the final agonies of his grandson Drusus (6.23–4); or *A.* 14.17.1, a spectacle put on by Livineius Regulus 'who, as I have mentioned [*rettuli*], had been expelled from the senate', in between the indignant descriptions of Nero's antics in the arena, the theatre and the dining room (14.14–16, 20).

An 'I' who speaks implies a 'you' who listens, just as in the preface to the *Histories* (above); and second-person verbs addressed to the reader duly tend to come close to such 'I's, though again not always in the same context. Thus *A.* 16.4.4, on the popular acclaim that greeted Nero in the theatre: 'you would have believed [*crederes*] they were delighted, and perhaps indeed they were so uncaring for the disgrace to the state that they did delight'; and a little later 'I would not believe [*neque ... crediderim*] that it was poison' that carried off Poppaea (16.6.1) – two different topics, but both extremely fraught. The effect of such second-person verbs is usually to draw readers more closely into visualising the events themselves, or to go some way beyond the visual.[13] Thus at *A.* 11.18.3 'you could tell [*scias*] that Corbulo was focused and would not be lenient with great misbehaviour, when he was believed to be so strict even in the case of trivialities', followed there by a different sort of first-person, a 'we' of 'we Romans':[14] 'our virtue swelled, the barbarians' ferocity was broken' (11.19.1). It is even as if we too knew Agricola: 'you would readily have believed [*facile crederes*] him a good man and gladly believed him a great one' (*Agr.* 44.2); or, less exuberantly, Flavius Sabinus: 'you would not have criticised [*non argueres*] his integrity or his sense of fairness: he talked too much' (*H.* 3.75.1).

Such addresses can draw the reader into the writing exercise too. When Tacitus reflects on his own themes,

> it does not matter to anyone if you have revelled more in your descriptions of Roman or of Carthaginian armies, but the descendants of many who were punished or shamed under Tiberius are still alive. Even if the families themselves have died out, you will find many who think other people's misdeeds a reproach to themselves because their characters are similar. (*A.* 4.33.4)

'You' are here someone who might be doing what 'I', Tacitus, am doing, and facing the same risks.[15] We are all in this together; author and reader are rhetorically bonded; and the personal engagement of both bonds them – 'us' – with the observers of the events themselves, all the more easily because 'other people's misdeeds' show so timelessly familiar a nature.

---

[13] Gilmartin (1975) treats such historiographic second-persons, discussing and refining [Longinus] *Subl.* 26.2 on the way such a figure 'makes you see what you hear': cf. Damon (2003) on *H.* 1.10.2.

[14] On that convention cf. Marincola (1997) 287–8. On the technique of 11.18.3 see Ash (2006b) 363: 'Tacitus ... raises the question of image versus reality and prompts readers to consider the layers of fiction and evolution of myth', especially relevant for actions in the east 'where perceptions often have more clout than the true state of affairs'. It is not coincidence that the reader's own potential perceptions – *scias* – become an important ingredient here.

[15] Sinclair (1995) 60–2 has good remarks on the use of 'we' and 'you' in this passage.

Insight shared

That technique recalls the way that readers were drawn in to be vicarious observers of the funeral of Junia (above, p. 148), in that case without an 'I' or a 'you' (though, typically, the previous paragraph had Ateius Capito 'whom I have mentioned', 3.75.1); but we also noticed that the ring of reader and writer need not always be so close, and that Tacitus can acknowledge that, at least at the outset, the reader is right to be sceptical (p. 149). Yet that too is a form of union: the implication is still that 'you' and 'I' both know what grappling with imperial history is like.

Narrative conveys a similar implication more subtly. 'I would not presume' (*non ausim*), says Tacitus – one of another cluster of authorial 'I's – to give the Vitellian battle order at the second battle of Bedriacum, 'even though others have conveyed' a detailed listing (*H.* 3.22.2). The narrative makes it clear why Tacitus is reluctant – everything in a night battle was simply too confused and confusing (cf. Thuc. 7.44.1). A non-committal authorial stance builds his own narrative authority by implying an insight into the way his predecessors had tried to build theirs – simultaneously showing that he knows better, and that his readers will understand why. A chapter later he tells of two brave soldiers who slipped through the lines and cut the cables tethering a lethal Vitellian catapult. 'They were immediately cut down and for that reason their names have been lost; there is no dispute over their deed' (3.23.2). Once again, it is assumed that we understand the confusion that attends such battles – it is no surprise that there might be such 'dispute' – but we are also taken as understanding the role of the historian to give glory when it is due and when he can.[16] So again several themes, some concerning the nature of battle and some the nature of historiography, are deftly insinuated. The same is true when Tacitus gives us 'on the authority of Vipstanus Messalla' the tale of a son killing a father (3.25.2): authority is needed, and the experienced reader understands why (these are the stuff of rhetorical battle descriptions, and they invite scepticism[17]); but Messalla was an eye-witness (3.18.2), and anyway – Tacitus claims – such things did happen, for, however much men relished the scandal of it all, they also relished the doing (3.25.3).[18]

---

[16] Similar assumptions can be seen at *H.* 3.54.3, noting variants on how a man died but stressing that all agreed on his honesty and resolution; at *A.* 15.67.3 it is other writers' neglect of an item (the final words of Subrius Flavus) rather than their unanimity that leads Tacitus to record something heroic.

[17] Cf. Woodman (1998) 13–16; Ash (1999a) 188 n. 93; also above, p. 93.

[18] Cf. *H.* 4.81.3, after the tale of Vespasian's miraculous cures at Alexandria: 'those who were present still tell of both cases, even though there is no longer any incentive to lie'. The reader is expected both to be sceptical and to know why and how such tales might arise; the narrator shares that mindset, but assures the reader that he has performed the proper investigative task.

As the battle reached its climax, who was it who turned its course by gesturing to Cremona, waiting there as the victors' prize? 'Whether this idea was due to the talent of Hormus, as Messalla says, or whether C. Plinius is a preferable author in accusing Antonius, I would find it hard to tell; the only indication is that, in the case of either man, not even the worst of crimes would have meant a decline of standards in reputation or behaviour' (3.28.1). Tacitus has done the historian's task of checking accounts, and again the confusion of it all is felt: the only way one can tell is to appeal to first principles of who might be expected to be the culprit, and here the characters of the two men do not allow one to decide.[19] A wider point is there, that at such a moment it is men like this who call the lethal tune; but there is a wider point still, for Antonius has come out very well from the last few chapters, but *as a general*, one who understands what warfare demands.[20] If indeed Antonius was rightly 'accused' for the fate of Cremona, it reminds us that the commendable and the outrageous can easily co-exist in such a man; indeed, that both sorts of act can be what such a natural understanding of warfare may demand.

So these few chapters show how complex a 'building of authority' can be. Yes, Tacitus has dutifully compared the sources: but the best way to evaluate them is to apply an understanding both of how false narratives can grow up and of how things are likely to have been. The historian understands historiography; he also understands how the world works, and particularly how the grim world of carnage works. And by now his reader understands it too, linked with the writer in a complicity of knowingness.

Another way in which the writer projects credibility is by adducing his own 'authorities' – his sources. These are not quoted just anywhere.[21] Citations are particularly required, and judgement in evaluating them is paraded, when the material is so momentous and so sensational as to invite scepticism: 'you'd hardly believe it, but ...'. Sometimes the reader is right not to believe, as when Tacitus warns against the sensationalised version of Drusus' murder (*A*. 4.10–12); more often the extraordinary turns out to be true – thus with the fraught exchange of Tiberius and Agrippina (*A*. 4.53.2), the atrocious story of the executioner raping Sejanus' young daughter (*A*. 5.9.2) or the 'wedding' of Messalina and Silius (*A*. 11.27).

---

[19] Cf. *H*. 1.42.1 and 2.100.3 for further cases when people's characters provide the only means of deciding what happened in a confused and violent episode.

[20] 'A villain in peacetime; in war, not to be dismissed lightly' (*H*. 2.86.2). On Antonius' portrayal see Ash (1999a) 147–65; on the distribution of blame for Cremona, Morgan (1996) 389–403.

[21] Whitehead (1979) 495 similarly notes that collections of alternative versions cluster at critical points in the narrative, including the descriptions of the fire and the Pisonian conspiracy in *Annals* 15.

More elaborate cases come at *A.* 13.20 and 14.2, where the discrepancies among authors – Fabius Rusticus, Cluvius Rufus and, in the first case, Pliny the Elder – are less striking than the points they are implied to agree about, firstly Nero's thoughts of matricide and secondly the narrow escape from incest of mother and son.

A certain amount of this assumed scepticism is based on a shared humanity: we do not need telling that tales of near-incest should not be lightly told or believed. But some cases are more a question of a *nurtured* scepticism, one encouraged in a reader by Tacitus' own narrative, and especially by earlier cases of his 'voiceprint'. One complex instance is the story of the conspiracy of Piso, again accompanied by a cluster of authorial 'I's.[22] There are also several source citations and notices of variants (*A.* 15.53–4, 61.3, 63.3, 74.3),[23] along with other markers of uncertainty: 'I would not find it easy to record' who started it all (15.49.1 *nec … facile memorauerim*); 'it is [or 'was'] uncertain how' Epicharis was brought in (15.51.1 *incertum quonam modo …*); perhaps Piso was nervous that L. Silanus would step in to take the fruits of a conspiracy in which he had no part, but 'several people believed' that it was the consul Vestinus who figured more in his apprehensions (15.52.2–3 *plerique … crediderunt*) – or perhaps Seneca might be the beneficiary (15.65.1). But there is a broader dubiety that might be felt about the whole thing:

> coeptam adultamque et reuictam coniurationem neque tunc dubitauere quibus uerum noscendi cura erat, et fatentur qui post interitum Neronis in urbem regressi sunt.   (*A.* 15.73.2)

> This conspiracy – its beginnings, its growth and its defeat – was not doubted at the time by people who took the trouble to find out the truth, and those who returned to the city after Nero's death admit that it was true.

That remark comes at the end; up to that point the doubts have concerned only the details. But the facts that are confidently retailed have included moves by Nero against people he knew, or should have known, were innocent: Vestinus, Seneca, Rufrius Crispinus and others (15.52.3, 56.2, 60.2, 68.2–69.3, 71.4). In some cases that was vindictiveness, in some cases nervousness (and 'after Nero's death' reminds us that there were only a few years to go, that plotting could well be as genuine now as it would be a little later, and Nero had reason to be afraid: those suggestions become firmer in the next chapter, with the mention of Vindex and other, subtler hints that the endgame is beginning[24]).

---

[22] *A.* 15.49.1, 50.3, 53.4, 54.1, 63.3, 67.3, 72.2, 74.3.
[23] Cf. n. 21.
[24] Woodman (1998) 215–17.

We have also seen people of the court rushing to denounce one another, however thin the basis (15.56.4, cf. 71.3; 58.1–4). Tacitus' readers would be failing in their duty if they were *not* by now suspecting that the whole thing might have been a sham: that too is part of our re-creation of the uncertainties of the times, where it was plausible that conspiracies might happen and also plausible that they might be pure fabrications. As with those battlefield fratricides, we hear the personal voice sounding the need both for scepticism and for a readiness, on this occasion, to lay that scepticism aside.

At such times wild allegations fly around, and the most sober might be tempted to believe them. That applies not just to contemporary observers but also to historians, even one so diligent as the elder Pliny:

> Meanwhile Piso was to wait at the temple of Ceres. The plan was for the prefect Faenius and the others to call him from there and take him to the camp; he would be accompanied by Antonia, daughter of the emperor Claudius, in order to gain the support of the people. That is what C. Plinius records. It has been our intention too not to conceal anything that has been passed down in any way, however absurd it might seem to think that Antonia should have lent her name and taken such a risk for a hopeless aspiration, or that Piso, whose affection for his wife was well known, would have committed himself to another marriage – unless, that is, lust for power flames brighter than all other affections.   (A. 15.53.3–4)

(Notice again how that Tacitean voiceprint of the final clause accompanies the preceding, rather different, projection of the historian at work.) This is not just an incidental sideswipe against a competitor for the historical market. It mattered that people at the time could believe the wildest claims, and Pliny has become a sort of surrogate for those contemporaries. Longer retrospect allows Tacitus a cooler head, but this is not the first time we have seen his technique priming us both to understand and to critique 'what people said'.[25]

And are there times where readers are primed both to understand and to critique, not merely Tacitus' predecessors, but also Tacitus himself? That is a good question: we will return to it.

Insight manipulated

Paradoxically, a personal voice can sometimes be sensed when it is someone else speaking. That can simply be a way of making us understand

---

[25] Above, p. 151. Cf. Levene (1997), an outstanding analysis of how readers of *H.* 3 become a 'meta-audience', engaged with but also judging popular reactions to Vitellius' fall.

that people are talking sense, as with the shrewd remarks of 'the older generation' contrasting Nero's rhetorical inabilities with the competence of his predecessors (*A*. 13.3.2). More interesting are those cases where the focus rests less on the insight itself, rather on what the speaker does with it. If Eprius Marcellus speaks impressively of the need for restraint under the Principate, 'to hope for good emperors but put up with whatever comes along' (*H*. 4.8.2–3), he may speak the same language as Agricola or Tacitus himself might have used,[26] but that does not make him a good man. The point is the *travesty* of insight and of rhetoric, itself a disturbing sign of the times.

Or consider Otho's words at *H*. 1.83–4. That is an impromptu speech provoked by an immediate crisis: hence, on this occasion at least, it is the emperor himself rather than his speech-writer (cf. 1.90) who is heard.[27] It is full of fine phrases about the senate: 'the eternal stability of the world, the peace of nations, your safety along with mine all rely on the safety of the senate' (1.84.4). We may take the authorial voice to approve such sentiments, given that by now the narrative has several times assumed a suite of traditional aristocratic values (comments, for instance, on the unpatriotic fickleness and greed of *plebs* and soldiery).[28] But of course this is not a matter of a speaker being the author's 'mouthpiece'. The validity of what is said is taken for granted – it is the reasons for saying it that matter. The first part of the speech has already radiated disingenuousness, with Otho ascribing to the soldiers motives that (at least in Tacitus' presentation at 1.80.2[29]) are over-generous, as if their turbulence is simply a symptom of their over-affection for himself; but that is the right, prudent thing for him to say. Now he gives the reasons why his soldiers ought to be polite about the senate: that is an important part of his window-dressing in the propaganda battle against Vitellius (1.84.3). The same reasons come into play when estimating why he himself is taking so complimentary a line – even if we also toy with a more favourable interpretation, given that there have

---

[26] Cf. e.g. Syme (1958a) 209, 547 and (1970) 138–9; Martin (1981) 94, 'it is one of the features of Tacitus' writing that the devil is given a fair share of the good tunes'.

[27] *Pace* Syme (1958a) 192 and (1970) 133.

[28] E.g. *H*. 1.50.1: 'not merely the senate and knights, people who had some concern for the *res publica*, but also the common people' lament the miseries of the present. Cf. *H*. 1.4.3, 5.1–2, 12.3, 23–6, 32.1, 40.2, 50, 51.3–4, 52.2, 57, 63.1, 67.1, 69, 82.1. Not that senators come out very well either: 1.35.1, 47.1, and now 85.3: cf. Keitel (1991) 2782. Pomeroy (2006) 189–91 observes that the empathy generated in readers can itself be seen as a 'class strategy', bonding readers and writers in the same value-scheme: participants in the action can attract pity in various ways, but this is not extended to the lower orders.

[29] Cf. Damon (2003) 261. A more generous interpretation of the soldiers' motives is possible, one more in line with Otho's own words: Shochat (1981) 373.

also been hints that Otho in power has taken some sort of turn for the better (1.71.1, cf. 2.11.3, 31.1).[30]

Certainly, no reader could be surprised that the senators themselves are nervous and bemused (*H.* 1.85). Our own critique of the speech is a version of what would be going through their minds, but for them it was a matter of life and death to get their own words right, and even their facial expressions. As the senate meets, they do not know quite what to say, 'lest silence seem rude, lest frankness arouse suspicion'; and a particular difficulty is that they know Otho can read them all too well, 'so recently a private citizen and so familiar with adulation through saying the same things himself' (85.3). One paradox is that we have just seen a sort of *adulatio* from Otho himself, this time an emperor disingenuously flattering the senate and the soldiers rather than the other way round. Those old skills of his are standing him in good stead. All comes together to reconstruct those uneasy days where no one can speak straight, even or especially when they are saying good things. And, if we did not sense that the narrator himself was presenting both the content as good and the speaker as untrustworthy, we would not find our own critique of the speech so suggestively re-creating the response of those who heard it, or heard of it, at the time.

Fact and impression – and impressions of perplexity

In her 1952 book *The Annals of Tacitus* Walker highlighted 'the discrepancy of fact and impression'[31] – the way that time and again, particularly in the Tiberian books, the interpretations given in the narrative seem at odds with the facts that the narrative itself recounts. Such a discrepancy is clearest with many of the impressions *of others*, rumours that circulated at the time or just the comments that contemporary observers passed on events. It was standard rhetorical practice to use such comments to influence an audience:[32] in his essay *On Herodotus' Malice*, more or less contemporary with Tacitus, Plutarch lists as one of the contemptible signs of a writer's malignity cases where they do not cast their charges openly but 'cast their slanderous shafts under cover, as it were, then turn about and draw back, saying that they do not believe things that they certainly want their audiences to believe' (856c). At first a reader, modern or ancient,

---

[30] Notice that Otho was 'concerned at the danger to the senate' – genuinely, it seems (*H.* 1.83.1, cf. Keitel (1991) 2782). Thus Shochat (1981) 374 is inclined to give Otho the benefit of the motivational doubt.
[31] Walker (1952) 82, etc.
[32] Cf. e.g. Cic. *Inv.* 2.46–7, 50; *Rhet. Her.* 2.9, 12; 4.53; Quint. *Inst.* 5.1.2, 5.3.

might indeed assume that the narrator 'wants his audience to believe' such barbs,[33] especially as there are occasions when those contemporary observers do seem to be talking sense, as, once again, with Nero's rhetorical inabilities (*A.* 13.3), given that Nero had preferred to turn his genuine intellectual gifts in other directions (and the narrator notes this in his own voice, §3).

Yet in so many cases the narrative gives us good grounds for rejecting the censure as baseless and malicious. People criticised Tiberius for ignoring the Gallic rebellion and 'spending his efforts on the depositions of accusers: was Sacrovir too to be put on trial for *maiestas* in the senate?' (*A.* 3.44.2–3). Yet events justified the emperor's inaction: within a few chapters he could give a single report that the war had come and gone (*A.* 3.47.1).[34] Events had similarly justified his decision not to go in person to confront the mutinies of 14, despite the strident criticisms (*A.* 1.46–7). They also justified the decision to withdraw Germanicus two years later: 'the Cherusci and the other rebel nations could be left to their internal wranglings, now that enough had been done to secure Rome her vengeance' (*A.* 2.26.3). However disingenuous Tiberius' motives (*A.* 2.26.5), his words were spot on: the later narrative dwells on those internal wranglings (*A.* 2.44–6, 62–3). Such censure, then, tells us more about the people doing the talking than about the person they are talking about, and that too re-creates the atmosphere of the time, as the narrative shows how hatred of the super-powerful can get in the way of fairness and insight. Gauging 'impression' against 'fact' is here an important part of the thoughtful reader's task.

Walker, however, meant a good deal more than that. She emphasised less these voices of others, more the personal voice of Tacitus himself and those cases where the interpretation embedded in the narrative seems clearly to be the author's own. Thus phrases like 'unmeasurable carnage' or 'unremitting slaughter' (*A.* 6.19.2 *immensa strages*,[35] 6.29.1 *caede continua*) are given in the author's voice, and summarise the feeling that the whole narrative leaves in a reader's mind; when one looks at the details, the numbers do not appear negligible, but do not add up to anything as bloodily

---

[33] Ryberg (1942), e.g. 384: 'they [traditional rhetorical techniques including the use of rumours] are the resources employed by Tacitus the artist to produce an impression for which Tacitus the historian is not willing to take the responsibility'.
[34] Cf. Woodman and Martin (1996) ad loc.
[35] The phrase may be borrowed from Silius Italicus 9.137–8 (above, p. 37), but, in a genre where the authorial presence is so strongly felt (above, n. 5), this does not reduce the 'voiceprint': a reader might well wonder what point is being suggested by the author (and so, in the terms of Hinds (1998), this is 'allusion' rather than 'intertext').

impressive as that.³⁶ The way that the first *maiestas* trial is introduced is also telling:

> It will not be unwelcome for me to record how in the cases of Falanius and Rubrius, insignificant Roman knights, charges were experimented with: this is to make clear what were the origins and how vast was Tiberius' skill in the way this most dreadful mode of destruction crept in, was then suppressed, then finally flared into flame and consumed everything. (A. 1.73.1)

Yet Tiberius' role in the first cases (1.72–4) turns out to be far more ambiguous and not so clearly discreditable, seemingly involving more repression of charges than encouragement.³⁷ Perhaps indeed that is what is meant by 'suppressed', *repressum* – but then, with an emperor so 'skilful', even a parade of moderation is likely to have a more sinister agenda. Here as elsewhere, '[t]he dramatic tension is sharpest, the rhetorical and poetic colouring most brilliant, the evocation of allusive associations most strong, where they have least relation to the events they are thought to describe', and it is no coincidence that such sparkling language is more frequent in the Tiberian than in the later books.³⁸ Or take the death of Germanicus. The facts of the case give scant reason for suspecting foul play; yet 'after reading Tacitus' account, it is very difficult to remember these facts, drawn from the account itself, and the simple hypothesis which fits them best – that Germanicus died of a fever or plague'.³⁹ That is part of a wider peculiarity of Books 1 and 2 of the *Annals*, which might seem to encourage intense enthusiasm for the young Germanicus and to contrast his easy attractiveness with the awkward unpleasantness of Tiberius; but there too Tacitus' own facts seem sufficient to give a reader pause, and make us wonder whether there is not another side to it.

Walker's own conclusion was couched in psychological language, as she analysed Tacitus' own mentality in Jungian terms. Tacitus, for her, is an 'intuitive' mental type, one who 'views the facts he describes in the light of a theory, a preformed judgement, or we may say more sympathetically a poetic and imaginative conception which gave them life, and sometimes transformed them';⁴⁰ but at the same time he is uneasy enough to lay bare the thinness of its support. If the style is most coloured when the tension is most apparent, '[a]n emotional conviction often grows most clamorous

---

³⁶ Walker (1952) 82–6.
³⁷ Walker (1952) 88–91 – though notice also the good remarks of Koestermann (1955) 85–6 on Piso's intervention at 1.74.4–6; cf. esp. Goodyear (1981) 163–4.
³⁸ Walker (1952) 158–61 (quotation from p. 158).
³⁹ Walker (1952) 116.
⁴⁰ Walker (1952) 187–96 (quotation from p. 195).

when facts will least support it'.⁴¹ His own 'inward conflict is fully and honestly expressed in his work',⁴² and there are signs that he himself 'became dissatisfied with his own reading of events' – a dissatisfaction that he 'was too honestly conscientious to muffle'.⁴³

Such psychological language is no longer in fashion, as scholars have grown squeamish about thinking they can gain such access to an author's mind. Yet it would not be difficult to rephrase Walker's argument in ways more in tune with contemporary critical taste. Instead of speaking as if we were penetrating *beneath* the text and working to expose the author's intentions, those sorts of clash can be regarded as embedded *within* the text, encouraging a reading experience where weighing judgements against their factual basis is part of our interpretative task. That, after all, is what we do with those contemporary rumours and comments, and, once a reader's critical scepticism is triggered, it is hard to make it stop: why not take the authorial comments too as encouraging a 'cross-grained narratee', one who is primed to listen but also, on occasion, to resist?⁴⁴ If we come to feel uncomfortable about any heroising of Germanicus, that too can be regarded as a matter of reading with the text instead of against it: both the idealising and its questionable basis are part of the history, and, if we feel both points empathetically, that is a reflection of the quality of the writing. If Germanicus is wrong but romantic and Tiberius is right but repulsive, all four adjectives capture historical points of the highest importance.⁴⁵

Perhaps we should take further the parallel with the comments of contemporary observers. Even once we have decided a comment is unfair or a rumour is false, we do not regard it as insignificant: it matters that people felt that way,⁴⁶ and we may ask why they should have felt so malign. Nor, in the case of the awkward, inscrutable and dislikeable Tiberius, is it hard to find an answer. The same can be true of the way we critique Tacitus' own

---

⁴¹ Walker (1952) 203.
⁴² Walker (1952) 234 n. 7.
⁴³ Walker (1952) 243.
⁴⁴ For the notion of the 'cross-grained narratee' cf. Pelling (2004) 417, discussing Plutarch. This, it should be stressed, is not the way Walker sees it: '[i]mperceptibly [the reader] comes to acquiesce in the storyteller's interpretation of events, and in the end, with chastened emotions, he offers no criticism' (Walker (1952) 8). Closer to the approach outlined here is Sinclair (1995) 59: '[Tacitus] provides the reader with opportunities to react to him as historical narrator and to assess his judgement, just as we judge other characters in his narrative' – but Sinclair is talking only of Tacitus' digressions.
⁴⁵ This, effectively, is the approach I adopted in Pelling (1993).
⁴⁶ Thus Ries (1969), esp. 8–10, 95–132, 172–3 ('ein Machtfaktor ersten Ranges'), and Gibson (1998) rightly emphasise the large consequences that often follow from rumours, false as well as true.

interpretations. We may feel uneasy with them, but Tacitus has built up sufficient authorial credit that we still pay them respect – and we respect, too, a writer who feels such emotional engagement with his story that he keeps wrestling so hard to expose a hidden truth. If Pliny the Elder served as a 'surrogate' for contemporary observers in what he said about Piso and Antonia (above, p. 158), so Tacitus' perceptible antagonism can become a surrogate for the cynical hostility felt by those who lived through the events – a converse counterpart of the way that earlier histories, so Tacitus claims (above, p. 149), had reflected adulation and fearfulness. Those writings reflected how contemporaries had spoken, these how they had really felt. We may even come to feel some of the mental struggle ourselves: if so, it is mimetic writing of the highest order, immersing reader as well as writer not merely in the horror but also in the bewilderment of the times, and the 'inward conflict' – as Walker put it – when participants and observers tried to make sense of it. And we may well be reluctant to write off those 'impressions' completely. Tacitus' own narrative has 'nurtured' a mentality where a reader understands that anything, particularly with an emperor like Tiberius, may not be what the surface facts might suggest. Impressions matter too, and a well-trained nose will not always be wrong in detecting, even at the distance of nearly a century, a suspicious smell.

Such a narrative certainly discourages complacency. When so many views and so many observations are proved wrong, no reader can feel that interpreting Tiberius is straightforward. These were riddling times.

When describing such a world, the personal voice can be most telling for being diffident, for that paradoxically builds a particular sort of authority in a historian, the authority of the interpreter who knows when it is right to be puzzled.

> In setting out the reasons for his departure [to Capri], I have followed most authorities in attributing his decision to the techniques of Sejanus. Still, I am often moved to wonder – given that he continued his stay in such a retreat for a full six years after contriving Sejanus' death – whether it might not be better to assign it to Tiberius' own character, producing savagery and lusts in his acts but concealing them by their location. There were some too who thought that he was embarrassed by his physical appearance in his old age: he was tall, very thin and stooping; his head was bald, his face covered in sores and often patched with medicaments; and at Rhodes he had grown accustomed to use seclusion to avoid crowds and keep his pleasures hidden. It is even said that he was driven out by the domineering behaviour of his mother, whom he spurned having as his partner in power but could not exclude from it, given that he had received the Principate itself as her gift. For Augustus had wondered about making Germanicus, his nephew and a man with universal approval, his successor, but he had been won over by his wife's argument to

make Tiberius adopt Germanicus while he adopted Tiberius himself. Augusta kept reminding him reproachfully of this – and claiming her reward.

(*A*. 4.57)

That is unexpected. The whole architecture of Book 4 has depended on the crucial role played by Sejanus; it looks, indeed, as if Books 4 and 5 are forming a unit tracking his rise and fall. Some of these other themes are also as under-prepared as that of Sejanus has been clear. The narrative has said little of Augusta; the startling item that Augustus had thought of making Germanicus his successor is also new, despite (we would think) its critical importance to the sketch of the succession issue at *A*. 1.3. One can understand why the chapter, or at least a part of it, has been taken to be an afterthought inserted in an already fashioned narrative.[47]

Yet the projection of an 'I'-voice can be seen as something subtler. It is precisely because Tiberius is both perpetually fascinating and perpetually perplexing that – so the narrator conveys – it is impossible to be satisfied even with so aesthetically fine-tuned a construct as he has just given us. There are too many ways of looking at Tiberius, and, whichever way one tries, one comes up against that final impenetrability. That is what makes the emperor so enigmatic, the historian so obsessive and the interpretative tussle so unending.

Then there is the famous final verdict on Tiberius (*A*. 6.51.3):

> His characteristic behaviour too had its different phases. That while he was a private citizen or in commands under Augustus was outstanding in life and reputation; secretive and crafty at giving an impression of virtues as long as Germanicus and Drusus survived; he was a mixture of good and evil during his mother's lifetime; he was loathsome in his ruthlessness but kept his lusts secret as long as he loved, or feared, Sejanus; finally he burst forth into crimes along with vices once, with the removal of all shame and fear, he had only himself to rely on [and/or 'was simply himself': *suo tantum ingenio utebatur*].[48]

Are these last words also the final, confident revelation of the historian's truth? Other ways of looking at the man have been frequent enough: 4.1.1

---

[47] Syme (1958a) 286, 695–6. See *contra* Luce (1986) 154–5, finding here the rhetorical figure of *reprehensio* ('self-correction') and pointing out that the explanations in 4.57 supplement rather than contradict those already in the narrative. Luce is followed by Martin and Woodman (1989) ad loc. It is true that Tacitus' phrasing presents these ideas as more of a 'self-correction' than he need: that underlines the projection of himself as one who is continually wrestling with and rethinking his material.

[48] On the contested interpretation of the final phrase see Woodman (1998) 155–67 (see also 240–1), arguing for 'had only himself to rely on'. I agree with Martin (2001) 199–202 that there is (also) a claim that his true character, one previously masked by successive phases of dissimulation, emerged at the end: cf. Pelling (1997) 122–3 n. 25.

and 4.6.1 had suggested a simpler division of the reign into two, with the death of Drusus as the watershed; nor is that positive view of Tiberius' virtue under Augustus quite what we heard in the early chapters (especially 1.4.3–5 and 1.10.7 – both admittedly given as the views of others rather than in the authorial voice, but 6.51.3 stresses Tiberius' early 'reputation' as well as his 'life'). If the final words are taken as 'was simply himself', implying that he had always been the same person at heart, a different interpretation has been put into the air only three chapters earlier, by the weighty figure L. Arruntius: 'after so much experience', Tiberius, for him, had still been 'convulsed and transformed under the pressure of rule' (6.48.2) – a change, then, in Tiberius himself, not just his behaviour. This ending may not be quite incompatible with anything we have heard before[49] (though it comes close to it), but it is not what we have been led to expect.

Perhaps we do take this as Tacitus' unequivocal verdict, a flash of understanding that has come to him at the last and is now to be taken as authoritative:[50] if so, looking back on all that has preceded will itself reinforce the need for provisionality, the alertness to the likelihood of discordant judgements. Perhaps, though, we cannot discard that earlier provisionality so easily, and we regard this as simply the latest guess, one given prominence by its finality but not deserving total confidence.[51] Can anyone really say the last word on Tacitus' Tiberius, even Tacitus himself?

One thing remains clear. Trying to understand such a man is central to reading and to writing history, just as it had been to living it. Obsessive worrying at the puzzle was not an intellectual quirk, something to be laid aside to allow the healthy-minded to get on with their lives. It was compulsory for those close to the powerful.

Conclusion

Syme entitled a chapter 'Tacitean Opinions'.[52] We have seen that the quest for such opinions is not wrong-headed: they can often be unearthed, sometimes

---

[49] The best case against incompatibility is put by Woodman (1998) 162–7, who again (cf. n. 47) profitably refers to rhetorical *reprehensio* and talks of 'adjustments' of earlier impressions. Notice also Walker (1952) 238 on the reconcilability of Arruntius' view with that of 6.51.3: 'it was quite possible for Tacitus to hold that as the evil in Tiberius' nature revealed itself there was progressively more evil for him to reveal'. Sage (1990) 978 observes that the phases of 6.51.3 fit Tacitus' book divisions more closely than they suit the earlier narrative emphases. See also below, pp. 182–3.
[50] Thus Martin (1981) 139–43 finds 6.51.3 more insightful than the earlier interpretations.
[51] Thus Koestermann (1963) 38 argues that Tacitus puts forward different views and allows the reader to choose: Woodman (1998) 160 finds this 'attractive' but ultimately rejects it.
[52] Syme (1958a) 520–33.

enticing a reader to remember the experienced consular man of the political world who was the 'author', sometimes leaving them at the level of the reflections that the events had suggested to the 'narrator' as they would to those hearing the narration. But, in this chapter, the purpose of the exercise has not been to categorise those opinions for their own sake; the political prejudices are not particularly interesting or original, and the commentary can convey befuddlement as much as interpretative insight – or even the insight that the best reaction is to be befuddled. 'He is not trying to present us with a Chinese box-puzzle or a masked costume-party in which we must strip away the deceptive or the superfluous to find the author underneath.'[53] Our purpose has rather been to see how the way in which 'the author underneath' sometimes pushes to the surface can affect the way the text works. The voice – or rather the voices, for they do not always say the same thing – is added to the voices we find of others in the text, all contributing to a polyphony that is part of the texture of the Principate, where imperial conduct was always something to talk about, where there were different explanations to weigh and to toy with, where later events could clarify earlier or could simply thicken the cloud of bemusement; and where talking about the most sensitive topics, if one were sensible, rarely meant talking straight.

FURTHER READING

On the whole, attention has focused more on disentangling Tacitus' opinions (and Luce (1986) is sound on the limitations of that approach) than on analysing what he does with them. Sinclair (1995), esp. ch. 2, is unusual in emphasising the personal voice and the response it implies in an imagined reader: he concentrates on Tacitus' use of epigrammatic *sententiae* as 'establishing a community of shared opinion with his audience' (16). Hutchinson (1993) 50–62 has fine remarks on the way Tacitus' self-projection conveys a 'commanding insight and authority' (56), particularly in a commitment to truthfulness and in an elevated moral stance that contrasts with the world he describes. As will be clear from the closing pages of the chapter, Walker (1952) is still extremely thought-provoking. Marincola (1997) ranges widely on historians' techniques for building 'authority'. There is of course much scintillating insight scattered in Syme (1958a), often presented obliquely: e.g. pp. 314–17 ('To render the action coherent, intelligible, and dramatic, he had to intervene all the time, unobtrusive and covering up his operations variously ...'), 411–19, and especially 534–46 ('The personality of Tacitus').

---

[53] Luce (1986) 149.

11

MIRIAM T. GRIFFIN

Tacitus as a historian

Many of the chapters in this book explore in their different ways the distinctive character of Tacitus as a historian. This one will sketch some of his general conceptions of history and show how he conveys them.

A philosophy of history?

Did Tacitus have a general philosophy of why things happen and, if so, does he make it explicit? Can we look to him for a theory of history, for systematic thinking about human life and its vicissitudes? The signs are not good, for no one who has considered these questions has emerged with a plausible picture of Tacitus as a thinker. On the contrary, opinions are divided between those who blame him for muddle-headedness and those who justify the muddle. 'Certitude is not given to mortals, and Tacitus is redeemed by his respect for the eternal ambiguities', writes Syme at the conclusion of his discussion. B. Walker, charitably, had pointed to a deep pessimism as the only unifying idea.[1]

In recounting events, Tacitus makes use of four different modes of interpretation, three of which are deployed to render what happens intelligible: (1) divine intervention; (2) fate, in the Stoic sense of an unalterable chain of natural causes;[2] this fate is perhaps related to the notion of a cycle of change in *A.* 3.55.5, 'unless perhaps there is in everything a kind of cycle, so that, just as the changes of season come round again, so do those of conduct'; (3) destiny, as determined by the time of our birth, i.e. by the stars; in one

---

[1] Syme (1958a) 521–7; Walker (1952) 244ff.
[2] At *A.* 6.22.2, Tacitus seems to allude to the Stoic doctrine of fate, though he is so unclear about how the tight nexus of cause and effect leaves room for human choice that it is not certain that he refers to the Stoic mode of reconciling free will and fate, or, if he does, that he understands it. See the excellent discussion in Martin (2001) 148–9. (Sometimes Tacitus uses *fatum* in a more colloquial way meaning 'chance', e.g. *A.* 6.46.3, or 'the common human lot', e.g. in the mouth of Germanicus at *A.* 2.71.1.)

place Tacitus calls this 'the lottery of one's birth' (*A.* 4.20.3 *sorte nascendi*).³ Of these, the first two can be detected through portents – natural disasters, examination of entrails (as in haruspicy), mysterious happenings that count as omens; the third, by casting horoscopes and observing the stars. But only the first leaves any real latitude for human determination of events, as Tacitus makes clear at *H.* 2.38.2, when, having traced all the Roman civil wars to human ambition, he then sees, in the wars of 69, conflicts caused by 'the same divine wrath, the same human madness'.

A fourth means of interpretation is 'fortune' or 'chance', which at *A.* 6.22.1 also carries a philosophical label and is apparently ascribed to the Epicureans. But, for Tacitus, it is a way of saying that things are inexplicable and unpredictable. Thus at *A.* 3.18.4 he says of the elevation of Claudius to the Principate: 'The more I consider recent events or those in the distant past, the more I am confronted by the mockery pervading human affairs in all their aspects. For in public opinion, expectations and esteem, no one was a less likely candidate for the throne than the man whom fortune was secretly holding in reserve.' Fortune serves to remove human control, if not over everything, at least over large areas of life. So at *H.* 1.4.1 the purpose of his sketch of the attitudes and motives of different sections of the population of the Roman empire is explained by saying: 'so that we may understand not only the occurrences [*casus*] and outcomes of events [*euentus ... rerum*], which for the most part are due to chance [*fortuiti*], but also their reasons and causes'.

Though Tacitus nowhere explicitly weighs the merits of the theory of divine intervention against the other three, he offers it as an explanation of events more often than any of them. Thus we are twice told that the gods have intervened benevolently: at *H.* 4.78.2, where the Romans win an unexpected victory against the Gauls and Germans, and again at *A.* 12.43.2, when there is a famine, and supplies unexpectedly come through quickly from others; and once Tacitus suggests (*A.* 14.5.1), without committing himself (*quasi*), that the clear starry sky and calm sea on the night of Agrippina's murder were the means by which the gods ensured that the crime would be detected. For the most part, however, he suggests a hostile role for the gods. Thus at *H.* 1.3.2, where he is summing up the character of the years from 69 to 96 that are to form the subject of his work, he says that no proof was ever offered by worse disasters for the Roman people or by clearer signs (apparently including the prodigies mentioned just before) that 'the gods do not care for our wellbeing but rather for our punishment'.

---

³ Tacitus carefully distinguishes this from *fatum* at *A.* 6.22.2, though some Stoics thought them compatible (see Martin (2001) 148).

And, again, at *A*. 4.1.2 Tacitus says that Sejanus' influence over Tiberius was achieved not so much by his own shrewdness as by the anger of the gods against the Roman state. Similarly Tacitus traces to the 'anger of the divinities against Roman affairs' the terrible string of deaths of those accused in 66, falsely or correctly, of participation in the Pisonian conspiracy the year before (*A*. 16.16.2). This divine malice, it is suggested, is a consequence of human wickedness. Though at *A*. 14.22.4 the anger of the gods is said to have been provoked against Nero by his own act of sacrilege, Tacitus leaves open what provoked the more general divine hostility against Rome. As Horace suggested that Roman vice and impiety provoked the gods to cause civil war, itself an expression of vice (*Carm*. 3.6.1–20, cf. 1.35.33–7), so Tacitus suggests, as we saw, that both divine wrath and human madness drive us to war – or, as he remarks more clearly about the burning of the Capitol in 69 (*H*. 3.72.1), no foreign enemy was to blame (it being a civil war) and the gods would have been propitious had human behaviour allowed it, but the disaster came about through the fury of the Roman leaders (here Vitellius and Vespasian).

As regards the practical applications of the three types of metaphysical explanation that imply an intelligible universe, Tacitus is cautious. In *A*. 6.22.3, after reviewing the philosophical theories of chance or fate, he says that most people have a rooted belief, both that their destiny is fixed by the stars at birth, and that the art of astrology, based on this belief, has proved itself impressively, in the distant past and in recent times; unfulfilled predictions arise from the deceptive behaviour of people ignorant of the art. Tacitus' sympathy for this popular view is demonstrated by the context in which his analysis appears, for it is framed by two true astrological prophecies of imperial power – concerning Galba and Nero respectively (6.20.2, 22.4) – and by the prediction of Tiberius' astrologer Thrasyllus about himself in Rhodes, which convinced Tiberius of his powers (6.21). But elsewhere Tacitus offers some striking examples of credulity on the one hand and of crookedness on the other, notably the story of the astrologer Ptolemaeus, who predicted that Otho would be adopted (by Galba), driving Otho, when this did not happen, to set out to make his imperial destiny come true, with the astrologer as his accomplice in crime (*H*. 1.22.2–3). Vespasian's belief in similar 'prophecies of seers and movements of the stars' is called superstition (*H*. 2.78.1). Tacitus clearly felt that the dishonesty and technical ignorance of the practitioners made it impossible to tell false from real predictions, though the latter did exist (*A*. 4.58.2–3).

The same is true of the prodigies that can be signs either from fate or from the gods, in the first case revealing what is unavoidable, in the second giving warnings that can lead to evasive action. On occasion Tacitus credits prodigies, such as atmospheric phenomena and strange births, as true signs of a change for the worse (*A.* 12.64.1; 15.47). He blames the general Caesennius Paetus for not heeding such warnings (*A.*15.7–8), and, in the case of Galba's adoption of Piso at *H.* 1.18.1, he first suggests that Galba was to blame for scorning the atmospheric portents when about to make his announcement in the praetorian camp, but then offers an alternative interpretation of the prodigies, as signs of a decree of fate that can be indicated but not avoided. At *H.* 1.10.3 Tacitus refers to the signs and oracles predicting the rise to power of Vespasian and his sons and implies that those who believed in them only after it had happened had failed to recognise what were in fact true revelations.[4] However, as with astrological predictions, there are phenomena that only seem to be portents, as at *A.* 14.12.2, when the various signs clearly do not reveal the concern of the gods, because Nero continued his reign, and his crimes, for years after.[5] Tacitus believed that people, when in an overwrought state, interpret natural or chance events as portents indicative of fate or the wrath of the gods (*H.* 4.26.1–2, cf. *A.* 4.64.1; 12.43.1). It can be argued that Tacitus' scepticism is 'that of a man who believes in the science in which he is an expert, but is also aware that not all interpretations proposed in its name are true'.[6] Yet the historian's scepticism about taking natural or fortuitous events as omens could operate even when a predicted disaster actually materialised, as when Otho's fatal defeat did in fact follow the Tiber flood that occurred as he departed to confront Vitellius (*H.* 1.86.2–3).[7]

It will be clear that Tacitus was consistent neither in adhering to any one metaphysical explanation for events (divine intervention, inexorable fate, astral determinism, random chance) nor in regarding portents and prodigies as reliable indicators of any one of these or, at times, as being of any real significance at all. On each occasion, Tacitus invokes the explanation that produces the effect he wants, and what he usually wants is a gloomy effect. Thus, if divine intervention is denied, it is usually intervention in a benevolent sense or in the interests of justice (in fact at *A.* 16.33.1 the

---

[4] At *H.* 5.13.2 Tacitus regards the ancient books of the Jewish priests, which foretold that the East would grow strong and that men from Judaea would come to power, as indicating the accession of Vespasian and Titus, though the Jews misunderstood them.

[5] Cf. *A.* 14.22.2–3, where a comet and a flash of lightning are falsely taken by the populace to be indications of a change of ruler.

[6] Liebeschuetz (1979) 194. As he goes on to say (196), a Roman senator who was also a priest would have learned to distinguish genuine from false signs. Tacitus, however, was not an *augur* or a *haruspex*, but one of the *quindecimuiri sacris faciundis*, so he would not have dealt with portents, only with oracles from the Sibylline books.

[7] Liebeschuetz (1979) 196 uses Otho's bad end as an argument for doubting that Tacitus was denying that these phenomena were signs, but his disbelief is patent in this passage.

'even-handedness of the gods towards good and evil' is explicitly asserted). Divine displeasure is adduced as an additional (and superfluous) explanation to darken the picture of human artfulness (*A*. 4.1.2) or madness (*H*. 2.38.2). When chance is involved, we are aware of lack of human control, but that does not remove human guilt: though Tacitus clearly regards a famine in 51 as fortuitous, Rome's reliance on foreign corn still comes in for blame (*A*. 12.43.2). And Tacitus, while crediting the control of 'fate *and* the lottery of one's birth' over all other events, can doubt whether the attitude of emperors is totally determined, or whether the judgement of an individual can make it possible to avoid both danger and dishonour (*A*. 4.20.3). He is clearly not a systematic thinker when it comes to natural philosophy. Mood prevails over analysis. We are convinced both of our helplessness and of our guilt. Goodyear reasonably regards Tacitus' references to fate and the gods as nothing more than 'devices of style, calculated to enhance his presentation of particular scenes and serving as convenient ways of expressing pathos and indignation'.[8] Less charitably, we may feel that, in the realm of abstract thought, brilliance of style triumphs over poverty of intellect.

The picture is not so different when we come to political theory. Tacitus was familiar with the classic works on the subject. A comparison of *A*. 3.26 with Seneca, *Letter* 90, shows that he knew the views of Posidonius on early human history. At *A*. 4.33 he mentions the traditional Greek analysis of basic forms of goverment, as rule by the one, the few or the many, and he makes a sour allusion to the theory of the mixed constitution, which shows his knowledge of Polybius' analysis of the Roman Republic in Book 6 of his history – or at least of Cicero's description of the Roman Republic as the embodiment of that ideal, in *De republica*. For Tacitus, the mixed constitution is easier to praise than to realise, and, if realised, it does not last long. So much for Polybius, who maintained that such a constitution was the most enduring sort; so much, too, for Cicero, who thought that such a constitution need never change (*Rep*. 1.65, 69).

An examination of Tacitus' outline of the history of government at *A*. 3.26–8 is enough to dispel the notion that we are dealing with an abstract thinker. We start with a golden age of equality in which restraint and shame prevail: there is no crime, and hence no need for punishment. Nor is there a need for rewards, as people spontaneously follow honourable aims. Only with the (mysterious) development of ambition and force came despotisms and – simultaneously (with the Roman kings after Romulus)

---

[8] Goodyear (1972) 276 on *A*. 1.39.6.

or subsequently (as in the case of other nations) – the feeling that laws were needed. Now Tacitus' subject here is the origin of legislation, and the context is a commission set up by Tiberius to make it harder for people to be victimised under the Lex Papia Poppaea, the Augustan marriage law of 9. So, whereas in Sallust (*Cat.* 6.6-7), Cicero (*Off.* 2.41-2) and Lucretius (5.1105ff.) the kingship serves a useful function until its degeneration into tyranny, for Tacitus the very appearance of government and law is a sign of moral degeneration. Then, with the expulsion of Tarquin, comes the early Republic, with the Struggles of the Orders culminating in the XII Tables: 'the last time when law was an instrument of fair legislation'.[9] After this, laws under the Republic are mostly a weapon serving the rivalry of the Orders and the ambition of individuals. 'When the infection of the state was at its greatest, so was the number of laws.' With the civil conflicts of 48 BC onwards there was 'no morality, no legality', until finally Augustus established the laws of the Principate. From then on the chains tightened, until the Lex Papia Poppaea unleashed a reign of terror. There can be no doubt that Tacitus meant this recital of moral decay and decline to be reminiscent of Sallust, who is mentioned two chapters later when his grand-nephew dies in this same year (*A.* 3.30.2); but, whatever weaknesses the earlier historian exhibited, this history of legislation is certainly more naive.

However, an interesting point does emerge: Tacitus was no uncritical admirer of the Republic. In fact, the dissensions of the Republic, which Sallust too traced to human vice, begin, not at Sallust's date of 146 BC, but right at the start of Republican history. No wonder Tacitus records that the provinces had no objection to the change of constitution, 'since they distrusted the rule of the senate and people [i.e. the Republic] because of the rivalries of factions, the avarice of magistrates and the impotence of the laws to help, given the violence, partiality and corruption that affected their implementation' (*A.* 1.2.2). But, if the Republic lost true equality early, it still had freedom at its end. On the other hand, as Tacitus points out at *A.* 3.55.4, under the Principate moral behaviour, at least among the upper classes, tended to follow the example of the *princeps*. Under a bad *princeps* standards would decline, but under a good one, like Vespasian, more could be achieved by deference and the desire to imitate than by fear of legal punishment.

[9] Woodman and Martin (1996) 250-1 take Tacitus to mean by *finis aequi iuris* the 'culmination of fair legislation', not its 'end'. However, the sequel treats all subsequent legislation in the Republic as unfair and partisan. Of course, this is absurd, but that does not mean that Tacitus did not say it.

Tacitus on writing history

In the passage that mentions the mixed constitution (*A.* 4.33), Tacitus is surprisingly deadpan about the change in constitution from Republic to Principate: political power must be in the hands of the people, or of the leaders of society, or of individuals; the old system was not a mixed constitution but meant control, at times by the people, at others by the senate and aristocracy; the current system is rule by one man, which is necessary for the preservation of Rome (the alternative being civil war). Tacitus' real focus here is on the role of the historian. He explains that what is useful to readers relates directly to the political system that obtains at the time of the events which the historian narrates. Thus, when the Roman Republic was in existence, those who understood the nature of the mob and how to handle it, and who understood the psychology of the senate and governing class, were held to be shrewd and wise; whereas, under the system of one-man rule in the Principate, it was important to understand the character of the emperor who manages everything. For Edward Gibbon, the great eighteenth-century historian of the Roman Empire, Tacitus was 'the first of historians who applied the science of philosophy to the study of facts'.[10] By 'the science of philosophy' he meant a knowledge of human nature, and he was referring to what readers have praised Tacitus for ever since the big revival of interest in him in the sixteenth century, namely, his interest in human motivation.

Tacitus refers only occasionally to the basic purpose of writing an account of the past, namely, to leave a record of memorable events – as Herodotus, the first extant Greek historian, laid down (1.1). Thus at *A.* 16.16.2 he says that to record the deaths of illustrious men is to leave a memorial to them (cf. *A.* 6.7.5). But the recording purpose is clearly more important for contemporary historians who are first in the field than for those, like Tacitus, who were treating a period already covered by earlier historians. Here the principal contribution to make to the record was an account that was more stylishly written, or more accurate, or both. Yet even near-contemporary history is not just a candid camera: so Tacitus' friend Pliny, supplying information for Tacitus' *Histories* about his uncle's conduct during the eruption of Vesuvius in 79, writes (*Ep.* 6.16.22): 'I have described in detail every incident which I either witnessed myself or heard about immediately after the event, when reports are likely to be accurate. It is for you to select the most important.'

Not everything is worth recording: the true usefulness of history, in the view of Greek and Roman historians, does not consist in supplying

---

[10] For Tacitus and Gibbon see below, Chapter 18. (Sailor (2008) 251 suggests an ulterior motive for *A.*4.32–3: flaunting political independence.)

a complete archive. In fact, at *A.* 3.65.1 Tacitus explains that he will *not* record individual opinions given in the senate, unless they show outstanding virtue or the reverse (cf. 14.64.3). The historian has a duty to teach, and that includes examples of good and bad conduct. But moral instruction is not the only kind of instruction that is useful. In the passage in Book 4 about constitutions (already discussed), Tacitus goes on to explain that his bleak recital of tyrannical acts is useful, 'because few people have the good sense to distinguish what is honourable from what is bad, or what is expedient from what is harmful: most people are taught by what happens to others' (4.33.2). In other words, most people judge good conduct by subsequent reputation, and advantageous conduct by success. Polybius had praised 'the lessons of history as the truest education and training for political life, and the study of what happened to others as the most effective, or indeed the only, school in which the right spirit can be acquired for enduring the changes of fortune' (1.1.2, cf. 3.118.12; 7.1.2; 12.15–18). Tacitus saw that, under an autocracy, history can teach us how to understand the character of the ruler, and thus how to save one's skin – and to achieve something worthy into the bargain.

Now the purpose of practical instruction, like that of moral persuasion, leads straight to a concentration on character and thus, as Gibbon saw, on motive. And this emphasis was enhanced by Tacitus' endorsement of the view, voiced by the now fragmentary historian Sempronius Asellio, that the historian must explain events, that history must be more than a mere record: 'I realise that it is not enough to make known what has been done, but that one should also show with what purpose and for what reason things were done' (fr. 1P = 1C, recorded by Gellius 5.18.8). Cicero, too, emphasises that history must show the causes of events, which comprise chance and the wisdom or rashness of men (*De or.* 2.63). Historical causation for ancient historians is a matter of human intentions, motives and decisions, not the kind of abstract economic or structural causes to which we have become accustomed ('need for markets', 'excess of supply over demand', 'technological limitations', 'insufficient checks on the executive'). Of course, these abstracts can be translated into terms of the group motivation of governments or of various classes of the population, but the difference in vocabulary is significant. Modern historians often speak as if men were just the passive victims of these causes; ancient historical writers thought in terms of the conscious attitudes and intentions of individuals or groups. So, when Tacitus at *H.* 1.4 comes to give the 'reasons and causes' for the events following Nero's death, what he does is describe how the different sections of the Roman community reacted to that death. For the interest in motive is to be conceived broadly. In order to know what people desire and fear, and why they act as they do, we need to know what they believe about their situation. Hence Tacitus has a great interest in rumour and popular belief, and this is perfectly legitimate, if there really were such rumours circulating at the time: for they are facts, if not about the state of affairs, then about the state of mind of those affected by them.[11]

Whether he was creating or improving a record, of course, the historian had an obligation to tell the truth.[12] Yet the relative weight of obligation to different kinds of truth was not the same for the historian recording events for the first time as for the historian treating a period already recorded. Thus, for Tacitus, the pursuit of truth – in the sense of recovering facts – only occasionally gets a mention in the *Annals* (e.g. 1.81.1; 6.7.4). The kind of improved accuracy that is his principal concern involves the pursuit of truth in the sense of impartiality. He felt that he could avoid the bias of writers of contemporary events, who were involved in politics under the autocratic system of the Principate and who succumbed to the temptation to flatter the living emperor and his associates and to vent their spite on him when he was dead. Hence both of Tacitus' great works start with declarations of impartiality. In the *Histories* he was including events belonging to his own early political career, so he was himself, in the latter part of his narrative, subject to some of the pressures that affected the writers contemporary with the events described: namely, to write with malice of emperors who injured him and with kindness of those who advanced him. Therefore, having declared that his political career had been advanced by the Flavian emperors, Vespasian, Titus and Domitian, he adds: 'But those who profess unblemished honesty must write of no man with affection or with hatred' (1.1.3). Tacitus specifically notes, at the end of Book 2, that the contemporary historians who wrote accounts of the civil war while the Flavians were in power falsified the motives of their partisans, and he sets out to correct the record (101.1). In the *Annals* he was further from the events, and he simply promises to write 'without resentment or partisanship, from the causes of which I stand far removed' (1.1.3). Naturally, he is not promising not to judge people and events, because, as we said, instruction is a basic purpose of writing history: he is promising to judge fairly, unmoved by personal prejudice. Two centuries earlier, Polybius had forcefully distinguished history from encomium, pointing out that history must distribute praise and blame impartially and give a strictly true account (10.21.8).

In the course of the *Annals*, Tacitus shows us that the bias requiring correction concerned not only what past writers had written but also the

---

[11] See esp. Gibson (1998).
[12] On this obligation see Brunt (1993) 181–209.

version given by official documents and the rumours spread at the time by those who were sceptical of the official version. So he mentions at the end of Book 15 that, after the suppression of the Pisonian conspiracy, many disbelieved Nero when, in a speech to the senate and an edict to the people, he presented the evidence against the condemned and the confessions elicited from them: they preferred to believe that the emperor invented the story, in order to get rid of people whom he envied or feared. But Tacitus notes that people returning to Rome after Nero's death confirmed that the conspiracy had really existed (15.73.1–2).

By good fortune, we now have the opportunity to see how, in the face of massive official obfuscation, Tacitus performed his tasks as a historian. This will be the first of three examples, chosen from his most mature work, the *Annals*, that illustrate the way in which Tacitus fulfills the aims he sets himself, through the narrative itself. For it is his skill in handling the material he had to work with, and the persuasiveness of his narrative, not his explicit and theoretical statements, that best reveal Tacitus' true merits as a historian.

Example 1: the trial of Cn. Calpurnius Piso

Between 1987 and 1990, in the neighbourhood of Seville in the Roman province of Baetica, metal detectors recovered a large bronze inscription and some fragments of other inscriptions recording a decree of the Roman senate of AD 20. As as result, in 1996 there was published the only complete decree of that body that we have.[13] Its value for us is enormous, because it overlaps substantially with the second and third books of Tacitus' *Annals* (2.43, 53–82; 3.1–19) and provides the only occasion when we can compare a lengthy and complete original document with an extended passage of Tacitean narrative. The decree gives the official version of the trial of Cn. Calpurnius Piso senior, who was accused of the murder of the young heir to the throne, Germanicus, and of acts of treasonable insubordination during 19, the year before the trial. Passed at the instigation of the emperor Tiberius, it gives a résumé of the judgements reached by the senate, in a composite decree circulated to the provinces of the Roman empire, for publication in the principal cities and in the headquarters of the legions.

What we have in Tacitus is a full account of the worsening of relations between Germanicus, who was on a mission to sort out various problems in the eastern provinces, and Piso, who was sent out by Tiberius as governor of Syria and assistant to Germanicus. The culmination of the struggle,

[13] Eck *et al.* (1996).

which went on after the death of Germanicus, between his loyal minions and Piso ended with the trial of Piso and his suicide, in the face of certain condemnation for treason, though not for murder. The document establishes that Tacitus did not exaggerate the importance of the events surrounding the death of Germanicus, which clearly convulsed Rome, nearly leading to the lynching of Piso (lines 155–8), and which had serious repercussions in the provinces and the armies, evoking the possibility of civil war (lines 45–9, 159–64).

In giving the reasons for its publication, the decree explicitly arrogates to itself two of the purposes of history as sketched above, recording and instruction (lines 165–8):

> in order that the course of the proceedings as a whole may be more easily transmitted to the memory of future generations, and that they may know what the senate's judgement was concerning the exceptional restraint of Germanicus Caesar and the crimes of Cn. Piso senior.

Future generations are to learn from this record and be instructed by the senate's judgement. Moral examples are offered to posterity: Germanicus a good example; Piso a bad one. Indeed the decree prohibits (lines 80–3) the wax effigy of Piso from being displayed in public, and such images served, as Sallust explains (*Iug.* 4.5–6), as an incentive to excellence for the family and others.[14] By contrast, the emperor and the members of the imperial house, who imitate him and learn from him (lines 133–6; cf. 149–50), exemplify many key virtues, set out in lines 13ff. and 123–51. In addition to recording and instructing, the decree explains the events in terms of motive: the cruelty, brutishness and inhumanity of Piso; the patience and moderation of Germanicus; the justice and clemency of Tiberius; the fairness, moderation and self-control of all the members of the imperial family in the face of overwhelming grief. This is, indeed, to tell stories to children.

The historian does better. The document demonstrates the historian's fundamental accuracy in recording the charges and the outcome of the trial. We can see that Tacitus was making available information he probably gathered from the records of the senate, to which senators, but not others, had access, and possibly from the published version of the senatorial decrees and the emperor's speech, which may still have been generally accessible. But the records of the senate also provided him with the evidence adduced by the defence at the trial, which did not appear in the official decree, and which probably did not feature in the accounts of these matters by earlier historians. For they were writing under the emperor Gaius, the son of Germanicus,

---

[14] On such masks see Flower (1996).

and the emperor Claudius, the brother of Germanicus. Indeed such historians are unlikely to have done justice to Piso's side of the story in general, any more than the contemporary official version in the decree. But Tacitus had a contrary, living, oral tradition, emanating from Piso's friends (3.16.1). Therefore the kind of truth that Tacitus must have been particularly eager to supply was impartiality, for the tradition was heavily biased in favour of the young prince.

As far as explanation goes, Tacitus' account is far superior to the decree, with its simple black and white motivation. It is also superior to the popular version that Tacitus recovered by reading between the lines of the decree, just as he implies that he did with Nero's public pronouncements about the Pisonian conspiracy. For Tacitus could see what the decree was intended to correct, namely, the popular belief that Tiberius, out of hatred, and Piso, out of malice, acted in concert to undo the gallant and popular Germanicus. Tacitus himself provides a far more nuanced account of the motivation of the principal actors in the tragedy. Germanicus was emotional, lacked judgement and could be high-handed and vindictive in wielding his authority; Piso was in a difficult situation, for the holder of his post was normally answerable only to the emperor, but now another layer of authority had been interposed in the person of Germanicus; yet Piso's selection by Tiberius for the job of accompanying the erratic prince was clearly the result of his well-known independence of mind and his loyalty to the emperor. Tiberius is shown to have had suspicions and reservations about his adoptive son, not entirely unjustified, but he was not guilty of his murder. He could appreciate, from his own experience, Piso's courage in standing up to Germanicus, but he was seriously concerned about Piso's attempts to attach the army to himself – so that he was called 'father of the legions' – and about his re-entering his province by force, causing Roman soldiers to fight each other. But he did *not* have Piso murdered, either, and he was eager to be generous to Piso's guiltless children when the senate, bowing to popular hysteria, would have been harsher. So Tacitus' explanation of the causes of these events is complex, like the situation itself.

Finally, this new document also enables us to see how truly instructive historical writing can be. Whereas the senate's decree is crudely moralising,[15] Tacitus shows us that, like the attribution of blame, the moral lessons to be learned are more subtle. Germanicus was not a paragon of virtue: his generosity and accessibility were mixed with paranoiac exhibitionism. Piso was not a paradigm of wickedness: his abrasiveness and pride were mixed with independence and courage. As to practical political instruction, Tacitus

---

[15] See Cooley (1998).

depicts for his readers the plight of high-ranking senators who become embroiled in the dynastic intrigues of this increasingly monarchic system, and also the plight of emperors trying to keep in line demagogic members of their own family.

More important, however, is another lesson: the lesson we ourselves learn, not from what we are explicitly told by the decree, or by Tacitus, but from comparison of the two. That comparison teaches us how sceptical we must be of official versions, especially those put about by totalitarian regimes, and reminds us how servile parliaments can become in only fifty years, even when they have a long tradition of freedom, like the Roman senate. Most important, however, and more heartening, the example of Tacitus reinforces what we have learned from the experience of eastern Europe and other tyrannical regimes in our time, namely, that living under a regime of propaganda and intimidation does not destroy in people their ability to see the truth, even if it may for a time hinder its expression.

Example 2: Claudius' speech on the admission of Gallic senators

We also have the opportunity to compare Tacitus' rendition of an imperial speech with the original, although the bronze tablet found at Lyon, on which Claudius' speech to the senate is inscribed (*ILS* 212), has unfortunately lost both its heading and a section from the middle of the speech. Tacitus divides the material of the speech between a statement of the opposition's case and the proposal of the emperor given in direct speech (*A.* 11.23-4). Tacitus would have been familiar with Claudius' speech, either from the verbatim report in the *acta senatus* or, perhaps less plausibly, through a reliable account in a literary source. Many of the discrepancies between the original and Tacitus' version spring from the historian's obligation to condense the speech and alter its style to harmonise with his own,[16] as well as his need to write an account that remains intelligible to generations of readers, whereas the emperor was seeking to persuade his immediate audience and could assume a grasp of the issues in hand.[17]

Claudius was reviewing the roll of the senate as censor in 48. He received a request from some leading men of Gallia Comata, the area of France added to the Roman empire by Caesar's conquests, for admission to the senate, with a view to standing for higher magisterial office. Up to then only the province of Narbonensis, the modern Provence, had been represented in that body. I can only summarise here the detailed comparison of

---

[16] Miller (1956).
[17] Wellesley (1954) 16 n. 1; De Vivo (1980) 29.

the original speech and the Tacitean version that I have given elsewhere.[18] Tacitus tightens the argument and improves the speech stylistically by omitting Claudius' feeble jokes and irrelevant digressions. But he also changes the arrangement and the emphasis. Claudius opens his argument with a collection of examples from Roman history, designed to prove that innovations such as his present proposal should not induce fear. The longest group of innovations consists of different constitutional phases through which Rome has passed (inspired by Livy 4.3–4). Tacitus omits all but the points directly related to the theme of new blood infusing the Roman governing class, just as he omits the change in size of the Roman empire through conquest. Moreover, Tacitus moves to the end of the speech the argument from innovation, suggesting a continuation of that process into the future. Claudius devotes the whole last part of his speech to Gallic leaders, making the climax his plea on behalf of Gallia Comata in particular, a plea supported by the loyalty shown by the Gauls to his father when he was taking the first provincial census. Tacitus omits the specific examples of men from Narbonensis, and the Gallic wars are put in the context of the Italian wars that preceded the incorporation of Italy. Tacitus also omits Claudius' concession to the opposition, that the final censorial list will reflect their preference for Italian senators over provincials. In sum, whereas Claudius' actual speech is an advocate's speech in favour of a particular proposal (namely, the acceptance of the petition from the Gallic notables), Tacitus' version is a coherent treatment of the thesis that Roman tradition sanctions the continual infusion of new blood into the citizen body and the governing class. He has sacrificed the depiction of Claudius' idiosyncrasies and risked contradicting his own portrayal of the emperor as politically naive and myopically obsessed with detail, investing the emperor here with dignity and far-sightedness. To what end? Tacitus takes advantage of the free conventions that obtained about reporting speeches in order to show the ultimate significance of steps such as those Claudius is taking, whatever the motives that inspired such individual acts. The historian points to a long process whereby the Roman governing class had been increasingly penetrated by provincials, to the extent that an emperor from Spain was ruling as Tacitus wrote. He himself may have originated in Gallia Narbonensis. In any case, the process was ongoing and had enabled Rome to avoid the loss of vitality that had afflicted Sparta and Athens. In view of the weakness of Tacitus' abstract excursus into the origins of law (above, pp. 172–3), we should be grateful that he opted for this indirect way of charting historical development.

[18] Griffin (1982a).

Example 3: the architecture of the *Annals*

The structure of the *Annals* as a whole combines an annalistic principle, which applies to the smaller organisation within each book, and a regnal principle, which groups the books according to the reigns of emperors and which ensures that the reigns of Tiberius and Claudius (and doubtless of Caligula) each close with the end of a book. This regnal principle is also apparent in Tacitus' definition of his subject matter at *Annals* 1.1.2–3, where he names the emperors, and in the title of his work, *Ab excessu diui Augusti*. It shows again in the fact that the books within a reign start or end at points of political significance for that reign. In the Tiberian books, all but the last of which end with a consular year,[19] that year is regularly chosen to correspond with the important stages of Tiberius' reign as outlined by Tacitus in his obituary of the emperor at the end of Book 6: the death of Germanicus (end of Book 2); the death of Drusus (start of Book 4); the death of Livia (start of Book 5); the fall of Sejanus (end of Book 5).[20] Tacitus indeed combines the two principles, annalistic and regnal, at the start of the crucial Book 4: 'In the consulship of C. Asinius and C. Antistius, when Tiberius was in his ninth year of power ...'.[21]

For Claudius and Nero, however, the regnal principle seems even more in control, for books end at significant events for the reign, even if that often means ending in the middle of a year. Thus Book 11 ends with the death of Messalina in the course of the year 48, and Book 12 opens with the preliminaries to Claudius' marriage to Agrippina, the change of wife being the key to developments in the government of this hen-pecked *princeps*. As for Nero, Book 14 opens with the plot to murder Agrippina in 59 and closes with the death of Octavia during 62, the year indicated as the turning point of the reign, when Tigellinus' influence replaced that of Seneca and Burrus (14.51–2, 57); Book 15 closes with the end of the Pisonian conspiracy during 65.

---

[19] But see n. 20 below.

[20] Tacitus' narrative of the end of 29, all of 30 and most of 31 is lost. Nor is there any indication at the end of the year 31 that a new book begins (cf. 5.11.1–2). Where Book 5 ended is therefore uncertain, and scholars are divided between two possibilities: 18 October 31, when Sejanus died, or the end of that same year.

[21] The match between the narrative, especially the sharp turning point at the start of Book 4, and the obituary has been much discussed (see particularly Woodman (1989) = (1998) 155–67; Martin (2001) 192–6 and 199–202). The importance of the deaths of Germanicus and Drusus in the evolution of Tiberius' conduct, which appears in the obituary, was clearly already in the tradition before Tacitus and appears in Suet. *Calig.* 6.2; *Tib.* 39 (cf. 42); Dio 57.7.1, 57.19. The fact that the sharp break in 23, marked at the start of Book 4, when an influence for good (Drusus) dies and an evil genius (Sejanus) gains influence, resembles the turning point of Nero's reign in 62, marked in Book 14 (see below), when Burrus dies and another evil praetorian prefect (Tigellinus) gains ascendancy, might suggest that this analysis is Tacitus' own contribution.

The book divisions thus serve to indicate Tacitus' understanding of how and why the reigns of individual emperors developed. But his tendency to adhere more strictly to the annalistic scheme within and between the Tiberian books is itself a means of historical interpretation. Goodyear suggested that his technique advanced, so that he became more willing to diverge from the annalistic framework as he became increasingly sure of himself.[22] And yet the *Histories* (what is left of them) already exhibit the looser arrangement: for despite his choice of 1 January 69 as the opening date, Tacitus marks the beginning of the year 70 in the middle of Book 4 (*H.* 4.38.1). A more attractive idea was suggested by Ginsburg.[23] Since the annalistic form of traditional Republican history, by stressing the assumption of office by the new consuls, fitted the emphasis on magisterial activity in domestic affairs and in the field, its adoption in the Tiberian books underlines Tacitus' insistence on the contrast between the Republican sham that Tiberius was concerned to maintain and the regnal reality of control by the emperor. In other words, Tacitus' emphasis on the magisterial year is in fact part of his way of revealing the hypocrisy of Tiberius.[24]

It is clear that the architecture of the *Annals*, and no doubt of the *Histories*, was used by Tacitus to indicate his historical interpretation of the period he was treating. As shown in the first two examples, his way of conveying his assessment of his sources, official and otherwise, was similarly implicit, on those occasions in his accounts of what was done and said. It is therefore in his works as a whole, in the carefully designed impact made on the reader by structure and narrative, that we must look for the genius of Tacitus, rather than in any theoretical excursus on the meaning of history.

FURTHER READING

On all aspects of Tacitus as a historian, Syme (1958a) is still the most learned and perceptive. Martin (1981) is very good at integrating historical and literary aspects. Liebeschuetz (1979) is an interesting discussion of Roman religion in connection with political ideology and historiography, and Barton (1994) discusses the importance of astrology in the early Principate. The *Senatus Consultum de Cn. Pisone Patre* has generated an enormous amount of scholarly discussion, much of which not unnaturally involves its relationship to Tacitus: see e.g. Woodman and Martin (1996) 67–77 and 110–98, Griffin (1997), Yakobson (1998), Damon and Takács (1999), Eck (2002a) and Mackay (2003), with some further references in Benario (2004–5) 307–9.

---

[22] Goodyear (1972) 45 n. 1.
[23] Ginsburg (1981).
[24] In Griffin (1995), I argued that Tacitus stressed the hypocrisy of Tiberius as a way of showing up the hypocrisy of the Principate itself.

12

S. P. OAKLEY

Res olim dissociabiles: emperors, senators and liberty

The relationship of the emperors to the senate is one of Tacitus' most important themes; and a striking feature of his writing, particularly of the *Annals*, is the large amount of space devoted to senatorial matters, especially the writing of obituaries[1] and the recording of motions, sometimes proposed by men of little consequence.

Power in the Roman Republic had been diffused between magistrates, senate and people. Polybius (6.10–18) saw an ideal, balanced constitution, but his and Livy's work allows the inference that after the Second Punic War the senate was the dominant force in the body politic. In the late Republic its power declined in the face of a resurgent populace and the ruthless ambition of magistrates and pro-magistrates. The Principate brought further decline, since Augustus' determination to remove the political conditions that had allowed his own rise meant that, *inter alia*, the collective will of the aristocracy had to be curbed. With him the senate made, almost unconsciously, a kind of Faustian pact: in return for massively enhanced dignity it surrendered much of its capacity to initiate actions of any real consequence.[2] Augustus and Tiberius[3] made much of consulting the senate, but their dominance rested more on an iron grip on the legions than on senatorial support.

Yet the senate still mattered. Although no *princeps* could hope to survive if he alienated his troops, it is equally true that, after Tiberius, no *princeps* who alienated the senate did survive: Gaius, Nero and Domitian are just the first names in a long list of those who were assassinated. The *princeps* needed the support of Rome's political elite, and that support depended

---

[1] For Tacitus' obituaries see conveniently Syme (1958b) = (1970) 79–90 and the indexes of Goodyear (1972) and (1981); Martin and Woodman (1989); Woodman and Martin (1996) under 'obituary notices' *vel sim*. (Tacitus is much more generous than Livy, his most famous extant predecessor, in his granting of obituaries to senators, this being part of his general interest in the senatorial order.)
[2] Tacitus' own view is not dissimilar (*A*. 1.2.1).
[3] At least before his retirement to Capri in 27.

on his allowing the senate sufficient freedom of action (*libertas*).⁴ For the aristocracy of the Republic *libertas* had meant the preservation of collective rule by the elite without domination by any one individual, and the right to voice one's own opinion on matters of import without fear of reprisal. Acting in this way had traditionally been regarded as a large part of correct behaviour (*uirtus*) in public life; the impossibility of such action could be regarded as slavery (*seruitus*), a condition that led naturally to sycophancy (*adulatio*) towards those in power.⁵ By the time of Tiberius' accession it was clear that Republican liberty had largely perished; it remained for senators under successive *principes* to determine what kind of *libertas* still existed, what kind of *uirtus* could still be displayed.⁶

A 'good' emperor, it was generally agreed, allowed some freedom of action to the senate. Dio Cassius (56.43.4) comments that the Romans grieved Augustus' passing because under him 'they were able to live, free from the licence of democracy and the insolence of tyranny, with restrained freedom ... ruled without servitude'. At *A.* 4.6.2 (cf. 4.15.2) Tacitus' assessment of the first half of Tiberius' reign is positive, largely because of the *princeps*' promptness in consultation of the senate and his readiness to promote its most talented members. When Tacitus' Nero proclaimed his ideas for his new reign, he duly said that the senate would have its traditional role (*A.* 13.4.2). Yet the notion of senatorial *libertas* remained fraught, and something of a charade: even under 'good' emperors senators never had freedom to decide really important matters such as the planning of wars or the imperial succession. Some *libertas* existed only if the *princeps* did not ostentatiously remind the senate of its inconsequence, only if senators did not try to recreate a Republican environment.

In the *Histories* and the *Annals* Tacitus' main preoccupations are much like those of other surviving ancient historians: politics and foreign affairs, with a particular emphasis in each case on the personalities involved; and much of his greatness as a historian of these themes rests upon his unerring grasp of how power was wielded and of its corrosive effect on the morals of those who possessed it. Tiberius and Nero dominate the books devoted to them because their personalities played a major role in the shaping of events; freedmen loom large when appropriate, especially under Claudius;⁷

---

⁴ The concept has often been discussed: see conveniently Wirszubski (1950); Vielberg (1987) 150–68; Brunt (1988) 281–350; Morford (1991).
⁵ For Tacitus' view of these two last concepts see Vielberg (1987) 80–128.
⁶ From Tacitus' own times, Pliny's *Panegyric* offers a classic example of this negotiation.
⁷ Since freedmen could be regarded as having usurped positions of power that belonged by right to senators, Tacitus tends to disapprove of them: for example, he never grants an obituary to a freedman. See further Damon (2003) 219 and 252–3.

and the mutinies in *A.* 1 and the extraordinary series of conflicts in *H.* 1–3 show the power of the army to make or break rulers. Since the senate had once directed Roman affairs, and since most earlier Roman historians had been senators, it was perhaps traditional to make the senate prominent in historiography.[8] If so, Tacitus, himself a leading senator, would conform to type.[9] But one may still ask why such a realist should be obsessed with the corporate role and behaviour of a body that no longer wielded real power.

Few who have read the closing paragraphs of the *Agricola* will think that Tacitus' interest in the behaviour of senators was not sharpened by his own extreme experiences (45.1–2):

> Agricola did not see [*non uidit*] the senate-chamber besieged and the senate shut in by force of arms, and, in the same massacre, the killings of so many consulars and the exiles and flights of so many very noble women. Carus Mettius was still reckoned with just one victory, the motion of Messalinus resounded only inside the citadel on the Alban Mount and Massa Baebius was still then conducting his defence. Yet soon our hands led Helvidius to prison,[10] the sight of Mauricus and Rusticus oppressed us and Senecio drenched us with his innocent blood. Nero at least averted his eyes [*subtraxit oculos suos*] and, although he ordered crimes, he did not watch them [*non spectauit*]; but a leading part of our wretchedness under Domitian was to see and be watched [*uidere et aspici*], when our breaths were recorded, when that fierce face and ruddy countenance with which he fortified himself against shame managed to record so many pale faces.

No other passage of ancient literature exploits so powerfully the effect of a domineering imperial gaze.[11] Tacitus' experiences of watching Domitian and being watched by him had made him acutely sensitive to the dynamics of the relationship between emperor and senate, and there is a real sense in which the role of the senate is a unifying theme of his whole work:[12] the *Dialogus* records the views of senators on oratory, and Tacitus' one biography, the *Agricola*, is of a senator.

---

[8] Although Livy takes comparatively little interest in the motions of senators, he was unusual among Roman historians in not being a senator.

[9] See further Syme (1958c) = (1970) 1–10.

[10] This is the younger Helvidius Priscus; all subsequent references are to his father.

[11] Roman culture was intensely visual: part of one's prestige or shame was to see others watching or to be seen by them. The concern about being watched surfaces again at *H.* 4.8.2, where Eprius Marcellus speaks of 'the mind of the *princeps* anxious at the beginning of his new reign and watching the faces and utterances of everyone'; also e.g. *A.* 1.7.1, 11.3 (the senators fearful of seeming to understand Tiberius (but *uiderentur* also has the sense 'be seen')). For other striking Tacitean uses of *uidit*, see *A.* 11.30.2; 14.64.2. On this theme see Bartsch (1994) 1–35, esp. 32–5.

[12] *H.* 1–3 are an exception, but, with the civil wars ended, *H.* 4 at once brings the senate to the fore.

The pronouncements of Tacitus' own characters show the importance of this relationship. Galba closes his exhortatory speech to Piso, his chosen successor, with words that are both cynical and wise (*H.* 1.16.4): 'you will rule over men who can endure neither complete slavery [*seruitutem*] nor complete freedom [*libertatem*]'. Eprius Marcellus (*H.* 4.8.4), arguing with an extreme proponent of *libertas*, speaks thus of rulers from the perspective of the ruled: 'in the same way as unending tyranny pleases the worst emperors, so a limit on freedom [*modum libertatis*] pleases even outstanding emperors'. Tacitus approves of *modus*, *moderatio* and their cognates,[13] and it is a great (but in Tacitus unsurprising) irony that the odious Eprius should utter such good sense. Tiberius too dislikes an extreme, this time of servitude (*A.* 3.65.3): 'it is recorded that Tiberius, whenever he left the senate-chamber, was accustomed to exclaim thus in Greek: "men ready for slavery": to be sure, even he, who did not want freedom in public life, was growing tired of the debased tolerance of the enslaved [*seruientium patientiae*]'.[14]

But no one in Tacitus' work is so interested in senatorial behaviour as the authorial voice itself. What constitutes *libertas*, whether it is real, and how its limits are to be established, these are the questions that it asks. The first part of Tiberius' reign may be commended (*A.* 4.6.2, mentioned above), his offering the senate jurisdiction to investigate privileges granted by its forbears and the decrees of kings may be hailed (*A.* 3.60–3, note 60.3 'great was the pomp of that day' and 'with freedom (*libero*), as in days of old'),[15] and the principates of Nerva and Trajan may offer a wonderful new dawn (*Agr.* 3.1); but such favourable comment is rare, and Tacitus' view of individual episodes in the senate is usually less positive. For example, when the new reign of Vespasian suggested the possibility of more freedom of senatorial action, Montanus (*H.* 4.42.2–6) called the senate to action against the informers, and Helvidius Priscus for the second time attacked Eprius Marcellus. However, after a few words from the powerful Mucianus, the senate backed down, and Tacitus comments acidly on its lack of constancy (4.44.1). When Tiberius attends trials, justice is improved but Tacitus seems to regret more that senators lose their freedom of action (*A.* 1.75.1 *dum ueritati consulitur, libertas corrumpebatur*), a remark that reveals much about his values. When senators argue early in the reign of Tiberius, some may have regarded the phenomenon as *libertas*, but Tacitus writes of

---

[13] See below, pp. 192–4.
[14] On *patientia* here see Vielberg (1987) 124.
[15] But note Tacitus' typically cynical introductory comment (*A.* 3.60.1): 'But Tiberius, strengthening for himself the power of the Principate, offered a semblance of days of old to the senate ...' (the sentence is not easy to interpret: see Woodman and Martin (1996) 432–3).

'the outward appearances of liberty' (*A.* 1.77.3 *simulacra libertatis*). When Tiberius allowed that those not nominated by him could stand for elections, Tacitus sees merely a charade of liberty (*A.* 1.81.4).[16] And just how fraught the establishing of boundaries could be under Tiberius is shown by his scornful refusal of some of the honours heaped on him after he had alleviated the corn supply (*A.* 2.87): 'hence speech was constricted and unsure under an emperor who feared freedom [*libertatem*] but hated sycophancy [*adulationem*]'.

Tacitus subjects his senators to a gaze and judgement as probing as that of the emperors from their curule chair, sifting their utterances for choice examples of *libertas* and *adulatio*. In his own words he says (*A.* 3.65.1–2):

> I have not set about enumerating motions, except those that are remarkable for their honesty or their conspicuous disgracefulness, because I regard it as a particular duty of history to ensure both that good deeds should not be passed over in silence and that those who speak or act wickedly should be afraid of the verdict of posterity and of public disgrace.[17] Yet those times were so tainted and so besmirched by sycophancy that not only the chief men of the state, who had to protect their own eminence by displays of deference, but all consulars, a great part of those who had held the praetorship and even many low-ranking senators stood up in competition with one another and proposed motions that were shameful and excessive.

After the killing of Nero's ex-wife, the innocent Octavia, Tacitus writes (*A.* 14.64.3):

> Up to what limit shall we record the gifts that were voted to the temples because of these events? Let whoever comes to know of the disasters of those times either from me or from other writers take it for granted that, whenever the emperor ordered exiles or killings, thanks were offered to the gods and that what were once indications of a happy state of affairs had become indications of public disaster. However, I shall not pass over in silence any decree of the senate that innovated in sycophancy or reached an extreme of submissiveness.[18]

The instances of servile behaviour that Tacitus chronicles are legion, and all readers will have their favourites; any selection that is not copious is false to the tone of his writing. For corporate servility one may cite

---

[16] It is significant for the importance of the theme that this is the final sentence of its book.

[17] The precise interpretation of this sentence is disputed: for an unorthodox interpretation see Woodman (1995) = (1998) 86–103 and Woodman and Martin (1996) 451–3; Kirchner (2001) 62–4 reasserts orthodoxy.

[18] By contrast, Tacitus invokes respect for their ancestors as his reason when he refuses (perhaps surprisingly) to name those senators who at Nero's behest disgraced themselves by racing chariots (*A.* 14.14.3).

the scenes at Tiberius' succession (*A*. 1.7.1): 'But at Rome consuls, senators, knights rushed into slavery [*seruitium*]; and, the more eminent men were, so the more hypocritical and hurried they were; yet with carefully devised expressions lest they should seem either cheerful at the death of one ruler or unhappy at the beginning of the reign of another, they mixed tears, joy, reproach, and sycophancy', for which Tiberius himself is partly blamed, since by behaving as *princeps* yet making a show of not wanting to hold this position he induced (hypocritically, in Tacitus' not necessarily correct judgement) this desperate behaviour. This scene is very important, since behaviour at Tiberius' accession, the point at which the reality of the Principate became evident, sets the tone for behaviour under future emperors. One may cite also decrees passed after the death of Drusus (*A*. 4.9.2), the vows of the priests for the safety of Tiberius' great-nephews/grandchildren by adoption (*A*. 4.17.1-2), the senate's response to Claudius' adoption of Nero (*A*. 12.26.1), its decrees in honour of the freedman Pallas (*A*. 12.53.2-3), its official welcoming of Nero when he had murdered his own mother (*A*. 14.12.1), or its conduct after the unmasking of the Pisonian conspiracy against Nero (*A*. 15.73.3).

As for individuals, few vignettes are more amusing than Dolabella's proposal that Tiberius be granted an ovation on his imminent return from Campania because his legate, Silius, had just crushed Sacrovir's rebellion in Gaul; Tiberius, both emperor and the last great Roman general to issue from the Republican nobility, witheringly responded that, after celebrating or declining so many well-earned triumphs in his youth, he had no wish to be rewarded for a holiday (*A*. 3.47.3-4). Tacitus describes Dolabella's sycophancy as ridiculous (*absurdam ... adulationem*). Many others disgraced themselves. Among *sententiae* uttered when tribunician power is decreed for Tiberius' son Drusus, Tacitus (*A*. 3.57.1-2) singles out those of M. Silanus and Q. Haterius as particularly shameful. A little later Ateius Capito is held up to judgement for a motion that barely hid sycophancy beneath a sham display of liberty (*A*. 3.70.1-3).[19] Cotta Messalinus, marked out earlier as the proponent of a harsh *sententia* that was implicitly a disgrace to his ancestors (*A*. 4.20.4), leads the senate in proposing the condemnation of Germanicus' widow Agrippina and his son Drusus (*A*. 5.3.2). After the fall of Sejanus and Livilla, the obscure Togonius Gallus provokes ridicule by speaking amongst the great names of the day and proposing that twenty senators be chosen as an armed guard for Tiberius when he enters the senate; Tiberius' response showed

---

[19] When Capito expires, Tacitus' obituary notes his over-eagerness to please those in power (*A*. 3.75.1).

that, whatever other breakdowns and ailments he had suffered in old age, his wit remained intact (*A.* 6.2.3–4):

> However Tiberius, prone to blending sarcasm and seriousness, thanked the senators for their kindness but asked who could be passed over, and who chosen? Always the same men, or different men on subsequent occasions? Men who had held offices of state or youths, private citizens or current magistrates? What would be the effect of men donning swords in the foyer of the senate-chamber? Nor did he place so high a value on his life, if it needed to be protected with arms.

Anicius Cerialis suggested the building of a temple to the Divus Nero (*A.* 15.74.3).[20] And Claudius Orfitus suggested naming May after Claudius, June after Nero (*A.* 16.12.2).

However, Tacitus approves of senators displaying *libertas* to good purpose. For example, when Cn. Piso points out to Tiberius that by voting he is bound to influence others, Tacitus comments (*A.* 1.74.5): 'some traces of dying freedom [*morientis libertatis*] remained'. He notes that Asinius Agrippa had not disgraced his famous ancestors (*A.* 4.61); that Memmius Regulus was famous for his constancy (*A.* 14.47.1); and that, when L. Vetus commits suicide, he does not compromise a life led with *libertas* (*A.* 16.11.1). Similarly, a senator (whose name is lost because of damage to the text), misled by Tiberius' actions into thinking that Sejanus should be cultivated, anticipated prosecution by committing suicide, which he announced with the words that he was free (*liber*) and could find no fault with his own actions (*A.* 5.6.3). A magnificent specimen of what the author regards as senatorial virtue in action is provided by *A.* 14.43–4: a slave had killed his master, which meant that under traditional Roman practice the whole household should be killed; many senators wanted something more lenient; but C. Cassius successfully argued for the ancestral custom. To highlight authorial approval, Cassius is given a speech.[21] The generally low standard of senatorial independence under Claudius and Nero makes Cassius all the more conspicuous, but a rare instance of corporate virtue is exhibited at *A.* 12.59.2, where the *delator* Tarquitius is expelled from the senate.

Perhaps surprisingly, given his general outlook, Tacitus is famously somewhat uncomfortable with the attitudes of those senators who were freely outspoken. Thrasea Paetus receives mixed treatment. His opening appearance is at *A.* 13.49.1–4, where Tacitus, solely in order to record Thrasea's objection to it, mentions a commonplace proposal to permit the Syracusans to break restrictions on numbers of gladiators. This in turn allows him

---

[20] Lest we are incredulous, Tacitus introduces this with 'I find in the records of the senate'.
[21] Most modern tastes are less likely to approve of the traditional practice.

to give voice to those who criticised Thrasea for lacking the courage to intervene on matters of consequence; carefully the authorial voice passes no final judgement. Thrasea's championship of *libertas* becomes a major theme in *A*. 14–16. At 14.48–9, when Antistius is threatened with death for reciting unpleasant verses about Nero, his intervention induces a milder senatorial decree (14.49.1 'the freedom of Thrasea broke others' bonds of servitude'). At *A*. 15.20.1–22.1, in a speech splendidly evoking old Roman standards, he speaks out against the habit of governors courting votes of thanks from the governed provincials: again Tacitus plainly approves. And our text of the *Annals* breaks off with a scene full of pathos, in which Thrasea prepares to commit suicide in response to an unjust prosecution instigated by Nero (16.21–35).[22] Yet at *A*. 14.12.1 his sharp comment on Thrasea's response to the senatorial decrees passed after Agrippina's murder insinuates that Thrasea's heroism was not devoid of egotism and futility: 'for himself he provided a reason for danger; for others he did not furnish a beginning of freedom'.[23]

Still more ambiguous is Tacitus' earlier treatment in the *Histories* of Thrasea's son-in-law, Helvidius Priscus, a rare senatorial death under Vespasian. Although the defective text does not offer us his end, Helvidius' appearances are all revealing. At 2.91.2–3 he disagrees with Vitellius, who, initially taken aback by his intervention, then observes that he himself had been accustomed to disagree even with Thrasea, a reference that pleased some senators but was regarded by others as impertinence on the lips of the once servile Vitellius.[24] At 4.4–5 Helvidius' failure to flatter Mucianus and the Flavians is greeted with an aphorism that Tacitus recalled in the context of Thrasea: 'this day above all began for him both great danger and great repute' (4.4.3).[25] Then a character sketch emphasises his rectitude, and by Tacitus' standards to be described as 'despising wealth, relentlessly righteous, and steadfast against fear' is a remarkable compliment. Yet Tacitus immediately offers a dissenting voice (4.6.1): some thought him too keen to acquire a reputation, a qualification entirely in line with the historian's

---

[22] Note esp. 16.21.1, where the authorial voice terms Thrasea 'virtue itself'.
[23] That Tacitus is basically favourable to Thrasea is certain, but I prefer the treatment of Liebeschuetz (1966) 128–30 to that of e.g. Syme (1958a) 559–61 and Vielberg (1987), esp. 48–75, because Liebeschuetz brings out more clearly Tacitus' reservation. Those who make light of this reservation often argue that in the years after writing the *Agricola* (and esp. *Agr*. 3.1) Tacitus had become more disillusioned with Trajan and Hadrian. That his views changed over some twenty years is not unlikely, but his treatment of Thrasea does not provide evidence for this.
[24] Tacitus' handling of the response of those present is perceptive: he sees that it is only Vitellius' general deportment that makes his offering of *libertas* absurd.
[25] At 4.9.2 comes another *sententia* of Helvidius that would long be held against him by Flavian partisans.

general attitudes to such men. When Tacitus refers to Helvidius' abandoning a prosecution of Eprius that he had planned under Galba, he comments that some praised his restraint (*moderationem*) but others criticised his lack of constancy (*H.* 4.6.2): when one behaved as Helvidius customarily did, it was difficult to win a reputation for *moderatio*, and Tacitus' reluctance to grant him this virtue (on which see below) is shown by his placing the charge of inconstancy in the more emphatic final position. And Helvidius does not always cut an impressive figure, since he is soon drawn into an unseemly squabble with the informer Eprius Marcellus. Nor is Tacitus unqualified in his praise of Helvidius at 4.43.1–44.1, where he tries once again to prosecute Eprius, but (by implication) abandons the prosecution after a few gently spoken words from Mucianus; we remember here the earlier charge of lack of constancy.

Between servility and Helvidian truculence there was a middle way, about whose practitioners Tacitus is unfailingly enthusiastic. When in the prologue to the *Agricola* he contrasts the times of Domitian with those of the late Republic (2.3), he implies an objection to extreme manifestations of liberty as well as to passive servility. When, two sentences later, he rejoices in the harmonisation of the Principate and liberty (3.1 *res olim dissociabiles miscuerit, principatum ac libertatem*),[26] he implies no objection to the tempering of liberty by the Principate. We have seen already that restraint is advocated by several of Tacitus' own characters, including Eprius Marcellus. The authorial voice offers its own counsel at *Agr.* 42.4:

> Let those who are wont to marvel at illegal acts know that even under bad emperors there can be great men and that deference [*obsequium*] and moderation [*moderatio*], provided that they are coupled with hard work and energy, can take one to the same level of praise as that attained by many men on a sheer course [*per abrupta*], men who have grown famous by an ostentatious death of no use to the country.

Note the claim that virtue is still possible for the energetic even under bad emperors, the criticism of the self-display and self-indulgence of those who became martyred, and his comparison of the careers and deaths of the martyrs to the climbing of a steep precipice.

Agricola is described as a classic exemplar of such *modestia*.[27] His mother tempered his early enthusiasm for philosophy so that he sought glory with more circumspection (4.3); then 'thought and advancing years mellowed him

---

[26] For the idea cf. Plin. *Pan.* 36.4.
[27] For the characterisation of Agricola, see e.g. Liebeschuetz (1966), esp. 126–7; Ogilvie and Richmond (1967) 16–20 (placing less emphasis on the apologetic features of the work); and, in particular, Vielberg (1987) 25–48. For *modestia* and its cognates, see Vielberg (1987) 134–50.

but he kept from philosophy, what is most difficult, a sense of proportion [*modum*]', a comment no one could have made of Helvidius; as a young soldier in Britain he learnt his profession under Suetonius Paulinus, a restrained (*moderato*) leader, and avoided bragging, fear and idle self-indulgence (5.1); as praetor he presided over games that steered a mid-course between economy and extravagance (6.4); back in Britain under Vettius Bolanus, Agricola again tempered action with circumspection (8.1); in Britain both under Petilius Cerialis (8.3) and after his opening campaign as governor (18.6) he increased his reputation by not exaggerating his achievements; and after his governorship of Britain he avoided Domitian's jealousy by eschewing contumacy and empty displays of freedom (42.3 *inani iactatione libertatis*), the passage which occasions the famous comment 'Let those …' (above, p. 192).

In the Tiberian *Annals* it is M. Lepidus who most obviously appears in the Agricolan mould. His suggestion at 4.20.2–3 that a punishment proposed by Asinius Gallus be moderated draws forth approving comment from the authorial voice: often Lepidus averted the murderous sycophancy (*saeuis adulationibus*) of others; he had a balanced disposition (*neque tamen temperamenti egebat*) that allowed even the friendship of Tiberius; and he showed that 'it is possible to steer a course between sheer impudence [*abruptam contumaciam*] and hideous compliance [*deforme obsequium*]'. Note that, as at *Agr.* 42.4, the flamboyant opposition to the *princeps* is described by the figure of a sheer cliff.[28] For this verdict the narrative of the *Annals* has provided ample evidence: we are told that Lepidus is described by Augustus as capable of being emperor but disdainful of the office (1.13.2); that he was prepared to defend Germanicus' enemy Cn. Piso (3.11.2); that he did not push his candidature for a governorship in face of rivalry from Sejanus' uncle (3.35.1–2); and that he spoke with restraint on the hapless Clutorius (esp. 3.50.3). His obituary notice (*A.* 6.27.4) makes clear that *moderatio* was the hallmark of his life.[29] Other men like Lepidus were Furius Camillus, whose success in war against Tacfarinas had gained him triumphal ornaments and a reputation that might have endangered him, were he not made safe 'because of the moderation [*modestiam*] of his life' (*A.* 2.52.5); Piso the pontifex, whose obituary (*A.* 6.10.3) records that he proffered no servile motion (*seruilis sententiae*), that he was prudently moderate (*sapienter moderans*) in times

---

[28] Martin and Woodman (1989) 150–1 well discuss the language of the passage.
[29] On the career of Lepidus see esp. Syme (1955) = (1970) 30–49; Syme discusses also Tacitus' portrait of him and shows how the historian takes an especial interest in the careers of the men whom Augustus regarded as *capaces imperii*. See also e.g. Martin (1981) 136–7; Sinclair (1995) 163–84.

of strife, and that he regulated (*temperauit*) the burgeoning power of the prefecture of the city; and Memmius Regulus (*A.* 14.47.1).[30]

To use one's military and civil talents energetically and thoughtfully when given the opportunity, to show restraint in advertising one's successes, to avoid initiating nauseating flattery of the emperor, to work against wrongdoing but to refrain from harrying those undeservedly exposed to the emperor's wrath, in short, to show decency and moderation – these are the qualities Tacitus advocates. The *Agricola* is an extended apology for a life of this kind, and, as has often been suggested, for the life Tacitus himself had led under Domitian. No doubt Tacitus was correct in his judgement that the principles of Thrasea and Helvidius were conjoined with a healthy dose of pride, that some of their gestures brought no good to anyone; but there were occasions when even moderate men were obliged to condemn the innocent, and Tacitus' readers have found it hard not to see passages like *Agr.* 45.1–2 (quoted above, p. 186) as reflecting his own guilt at not having taken a nobler course.[31] Did Tacitus really believe that the way in which he and Agricola behaved constituted *libertas*, that Nerva reconciled the Principate and senatorial liberty to each other? No reader of his later words will believe that he was so readily deceived.

Does the imperial senate deserve the prominence that Tacitus gives to it? Dio (himself a senator) and Herodian both concentrate on the personalities of emperors rather than the senate, and Tacitus' younger contemporary, Suetonius, chose to write imperial biography. Perhaps Tacitus' usual perceptiveness did desert him when he devoted so much space to an institution in terminal decline; but his sustained and passionate meditation on *moriens libertas* has given us some of Latin literature's most memorable pages.[32]

FURTHER READING

For the Roman imperial senate see the excellent studies of Brunt (1984) and Talbert (1984). Tacitus' views on the relationships of emperors to the senate, and on the manner in which senators should behave, have been discussed very often. The best study is now Vielberg (1987); good expositions in English include Wirszubski (1950) 124–71, Liebeschuetz (1966) and Morford (1991). Syme (1958a), esp. 547–65, regularly touches on these themes, as do several studies reprinted in Syme (1970), esp. chs. 1 and 10. Sinclair (1995) discusses many utterances in the Tacitean senate.

---

[30] For Memmius' characteristics see Woodman (1983b) 239–40.
[31] See e.g. Walker (1952) 196–203.
[32] And our best evidence for the workings of the senate in the early Principate.

13

S. P. OAKLEY

Style and language

Introduction

Tacitus' great reputation owes as much to his style as to the content of his writings, the two being fused in notable harmony. Yet the expression 'his style' is potentially misleading. First, just as a well-trained composer can compose in different genres and styles, so a well-trained Latin writer could write in more than one style. Most of this chapter will be devoted to discussion of the historical styles found in the *Histories*, the *Annals* and much of the *Agricola*, but Tacitus' splendid *Dialogus* is a virtuoso performance in a neo-Ciceronian style that is the equal of anything in Quintilian. Second, even in his historical works Tacitus' style varies: in particular, speeches tend to have more pointed phrasing and less grand vocabulary than narrative.[1] Third, Tacitus' style developed throughout his writing career, becoming more idiosyncratic as it progressed: compared to the later *Annals*, the earlier *Agricola* and the *Germania* are less taut, compressed and solemn. Even the most distinctive of artists owe much to their predecessors and the fashions of the age in which they worked; we shall see that earlier historians, especially Sallust,[2] and the pointed style fashionable in his own times are the dominant influences on Tacitus' historical style.

---

[1] See Adams (1973).
[2] The classic treatment of Sallust's style is Kroll (1927). His influence on Tacitus has been much studied: a good starting point is provided by Syme (1958a) 728–32, but there is much material in the commentaries of Gudeman (1914), Ogilvie and Richmond (1967), Heubner (1963–82) and (1984), Goodyear (1972) and (1981), Martin and Woodman (1989), Woodman and Martin (1996), Damon (2003) and Ash (2007b). Most have useful index entries under 'Sallust'. However, Tacitus' debt to Livy in stylistic matters should not be underestimated. Syme (1958a) 733–4 again provides the easiest starting point, and the commentaries listed above reveal numerous Livian parallels. Important too are Fletcher's works on Tacitus' vocabulary, especially (1964).

Vocabulary

Tacitus was exceptional for the manner in which he constantly refined his vocabulary,[3] with regard to both usual and less usual words, the process continuing even in his final writing.[4] Here we shall illustrate his use of archaisms, poetical colouring and metaphor.

The similarity exhibited by Sallust, Livy, Quintus Curtius Rufus (in his *History of Alexander the Great*) and Tacitus in their choice of vocabulary allows the generalisation that Latin historical style was marked by frequent employment of archaisms: e.g. the use of *cunctus* for the more mundane *omnis* ('all'), *glisco* for *cresco* ('grow') and *metuo* for *timeo* ('fear').[5] With such words the historians evoked the dignity of both olden times and their own subject. Sallust famously took the cult of archaism to an extreme, allegedly ransacking Cato's works,[6] and Tacitus sometimes follows him. A classic example is his use of *torpedo* for the more usual *torpor* ('sloth') at *H.* 3.63.2 (quoted below, p. 202);[7] combined with the devastating *sententia* in the same sentence, it powerfully evokes the exceptional inertia of Vitellius.

Poetic colour could be achieved in various ways. One was by incorporation of a scene that might in general seem poetical, for example the description of the storm off the coast of Germany that afflicts the Romans at *A.* 2.23–4.[8] Another was direct allusion to a poet: an uncontroversial example is Tacitus' description of Nero's playing of the female role in a mock marriage to the eunuch Pythagoras, who is described (*A.* 15.37.4) as 'one from that herd of polluted individuals' (*uni ex illo contaminatorum grege*); Horace (*Carm.* 1.37.9–10) had described Cleopatra as trying to bring doom to Rome 'with a polluted herd of men disfigured by disease', i.e. eunuchs (*contaminato cum grege turpium | morbo uirorum*).[9] A third was the use of words associated particularly with poetry, e.g. *senecta* for *senectus* ('old

---

[3] Much scholarly work of a very high standard has been devoted to the study of Tacitus' vocabulary. See e.g. Degel (1907); Löfstedt (1933) 2.276–90; Syme (1958a) 711–45; Adams (1972) and (1973). Detailed material, especially on archaisms and poeticisms, may be found in the commentaries listed in n. 2.

[4] See conveniently Goodyear (1968) = (1992) 125–37.

[5] See, respectively, Adams (1973) 129–31 (and *A.* 4.25.2, quoted below); Oakley (1997) 516–17; Adams (1973) 135.

[6] See e.g. Suet. *Aug.* 86.3; *Gram.* 10.2, 15.2.

[7] Elsewhere in classical Latin this usage is found only in Sallust (*Hist.* 1.77.19; 3.48.20, 26; cf. [Sall.] *Ad Caes. sen.* 2.8.7), who had found it in Cato (*Carmen de moribus* 3). For the evidence see Heubner (1972) 146.

[8] See above, pp. 5–6.

[9] That Tacitus sometimes alludes to Virgil is generally accepted, but the frequency, extent and import of these allusions are disputed; at the extremes are Baxter (1972) (enthusiastic) and Goodyear (1981) (over-sceptical). For an example see below, p. 210, and see further above, pp. 6–7.

age'); again, Sallust was a particular model, for example in his use of *sonor* for *sonitus* ('noise').[10]

The power of Tacitus' writing owes much to his vivid use of metaphor,[11] in which he far surpasses Sallust and Livy. Part of Calgacus' speech before the battle of Mons Graupius provides illustration (*Agr.* 30.4–5):

> raptores orbis, postquam cuncta uastantibus defuere terrae, mare scrutantur; si locuples hostis est, auari, si pauper, ambitiosi, quos non Oriens, non Occidens satiauerit; soli omnium opes atque inopiam pari adfectu concupiscunt. auferre trucidare rapere falsis nominibus imperium, atque ubi solitudinem faciunt, pacem appellant.

> When the lands have failed them in their devastation of everything, the ravishers of the world scour the sea. If their enemy is affluent, they are greedy; if he is poor, they are eager for glory. These are men whom neither the East nor the West has satisfied; alone among mankind they lust after wealth and poverty with equal passion. Using false names they both term looting, butchering and ravishing 'rule' and, when [or 'where'] they make a desert, they call it 'peace'.

In the most obvious reading of the passage the Romans are viewed as violent highwaymen (*raptores*, *auferre*, *rapere*), men whose unbridled appetites (*satiauerit*, *pari adfectu*, *concupiscunt*) empty the world (*defuere*, *solitudinem*); but *raptor*, *concupisco* and *satio* may be used also in erotic contexts: the Romans rape the world.[12]

Sentence-structure: the influence of Sallust

In sentence-structure Latin historiography bequeathed Tacitus no fixed pattern: Sallust, Livy and Curtius all write in ways very different from one another. Sallust's sentences exhibit brevity, extreme variation of construction and a taste for aphorism; although Tacitus has a higher proportion of long sentences than Sallust, it is easy to illustrate all these features in his work.

Three different ways in which Tacitus achieves brevity may be noted here. First, the use of three words in asyndeton, as exemplified by *auferre trucidare rapere* at *Agr.* 30.5, quoted above. Though used by many Latin writers, this figure is particularly common in Sallust and Tacitus.[13] Second,

---

[10] See further Oakley (1997) 464–5 and Goodyear (1981) 112.
[11] Again, see the commentaries listed above in n. 2, especially Martin and Woodman (1989) and Woodman and Martin (1996); also e.g. Walker (1952) 62–6.
[12] Tacitus sometimes employs imagery over a longer span of text: see e.g. Woodman (2006b) on Tiberius, food and taste.
[13] Other instances include: *Agr.* 21.1; *G.* 20.3; *H.* 3.2.2, 13.3, 22.3, 25.3 (quoted below, p. 202), 36.1, 58.3; *A.* 1.71.2, 74.2; 2.15.3, 17.4, 19.1, 27.1, 33.1, 33.3, 36.3; 3.18.4, 55.2;

the omission of a verb, as exemplified by *H.* 2.42.2 *et per locos arboribus ac uineis impeditos non una pugnae facies* ('and throughout places obstructed by trees and vineyards, no uniform spectacle of battle'): supply *erat* ('there was').[14] Third, zeugma, as exemplified by *A.* 15.34.1 (on Nero) *per compositos cantus grates dis atque ipsam recentis casus fortunam celebrans* ('extolling, through songs that he had composed, thanks to the gods and his good fortune in the recent collapse'): *celebrans* does not go well with *grates*, with which one needs to understand a participle such as *agens*, 'performing'.[15] We shall see that brevity was encouraged also by Tacitus' rhetorical training.

uariatio, the deliberate changing of grammatical or syntactical construction without there being any need to do so, was not a phenomenon on which Sallust had a monopoly,[16] but Tacitus' very extreme affectation of it owes more to him than to any other writer.[17] For both writers style here reflects subject matter: the times about which they wrote were uncomfortable, and this device shakes readers out of too easy reading. *Agr.* 30.5, quoted above, provides a good example: although *imperium* and *pacem* are parallel to each other, the overall structure is made harder to grasp by the shift from infinitives (*auferre trucidare rapere*) to *ubi*-clause (*ubi solitudinem faciunt*). For a simpler example see *G.* 32 *nec maior apud Chattos peditum laus quam Tencteris equitum* ('nor is praise of infantry greater among the Chatti, than of cavalry for the Tencteri'), where a dative corresponds to *apud* and the accusative.[18]

4.25.2, 46.3, 49.2, 49.3, 60.2; 11.19.1; 12.1.1, 6.1, 51.3, 64.3 (two instances), 65.2; 13.57.3; 14.47.1, 55.3; 16.28.3, 29.1. Variously somewhat different are: *H.* 3.1.2, 17.2, 77.1; *A.* 2.19.1, 23.4, 64.2; 3.33.3; 4.48.1; 11.24.6; 14.33.2; 15.34.2.

[14] Tacitus' willingness to strain language can very often make it difficult to discern whether brevity and abruptness are due to his pen or to textual corruption. At *A.* 4.57.1 the paradosis offers *inter quae diu meditato prolatoque saepius consilio tandem Caesar in Campaniam, specie dedicandi templa apud Capuam Ioui, apud Nolam Augusto, sed certus procul urbe degere*. This is accepted by Heubner (1994) in his standard but conservative Teubner text; Martin and Woodman (1989) 223 argue with good reason that the ellipse is intolerable and accept Otto's supplement *concessit* after *Campaniam*.

[15] In general on Tacitus' brevity see Clemm (1881); Furneaux (1896) 68–9; also the entries under 'compressed expressions', 'ellipse', 'syllepsis' and 'zeugma' in the indexes to Goodyear (1972) and (1981); Martin and Woodman (1989); Woodman and Martin (1996); Damon (2003). Clemm discusses omission of verbs at 43–66, zeugma at 124–52.

[16] For Livy see Caterall (1938).

[17] See the full study of Sörbom (1935); also the indexes of Martin and Woodman (1989); Woodman and Martin (1996).

[18] As a pendant to these remarks, it should be noted that Tacitus' desire to surprise included stretching the grammatical structures of the Latin language beyond normal limits. As good an example as any is provided by his exceptionally bold use of the genitive of the gerund as an infinitive, found thrice in the final books of the *Annals*: 13.26.3 *nec graue manumissis per idem obsequium retinendi libertatem* ('nor was it a burden for the manumitted to keep their liberty by means of the same deference'); 15.5.3, 21.2; see e.g. Furneaux (1896) 52.

Style and language

As for aphorism, several instances of *sententiae* will be given below. Here the declamatory style was the main spur for Tacitus' practice, but Sallust's influence too must again have played its part.

The pointed style

Declamation was the practice of making imaginary speeches, whose unreal situations encouraged a quest for 'point', with short sentences and *sententiae* very prevalent. No other phenomenon so much influenced the literature of the years from Augustus to Hadrian, and Tacitus' pointed style owes much to it.[19] Its characteristics include: brevity (already discussed), parallelism and balance, antithesis, and a desire for abstraction (under which the *sententia* may be counted, as indeed may some instances of zeugma).

Scholars do not emphasise sufficiently Tacitus' love of balance, which often involves asyndeton and sometimes anaphora. The following example is typical: *A.* 2.14.3 *sine pudore flagitii, sine cura ducum abire fugere* ('they departed, fled, without shame at their disgrace, without a thought for their leaders'). Writing of this kind is highly characteristic of Tacitus, since in his extraordinary style variation and inconcinnity are often placed in the context of otherwise balanced phrasing. A simple example may illustrate this fusion: *A.* 2.20.3 *utrisque necessitas in loco, spes in uirtute, salus ex uictoria* ('for both sides there was compulsion in their position, hope in their bravery, and safety from victory') – three balanced members, but with *ex* rather than *in* in the third.

Antithesis, a dominant trait in Tacitus' pointed style, may be created by comparative clauses or phrases, as e.g. at *A.* 1.65.1, where Caecina and his army await a German attack:

> nox per diuersa inquies, cum barbari festis epulis, laeto cantu aut truci sonore subiecta uallium ac resultantes saltus complerent, apud Romanos inualidi ignes, interruptae uoces, atque ipsi passim adiacerent uallo, oberrarent tentoriis, *insomnes magis quam peruigiles.*

> For different reasons the night was restless: at their celebratory feasting the barbarians filled the low-lying valleys and the re-echoing defiles with cheerful song or fearful sounds; on the Roman side, there were intermittent fires and halting voices, and the troops themselves lay next to their palisade or wandered around their tents, sleepless rather than alert.

Preparatory to the sentence's four-word climax is an antithesis built around *diuersa ... cum barbari ... apud Romanos*, the activities of the two sides broadly

---

[19] On declamation see Bonner (1949), esp. 149–67; Fairweather (1981). Voss (1963), to which I owe many of the passages cited, is the best discussion of Tacitus' pointed style.

contrasting (e.g. *laeto cantu aut truci sonore ~ interruptae uoces*).[20] Again, the splitting of a wider entity can create antithetic point, as at *H.* 2.7.2:

> igitur arma in occasionem distulere, Vespasianus Mucianusque nuper, ceteri olim mixtis consiliis, optimus quisque amore rei publicae, multos dulcedo praedarum stimulabat, alios ambiguae domi res: ita boni malique causis diuersis, studio pari, bellum omnes cupiebant.

> Therefore they deferred their revolt until a suitable opportunity, Vespasian and Mucianus having recently come to an agreement, the others long since: the best acted with love for the state; many the inducement of plunder goaded, others their doubtful domestic circumstances. Accordingly for different reasons but with equal enthusiasm all, both good and evil, desired war.[21]

Likewise effective are:

(a) abrupt asyndeton, as for example at *A.* 1.53.5 (on Sempronius Gracchus) *ceruicem ... percussoribus obtulit, constantia mortis haud indignus Sempronio nomine: uita degenerauerat* ('he offered his neck to the executioners, in the steadfastness of his death not unworthy of the name Sempronius: his life had failed to live up to it [or 'in life he had failed to live up to it']') (note the appendage after the main clause);[22]

(b) the pointed use of *et*, as at *A.* 12.52.3 *de mathematicis Italia pellendis factum senatus consultum atrox et irritum* ('with regard to the expulsion of the astrologers from Italy, a decree of the senate was passed that was fearful – and ineffectual');[23]

(c) oxymoron, as at *H.* 1.47.1 *exacto per scelera die nouissimum malorum fuit laetitia* ('after the day had been passed in crimes, the last of the evils was happiness') and *H.* 4.70.3 *honesto transfugio rediere* ('they came back by means of an honourable desertion') (note that in each case the oxymoron involves an abstract noun, and hence some generalising[24]).

An excellent example of the combined effect of parallelism and antithesis is provided by *G.* 27.1, on funerals:

> Funerum nulla ambitio: id solum obseruatur, ut corpora clarorum uirorum certis lignis crementur. struem rogi nec uestibus nec odoribus cumulant: sua cuique arma, quorundam igni et equus adicitur. sepulcrum caespes

---

[20] For a full collection of examples see Voss (1963) 126–8.
[21] This passage provides also a good instance of Tacitean variation and inconcinnity, *optimus quisque amore rei publicae* not sharing a construction with what follows and being awkward with what precedes. Other good examples of the splitting of a corporate entity to make point may be found at *A.* 1.2.1 (*ferocissimi ... ceteri*), 18.1; 11.29.2; 14.49.3.
[22] See Voss (1963) 32, 58–9, 65. Other examples: *G.* 5.1; *H.* 1.45.2; 4.15.1.
[23] See also e.g. *H.* 2.49.4; 3.34.2; *A.* 13.45.3; Voss (1963) 20.
[24] See also e.g. *H.* 2.45.3; *A.* 1.8.5; Voss (1963) 22–3.

erigit: monumentorum arduum et operosum honorem ut grauem defunctis aspernantur. lamenta ac lacrimas cito, dolorem et tristitiam tarde ponunt. feminis lugere honestum est, uiris meminisse.

In the case of funerals there is no competitiveness: the only special custom is that the bodies of famous men should be burnt with particular kinds of wood. Nor do they heap up the bulk of the pyre with clothes or scents: each is given his own arms, and to the flames of some their horses are added. A sod of turf marks the grave: they despise the lofty and elaborate honour of a funeral monument as burdensome to the deceased. They dispose fast of wailing and weeping, slowly of grief and sorrow. For women it is honourable to mourn, for men to remember.

Tacitus builds this paragraph to its climax through a series of sentences in which the parallelisms and antitheses become ever sharper. First, the introductory sentence, in which the minor antithesis is brought about by *nulla ... id solum*. Then *struem ... adicitur* contains two sentences in contrast with each other (note too the antithesis articulated by *cuique* and *quorundam* in the second). *sepulcrum ... aspernantur* constitute another pair of contrasting sentences. The next antithesis is contained in just one sentence (the penultimate), the alliteration in *lamenta ac lacrimas* drawing attention to the point. Finally the climactic six-word sentence contains an even sharper antithesis. Some redundancy of expression (*arduum et operosum, lamenta ac lacrimas*) is typical of the style of this early treatise, but Tacitus has taken pains to ensure that the parallelism is not too monotonous or cloying: the sentences either side of the three colons[25] are of different length. In the penultimate sentence *ponunt* comes with the second of the contrasting ideas, in the last *honestum est* with the first. In his later works Tacitus uses such parallelism more sparingly, and most often in his speeches.[26]

Generalising abstract nouns help Tacitus point the moral lessons that could be learned from his history. At *H.* 4.11.1 the king-maker Mucianus effortlessly tightens his grip on Rome: *nec deerat ipse, stipatus armatis domos hortosque permutans, apparatu incessu excubiis uim principis amplecti, nomen remittere* ('nor did he himself, surrounded with armed men as he bartered houses and gardens, fail to embrace the essence of imperial power in his pomp, progress and guard, though eschewing the name'). The powerful effect of the final five words comes both from their taut antithetical balance and the contrast between the acts of Mucianus described previously and the more abstract *uim* and *nomen*.[27]

[25] By colon I mean here the modern punctuation mark, not the ancient rhetorical term.
[26] See e.g. *A.* 2.38.3.
[27] Note too *H.* 4.28.2, where the final words generalise from an earlier antithesis. See further Voss (1963) 57, 104.

Epigrammatic *sententiae* are the most famous characteristic of the declamatory and pointed style, serving often to mark the climax of an argument or the end of a paragraph.[28] Many *sententiae* in surviving declamations and in literature influenced by declamation are puerile in the extreme, and Quintilian and others were merciless in their criticism of the cult of the figure. In his first published writings Tacitus was undeterred, and his flamboyant use of the paradoxical *sententia*, especially in *Agricola* and *Histories* 1–3, makes his aphorisms far more pointed than those of Sallust. Here are four very famous examples:

> *H.* 1.2.3 (on the subject matter of the *Histories*) *corrupti in dominos serui, in patronos liberti; et quibus deerat inimicus, per amicos oppressi* ('slaves were bribed against their masters, freedmen against their patrons, and those who lacked an enemy were suppressed by their friends');
>
> *H.* 1.49.4 (on Galba) *et omnium consensu capax imperii, nisi imperasset* ('by general agreement well able to rule, if only he had not ruled');
>
> *H.* 3.25.3 (on the killing of relatives in civil war) *nec eo segnius propinquos adfinis fratres trucidant spoliant: factum esse scelus loquuntur faciuntque* ('nor for that reason did they more idly butcher and fleece relations, in-laws, and their brothers: they said that a crime had been committed and they committed it');
>
> *H.* 3.63.2 *tanta torpedo inuaserat animum ut, si principem eum fuisse ceteri non meminissent, ipse obliuisceretur* ('such sloth had seized his soul that, if the others had not remembered that he had been emperor, he himself would have forgotten').

In all these an antithesis points the *sententia*,[29] and often this point is enhanced by extreme brevity (especially *H.* 3.25.3) and word play: in the first three examples note *inimicus ~ amicos* (here the word play pointed further by the chiasmus), *imperii ~ imperasset, factum ~ faciuntque*. In the

---

[28] Both ancients and moderns have used the term *sententia* ambiguously, to refer either to a gnomic remark that offers a generalisation based on what has been said or written or to a phrase that exhibits extreme paradox or epigrammatic point, this latter kind being especially fashionable in the early Principate; see e.g. Quint. *Inst.* 8.5. Some gnomic utterances are phrased with point and may count as *sententiae* on either definition; but others do not, and many epigrammatic phrases offer no generalisation. Kirchner (2001) provides an excellent discussion of ancient definitions at 9–48 and of Tacitus' use of gnomic generalisations at 49–192; note too Stegner (2004), esp. 7–19. Unfortunately, Kirchner's decision not to discuss Tacitus' employment of non-generalising *sententiae*, such as those quoted here, means that his book offers no comment on many of Tacitus' most celebrated pointed utterances. Sinclair (1995) discusses *sententiae* in *A.* 1–6 more from the perspective of political thought than of style. Many *sententiae* feature in the discussion of Tacitus' wit in Plass (1988).

[29] On this feature of Tacitus' *sententiae* see esp. Plass (1988) 26–55.

Style and language

Annals Tacitus himself became sparing in his use of *sententiae*, often confining them to speeches and integrating them more securely into their surrounding context.[30]

Differing shapes of sentence

Tacitus was more interested than Sallust in sentences with longer structures. Only rarely does he use periodic structures familiar from, for example, Caesar and Livy (that is, a long sentence that reaches its climax in a main clause after the preliminary thoughts and actions have been dispatched in subordinate clauses or participial phrases);[31] perhaps the most interesting instance in his work is *A*. 11.3.1:

> sed consultanti [*sc*. Claudio] super absolutione Asiatici flens Vitellius, commemorata uetustate amicitiae utque Antoniam principis matrem pariter obseruauissent, dein percursis Asiatici in rem publicam officiis recentique aduersus Britanniam militia quaeque alia conciliandae misericordiae uidebantur, liberum mortis arbitrium ei permisit.

> But when Claudius was discussing with him the possibility of acquitting Asiaticus, Vitellius in tears first recalled the length of his friendship with him and how both of them had been respectful to Antonia, the emperor's mother, and then, after running through Asiaticus' services to the state, his recent military service against Britain and other matters which seemed suitable for procuring pity – he granted him free choice in the manner of his death.

In this artful sentence the climax in the main clause is enhanced by an element of surprise: we expect Vitellius to argue for sparing Asiaticus. Its final word, *permisit*, well conveys Vitellius' hold over his emperor.[32]

In contrast to the narratives of, for instance, Caesar and Livy, Cicero is usually engaged in argument, and therefore his periods are rounder and smoother and often fall into two parts articulated by such structures as *quamquam ... tamen ...* ('although ... nevertheless') and *non ... sed ...*

---

[30] See e.g. *A*. 3.6.3; 12.14.1, 67.2; Goodyear (1972) 41 n. 4; Martin (1981) 219–20; Kirchner (2001) 78–83. By contrast, Stegner (2004) 16 argues that the *sententiae* in the *Histories* are more integrated than is generally believed.

[31] The periodic sentence is notoriously difficult to define, and there is no entirely satisfactory modern discussion. For recent comment see e.g. Reinhardt *et al*. (2005) 7–14; Mayer (2005). Wilkinson (1963) 167–88 writes for beginners but is better on the periods of oratory than those of writers of narrative. For these Spilman (1932) provides much material. For more recent discussion of Livy's periods see Oakley (1997) 128–36.

[32] Other examples of this kind of periodic writing may be found at *Agr*. 35.4 (an excellent example, with both subordinate clauses and participles); *H*. 1.5.1 (another good example), 40.2; 3.14.1, 47.2; *A*. 4.67.1; 12.12.2, 15.1, 15.2, 17.2; 15.1.1–2, 26.1; 16.14.1; add perhaps *Agr*. 29.2 and *A*. 13.36.2.

('not ... but'). In the *Dialogus* Tacitus works in this style, and the following is one of his more elaborate periods (7.1):

> equidem, ut de me ipso fatear, non eum diem laetiorem egi quo mihi latus clauus oblatus est, uel quo homo nouus et in ciuitate minime fauorabili natus quaesturam aut tribunatum aut praeturam accepi, quam eos quibus mihi pro mediocritate huius quantulaecumque in dicendo facultatis aut reum prospere defendere aut apud centumuiros causam aliquam feliciter orare aut apud principem ipsos illos libertos et procuratores principum tueri et defendere datur.

> For my part, if I may talk about myself, I did not pass more cheerfully that day on which the broad band [on the toga] was conferred on me or those on which I (a new man and born in a town of no consequence) was elected to the quaestorship or the tribunate or the praetorship than those on which, because of the modest attribute of being able to speak reasonably well, it was granted to me either to defend an accused man successfully or to plead some case with good fortune in the centumviral court or to protect and defend those very freedmen and procurators of the emperors in front of the emperor.

This is a fine example of a massive sentence in which the main clause comes early but the sense is never complete before the (modern) full stop at the end.[33] The main verb (*egi*) is the eleventh word in the sentence, but *laetiorem* has already made the reader look forward to the object of the comparison. For this, however, we have to wait, since Tacitus takes us through two relative clauses, each introduced by *quo*. Finally *quam* arrives as the thirty-fourth word. Yet the next word again causes anticipation: *eos* is in the accusative and the ear and eye await an explanation of the kind of days that Tacitus has in mind. The days are characterised in a long relative clause expanded by three *aut*s, in which the sense is complete only with *datur*, the final and sixty-eighth word of the sentence.

Since little is said here about the *Dialogus*, it will be worthwhile to examine a further feature of this sentence, its amplitude in phrasing. The first part is expanded around the structure *quo ... uel quo* and contains one instance of varied doubling (*homo nouus et in ciuitate minime fauorabili natus*) and one of trebling (*quaesturam aut tribunatum aut praeturam*). In the second part there is an expanding tricolon:

> aut reum prospere defendere
> aut apud centumuiros causam aliquam feliciter orare
> aut apud principem ipsos illos libertos et procuratores principum tueri et defendere datur,

[33] Such a 'pure' period is doubtless beloved more by a modern analyst searching for types than it ever was by ancient practitioners.

with two instances of doubling (*libertos et procuratores*; *tueri et defendere*). Such amplitude of phrasing is typical of the *Dialogus* and is also the most notable hallmark of Cicero's style. It is found more often than one might expect also in Tacitus' other early writings but is rarer in the lean *Annals*.[34]

Tacitus used another kind of sentence very much more extensively, that in which the main clause comes early and after it comes an appendage.[35] Structures of this kind are not rare in earlier Latin writers,[36] but in Tacitus they are exceptionally common, and result, as Martin well writes, 'from looking at events and their surrounding circumstances in a way different from that of the writers of orthodox classical prose'.[37] In Tacitus' hands the appendage may take varying forms, but by far the most common is that in which a structure involving an ablative follows the main clause. Precise definition of types of Latin ablative is often difficult, but many of those which Tacitus uses for this purpose may be regarded as 'ablatives of attendant circumstances' or 'ablatives absolute'. Sentences of this kind allowed him first to state and then comment (often cynically or subversively) on an action. They are present right from the outset of his historical work: at *Agr.* 14.1–2 three are found in swift succession, the second being notably cynical. A good, short example of cynicism is *A.* 6.14.2 (on Rubrius Fabatus, who had tried to flee the horrors of Tiberian Rome): *mansit tamen incolumis, obliuione magis quam clementia* ('he nevertheless remained unscathed, because of [Tiberius'] forgetfulness rather than forgiveness'). Sometimes the appendage can be very extensive, as, for example, at *A.* 14.1.1:

> C. Vipstano C. Fonteio consulibus diu meditatum scelus non ultra Nero distulit, *uetustate imperii coalita audacia* et flagrantior in dies amore Poppaeae, quae sibi matrimonium et discidium Octauiae incolumi Agrippina haud sperans crebris criminationibus, aliquando per facetias incusare principem

---

[34] Some examples of doubling from the *Germania*: 6.3 **apta et congruente** *ad equestrem pugnam* **uelocitate peditum** ('the speed of the foot-soldiers being apt and suitable for a cavalry battle'); 7.2 *non* **casus nec fortuita conglobatio** *turmam aut cuneum facit sed* **familiae et propinquitates** ('neither chance nor a random grouping, but families and relatives, make up a squadron or platoon'); 8.1 *acies* **inclinatas iam et labantes** ('battle lines that had been forced back and were now losing cohesion'); 8.2 *inesse quin etiam* **sanctum aliquid et prouidum** *putant* ('indeed, they think that a holy and provident power is within them'); 16.1 *discreti ac diuersi* ('separate and unconnected'). That the words in bold are not always precisely synonymous does not detract from the redundancy of expression: in every passage Tacitus could have removed one word without much detriment to his sense.

[35] For this kind of sentence see esp. Kohl (1959); also Courbaud (1918) 244–9; Martin (1981) 221–3; Martin and Woodman (1989) 24; O'Gorman (2000) 3–5; Damon (2003) 16–19; Ash (2007b) 19–20.

[36] See Chausserie-Laprée (1969) 283–336.

[37] Martin (1981) 223.

et pupillum uocare, qui iussis alienis obnoxius non modo imperii, sed libertatis etiam indigeret.

When Gaius Vipstanus and Gaius Fonteius were consuls, Nero postponed no longer the crime that he had long planned, his boldness strengthened by the length of time in which he had been ruling and his passions being aflame more each day with love for Poppaea, who, not expecting that Nero would marry her and divorce Octavia while Agrippina was alive, criticised the emperor with frequent reproaches and sometimes with witticisms calling him a ward, who, beholden to someone else's orders, lacked not only the authority to rule but his own freedom of action.

Here the main clause, in which it is stated that Nero no longer deferred his crime, comes right at the beginning of the sentence. It is followed by an appendage of forty-one words, introduced by an ablative absolute that explains why Nero no longer deferred; after the ablative absolute comes a nominative (*flagrantior*) that agrees with Nero, the subject of the sentence, and after *Poppaeae* comes a relative clause that makes Poppaea the main focus of the end of the sentence.

Tacitus and Suetonius on the end of Vitellius

To supplement and bring together results achieved from analysis of many sentences and short extracts, this chapter will close with a full analysis of Tacitus' account of the death of Vitellius, the climax of the most exciting historical writing in extant Latin, namely *Histories*, Books 1–3.[38] A comparison with the account of Tacitus' contemporary Suetonius, who clearly had very similar material at his disposal, reveals much that is typical of his writing. First, Suetonius (*Vit.* 16–17):

> postridie responsa opperienti nuntiatum est per exploratorem hostes appropinquare. continuo igitur abstrusus gestatoria sella duobus solis comitibus, pistore et coco, Auentinum et paternam domum clam petit, ut inde in Campaniam fugeret; mox leui rumore et incerto, tamquam pax impetrata esset, referri se in Palatium passus est. ubi cum deserta omnia repperisset, dilabentibus et qui simul erant, zona se aureorum plena circumdedit confugitque in cellulam ianitoris, religato pro foribus cane lectoque et culcita obiectis. [17] irruperant iam agminis antecessores ac nemine obuio rimabantur, ut fit, singula. ab his extractus e latebra, sciscitantes quis esset (nam ignorabatur) et ubi esset Vitellius num sciret, mendacio elusit; deinde agnitus rogare non destitit, quasi

[38] On this passage see Courbaud (1918) 157–61; Löfstedt (1958) 165–7; Heubner (1972) 184, 196–8; Goodyear (1970) 27–8; Wellesley (1972) 186–8; Levene (1997) 144–6; Ash (1999a) 124.

quaedam de salute Vespasiani dicturus, ut custodiretur interim uel in carcere, donec religatis post terga manibus, iniecto ceruicibus laqueo, ueste discissa seminudus in forum tractus est inter magna rerum uerborumque ludibria per totum uiae Sacrae spatium, reducto coma capite, ceu noxii solent, atque etiam mento mucrone gladii subrecto, ut uisendam praeberet faciem neue summitteret; [2] quibusdam stercore et caeno incessentibus, aliis incendiarium et patinarium uociferantibus, parte uulgi etiam corporis uitia exprobrante; erat enim in eo enormis proceritas, facies rubida plerumque ex uinulentia, uenter obesus, alterum femur subdebile impulsu olim quadrigae, cum auriganti Gaio ministratorem exhiberet. tandem apud Gemonias minutissimis ictibus excarnificatus atque confectus est et inde unco tractus in Tiberim.

On the next day, as he was awaiting answers, it was announced by a scout that the enemy were drawing near. Therefore, hidden forthwith in a portable chair, his only two companions a baker and a cook, he secretly sought the Aventine and his father's house, so that he could flee from there to Campania. Soon, on an idle and dubious rumour that peace had been reached, he allowed himself to be carried back to the palace. After he found that everything there was deserted, while even those who were with him were slipping away, he girdled himself with a belt full of gold coins and fled into the small cubicle of the door-keeper, tying up a dog in front of the door and propping a bed and cushion against it. [17] Already the advance guard of the invading force had burst in and, finding no one in their way, they were, as one would expect, peering everywhere. By these he was dragged out of his hiding place. When they asked him who he was (for he was not recognised) and whether he knew the whereabouts of Vitellius, he tricked them with a lie; but after he had been identified he did not stop requesting, on the ground that he would say things pertaining to the safety of Vespasian, that for the time being he should be placed in custody, even in a gaol. Eventually, with his hands tied behind his back, a noose put round his neck and his clothes ripped, he was dragged halfnaked into the forum amidst both verbal and physical abuse, then along the whole distance of the Sacred Way with his head held back by his hair (as is the way with criminals) and with his chin kept up by the tip of a sword in order that he should offer his face for inspection and not lower it. [2] Some pelted him with dung and mud, others called him an incendiary and a glutton, and part of the crowd made fun of his bodily defects (for he was exceptionally tall, had a red face largely from drinking wine, a pot-belly, and a thigh that had been damaged in an old chariot crash while he had been attending on Gaius). Finally at the Gemonian Steps he was tortured by many small thrusts, finished off, and then dragged on a hook into the Tiber.

Next, Tacitus (*H.* 3.84.4–85):

Vitellius capta urbe per auersam Palatii partem Auentinum in domum uxoris sellula defertur, ut si diem latebra uitauisset, Tarracinam ad cohortis fratremque perfugeret. dein mobilitate ingenii et, quae natura pauoris est, cum omnia metuenti praesentia maxime displicerent, in Palatium regreditur uastum desertumque, dilapsis etiam infimis seruitiorum aut occursum eius declinantibus. terret solitudo et tacentes loci; temptat clausa, inhorrescit uacuis; fessusque misero errore et pudenda latebra semet occultans ab Iulio Placido tribuno cohortis protrahitur. [5] uinctae pone tergum manus; laniata ueste, foedum spectaculum, ducebatur, multis increpantibus, nullo inlacrimante: deformitas exitus misericordiam abstulerat. obuius e Germanicis militibus Vitellium infesto ictu per iram, uel quo maturius ludibrio eximeret, an tribunum adpetierit, in incerto fuit: aurem tribuni amputauit ac statim confossus est. [85] Vitellium infestis mucronibus coactum modo erigere os et offerre contumeliis, nunc cadentes statuas suas, plerumque rostra aut Galbae occisi locum contueri, postremo ad Gemonias, ubi corpus Flauii Sabini iacuerat, propulere. una uox non degeneris animi excepta, cum tribuno insultanti se tamen imperatorem eius fuisse respondit; ac deinde ingestis uulneribus concidit. et uulgus eadem prauitate insectabatur interfectum qua fouerat uiuentem.

After the city had been captured, Vitellius was carried in a chair through the opposite side of the palace into his wife's house on the Aventine, so that, if he avoided the daytime by hiding, he might escape to his cohorts and his brother at Terracina. Then, because of the fickleness of his nature and since (such is the nature of panic) his present circumstances were particularly displeasing to one who feared everything, he went back into the palace which was desolate and empty, with even the lowliest of slaves slipping away or avoiding an encounter with him. The loneliness and the silence of the place were terrifying. He tried closed doors; he shuddered at the emptiness; and tired with his pitiable wandering and trying to conceal himself in a shameful hiding place he was dragged forth by Julius Placidus, a tribune of the cohort. [5] His hands were tied behind his back; he was led with his clothing ripped, a disgusting sight, with many taunting him but no one bewailing him: the hideousness of his end had removed pity. One of Vitellius' German troops who happened to pass aimed a hostile blow at him, perhaps in anger, or perhaps to remove him more swiftly from the taunting; or he may have been aiming at the tribune. At any rate, he cut off the ear of the tribune and was swiftly run through. [85] They compelled Vitellius with hostile sword-points now to lift up his face and offer it to insults, now to see his own statues toppling over, and often to look at the speakers' platform or the place of Galba's slaughter; finally they drove him on to the Gemonian steps, where the body of Flavius Sabinus had lain. A sole utterance indicative of a not degraded spirit was heard, when to the tribune who insulted him he replied that he had been his commander; and then, under a shower of wounds, he collapsed. And the crowd harried him when killed with the same perversity with which it had cherished him when alive.

All Suetonius' biographies are marked by their attention to detail; here the accumulation of both the sordid and the unusual gives the writing its power.

Style and language

Vitellius is a Roman emperor – but accompanied by a baker and a cook, and hiding in the janitor's cubicle with a money-belt, dog, bed and pillow. Who can forget the picture of the Flavian advance guard peering into every nook and cranny or the dung and mud that is then hurled, or the taunts of incendiary and glutton, or the parenthesis in which Suetonius portrays his height, wine-soaked face and pot-belly, or the marvellously evocative *minutissimis ictibus excarnificatus est*? Suetonius never wrote better.

Tacitus' approach is different: all is less precise and more dignified, and he avoids these sordid details; indeed, nowhere in his work can Tacitus' striving for grandeur and dignity be better illustrated.[39] The *gestatoria sella* has became the *sellula*, the baker and the cook merely *infimis seruitiorum*, the hiding place (evoked so memorably by Suetonius) a *pudenda latebra*, the precise taunts *contumeliis*, the butchery *ingestis uulneribus*.

Tacitus' opening sentence is straightforward and purposeful: Vitellius plans to take action in the only way possible in his desperate situation. The main verb (*defertur*) is in the 'historic present' tense, used regularly by Latin writers to make narrative more vivid. Tacitus uses it elsewhere in this section (*regreditur, terret, temptat, inhorrescit, protrahitur*); Suetonius does not.[40] In both writers Vitellius is at the mercy of events (note Suetonius' *referri se ... passus est*), but by attributing the subsequent change of plan to a rumour, albeit insubstantial, Suetonius makes Vitellius' vacillation not entirely irrational. By eschewing the rumour, Tacitus points to causes internal to Vitellius. His inertia and indecisiveness have been to the fore earlier in the narrative;[41] they are emphasised here by the appearance of *mobilitate ingenii* immediately after the connecting *dein*, and by the generalisation in *quae natura pauoris* (characteristically for a Roman historian Tacitus seeks to draw a general moral about human behaviour).[42] The end of this sentence is splendidly evocative: the placing of the predicative *uastum desertumque*, with its five successive heavy syllables, after *regreditur*

---

[39] How far the differences between Tacitus and Suetonius are to be explained by the differences in genre between annalistic history and biography cannot be determined because of the loss (the *Agricola* apart) of the other Latin historical and biographical writings of the period. Since Livy too displays some of the dignity in narrative to which Tacitus here aspires, generic differences perhaps did play their part, but they should not be exaggerated: a genre lives only by being flexible and capable of adaptation, and Suetonius may have derived his material from annalistic history (note that Dio 64.20.1–3, which contains many of the sordid details found in Suetonius, may well be independent of Suetonius).

[40] *petit* (16) is ambiguous in form and could conceivably be present.

[41] See e.g. *H.* 3.63.2, quoted above, p. 202; Ash (1999a) 118–25.

[42] See above, p. 202, for Tacitus' generalisations; Kirchner (2001) 166–7 for his generalisations about fear and 182 for clauses beginning *quae natura*. Note too Walker (1952) 191 '[t]his power of diffusing an emotion without diminishing its intensity is a rare gift which Tacitus possesses to an extraordinary degree'.

emphasises the emptiness of the palace (contrast Suetonius' plainer *deserta omnia*); *uastum* (the connotations of which suggest both 'emptiness' and 'awesomeness' and perhaps also 'devastation')[43] itself enhances the mood; then a characteristic ablatival appendage brings out by way of reflection the true nature of Vitellius' fall (even his slaves avoid him); and, whereas Suetonius contents himself with *dilabentibus et qui simul erant*, Tacitus' additional *aut occursum eius declinantibus* shows his greater interest in the psychology of the situation. The emphasis on Vitellius' psychological state continues in *terret solitudo et tacentes loci; temptat clausa, inhorrescit uacuis*: the short sentences and initial verbs bring out the urgency of the situation; the neuter plural participle and adjective serve to generalise the emptiness; the final four words are an excellent example of Tacitean balance (each colon has two words in the order verb, adjective) with variation (*clausa* and *uacuis* are in different cases);[44] and the description of Vitellius' plight is deepened by echoes of Virgil's *Aeneid*.[45] Suetonius' narrative voice achieves its effects by a dispassionate gaze: Tacitus' narrative is both more impassioned (note *misero*) and judgemental (note *pudenda*).

Tacitus deals briefly and incisively with the discovery of Vitellius and his being dragged across Rome: note the omission of the auxiliary with (§5) *uinctae*, the prominent initial place of this participle in its four-word sentence, and the emphasis given to the striking *laniata* by its initial position in the ablatival phrase *laniata ueste* (Suetonius' *ueste discissa* offers a less striking verb in a more normal position). Like Suetonius, Tacitus takes an interest in the effect of the scene on bystanders, but with *foedum spectaculum* he evokes it more explicitly through their eyes. Again he passes judgement – that of the authorial voice in these two words and in the generalising *deformitas exitus misericordiam abstulerat* (almost a *sententia*), that of the bystanders in the appendage after *ducebatur*, which consists of two ablative absolutes, perfectly balanced with each other, bound by assonance of *in-*, reflecting on the scene and, in typically Tacitean manner, splitting up the actors.[46] The scene with the soldier from Vitellius' German army is not present in Suetonius; in Tacitus it is notable

---

[43] It is used regularly with *silentium*: see e.g. Oakley (2005) 360.
[44] On balance, see above, p. 199.
[45] See *Aen.* 2.755 *horror ubique animo, simul ipsa silentia terrent* ('everywhere fear is in my soul, and at the same time the silences themselves frighten me'), 6.265 *loca nocte tacentia late* ('places silent far and wide with night'), and perhaps 2.728 *nunc omnes terrent aurae* ('now all the breezes frighten me'). Most obviously, these echoes enhance the pathos of Vitellius' meandering by recalling the sack of Troy and Aeneas' visit to the Underworld; Keitel (2008), in a full discussion of them, argues additionally that Tacitus underlines Vitellius' unfitness to rule by encouraging his readers to contrast him with Aeneas.
[46] On this splitting, see above, p. 200.

Style and language

for the compression achieved in his discussion of the possible motivations for his action.

Chapter 85 begins with a long piece of subordination (*Vitellium ... iacuerat*) that contains a typical example of Tacitean variation (*modo ... nunc ... plerumque*).[47] With his references to Galba and Flavius Sabinus, Tacitus integrates the scene firmly with earlier events in the *Histories*. He describes Vitellius' one not ignoble utterance briefly (after *excepta* the auxiliary is again omitted). Yet his masterstroke is the last sentence of the chapter, which brings to a climax the theme of the behaviour of the urban plebs that has been running through the final chapters of the book: in chapter 83 we have been told how it watched the fighting between the two sides as though at the games (83.1 *spectator populus*, 'the watching people'); with Vitellius' being dragged out into the open at 84.5 the theme continues, as illustrated above (note in particular *foedum spectaculum*); now Tacitus uses it to bring the scene to a close with a typically pointed contrast between *interfectum* and *uiuentem* and with the abstract and censorious *prauitate*.

FURTHER READING

The most balanced account of Tacitus' style in English is Martin (1981) 214–35, but the distinctively solemn voice and tone of Tacitus are evoked more forcefully by Syme (1958a) 340–63. Goodyear (1970) 35–42 remains very judicious; unlike this essay it concentrates more on vocabulary and syntax than sentence-structure. Löfstedt (1958) 157–80 on 'The style of Tacitus' is likewise sympathetic but is much less detailed in its range of linguistic observation than his famous philological studies and concentrates on style in its widest sense. Several commentaries on individual books have excellent discussions in their introductions: see in particular Ogilvie and Richmond (1967) 21–31, Martin and Woodman (1989) 19–26, Damon (2003) 12–20 and Ash (2007b) 14–26. The theoretical assumptions of Draeger (1882) are dated, but it remains an extremely useful collection of material on Tacitus' syntax, being the summation of much earlier research conducted by German scholars. Draeger's book is easily used even by those without German, but much of his material was presented in English by Furneaux (1896) 38–74. See also the 'Further reading' section of the Introduction.

---

[47] The variation is found first in Tacitus: see Heubner (1972) 198.

14

D. S. LEVENE

Speeches in the *Histories*

I

Virtually all ancient historians give a high prominence to speeches. This is a complex reflection of various related strands of the societies of Greece and Rome. For one thing, in antiquity persuasion through speeches played a central political role, and hence speeches needed to be represented as a significant causal factor in history. But there is a second aspect too: precisely because of the key political role of oratory, rhetoric was central in the education of the upper classes from whose ranks historians were invariably drawn. Hence historians found it very natural to interpret history through the presentation of speeches that both discussed and putatively influenced that history, and indeed to insert speeches largely or entirely of their own composition to illustrate key themes underlying historical events.

Such speeches were often constructed to appear realistic – they were presented in direct speech and thus strongly mimetic, purporting to represent the speaker's actual words. But that formal similarity to real speeches is to some degree an illusion, for it is surprisingly rare for a political speech that appears in an historical text genuinely to be something that could actually have been delivered on the purported occasion. The most obvious point is that real speeches, such as those published by Demosthenes or Cicero, tend to be considerably longer than their counterparts in historians. The latter, though sometimes following a traditional oratorical format in outline, are typically far more terse and selective in developing their arguments. Sometimes the historian tacitly alerts the reader to the process of abridgement by, for example, beginning in indirect speech as if to illustrate the general lines of the argument before moving into direct speech for the climax; but other speeches that are in direct speech throughout are manifestly not actual representations of reality. This observation does not merely make the familiar point that ancient historians are not always accurate in their

---

Thanks to Rhiannon Ash for her useful comments on an earlier draft.

reproduction of speeches (or indeed of other events), but also suggests something more noteworthy: that an attentive ancient reader, familiar with actual speeches, would have been aware of the artificiality of their historical representation.[1]

All this applies to ancient historiography in general, but speeches in Tacitus to some degree constitute a special case. *Speaking* in Tacitus is constantly represented in all sorts of contexts: people are described talking, persuading or discussing issues. But this is not the same thing as saying that *speeches* are constantly represented. Formal speeches in Tacitus are somewhat rarer than in most of his historical counterparts. While there are naturally a number of set speeches in his works, often such speeches are represented only summarily and in indirect speech, or else the speeches that are represented are closer to conversation than to speeches delivered to audiences on formal occasions.[2] The boundaries of this are fluid. It is common in historians, as I noted above, to abbreviate speeches to some degree, and so Tacitus' own abbreviations are not transgressing any generic rules; nor is there a precise definition of what constitutes 'a formal occasion' that puts speeches clearly inside or outside the category. Tacitus' speeches, however, are removed from traditionally formal speeches more regularly and to a greater degree than those in Thucydides or Sallust, Livy or Polybius. In place of the regular run of speeches – those delivered in the course of properly constituted debates in assemblies and senates, generals' pre-battle speeches to armies or negotiations between ambassadors, for example – Tacitus often, especially in the *Annals*, represents people speaking either in a more abridged way or in less traditional contexts. Thus at the opening of *Annals* 13, for instance, Nero gives formal speeches at Claudius' funeral and to the senate at 13.3–4, but they are presented only briefly in indirect speech, as are the senatorial debate over Parthia (13.8.1), the embassies (13.9.1) and Nero's decree after Britannicus' death (13.17.3). Instead one has longer accounts (though still represented in indirect speech) of the popular gossip of Nero's capacity to rule (13.6) and of Agrippina's quarrel with Nero (13.13–14); the latter in particular is a complex set of exchanges involving multiple charges, counter-charges and shifts in approach rather than arguments laid out in the manner of oratory. In these chapters there is only one direct speech: Agrippina's self-defence before Burrus and Seneca, which is presented more formally and at greater length (13.21.2–5) – but it is delivered on an occasion that has no regular legal or constitutional standing and whose result is simply to obtain her an

---

[1] Compare the discussion in Laird (1999), esp. 111–15 and 121–52.
[2] Ullmann (1927) 18; Miller (1964), also (1975) 54–5.

interview with the emperor. While it is certainly true that the dominance of rhetoric and rhetorical training in Roman culture meant that rhetorical influences could be expected in private as well as public speech, it is rare in earlier Roman historiography to find so formal a speech in a context that is directly marked as a private occasion; it is rarer still for this to substitute for the representation of formal speeches on public occasions.

The obvious explanation for this change in balance from earlier literature is that it mirrors Tacitus' picture of the structure of power at Rome: speaking is still represented because of its political effectiveness, but in the context of a world in which political structures have been overturned. There is less need for him to report public speeches or senatorial debates, since it is not primarily through such debates that decisions of consequence are being made (a point that Tacitus famously puts into the mouth of Maternus in *D.* 36, 40–1);[3] the greater emphasis on private conversations or quasi-judicial but still private hearings marks the fact that power resides more behind closed doors, rather than being derived from public persuasion. A secondary point is that speeches presented in such a fashion are – at least potentially – able to mirror reality more closely than are the unnaturally abbreviated speeches of most historians. It would after all not be unexpected if speeches delivered on informal occasions were shorter or less formally structured than those typically delivered on formal occasions; so, if such speeches in Tacitus appear short and informal, that simply fits what one would expect, given the circumstances of their delivery.

But while this goes some way towards explaining the distinctive features of the *Annals*, it leaves the *Histories* now looking anomalous. Speeches in the *Histories* appear on the face of things more traditional than do those in the *Annals*.[4] Even though the surviving work is shorter than the surviving portion of the *Annals*, a higher proportion of it consists of substantial set-piece speeches: Book 1 alone contains no fewer than four, one by Galba (1.15–16), one by Piso (1.29.2–30.3), and two by Otho (1.37.1–38.2, 1.83.2–84.4); there are also shorter reported speeches and discussions, such as Galba's formal adoption of Piso (1.18.2), or the debate over how to deal with Otho's coup (1.32.2–33.2). One possible explanation for this is that at the time when he wrote the *Histories* Tacitus had not yet developed the distinctive analysis of Roman power that he explores in his later work; a further, though related, answer would be to suggest that the *Histories* is more conventional in its handling of historiographical structure, and it was

---

[3] Compare Dio 53.19.3–4 for the difficulties of writing history under the Empire, where decisions are made in private rather than in public debate.

[4] Ullmann (1927) 217–18; Miller (1964) 292–4; Sage (1990) 921.

only in the *Annals* that Tacitus experimented with more radical techniques to mirror his more radical interpretation of Roman history. But though this may appear plausible at first sight, a closer reading of the *Histories*, and the role that speeches play in it, can lead us to a different conclusion.

II

Let us examine as an example the first speech in the work. Galba's speech defending his plan to adopt Piso at *H.* 1.15–16 is significant, since its position and subject matter reveal it as in some ways programmatic for the whole of the first three books.[5] For our purposes we can observe that it bears more than a passing resemblance to a deliberative speech such as might have appeared in any earlier historian. It is spoken from a position of authority, and opens with an exordium of a type recommended in the rhetorical handbooks (1.15.1), beginning the speech from the persons of the speaker and the addressee, and the specific situation under which Galba is speaking;[6] it ends with a clearly marked conclusion (1.16.4), in which he draws the threads of his argument together while denying the necessity for a long speech. In between he presents a long and carefully reasoned set of arguments:[7] a citation of precedent (1.15.1) to explain why he chooses to adopt a successor at all; praise of Piso to demonstrate his superiority to other possible candidates (1.15.3–4), while warning him of the danger that he will be corrupted through flattery; an explanation of the necessity to the stability of Rome of maintaining an emperor rather than restoring the Republic (1.16.1); and arguments why that stability is best ensured by adoption of a distinguished outsider rather than remaining within a single dynasty (1.16.2).[8]

But this speech, apparently conventional in form, is delivered in a strange context. Whereas in the parallel narratives of Plutarch (*Galb.* 23.2) and Suetonius (*Galb.* 17) the adoption takes place before the soldiers in a *contio* or public meeting, in Tacitus that *contio* is merely a public announcement of something that has already occurred (1.18.2). The actual adoption had taken place at what Tacitus refers to as *comitia imperii* – 'imperial elections' (1.14.1). This is a unique and ironic phrase. Under the Republic *comitia* had been the assemblies at which elections were held for the annual magistrates,

---

[5] See Keitel (1991) 2775–6; (2006) 220–3.
[6] For the topics of exordia in deliberative oratory see e.g. *Rhet. Alex.* 1436b1–1438a1; Quint. *Inst.* 3.8.6–8.
[7] Which is not to say the reader is necessarily to accept their validity: for some of the weaknesses in Galba's arguments see Welwei (1995) 359–61; Damon (2003) 136–41.
[8] See the analysis of Ullmann (1927) 202–3.

the properly constituted authorities who were the official possessors of *imperium*, the legal right of command. Here the *comitia* are elections in nothing more than name, and the *imperium* that is acquired through them gains its force simply through the emperor's ability to maintain it. The participants at this 'assembly', and hence the audience for Galba's speech, are merely four of Galba's political associates along with Piso himself. This is not in reality an unusual situation – upper-class Romans would regularly take decisions after convening an advisory group of friends – but the sense that Galba is transgressing a traditional boundary is accentuated because Tacitus transfers the language and formal structure of an official occasion to a private one.

The opening words of the speech draw out precisely that disparity between form and occasion (1.15.1):

> si te priuatus lege curiata apud pontifices, ut moris est, adoptarem, et mihi egregium erat Cn. Pompei et M. Crassi subolem in penatis meos adsciscere, et tibi insigne Sulpiciae ac Lutatiae decora nobilitati tuae adiecisse; nunc me deorum hominumque consensu ad imperium uocatum praeclara indoles tua et amor patriae impulit ut principatum, de quo maiores nostri armis certabant, bello adeptus quiescenti offeram.

> Were I a private citizen, and were I to adopt you in the presence of the pontiffs by the usual formality of a curial statute, it would be an honour for me to introduce into my family a descendant of Gnaeus Pompey and of Marcus Crassus, and for you it would be a distinction to add to your noble ancestry the glories of the Sulpician and Lutatian houses. As it is, I have been called by the consent of gods and men to be an emperor. Your distinguished qualities and your patriotism have persuaded me to offer to you peacefully the throne for which our ancestors fought on the field of battle, and which I too won by war.

The basic contrast that Galba is drawing here is between the qualities of ancestry that a private citizen might seek in an adopted son and the personal qualities that an emperor seeks in adopting an heir. But in the course of making that contrast he introduces a secondary contrast as well: between the legal adoption in which a private citizen would engage and that which Galba is performing here. This point is on the face of things superfluous to Galba's main argument, but highlights the occasion for the speech in a way that draws out its paradoxes. As a private citizen Galba would have adopted Piso in public through a traditional legal process in front of a properly constituted group; yet as an emperor choosing his successor he does so privately, by personal fiat in front of an *ad hoc* assemblage of a few associates.[9] In exactly

---

[9] Haynes (2003) 52. See also Welwei (1995) 356–63 and Haynes (2003) 50–3 for the wider tension in the speech between Galba's Republican-sounding language and the imperial ideology that he is articulating.

the same fashion, the form of the speech seems to belong to the traditions of public Roman oratory, a form which the vital political subject matter of the speech would appear to warrant – it is after all concerned with the future rule of the entire empire. Indeed, Galba's chief point in the speech is that, unlike the Julio-Claudians, he sought an heir not merely in his own house but with the entire country to choose from (especially pointed is 1.15.2 *Augustus in domo successorem quaesiuit, ego in re publica*, 'Augustus sought his successor in his household, I in the state'; cf. also 1.16.1–2). Yet that format and subject matter seem out of keeping with the privacy and informality of its occasion and audience.

The other side of the coin is that with the public announcement of the adoption (1.18.2), which could itself have been the occasion for a representation of formal oratory, Tacitus emphasises its lack of oratorical form. Not only does he not give Galba's words directly, the speech is not even treated as a traditional oratorical product in outline. It is summarised by Tacitus in a bare couple of sentences: it is said to be spoken 'with imperial brevity' (*imperatoria breuitate*), and Tacitus adds that Galba failed to include in his speech any 'pandering' (*lenocinium*)[10] or reward; likewise his address to the senate is said to be 'a talk no finer or fuller than to the soldiers' (1.19.1 *non comptior ... non longior quam apud militem sermo*). Cynthia Damon suggests that 'imperial brevity' evokes stereotypes about the taciturnity of the traditional Roman general,[11] but those stereotypes, while they certainly existed, were not part of the standard historiographical representation of even idealised Romans. Roman military commanders – including those who claimed the stereotype applied to them – were rarely represented as eschewing lengthy oratory when oratory was necessary (Livy regularly represents his central characters from Camillus to Aemilius Paullus as eloquent speakers). Moreover, Tacitus elsewhere implies that oratorical eloquence was a quality expected of emperors – most famously in his criticism of Nero for lacking it (*A.* 13.3.2–3) – and Galba's actual 'adoption speech' a few chapters earlier is not marked by laconicism. 'Imperial brevity' as practised by Galba appears to be a function of the superfluity of the occasion – that is the way that emperors speak when they are merely transmitting a previous decision and their audience does not need to be aware of their reasons. When the real decision was made, it was done with all the traditional verbosity of the speaking ruler.[12]

---

[10] In this context the word has specific connotations of rhetorical ornamentation: see Quint. *Inst.* 4.2.118, 8 *praef.* 26, 12.1.30, and cf. *TLL* s.v. *lenocinium* I B.3; cf. Morgan (1993) 579.
[11] Damon (2003) 143.
[12] Cf. Münkel (1959) 62–3, 68.

But there is one further problem: Galba's private speech, nominating Piso as his heir, does not succeed in forestalling Otho's rebellion. Power is slipping from Galba's hands even while he exercises it: merely employing his authority as emperor in private does not seem to be adequate – he would have done better to address his arguments to a larger group, always assuming that he was capable of persuading them. The contrast between Galba's private and public oratory might seem to imply that the public has ceased to be relevant, but Tacitus in his presentation of subsequent events demonstrates how partial and inadequate that is as an understanding of power within the Empire – especially since the 'public' in this case are not random Roman citizens, but the troops on whose will imperial authority is frequently in the *Histories* shown to rest.[13] It had been a deliberate decision to honour them by choosing the camp rather than the senate or the forum to announce the adoption (1.17.2): that instinct may have been correct,[14] but the rhetorical execution fails to match it.[15] The troops' response to Galba's words is mainly sullen silence – though Tacitus does note that it is primarily the absence of any promise of money that is angering them (1.18.3): Galba's parsimony towards his troops is a leitmotif of his reign.

So the very first speech in the work shows that the existence of the Empire has caused a fundamental shift in the location of power and hence in the rhetorical situation envisaged: in this it resembles the *Annals* more closely than might have been suspected. The difference from the *Annals* comes in the maintenance of the traditions of the representation of Republican rhetoric – a deliberative speech spoken by an authoritative speaker – within the new political framework, while simultaneously demonstrating that the emperor's attempt to confine himself to that framework is itself to fail to understand the nature of power at Rome.

This is not a universal pattern in the *Histories*, in which most extended speeches are delivered at more formal and structured occasions. Even here, however, Tacitus challenges the traditional relationship between public speech and official power in different ways. For example, Otho's first speech begins, rather like Galba's, with a personal reflection on the occasion and hence on his own authority to speak. But here, instead of assuming his claim to the throne, he starts by noting the ambiguity of his own position between emperor and private citizen (1.37.1).[16] He owes his claim to be emperor

---

[13] Keitel (1991) 2773 observes that three of the four speeches in *Histories* 1 are addressed to the praetorians as the true location of power at Rome. The fourth is Galba's here, which Tacitus implies might have been better advised to be addressed to them: cf. Syme (1958a) 155–6.
[14] But note Morgan (1993) 578–9 on the insult to the senate that this represented.
[15] See Ash (1999a) 24–5.
[16] Cf. Keitel (1987) 73–4.

to his nomination by the very soldiers whom he is addressing, yet in fact, were he unambiguously emperor, he would not need to address them at all, since it is only the rival claimancy of Galba that puts his position in doubt and demands his further encouragement of his troops. Another example is Mucianus' speech to Vespasian at 2.76–7. This is said to be a public speech, though it follows a number of earlier conversations that they had had in secret (2.76.1 *multos secretosque sermones*). But the phrase used to indicate that it was in public – *corona coram* ('in the presence of a crowd') – highlights once again the oddity of the occasion.[17] In a Roman oratorical context, the *corona* is not the audience to whom a speech is addressed, but a crowd of (typically) casual bystanders. And indeed, Mucianus addresses his speech directly to Vespasian alone, employing precisely the sort of arguments that he (presumably) could equally have used on those earlier private occasions which Tacitus has informed us about but not described – though those are said to have been conversations (*sermones*), a term that implies something less formal than the speech Mucianus delivers here. On the face of things this is the reverse of the situation in Book 1 with Galba, who speaks formally when making the true decision in private and laconically when reporting it in public; but it pushes at the boundaries of public and private speech, and their relationship to imperial power, no less than Galba's did – for while the formality of the speech fits the public occasion, the ostensibly public nature of the speech appears to be a facade, since the only named addressee is Vespasian and the audience appears to be there only to observe his decision.

Of course here, as elsewhere in Roman historiography, there is also a constant awareness of another, external audience, namely Tacitus' readers. They are not being persuaded to join Vespasian in his campaign, but may be alert to other elements in the arguments deployed whose implications are more far-reaching within the wider Tacitean narrative and indeed sometimes have contemporary overtones. Examples are the role of the army in creating and maintaining an emperor (2.76.4), or the qualifications of Vespasian to take the throne and Titus to inherit it – a prominent theme since Galba's opening speech, but one which had a particular pertinence in Tacitus' day, in the wake of the accession of Trajan, who achieved the throne by adoption thanks to his personal qualifications and despite his lack of distinguished ancestry. All ancient historiography contains speeches with such a double effect. One reason the role of oratory in historiography is often controversial

---

[17] *corona coram* is Wellesley's emendation (in his Teubner edition) of the meaningless MS reading *coronam*. Other editions emend to *coram*, the sense of which is similar though less pointed.

is that it is difficult to untangle the aspects of speeches that simply serve to show the speaker's persuasive techniques at work from those aspects that explore broader themes that can be understood only within the context of the narrative. And to the latter, of course, the speaker and the internal audience have no access.

There is yet one further – and more far-reaching – complexity about this occasion. The *Histories* regularly complicates the relationship between the addressee of the speech, the wider audience of the speech and the success or otherwise of the speech in persuading. The ostensible point of Mucianus' speech is to persuade Vespasian to claim the throne – something which of course Vespasian is shortly to do. Yet the connection in Tacitus between Mucianus' persuasion and Vespasian's decision is far from straightforward. First he describes at length Vespasian's desire to be emperor, but also his hesitation (2.74–5). Tacitus then introduces Mucianus' speech (2.76.1): 'his pauoribus nutantem et alii legati amicique firmabant et Mucianus post multos secretosque sermones iam et corona coram ita locutus' ('While these anxieties were making Vespasian hesitate, the other generals and his friends continued to encourage him. At last Mucianus, after many private interviews, now even addressed him before bystanders, as follows'). The implication is that Mucianus saw private encouragement as inadequate: what is left unclear is why. One possibility is that Vespasian is less likely to be able to back away from his ambitions if challenged in public to act on them, since he could not admit to the fear of assassination which is a major cause of his hesitation (2.75); another is that Mucianus is publicly affirming his own support for Vespasian.[18] But a third point is that the bystanders, for all that they are ostensibly not being addressed, are meant to strengthen his resolve by adding their encouragement to Mucianus', which is indeed what happens (2.78.1). The oddity in this latter passage is that the bystanders add a further argument that Mucianus has failed to mention – the prophecies and omens portending Vespasian's rule – and this indeed seems to be what finally sways him: Tacitus describes at some length the omens and their effect on Vespasian, concluding (2.78.4): 'haud dubia destinatione discessere' ('having come to a definite decision they departed').[19] Mucianus, in other words, appears to have been effective in his aim, yet his arguments are presented as being largely irrelevant to that, except perhaps indirectly through their encouragement of the bystanders to approach Vespasian with their own brand of encouragement.

---

[18] So Ash (2007b) ad loc., who notes that Mucianus' admiration for Titus made him a possible alternative candidate (2.5.2, 74.1).

[19] Cf. Ash (1999a) 129–32 on Tacitus' characterisation of Vespasian as a commander whose superstition is uncomfortably close to that of his ignorant troops.

So the bystanders, who are not addressed by the speaker, nevertheless seem to be intrinsic to explaining the speech's outcome. It is for this reason that Mucianus' speech, like others in Tacitus, has an oddly destabilising effect. The speech is so constructed as to respond systematically to the reasons that were said to be causing Vespasian to hesitate,[20] and some of these arguments make perfect sense in a speech addressed to Vespasian alone, such as 2.76.3, where Mucianus responds indirectly to Vespasian's private fear of assassination by arguing that Vespasian's distinction makes him a target for Vitellius even if he does not claim the throne, or 2.77.1, in which he requests a senior though not precisely specified position in return for his support. Other points that Mucianus makes, however, while not irrelevant to Vespasian's position, have broader appeal, such as the constant hints at the disasters that Vitellius as emperor will bring on Rome, and the suggestion that the Flavian troops are superior enough to the Vitellians to ensure a comfortable victory. That appeal to a double audience would be unexceptional in other contexts, but the way Tacitus sets up the occasion of the speech, and the oblique way in which it achieves its aim, gives an unexpected prominence to those elements in it that appeal to the bystanders whose presence Mucianus deliberately sought. And once again, as with Galba, the complex relationship between speaker, speech and addressee points to an analysis of Roman power where on the surface power resides with a few individuals, yet where those outside the ruling circles nevertheless play a central role in its acquisition and maintenance.

This is entirely typical of the *Histories*: while it contains numerous speeches, the great majority are speeches which do not have the desired effect on their audience, or which have an effect on the wrong audience, or which have an effect for reasons that have little to do with the arguments in them. One example is the speech of Piso attempting to enlist the support of the troops for Galba against Otho (1.29–30). This is a speech with a strong ethical focus, the strongest of any in the surviving work. Yet such effect as it has seems to have little to do with its ethics, and rather more with the hint that Piso offers in his final sentence that the troops will be rewarded financially for their loyalty (1.30.3) – the speech's rhetoric and its ability to persuade its hearers appear entirely mismatched. Moreover, even the support Piso achieves as a consequence is desultory and soon melts away (1.31.1).[21]

Or one may consider the debate in the senate over the punishment of the *delatores* at 4.40–4. This centres on a speech by Curtius Montanus

---

[20] Heubner (1968) 251–2, though his analysis oddly overlooks Mucianus' response to Vespasian's fear of assassination which I discuss in the text.
[21] Levene (1999) 208–9.

attacking the *delator* Regulus (4.42.2–6). Montanus' speech is eloquent and persuasive, moving from an ironic analysis of the brilliance of Regulus' denunciations to a warning to the senate not to assume that the mild rule of Vespasian precludes future tyrants: the implication is that Regulus, like the other *delatores*, should be treated as an example to deter those who would act similarly in future.

This speech is presented in a way that, within the usual generic framework of Roman historiography, leads the reader to expect that it will be effective. It is in response to another speech, albeit one not recounted in full, and within the usual structure of debates in historians the second speaker rarely loses. Moreover, in this particular case Tacitus describes the response in a way that suggests that the speech is successful (4.43.1): 'tanto cum adsensu senatus auditus est Montanus ut spem caperet Heluidius posse etiam Marcellum prosterni' ('the senate listened to Montanus' speech with such sympathy that Helvidius began to hope that even Marcellus might be brought down'). In other words, the principle of the condemnation of Regulus, which formed the heart of Montanus' argument, seems to have been accepted, and the hope is that this can be used also against the more senior prosecutors, above all Eprius Marcellus, who had been a subsidiary target of Montanus' speech (4.42.5), and who has been in Helvidius Priscus' sights since their debate over the approaches to be made to Vespasian at the start of the book (4.5–8). Tacitus' description of the senate's response supports this interpretation. The conflict between the 'few good senators' and the 'many bad' has been a standard theme in Roman historiography since Sallust;[22] but here we find the opposite: the majority are on the side of the angels (4.43.2), and for once we may reasonably expect right to triumph.

Yet the following chapter reverses these expectations: Domitian and Mucianus move, albeit in the mildest terms, to have the cases against the *delatores* dropped, and the senate instantly caves in (4.44.1), though Mucianus arranges for the exile of two senators punished for their actions under Nero (4.44.2–3). The eloquence of Montanus and his ability to persuade the senate has proved irrelevant, because there is, as before, another audience for his speech, namely the Flavians who are actually controlling the senate: none of his arguments is addressed to that end, and this retrospectively changes the significance of what he says. Even when the reader first encounters his speech, it is not hard to see in his final warning against future tyrants Tacitus' covert glance forward to Domitian, but that proves to have an immediate relevance to its internal audience as well as broader interest to Tacitus' readers. Domitian's actions now turn that into the major

---

[22] See e.g. Sall. *Iug.* 15.2–3; for later examples see e.g. Livy 42.47.4–9.

theme of the speech: in his protection of the *delatores* he prefigures their sinister role in his own reign.

There is yet a further twist, because the senators fail to recognise Domitian's significance even when he acts. They have, it appears, taken the lesson from Montanus that the *delatores* need to be punished, since they resent the fact that they have escaped punishment (4.44.3). But in their inability to act on their resentment they prove Montanus right in his accusation of their pusillanimity (4.42.6), and they have also failed to notice that the greatest source of danger lies not in the present dominance of Mucianus, the object of attention throughout the book (4.4.1–2, 11.1, 39.2, 68.1, 85.2), but in Domitian, who is destined to inherit, as Mucianus himself had implied in his speech in Book 2 (2.77.1), and whose future role is also repeatedly hinted at in Book 4;[23] yet it is on Mucianus rather than Domitian that their resentment is focused.[24] Montanus' speech looks prescient in its warnings, but also misjudged and politically impotent, since it is addressed to the wrong audience and is misunderstood by the audience to whom it is addressed. Here as before, identifying and addressing the proper audience is crucial to achieving effective oratory and the power that accompanies that – but here the crucial addressee is not those outside the imperial circle, but a neglected member within it.

III

The speeches in the *Histories* are thus closely bound up with Tacitus' analysis of imperial power, not merely in their content (although they frequently raise vital questions about the nature of political authority), but even more acutely in the complexity of their rhetoric when viewed against the backdrop of the occasions when they are spoken. It is not simply that the location of power has shifted since the Republic, though that is certainly part of the point that Tacitus is making. It is also that the ostensible holders of power are acting on an illusion of personal authority that they can in fact maintain only with the support of others. The *Histories*, even more than the *Annals*, shows a world in crisis, in which the illusions on which imperial power rests are regularly exposed.[25] The speeches are essential to that picture, because of the constant tension between their formal gestures to political and rhetorical

---

[23] Schäfer (1977).
[24] Cf. 4.4.1, where the senate likewise criticised Mucianus and failed to recognise the responsibility of the Flavian rulers themselves: on the significance of this passage see Haynes (2003) 152–5.
[25] See Haynes (2003) for an extended and sophisticated analysis of the relationship between the illusion of power and actual possession of power in the *Histories*.

tradition and their need to influence a world where power is maintained in quite untraditional ways.

FURTHER READING

Speeches in Tacitus as a whole and the *Histories* in particular have often been studied; there are many articles on individual passages and broader studies of their significance. The major study of speeches in Roman historiography by Ullmann (1927) covers Tacitus in detail and is still worth reading, though its methodology is nowadays seen as problematic. For more recent scholarship on the role of speeches in ancient historiography see Miller (1975), Keitel (1986–7), Hansen (1993) and Brock (1995). Laird (1999) is a fundamental study of the representation of speech in Latin literature, and at 116–52 he specifically discusses the issues raised by historiography with particular attention to Tacitus; a narrower approach to some of the same questions is found in Utard (2004).

On Tacitus in particular, central studies include several on the *Histories* by Elizabeth Keitel: (1987), (1991) and (1993). Also relevant are Münkel (1959), Miller (1964), Adams (1973), Dangel (1989) on Tacitean speeches in general, Levene (1999) on the speeches in the *Histories* and Devillers (1994) 195–261 on those in the *Annals*. Other studies of particular speeches include Martin (1967), Bastomsky (1988), Pigoń (1992), Welwei (1995) on the *Histories*, Miller (1956) and (1968), Schillinger-Häfele (1965), Griffin (1982a), Ginsburg (1986) and (1993) and Epstein (1992) on the *Annals*. Aubrion (1985) and, more briefly, (1991) addresses a number of wide-ranging issues about the role of rhetoric in Tacitus' work, including an extended analysis of his speeches ((1985) 491–678).

15

D. S. LEVENE

Warfare in the *Annals*

The work of Tacitus most single-mindedly focused on war (at least in its surviving portion) is unquestionably the *Histories*.[1] From the point when Vitellius begins his invasion of Italy (1.51) war stands consistently at the centre of the narrative, as the war between Vitellius and Otho gives way to one between Vitellius and Vespasian, which is almost immediately succeeded by the narrative of the revolt of Civilis, punctuated in Book 5 by the beginning of the Jewish War. Although this may be part of what has made the *Histories* considerably less popular than the *Annals* among modern readers – military history appealing to a narrower audience than political and dynastic intrigue – it is entirely expected of a historical narrative in the ancient world. Indeed it was commonplace for an entire history to focus on (as it might be) 'the Peloponnesian War' or 'the Jugurthine War'; and even when (as with Livy) the history purported to cover all the events, domestic as well as foreign, of a state over a longer period, war was often used for the purposes of structural articulation within the narrative (so Livy groups many of his books in 'pentads' and 'decades' according to the wars that were taking place in them).

The *Histories* in this respect is a highly conventional work, and Tacitus' introduction – which is of course an introduction to the entire work, not merely the section that survives – accordingly advertises its attractions in highly conventional terms, focusing first of all on the wars that it will contain (*H.* 1.2.1). Moreover, it is above all through war that the qualities of leaders and armies, Romans and foreigners alike, are seen. The unpleasant twist, of course, is that most of the wars that appear in the first books are civil wars, and thus the finest military successes can occur only at the expense of one's own country, a grim paradox that Tacitus repeatedly explores: traditional

---

Thanks to Rhiannon Ash and Christina Kraus for their useful comments on an earlier draft.

[1] On warfare in the *Histories* see in particular Herzog (1996); Ash (1999a).

virtue is inextricably bound up with the worst of vices. Even the revolt of Civilis does not provide relief. Civilis' own identity is partially Roman and partially foreign, and Tacitus accordingly twice refers to the war as a mixture between a civil and a foreign one (*H.* 2.69.1; 4.22.2), offering some acute explorations of the ambiguities of national identity – though with the advent of Petilius Cerealis the boundaries are reasserted, and Cerealis is able to win not least by dividing the 'Romanised' Gauls from the 'Germanic' Civilis (4.73–4).[2]

The *Annals* on the other hand is rather stranger. While its greater domestic focus gives less scope for warfare in terms of space, it might be thought to offer more opportunities for the display of uncomplicatedly patriotic heroism, since the wars that it does include are invariably against foreign enemies. However, Tacitus himself presents it in quite another way. In what is perhaps the most self-consciously programmatic passage in the work he contrasts, surprisingly unfavourably, his own history with those of his predecessors: 'Those men with free elaboration recounted vast wars, the storming of cities, kings routed and captured … but my labour is inglorious and in a narrow compass: peace was untroubled or only moderately challenged, the affairs of the city were miserable, and the *princeps* was uninterested in expanding the empire' (4.32.1–2). He goes on to explain that his history is nevertheless useful, but he accepts that it will be less enjoyable: 'For it is foreign geography (*situs gentium*), the vicissitudes of battles (*uarietates proeliorum*), the renowned fates of generals that keep and revive readers' minds; we are linking together savage orders, endless prosecutions, deceitful friendships, the destruction of the innocent, with always the same reasons for their downfall' (4.33.3).

This passage has understandably attracted the attention of many scholars, who have explored in particular the political implications of Tacitus' self-declared focus on the miseries of the early Empire, and the relationship to the trial of the historian Cremutius Cordus immediately afterwards. Less often discussed, however, is the apparent mismatch between what is claimed in this passage and the actual texture of the *Annals*, for the work does not in fact seem at first sight to lack grand wars and sieges, or the capture of kings and deaths of generals. Tacitus frequently punctuates his accounts of Tiberius, Claudius and Nero with significant foreign wars: Germanicus' battles in Germany in Books 1 and 2, Corbulo's campaign in Mesopotamia in Books 13–15, and the aftermath of Claudius' conquest of Britain in Books 12 and 14 are merely the best known. Indeed he later (6.38.1) concludes one such episode with a comment that it allowed the reader a respite from

---

[2] On the question of identity in the *Histories* see above, Chapter 6.

the evils at Rome (*quo requiesceret animus a domesticis malis*) – in other words, he claims to be introducing there precisely the sort of entertaining episode that he had earlier said was lacking. This mismatch requires an explanation.[3]

One way of accounting for it is to question whether Tacitus' battles are in fact comparable with those in earlier writers. One noticeable point is that, although Tacitus regularly offers extended accounts of campaigns, the descriptions of the actual fighting in most of the *Annals* tend to be highly abbreviated by comparison with those in Herodotus, Thucydides or Xenophon, Caesar, Livy – or indeed with those Tacitus himself had offered in the *Agricola* and *Histories*.[4] Of course, all of those authors at times describe battles merely in brief summary, without providing a detailed blow-by-blow account of the various tactical manoeuvres. But in earlier historians such abridged narratives are found alongside large-scale set-piece battle scenes in which the dispositions of the armies, the various movements of the battle lines, and the charges and melees in which the battles are decided are recounted in vivid detail. In most of the military campaigns in the *Annals* heavily abridged battle descriptions are the norm, and the bulk of the narrative is occupied with quite different matters.

So, for example, if we take the lengthy account of the campaign of Corbulo that occupies the opening fifth of *Annals* Book 15 (15.1–17),[5] although the narrative keeps appearing to prepare us for a large-scale conflict between Parthia and Rome under her leading general, those expectations are constantly defeated.[6] In the opening lines of the book the Parthian

---

[3] One of the few to address the issue directly is Woodman (1988) 180–96. His explanation is that Tacitus' disclaimer applies particularly to the later part of the reign of Tiberius (and hence its appearance here): that Tacitus deliberately introduced the *Annals* with the apparently traditional wars of Germanicus, only then to reject that model in favour of a new kind of history. Woodman further suggests that Tacitus' account of Tiberius metaphorically incorporates the traditional ethnographic and military themes that (according to what he says here) will have no place in his unconventional history. This interpretation of the role of Germanicus' campaign in the work, and hence of the belated appearance of Tacitus' disclaimer, is a powerful one, as I shall discuss below. But it seems more natural to understand this passage as a description of his work as a whole, not merely one section of it (4.32.1 'I am well aware that most of the things I have told and will tell [*quae rettuli quaeque referam*] perhaps seem petty and trivial to recount; but no one should compare my annals [*annales nostros*] with the writing of those who compiled the ancient affairs of the Roman people'); indeed even on Woodman's interpretation there is a problem (as he acknowledges) about explaining why Tacitus included the Thracian war at *A*. 4.46–51 (Woodman (1988) 195–6).

[4] Noted by Wellesley (1969) 64; but he attributes it merely to the general abbreviation of the narrative in the *Annals*, a suggestion that, as I shall explain below, is inadequate.

[5] The classic study of the episode is Gilmartin (1973) 604–19.

[6] Corbulo is provocatively described as 'preferring to have a war than to wage one' (15.3.1 *bellum habere quam gerere malebat*).

king Vologeses and Corbulo are placed in close juxtaposition, but then it emerges that Vologeses is avoiding war rather than the opposite (15.1.1). He is provoked by the attacks on his allies by the Roman-allied king of Armenia, Tigranes, and after long consultations launches a war in support of his own candidate for the Armenian throne (15.1.2–2.4), 'threatening the Roman provinces' (15.2.4 *prouinciis Romanis minitans*). But here too no direct conflict results: Corbulo's immediate response is merely to consolidate the Roman province of Syria, and even the legions he sends to Tigranes are under secret instructions (15.3.1 *occulto praecepto*) to act calmly (*compositius*). The Parthians briefly attempt a siege of a Roman-controlled city, but are temperamentally incapable of accomplishing it and are quickly slaughtered (15.4). Even this does not encourage Corbulo to open battle; instead he sends angry messages to Vologeses, who retreats (15.5.1–6.2).

At this point a new commander, Caesennius Paetus, arrives to take command in Armenia (15.6.3–4), and we are told that 'war was openly undertaken by the Parthians' (15.7.1 *bellum ... propalam sumptum a Parthis*). Paetus receives bad omens (15.7.2), implying that a major defeat is in the offing, though he immediately captures some forts (15.8); meanwhile Corbulo briefly repels a Parthian attack, and the Parthians decide henceforward to concentrate on Armenia (15.9). The Parthians attack Paetus (whose forces are divided), and he retreats after a brief skirmish (15.10.1–2); Vologeses attacks again and beats him – but the battle is given only the briefest summary (15.11.1). Paetus appeals for aid to Corbulo (15.11.3; cf. 15.10.4), but here too the promised battle never materialises: for, while Corbulo is still on the way, Vologeses besieges Paetus' positions without enticing him to battle: instead, after extended negotiations, Paetus persuades Vologeses to allow him to retreat under terms (15.13.1–16.3). Finally Paetus proposes to Corbulo that they attack Parthia jointly (15.17.1); but yet again nothing happens: Corbulo refuses the suggestion, and instead he and Vologeses negotiate a mutual retreat (15.17.3).

It should be noted that Tacitus' account does not deny that fighting took place, nor indeed does he minimise its results in a purely quantitative sense. In the course of this narrative we are told of cities stormed, and in particular of two sieges, one failed, one ultimately successful, both of which are said to involve large-scale losses by the losing side; there are also two significant battles in open country. When Vologeses takes the Roman camp after the negotiations with Paetus Tacitus refers (15.15.3) to 'heaping up the weapons and bodies of the slain to bear witness to our disaster' ('armis et corporibus caesorum aggeratis quo cladem nostram testaretur'). But such gestures towards major events are undercut by a narrative where the descriptions of actual fighting are so perfunctory, and the focus is constantly thrown on to the avoidance and deferral of battle. Indeed the absence of significant warfare is something that Paetus himself notes when he arrives, in a comment that could virtually stand as a description of Tacitus' narrative as well as a criticism of Corbulo in particular (15.6.4): 'despiciebat gesta, nihil caedis aut praedae, usurpatas nomine tenus urbium expugnationes dictitans' ('he scorned his deeds, saying that there was no slaughter or plunder, and that the claims of storming cities were merely nominal'). The contrast with earlier historical narratives becomes even more apparent when Tacitus repeatedly alludes, in the context of Paetus' negotiated defeat, to the famous stories of the Caudine Forks and Numantia (15.13.2, 15.2). In the former case at least, Livy (whose language is directly recalled here) had given considerably more space to the military circumstances that had led to the humiliation,[7] and the characters in Tacitus self-consciously replay those events (15.15.2). Yet the balance of his narrative is shifted markedly away from providing military detail comparable to that in his model.

It might be thought that this is because Tacitus lacked source material for detailed battle accounts, but this episode is entirely typical of the abridgement of his battle narratives, and detailed sources cannot have been absent for the entire period. Moreover, he claims to have used Corbulo's own memoirs (15.16.1): Corbulo is probably unlikely to have eschewed military detail in recounting a sequence of events that he handled successfully and that left his rival Paetus humiliated. In any case Tacitus was perfectly capable of taking the initiative for himself in imaginatively elaborating his descriptions of military campaigns, even in the absence of details in his sources.[8] Rather this appears to be a systematic attempt to shift the focus self-consciously away from the actual fighting that the dynamic of the narrative leads us to expect, and instead towards the plans and negotiations worked out between the various parties.

There is a related but separate issue that should be considered as well: that Tacitus' accounts of military victories and defeats are not merely perfunctory, but are also extremely simple. Battles in Caesar or Livy, even those narrated briefly, are often decided by a complex interplay of factors such as tactics, troop morale, terrain or weaponry, with different factors carrying weight on either side. But the great majority of battles in the *Annals* are

---

[7] The Caudine Forks did not involve actual fighting, since the Roman army was trapped without a battle; nevertheless Livy provides a detailed account of the military moves that brought them to that state and the terrain in which they were trapped (9.2.1–3.4). Livy's account of the defeat at Numantia was in Book 55, which is lost: hence we cannot be certain how he described it, though from *Per.* 55 it seems that the episode might have occupied a fair proportion of the book.

[8] The classic demonstration of this is in Woodman (1979).

one-sided, decided more or less immediately in favour of the victors, with little or nothing suggested to work in favour of the defeated side. This applies no less to victories by foreigners than to those by Romans. Let us take, for example, the description of the revolt of Boudicca at *Annals* 14.29–39.[9] The sequence starts with Suetonius' attack on Mona (14.29.2–30.3), followed by the Britons' sack of Camulodunum (14.31.3–32.3), London and Verulamium (14.33), as well as their defeat of Petilius Cerealis (14.32.3); finally Suetonius' defeat of Boudicca's army (14.34.1–37.2) is followed by his mopping up the remaining British forces (14.38).

Each of these fights is decided straightforwardly.[10] The Britons overwhelm Cerealis instantly (14.32.3); of the three towns they capture, Camolodunum is unfortified (14.31.4, 32.2) and all three lack defenders (14.32.2, 33.1, 33.2), leading in each case to immediate defeat.[11] On the Roman side Suetonius' troops are initially paralysed by the strange sight of the Druids at Mona, but, after Suetonius reminds them that their enemies are merely 'a womanly and fanatical column' (14.30.3 *muliebre et fanaticum agmen*), they cut them down without a problem; and at the end the remaining British forces are worn out by a combination of devastation and hunger (14.39.2), though Suetonius is denied a final victory when he is recalled following internal dissension among the Romans (14.39.3). Much as with Corbulo, the final peace is achieved by giving up on war rather than demonstrating military superiority. Even the victory over Boudicca, which is described at rather greater length, is achieved unproblematically.[12] The bulk of the narrative consists of the speeches made by the leaders on each side, and the actual fight is entirely one-sided: the Romans are positioned on terrain that protects them from ambush (14.34.1, 37.1), hold their line, discharge their weapons, and then charge and massacre the enemy, who attempt to flee but are trapped by their own wagons (14.37.1), exactly as Suetonius had predicted in his speech (14.36.1–2). By contrast, in Dio 62.12 (as abridged by Xiphilinus) the final battle is much closer, with complex tactical movements on both sides before the Romans achieve victory.

In each case, then, the battle is one-sided, and victory or defeat is the straightforward consequence of one or two clearly defined factors. The

---

[9] On the episode see Roberts (1988); cf. Miller (1969) 107–12.

[10] Mommsen's comment is notorious: 'A poorer account than Tacitus' on this war in 14.31–39 is hard to find even in this most unmilitary of all authors' (Mommsen (1919) 5.165 n. 1).

[11] It may be relevant that the fall of Camolodunum is presaged by several omens (14.32.1), the first of which is a statue of Victory falling over *sine causa* ('without cause'): the inability of the Romans to offer more than a token resistance to the British revolt is thus heralded on the divine level.

[12] Cf. Miller (1969) 111: 'It is the fact of victory rather than the process of obtaining it that Tacitus describes'.

partial exception is Cerealis' defeat, where no clear reason is given at all, though there is a hint that it happens simply because the Britons already have the momentum of victory behind them (14.32.3 *uictor Britannus*). While of course individual battles in earlier historians had sometimes been equally simple and one-sided, in the *Annals* such simplicity is the norm rather than the exception, even when the battle is given more than a summary description. When Tacitus at 14.37.2 refers to Suetonius' gaining praise (*laus*) equal to ancient victories (*antiquis uictoriis par*), there is a hollow irony to it: the praise he received may match that of the ancients, but the narrative hardly makes the achievements appear comparable.

So here too Tacitus seems to be justifying his statement in his 'manifesto' about the relative lack of significant and exciting warfare, but does so by deliberately slanting his narrative in such a way as to make the warfare appear less significant and less exciting. It is interesting to note that at *A*. 4.33.3 one of the things that he suggested was lacking in his history was 'vicissitudes of battles' (*uarietates proeliorum*): while his narrative might be thought to have *uarietas* in the sense of different sides winning different battles, the phrase implies *uarietas* within an individual battle[13] – yet that is precisely what he tends to exclude. In other words, Tacitus 'proves' the truth of his own complaint about the restricted compass of his subject matter, but his 'proof' is merely in his own manner of telling the story: he avoids deploying the features that might have made his war narratives attractive and entertaining in the way that he purports to think desirable.

Why does he do this? The 'manifesto' in *A*. 4.32–3 implies the answer: by narrating his wars in a manner that was unattractive by conventional historiographical criteria, he reinforces the sense of the corrupt state of Rome under the Julio-Claudians, partly by focusing the reader's attention on domestic affairs, and partly by suggesting that the emperors, among their other crimes and flaws, were no longer running the Empire according to the canon of traditional military glory. Even when, as with Suetonius, military victories in a conventional sense are achieved, those victories are not presented as coming in hard-won fights. Moreover Suetonius is not allowed to stamp out the rebellion: he is replaced by Petronius Turpilianus at Nero's insistence, and Tacitus cynically comments that 'he put the honourable name of "peace" on to sluggish inactivity' (14.39.3 *honestum pacis nomen segni otio imposuit*). The criticism of emperors for failing to accomplish victories through war is a recurrent theme in the *Annals*.[14] While to most modern

---

[13] See Koestermann (1965) and Martin and Woodman (1989) ad loc.
[14] See e.g. 2.26.2–5, 64.1; 4.74.1; 6.32.1; 11.19.3; cf. 4.32.2 (quoted above), and also *Agr*. 39.

readers the preference of Tiberius, Claudius or Nero for diplomacy, and their reluctance to give a free hand to glory-seeking commanders, would appear, if anything, to be points in their favour, Rome's militaristic and honour-based culture set a high premium on success through conquest.[15] Tacitus portrays a world in which, though the cultural value attached to military conquest remains intact, military action itself has ceased to matter: either the expected battles are deferred and the wars cut short, or else they are treated as a perfunctory side-issue, for all that in terms of purely quantitative criteria, such as the number of cities taken or people killed, they might seem comfortably to match the great events of the Republic. Nor is this simply a criticism of the emperors, for the generals appear all too often to share the imperial temperament and engage in political manoeuvres instead of frontal warfare – Corbulo in Mesopotamia again stands as a good example.[16] In imperial society the military virtues of Rome's great period have become attenuated and corrupted.

But there are exceptions. One may be mentioned briefly: the Parthian-Armenian war at 6.31–7. This is the episode that Tacitus describes in 6.38.1 as an attractive respite in his narrative (above, pp. 226–7); and indeed it does present many of the features of traditional military history that his work generally seems to lack. The central battle narrative is not only relatively extended and detailed, but also presents the sort of complex and balanced tactical considerations familiar from earlier historians. But the difference here is clear: the Romans are not fighting directly, but merely working through foreign proxies, with the Roman commander Vitellius sitting on the sidelines. In other words, far from undermining the picture of the decline in Roman warfare, it seems to reaffirm it, with foreigners providing a graphic demonstration of what is missing in most of the campaigns in which Romans are directly involved.[17]

A more significant exception comes with Germanicus' campaigns in Germany in Books 1 and 2. Here, in a number of campaigns spread over several separate episodes, the fighting is narrated at some length and with the sort of complex and balanced military detail that later mostly disappears from the narrative. Noteworthy is the major conflict between Germanicus' subordinate Caecina and Arminius' Germans at 1.63.3–68.5, a fight which fluctuates through several dramatic episodes, with the balance finally

---

[15] On this see Mattern (1999), esp. 81–122, 162–210; on the importance of honour in Roman culture more generally see Lendon (1997).
[16] Delpuech (1974) suggests that Tacitus admires Corbulo's employment of diplomacy rather than warfare; but see *contra* Ash (2006b) for the ways in which Tacitus undercuts Corbulo's claims to glory.
[17] On this episode see Ash (1999b).

ending in the Romans' favour.¹⁸ Likewise Germanicus himself fights a pair of extended battles back to back at 2.15–21, both of which are recounted in detail and with close attention to the tactical moves on both sides. The second battle, like that of Caecina, is relatively even-handed, and though the Romans eventually come out on top they do so only on balance – the final words (2.21.2) are *equites ambigue certauere* ('the cavalry fought to a draw'). The first battle is especially interesting: on the face of things it is no less one-sided than the summarily described battles of the later books, since Germanicus wins swiftly and without significant loss.¹⁹ Yet Tacitus makes a point of describing the Germans' attempted counters as well. He explains the disposition of their army, with the Cherusci placed to attack the Romans from above (2.16.2), which indeed they do, though prematurely (2.17.1), and when they are forced from their position they are rallied by Arminius (2.17.4). Tacitus, in other words, gives Germanicus' battles the characteristics that he later ascribes to Republican historiography, and they bear relatively little resemblance to his general presentation of warfare under the Principate – even though the distinction in fact rests less in the events of the battles themselves, and rather more in the manner in which he chooses to portray them.

Why should this be? One explanation has already been mentioned:²⁰ that Tacitus begins the *Annals* as if he were offering a relatively conventional narrative, only to change tack later and propose a new sort of historiography more appropriate for an imperial age. This is a plausible explanation as far as it goes, and indeed fits with other aspects of the portrait of Germanicus in the work. He is depicted as a man who is in many ways out of his time: a Republican hero anachronistically marooned in the Principate.²¹ It is little surprise that his campaigns would conform so unusually closely to the style of warfare expected in Republican historiography. Once he is dead the corruption of imperial warfare can be seen truly to have set in, and this is marked by Tacitus' belated 'manifesto', along with the actual manner in which wars are henceforward narrated.

This reasonable explanation may itself, however, be oversimplified. Germanicus does not appear to be the only character in the work whose wars are treated in this fashion. Even if we leave aside Caecina, who is acting under Germanicus' orders (albeit as an ex-consul and military governor in his own right), the campaign of one other Roman general is narrated in

---

¹⁸ For detailed discussion of the episode see Woodman (1988) 172–6.
¹⁹ Esp. 2.18.1 *magna ea uictoria neque cruenta nobis fuit* ('that was a great victory and not bloody for us').
²⁰ See above, n. 3.
²¹ So especially Pelling (1993).

a 'Republican' manner. The Thracian campaign of C. Poppaeus Sabinus at 4.46–51, though hardly possessing the significance of Germanicus' victories earlier or Suetonius' and Corbulo's later, is described with all the dramatic vicissitudes that one would associate with a major set-piece war. The Thracians are initially entrenched on high ground, where Sabinus attacks them, but after a counter-attack he encamps nearby. The Thracians attack the camp at night and massacre the auxiliaries, in response to which Sabinus, after failing to draw them to open battle, blockades them until they die of thirst. Some surrender, some commit suicide; the remainder attack the Romans at night, but in a close battle fail to break through.

This episode appears highly anomalous in terms of the discussion above. Sabinus is not a Germanicus, a Republican leader out of his time. On the contrary, both in his introduction at 1.80.1 and at his death at 6.39.3 he is treated as an iconic figure of quite a different sort – the quintessential Tiberian commander, a mediocrity who owed his extended period of command to his friendship with the emperor. Nor does it seem likely that Tacitus simply overlooked the contradiction: this is, after all, the first military campaign he has described since his claim at 4.32–3 that dramatic military campaigns no longer existed.

It is, of course, typical of Tacitus' destabilising technique to defeat the reader's expectations in this fashion,[22] and it may be that there is little more to it than that – an unexpected final triumph of traditional Roman warfare before the promised decline into imperial torpor takes hold. But it is worth observing that Sabinus' campaign has another part to play as well in the dynamics of battle narratives in the *Annals*.

Among the 'traditional' themes that Tacitus claims in his 'manifesto' to be eschewing is *situs gentium* – 'foreign geography' (*A.* 4.33.3). This could simply be a reference to the sort of ethnographic and geographical digressions that one finds scattered through ancient historiography,[23] but (as Woodman indicates) geography had direct relevance to warfare, since foreign terrain was one of the things that a successful general had to master, and accordingly historians often elaborate their accounts with geographic information even in the absence of formal digressions. Indeed, one noticeable feature of Germanicus' campaign in Germany is the central role played by the terrain in the battles. In his first direct fight against Arminius at 1.63.1–2 the Germans, in the space of a few lines, lead him into pathless country (*auia*) and conceal troops in wooded defiles to lure the Romans into an ambush: in the resulting confusion the Roman cavalry and auxiliaries

---

[22] So Martin and Woodman (1989) 207.
[23] So, implicitly, Woodman (1977) 107, who gives numerous other examples of the trope.

almost end up in a marsh before Germanicus turns the tide by drawing up the legions, though even that only allows the battle to end on terms of equality. The Germans' superior acquaintance with and suitability to the alien terrain is from the first moment tactically crucial. The same applies to Caecina's battle, which immediately follows. The scene is set among a detailed description of marshes and wooded hills (1.63.4), and the marshes hinder the Romans from the very start – Tacitus suggests that they, unlike the Germans, are unsuited physically and in their weaponry for fighting under those conditions.[24] Indeed the Germans are actually able to create marshes at will (1.64.3). On the following day the Romans do succeed in breaking through to solid ground, but not before once again getting caught in the marshes (1.65.4–5). Caecina had planned to use the terrain against the Germans and trap them in the forest (1.64.4), but that plan manifestly fails:[25] Arminius is able to attack when he likes, and the Romans escape only because the Germans get involved in plunder (1.65.6). Caecina's ultimate victory comes because the Germans fail to follow Arminius' sensible advice to draw the Romans back into the marshland and forests and instead follow Inguiomerus in attacking the camp on solid ground (1.68.1–3).

A major component, therefore, of the Romans' problems against the Germans is their inability to master foreign landscape. The same point emerges in a slightly different way immediately afterwards (1.70), when P. Vitellius is caught in a chaotic tide in which land and sea are dramatically confounded and he escapes only with difficulty. But, when the German narrative is resumed in Book 2, the Roman situation appears to be ameliorating. Germanicus decides that the way to compensate for the Germans' advantage in the terrain is to use the rivers (2.5.3–4): here indeed Tacitus has a direct geographical description of Batavia that stresses its suitability for his plan (2.6.3–4). Accordingly, Germanicus crosses the sea and lakes comfortably, though he subsequently disembarks his troops on the wrong side of the river Amisia[26] and is forced to ford it (2.11.2–4).

With his last major battles, however, Germanicus shows his mastery of the whole of the German terrain. He assures his troops that they will find that not only plains but also woods and defiles would benefit them – indeed he suggests that the Germans' weaponry is less suited to such conditions

---

[24] 1.64.2. Goodyear (1981) ad loc. notes that Tacitus' claim about German weaponry does not match his earlier description of that weaponry at G. 6.1, and at A. 2.14.2–3 it is significantly qualified. This suggests that Tacitus' account is based less on the actual weapons the Germans used, and rather more on the changing needs of his narrative, for in the latter passage, as we shall see shortly, exactly the opposite conclusions are drawn about the suitability of German weaponry for the terrain.

[25] Overlooked in Woodman's otherwise compelling analysis of the passage ((1988) 173–4).

[26] Or so it appears: the text is extremely problematic (see Goodyear (1981) ad loc.).

than the Romans' (2.14.2). The landscape is described in detail, along with the Germans' disposition in relationship to it, holding the edge of the woods and cliffs to attack the Romans from above (2.16.1–2). And the battle – apparently – bears Germanicus' prediction out. The woods do indeed work against the Germans: they flee into them and try to climb the trees, but are shot or cut down; those who attempt to flee across the river likewise are overwhelmed (2.17.6). It is true that the Germans do themselves no favours by attacking prematurely and losing their command of the high ground (2.17.1). Moreover, the battle appears to be decided as much by divine will as by direct strategy, since there is a favourable augury of eagles entering the forest (2.17.2), and Germanicus encourages his troops to do the same; this is followed by an apparent miracle (2.17.3 *mirumque dictu*), when the German troops inexplicably flee in opposite directions to the plain and to the forest. But that implicit attribution of the result of a battle to the miraculous is itself something Tacitus draws from the historiographical tradition (Livy often handles his battles in similar ways). It suggests Germanicus as favoured, and the specific connection made to Romans successfully entering the forest while the Germans are destroyed there suggests that not only has Germanicus learned to master German territory, but he has done so with divine sanction. The battle that immediately ensues demonstrates the practical effects of that mastery: the Germans once again draw themselves up in woods and marshes for an ambush (2.19.2), but Germanicus is not only aware of this but plans to use it against them (2.20.1). And indeed ultimately the Romans win because the Germans are caught and unable to use their weapons in the confined space (2.21.1). Germanicus' control of the physical landscape of Germany is now complete – though when he attempts to sail on the ocean he is overwhelmed in a spectacular and symbolically resonant episode. There still remain areas beyond imperial control into which the Romans cannot safely move.[27]

The Thracian war at 4.46–51 is the only other battle in the *Annals* where terrain plays a significant role. The Thracians make a point of their impregnability on their cliffs (4.46.3), and they hold their troops in narrow defiles (4.47.1). But Sabinus has no difficulty dealing with this: he himself uses the mountain to attack (4.47.2) and ultimately forces the victory by trapping the Thracians on the mountain itself, where they have no water or pasturage (4.49). From here onwards the Romans are never again in the *Annals* seriously hampered in battle by the terrain: on the rare occasions it is mentioned it is either irrelevant to the final outcome (e.g. 12.35.1–2) or works

---

[27] See especially Pagán (1999) on the transgressive side to Germanicus of which this episode is an example.

entirely in the Romans' favour (e.g. 13.38.3; 14.37.1). It is important to note that this is not a reflection of historical reality. Topographical descriptions in Tacitus, as in other Roman writers, are generally formulaic and governed by the needs of the narrative rather than the actual geography of the locations;[28] it is noticeable that when the German campaigns resume at 4.72–3 and 11.16–21 landscape now has little role to play, and that little is in the Romans' favour.[29] Tacitus concentrates such features of his battles in particular episodes, and does so by choice.

Germanicus' battles, with which the *Annals* begin, are indeed in the traditional historiographic manner, partly in their dramatic mode of narration, partly in the complex interplay of factors that decide defeat or victory. That suits Germanicus' status as the last of the traditional heroes. However, they perform another function too, for through them the Romans acquire a physical mastery over the actual terrain of the empire that they will never subsequently lose. When Tacitus in his 'manifesto' in Book 4 decries the absence of dramatic battles from his history and then – for the last time, at least involving Roman participants – immediately includes one, he may be destabilising the reader, but he is also doing something else. Having alerted the reader to the significance of topography, the Thracian narrative then shows how topography has ceased to matter: the Romans can win comfortably even in the most alien terrain, and even under Poppaeus Sabinus, the most perfectly Tiberian commander of all. If the Empire no longer involves grand wars and conquests, it is only partly the fault of the imperial system. It is no less the result of the success of Germanicus, who has made control of the Empire all too easy.

FURTHER READING

Studies of war in Tacitus as a topic in its own right are not that common. The best general account of Tacitus as a military historian is still Wellesley (1969); Kajanto (1970) discusses Tacitus in terms of his general sympathy for martial and imperial qualities, while on the other hand Olshausen (1987), looking at the antithetical presentation of war and peace in the works, detects in Tacitus a more nuanced and critical attitude towards war. Laederich (2001) goes in detail through Tacitus' narratives of foreign campaigns, though with more description than analysis. Woodman (1979) is a short but fundamental study of Tacitus' technique of constructing a military narrative, while Poignault (2001) examines issues of topography in Tacitus' battle

---

[28] Horsfall (1985); on Tacitus in particular see Malissard (1991).
[29] Corbulo at 11.18.2 replays Germanicus' successful invasion by river, without Germanicus' final mishap (Ash (2006b) 360–1). Furthermore, at 11.20.2 he has his troops construct a canal to bypass the ocean: Tacitus attributes this mainly to his desire to keep them active, but it does mean that Germanicus' extraterritorial transgressions can henceforward be avoided.

scenes. More attention has been paid to the military narratives in the *Histories* in particular, for reasons explained in this chapter: the most important general studies of this side to the *Histories* are Syme (1958a) 157–75, Herzog (1996) and Ash (1999a).

In addition there have of course been numerous studies of individual battles and campaigns in both works. In the *Histories* these include several articles by Gwyn Morgan (especially Morgan (1994), (1996), (1997), (2005)); also Ash (1998). Studies on the *Annals* include Koestermann (1958), Gilmartin (1973), du Toit (1977), Roberts (1988), Pagán (1999) and Ash (1999b) and (2006b).

PART IV

Transmission

16

R. H. MARTIN

From manuscript to print

The dates at which each of Tacitus' works was published is not known for certain, but it is generally accepted that they were written and published in a period of roughly twenty years, beginning in 98 (the year after his consulship) and in the order *opera minora* ('lesser works': *Agricola*, *Germania*, *Dialogus*),[1] *Histories*, *Annals*. Though Tacitus was well known in his lifetime as a public figure, the prophecy of his friend, Pliny the Younger, that his histories would be immortal (*Ep.* 7.33.1) seemed unlikely to be fulfilled, for Tacitus was never a popular author, and during the next four centuries there are only a few references to him by name and an even smaller number of quotations from him. According to a statement in the fourth-century *Historia Augusta* the emperor Tacitus (275–6) ordered that copies of all Tacitus' works were to be made and placed in public libraries. Though that statement may not be literally true, a germ of truth may lie behind it, namely, that at that time works of Tacitus were scarce and hard to come by. The only significant sign of a Tacitean influence in this period is that the late fourth-century historian, Ammianus Marcellinus, a Greek by birth, but writing in a highly individualised Latin style, proclaimed that his work continued the narrative of events from where Tacitus had left off.[2]

However, one statement from late antiquity is of importance for the manuscript tradition. In his commentary on Zacharias (3.14.1–2) Jerome wrote, 'Cornelius Tacitus, qui post Augustum usque ad mortem Domitiani uitas Caesarum triginta uoluminibus exarauit' ('Cornelius Tacitus, who in thirty volumes wrote the lives of the Caesars after Augustus up to the death of Domitian'): that is, the combined total of books for *Annals* and *Histories* was thirty. It is not known how that total was divided between the two

---

[1] See Brink (1994a); also above, Chapter 2.
[2] Amm. 31.16.9 'haec ... a principatu Caesaris Neruae exorsus ad usque Valentis interitum pro uirium explicaui mensura' ('These events, ... beginning from the principate of Caesar Nerva up to the death of Valens, I have set out according to the measure of my powers'), the last paragraph of the work. See Barnes (1998) 192–5.

241

works,[3] but since Jerome was educated at Rome under the distinguished grammarian, Donatus, the figure is likely to be correct. As the number of books that have survived is only four and a quarter for *Histories* and (roughly) twelve for *Annals*, Jerome's figure must signify (and perhaps indicates access to) the complete total of Tacitus' two major works. By contrast, the total of the surviving books is that of our earliest manuscripts of Tacitus, which owe their preservation to Benedictine monasteries, in which the copying of manuscripts – pagan as well as Christian – was standard: Montecassino, founded in the sixth century in southern Italy, and Fulda and Hersfeld, both founded in the eighth century in northern Germany east of Cologne, were particularly important as repositories of classical manuscripts.[4]

From the time of Tacitus' death (possibly early in Hadrian's reign: 118–37)[5] until the first printed edition of any of his works (c. 1470 by Vindelin de Spira in Venice) there elapsed a period of over 1,300 years, during which time every copy of every work had to be transcribed by hand, a process subject to scribal errors caused by tiredness, carelessness, illegibility of the text that was being copied, or failure to understand Tacitus' difficult Latinity. In view of these circumstances readers may wonder how sure they can be that the modern Latin text that faces them reproduces the author's *ipsissima uerba*. In the following pages the reader is offered, first, an account of the manuscript tradition (as far as it is known) and, second, a brief survey of the history of the printed text to 1607, a year which saw the publication of the edition of Curtius Pichena and the death and publication of the last (and posthumous) edition of Justus Lipsius, rightly proclaimed by Goodyear to be 'indisputably first of all Tacitean scholars'.[6]

Manuscripts

The five works of Tacitus that survive in whole (the *opera minora* apart from a lacuna at *D.* 35.5) or in part (*Histories* and *Annals*) descend through three separate manuscript traditions. Paradoxically, it is the *opera minora* whose manuscript tradition is most complicated, while *Annals* 1–6 (covering the reign of Tiberius, and the last to be printed, in 1515) have the most straightforward tradition. Consequently, it is with this group rather than the *opera minora* that I begin.

---

[3] For a full discussion of the question see Syme (1958a) 686–7 (Appendix 35, 'The total of books').
[4] See Reynolds and Wilson (1991), esp. 90 and 99.
[5] Birley (2000a) argues that Tacitus died later in Hadrian's reign.
[6] Goodyear (1972) 8.

Annals 1–6

The first six books of the *Annales* (or *Annals*, as it is known in English) survive in a single manuscript, the so-called 'First Medicean' (commonly abbreviated as M or M1), now in the Laurentian Library in Florence (plut. 68.1), written in Caroline minuscule in the middle of the ninth century, probably at the monastery of Fulda. There are some corrections both in the text and in the margins by the original hand and by a slightly later hand. The manuscript's legibility indicates that it was copied with considerable care: accordingly, in addition to errors that the scribe may himself have made inadvertently, it contains errors that the scribe has faithfully transcribed from the manuscript he was copying. Though it is unlikely (as Tacitus was never a popular author) that his works were ever subject to numerous copyings, palaeographical examination indicates that M had passed through at least two earlier stages – a more recent stage, when it was copied from a minuscule script, and an earlier stage, when the minuscule manuscript was copied from a rustic capital predecessor in which there was no division between words.

A number of preliminary points may be made, though they do not materially affect the text as it is now printed. It is uncertain whether Tacitus' *praenomen* was Publius (P.), which the Medicean manuscript exhibits, or Gaius (C.), which the fifth-century Sidonius uses (*Epist.* 4.14.1, 22.2), though the former is more likely to be right;[7] and, before the famous words *Vrbem Romam* with which the *Annals* opens, the manuscript has *Ab excessu diui Aug.*, which modern editors therefore regard as a form of title.[8] Two further points may be mentioned. First, M does not mark a book division between *testarentur* and *quattuor et quadraginta orationes*, which in modern notation are 5.5 (where Book 5 breaks off) and 5.6.1 (where the surviving portion of Book 6 begins) respectively: in fact, at this point there is a gap of over two years between events belonging to the early months of 29 and the last months of 31.[9] Second, whereas M marks book divisions (apart from its failure to separate Books 5 and 6), divisions within books are additions made by editors of the printed text. Divisions into chapters or paragraphs were first introduced in the seventeenth century,[10] while divisions into sections within chapters are an innovation of the twentieth century: their usefulness for giving references is obvious.

---

[7] See Birley (2000a) 231 and n. 4.
[8] See Oliver (1951) and the judicious discussion of Goodyear (1972) 85–7.
[9] See Syme (1958a) 267 n. 2; Martin (2001) 102 discusses fully the point at which Book 6 begins.
[10] See Goodyear (1972) 11.

After the Medicean codex had been copied at Fulda, it was transferred to the nearby monastery of Corvey, where it remained until the beginning of the sixteenth century, when, at the request of Pope Leo X (Giovanni de' Medici, Pope 1513–21), it was 'borrowed' and brought to Rome. It was then lent to the younger Beroaldus (Filippo Beroaldo), who used it as the basis of his edition, published in 1515. The manuscript was not, however, returned to Corvey, which received instead a bound volume of Beroaldus' edition. Later, the manuscript passed to the Laurentian Library in Florence,[11] where it remains.

Annals 11–16 and Histories 1–5

Books 7–10 of the *Annals* (covering the whole of the reign of Caligula) and the first half of Book 11 (covering the early years of Claudius' reign) are lost, and only the first four and a quarter books of *Histories* survive (taking the narrative only from 69 into 70). These books are contained in a single manuscript in the Laurentian Library (plut. 68.2): it is generally referred to as the 'Second Medicean' or M2 to distinguish it from M1, the manuscript of *Annals* 1–6, described above. Though the *Histories* were written *before* the *Annals*, they deal with a chronological period *later* than the *Annals*, and in M2 the subscriptions to *Histories* 3 and 4 show that the *Histories* were listed as Books 17 etc., following *Annals* 16, which, though incomplete, must have ended with the death of Nero in 68.

M2 was written in the middle of the eleventh century in the monastery of Monte Cassino in a Beneventan script.[12] The manuscript was already known to Boccaccio in the middle of the fourteenth century, and he may (or may not) have been instrumental in arranging its transfer to Florence. Correspondence between Poggio and Niccolò Niccoli confirms that the latter, perhaps by dubious means, had acquired the manuscript by 1427, and on his death in 1437 it came to the Laurentian Library. The distinctive Beneventan script, which Italian scholars, including Poggio, found difficult to read, may have led to the fact that during the fifteenth century almost forty copies were made, while the Beneventan manuscript itself was neglected until 1607, when Curtius Pichena's edition was the first printed text to draw directly on both Medicean manuscripts.

Scholars had always believed that all the fifteenth-century manuscripts of *Annals* and *Histories*, in spite of their multiplicity, were derived from

---

[11] For the likely date (early in the sixteenth century) see Tarrant in Reynolds (1983) 407 n. 3.

[12] The standard work on this script is that of Lowe (1980); for M2 see p. 43 of the Addenda.

M2. However, that consensus was called into question in the middle of the twentieth century, when a concerted attempt was made to establish that one or other of these humanistic copies contained readings that were independent of M2. A particularly strong case was advanced for believing that a Leiden manuscript (BPL 16B) had numerous genuinely Tacitean readings independent of M2. The case for believing in the independence of the Leiden manuscript (L), advanced by the American scholar, C.W. Mendell,[13] was strengthened when it was endorsed by E. Koestermann in his Teubner editions of the *Annals* (1960) and *Histories* (1961), but has been progressively rejected by scholars (including Koestermann himself), who accept that the allegedly independent Tacitean readings are all within the competence of fifteenth-century scholars.

Opera minora

Tacitus' three *opera minora* (*Agricola*, *Germania*, *Dialogus*) were published in a period of five or six years from 98, the year after his consulship. The *Dialogus*, to which Pliny the Younger seems to make allusion (*Ep.* 9.10.2),[14] leaves no trace until knowledge of it surfaces during the Renaissance, but there are a few indications that the *Agricola* and *Germania* were known during the Middle Ages, including some detailed knowledge of the latter work shown in the ninth century by Rudolf of Fulda in the annals of the monastery.

But it was in the early fifteenth century that an intensive search for manuscripts of the minor works of Tacitus began in earnest and, once more, Poggio was involved, as his correspondence reveals. In 1425 in a letter to Niccoli he writes that a monk from a German monastery had discovered some works of Tacitus that he describes as 'nobis ignota'. The letter was accompanied by an inventory of the works in question, and, though the inventory is now lost, a letter in the next year from Panormita to Guarino not only names the works but also gives the *incipit* of each of them. For the *Germania* and *Agricola* the author is named as 'Cornelius Tacitus' and that is followed by 'quidam dyalogus de oratore ... et est, ut coniectamus, Cor. Taciti'. Though Poggio's attempts to persuade the monk, now revealed to come from Hersfeld, to bring these works to him proved unavailing, a list compiled by Niccoli for two cardinals who were to visit monasteries in Germany and France contains, among other works, the three Tacitean *opera*

---

[13] See e.g. Mendell (1954) for his part in reviving the belief that the Leiden manuscript preserved readings independent of the Medicean codex; for the (?) final abandonment of that belief see Römer and Heubner (1978).

[14] See above, p. 33.

minora in the same order as the 1425 inventory, as well as longer versions of their *incipit*s and some other details. There is no evidence that the cardinals brought any of these manuscripts back to Rome, but in 1455 Pier Candido Decembrio wrote of seeing in Rome a manuscript containing the three *opera minora* in the order listed above. By the end of the fifteenth century numerous copies of one or more of the three works had been made, but via two, or three, (lost) hyparchetypes.

At the beginning of the twentieth century there existed roughly forty manuscripts, all written in the second half of the fifteenth century and containing one or more of Tacitus' *opera minora*. At that juncture there was general agreement among scholars that the manuscripts could be divided into two subclasses derived from two (lost) hyparchetypes, X and Y, which in turn were assumed to be derived from an earlier manuscript, housed at either Hersfeld or Fulda. But in 1902 the discovery of a hitherto unknown manuscript in a private library at Jesi in central Italy made it necessary to reconsider the accepted view.

The Jesi manuscript (*codex Aesinas*) is a composite volume, containing three works: the *Bellum Troianum* by the so-called 'Dictys of Crete'[15] and the *Agricola* and *Germania* of Tacitus. More importantly, it is not all written in hands of the same period: a readily accessible account is given by Ogilvie and Richmond in their edition of the *Agricola*.[16] The major surprise is in the manuscript of the *Agricola*, which extends from f. 52 to f. 65. While ff. 52–5 and 64–5 are in a fifteenth-century hand (which has been identified as that of Stefano Guarnieri, founder of the Jesi library), ff. 56–63 are a quaternion written in a Carolingian minuscule of the ninth century; ff. 69 and 76 are a *unio*, of which the former is a palimpsest of which enough can be deciphered to show that it continues exactly where the Carolingian quaternion ended, while f. 76 is blank, but with Carolingian minuscule erased. The *Germania* throughout (ff. 66–75) is in the fifteenth-century hand of Guarnieri. A further feature of the Carolingian quaternion of the *Agricola* remains to be noted: there are numerous marginal variant readings by a contemporary hand. These variants are of a vastly differing quality, but a number are of such excellence that they cannot reasonably be ascribed to a ninth-century copyist. From this only one of two conclusions can be drawn: either the scribe had by him another manuscript which contained these variants in its text or he was copying a manuscript that already had these variants in *its* margins. Whichever of these alternatives is correct, the dichotomy of two

---

[15] See *OCD* s.v. 'Dictys Cretensis'.
[16] Ogilvie and Richmond (1967) 84–6, though the statement three lines from the end of 84 that ff. 11–40 'are in Carolingian minuscule' should be emended to read that ff. 11–50 are in Carolingian minuscule.

lost hyparchetypes (X and Y) seems to be either untenable or increasingly elusive.

The Carolingian pages of the Jesi *Agricola* offer a Latin text that is different from, and in some cases superior to, that of any of the fifteenth-century manuscripts. But they also pose a question: are those pages part of the Hersfeld manuscript that the German monk claimed to be able to produce for Poggio? Scholarly opinion is still divided over the answer to that question, and, though it is attractive to believe that the Jesi pages come from the Hersfeld manuscript, there are arguments of some importance to the contrary. First, in none of the lists known to the fifteenth century is there any mention of Dictys' *Bellum Troianum* being associated with any of the works of Tacitus. Second – though this may not be an insuperable objection – all of the fifteenth-century lists put the *Germania* and the *Agricola* in that order, whereas the Jesi manuscript has them in the reverse order. Lastly, there is a highly technical point, set out in an important article by D. Schaps,[17] namely, that the outer marginal prickings of the ninth-century pages of the *Bellum Troianum* and of the *Agricola* are identical; in that case the junction of the two works goes back to the ninth century and antedates the various fifteenth-century lists that itemise Tacitus' *opera minora* among the contents of the Hersfeld manuscript, but none of which mentions the *Bellum Troianum*.

During the Second World War, the Jesi manuscript seemed to have disappeared after being taken to Germany, where a photographic reproduction of the *Agricola* and *Germania* sections was published in 1943.[18] Immensely valuable though that reproduction is, it does not show the marginal prickings, for which Schaps was able to use original photographs. Though the Jesi manuscript has reappeared more recently in Rome,[19] the majority opinion among scholars is that the ninth-century pages in the Jesi manuscript *are* part of the Hersfeld manuscript.[20] If they are not, it must be assumed that they are the remnants of an otherwise unknown ninth-century manuscript, while the Hersfeld manuscript, which was seen in Rome in 1455 by Pier Candido Decembrio (who left a detailed list of its contents),[21] has disappeared completely. But, whatever the case for the *Agricola*, it is from the *Hersfeldensis* that our surviving texts of both the *Germania* and the

---

[17] Schaps (1979).
[18] Till (1943). For a gripping account of the historical background see Schama (1995) 75–81.
[19] See Mayer (2001) 48 n. 109.
[20] See Murgia and Rodgers (1984).
[21] The text of Pier Candido's 1455 list is given in Römer (1991) 2325 and e.g. Robinson (1935) 8–9.

Dialogus descend. Though attempts have continued to construct stemmata for both these works, there is no agreement whether they lead to a two-pronged or to a three-pronged hyparchetype.[22] That exercise, at best, could take us back only to one or more lost hyparchetypes of the ninth century, whereas the marginal variants in the Jesi manuscript point to the existence of two or more lost manuscripts of either the ninth century or (probably) earlier; stemmatics alone cannot produce a solution to that question.

Early printed editions

The *editio princeps* of Tacitus' works was printed c. 1472–3 in Venice by Vindelin de Spira. It contains what we know as *Annals* 11–16, followed by *Histories* 1–5, then by the *Germania* and the *Dialogus*, which it ascribes unequivocally to Tacitus. Neither the *Annals* nor the *Histories* has title or book division. As numerous manuscripts of all these works survived from about 1420, the printer was not introducing to the public works that were hitherto unknown to scholars. Accordingly, the *editio Spirensis* is devoid of scholarly merit, and the manuscript the printer used is lost and unknown, though the fact that its text of the *Histories* ends with *nauium magnitudine potiorem* (= *H.* 5.23.2) might suggest that it belonged to a group of manuscripts, now designated as Class II, all of which ended at the same point.[23]

The second printed edition of Tacitus was published in Milan, probably in 1476 or 1477. Its editor, Puteolanus, set out to remedy the imperfections of the *editio princeps*, but his edition is more noteworthy for having added the *Agricola* to its contents. It also added three further chapters at the end of the *Histories*[24] and at the beginning of its text of the *Annals* gives the title 'Cornelli Taciti Historiae Augustae Li. XI'. A second edition by Puteolanus was printed in Venice in 1497 and has the distinction of being the first dated edition of a work by Tacitus.

The hundred years from early in the sixteenth century saw a Golden Age of Tacitean scholarship. In addition to editions of his works by four distinguished scholars there were published several volumes of notes on Tacitus that directly or indirectly contributed to the improvement of his text. In 1515 Philippus Beroaldus (the Younger) had the good fortune to be

---

[22] Winterbottom (1972) and (1975); Brink (1994b).
[23] The humanistic manuscripts can conveniently be divided into three classes, depending on the point at which their text of the *Histories* breaks off. Class I ends with *Flauianus in Pannonia* (5.26.2), Class II with *potiorem* (5.23.2), Class III with *euenerant* (5.13.1). For a more critical analysis of the inter-relationship of all these manuscripts see Römer (1976) xi–lxix.
[24] As do also a number of fifteenth-century manuscripts: see n. 23 above.

commissioned by Pope Leo X to publish *Annals* 1–6, whose text had come into the hands of the Vatican a few years earlier.[25] Though Beroaldus' scholarship was surpassed by that of his two successors, Beatus Rhenanus and Justus Lipsius, the quality of his work can be seen from the apparatus criticus of Goodyear's edition of *Annals* 1 and the additional apparatus thereto at the end of that volume.

Beatus Rhenanus, a pupil of Erasmus, produced two editions of Tacitus, in 1533 and 1544. Rhenanus is better known as the editor of the *editio princeps* of Velleius Paterculus (1520–1), but his editions of Tacitus have a number of important features. He argued that the title of all the historical works should be *Annales* and he included a *Thesaurus constructionum locutionumque et vocum Tacito sollennium* and an index *rerum memorabilium*. For *Annals* 1–6 he did not have direct access to the first Medicean manuscript, but was able to use Beroaldus' edition for those books, while for *Annals* 11–16 and *Histories* 1–5 he used a manuscript now identified as Y 01 (Yale University Library). His professed aim was not to depart from the manuscript reading without good reason, and Goodyear correctly says of his conjectures that they 'are not often ... brilliant and exciting, but they possess the more valuable quality of often being right'.[26] It would be easy to quote numerous examples that confirm Goodyear's assertion, but two may be given. In a well-known phrase of Tacitus, where he seems notoriously to refuse to call a spade a spade, most scholars accept an emendation of Rhenanus, viz. *A.* 1.65.7 *per quae <e>geritur humus* ('[things] by which earth is removed');[27] or, to give an example that is both simple and certainly correct: *A.* 16.29.1 *crebritate periculorum* (where all manuscripts have *celebritate*).[28]

Despite the substantial contribution that Rhenanus made to the text of Tacitus and its understanding, his work was overshadowed in the last quarter of the sixteenth century by that of Justus Lipsius (1547–1606) with a succession of editions from 1574 to his last edition, published posthumously in 1607. Lipsius' pre-eminence as a Tacitean scholar was based, above all, on an unrivalled knowledge of Tacitus' language and style, underpinned by an exceptional learning in the fields of Roman history and institutions. However, his enduring fame as a classical scholar rests upon the contribution he made to the text of Tacitus' major historical works, above all the *Annals*. The immense volume of his published works – editions and separate commentaries – and the fact that each new edition

---

[25] See above, p. 244.
[26] Goodyear (1972) 7.
[27] Sceptical are Lenchantin de Gubernatis (1940) and Woodman (2004) ad loc.
[28] For Rhenanus see also below, pp. 287–8.

of the text included numerous new conjectures and some alterations to, or rejection of, emendations that he had previously proposed makes the appraisal of his work a daunting task. That task, fortunately, was undertaken by J. Ruysschaert in a book published in 1949, *Juste Lipse et les Annales de Tacite*. Though the work has some shortcomings,[29] it gives a list, with dates, of over a thousand emendations proposed by Lipsius for the *Annals* alone. A relatively small number of those emendations (perhaps fifty or sixty in all) seem to have been taken, without acknowledgement, from learned contemporaries such as Muretus and Chifflet,[30] but the accusations of plagiarism that this evoked may perhaps be excused. A more serious fault is indicated by the subtitle 'Une méthode de critique textuelle au XVIᵉ siècle', by which Ruysschaert implied that Lipsius' approach to the handling of manuscripts was essentially the same as that used by modern scholars (often called, inaccurately, the 'Lachmann method'),[31] who seek to establish an ancient author's text by constructing a family tree (*stemma codicum*), but only after all known manuscripts have been collated and their interrelationship established. Lipsius' own words and practice clearly disprove Ruysschaert's assertion. So Ruysschaert's diligent examination of Lipsius' sources demonstrates that, when Lipsius refers – in a variety of ways – to the manuscripts that he has consulted, those manuscripts were, principally, three fifteenth-century manuscripts, namely, Vaticanus 1863, Vaticanus 1864 and Neopolitanus IV.C.21.

Though Lipsius died before the publication of Pichena's edition in 1607, he knew, from the two volumes of notes that Pichena had published in 1600 and 1604, the results of Pichena's collations of the two Medicean manuscripts. Lipsius had welcomed Pichena's collation because, in his own words, the ancient manuscript had confirmed in roughly a hundred passages 'conjectures that he [Lipsius] had made by his own unaided native talent' ('coniecturas nostras, quas solo ingenio duce ... ponebamus').[32] Yet, although he accepted Pichena's mistaken dating of the Second Medicean as written more than 1,200 years before his time,[33] he never entertained the possibility that the two Medicean codices might, directly or indirectly, be the sources of all surviving manuscripts of Tacitus.

Clearly, among the extensive list of Lipsius' proposed emendations there is a considerable variation in the merit of individual examples, and indeed Lipsius himself, in the course of many years, withdrew or replaced a

---

[29] See esp. the review by Brink (1950).
[30] Ruysschaert (1949) 144–63.
[31] See Kenney (1974) 110–14; Timpanaro (2005).
[32] Ruysschaert (1949) 139 n. 2.
[33] Ruysschaert (1949) 139 n. 3.

number of them. Fortunately Brink, who in his review had commented on the absence in Ruysschaert's book of any attempt to give a critical assessment of any Tacitean passage, followed up with just such an assessment of Lipsius' emendations in *Annals* 1.[34] Brink considers the emendations under a number of headings, including cases where Lipsius is right as against the vulgate reading of his time, cases where he defended the vulgate, cases where he departed from both the Medicean codex and the vulgate, cases of erroneous conjectures (many of them later retracted by Lipsius himself), and consideration of Lipsius' suggestions on unsolved *cruces*. At the end of his article Brink draws a number of general conclusions. For *Annals* 1 he concludes that, of forty-seven passages where Lipsius attempted to correct or defend the text, thirty-four are correct or probable (twenty-six being conjectures). That is a remarkably high percentage, and, when Brink goes on to say 'the position in the rest of the first part of the *Annals* is not dissimilar', that may somewhat overstate Lipsius' 'success rate', but it is clear that Lipsius was a giant among Tacitean scholars, and it need occasion no surprise that for over half a century after his death editions of his work continued to be printed.[35]

Though, by contrast with Beroaldus, Rhenanus and Lipsius, Curtius Pichena was a less notable figure, his role in Tacitean scholarship was not insignificant. His edition of 1607 was the first to insist that both the First and Second Medicean codices (of which he had already published careful collations) had to be used by an editor of Tacitus' *Annals* and *Histories*. Strangely enough, he also drew heavily on Puteolanus' second edition (1497), as if it were an independent authority for the text of Tacitus. But one other feature of his edition, the division of the historical books into chapters, was to set a precedent that all successive editors have followed.

FURTHER READING

Brief discussion of manuscripts and printed texts may be found in Goodyear (1972) 3–11; greater detail may be found (by using the General Index and Index of Manuscripts) in Reynolds and Wilson (1991).

The photographic facsimiles of M1 and M2 by Rostagno (1902) and of the *codex Aesinas* (the Jesi manuscript) by Till (1943) are out of print. For the Leiden manuscript see Mendell and Hulshoff Pol (1966), published at a time when there was still a widespread belief that the manuscript might preserve independently a number of

---

[34] Brink (1951).
[35] An indication of Lipsius' dominance is given by the editions published during his lifetime by the Plantin Press and for almost a century after his death by reprints by the Elzevir Press. For the former see items 2276–81 in Voet (1980–3); for seventeenth-century editions of Tacitus by the Elzevir Press see the Index of Willems (1880).

genuine Tacitean readings. In Reynolds (1983) 406–11 there are general surveys of the Tacitean manuscript tradition by R.J. Tarrant (on the *Annals* and *Histories*) and M. Winterbottom (on the minor works). On a much larger scale is the invaluable survey by Römer (1991), which has an extensive bibliography of over a hundred items up to 1989.

The only separate work that covers the field of early printed texts is Kenney (1974), whose wide-ranging and critical survey focuses more on Latin scholarship than Greek and more on verse than prose.

17

ALEXANDRA GAJDA

Tacitus and political thought in early modern Europe, c. 1530–c. 1640

Readers of Roman history in early modern Europe showered praise on the timeless universality of Tacitus' wisdom: 'In iudgement there is none sounder, for instruction of life, for al times', wrote the author of the English translation of the *Annals* and *Germania*.[1] But students of Tacitus in the sixteenth and seventeenth centuries also believed that his writings communed directly with their own present; that Tacitus revealed political truths to all ages, but most especially 'to these our times'.[2]

Tacitus had been largely forgotten or overlooked in the medieval and early Renaissance periods, and, despite the print publication of his works in various editions from the 1470s, his relative obscurity persisted in the sixteenth century. The magisterial editions of Justus Lipsius (1547–1606) from 1574 to 1607, however, anticipated a change in scholarly and political culture in the later sixteenth century, when Tacitus enjoyed an overwhelming and unprecedented popularity.[3] Between 1600 and 1649 at least sixty-seven editions of the *Annals* and *Histories* were printed.[4] The major works were translated into various vernacular languages, widening the readership of an author whose prose was deemed difficult even in a Latinate culture.[5] Writers modelled the style, content and structure of their own histories on Tacitus, whilst the *Annals* in particular supplied dramatists with the most lurid of plots to realise on the stage. Appreciation of the themes and epigrammatical style of Tacitus' writings also spawned a new type of political commentary: sets of observations and aphorisms based around Taciteanquotations,

---

[1] Richard Greneway (trans.), *The annales of Cornelius Tacitus. The description of Germanie* (1598), unpaginated.
[2] 'Cornelio Tacito, Autor ... per tutto il mondo, e particularmente ne' tempi nostri' (Malvezzi (1635) d2ᵛ).
[3] For these matters see above, pp. 249–51.
[4] Burke (1990) 485.
[5] Schellhase (1976) 14–17.

253

all of which emphasised the utility of Tacitus as a guide to contemporary politics.[6]

In a famous lecture delivered in 1580, the French scholar Marc-Antoine Muret declared that the utility of Tacitus, historian of the Principate, was his topicality for the present age, when most European peoples lived in monarchies rather than republican states.[7] Muret's comment signals a consciousness of change in European politics in the sixteenth century and the related transformation of Renaissance political culture. 'Civic humanist' political thought of the Quattrocento celebrated the ideal of the *vivere civile* – the ability of virtuous men to play an active role in politics. The vocabulary and preoccupations of humanist political thinking were forged in Italy, where the city-republics of the north developed an ideology that celebrated the sweetness and benefits of liberty that derived from communal self-government – the equality of citizens united in government under the laws, and the fulfilment of man's potential through the exercise of virtue in political life in free states.[8] Renaissance political thought had Aristotelian and jurisprudential foundations, but Cicero was the most admired and influential author. Cicero's account of the relationship between the exercise of the moral virtues and political success in the third book of *De officiis* – the *honestum* and the *utile* – had obvious appeal for Christian explanations of the operation of politics.[9] Ciceronian ideals and vocabulary were also applied to the beneficial properties of monarchy: humanist writers at the princely courts of Europe argued that monarchy was the best form of government, provided that rulers exercise the traditional cardinal virtues of prudence, temperance, fortitude and justice, took counsel from similarly virtuous subjects, and ruled only for the common good.

These certainties were vigorously challenged in the sixteenth century. By 1500 most republican governments in northern Italy had succumbed to hereditary rule by *signorie* or princes. The invasion of Italy by Charles VIII of France in 1494 heralded a century of intensive warfare. France and Spain battled in the early sixteenth century for dominance over Italy, a battle won by Habsburg Spain, which had achieved hegemony over almost all Italian provinces by 1559. (Venice, which retained its aristocratic republican government *and* independence from Spain, remained a remarkable exception.) After 1517, the religious schism of Martin Luther rent the unity of western Christendom, as Europe divided along the confessional lines of Catholic and Reformed churches. Religious division catalysed civil war in France and the

---

[6] Burke (1990) 484–90.
[7] Muret, 'Oration on Tacitus', in Mellor (1995) 33.
[8] Viroli (1992) 71–124.
[9] This is – and was – to simplify Cicero's position. See Salmon (1980) 310 and n. 12.

Netherlands in the late sixteenth century, watched with horror by the rest of Europe. War and fear of sedition and disorder contributed to the painful process whereby early modern rulers attempted to intensify the legal, military and fiscal powers of government. Monarchs and states impressed on subjects the necessity of obedience to superior powers, whilst the size, grandeur and glitter of princely courts made potent statements of might and power, both real and aspired.

Within the context of the development of the European dynastic state political thinking was transformed, as the concepts and vocabulary of civic humanism no longer seemed to reflect political reality. In a brilliant engagement with Ciceronian humanism Machiavelli (1469–1527) famously challenged the assumption that virtuous conduct in the conventional sense equated to political success and coined his own distinctively secularised conception of *virtù*, which acknowledged the role that craft, deception and other expedient forms of conduct played in attaining political ends. But Machiavelli's slightly younger contemporary, Francesco Guicciardini (1483–1540), was a more representative transitional figure between 'Renaissance' humanism and the world of the late sixteenth century. He also happened to be the most influential early reader of Tacitus.

A Florentine aristocrat, Guicciardini lived through the wars of France and Spain for domination of the Italian peninsula. He experienced at first hand the final decline of Florentine independence, the transition of government from republic to principality and the eventual establishment of the Medici dukedom of Tuscany through Spanish support.[10] Guicciardini's early writings addressed the difficulties in governing a republic and in protecting republican liberty. His later writings reflect his disillusionment with the ideology of the *vivere civile*, and his pessimistic view of the forces that shaped human history.

Tacitus strongly influenced the colour, content and style of Guicciardini's mature writings about politics, his famous *Storia d'Italia* (*History of Italy*), composed in his enforced retirement, and his *Ricordi politici*, or political aphorisms, a series of private observations and maxims that he periodically revised throughout his career. The *Storia* chronicled the devastation of the liberty of Italy through the invasion of foreign powers. Tacitus' influence is evident in the work's ambitious scope and intricate attention to detail, as the narrative weaves between dense accounts of court politics and the wider effects of intrigue and diplomacy, bloody battles and life-sapping sieges. Guicciardini's understanding of historical causation was the particularity

---

[10] Florence was established as an hereditary dukedom in 1537. The Medici were titled Grand Dukes of Tuscany in 1569.

of the interplay of human factors with Fortune, irresistible and unknowable. His depiction of the operation of power was relentlessly cynical: in his excoriating character portraits, statesmen and rulers are motivated by self-interest and ambition, rather than virtue or the public good. Like Tacitus, Guicciardini was fascinated by the psychology of rulers, and sought to prise open the gulf between the public speech and private thought, and to lay bare the hidden motivations of the powerful. Throughout his life Guicciardini's understanding of human nature grew ever gloomier, and he placed increasing emphasis on man's propensity for corruption. In the world of the *Storia d'Italia*, republican liberty and the virtues of the *vita activa* are an arcane political language, empty slogans in a world where political success is guaranteed by might, wealth and cunning. The young Guicciardini had written historical accounts of his native Florence. The *Storia d'Italia* recognised the changed scope of his political horizons: from the self-governing city-state to the world of the princely courts, where the monarchs who controlled the destiny of Italy and Europe resided. His writings reflected Tacitus' distinction between the material of his own narrative, the world of the Principate, and an earlier, glorious, but distant, history of Republican Rome.

The final version of Guicciardini's *Ricordi*, revised in 1530, outlines more crisply not only the patterns of his thought but also his engagement with Tacitus in ways that strongly anticipated the methods and concerns of later Tacitean scholars. Guicciardini's understanding of Tacitus (the only author cited by name in the late version of the *Ricordi*) is summarised in his famous pronouncement: 'Cornelius Tacitus teaches well those who live under tyrants how to live and behave prudently; just as he teaches tyrants ways to establish their tyranny.'[11] Many of the maxims collapsed the distinction between tyrants and monarchs and emphasised the ways in which princes secured their own 'state' and power. 'Ambition' produces excellent deeds in those who seek honour 'by honest and honourable means'. It is 'pernicious and detestable when its only end is power, as is usually the case with princes'.[12]

Guicciardini shared with Tacitus a fascination with the methods of successful tyrants – in particular the political techniques of Tiberius – and crucially distinguished between 'prudent' and 'rash' tyranny. For the subjects of a 'bestial' and 'cruel' tyrant Guicciardini advises the same remedy as for

---

[11] 'Insegna molto bene Cornelio Tacito a chi vive sotto a' tiranni el modo di vivere e governarsi prudentemente, così come insegna a' tiranni e' modi di fondare la tirannide' (Guicciardini (1994 [1530]) 60).

[12] 'La ambizione non è dannabile, né da vituperare quello ambizioso che ha appetito d'avere gloria co' mezzi onesti e onorevoli ... Quella è ambizione perniziosa e detestabile che ha per unico fine la grandezza, come hanno communemente e' príncipi' (Guicciardini (1994 [1530]) 67).

avoidance of the plague: 'Flee from him as far and as fast as you can.'[13] A 'prudent' tyrant, however, would secure stability by forging relationships with 'bold' as well as 'timid' supporters and by recognising the utility of the support of powerful subjects. The subjects of prudent tyrants must learn how to act prudently themselves: by maintaining their own secret counsel, by learning to understand the ruler's psychology and by engaging in conduct that might involve the suspension of ordinary virtue. Deception, in particular, is an advantageous political technique, that would necessarily be practised by princes and their subjects in the modern world. For Guicciardini insisted that accommodation with a prudent tyrant was not only possible but was the *duty* of public-minded subjects and citizens, who must 'try to cooperate' with a tyrant, and 'counsel him to rule well and to renounce evil deeds'.[14]

The problems of balancing conscience and political engagement under tyranny were ones that Guicciardini obviously shared with Tacitus, as was the recognition that republican and Ciceronian codes of virtue and political conduct were inadequate guides for the subjects of tyrants. In particular Guicciardini's notion that a tyrant could be 'prudent' represents a development in political vocabulary. In traditional 'humanist' and Aristotelian terms prudence was a cardinal virtue, a quality that a tyrant could not possibly possess; Guicciardini's application of the term to tyranny and to the conduct of subjects under tyranny unmoored the word from its conventional ethical meaning. Prudence could be re-translated as 'statecraft'.[15]

Guicciardini's reading closely foreshadowed the ways in which Tacitus would be read in the late sixteenth century. Guicciardini's *Storia d'Italia*, however, remained unpublished until 1561, his *Ricordi* until 1576. By the 1570s the political climate of Europe was more fertile for the reception of Tacitus. To admiring and hostile observers alike the Spanish crown, with its sprawling dominions, seemed poised to realise ambitions to recreate the 'universal monarchy' of the Roman Empire. Standing in the way of this ambition, though, the Spanish Netherlands rose in revolt against the oppressive religious and secular policies of the Habsburg regime. In France religious violence between Huguenot and Catholic reached a horrific climax on St Bartholomew's Day 1572, when a Catholic mob murdered thousands of

---

[13] 'A salvarsi da uno tiranno bestiale e crudele non è regola o medicina che vaglia, eccetto quella che si dà alla peste: fuggire da lui el più discosto e el più presto che si può' (Guicciardini (1994 [1530]) 95).
[14] 'Credo sia uficio di buoni cittadini, quando la patria viene in mano di tiranni, cercare d'avere luogo con loro per potere persuadere el bene e detestare el male' (Guicciardini (1994 [1530]) 135).
[15] See the important discussion by Viroli (1992) 178–200.

Huguenots in Paris. As violence in the Netherlands and France spiralled into bloody civil wars, the spectre of assassination plots both real and imagined dogged the government of Elizabeth I, fears made worse for all European monarchs by the actual assassinations of William the Silent (leader of the Dutch rebels) in 1584, and King Henry III of France in 1589. In a conscious repudiation of the certainties of Ciceronianism Montaigne declared the influence of Tacitus to be 'proper in a sick and troubled state, as ours is in the present age'.[16]

Italian émigrés at the court of the Queen Dowager of France, Catherine de' Medici, became notorious in the 1570s and 1580s for their modish interest in Machiavelli, Guicciardini and Tacitus.[17] In 1580 Carlo Pasquale (or Pasqualius), a Piedmontese writer living in France, published a commentary on the first four books of the *Annals* in Paris, an aphoristic commentary using Lipsius' edition of 1574.[18] Where Pasquale trod, the literati of Europe rushed in. Peter Burke has estimated that between 1580 and 1700 over a hundred authors wrote commentaries on Tacitus, many recycling similar *topoi*, tone and style.[19]

Readers and commentators agreed that Tacitus was an unparalleled repository of *arcana imperii*, secrets of state that opened up to the reader the hidden workings of high politics. They explored the techniques of political manipulation used by rulers of ancient Rome and the present day, drawing parallels between life at the imperial and early modern court, where the *utile* was often far from the *honestum*. Certain features of Tacitus' writings had particular resonance for an early modern audience. In the late sixteenth century France and England were governed by childless monarchs, prompting a major political and military crisis in France in 1589 (after the assassination of Henry III), and severe anxiety about the succession to Elizabeth I's throne. Commentators often focused on Tacitus' descriptions of imperial succession, and the role (or lack of role) of the senate or the army in choosing and legitimising new emperors. Understandably the example of the rise and fall of Sejanus was applied with vivid enthusiasm to the story of men who fell from positions of power, his story invoked as a warning to all who sought their fortune at court. Governments also pursued more vigilant control over the power of the written word, especially wary of the potency of the printing press. Tacitus' hostility to censorship struck a particular note with writers, and his sympathy with the fate of Cremutius Cordus, the censored historian, was one of the most cited passages of the *Annals* (4.34–5).

---

[16] Cited in Salmon (1980) 327.
[17] Tuck (1993) 40–5.
[18] Momigliano (1947).
[19] Burke (1990) 485.

The flood of Tacitean commentaries that professed to lay bare the 'realities' of political conduct, however, shaped a new strain of political thinking that interpreted Tacitus' writings in ways that at first seem unlikely. The instability of the late sixteenth century, this 'sick and troubled state', engendered a desire to remedy the sickness: a yearning for security, civil peace, the suppression of disorder and the need to discipline the unruly masses. There sprang up a new set of apologists arguing for the necessity of strong or 'absolute' government to achieve these goals. Tacitus' account of Rome's bloody civil wars in the *Histories*, and the methods used by Augustus and Tiberius to create and sustain the Principate in the *Annals*, were pressed into demonstrations of the ways that a state – almost always a monarchical state – must establish strong, stable rule over subjects.

No scholar had a more comprehensive knowledge of Tacitus than Justus Lipsius, Tacitus' superlative editor. He was born in Brabant in 1547, and his thought was forged by his experience of living through the Dutch Revolt. In his first lectures delivered at the University of Jena in 1572, Lipsius made an explicit parallel between the tyranny of Tiberius and the bloodthirst of the Duke of Alba, the Spanish governor of the Netherlands who had been reviled for his draconian persecution of rebels in the early years of the revolt. But, as the conflict in the Low Countries drew on, Lipsius developed a far more conciliatory attitude towards Spain. By the 1590s, Lipsius' sympathy for the rebels' resistance to tyranny had been replaced by a more strongly articulated desire that order and peace be restored to the Netherlands and to Christendom. His political works examined the mechanisms of state that founded strong powers, and the qualities that rulers must cultivate to secure effective government.[20]

Lipsius' major political treatise, the *Politicorum ... libri sex* (*Six Books of Politics*), first published in 1589, wove a dense series of quotations into a defence of the means of achieving strong princely rule: the prefatory material declared, unsurprisingly, that of the authors cited in the treatise 'Cornelius Tacitus stands out', being more full of useful material than any other writer.[21] In Lipsius' interpretation, Tacitus 'proves' with historical examples his own preference for powerful monarchy – 'the straight and princely path to stable Authority'.[22] Tacitus is cited as a sage who disavows the likely longevity of mixed monarchy (cf. *A.* 4.33.1) and approves that a prince handle the most weighty matters of state himself, 'lest he should weaken the force of

---

[20] Tuck (1993) 45–64; Oestreich (1982).
[21] 'Inter eos eminet CORN. TACITVS extra ordinem dicendus: quia plus unus ille nobis contulit, quam ceteri omnes' (Lipsius (1589) sig. [***4ʳ]).
[22] 'Viam primam vides: alteram tibi POTENTIAE ingredior, quae est illa ipsa directa & Regia ad solidam Auctoritatem via' (Lipsius (1589) 140–1).

Monarchy by referring all things to the Senate'. This particular citation is scrounged from Sallustius Crispus' advice to Livia at Tiberius' accession, as to how Tiberius ought to secure his power; Sallustius' advice is stained by his fear at the repercussions of his own complicity in the murder of Agrippa Postumus and it hardly represents Tacitus' own opinion.[23] For Lipsius, however, the phrase is typically decontextualised, plucked from the text and marshalled in support of his argument that rulers should bypass or undermine constitutional shackles on monarchical authority.

'Politics', in Lipsius' terminology, was the princely art of ruling the people, 'by nature fierce, wild, and impatient even of what is just', whose dangerous desire for liberty needed to be tamed and repressed for the common good.[24] Lipsius emphasises that prudence cannot be divorced from the exercise of traditional virtues, especially piety. However, the exercise of virtue itself is a political technique, establishing the goodly *reputation* necessary to maintain the love of a prince's subjects. Lipsius' authoritative prince would build the solid bases of his power, finance and military might, whilst not *appearing* to tax his subjects excessively. Augustus' and Agricola's methods of pacifying the Roman people and the Britons respectively with bread, circuses and the trappings of civility are approvingly cited to demonstrate that 'more violent' subjects, 'prone to war, are through pleasures accustomed to peace and ease'.[25] Tacitus' descriptions of the networks of spies and informers spun through imperial Rome were vilified as the instruments of tyranny by other Tacitean commentators: in Lipsius' estimation, they were necessary supports of princely governments, allowing rulers to snuff out sedition.[26] Lipsius' concept of princely 'prudence' concurred notoriously with that of Machiavelli, that the *utile* and *honestum* might conflict. In one of the most influential passages of the *Politicorum* Lipsius distinguished between different degrees of 'simulation' and 'dissimulation', admitting that for princes moderate amounts of deception were acceptable. Against detractors of 'an upright mind', who would object to the immorality of deception, Lipsius cites Tiberius' mastery of dissimulation as proof that moderate deception is an absolutely necessary aspect of princely prudence.[27]

---

[23] 'A te quidem, vt maxima rerum aut agas ipse, aut firmes: neu vim Principatus resolvas, cuncta ad Senatum revocando' (Lipsius (1589) 140); cf. *A.* 1.6.3.

[24] 'Naturâ nos feroces, indomiti, aequi impatientes' (Lipsius (1589) 73–4).

[25] 'Vsus enim aliquis in istâ re: cum ita ferociores populi, eoque bello faciles, quieti & otio per voluptates assuescunt' (Lipsius (1589) 132); see *A.* 1.2.1; *Agr.* 21.

[26] 'Ab illâ primum: quoniam omnino vtile habere te Speculatores quosdam sive Auricularios ... conari ne te lateat, quid quisque subditorum faciat aut dicat' (Lipsius (1589) 154–5).

[27] 'Displicebit hoc ingenuae alicui fronti, & clamabit: Ex omni vitâ Simulatio, Dissimulatioque tollenda est. De priuata, fateor: de publicâ, valde nego. Numquam regent, qui non tegent' (Lipsius (1589) 210).

Though Lipsius commends the methods of establishing strong government, he makes a sharp distinction between that and a tyrant, a ruler who subverts laws through the use of force for private and selfish ends, rather than for the common good. But he allows only princes the power to determine the needs of the 'common good', and even more strongly refutes the notion that subjects may resist tyrants actively: the tyranny of the multitude was far more deadly than the tyranny of one. Tacitus again provides Lipsius' justification of non-resistance: 'And how could my advice that we must bear [tyranny] not be more worthy of praise? That we must remember the times in which we were born, and pray to God to send us good Princes, and to tolerate them however they are.'[28] In Lipsius' handling, Tacitus' phrase becomes a hallowed injunction, repeated time and again in early modern commentaries on Tacitus. Again, however, Lipsius ignored the context of the phrase, which was plundered from a speech made by the slippery Eprius Marcellus as he defended his questionable integrity in a debate in the senate.

Unlike Guicciardini, Lipsius did not claim that tyrants could be 'prudent'. But his notion that politics largely encompassed an analysis of the prudence of the public conduct of rulers characterised a burgeoning literature on the 'art of the state', in which interpretation of Tacitus was central. In the late sixteenth century the increased popularity of Tacitus was directly proportional to the significance of the newly ubiquitous phrase 'reason of state'.[29] Guicciardini – early influence on the study of Tacitus – is also credited with coining the term *la ragione e uso degli stati* ('reason and profit of states').[30] It was common to the political lexicon by 1589, when Giovanni Botero (1544–1617) published his *Della Ragion di Stato*, his own interpretation of the phrase. A deluge of similar treatises followed, many of which took the form of commentaries on Tacitus.

Reason of state referred to the means used by rulers to secure and preserve existing governments – their own 'state', which was equated with the abstract notion of the commonwealth or polity. Commentators on reason of state tended not to concern themselves with the legitimacy of constitutional arrangements, choosing to explain rather than to justify the ways that princely authority might be elevated and enforced.[31] Reason of state was sometimes described as the special knowledge of statecraft or 'prudence' required for successful government; otherwise it referred to the circumvention of ethical or legal standards and processes by rulers in times of necessity,

---

[28] 'Quidni ergo laudabilius, nostrum Ferre? meminisse temporum, quibus nati sumus, & bonos Principes voto expetere, qualescumque tolerare' (Lipsius (1589) 365); cf. H. 4.8.2.
[29] See Burke (1990) 479–80.
[30] Viroli (1992) 194.
[31] But see Rubiés (1995).

for the security of the state. Tacitus' writings were deemed to be the richest treasury of *arcana imperii*: he was esteemed as *un grand Homme d'Estat*, a great man of 'state' or 'policy'.[32]

In the preface to his *Della Ragion di Stato* Botero denounced both Machiavelli and Tacitus as teaching a false reason of state, which allowed men to legitimise behaviour that clashed with Christian ethics.[33] But Botero's subsequent discussion of statecraft – the techniques of political manipulation and the fiscal and military foundations of a strong monarchy – bore strong similarities to that of Lipsius, and the text, too, was larded with quotation from Tacitus.

It was no coincidence that the earliest printed treatise to explore systematically the concept of reason of state was penned by an Italian. After the Treaty of Cateau-Cambrésis between France and Spain in 1559, Spanish hegemony in the Italian peninsula was maintained by alliances with Italian rulers, who in the subsequent years of peace intensively developed their own fiscal and military powers. Scipione Ammirato (1531–1601), a scholar from Lecce in southern Italy, who wielded his pen at the court of Grand Duke Cosimo I of Tuscany, most keenly appropriated Tacitus as the chief authority for an understanding of reason of state in a Christian world. Grand Duke Cosimo, allied to the Spanish Habsburgs, typically magnified his 'absolute' authority in his own principality: Ammirato's writings, like those of Lipsius, praised this amplification of the authority of the ruler and the state within a religious and conventionally ethical framework.

Ammirato's *Discorsi ... sopra Cornelio Tacito* (1594) was one of the most influential and widely read commentaries on Tacitus and reason of state in early modern Europe, reprinted eight times before 1619 and translated into Latin and French.[34] He sought to reclaim Tacitus as an ethical source of wisdom about reason of state, distanced from the irreligion of Machiavellianism. The very title of the work was a response to Machiavelli's *Discorsi sopra la prima deca di Tito Livio* (*Discourses on the first ten books of Livy*), making a deliberate contrast between Machiavelli's defunct, suspicious enthusiasm for republican government and Tacitus' legitimate and profoundly useful source of wisdom about monarchies. Ammirato's discourses are hung from Tacitean quotation, mostly extracted from the *Annals*. But, like Lipsius' *Politicorum*, Tacitean maxims awkwardly illustrate rather than illuminate Ammirato's text, the purpose of which is to demonstrate that Christian religion, virtue and princely rule are necessarily

---

[32] Melliet (1619) frontispiece; the work is a translation of Ammirato (1594).
[33] Botero (1589) xiii–xiv.
[34] De Mattei (1963).

compatible. It is significant that in a discourse concerned with *le vere regger i popoli*, the best means of governing the people, Ammirato lauds Agricola's government of the Britons (rather than the government of one of the emperors) through education and the fair administration of justice and taxes as the finest example of that art.[35]

Ammirato defined reason of state as the extraordinary means that a ruler might use to preserve the common good – *il publico beneficio*. For example, he insisted that it was legitimate to break human rather than divine or natural law in the case of severe threats to the state: Tiberius legitimately suspended due legal process when he executed Sejanus without trial.[36] But his understanding of the common good was unequivocally strong monarchical rule. Ammirato read Tacitus' description of the transformation of Rome's constitution under Augustus and Tiberius with admiration. The people's love of *libertà* was defined as a dangerous and brutal passion, sapped and repressed by Augustus' wise policies of building the institution of the Principate in a covert and sensitive way.[37]

Ammirato's and Lipsius' palatable application of Tacitean history to a reason of state for Christian princes shaped many other readings of Tacitus in the early seventeenth century, especially in France, Spain and Spanish Italy.[38] The darker tone of Guicciardini and his belief in man's basic self-interest and propensity for corruption, however, continued to be an important characteristic of Tacitean scholarship, as did Guicciardini's ambivalence about monarchy. Virgilio Malvezzi (1595–1653), a Bolognese scholar wrote a commentary also entitled *Discorsi sopra Tacito* (1635), which rekindled the qualities of an older Italian Tacitism. Malvezzi dedicated his treatise to another Tuscan Grand Duke, Ferdinand II de' Medici, but his treatise diverged from Ammirato's in significant ways.

The outlook of Malvezzi's *Discorsi* was altogether bleaker. The *sententiae* on which the discourses were based are taken from Books 1–6 of the *Annals*, and many deal with the traditional hobby horses of Tacitean commentaries – the achievement of political stability and the grubby behaviour of those who swarm round the nest of power. But Malvezzi also focused intensely on the opening paragraphs of *Annals* 1, the transition of the Roman state into the Principate, engaging closely both with the meaning of Tacitus' words and vocabulary and with Machiavelli's discussion of the rise and decay of republican states, the *Discorsi sopra … Tito Livio*. Augustus had been able to establish the 'rule of one' because of the people's preference for security

---

[35] Ammirato (1594) 540–2.
[36] Ammirato (1594) 239–40.
[37] Ammirato (1594) 300–5, 525–7.
[38] Tuck (1993) 65–119; Bireley (1990); Salmon (1980).

and luxury rather than 'courageous' liberty.[39] Unlike Ammirato, Malvezzi's concept of *libertà* is a desirable state of being, but one that is unattainable in the modern age. Malvezzi accepted the inevitability of monarchy in the contemporary and Roman worlds, but in far less positive terms: the decline of the republic was the result of *l'imperfettione de' Cittadini*, the imperfection of the citizens, who had fallen away from the virtue necessary to maintain states in strenuous liberty.[40] Malvezzi consciously invoked the terminology of humanist vocabulary to show its inoperability in the world of the monarchical state. Neither *la Libertà* nor *l'egualità*, equality, could exist in a state governed by one ruler.[41]

The darker spirit of Guicciardini's and Malvezzi's Tacitism was more brilliantly developed in the writings of Traiano Boccalini (1556–1613), the author of the most viciously entertaining writing about contemporary political culture, the *Ragguagli di Parnasso* (*News from Parnassus*). Many passages of the *Ragguagli* (the first parts of which were published in 1612–13) were drawn from Boccalini's own Tacitean commentary, *Commentarii sopra Cornelio Tacito*, which remained in manuscript until parts were printed in 1669. In Boccalini Tacitus found a student who combined an irony and cynicism that matched his own. The *Ragguagli di Parnasso* is written as a series of newsletters or advertisements from the court of Apollo on Mount Parnassus, where European writers of ancient and modern times gathered, jostling for pre-eminence. The new politics of reason of state is brilliantly satirised as the base commodity of a 'Society of Polititians', who sell their wares at a marketplace on the hillside, hawking not only spectacles that illuminate or distort the wearer's perception of virtue and vice but also pencils that sketch the vicious deeds of rulers as glorious triumphs. The Polititians' wares are the 'Stuffing, or Bombast', which serves to 'stuff up the Pack-Saddles of Slavery'.[42] Boccalini flatly correlated reason of state with the self-interest of rulers. When Apollo visits the prisons of literati he finds Scipione Ammirato, a 'Polititian', imprisoned for having redescribed the vices of tyrants as the policies of strong monarchs. Apollo is so disgusted with this dangerous example of redescription that he orders Ammirato to be thrown from the Tarpeian rock.[43]

Boccalini's admiration for Tacitus in the *Ragguagli* is double-edged, because of his critical hostility to those who read Tacitus not as the scourge

---

[39] 'Percioche è tanto gustosa la sicurezza, che il Popolo più tosto elege la servitù pur che sia sicuro, che esporsi a pericolo per la Libertà' (Malvezzi (1635) 90–1).
[40] Malvezzi (1635) 21.
[41] Malvezzi (1635) 93.
[42] Boccalini (1656) 1. The translation is that of Henry Carey, 2nd Earl of Monmouth.
[43] Boccalini (1656) 185–6.

of tyrants, but as an apologist for absolute monarchy. In a famous episode, Boccalini imagines that Tacitus himself puts into practice the methods of government exhibited by Augustus and Tiberius. Tacitus is chosen prince of Lesbos, a country with an elective monarchy. There are high expectations of his success, because most of the world is 'governed by the modern Princes, according to the rules of his Politicks'. Once Tacitus is established on Lesbos, however, he immediately and disastrously begins to seek 'absolute dominion'. He nourishes discord between nobles and commons, whilst posing as the friend of the people. He raises a party of partisans and a personal militia, and disarms his subjects with luxury and entertainments. Fortunately for the elective monarchy of Lesbos, Tacitus is ousted by a conspiracy and flees back to Parnassus, licking his wounds. Upbraided by Pliny the Younger for this tyrannical behaviour, Tacitus explains that, although he had condemned tyranny as a private citizen, once in power his 'wholsom resolutions' were 'so grub'd up and eradicated by the cursed power of Rule'.[44] The conceit operates on several levels. First, Boccalini fictionally puts into practice Tacitus' warning that power corrupts individuals, by making Tacitus illustrate his own admonition, a brilliant irony. Second, he illustrates the propensity of monarchs to suppress existing constitutional forms of government. In other words, monarchs who govern according to Tacitean reason of state do so absolutely and tyrannically.

As Boccalini implied, the association of Tacitus with 'reason of state' and the 'policy' of prudent princes hardly flattered the institution of monarchy. Tacitus' writings were perhaps some of the least obvious historical narratives to bolster confidence in princely government. In his tract on kingship, *The Trew Laws of Free Monarchies* (1598), James VI, king of Scotland and future king of England and Ireland (1566–1625), conventionally described kings as gods on earth. Tacitus showed that the deification of Roman emperors was a technique of political manipulation.

Other treatments of Tacitus focused more explicitly on Guicciardini's first observation about the utility of Tacitus: that Tacitus exposed the tyranny of rulers, and instructed the subjects of tyrants how they might accommodate themselves to tyranny. Resistance to tyranny was almost always condemned: the injunction that subjects could only pray for good emperors was cited repeatedly.

Without question, however, the passages from Tacitus that held the greatest fascination for contemporary Europeans were his brilliantly succinct, cyclical account of the mutation of the Roman state from monarchy to Republic to Principate and his summary of the reign of Augustus at the

[44] Boccalini (1656) 47–50.

very beginning of the *Annals* (1.1–10). No reader or commentator on these passages could ignore the language used in Tacitus' description of the transition of the people from the condition of *libertas* to *servitium*, from the freedom of the consulate established by Lucius Brutus to 'slavery' or 'bondage' under the Principate.[45] Malvezzi described the transition from republic to monarchy as an inevitable phenomenon, because the virtue of the Roman people had been corrupted. But he too picked over at length the first sentence of the *Annals*, and described the assassination of Tarquin by Lucius Brutus as a positive and glorious act for the then liberty of Rome, an act deemed legitimate because it was carried out with the consent of the Roman people in a state not yet settled into monarchy.[46]

Quentin Skinner has recently argued that translations of Roman history – of Sallust, Livy and Tacitus – in the Elizabethan and Jacobean periods sharpened awareness of the absolute distinction in Roman Law between freedom and slavery in early modern England. This awareness in turn exacerbated Englishmen's perception that the early Stuart monarchs, James I and Charles I, were eroding constitutional liberties in the years preceding the English civil war.[47] Certainly readers of Tacitus in early modern England do appear to have been particularly sensitised to Tacitus' account of the eradication of the virtue, senatorial privileges and legal norms of the Republic by Augustus and Tiberius, drawing parallels with their own experience. In England in particular Tacitus seems to have been interpreted in a way that was actively critical of contemporary monarchs.[48]

Constitutionalist thought in England, in particular the conception of England as a mixed monarchy, continued to be the dominant way of describing the polity in the Elizabethan and early Stuart periods, where there was no strong native equivalent of Continental 'reason of state' literature. Tacitism came to England in the late years of the reign of Elizabeth I (especially following Henry Savile's translation of the *Histories* and *Agricola* in 1591). When English attention was drawn to Tacitus during the final decade of Elizabeth's reign, there were several who made explicit parallels between the queen and Tiberius.[49] Robert Devereux (2nd earl of Essex) and his immediate circle, keen scholars of Tacitus, believed that the earl's estrangement from the queen represented Elizabeth's jealousy of Essex's virtue and her willingness to be led by evil counsel, characteristics of the fearful government of

---

[45] Skinner (2002) 316.
[46] Malvezzi (1635) 21–2.
[47] Skinner (2002) 308–43.
[48] See also comments by Burke (1990) 489–90.
[49] Smuts (1994).

weak tyrants. Essex's perception of Elizabeth's tyranny catalysed his rising in 1601, a pathetic failed coup.[50]

In the 1620s the language of Tacitus was aired in more public spaces. Sir John Eliot (1592–1632), who in parliament famously likened the duke of Buckingham, Charles I's unpopular favourite, to Sejanus, protested more significantly against what he perceived to be the infringement of parliamentary and constitutional privileges by Charles's government. Imprisoned in the Tower of London, Eliot wrote the *Monarchie of Man,* a large part of which is an account of the distinction between monarchy and tyranny. The former is defined as a government where monarch and 'Senate' govern together, in other words a mixed monarchy – the implication being that Charles's government increasingly resembled a tyranny. Eliot's discussion of government drew extensively on Tacitus.[51]

The most 'radical' use made of Tacitus in early modern England, however, was by the Dutch scholar, Isaac Dorislaus (1595–1649) in 1627, after his appointment to a lectureship in history at Cambridge. Dorislaus was commissioned to deliver a lecture series on Tacitus, which was closed down after he had delivered only two (the substance of which has to be discerned from a series of excerpts rather than a full text). Malvezzi had praised the killing of Tarquin by Lucius Brutus as a virtuous act in a free state – but he denied the legitimacy of a similar deed in the context of the Principate, or any settled monarchy. Dorislaus' meditations on Tacitus considered more deeply the foundations of the power of the Roman Republic and Principate, and drew daring parallels with politics in the contemporary world. Dorislaus insisted that the Roman monarchy, and therefore the Principate also, was from its foundation a mixed monarchy, where sovereignty had resided with the people. Even in the era of the Principate the people's sovereignty had not been annulled, because they had never officially conferred the powers wielded by the emperors, who therefore ruled as usurpers rather than legitimate, absolute monarchs. Dorislaus also argued that in a mixed monarchy the chief magistrates and representative institutions might lawfully resist rulers who attempted to undermine their own constitutional powers.[52] Charles's government's fear of this radical Tacitism was realised in 1649, when Dorislaus was appointed to the counsel for the prosecution at the king's trial, drawing up the charge of high treason which sentenced Charles to death.[53]

[50] Worden (2006).
[51] Eliot (1879) 1–80; Skinner (2002) 321–2.
[52] National Register of Archives, London: State Papers 16/86/87 I; a translation can be found in Mellor (1995) 118–21; also see Todd (2003).
[53] Todd (2004).

Despite the direct relationship between scholarship and action in Dorislaus' radical example, by 1650 the influence of Tacitus on the major direction of political thought was in decline. The late humanist fascination with the 'art of the state' was superseded by political philosophy, which sought – through reason rather than the patterns of history – to elucidate the natural laws that governed the origins of political societies. Natural law theorists, however, such as Hugo Grotius (1588–1679) and Thomas Hobbes (1588–1645), owed much to the legacy of the Tacitists.[54] Tacitean scholarship had questioned the certain existence of absolute ethical and political values. This emphasis on moral relativity stimulated attempts to define the minimal natural laws governing the interaction of individuals and their collective formation into states. By the mid-seventeenth century, Tacitus had an unshakeable place in the historical and literary canon. The imperial Rome of Tacitus would maintain its fascination for the political imagination of men and women in the Enlightenment and beyond.

FURTHER READING

The influence of Tacitus in early modern Europe has an enormous bibliography, covering reception in many European nations which for reasons of space are not treated in this chapter. The best recent general discussion of the deep impact of Tacitus on early modern European political thought is the masterly discussion by Tuck (1993). A useful starting place, with much material relating to editions and commentaries, is also Burke (1969). For general introductions to reason of state literature in the early modern period see De Mattei (1979) and Bireley (1990).

---

[54] The authorship by Hobbes of a Tacitean discourse published anonymously in 1620 is still disputed: Malcolm (2004).

18

PAUL CARTLEDGE

Gibbon and Tacitus

Edward Gibbon (1737–94) is today not often read as a 'colleague' by professional historians of Roman or Byzantine history. He is read rather, if at all, as a 'classic' of English literature, of which he is unquestionably an ornament. His luminous and eminently parodiable style has not pleased all his readers equally, however.[1] But its intricate subtleties demonstrate time and again the truth both of Buffon's adage that 'le style c'est l'homme même'[2] and of A.D. Momigliano's mantra that a history – *any* history – cannot be understood apart from the historian who composed it.[3] Gibbon was besides an outstanding Latinist, and did not merely parade but made consistently excellent practical use of his 'seraglio' (his personal library) of 6,000–7,000 volumes.[4] Though judged weak in source-criticism by the highest contemporary standards applied at Göttingen,[5] Gibbon more than justifies the place he claimed – with David Hume (for some others, the first truly modern historian) and William Robertson – among the triumvirate of leading English-language historians of the second half of the eighteenth century.[6]

The present essay is heavily indebted to my three previous Gibbonian forays (Cartledge (1977), (1989) and (1995)), and economises on space (but not, it is hoped, truth) by not citing anything like all the ancient and modern documentation given there. Yet rather to my surprise I have found myself altering at least the emphases and nuances of those earlier papers, as I re-read them and Gibbon in the light of later research.

[1] The hugely wealthy William Beckford – of Fonthill Abbey fame (or infamy) – acquired a good chunk of Gibbon's personal library, but was far from being a fan of his work, and notoriously squeamish in his disapproval of Gibbon's style (Keynes (1980)).
[2] Or, as Gibbon rephrased it in his *Autobiography*, 'the image of character' (p. 1). (This and subsequent references to the *Autobiography* are to the 1966 edition by Bonnard (see below, p. 278).) See further below on Gibbon's own style – or styles.
[3] Momigliano (1994) offers an excellent sampling of that scholar's extraordinary oeuvre.
[4] 'Seraglio': *Autobiography* 183; for the library see Keynes (1980). Bowersock (1977) 29 rightly speaks of Gibbon's 'bookish temperament'.
[5] Butterfield (1955) ch. 1.
[6] *Autobiography* 98–9.

The subject of this chapter is Gibbon's 'Tacitism'. The quotation marks are necessary, since Tacitism (without them) is a technical term for early modernists, referring to the (especially seventeenth-century) European conception and reception of Tacitus as a master of *raison d'état*, the politician's wise adviser, in short a Machiavelli-substitute. As such, he was found particularly useful at times and in places where the Florentine himself was listed on the prohibited Vatican Index, and scholars thought it prudent not to risk the fate of expurgation – or worse. The rediscovery of Tacitus in the Renaissance had come relatively late. But, once humanists had rediscovered him, they and their 'antiquarian' or 'erudite' successors were in thrall to what was considered Tacitus' unique capacity to penetrate the innermost recesses of human motivation, and they ransacked Tacitus' writings for quotable *sententiae* (epigrams, maxims) to adorn a moral or point a tale. For our purposes here, however, 'Tacitism' denotes the peculiar admiration and empathy that Gibbon displayed, even to the point of self-identification, for one of his own earliest masters of thought. That part of my argument is perhaps relatively straightforward and uncontroversial, but I wish also to suggest that in crucial ways it was Gibbon's reading and reception of Tacitus that crucially helped make him the sort of historian he became, that is, a Gibbonian as well as a 'Tacitist', as it were.

Enlightenment in Lausanne

Gibbon's education, for health reasons among others, was largely autodidactic. The despised monks of Magdalen College, Oxford, did him no lasting damage, perhaps, but it was an imposed exile in Lausanne (1753–8) that formed him as a scholar, writer and, above all, historian. This was the foundation of all his future improvements, as he himself later reflected: 'Such as I am in Genius or learning or in manners, I owe my creation to Lausanne.'[7] Retrospectively, and with typical self-deprecation, he also allotted a considerable formative role to his modest experience as a captain in the Hampshire militia during the Seven Years War.[8] In his contemporary journal for 26 July 1761, however, written in camp at Winchester, he had mused, more revealingly: 'Am I worthy of pursuing a walk of literature, which Tacitus thought worthy of him?'

That same year Gibbon did nevertheless publish his own first work, begun at Lausanne and also completed originally in French: an *Essai* on the critical study of literature, on how literature, including then historical literature

---

[7] *Autobiography* 86; cf. 209–10.
[8] *Autobiography* 117.

(not yet separated from *belles lettres*), should be written. Also, arguably, the *Essai* was intended as a late blow in the battle between the Ancients and the Moderns, struck decisively in favour of the former, and especially of Tacitus. For it is here that Gibbon adumbrates his ideal of the 'philosophic historian', or historian as philosopher in the enlarged non-technical sense, although he does so in a characteristically esoteric, if not idiosyncratic, way. While allying himself with the French *philosophes* – thinkers such as Montesquieu and Voltaire – against the dry-as-dust antiquarian pedants whom they dismissed as mere *érudits* (something like 'stamp-collectors' or 'train-spotters'), Gibbon yet claimed to have found the perfect instantiation of his philosophic ideal not in a Modern but in an Ancient writer: 'je ne connois que Tacite qui ait rempli mon idée de cet historien philosophe' (ch. 52).

Erudition and philosophy

The sources of this youthful admiration were various, both erudite and philosophical. He seems to have felt almost a spiritual kinship with some of the humanist Tacitists of a bygone age, such as the Dutch founder of Tacitism himself, Joost Lips (Justus Lipsius), who in the 1570s had produced famously scholarly editions of the master's works and specifically praised Tacitus for his acuity in unmasking hidden causes.[9] Moreover, it was no obstacle whatsoever that Montesquieu, by whom Gibbon's thought and historiography were very deeply influenced from early on, was himself suffused with Tacitus' ideas,[10] or that another leading *philosophe* for whom Gibbon evinced extreme admiration, the Scot David Hume, had written in his *Enquiry Concerning Human Understanding* (1748) that Tacitus was 'the greatest and most penetrating genius perhaps of all antiquity'.[11]

Gibbon's 'Damascus Road' experience in the Roman Forum on the Ides of October 1764 (as he retrospectively viewed it, at any rate) at last afforded him the opportunity to give his special brand of 'Tacitism' its head. He constantly read and re-read Tacitus (he was never to devote as much attention to, or attain as great fluency in reading, his Greek sources), and this devotion played a major role in forming his mature conception and treatment, from 1768 on, of what was to become the six-volume *Decline and Fall* (published between 1776 and 1788). From one standpoint, it may be thought rather

---

[9] For Lipsius' editions of Tacitus see above, pp. 249–51; more generally cf. Morford (1993).
[10] Volpilhac-Auger (1985). For a recent discussion of Tacitus and Montesquieu see Hammer (2008) 132–79; also below, pp. 289–90.
[11] In his essay 'Of miracles', repr. from his *Enquiry Concerning Human Understanding* (1748); cf. Cartledge (1995) 270 n. 64.

diminishing of Gibbon's achievement to label the first thirty-eight chapters (volumes I-III) 'a splendid elaboration of Tacitus', since there is so much more to them than that.[12] From another standpoint, however, that label does arguably capture the essence of the matter.

Indeed, this is one of those rare cases where I believe a hypothesis about a writer's intellectual proclivities and emotional state is capable of demonstrative proof. Probably in the winter of 1790/1, when Gibbon was reeling under the impact of the hated French Revolution and seeking solace, Livy-like, in the comforting distance of Antiquity,[13] he added several substantial marginalia to a printed text in his possession of the six-volume quarto edition of the *Decline and Fall*. The first of these, and the most relevant for my purposes, runs as follows (orthography original):

> Should I not have given the history of that fortunate period which was interposed between two Iron ages? Should I not have deduced the decline of the Empire from the civil Wars, that ensued after the fall of Nero or even from the tyranny which succeeded the reign of Augustus? Alas! I should: but of what avail is this tardy knowledge? Where error is irretrievable, repentance is useless.[14]

This is an object lesson in civil prudence, no doubt, but also more relevantly in historiography. By 'that fortunate period' Gibbon meant the so-called Antonine age (96–180) during which – in his neat inversion of a judgement passed on another age by another of his mentors, William Robertson – 'the condition of the human race was most happy and prosperous', and of which his beloved Tacitus was a conspicuous ornament.[15] And the error he was confessing was that of not having (as it were) re-done Tacitus' *Histories* (which commenced in 69, after Nero's suicide in 68) and *Annals* (the narrative of which commences in 14, the year of Augustus' decease). For, had he done so, he could have developed and corroborated his underlying explanatory thesis – itself derived from a reading of Tacitus – as to the original sources of the Roman Empire's 'Decline'. Why, then, had he not?

I suggest that here his commitment to the ideals of 'erudition' got the better of his 'philosophy', or rather that it was precisely because Tacitus had already so far 'fulfilled this ideal of the philosophic historian' that he did

---

[12] Jordan (1971) 177. This is a key element indeed of the unresolved debate over whether and how far Gibbon was an 'ancient' as opposed to a 'modern' historian, to which we shall return in the Conclusion.

[13] For Gibbon on the French Revolution see Cartledge (1977) 77–8. For Livy's attitude to historiography as solace see his preface (*praef.* 5); note also 43.13.2.

[14] Quoted in Craddock (1972) 338; cf. Cartledge (1995) 266 n. 20.

[15] The Robertson passage ('most calamitous and afflicted') is from his *History of the Emperor Charles V* (London 1769) vol. I, 10; cf. Bowersock (1977) 35 n. 54.

not think to improve upon his model's own works (incompletely preserved though they were). For Gibbon, not only Tacitus' matter but also his manner did not allow of direct imitation, let alone emulation. The events and processes that Tacitus had chosen to record had been already interpreted, by him, most satisfactorily. It followed from those calculations that Gibbon more or less had to start his detailed narrative after 70 (where the extant *Histories* breaks off). In practice, although he treated the first two centuries of the Principate in his systematic third chapter, he began the consecutive narrative very much later, after the death of Marcus Aurelius. This was partly no doubt because it would have been awkward to accommodate the happy Antonine age to a schema of continuous post-Augustan 'decline', but partly also, I suggest, to distance himself from any invidious or odious comparison with his historiographical exemplar. Besides, if one follows Ronald Syme, that *recusatio* had a most compelling precedent – that of Tacitus himself, who had claimed that he would in time memorialise the age of Augustus (pre-14) if he should only live long enough to do so.[16]

This point about Gibbon's privately self-confessed debt to the old Roman historian has been noticed also by the ancient historian and historiographical connoisseur Glen Bowersock, who indeed on that very basis has dubbed Tacitus 'Gibbon's great evil genius'.[17] More neutrally and cautiously, another distinguished ancient historiographer has written, too tentatively I believe, that 'perhaps the historian who influenced [Gibbon] most was Tacitus'.[18] The issue, however, is not only or so much the amount, but also and rather the duration, of Tacitus' hold over Gibbon. This, therefore, is an element – and not an inconsiderable one – in the debate over whether Gibbon's historiography in general changed markedly and significantly over the course of the six volumes of the *Decline and Fall*.

Some Gibbon specialists have detected just such a change in Gibbon's historiographical outlook and manner.[19] Others, with (to me) greater persuasiveness, have argued that Gibbon remained the historian he established himself as in the first, separately issued, volume of 1776. For example, an amateur contemporary reader, Mme Suzanne Necker (*née* Curchod), who was also an old flame of Gibbon's from his Lausanne days, appears to me to have got it just right. In the first volume, she wrote to the author, Tacitus seemed to her to have been Gibbon's 'model and perhaps the source of your

---

[16] *A*. 3.24.3; cf. e.g. Syme (1958a) 367–71; also below, p. 326.
[17] Bowersock (1977) 31.
[18] Evans (1973) 252.
[19] Womersley (1988) to the fore. His chapter 6 (pp. 80–8) acutely explores Gibbon's – for Womersley, ambiguous – relationship to Tacitus. Against any significant change, see Cartledge (1995) 146–7 n. 43.

work'; yet already that putative source had been 'enlarged by the torrents of thought of all the ages'.[20] To demonstrate the truth of the first half of that two-fold claim with respect to the whole of the *Decline and Fall* will be the task of the remainder of this chapter, though illustration and quotation will necessarily be selective. I shall consider in turn the following: Gibbon's expressed objectives, his theme and subject matter, his style and his (other than stylistic) interpretations.

Objectives

The notorious concluding fifteenth and sixteenth chapters of the first quarto volume laid Gibbon open to accusations of 'infidelity', in other words, what would today be called irreligion or more bluntly atheism. Gibbon chose to respond not in the religious terms of his critics, but on secular intellectual grounds, vindicating his good faith as a historian rather than his subscription to any articles of religious dogma.[21] The historian, he asserted programmatically, 'owes to himself, to the present age, and to posterity, a just and perfect delineation of all that may be praised, of all that may be excused, and of all that must be censured'. The tricolon is typically Gibbonian, but the sentiment virtually reproduces Tacitus' own programmatic statement of *Annals* 3.65.1.[22] This does not necessarily mean that Gibbon agreed with Tacitus that history's chief office was to teach lessons of moral philosophy through historical examples, and he seems to have been quite sceptical of the extent to which 'mankind' could learn from history. Yet, if there was a single guiding ideological thread to his work, it was his commitment to liberty in all its guises, religious, intellectual, political or economic. Of course, the 'firm friend to civil and ecclesiastical freedom' did not imperatively need to look to Tacitus to discover this commitment in the first place, but Tacitus' preoccupation with *libertas* will have been at the very least utterly congenial to him.[23]

Theme and subject matter

Again, Gibbon did not need to look to Tacitus for the choice of his major theme. The decline and fall of Rome specifically had become almost a trite

---

[20] See Cartledge (1995) 255 and n. 23.
[21] Cartledge (1995); for the critics, cf. Womersley (1997b).
[22] Interpretations of this key Tacitean passage (e.g. Syme (1958a) 520 and n. 3) differ quite sharply; for a critical survey of them, and a heterodox reading of his own (as apologia for the content of the surrounding narrative), see Woodman (1995) = (1998) 86–103.
[23] *Vindication* 1158 in Womersley (1994); cf. Cartledge (1995) 260–1 n. 58. See Syme (1977) = (1984) 962–8.

topic since the fifteenth-century treatment by Flavio Biondo, and it had been addressed much more recently by Montesquieu himself.[24] Moreover, Gibbon's approach was genuinely universalist, integrating subjects other than war, politics and diplomacy, especially of course religion, into his overall framework of narration and explanation. One of the most striking instances of this integrative approach is the famous fiftieth chapter, devoted to the rise of Islam, which marks a pivotal moment in the mechanics of the work as a whole:

> The genius of the Arabian prophet, the manners of his nation, and the spirit of his religion, involve the causes of the decline and fall of the eastern [Roman] empire; and our eyes are intent on one of the most memorable revolutions, which have impressed a new and lasting character on the nations of the globe.

Yet we note that, for all that Gibbon is writing avowedly global history, employing the most up-to-date conceptual tools of Voltaire ('manners') and Montesquieu ('spirit') to do so, still he is also preoccupied – no less than Tacitus would have been – with the 'genius' of Muhammad.[25]

Style

In one major respect Gibbon's famous style was radically un- or even anti-Tacitean: for both objective and idiosyncratic reasons alike, Gibbon opted for Ciceronian amplitude over Tacitean laconic brevity.[26] Moreover, although the famous Gibbonian irony might be thought to bear a Tacitean stamp, actually Gibbon himself ascribed it explicitly to his reading of Pascal's *Lettres provinciales*.[27] There are, however, several other points of contact, of varying degrees of centrality. 'Amrou divulged the dangerous secret, that the Arabian caliphs might be created elsewhere than in the city of the prophet' knowingly echoes Tacitus' famous *arcanum imperii*,[28] while the

---

[24] Bibliography in Cartledge (1989) 268 n. 38. Montesquieu's *Considérations sur les causes de la grandeur des Romains, et de leur décadence* appeared in 1734 (Cartledge (1989) 257 and n. 40).

[25] Voltaire, *Essai sur les moeurs* (1756); cf. Cartledge (1989) 268 n. 44. Montesquieu, *De l'esprit des lois* (1748); cf. Cartledge (1977) 80 and nn. 62–4. 'Genius' could be applied by Gibbon to an 'age' as well as an individual, as, for instance, in his judgement that Montesquieu's 'energy of style, and boldness of hypothesis, were powerful to awaken and stimulate the Genius of the age' (*Autobiography* 78).

[26] Cartledge (1989) 256–7.

[27] *Autobiography* 79. Note also that Schmal (2005) 10 views Tacitus' character and outlook as 'sceptical, mistrustful, and strongly misanthropic'; this last at least Gibbon could not possibly be accused of being.

[28] *Decline and Fall*, ch. 4; cf. Tac. *H.* 1.4.2.

characteristically Tacitean devices of elevation combined with bathos, and the 'loaded' or 'weighted' alternative, are consciously deployed by Gibbon to Tacitean effect.[29] There is even a case for claiming that Gibbon's 'whole intellectual style' was owed to Tacitus, besides remarking the more specific debts.[30]

Interpretations

Gibbon's style has been studied perhaps even more assiduously than his content and interpretations. But that disjunction may mislead. For his style was not a mere varnish overlaid upon his interpretation. It was in and of itself a means of interpretation, and vitally so. For it was the appropriate weapon of a 'philosophic historian', that paragon and ideal of which Tacitus was for the young Gibbon the sole exemplar, and it remained for the later Gibbon a pre-eminent one, alongside Hume and Robertson. Gibbon's interpretation of his 'awful revolution' outstripped in comprehensiveness the causal thinking of Tacitus, who in any case could not have provided a direct model for explaining Gibbon's 'fall'. Yet, as in the case of Muhammad above, in some key respects Gibbon never advanced beyond the sort of crude causal thinking contained in the 'General Observations' appended to volume III (published in 1781, but mainly composed perhaps as early as 1772).[31] Thus, of Septimius Severus, Gibbon could confidently write that 'Posterity ... justly considered him as the principal author of the decline of the Roman empire'.[32] Likewise, his constant search for the one big all-encompassing explanation was at best reductionist, at worst naive.

But if causality on the broadest historical scale was not Gibbon's strongest suit, that throws into even greater relief the other elements of Tacitus' 'philosophy' that Gibbon gratefully acknowledged as his legacy. These would have included at least Tacitus' self-proclaimed (if dubiously grounded) freedom from exclusive and prescriptive political allegiance or any other angry attachments,[33] his obedience to the 'cool dictates of reason',[34] and his discernment of the hidden motivations underlying the superficial froth of

---

[29] Cartledge (1989) 256 and n. 29.
[30] Gay (1966) 157; cf. Gay (1974) 26; Cartledge (1977) 85.
[31] Ghosh (1983), (1991).
[32] *Decline and Fall*, ch. 5.
[33] Tacitus' *sine ira et studio* manifesto – on which see sceptically Syme (1958a) 204, 420 and n. 1 – was appropriated by Gibbon, declaring himself 'attached to no party, interested only for the truth and candour of history' (*Decline and Fall*, ch. 44).
[34] *Decline and Fall*, ch. 52.

propaganda and seemingly disconnected episodes. 'Few observers', Gibbon slyly observed, 'possess a clear and comprehensive view of the revolutions of society'[35] – few, that is, besides himself, and Tacitus.[36]

Conclusion

In short, Gibbon remained – very largely – the devoted but not slavishly devoted follower of Tacitus that he had proclaimed himself to be in his maiden publication of 1761, ever alert to the hypocrisies and deceits of public, especially imperial, power. Yet Gibbon's Tacitean allegiance, his 'Tacitism', should not in my view reduce Gibbon to being seen merely as an 'ancient' historian: that is, as a historian who, though living and writing in the second half of the eighteenth century, could, as it were, have been writing in the early part of the second. Rather – even leaving on one side Benedetto Croce's surely correct insight that all historiography is in some sense and to some degree contemporary historiography[37] – Gibbon's skilful grafting of sociological, intellectual, religious, social and economic history on to the traditional stock of political-military-diplomatic narrative and interpretation, together with his unusual (if not indeed unique) combination of the erudition of the Renaissance humanists with the broadly sociological interpretative frameworks advocated by Montesquieu and his other eighteenth-century followers such as Adam Ferguson, make Gibbon a historian of his own, enlightened age – and still, therefore, of our own age too.[38]

GIBBON'S WORKS

I have cited and/or consulted the works of Gibbon (listed in chronological order of original composition or publication) in the following editions:

The English Essays of Edward Gibbon, ed. P.B. Craddock (Oxford 1972)
Essai sur l'étude de la littérature (1761; English trans. 1764); repr. with intro. by J.V. Price (London 1994)

---

[35] In full: 'There are few observers, who possess a clear and comprehensive view of the revolutions of society; and who are capable of discovering the nice and secret springs of action, which impel, in the same uniform direction, the blind and capricious passions of a multitude of individuals' (*Decline and Fall*, ch. 27, in a section labelled 'Corruption of the times', sc. of Theodosius I).
[36] Cartledge (1995) 259 and n. 47.
[37] Momigliano (1961b) = (1966) 40–55.
[38] Momigliano (1954) = (1966) 221–38.

GIBBON'S JOURNALS

Gibbon's Journal to January 28th, 1763, ed. D.M. Low (London 1929)

'Journal de mon voyage dans quelques endroits de la Suisse' and 'Le séjour de Gibbon à Paris du 28 janvier au 9 mai 1763', in *Miscellanea Gibboniana*, ed. G. de Beer, G.A. Bonnard and L. Junod (Lausanne 1952)

Le Journal de Gibbon à Lausanne, 17 août 1763 – 19 avril 1764, ed. G.A. Bonnard (Lausanne 1945)

Gibbon's Journey from Geneva to Rome: His Journal from 20 April to 2 October 1764, ed. G.A. Bonnard (London 1961)

The History of the Decline and Fall of the Roman Empire, 6 vols. (London 1776–88); ed. D. Womersley, 3 vols. (London 1994) (=Womersley (1994))

A Vindication of Some Passages in the Fifteenth and Sixteenth Chapters of the History of the Decline and Fall of the Roman Empire (London 1779), reprinted in its revised and enlarged version in Womersley (1994) (vol. 3, Appendix 3, 1106–84)

The Miscellaneous Works of Edward Gibbon, Esq. with Memoirs of His Life and Writings, Composed by Himself: Illustrated from His Letters, with Occasional Notes and Narrative, by the Right Honourable John, Lord Sheffield, 5 vols. (London 1814); first publ. 3 vols. (London 1796)

The Autobiographies of Edward Gibbon, ed. John Murray (London 1896)

Memoirs of My Life, ed. G.A. Bonnard (London 1966); ed. with intro. by B. Radice (Harmondsworth 1984)

Memoirs of My Life and Writings, ed. A.O.J. Cockshut and S. Constantine (Keele 1994)

The Letters of Edward Gibbon, ed. J.E. Norton, 3 vols. (London 1956)

I have also found indispensable J.E. Norton, *A Bibliography of the Works of Edward Gibbon* (Oxford 1940; repr. Port Talbot 1970)

FURTHER READING

In the last two decades English-language Gibbonian studies have been advanced principally by David Womersley, now Warton Professor of English at Oxford University: Womersley (1994) is now the standard edition of the *Decline and Fall*, invaluable also for its indexes and for reprinting the *Vindication*; see also Womersley (1988). On Gibbon's life and writings, see Craddock (1982) and (1989), as well as her edition (above) of the *English Essays* (1972). For an attempt to reconstruct his library, see Keynes (1980). On the genesis of the *Decline and Fall*, particularly the place therein of the 'General Observations', see Ghosh (1983) and (1991). On his historiography generally, I have learned most from Momigliano (1994) and Bowersock (1977). See also Bowersock *et al.* (1977); Womersley (1997a). On his style see Bond (1960) and Gay (1974). Further recent bibliography is helpfully collected in Nippel (2003).

On Tacitus' *Nachleben* generally, from antiquity to the twentieth century, see Mellor (1995); cf. Benario (2004–5) 325–31. On humanist Tacitism see Antón Martínez (1992), Burke (1969), Cartledge (1995), Malcolm (2007), Rubiés (1994),

Schellhase (1976), Skovgaard-Petersen (1995) and Syme (1960) = (1979) 470–6. On Tacitus in the (especially French) Enlightenment, Volpilhac-Auger (1993). On the Enlightenment as such, Pocock (1999–2003). On Tacitus' *praecipuum munus*, Woodman (1995) = (1998) 86–103; on his historiography generally, Clarke (2002); cf. Benario (2004–5) 285–323.

19

C. B. KREBS

A dangerous book: the reception of the *Germania*

> But a German may drink beer; indeed, he should drink it as a true son of *Germania*, since Tacitus mentions specifically German *cerevisia*.
> (Heinrich Heine, *Über Ludwig Börne. Eine Denkschrift.* 1840)

The *Germania* was praised as a *libellus aureus* ('golden booklet') upon its rediscovery in the fifteenth century. Following centuries saw it compared to the 'dawn' of German history, a gift of a 'benign fairy' and 'a bible'. After the collapse of the National Socialist (NS) regime, however, from the vantage of hindsight, Arnaldo Momigliano gave it high priority among 'the hundred most dangerous books ever written', and added that it was 'fortunately' not his task to speak about its influence.[1]

The influence of Tacitus' *Germania* spans 450 years, starting with German humanists in the sixteenth century and ending with the NS downfall in 1945. Germany as a nation-state began to exist with the declaration of the German Empire in 1871. Before then, in the absence of political unity, a common past, culture and language were called upon to substantiate the German nation. But such a cultural nation has proved elusive too: the people within the Holy Roman Empire of the German Nation[2] lived mostly in their communities with their regional traditions and local dialects and quite unaware of 'Germany'. 'What is German history?' is therefore a difficult question.[3] Yet ever since the days of humanism north of the Alps there were writers who spoke of themselves as Germans and their *patria* as Germany. It thus existed in a paradoxical state of anticipation for centuries

---

[1] Momigliano (1966) 112–13. 'libellus aureus' occurs for the first time in the title of the *editio princeps* (Bologna 1472). The comparisons are those of J. Grimm, E. Norden and R. Benze.

[2] The *Heiliges Römisches Reich Deutscher Nation* originated in the wake of the rule of Charlemagne and had the German 'nation' as its centre (while comprising various and varying substates from the Netherlands to the northern parts of Italy); it was officially dissolved during the Napoleonic Wars.

[3] See Sheehan (1981) for this question.

A dangerous book

before its realisation; Ernst Moritz Arndt expressed this paradox in the early nineteenth century: 'German people? What are you, and where are you? I seek and cannot find you.'[4] The *Germania* time and again provided a normative answer to this question (a fact that drew Heinrich Heine's sarcasm, as quoted above). This use of Tacitus' text also accounts for its twofold significance for the NS discourse: a 'magnificent monument', 'a particular stroke of luck',[5] it inspired NS writers; and, more importantly, it contributed to the formation of those traditions that would ultimately fuse and culminate in NS ideology. The *Germania* fitted the frame it had helped to form: Hans Friedrich Karl Günther, the NS 'expert' on race, could cite G. 4 affirmatively, as it had figured within the European race discourse right from its beginnings.

After early inconsequential receptions prior to its rediscovery, the *Germania* served as the foundational text for German humanists, who formed 'Germany' as an 'imagined community', actively 'inventing traditions' set in the Germanic past.[6] Subsequent generations followed their lead, their modifications owed mainly to specificities of contemporary discourses, such as racist interpretations in the nineteenth and twentieth centuries. The paradigmatic role of the Germanic past, however, remained mostly unchanged and unquestioned: the 'Germanic revolution' that National Socialists demanded was conceived of as a 'homecoming' to former shores.[7] For them, as well as for generations of Germanophiles before them, Tacitus was the involuntary helmsman.

Early inconsequential receptions

The circle of Tacitus' readers in late antiquity and the Middle Ages was limited, and traces of the *Germania* are few, though sweeping statements about dead silence seem exaggerated and affected by preconceptions.[8] In addition to explicit references, traces of one *opus minus* may indicate the presence of the others, since it is likely that the *opera minora* were transmitted in one manuscript (especially in the Middle Ages).

The most extensive use of the *Germania* appears in the ninth century in Fulda, near to which, in Hersfeld, the only extant codex would be

---

[4] See Petersen and Ruth (1934) 62.
[5] See *Der Schulungsbrief* 2 (1935) 169; *NS Bildungswesen* 1 (1936) 41. Translations are my own.
[6] See Anderson (1991), esp. ch. 2–3; Hobsbawm (1992) 6–7, 13–14.
[7] See *NS Bildungswesen* 1 (1936) 38.
[8] For the most comprehensive overview, see Perl (1990) 50–6; in addition, for reminiscences in Ambrosius, Eccehard and Widukind of Corvey, see Jacobi (1993); Mertens (2004) 46.

rediscovered in the *Quattrocento*.⁹ Rudolf of Fulda in his part of the *Translatio S. Alexandri*¹⁰ describes the Saxons, whose past is rendered with the help of the *Germania* (esp. 4, 9 and 10). What Tacitus, who is unnamed,¹¹ says there about the contemporary *Germani* is here in long literal quotations simply transferred to the *gens Saxonum*: noble heathen, who were freed of their dark errors (*a quantis errorum tenebris*) by the grace of God; who had come from Britain (*gens ... ab Anglis Britanniae incolis egressa*) and then tried to turn themselves into 'a people resembling only itself' (*tantum sui similis gens*), a characteristic which the author considers positive. Although the Saxons are said to belong to those people who live in a territory the author calls 'Germania' (*Germaniam incolentes nationes*), there is no mention of *Germani* and apparently no notion of them as a cohesive ethnic group. The regional and 'tribal' specificity of this adaptation differs from those in the fifteenth century and caused no repercussions; for that, very different circumstances were needed.

The rediscovery of the *Germania* and the discovery of the *Germanen*

Four factors were particularly conducive to the ideological impact of the *Germania* in the sixteenth century: the Holy Roman Empire of the German Nation was losing its centripetal force, and the notion of a German nation correspondingly became more appealing and integrative. This emerging national consciousness rose further in the confrontation between German electors and the Curia in Rome as well as German and Italian humanists – the former all too aware of their *barbara tellus*, the latter scornful of it.¹² Finally, a classical text of unquestionable authority to humanistic eyes, the *Germania* fulfilled deep desires: the obstinate German search for a national identity in its own right found a past characterised by specific values very different from Roman ones, a past that in present times of instability offered a stable foundation for nation-building. The rediscovery of the *Germania* is tantamount to the discovery of the *Germanen* as the Germans' forefathers.¹³

This first significant phase of reception and adaptation determined the parameters for usages to come: it set the categories that would inform future

⁹ See above, pp. 245–7.
¹⁰ Meginhart wrote the latter part. Quotations (§§1–3) are from the reproduction of Krusch (1933) 423–36.
¹¹ Thus authors copying Rudolf unwittingly passed on Tacitus (see Mertens (2004) 46).
¹² For these issues, see Krebs (2005) 112–16.
¹³ See Joachimsen (1970a) 282 and Muhlack (1989) 138.

reflections on the past; posed the ethnic continuity – from now on mostly unquestioned – between the *Germanen* and the Germans; extrapolated the *Germania*'s implicit antithesis; and finally established the German(ic) virtues, their autochthony and ethnic purity. However, in striving for cultural independence German humanists depended on Italian stimulation.[14]

Italian intermediation, provocation and fiction

Although the *Germania* would become a predominantly German affair, Italian intermediation was needed to initiate the reception. At the beginning stood the cardinal and later pope Enea Silvio Piccolomini (1405–64), who in 1457 received a letter in which he was warned of widespread dissatisfaction with curial politics (the *gravamina*) amongst the Germans: they felt pressed for money just as if they were barbarians (*tamquam ... barbaris*), and their country, once so powerful, was now brought low.[15] In response Piccolomini produced an epistolary treatise in three volumes, in which he refuted the charges, lauded curial politics and presented himself as a suitable candidate for the papacy. In the second volume he demonstrated how much, contrary to the German impression, Germany had changed for the better owing to the civilising influence of the Roman church. In his argument the barbaric heathen past was replaced by the civilised Christian present.[16] Among other ancient authorities Tacitus was called upon as the prime witness of a Germanic past in which 'everything was barbaric, wild and bestial' (*omnia ... barbara, ... ferina ac brutalia*).[17] Piccolomini's version of the Germanic past was simply bleak, and positive traits were omitted,[18] so that the subsequent scenery of the abundant present could stand in starkest contrast and the ancient Germans would not recognise their own land. The opportunism of this version is clear from a comparison with the positive image of the German(ic) past which he deployed in an earlier speech in Frankfurt.[19]

Piccolomini's impact on German humanism can hardly be exaggerated; he spread humanism in the northern hemisphere and stirred anti-Italian sentiments and anti-papist rancour.[20] His provocative account of Germany,

---

[14] For the reception of the *Germania* in this period, see Ridé (1977).
[15] Picc. *Germ.* 2.4. The original letter is lost (see Krebs (2005) 142 n. 75).
[16] He had already written three letters, similar in argument, different in tone, not mentioning Tacitus.
[17] *Germ.* 2.4. Doubts about his knowledge of the *Germania* are unfounded: see Mertens (2004) 67–71.
[18] The two exceptions are Germanic fortitude and morality; both are, however, qualified and rendered irrelevant.
[19] *Oratio de clade Constantinopolitana et bello contra Turcos congregando*, 1454.
[20] See Paparelli (1950) 146–7; Joachimsen (1970b) 342; and Stadtwald (1996) 46.

the title of which clearly addressed German readers, was widely read by German humanists and seems to have brought Tacitus' *Germania* to their attention.[21] Ironically, it was another Italian who opened a very different perspective on Tacitus' *libellus*: in 1471 Giannantonio Campano (1429–77) was dispatched by Pope Paul II to Regensburg to participate in the Diet, which was held there in order to enlist German military forces for a papal crusade against the Ottoman threat, as announced by the programmatic title.[22] As suited his intention, Campano praised German military skill and fortitude, using the *Germania* to evoke a heroic image of the Germanic past, to which the German present should aspire (*facite et Germania Germania sit et eos nunc habeat propugnatores quos olim habuit*). The unacknowledged debts to Tacitus are many;[23] two are of particular importance. Wishing to stress the continuity between past and present, the versatile speaker adduced Germanic autochthony (*semper indigene Germanie hoc in coelo nati*), their purity (*impermixti aliis*) and the fact that their forefathers' way of life was also theirs (*mores, quos vestri maiores ab initio habuere, ad ultimum retinetis*). Secondly, Tacitus' physiognomic description was simply transferred to Campano's contemporaries: they have the same huge bodies (*corpora ... eximia atque extantia*), threatening eyes (*oculos in pugna minaciores*) and terrifying voices (*voces ad perterrefaciendum pleniores*). The Germans were obviously their forefathers' sons; the Germanic past was laudable and imitable. Campano's speech was widely read and welcomed among German humanists, who seem to have come to an appreciation of specific Germanic values only because of Campano's intermediation.[24]

A fictional account of great, but comparatively short-lived, influence appeared in 1498: the *Antiquitates*, fabricated by the veteran forger Annius of Viterbo (Giovanni Nanni) on the basis of the *Germania* (*inter alia*), but presented by him as fragments of the Chaldean historian Berosus. He added notes, which often contain references to and quotations from those in fact foundational texts. Although its author was soon denounced by Beatus Rhenanus, it remained influential until the late seventeenth century.[25]

---

[21] *De ritu, situ, moribus et condicione Theutonie descriptio* (thus the *editio princeps* of 1496, Leipzig; the much used edition from Basle has 'Germanie'). See Paul (1936) 34–58 for its reception.

[22] *In conventu Ratisponensi ad exhortandos principes Germanorum contra Turcos et de laudibus eorum oratio* (it became a classic of its kind: see Paul (1936) 60–5). The printed versions of the *oratio* (by itself: Rome 1487; within the *opera omnia*: Rome 1495) are faulty; I have corrected apparent mistakes in subsequent quotations.

[23] For a collation, see Perret (1950) 151 n. 5.

[24] For his role, see Tiedemann (1913) 43.

[25] *Commentaria super opera diversorum auctorum de antiquitatibus loquentium* (Rome 1512). For his denunciation as a 'fabulosi auctoris fabulosior interpres', see B. Rhenanus, *Rerum Germanicarum libri tres* (Basle 1551) 39.

German awakening and the durable formation of stereotypes

German humanism at the start was patriotic, occasionally outright chauvinistic; competing with Italian writers in the *res publica litteraria*, it considered fluency in Latin a question of national responsibility and using one's literary skills a moral duty. In this spirit Heinrich Bebel (1472–1518) promoted the mastery of Latin and promised to devote whatever and however little talent and erudition he possessed (knowing, he said, how meagre it was) to defending and praising his *patria*. This pledge showed him to be aware of the rhetorical *topos* of modesty and versed in the classics, since he alluded to Cicero's opening in *Pro Archia poeta*, thus elegantly undermining his own assurance.[26] Like Jacob Wimpheling (1450–1528) and many others, he was a 'true lover and defender of his country' (*verus patriae ... amator ac defensor*).[27]

The most important *amator ac defensor* was Conrad Celtis (1459–1508). In one of German humanism's foundational texts,[28] he encouraged the youth to master the Latin language so that, the maligned shortage of German writers remedied, Germans might write their own accounts of Germany. A *Germania illustrata* ('description of Germany') from a German pen was needed to rectify the foreign images of the dimmed present and the blackened past.[29] Since their ancestors had tended to be virtuous rather than studious (and German humanists had Sallust, *Cat.* 8.5 in mind), the main obstacle on the way to the past was the lack of evidence; the *Germania* of Tacitus, a foreigner,[30] became the highly esteemed guidebook.[31] The ideological (as distinguished from the merely philological) interest it raised among German humanists can be inferred from the number and distribution of editions: starting with the *editio princeps* in Bologna in 1472, for almost three decades the *Germania* remained an 'Italian' affair (with the exception of Nuremberg in 1476);[32] but the appearance of Celtis' edition in 1500 marked

---

[26] *Quicquid et quantulumcumque est in me ingenii ... quod sentio perquam exiguum esse* ('Apologia pro defensione imperatorum contra Leonhardum Justinianum', in Schardius (1673) 108). Cf. Cic. *Arch.* 1. On Bebel's writing and teaching, see Classen (1997).

[27] Trithemius' praise of Wimpheling is quoted from Ridé (1977) vol. 2, 304.

[28] *Oratio in gymnasio in Ingelstadio publice recitata*, 1492.

[29] Celtis attempted such a *Germania illustrata*.

[30] The apparent irony that in defending their 'country' against Italian writers they were dependent on a Roman was suspended by differentiating the classical Romans from the contemporary Italians (in the verse of Ulrich von Hutten: *Romanum invenies, hic ubi Roma, nihil*); or it was turned into an asset: a foreigner's praise was particularly valuable, and Tacitus a eulogist *à contrecoeur*.

[31] To give one example: Heinrich Bebel quotes the following passages from the *Germania* (for the works in which these quotations occur see Krebs (2005) 239 n. 13): 1, 2.1, 2.3, 3.1, 4, 5.2–3, 18.1, 19.1–2, 20.2, 21.2, 22.5, 26.1, 28.2, 28.4, 37, 37.5, 38.1.

[32] Since this first German edition did not cause much stir, it may reasonably be conjectured that Piccolomini's *Germania* (cf. n. 21) was needed as a stimulus.

a turning point, and in subsequent decades the *Germania* was printed mostly in German-speaking countries. Over five decades a staggering 6,000 copies may have been produced,[33] supplemented by a German translation (1535 by Jacobus Micyllus), which was the first into a vernacular and was meant to appeal to a broader audience.[34]

The Tacitean emphasis on Germanic customs and morals was particularly welcome, since the majority of humanists intended history to reveal the morally superior past and teach its readers to embrace lost values. 'Unser vorfordern warn ander leut', in the vernacular words of Johannes Aventinus (1477–1534): 'our forefathers were different' – better.[35] In reaction to the Germanic cultural shortcomings, apparent even to patriotically blinded eyes, their simple life (in contrast to Roman/Italian decadence) and morality were emphasised, and weakness was turned into strength.[36] However, the re-evaluation of the German past relied on a second strategy, namely, the demonstration that it was not as primitive as Italians liked to assert (this foreshadowed attempts in the late nineteenth and early twentieth centuries to raise the cultural level of the Bronze Age): Celtis' promotion of the learned Druids, Bebel's collection of *proverbia* and Jacob Wimpheling's characterisation of the Germans as supreme inventors and crafters are merely three examples of this endeavour.[37] Overnight the ancient Germans became Promethean warriors; and, for centuries to come, disappointing realities would yield to gratifying fiction.

Conrad Celtis, though now mostly forgotten, was celebrated by contemporaries, and later declared the 'arch-humanist' and cast as a *völkischer* in the early days of the Nazi regime.[38] He supplemented his edition of the *Germania* by hexametric *additiones* (later published as *Germania Generalis*), the two texts revealing the continuity of location, name and morals and the discontinuity of cultural sophistication. Celtis' use of the *Germania* is representative of his time and formative for later times, which the following anachronisms are intended to anticipate. At the

---

[33] For the calculation, see Mertens (2004) 61.
[34] Johann Eberlin von Günzburg's translation in 1526 was not printed; the first German translation of Tacitus' complete works would appear more than a century later (1675).
[35] See Laurens (1979), esp. 343.
[36] See e.g. Celtis, *Oratio* (see n. 28) 66: 'Ita nos Italicus luxus corrupit ... ut plane sanctius et gratius fuisset nos agere rudi illa et silvestri vita'.
[37] See Krebs (2005) 200, 237; add *Epitoma rerum Germanicarum Jacobi Wimphelingii Selestadiensis*, in Schardius (1673) 197.
[38] For 'arch-humanist', originally a term of D. F. Strauss, see Spitz (1957). For the *völkisch* Celtis, see Sponagel (1939). 'Völkisch' includes an emphasis on features typical of the German people and their 'spirit' and the rejection of other peoples' influences; no translation is quite accurate.

beginning of his characterisation stood fortitude and indigenousness (*gens invicta manet ... indigena*). In general, fortitude seemed the most important Germanic characteristic in this period (and parts of G. 37 were frequently quoted[39]), and fellow humanists liked to add that German stamina had sustained the Roman Empire and struggled and faltered only when opposed by Germans fighting on the other side: the bravest Polish officers would be of German blood.[40] German autochthony was an alternative to the dominant genealogical (Trojan) paradigm and contrasted with the Roman ethnic potpourri: the Germans were no 'dregs of a people' (*populi colluvies*) but *rasserein*, racially pure (*sine advenarum mixtura*), and still running through their veins was the blood of their forefathers (*sumus illorum sanguis*),[41] with whom they also shared the Aryan-Nordic racial characteristics: blond hair, bright eyes, and light and well-proportioned limbs. Celtis' 'patriotic etymology' of 'Germanus' was one among a standard set, and represented a linguistic interest particularly pronounced in Aventinus' work and blossoming later in the seventeenth century. When, finally, Heinrich Himmler avowed that 'one thing can never be excused amongst us Germanen, that is disloyalty',[42] he called upon one of the Tacitean virtues (G. 6.4, 14.1), copied by Celtis (esp. lines 91–8) and celebrated by German humanists in general: integrity, honesty and righteousness, loyalty, fidelity and spiritedness. Simplicity of mind and circumstances was only hinted at in this poem, and generosity (as expressed in Germanic hospitality) omitted, but both were elaborated elsewhere and are important parts of the Germanic inventory (German *Einfalt*).[43]

Other long-lasting ideas sprouting at this time, growing over centuries, and blossoming and withering in the twentieth century included the attribution of other peoples' achievements to the ancient Germans, the idea that noble and outstanding individuals and families were of German, later Aryan, blood (and for some NS readers Tacitus himself would become an Aryan peasant), and that a demographic surplus caused German migrations – this last an explicatory notion that within NS ideology served as a justification of the necessary expansion of *Lebensraum*.[44]

---

[39] So by Bebel (in Schardius (1673) 99) and Wimpheling (in Schardius (1673) 172).
[40] Himmler (1974) 27.
[41] For the Trojan genealogy, see Garber (1989). The quotations are from Bebel (in Schardius (1673) 105, 101, 139).
[42] See Fest (1996) 173.
[43] Celtis, *Quattuor libri amorum* 2.9, lines 33, 127–30.
[44] *Webster's Dictionary*, s.v.: 'territory that is held to be necessary for the existence of a state'.

While similarly chauvinistic readings of the *Germania* – like Jacob Wimpheling's *Epitoma* – were hugely influential, the greatest philologist of his times was hardly heeded: Beatus Rhenanus (1485–1547) stood apart, representing the above mentioned philological reading in this early phase and refusing to sacrifice scholarly conscientiousness on the altar of patriotism. On the contrary, drawing on a comparatively comprehensive historical inquiry and commanding a philological acumen that enabled him to produce the standard edition of Tacitus' work prior to Justus Lipsius', he problematised the generally unquestioned assumption of a German(ic) continuity – with wide-ranging consequences: the Swabians could not simply be identified with Tacitus' *Suebi*, and the past could not simply serve as a foil for the present. He took an equally solitary path when he rejected attempts at attributing to the Germans the achievements of other people.[45] Needless to say, Rhenanus' refusal to chime in with his panegyrically inclined fellow humanists made him a lonely figure – no students of his are known.[46]

Languages and mores: the seventeenth century

It is often said that the impact of the *Germania* abates after the stormy first half of the sixteenth century, or, less categorically, that baroque authors adapt this booklet 'by the most distinguished writer' (*scriptor eminentissimus*) in much the same way as the humanists had. A cursory survey of the topics they predominantly address with the help of the *Germania* seems to confirm this contention: legends of origin, religion, mores and customs, language and heroes had already been discussed in more or less detail.[47] Like their humanistic predecessors, baroque authors also felt threatened by an overwhelming foreign culture, and buried their cultural fears in the glorious Germanic past, naturally considered morally superior.[48]

Yet four developments distinguish the seventeenth century. The cultural antagonist was now French rather than Italian: *dramatis personae* like Arminius and other born-again Germanic heroes (*redivivi*) did not recognise their alienated country and could not understand their countrymen who spoke *à la mode*.[49] The *Germania* was used to sharpen the Germanic,

---

[45] Tacitus, *De moribus Germanorum* (Basle 1519) 45–6, quoted in Mertens (2004) 93, and *Rerum Germanicarum libri tres* (Basle 1551) 81.
[46] The use of the *Germania* in the context of the Reformation does not seem to add anything different. For Rhenanus see also above, p. 249.
[47] For the topics, see Frenzen (1937). In a forthcoming paper I shall discuss in more detail the little-studied reception of the *Germania* in the seventeenth century.
[48] See e.g. the *Sinngedichte* by Friedrich von Logau (Breslau 1654) (= von Logau (1984)).
[49] See J.G. Schottelius, *Friedens-Sieg* (Wolfenbüttel 1648) (= Schottelius (1900)).

sword-wielding warrior in the face of the effeminate French knight, the former a characterisation that led to (what would later be perceived as) the caricature of the *Theatergermane*: wearing a winged helmet, hides, long braided hair, an unclipped beard and a huge sword.[50] Thirdly, while in the sixteenth century the *Germania* figured mostly in historiographical work, the seventeenth century was marked by a diversification of genres: not only in histories (like the first book of Philippus Cluverius' influential *Germaniae antiquae libri tres*), but also in plays, satires, historical novels and linguistic treatises.[51] The last genre indicates the fourth and most significant novelty of the *Germania* reception in the seventeenth century.

Etymology and occasional assertions of the value of the vernacular reflect the humanists' linguistic awareness, but baroque authors, weary of their contemporaries' *frömdgierigkeit* ('greed for the foreign'), went much further. They organised themselves in language societies, the most famous being the *fruchtbringende Gesellschaft* ('Fruitful Society'), and undertook to purify the German language.[52] Since 'changes of language are followed by changes of morals', linguistic purification implied ethical elevation (and the production of a dictionary improved the German stamina).[53] To baroque ears, German was particularly worthy of protection, as it was widely held to be a pure language, as distinguished from French, 'the child of a whore'.[54] This Ur-language carried essential meaning (a notion that would be echoed in the twentieth century by Martin Heidegger, who did not have much respect for the French language, either) and provided access to God. In consequence, Tuisto (G. 2.2) was not only the Ur-father of the Germanic people and their laws, but also of their Ur-language. Johann Gottlieb Fichte (among many others) famously elaborated this at the beginning of the nineteenth century – with the *Germania* in mind, as we will see.

Montesquieu's *esprit général* and Herder's *Geist der Nation*

In the eighteenth century the *Germania* served to form a set of abiding interrelated ideas: the 'Germanic spirit' (as Houston Stewart Chamberlain would

---

[50] E.g. in J.M. Moscherosch, *Gesichte Philanders von Sittewald* (Darmstadt 1964; orig. Strasburg 1640).
[51] Von Lohenstein's monumental novel *Grossmüthiger Feldherr Arminius* (Leipzig 1689–90) must at least be mentioned.
[52] See Borchardt (1968); Smart (1989).
[53] 'Auf die Enderung der Sprache folget eine Enderung der Sitten' (Schottelius (1900) 50).
[54] 'Hurenkind': von Logau (1984) 164.

call it a century later), Germanic freedom and the North. One major influential contributor to this discourse was Baron de Montesquieu with his work *L'esprit des lois* (*The Spirit of the Laws*).

Montesquieu knew his Tacitus well – as indicated by slipshod quotations retrieved from memory – and made ample use of his authority. There are fifty-three references (mostly quotations) to the *Germania* alone: 'a short book', he writes, but by an author 'who summarised everything because he saw everything'.[55] One of the influential concepts he presented, especially in the fourteenth book of his *chef d'oeuvre*, was the theory that a people is formed by its environment (a theory which in fact dated back at least to the fifth century BC but which experienced a renaissance in the eighteenth).[56] 'Many things govern men: climate, religion, laws ... mores, and manners; a general spirit is formed as a result' (19.4). Due to specific Northern circumstances the German *esprit général* was characterised above all by liberty;[57] studying the origins of the political system in England, which in Montesquieu's opinion had established liberty by its laws, he refers to the *Germania* (11.22): 'whoever shall read [this] admirable treatise ..., will find that it is from [the Germans] that the English have borrowed the idea of their political government. This beautiful system was invented first in the woods.'[58] *Libertas* had been a Germanic hallmark since the fifteenth century, but it was now no longer primarily conceived of as mere independence from the Roman (or any other aggressor's) Empire – rather, it was seen as the organising principle of the Germanic 'constitution'. By locating the 'beautiful system' in the North, Montesquieu, who believed in the Germanic origin of the French, also changed the traditional semantics of geography: politically, the formerly abhorrent North, hitherto contrasted unfavourably with the superior median, moved from the fringes to the centre.[59]

L'esprit des lois was published in 1748, and its German reception began in 1753 with the translation by A. G. Kästner,[60] swiftly followed by German adaptations, such as that of F. K. von Moser (*Von dem deutschen National-Geist*, 1765), around which the debate about the national spirit

---

[55] Montesquieu, *The Spirit of the Laws* (Cambridge and New York 1989; orig. Geneva 1748) 30.2 (book and chapter); for him as a reader of Tacitus, see Volpilhac-Auger (1985), esp. ch. 6 and 192 (for references to the *Germania*).
[56] See Fink (1987).
[57] For a short overview of the debate on the *esprit général*, see Kra (2002).
[58] This expression ('in the woods') would become common currency: see Poliakov (1977) 17–36.
[59] See Hölzle (1925) for the idea of Germanic liberty before Montesquieu.
[60] For the reception of Montesquieu in Germany, see Herdmann (1990).

centred.⁶¹ (The translation 'Geist' would have an interesting history in its own right, figuring in Hegel's *Weltgeist*, Arndt's *Zeitgeist* and Dilthey's *Geistesgeschichte*.) Montesquieu was also read by Johann Gottfried Herder (1744–1803), who slightly modified the former's anthropo-geographical theory and elaborated the implied notion of a people's general character, which to him appeared purest in its original form and most fundamentally expressed in a people's language.⁶² Herder, whose life extended from the dusk of the Enlightenment to the dawn of Romanticism and comprised the *Sturm und Drang* and the German *Klassik*, defies categorisation, and scholarship on him is highly controversial; undoubtedly, however, there are passages that lend themselves facilely to nationalistic misinterpretation and appear to anticipate Romanticist and *völkisch* ideas:

> A nation can suffer no greater injury than to be robbed of its national character, the peculiarity of its spirit and language ... Look around in Germany for the character of the nation ...; where [is it]? Read Tacitus; there you will find its character: 'The tribes of Germany, who have never degraded themselves by mingling with others, form a peculiar, unadulterated, original nation, which is its own archetype ...'. Now look around and say: 'The tribes of Germany by mingling with others are degraded.'⁶³

Read in its larger context of Herder's thought, which was defined by an understanding of history as an organic whole and the higher notion of a common humanity (*Humanität*), this statement loses much of its nationalistic ring. However, in the form of the Romanticist striving for origins and the *völkisch* obsession with the *Volkstum* (national essence) as expressed in folklore art and fairy tales, its core themes, here as elsewhere linked to the *Germania*, would live on through subsequent decades. Even if, as has been suggested, Romanticism commented on Herder's work with icy silence and no *völkisch* voice mentioned his name, his ideas circulated within the *res publica litteraria*. As Goethe knew, ideas do not have to be transmitted under their author's name in order to be influential: Herder would be called upon in the context of National Socialism – undeservedly but not fully unreasonably, like many others.

---

⁶¹ For the 'Nationalgeist Debatte', see Vazsonyi (1999).
⁶² *Gedanken bei Lesung Montesquieus* (in *Sämtliche Werke* (Hildesheim 1967–8) vol. 4, 464–8).
⁶³ *Fragmente über die neuere deutsche Literatur*, 1767 (in *Werke* (Frankfurt 1985) vol. 1, 376).

Nationalism, racism and the *völkisch* movement: the nineteenth century

> We see the old German nationalism ... after its deepest foundation by Fichte, after its explosive rise through Stein and Arndt.   (Alfred Rosenberg)[64]

Writers of the nineteenth century suffered the most from what Ernst Bloch called the 'Nazification of the past': Nazis, who read between the lines rather than the text itself, misappropriated them, and critics of fascism followed suit.[65] Yet the nineteenth century was marked by an unprecedented nationalistic movement and by a systematisation of racism, both of which are detectable in their writing; both would merge into the *völkisch* ideology from which National Socialism would emerge. The 'Germanomania' so increased that it earned Heine's ridicule.

At the turn of the century German consciousness was piqued by the experience of the Napoleonic wars, as is illustrated by the case of Johann Gottlieb Fichte (1762–1814), a student of Kant's, controversial teacher of several Romantics and figurehead of German idealism. In Berlin under French occupation he delivered fourteen *Addresses to the German Nation* from December 1807 to March 1808, which were received by Prussian ministers, praised by (amongst others) Johann Wolfgang von Goethe and Ernst Moritz Arndt and made a considerable impact, not least because of their speaker's notoriety.[66] They were meant for 'the whole German nation', which he perceived to be 'threatened by its fusion with foreign people', and he promised a 'German national education' in line with 'the German national characteristics', thereby 'mould[ing] the Germans into a corporate body' so that this nation could realise its destiny as the 'regenerator and re-creator of the world'. Even when considered in their larger transnational context, these statements, frequently repeated during the fourteen speeches, hardly lose their nationalistic tone.[67] As nationally defining characteristics Fichte proposed two: Germans had 'remained in their original dwelling places' and 'retained and developed their original language'.[68] This, inspired by Tacitus, whom he had read during the preparation of his speeches and quoted elsewhere, was subsequently qualified: naturally, Germans had lost their ethnic purity; more important, the speaker added, was the continuity of the German language, which maintained the purity of its 'spirit' despite the acceptance of foreign words. The long-established delusion of

---

[64] A. Rosenberg, *Mythus* (Munich 1938) 539–41, quoted from Viereck (1961) 48.
[65] 'Nazifizierung der Vergangenheit': E. Bloch, *Politische Messungen* (Frankfurt 1977) 300.
[66] See Reiss (2006). Accessible and informative, though occasionally inaccurate, is Kelly's introduction to Fichte (1968).
[67] See Baumann (2006) for a slightly different position.
[68] Fichte (1968) 47.

A dangerous book

the superiority of the German language[69] was here emphatically moved into the centre of the nationalistic debate, embedded, as it is, in an idealistic philosophy. Less often noted, but also highly resonant with the *Germania*, were the national virtues that the sixth lecture traced through history, 'loyalty, uprightness, honour and simplicity', not to mention the concession of the German ancestors' comparatively low intellectual achievements, ultimately owed to the fact that their 'dwellings were scattered'.[70]

Ernst Moritz Arndt (1769–1860), who held Fichte in high esteem, and Friedrich Ludwig Jahn (1778–1852), who held abstract philosophy in general in low esteem, would also be called upon by National Socialists: Jahn was 'the natural starting point for every analysis of the concept of *Volk*', a portrayal so readily and uncritically accepted by post-war historians that Jahn became 'the first storm trooper'.[71] Both were highly influential – the former primarily as a writer of, for example, *Geist der Zeit* ('The spirit of times') and *Das deutsche Vaterland* ('The German fatherland'), the latter as an agitator, whose organisations, the most famous being the *Turnverein* ('gymnastic movement'), revolutionised German society. Both had of course read Tacitus, the 'greatest man who ever lived', and both sounded the familiar nationalistic themes: Jahn's *Das deutsche Volkstum* ('The German national essence') established a concept and its term that would be central in the *völkisch* movement and racism. The beginning of such a racist interpretation can be detected in Arndt's elaboration of Tacitus (*G.* 4):

> The Germans are not *bastardised* ..., they have remained more than many other peoples in their original purity and have been able to develop slowly and quietly from this purity ...; the fortunate Germans are an original people[, as evidenced by] the Roman Tacitus ... [H]e saw most clearly how important it was for the future greatness and majesty of the German people that they were pure and resembled only themselves.[72]

Intimations of racist thinking, defined as an evaluative belief in inherent racial differences and a correlation between biological and cultural / intellectual characteristics that elevate one race to superiority, have been traced back to the Renaissance,[73] but the first comprehensive theory appeared in the middle of the nineteenth century: Arthur de Gobineau's hefty *Essai sur*

---

[69] Martyn (1997) gives a stimulating deconstruction of Fichte's purely 'German' words.
[70] Fichte (1968) 81, 89.
[71] B. Theune, *Volk und Nation bei Jahn, Rotteck, Welcker und Dahlmann* (Berlin 1937) 13, quoted from Viereck (1961) 63, who refers to Jahn as 'storm trooper'.
[72] *Fantasien zur Berichtigung der Urteile über künftige deutsche Verfassungen* (orig. 1815), in *Ausgewählte Werke*, ed. H. Meisner and R. Geerds (Leipzig, n.d.) pt. 15, 115. Quotation and trans. are taken from Kohn (1949) 791–2, with whose interpretation Vick (2003) should be compared.
[73] Mosse (1985).

l'inégalité des races humaines. He posited three races – the black, the yellow and the white – and conceived of history racially: a decrease of racial purity (*bastardisation*) caused cultural decline. The white race was defined as beautiful, honourable and destined to rule; within it the Aryans are 'cette illustre famille humaine, la plus noble'.[74] Originally a linguistic term synonymous with Indo-European,[75] 'Aryan' became, not least because of the *Essai*, the designation of a race, which Gobineau specified as 'la race germanique'. He makes frequent use of the *Germania*, which curiously also figured in the context of the controversial 'Aryan question' of whether the Aryan race originated in Asia or in Europe. One of the first advocates of a European cradle – and the authority repeatedly referred to – is Robert Gordon Latham, who pronounced on this question in his 'The *Germania* of Tacitus with ethnological dissertations and notes'.[76]

Although the *Essai* was translated into German by Ludwig Schemann[77] and its tenets promulgated by the Gobineau Society, its immediate impact was limited – and yet significant, especially on Houston Stewart Chamberlain. Like Schemann a member of Wagner's 'circle at Bayreuth',[78] Chamberlain authored the hugely influential *Die Grundlagen des 19. Jahrhunderts* (*The Foundations of the 19th Century*), which went through thirty editions by 1944. He reconstructed history as a mortal battle between the Germanic and the Jewish race, the latter having 'established as its guiding principle the purity of the blood'.[79] Ultimately, he aimed at demonstrating the 'superiority of the Teuton family', which would lead to a 'new, splendid, and light-filled future' – or such was his utopian hope. Needless to say, Germanic talent was also to be found behind every major cultural achievement. Again, the *Germania* was called upon frequently, especially in the part concerning 'The entrance of the Germanic people into history'. Chamberlain, who did not hesitate to deviate from the Latin for the sake of emphasis, approvingly commented on Tacitus' remark about the purity and self-similarity, and praised him for his 'intuitively accurate observation'.

Since the authenticity of the *Germania* was needed for all these purposes, scholarly work that exposed its realism to doubt drew heavy criticism. Towards the end of the nineteenth century voices could be heard that emphasised its literariness and its author's 'creative powers of imagination'.[80] The

---

[74] A. de Gobineau, *Essai sur l'inégalité des races humaines* (Paris 1853–5) book iii, ch. 1.
[75] For the *Germania* in the linguistic debate, see F. M. Müller's *Lectures on the Science of Language* (London 1861). For the 'Aryan myth', see Poliakov (1977).
[76] London 1851, cxlii. For the 'Aryan question' see e.g. Vacher de Lapouge (1899) with 332 for the reference to Latham.
[77] *Versuch über die Ungleichheit der Menschenracen* (Stuttgart 1898). See Fortier (1967).
[78] It should at least be mentioned that this circle was a melting pot of *völkisch* ideas.
[79] I have used the 2nd edn (New York 1912); quotations: vol. 1.253, 1.xlix, and Mosse (1998) 97.
[80] Baumstark (1875) xiii.

two most important studies, however, appeared after the Great War: Karl Trüdinger revealed Tacitus' formal debt to the standardised set of questions and interpretations in the ethnographical tradition, and Eduard Norden demonstrated that various aspects of Tacitus' *Germani* could be traced back to other peoples, and spoke of *Wandermotive* ('tralatitious motifs').[81] Norden's monograph met with outrage from *völkisch* readers, so he felt compelled to reassert its historical value in the preface to the second edition.[82]

The nationalistic *völkisch* movement combined many of the attitudinal tendencies of the first half of the nineteenth century: originality and peasantry, *Volkstum*, racism and anti-Semitism, and *Germanentum* ('Germanicness') were its central characteristics; it culminated during the German Empire (1871–1918), when it was the most important subculture.[83] It pervaded German society: its literature (mostly in the form of historical novels like Felix Dahn's *Kampf um Rom*), art and the humanities, especially studies in German language and literature and history, which the pioneer Gustav Kossinna elevated to 'a pre-eminently national science' (*eine hervorragend nationale Wissenschaft*).[84] It aimed at illuminating and raising the profile of German pre-history, the Bronze Age – just as German humanists had demanded. Needless to say, the *Germania* was once again a cornerstone of the ideological edifice: in 1904 the 'Germanic Bible' (*Germanenbibel*) appeared, soon to reach an edition of 20,000, and introduced by the *libellus*, 'this eulogy'.[85] A recruitment flyer of the Germanic Order, the umbrella organisation whose political programme was by and large identical with that of the famous Thule Society, warned in apocalyptic tones of the imminent extinction of the 'blond heroic race', wistfully evoking the times 'in which the Roman Tacitus still spoke of the old Germans as racially pure'. In their message for *Germanen* they pleaded for a systematic 'breeding to former heights' (*Wiederhochzüchtung*);[86] NS eugenicists would heed their call.

'Thus shall we be again': National Socialist readings of the *Germania*

In a melodramatic scene, duly photographed and publicised, Hitler visited the bedridden Chamberlain and kissed his hands. The encounter of a leading

---

[81] Trüdinger (1918); and Norden (1920), esp. 54.
[82] For reactions to Norden's *Urgeschichte*, see Canfora (1979) 38–42.
[83] The classic study is Mosse (1998).
[84] G. Kossinna, *Die deutsche Vorgeschichte: eine hervorragend nationale Wissenschaft* (2nd edn, Würzburg 1914).
[85] W. Schwaner (ed.), *Germanen-Bibel* (6th edn, Berlin and Stuttgart 1934); quotation from the preface to the 4th edn.
[86] The flyer is printed in Rose (1994) 90–1.

figure in the *völkisch* movement and the leader of the NSDAP represents the relationship between the two ideologies: 'National Socialism was a *Völkish* movement'.[87] Yet NS ideology, as embraced by its leaders, was far from monolithic, and there were always discordant voices: Hermann Göring (the field marshal of the air force and later Hitler's official successor) privately discarded it as 'junk'; and Hitler felt compelled to contain the widespread Germanic element in his party (though he had considered 'Germanic Revolution' as a title for *Mein Kampf*).[88] Among the NS leadership, Heinrich Himmler, who upon reading the *Germania* in his youth vowed 'thus shall we be again', stands apart as a genuine believer and powerful promoter of the Germanic cause, joined only by his intermittent rival Alfred Rosenberg (the chief ideologue of the NSDAP).[89] While not representative of Hitler's highest-ranking paladins, the *Reichsführer SS* embodies a mainstream trend within NS culture, of which the party apparatus, despite its leader's hesitations, took advantage so that at the party convention in 1936 in Nuremberg a 'Germanic room' (*Germanenraum*) was decorated with Tacitean quotations.[90] And when Cardinal Michael von Faulhaber in his New Year's Address in 1933 followed in the footsteps of Enea Silvio Piccolomini and used the *Germania* as evidence of Germanic barbarism, his speech was burned by members of the Hitler Youth, and two shots were fired on his residence.

For many NS foot soldiers the *Germania* was a 'bible', and the election in 1933 was considered a promise that the Germanic element would be valued more highly than ever before.[91] It figured in numerous doctrinaire articles in ideological journals like the SS' 'The Black Corps' (*Das Schwarze Korps*), 'National Socialist Education' (*Nationalsozialistisches Bildungswesen*) and 'The National Socialist Monthly' (*Das Nationalsozialistische Monatsheft*). Ultimately, it also lay behind the Nuremberg race laws, Himmler's SS and Walther Darré's concept of 'blood and soil' (*Blut und Boden*).

One Nuremberg race law, passed in 1935, forbade marriages between Jews and Germans 'out of the deep conviction that the purity of the German blood is the prerequisite of the survival of the German people'. A few days earlier, Hans F. K. Günther (1891–1968), the NS 'expert' on questions of race, had been honoured for having established 'the spiritual basis for … the legislation of the National Socialist state'.[92] Günther was a fervent

---

[87] Mosse (1998) v. 'NSDAP' is the acronym of *Nationalsozialistische Deutsche Arbeiterpartei* ('National Socialist German Workers' Party').
[88] For 'junk', see Fest (1996) 105; for the discarded title, see W. Maser, *Adolf Hitler. Mein Kampf* (6th edn, Esslingen 1981) 160 (photo 6).
[89] Bundesarchiv Koblenz, NL Himmler, N 1126/9, no. 218.
[90] For the Germanic room, see *Germanenerbe* 1 (1936) 194.
[91] Benze (1936) 20; H. Schneider, in *Forschungen u. Fortschritte* 15 (1939) 1–3.
[92] Quoted from E. Weisenburger, in M. Kissener and J. Scholtyseck (eds.), *NS-Biographien aus Baden und Württemberg* (Konstanz 1997) 162, 188–9.

admirer of the Nordic race and an advocate of 'breeding to former heights' (*Wiederhochzüchtung*) of Nordic purity. 'A race', in Günther's often-quoted definition, 'manifests itself in a group of people that through a specific combination of characteristics of the body and the soul differs from any other group and produces always and only those like itself.' The last characteristic, the reproduction of identity, was an audible echo of Tacitus' 'resembling only itself' (*G.* 4), which Günther quoted frequently. In his view, Tacitus' *Germani* had practised what he advanced: selection and eradication in the name of racial purity. The third chapter of his 'Origin and racial history of the *Germanen*' was entitled 'The Germanic care of race and the health of their [genetic] heritage'. When he discussed the various measures undertaken by the Germanic tribes for the sake of their genetic health, he mentioned Tacitus' description of crimes and punishment (*G.* 12.1), and then elaborated on 'how the *Germanen* hung up or drowned in the marshes those who were inferior or predisposed to perversion' (homosexuals, in Günther's opinion). He concluded that this practice guaranteed a continuous purification of the people, 'since the genes of those people would not be passed on to future generations'.[93] To his eyes, Tacitus' *Germani* practised NS euthanasia. In another instance of NS misappropriation the *Germanen* forbade 'mixed marriages' in an effort to retain their racial purity – in the same way as the NS legislation took measures to prohibit 'mixed marriages' between Jews and Germans. One avid NS reader of the *Germania* considered the laws concerning the 'Jewish question' as the most recent effort to restore the racial purity mentioned in the fourth chapter.[94]

Another fervent reader was Himmler, who embraced Günther's Nordic ideals and followed him in his interpretation of the punishment of homosexuals in one of his secret speeches for members of his SS. He had vowed to resuscitate Germanic virtues and lifestyle, and within his SS he tried to live up to his word. It presented itself as an elite of 'German men of Nordic determination selected on special criteria', all but one of which were the Tacitean virtues: racial purity, will to freedom and bravery, loyalty (often including camaraderie) and honour, and obedience.[95] Before a young man entered this 'new nobility', he would have been a member of the Hitler Youth, where he was indoctrinated with the help of manuals like 'The followers – the Germanic combat unit'.[96] For this doctrinaire collection of passages

[93] H.F.K. Günther, *Herkunft und Rassengeschichte der Germanen* (Munich 1937) 148–9.
[94] M. Schlossarek, *Die Taciteische Germania als Künderin eines urdeutschen Heroismus* (Breslau 1935) 18–19.
[95] H. Himmler, *Die Schutzstaffel als antibolschewistische Kampforganisation* (München 1936) 20–4.
[96] H. Wagenführ, *Gefolgschaft – Der germanische Kampfbund* (Hamburg 1935).

concerning Germany and the Germans the *Germania* supplies the motto: 'It is the greatest honour ... to be ... surrounded by a huge band of chosen young men' (cf. G. 13.3). Towards its end the adolescent learns about 'combat honour and courage of the followers' from a rather literal translation of two Tacitean paragraphs (G. 13–14), noteworthy for its adjustment to Nazi jargon, but above all for its dark resonance with the cult of the *Führer*. The translation relates how the Germanic forebear would fall in with the followers of the leader, competing with the others for the place of honour at the *Führer*'s side (the Latin is *princeps*, G. 13.2). In Himmler's SS the entering 'followers' had to swear: 'We swear by you, Adolf Hitler, *Führer* and chancellor of the German Reich, loyalty and fortitude.' Germanic loyalty (along with other Germanic virtues) also figured prominently in school texts: 'never will the German people perish as long as this manly loyalty persists ... [I]s not the *Führer* also surrounded by a loyal following? ... These German compatriots embody Germanic loyalty and heroic spirit and are your shining examples.'[97] Tacitus' description of Germanic loyalty (G. 13–14.1) is the most quoted in NS discussions of Germanic values, second only to that of the Germanic race's purity and physiognomic characteristics (G. 4).

Walther Darré (1895–1953), appointed by Himmler, served as director of the 'SS office of race and settlement', which was responsible for preserving and increasing the purity of the Aryan race and the acquisition of *Lebensraum* and its Germanisation. He had established himself with a number of *völkisch* books, one of them being *New Nobility from Blood and Soil* (*Neuadel aus Blut und Boden*), published in 1930. Contemporaries characterised National Socialism as the 'ideology of blood and soil', and Darré promoted it throughout his career. Stripped of its mystical embroidery, it deployed an antithesis between the city and the land to elevate the countryside as the place of the Nordic race's health, morals and genuineness. According to that view, farming was not just work, it was the lifestyle of endurance, seriousness and responsibility, as opposed to the uprooted existence of the city *flâneur*. Summing up his doctrine of blood and soil, Darré spoke of the countryside as the 'bloodstream of the people' and source of rejuvenation of the Nordic race.[98]

The metaphorical language, such as the 'stream of blood', the *Volkskörper* (literally, 'the body of the people', not quite corresponding to the 'body politic'), and the notion of the people as an organism, lent itself to a more fanciful and mystical elaboration and fuses with the Tacitean myth of Germanic

---

[97] C. Schütte and O. Gaede, *Geschichtsbuch für die Jugend des Dritten Reiches* (2nd edn, Halle 1934), esp. 3, 10–16 (quotation from p. 14).

[98] 'Ideology': *NS Bildungswesen* 1 (1936) 16. Darré, *Um Blut und Boden* (5th edn, München 1942) 180.

indigenousness. When Darré wrote that it was the 'farms and estates where the body of the people penetrates the home soil [*Heimatboden*] with its roots', the metaphorical expressions are easily associated with the Tuisto-myth (*G*. 2.2). Darré, though intimately familiar with the Roman historian's little book, does not seem to have embraced this myth. Others, however, did: one of the many translators and editors of the *Germania* in the 1930s inserts the NS doctrine in the title: 'Tacitus: Germania. Of blood and soil, mores and customs in the Germanic sphere', and later, in his annotations to the fourth chapter, states that 'race and soil formed the Germanic man, blood and soil are the roots that supply him with strength'. And drawing a direct line between the 2,000-year-old text and the politics of the NS regime, the prophet of 'new heroism' supplied his comments on the myth of Tuisto: 'from the beginnings, the German[ic] people drew its strength from the soil, and it is no wonder that in the new Germany, the Third Reich, the peasantry, lovers of the clod, are the most important basis of the people'.[99]

More than anybody else, Himmler believed in the ideas that had been developed over centuries with the help of Tacitus' *Germania*. It seems only natural that in 1943 he authorised a special SS mission to Italy to retrieve its oldest extant manuscript, the *codex Aesinas*; but to no avail.[100] It did not matter: the most dangerous book had done its damage already.[101]

FURTHER READING

Studies of the reception of the *Germania* have been limited to specific epochs:[102] Lund (1995) has documented its relevance within the context of NS ideology; Canfora (1979) has focused on the German Empire, and Krapf (1979), Mertens (2004) and Krebs (2005) have looked at its use by Italian and German humanists. Study of these works brings to light a recurrent set of ideas and notions drawn from the *Germania* and coherently developed over the centuries, often within the (inter-changing) discourses of *Germanentum*, the myth of the Aryan race and the simple original life. Intellectual histories of these discourses have been written by Mosse (1998), Poliakov (1977), Ridé (1977) and von See (1986), all of whom repeatedly point to the importance of Tacitus' *libellus*.

---

[99] J. Weisweiler, *Tacitus: Germania. Von Blut und Boden, Sitte und Brauch im germanischen Raum* (Bielefeld – Leipzig, ca. 1936), 8–9 and n. 40; Schlossarek (as in n. 94) 10.
[100] For this episode, see Schama (1995) 75–81.
[101] For Tacitus' *Germania* as *the* most dangerous book, see Krebs (forthcoming).
[102] Von Stackelberg (1960) is not particularly concerned with the *Germania*.

20

MARTHA MALAMUD

Tacitus and the twentieth-century novel

Opus adgredior opimum casibus, atrox proeliis, discors seditionibus, ipsa
etiam pace saeuum   (H. 1.2.1)

I am entering on a work rich in disasters, ferocious in its wars, ripped apart
by civil strife, savage even in peace

Tacitus frames his histories as an account of catastrophic and historic change at home and abroad. In both the *Histories*, the extant books of which cover the civil wars of 69, and the *Annals*, which recount the history of the Julio-Claudian emperors, he anatomises the consolidation of and struggle for imperial power and the consequences of Empire for Romans and the peoples they conquered. This grim history offered obvious analogies with the fraught political and social issues of Europe in the 1920s, 1930s and 1940s, when the uneasy peace achieved after the First World War degenerated into economic collapse, social upheaval, the rise of totalitarianism and the cataclysm of the Second World War. The conflagration of Rome, the Pisonian conspiracy and the persecution of the Christians, the paranoia and murderous struggle for power within the Julio-Claudian house, Rome's relentless push for Empire, pitting the imperial might of Rome against freedom-loving but savage natives – these Tacitean motifs provided powerful material for writers of the twentieth century. This essay examines three novelists who based their historical fiction on the works of Tacitus: Robert Graves, Naomi Mitchison and Lion Feuchtwanger. Each draws on Tacitus to expose corruption and abuse of power, explore the difficulties of political action or inaction, and project contemporary political problems on to Julio-Claudian Rome.

Coming badly unhinged: Robert Graves

Peter Quennell recalls a visit from the young Robert Graves, who 'still exhibited the wounded features of a shell-shocked public schoolboy, who had gone straight from Charterhouse to a line regiment, had been shot through the body on some Flemish battlefield and temporarily left for dead. In common with many survivors of the battle, he wore the strained and troubled expression of a young man who had lately emerged from an inferno'.[1] Virginia Woolf paints a similar picture of an odd and damaged young man: 'Graves has come to London after 6 years; cant travel in a train without being sick; is rather proud of his sensibility. No I don't think he'll write great poetry: but what will you? The sensitive are needed too, the halfbaked, stammering stuttering, who perhaps improve their own quarter of Oxfordshire.'[2]

This 'shell-shocked public schoolboy', whose patriotism and religious beliefs had been shattered by trench warfare, created a fictional Rome as iconoclastic as *Goodbye to All That* (1929), his lacerating memoir of his English childhood and his experience in the trenches in the First World War.[3] Like Naomi Mitchison's historical fiction, the Claudius novels go against the grain of such popular historical romances about Rome as *The Gladiators* (1863) and *Quo Vadis* (1896), whose plots celebrate the uncomplicated triumph of Christian morality over Roman decadence and/or glorify the merging, often through marriage, of the strength and vigour of conquered natives with Roman self-control.[4] In his novels Graves projected a Tacitean world view very different from his predecessors' generally unambiguous and morally didactic narratives of Rome, and his protagonist is startlingly unlike the typical historical romance hero. There are obvious affinities between the narrator Claudius and his 'halfbaked, stammering stuttering' creator. Both were physically clumsy with nervous tics, both were dominated by powerful females, both were experts in ancient history and literature and both presented themselves as cynical observers able to see through cant and hypocrisy to an underlying truth. Graves's Claudius inhabits a Rome that is a stagnant sewer of vice and intrigue; the few decent characters in the narratives can do little more than attempt to survive amid betrayals, bribery, murder and other crimes. He is a Tacitean creature *par excellence*, a closet Republican who survives by diligently searching out truth among conflicting sources and by playing a role so perfectly that no one realises that he is acting. Graves sets the atmosphere of his novel and signals his debt to the historian's world view in the epigraph to *I, Claudius*:

---

[1] Kersnowski (1989) 6.
[2] Kersnowski (1989) 8.
[3] *I, Claudius* and *Claudius the God* were first published several months apart in 1934. Page references in the present chapter are to the 1965 edition of *I, Claudius* and the 1966 edition of *Claudius the God*.
[4] Hoberman (1997) 120.

... A story that was the subject of every variety of misrepresentation, not only by those who then lived but likewise in succeeding times; so true is it that all transactions of pre-eminent importance are wrapt in doubt and obscurity; while some hold for certain facts the most precarious hearsays, others turn facts into falsehood; and both are exaggerated by posterity.

The source of the epigraph is *A.* 3.19.2, a description of the attempts by contemporaries and posterity to understand the swirl of rumours around the death of Germanicus. Tacitus' characters are constantly watching, reading and attempting to interpret the actions, expressions and motives of others.[5] Like Tacitus, Graves is fascinated by the difficulty of arriving at a truthful account and he uses various devices to build 'doubt and obscurity' into his novels, challenging the reader to interpret the truth of a scene or statement and to question the reliability of sources, rumours, interpretations and even the narrator. Throughout the novels, the character Claudius attempts to sort out the truth behind the confusion of events, and various elements within the novel reflect this struggle to attain an impossible clarity.

Graves's style differs from both the archaising language common to nineteenth-century historical novels and the tortured, fragmented prose of Tacitus.[6] His characters speak in a contemporary idiom and he modernises Roman expressions in a way that occasionally sounds odd – for example, 'manly-gown' for *toga uirilis* (*Claudius the God* 483). He draws attention to his anachronistic style early in *I, Claudius,* when he says 'my hope is that you, my eventual readers of a hundred generations ahead or more, will feel yourselves directly spoken to as a contemporary' (5). But while his modern-sounding prose style creates the illusion of transparency, Graves complicates the apparently straightforward relation of reader to text by various devices, including the narrator's revelation that the text is written not in Latin, as one might expect, but in Greek.[7] 'I have chosen to write in Greek', remarks Claudius, 'because Greek, I believe, will always remain the chief literary language of the world, and if Rome rots away as the Sybil has indicated, will not her language rot away with her?' (*I, Claudius* 14). If Claudius was so inept an interpreter of history as to predict that Greek, not Latin, would become the world's *lingua franca*, how can readers trust his other conclusions and conjectures? Other questions about Claudius as narrator are

---

[5] E.g. *A.* 1.11.2–3, where the senators attempt to weigh the credibility of Tiberius' proposal to share power with them.
[6] Mitchison (1979) 163–4 claimed to have been the first British author to write historical novels in a contemporary style: 'Oddly enough I was the first to see that one could write historical novels in a modern idiom: in fact, it was the only way I could write them. Now everybody does, so it is no longer interesting.'
[7] Du Pont (2005) analyses the phenomenon of 'pseudotranslation' in the Claudius novels.

raised by a passage that describes another of his literary ventures, a public history of his life which he dictated to a Greek slave who 'modelled his style so accurately on mine, that really, when he had done, nobody could have guessed what was mine and what was his'. He himself, he claims, could not remember writing entire chapters of this volume, but the style was clearly his own. He adds, 'Reading over what I have just put down I see that I must be rather exciting than disarming suspicion, first as to my sole authorship of what follows, next as to my integrity as an historian, and finally as to my memory for facts' (5).

Graves conveys some of the ambiguity and difficulty of Tacitus' writing through his presentation of Claudius' repeated attempts to come to grips with the raw materials of history.[8] In a scene set in the Palatine library, Pollio and Livy argue over the best way to write history. Claudius comments that Livy 'makes the people of Ancient Rome behave and talk as if they were alive now'. Pollio then says to Livy, 'You credit the Romans of seven centuries ago with impossibly modern motives and habits and speeches. Yes, it's readable all right, but it's not history' (107). Asked to choose sides, Claudius comes down on the side of Pollio: 'As I am sure that I can never hope to attain Livy's inspired literary elegance, I shall do my best to imitate Pollio's accuracy and diligence' (110–11). The irony, of course, is that while the *narrator* Claudius adopts the 'Livian' device of crediting Romans with 'impossibly modern motives and habits and speeches', the *character* Claudius endorses Pollio's model of diligent historical accuracy.[9] He struggles to interpret conflicting, biased, incomplete and sometimes deliberately deceptive sources of all sorts: the City archives, an oral prophecy from the Cumaean Sibyl and a copy of 'such prophecies found incorporated in the original canon as have been rejected as spurious by the priests of Apollo' (10), a full account of her crimes from the dying Livia, the contents of the Palatine library, letters and notebooks of various members of the royal family, testimony from slaves, etc. From these disparate, biased and possibly untrustworthy sources, he pieces together his history.

Paul Fussell has noted that Graves used much the same technique in his wartime memoir, *Goodbye to All That*, a book Fussell characterises as rich

> in fatuous, erroneous, or preposterous written 'texts' and documents, the normal materials of serious 'history' but here exposed in all their farcical ineptitude and

---

[8] On the difficulty of reading Tacitus, see O'Gorman (2000) 1–10.
[9] At the end of this scene, Claudius attempts to reconcile the two kinds of history, saying to Pollio, 'there are two different ways of writing history; one is to persuade men to virtue and the other is to compel men to truth. The first is Livy's way and the other is yours: and *perhaps they are not irreconcilable*' (113–14, my italics). See Furbank (2004) 102–3.

error. Almost all of them ... have in common some dissociation from actuality or some fatal error in assumption or conclusion. Their variety is striking ... There are the propaganda news clippings about the priests of Antwerp, hung upside down as human clappers in their own church bells. There is the laughable Loos attack order, and the optimistic orders, all based on false premises, written on field message forms. There is the colonel's letter deposing not merely that Graves is dead but that he was 'very gallant'... The point of all these is not just humankind's immense liability to error, folly, and psychosis. It is also the dubiousness of a rational – or at least a clear-sighted – historiography. The documents on which a work of 'history' might be based are so wrong or so loathsome or so silly or so downright mad that no one could immerse himself in them for long, Graves implies, without coming badly unhinged.[10]

Graves did come badly unhinged after his immersion in the loathsome madness of the First World War. Like so many who experienced trench warfare, he returned to civilian life feeling betrayed, stripped of illusions and shattered by post-traumatic stress disorder. His response was to leave England for voluntary exile on the island of Majorca, where he lived a semi-isolated life free of the bourgeois society he had come to despise. At the conclusion of *Claudius the God* Claudius similarly dreams of an external alternative to the corruption and vice of Rome for his beloved son Britannicus – Britain, the last place on earth where a life of heroic virtue is possible (485–6):

'But the world is now wholly Roman, with the exception of Germany, the East, the Scythian deserts north of the Black Sea, unexplored Africa, and the farther parts of Britain: so where can my Britannicus be safe from Nero's power?' I asked myself. 'Not in Parthia or Arabia: there could be no worse choice. Not in Germany: I have never loved the Germans. For all their barbaric virtues they are our natural enemies. Of Africa and Scythia I know little. There is only one place for a Britannicus, and that is Britain.'

Claudius clings to the hope that Britannicus will stain his skin blue and become one of the 'brave and courteous warriors' who serve the British Queen Cartimandua. As Joshel remarks, 'Having debunked Roman versions of such heroes in Livy, Graves projects their purity onto the ancient Britons, his own putative ancestors.'[11]

Speaking for the conquered: Naomi Mitchison

The romantic vision of Britain and the Britons was a manifestation of an idea of British antiquity that has persisted in the popular imagination

---

[10] Fussell (1987) 123–4.
[11] Joshel (2001) 124.

since the sixteenth century and that has its roots in classical sources like this description of Calgacus, rallying his troops before the pivotal battle of Mons Graupius (*Agr.* 30.3–5):

> 'But there are no longer any nations beyond us; nothing but waves and rocks and the Romans, even more deadly these – for you can't escape their arrogance through obedience or good behaviour. Pillagers of the world, they have exhausted the land by their comprehensive ravaging and now they ransack the sea. A rich enemy excites their greed; a poor one, their lust for power. East and West alike have failed to satisfy them. They are the only people on earth so greedy as to be tempted by both riches and poverty. They use lying names: robbery, slaughter and plunder they call "government"; they create a desert and call it "peace".'

Tacitus' vivid narratives of resistance to Roman rule, centred around Calgacus and the heroic British leaders Boudicca (Boadicea) and Caractacus, helped shape a romantic, patriotic view of ancient history. The ancient Britons were imagined as strong and noble savages, hardened by the harsh climate of their island country and ferociously determined to defend their freedom. This romanticisation of the early Britons culminated in the nineteenth century in Tennyson's lurid Boadicea, 'mad and maddening all who heard her in her fierce volubility', stirring a 'wild confederacy' of native tribes to battle against the Roman oppressors.[12] Tennyson's Boadicea is both an avatar of and a foil for Victoria, the British queen whose discipline and restraint were legendary, and who would avenge the Britons' defeat by establishing England as an imperial power.[13] The identification between Victoria and the warrior queen was actively encouraged by Prince Albert, who advised the sculptor Thomas Thornycroft on the design of the monumental bronze statue of Boadicea that is now to be found at the end of Westminster Bridge in London. Boadicea stands in a regal war chariot, arms uplifted, gripping a spear in one hand, flanked by her half-naked daughters. In the Victorian and Edwardian periods, Boadicea and Caractacus transcended their historical defeat at the hands of the Romans and became proleptic indicators of the future glory of imperial Britain.[14] Mythical Britain, land of freedom and refuge from corrupting civilisation, was a popular setting for such works of historical fiction as Bulwer-Lytton's *The Last Days of Pompeii* (1834), Macaulay's *Lays of Ancient Rome* (1842), Whyte-Melville's *The Gladiators* (1863), G.A. Henty's *Beric the Briton* (1897) and Kipling's *Puck of Pook's Hill* (1906).

[12] Tennyson, *Boadicea*, lines 4 and 6.
[13] Lovelace (2003) 67–9.
[14] Smiles (1994) 164.

These works shaped the imagination of Scottish writer Naomi Mitchison, a member of the intellectually prominent and politically active Haldane family. Educated at home after the age of twelve, she read Latin and Roman history and was fascinated by Roman Gaul and Britain. Tales of Gauls and Britons conquered by – yet resistant to – Roman tyranny featured repeatedly in her own historical fiction, which was firmly grounded in contemporary events and intended to promote her political views. Her first historical novel, *The Conquered* (1923), is set in Roman Gaul and inspired by the Irish War of Independence (1919–21), a revolt against British rule that resulted in rebellion, a bitter civil war and the partitioning of Ireland. In the novel, the Romans play the role of the British and impose their rule on the rebellious indigenous population. The novel's epigraph, *Victrix causa deis placuit sed victa puellis* ('The winning cause was pleasing to the gods, but the conquered was pleasing to girls'), epitomises Mitchison's reaction as a schoolgirl to reading Roman history: a fierce, Lucanian sympathy for the victims of Empire. Recalling these early encounters with ancient history, she remarked, 'Not unnaturally, one always sided with the barbarians against Rome.'[15]

Just as her depiction of conquered Gaul was shaped by her reaction to the troubles in Ireland in the early 1920s, so Mitchison's grim narrative of Nero's Rome, *The Blood of the Martyrs,* was wrung out of her by a combination of political despair – her fears of where contemporary politics would lead – and her own desolation after the loss of a child.[16] Among her most despairing works, *The Blood of the Martyrs* is both an allegory of the rise of totalitarianism and an outspoken affirmation of her socialist beliefs. The slaughter of the First World War and signs of the coming conflict with Hitler shaped Mitchison's political views. For many writers of her generation, the nostalgic dream of a return to an Arcadian pre-war England was shattered by the horrible realities of the Second World War and the subsequent political disintegration of Europe. For some writers during the ominous 1930s, the Arcadian dream was displaced by utopianism, 'an orientation towards the future rather than the past, and a conviction that the solution to society's ills lies not in restoring a Golden Age but in creating a brand new kind of social organization'.[17] Among the utopian thinkers of the period were socialist writers who used the historical novel as a critique of Fascism in the 1930s, most notably Sylvia Townsend Warner, Jack Lindsay,

---

[15] Mitchison (1924) 316.
[16] The novel was first published in 1939. Page references in the present chapter are to the 1948 edition.
[17] Rae (2003) 246.

Leopold Myers and Mitchison herself.[18] In *The Blood of the Martyrs,* she underlines her socialist message with chapter titles like 'The bosses', 'Ends and means', 'The individual and the state', and 'The doctrine of efficiency'. The dedication thanks friends, editors, consultants and 'Austrian socialists in the counter-revolution of 1934, share-croppers in the named and unnamed host of the witnesses against tyranny and superstition and the worship of the State, witnesses for humanity and reason and kindliness, whose blood is crying to us now'.

The Blood of the Martyrs returns to the themes of power and conquest, assimilation and identity raised in *The Conquered* and in *Barbarian Stories* (1929), but the setting this time is in the heart of Nero's Rome. Mitchison reworks the plot of G.A. Henty's novel *Beric the Briton,* calling attention to the borrowing by using the name of Henty's hero, Beric, for her own protagonist. Both novels are set in Neronian Rome and in both Rome is split between the old aristocrats, who embody old Roman virtues, and the corrupt followers of Nero. Henty's Beric follows in the footsteps of Calgacus, Boudicca and Caractacus in his bravery and love of liberty, but he inhabits a plot with a more optimistic trajectory. Beric the Briton falls in love with Roman Aemilia, who unites old-fashioned Roman virtue with Christian morality; she persuades him to convert to Christianity. After the death of Nero, they marry and he becomes the governor of Britain, bringing enlightened rule to the country and foreshadowing the civilising mission of the British Empire. As Hoberman puts it, the romance plot found in *Beric the Briton* and similar fictions of Rome 'depicted Roman imperialism as a happy ending to a fairy tale, in which the conquered Britons merge their energy with Roman self-control and live happily ever after. The merging often takes literal form in the marriage of Roman and Briton, channeling all of the reader's romantic voyeurism into a desire for this marriage to take place.'[19]

Mitchison's Beric, however, finds himself in a much more complicated situation than that of his namesake. Beric, the son of a British chieftain, raised in the household of the aristocrat Flavius Crispus, discovers that, although he has been treated like a son by his kind patron, he has neither the status nor the privileges of a Roman citizen. He has been carrying on an affair with Flavia, the daughter of the house, but in the banquet scene that launches the novel, she humiliates him in public and becomes engaged instead to Aelius Candidus, a vicious subordinate of Tigellinus.

---

[18] See Montefiore (1996) ch. 5: 'Parables of the past: a reading of some anti-Fascist historical novels'.

[19] Hoberman (1997) 120.

Disoriented by this turn of events, Beric is befriended by a dancing girl named Lalage and some of the slaves from Crispus' household. They begin to undermine his automatic identification with the Roman masters, and lead him to question the mechanisms of oppression that maintain the class structure in Rome. These egalitarian slaves are Christians – proto-Socialist Christians who preach a gospel of social equality and believe their Messiah will bring about a revolution on earth. Mitchison's Christians, like their author, show little interest in religion *per se*; Beric is attracted not by the promise of salvation but by their message of equality and the joy of fighting for a cause greater than the individual.

Both the structure and characters of the novel reflect Mitchison's socialist ideals. The novel opens with a focus on the Roman aristocrats with whom Beric identifies and associates. Three noble senators, Crispus, his friend Balbus and Gallio (brother of the philosopher Seneca), discuss emperors past and present in a dinner party conversation that reads like a cross between an epitome of Tacitus' *Annals* and Graves's Claudius novels (22):

> 'There was that unhappy madman [Tiberius], betrayed by his wife and his friends, and last by his own scholarship, glowering and pouncing between here and Capri. And then when he died and young Gaius took over – Caligula they called him, remember, Crispus? – it seemed like the good old days. Yes, the exiles came back, there were free elections and free speech again; we thought Rome could be Rome … But it was hardly a year before the prosecutions and the tyranny came back; Gaius was as mad as Tiberius. The things we had to put through in the Senate! Enough to make one ashamed to bear one's grandfather's name. And then Gaius was murdered and the Divine Claudius came shambling and stammering; but still, he was no tyrant. No, Gallio, he kept the Provinces together and he might have done well for Rome, but for trusting his wives and his freedmen. It didn't send him mad, being Caesar, but whether Nero is going the same way as Tiberius and Gaius – what do you think, Gallio?'
>
> 'He's not mad, he's bad,' Gallio answered. 'It would take more than my poor brother and Burrus to hold a boy like that. He took after his mother. And she was a devil. But he only murdered her for a worse woman yet. Women and slaves!'

The 'good Romans' in the novel are stuck in a nostalgic longing for the past, vainly dreaming of restoring the virtues of an earlier Rome. Beric's mentor, the kindly Crispus, is described as going 'along to bed, still sighing and shaking his head and wondering if it could be true that the Emperor was no better than the rest, that something was really wrong, so badly wrong that it could not be put right by going back – back to the manners and decencies and truthfulness and civilisation of Augustus – or farther' (25). But, while

Crispus and the uncorrupted senators dream of a vanished golden age, Nero and his court presage a dystopian future. His egotism, the cult of personality that he encourages, and his demonisation of the Christians for political purposes clearly evoke Hitler, and he speaks in a fascist idiom, using slogans like 'Strength through joy!' and 'I am the Will of Rome'.

As the novel progresses, however, Mitchison creates a narrative that deliberately inverts the Rome depicted by Tacitus, who, like most surviving classical authors, was primarily preoccupied with the social and political interactions of the elite and the intrigues of the imperial court. Thus, though her story depends on characters (Nero, Lucan, Seneca, Claudia Acte, Poppaea, Tigellinus, etc.) and events familiar to us from the pages of Tacitus, Mitchison's main characters are the slaves and foreigners who have so little voice in classical texts. As Beric becomes more and more alienated from the Romans with whom he has grown up and identified, the narrative focus shifts away from the elite senators and members of the Neronian court and towards the 'women and slaves' that the aristocratic Gallio sees as the cause of Nero's bad character. These characters seek neither to restore the golden age of senatorial rule nor to succumb to the emperor's totalitarian rule, but represent instead the dream of a utopian society. They imagine a world in which people 'loved and trusted and understood each other without too many words; they were no longer separated by fear and suspicion and competition and class' (34).

Mitchison's anachronistic projection of the political situation in Europe of the 1930s on to the backdrop of Neronian Rome creates a rather disorienting reading experience that has put some readers off. A contemporary review in the *New Statesman* compared Mitchison's Christian proto-Socialists to 'a Fabian summer school captured by white slavers'.[20] However, the anachronistic juxtapositions are part of a deliberate strategy meant to force the reader, like Beric, to undergo an alteration of consciousness, discover a new identity and, ultimately, 'to align herself with the progressive, egalitarian, and solidarity-steeped early Christians of the narrative and thereby with the oppressed and dispossessed of her own time and place'.[21]

The Blood of the Martyrs raises unsettling questions about martyrdom – the same questions Tacitus raised in the conclusion of *Agricola*, when he weighed the life of Agricola, a good man who loyally served under a bad emperor, against the exemplary deaths of those who openly resisted Domitian (*Agr.* 42.3–4):

> Domitian was by nature prone to anger and, the more he hid it, the less it was possible to suppress it; yet even he was softened by the self-restraint and

---

[20] Mair (1939), cited by Calder (1997) 146 and Castelli (2006) 4.
[21] Castelli (2006) 8.

prudence of Agricola, who did not compete for fame or challenge fate out of stubbornness and a futile parade of independence. Let it be clear to those who admire disobedience that even under bad emperors men can be great, and that obedience and restraint, if backed by industry and energy, can reach that high degree of reputation which most men attain only by following a perilous course, winning fame by an ambitious death without benefiting their country.

Beric struggles throughout the novel with the question of whether to embrace Christian pacifism and submit to martyrdom or to choose violent resistance. Mitchison, who was herself passionately committed to political transformation through civic action, appears to be not entirely at ease with the Christian paradigm of martyrdom, and the conclusion of her novel is hardly an unambiguous endorsement of it. Its conclusion evokes several texts: Henty's *Beric the Briton*, Mitchison's own *The Conquered* and Tacitus' *Annals*. Beric the Briton triumphed in the arena, and lived to marry his Christian Roman wife and establish Roman governance in Britain. Mitchison's Beric suffers an inverse fate. His Flavia proves to be a decadent slut, he fails in his attempt to murder Tigellinus and he dies in the arena. His death scene rewrites in a more uncertain register the resolution of the issues of identity and resistance that Mitchison had offered in *The Conquered*. That novel ends in a metamorphosis: its hero, Meromic, is transformed into his totem animal, a wolf, and heads north into the untamed woods, away from the constraints of Roman rule. In *The Blood of the Martyrs*, the totemic wolf again appears, but this time, instead of being a vehicle of transformation, it tears Beric apart in the arena. Optimists could read the wolf as a liberator, like the wolf in *The Conquered*, that brings an end to Beric's suffering and ultimately frees him from the power of Rome. But the wolf was also the totem animal of the Romans and carried special political resonance in the 1930s, when the she-wolf who nurtured Romulus and Remus was adopted by the Italian fascists as a symbol of resurgent Roman might.[22]

The last chapter of the novel describes a meeting of the remaining Christians, who are comforted by their belief that their friends' martyrdom and suffering will bring about the social transformation they long for. In the novel's concluding gesture, Eunice, who bakes the bread for the Eucharist, prepares to give a piece of cake and a hot drink to visiting strangers. 'So ends

---

[22] Mussolini even had copies of the statue of the Capitoline wolf sent to several American cities, including Rome, Georgia. Georgians found the nursing wolf and bare-bottomed children so offensive that on public occasions they draped the wolf and diapered the twins, according to the Greater Rome Convention and Visitors Bureau (www.romega.us/index.asp?NID=223). The wolf has connections to Hitler as well; his nickname was Wolf.

The Blood of the Martyrs, with an image of domestic service that seems all too familiarly feminine', remarked one critic.[23]

But, in fact, the novel does not end with that image of domestic service. It ends with a return to Tacitus, a historical note that summarises the Pisonian conspiracy. Significantly, the historical note does not look beyond the incomplete text of the *Annals*. It recounts the failure of the Pisonian conspiracy, but not the later plot that culminated in the death of Nero. While the novel's concluding chapter holds out hope that the cause of social justice can be advanced through pacifism, witness and suffering, that hopeful vision is balanced by the evocation of the Pisonian conspiracy.[24] Are readers to interpret the reference to the Pisonian conspirators as a step along the path to the eventual overthrow of Nero? Or does Mitchison's decision to end the novel with Nero triumphant suggest that overwhelming power can crush resistance? The ending reflects Mitchison's own ambivalent state of mind about the historical and political situation of Europe on the eve of war. At times in her portrayal of the Christian underground she projects the tremendous optimism and feeling of solidarity she felt when swept up in the socialist cause.[25] But, as she completed the novel in 1939, her mood was more despairing. Reflecting on that year in her memoir, she recalls: 'For all of us international socialists, whatever the outcome of the war, we felt ourselves, deep inside, already defeated. Stalin and Chamberlain had seen to that'.[26]

Losing memory as well as voice

The *Agricola* is, among other things, a meditation on *libertas* (freedom). Early in the text Tacitus remembers senators killed for their opposition to Domitian and mourns the loss of *libertas*, freedom of speech and thought, among the men of his age (*Agr.* 2.1, 3):

> We have read that when Thrasea Paetus was praised by Arulenus Rusticus and Helvidius Priscus by Herennius Senecio, it was a capital crime, and that not only the authors but even their books were objects of rage, and the triumvirs were commissioned to burn these reminders of the noblest characters in the

---

[23] Hoberman (1997) 133. She goes on to say that the novel shows 'the limits of Mitchison's power to imagine a transformative role for historical fiction'.
[24] See Hoberman (1997) 133–5 for a discussion of Mitchison's use of myth 'as a refuge from history'.
[25] 'Looking back on it all, what is so strange and striking was the feeling we all had that, if we tried hard enough, the millennium – the revolution or whatever we called it – would come into being. Where there was a choice, the signposts were clear. We knew which side we were on. Moreover, we felt we had a cause worth living for, even worth dying for' (Mitchison (1979) 205).
[26] Mitchison (1979) 221.

comitium and the Forum.... Certainly we showed great proof of submissiveness; and just as a former age had witnessed the extreme of liberty, so we witnessed the extreme of servitude, when even the exchange of speech and listening was stolen from us by informers. If it had been as much in our power to forget as to keep silence, we would have lost memory as well as voice (*memoriam quoque ipsam cum uoce perdidissemus, si tam in nostra potestate esset obliuisci quam tacere*).

He returns to this theme at the end of the *Agricola*, but this time, instead of praising the *libertas* of men like Arulenus Rusticus and Herennius Senecio, he makes the case that it was the duty of good men to survive and that Agricola's refusal to risk his life by speaking out against the emperor was the only rational choice (*Agr.* 42.3–4, cited above).

The interlocking issues Tacitus explores at the beginning and the conclusion of the *Agricola* – what room is there for right action under a tyranny? Is it better to die a martyr and be useless to the state, or to submit, survive and ensure that the memory of events lives on? – mattered to Lion Feuchtwanger, a prolific German writer and novelist. Like Mitchison, he used historical novels as a means of spreading his political and social views. In an essay on the historical novel published in 1935, he remarked:

> Both the historian and the novelist view history as the struggle of a tiny minority, able and determined to make judgments, which is up against a vast and densely packed majority of the blind, who are led by their instincts and unable to think for themselves.
>
> I believe it is important to depict episodes from earlier phases in this struggle. Reminders of earlier victories and defeats, legends, and historical novels seem to me to be a weapon we can well use at our present stage in this eternal struggle. Our opponents, incidentally, are aware of the value of this weapon; they are recasting human history in the form of sentimental myths, according to their ideological precepts, and they are also busy heating up the historical novel in some of its stalest forms.[27]

Feuchtwanger, a German Jew, was an outspoken critic of the Nazis, the 'opponents' he mentions in his essay. His 1930 satirical novel, *Success* (*Erfolg*), parodied the rapidly growing National Socialist movement; its leader, Rupert Kutzner, a pale, thin-lipped man with a small moustache and slicked-back hair, addressed the masses in a high, hysterical voice and blamed Jews, the Pope and international banking systems for the sad state of Germany. Feuchtwanger's outspoken criticism attracted the attention of Goebbels, who, when Feuchtwanger remarked that Berlin was becoming a city of future exiles, ominously responded that Feuchtwanger had

---

[27] Feuchtwanger (1935).

earned his place among them. On 1 February 1933, the day after Hitler was sworn in as Chancellor, the German ambassador to the United States called Feuchtwanger, who was there on a lecture tour, and warned him not to return to Germany. In August that same year, Feuchtwanger's German citizenship was revoked because of disloyalty to the state. In exile in France, he continued to write overtly anti-Nazi novels, including *Der Falsche Nero* (*The Pretender*) and the Josephus trilogy, throughout the 1930s. After the Wehrmacht invaded France in 1940, he was put in an internment camp, Les Milles. With the assistance of the American consulate, Feuchtwanger's wife engineered his escape from Les Milles to Marseille. The couple sneaked their way on to a train that took them to a village near the Spanish border and they hiked over the mountains into Spain, where they gained entry by bribing the border guards with cigarettes. From there they departed for the United States and settled in Los Angeles, where they lived for the rest of their lives.

In *Josephus and the Emperor*, the concluding novel of his trilogy based on the life of the historian Josephus (its German title is *Der Tag wird kommen*, *The Day Will Come*), Feuchtwanger explores the difficulty of reconciling conflicting elements of Josephus' identity: devout Jew and Roman citizen; patriot devoted to his native land and passionate believer in the need to create a cosmopolitan, international culture. In the words of one reviewer, 'Here is one of the most tragic figures of modern society, the assimilated European Jew, the good German of Jewish ancestry.'[28] For Feuchtwanger the dilemma of whether and how to speak out against oppression had particular urgency. His own outspokenness resulted in loss of citizenship and exile; Jews and other opponents of the Nazis who remained in Germany during the rise of the Third Reich had to weigh the moral imperative to protest and the danger of imprisonment or death. Feuchtwanger dramatises this issue in *Josephus and the Emperor* by using Tacitus himself as a character in a subplot that recounts one of Domitian's most notorious deeds, the sentencing of the Vestal Virgin Cornelia to be buried alive for alleged unchastity.[29] Characters representative of the 'ancient aristocracy' react to the news of her trial and condemnation in different ways; the characters are drawn from historical accounts, but Feuchtwanger has made some changes. His Fannia and Gratilla are presented here respectively as the widow and the sister of Caepio, who was executed by Domitian after participating in Lucius Antonius Saturninus' failed revolt against Domitian in 89. Caepio is a fictional character: the historical Fannia was the wife of Helvidius Priscus

---

[28] Apsler (1947) 23.
[29] Plin. *Ep.* 4.11, Suet. *Dom.* 8.

the elder and stepmother of the younger Helvidius; Gratilla was probably the wife of Arulenus Rusticus, another victim of Domitian's treason trials. Fannia (both the character and the historical figure) was the descendant of two celebrated suicides: her grandmother Arria, who famously remarked to her husband before he too committed suicide, 'It doesn't hurt, Paetus' (*Paete, non dolet*), and her father Thrasea Paetus, whose forced suicide, by the luck of textual transmission, is where the extant text of Tacitus' *Annals* comes to its abrupt end. The other characters in this subplot are Senator Helvidius (presumably Helvidius Priscus the younger); Decian, a fictional character based on the addressee of one of Martial's poems;[30] Priscus, a fictional character resembling Arulenus Rusticus;[31] and Publius Cornelius (Tacitus himself, whom Feuchtwanger makes a cousin of the condemned Cornelia). They are stunned by the rumour of Cornelia's sentence, and their first reaction is to deny that it could be true (165):

> 'He will not dare it.' With that they had comforted themselves from the first day on which they had heard about the rumour. But in how many cases had they comforted themselves with similar words. As often as there was talk of some new, shameless intention of the Emperor's they had muttered between clenched teeth: He won't dare that; the Senate and the people won't stand for that. But, especially since the unfortunate uprising of Saturninus, he had dared everything, and the Senate and the people had stood for everything.

Publius Cornelius reacts first, with words that recall Tacitus' praise of Agricola's obedience at *Agricola* 42.3–4: '"He will dare it", he said, "and we shall be silent. Shall accept it and be silent. And we shall be right in doing so; for it is the only thing left for us to do in these times"' (166). He is sharply contradicted by the elderly Fannia, a living personification of Republican resistance to the Principate, who makes the future historian doubt his caution (166):

> Whenever Fannia spoke, doubts overcame Cornelius whether perhaps after all he was not wrong in calling heroic that silence which he recommended with so many reasonable arguments. Perhaps, in the last analysis, the demonstrative martyrdom of a Fannia was the better virtue.

In an argument that pits the virtue of reason against the virtue of heroic protest, Decian takes the side of Cornelius. He is a quiet man, silently in love with the Vestal, who, despite his anguish, sees no useful action

---

[30] His character and the side he takes in the discussion suggest that he is modelled on the Decianus of Martial 1.8, whom Martial congratulates for being able to combine praiseworthy action with survival.

[31] The character Priscus is said to be composing a historical work about Fannia's father, Thrasea Paetus; Arulenus Rusticus was put to death for writing a panegyric of Paetus.

that can be taken. Another character, Priscus, characterised as the 'greatest lawyer of the Empire', tries to find a third way between speech and silence (169):

> He had now found a personal solution for himself. He was silent, and yet he was not silent. He vented his resentment in a historical work, in a representation of the life of the great Paetus Thrasea, Fannia's father. It fascinated him to set down the life of this republican (whom Nero had had executed for his liberal views) with the greatest objectivity, stripped of all legendary traits, and to present him so, that this Paetus Thrasea, even without the mythical accessories, appeared as a great man and worthy of the highest veneration ... This work, however, now almost finished, was intended only for the author and his closest intimates, especially for Fannia. To publish such a book under Domitian's regime meant risking position and income, even life, and he had never thought of doing that.

Fannia's call to action proves more persuasive than Cornelius' caution. Priscus decides to publish his biography of Paetus, and Helvidius is emboldened to move openly in the senate against Domitian. The result is, as Cornelius predicted, catastrophic for the individual actors and for their cause. Domitian decides to purge the Republican resistance. Fannia and Gratilla and Decian are convicted of treason and sentenced to exile; Priscus' books are burned, and he and Helvidius are executed. Of the group of friends who gathered to discuss the fate of Cornelia, only Cornelius, who refuses to be drawn into open protest against the emperor, remains to witness the end of Domitian's reign. In Cornelius' last appearance in the novel, he prepares to write the introduction of the *Agricola* (407–8):

> The day had come. In his study Senator Cornelius, the historian, sat and thought over what had happened. The heavy furrows in his sombre, earth-coloured face[32] had grown even deeper; he was only in his early forties, but he had the face of an old man ... He thought of the faces of his friends who had gone to their death, of the women who had gone into exile. They had been grim faces, yet the faces of people who were resigned. They had been heroes; he was only a man and a writer. They had only been heroes; he was a man and a writer ... In powerful, sombre sentences, like towering blocks of stone, he re-created the horrors and crimes of the Palatine; and for the heroism of his friends he found words large and bright as the skies of an early summer day.

Feuchtwanger uses Tacitean material and the character of Tacitus himself to explore the possible consequences of action and inaction, speech and

---

[32] The description of his 'sombre, earth-coloured face' suggests that Cornelius, as he prepares to bear witness to history, has taken on the role of Fannia, described earlier as having an 'earth-coloured face hardened from suffering and severity' (168).

silence, for people caught in a historical moment that leaves them faced with impossible choices. He drew on the 'horrors and crimes' of imperial Rome to expose the horrors and crimes of his own day, using the historical novel as a political weapon. One suspects he took to heart the last words of Thrasea at the end of the text of Tacitus' *Annals* (16.35.1). Offering to Jupiter the blood pouring from his slashed wrists, he said to the young quaestor who had brought him the order to commit suicide, 'you have been born into times when it is necessary to strengthen the spirit with examples of fortitude' (*in ea tempora natus es quibus firmare animum expediat constantibus exemplis*). Despite great differences in class, nationality and political beliefs, Robert Graves, the shell-shocked poet in exile, Naomi Mitchison, the Scottish feminist and socialist, and Lion Feuchtwanger, the outspoken German Jewish writer, all looked to Tacitus to provide 'examples of fortitude' in troubled times.

FURTHER READING

For an overview of the later reception of Tacitus, see Mellor (1993). Montefiore (1996), Joannou (1999) and Rae (2003) offer good discussions of British writers' reactions to the First and Second World Wars. Hoberman (1997) focuses on the use of the ancient world by twentieth-century women writers and has a good discussion of Naomi Mitchison's novels. Joshel (2001) remains the best analysis of both the novel *I, Claudius* and the BBC television series.

The list of novelists who have used the events related by Tacitus for plot material is enormous. Especially influential, though they were written in the late nineteenth century, are H. Sienkiewicz, *Quo Vadis* (1896) and L. Wallace, *Ben-Hur: a tale of the Christ* (1880): see Fitzgerald (2001) and Winkler (2001) for discussions of Hollywood adaptations of the novels. J. Hersey, *The Conspiracy* (1972), satirised Richard Nixon's secretive White House in his novel about the Pisonian conspiracy. Albert Bell, *All Roads Lead to Murder* (2002), perhaps inspired by the phenomenal success of Lindsey Davis's series of detective stories set in Vespasian's Rome, offers the unlikely pairing of Pliny the Younger as detective with Tacitus as his hard-drinking sidekick. The lure of the rebellious Boudicca has not faded with time: H. Treece, *Red Queen, White Queen* (1958), P. Gedge, *The Eagle and the Raven* (1978) and R. Sutcliff, *Song for a Dark Queen* (1978), offer very different fictional treatments of the warrior queen. Perhaps the least recognisable to Tacitus would be that featured in the popular fantasy novels by Manda Scott in her Boudica series: *Dreaming the Eagle* (2003), *Dreaming the Bull* (2004), *Boudica: Dreaming the Hound* (2006) and *Dreaming the Serpent Spear* (2007).

21

MARK TOHER

Tacitus' Syme

Only two ancient historians, Tacitus and Thucydides, have had a direct and enduring influence on how modern historians understand and write history. While Tacitus does not enjoy the status of Thucydides as required reading still in philosophy and politics courses, his influence is clearly evident on the two greatest historians of imperial Rome, Edward Gibbon and Sir Ronald Syme.[1] Indeed, it is this triumvirate of an ancient, early modern and modern historian that is responsible for the prevalent pessimistic view that, for all its achievements in so many realms, Rome under the emperors was an environment of ambition, deceit and violence.

Syme (1903–89) was a New Zealander but from the age of twenty-two Oxford was his home, first as an undergraduate at Oriel College (1925–7),[2] then from 1929 as Fellow of Trinity College. He moved to Brasenose College in 1949 when elected Camden Professor of Ancient History, was knighted in 1959 and, upon his retirement in 1970, was elected a Fellow of Wolfson College. In 1976 he was appointed to the Order of Merit, one of the highest honours bestowed by the monarch in the United Kingdom and restricted to twenty-four members at any one time. The author of more than a dozen scholarly books and over two hundred articles and essays on the history, historiography and prosopography of Rome, Syme, along with Theodor Mommsen, is generally recognised as one of the two greatest Roman historians of the modern era.

Of all his publications over the course of sixty years, Syme's two great works were *The Roman Revolution* (1939) and *Tacitus* (1958). Written in a

---

Given the topic of this essay, acknowledgement of debt and gratitude to others is more than pro forma. A.R. Birley, Miriam Griffin and Fergus Millar provided illuminating comments on an early draft, and Professor Birley was especially kind in allowing me to read correspondence and unpublished work of Syme that was previously unavailable to me. The standard acknowledgement concerning any remaining error applies.

[1] For Tacitus and Gibbon see above, pp. 269–79.
[2] Syme had taken a BA in Classics at Victoria University College in Wellington (1923) and an MA in French at Auckland (1924).

style and from a perspective that clearly betray the influence of Tacitus, *The Roman Revolution* is an account of the violent transition to autocratic rule at Rome between 60 BC and AD 14. Syme took an avowedly hostile view of Augustus and his regime, and he analysed the composition of the oligarchy that maintained and competed for power during the era that was the binding link between the Republic and the Empire. *Tacitus* is a two-volume appraisal of Tacitus that interweaves a substantial social history of his era. Thought by many to be Syme's most important work, *Tacitus* 'established a model for the study of an ancient author in his historical context'.[3] Fifty and more years on, these two works remain the most important studies of their respective topics, and both are admired as much for the compelling style in which they are written as for their scholarship. Together they show how deeply Tacitus influenced the way Syme thought about Roman history and its composition.

It seems that Syme had an early interest in Greek epigraphy, which may explain why he came to Oriel College, where Marcus Tod was the tutor in ancient history.[4] Upon reading Tacitus as an undergraduate at Oxford, however, he turned to Roman history as his life's vocation. Syme recalled the approach to Roman history in Oxford in the 1920s as unsatisfying. The concentration was on the late Republic, a period then over-analysed and circumscribed by constitutional history and biography. Syme always distrusted an approach to history that relied on abstract principles to explain the behaviour of individuals or parties, and he had a very low estimate of the value of biography to a real historian. In faculty lectures, ancient historians were treated as sources of facts, 'not in and for themselves' as authors of literary works, and there were no sets of lectures that had Tacitus, Sallust or Livy as their topics. What appealed to Syme was Tacitus, especially the *Histories*.[5] Apparently that historian's abrupt, incisive narrative of imperial intrigue provided an escape from the elegant and anodyne observations on the death throes of the Republic found in the rotund Latin of Cicero.

Although he had an inclination to compose a book on Domitian after taking his undergraduate examinations in 1927,[6] Syme's earliest attempt at a monograph seems to have been a short work entitled *The Germania of Tacitus*, which won the Charles Oldham Prize in 1929.[7] The work is seventy-two pages in manuscript and is essentially an exercise in source-criticism

---

[3] Bowersock (1993) 556.
[4] Devine (2004) 941; although the set syllabus for the BA degree at the time would not have permitted an undergraduate to specialise in epigraphy.
[5] Syme archive, Bodleian Library, Oxford: notes from a lecture entitled 'Rom. Hist. 50 or 60 Years Ago'.
[6] Bowersock (1993) 545.
[7] Birley in Syme (1999) xii n. 4.

(*Quellenkritik*), then much in favour among German scholars. It is imaginative and sharp in its argument, but without any revolutionary conclusions about Tacitus. What is striking is an occasional dismissive attitude toward Tacitus that is not evident in Syme's mature work. The young Syme judged Tacitus in the *Germania* to be 'vague and grandiose' at the expense of precision in his terminology: '[H]is account is not of a kind to inspire any confidence in his critical powers when he deserts his sources and stands by his own opinion and judgement alone ... It is in precisely these passages where he is most himself that he is most unsatisfactory as an historical authority.'[8] This low assessment of Tacitus' acuity can be explained by the method of source-criticism that Syme employed in this work. Its iron laws of deduction reduced an extant text into a collage of its 'sources' and the author into a mindless medium of lost predecessors now resurrected through autopsy of his text. There is no evidence that Syme ever submitted this first study of Tacitus for publication, and that, combined with the fact that Syme never again engaged in elaborate *Quellenkritik*, suggests that he soon progressed beyond a method of text analysis that he dismissed with mild derision in *Tacitus*.[9]

It would be another thirty years before Syme would present his comprehensive judgement on Tacitus, but, when it came, it revealed how deeply Syme was affected by the ancient historian in his conception of what Roman history was and how it should be written.

First and foremost, Syme adopted Tacitus' focus on the governing class and the personal relations of senators and emperors as the primary topics of a Roman historian. The individuals who wielded power and those who competed for it were the subjects of Syme's historical narrative, since 'power is the essential subject of political history' ((1958a) 375):

> When the Caesars ruled, Rome remained the seat and domicile of power, even if power was exercised by an imbecile or by a group at court. The Roman government is therefore the historian's subject. The main concern of the government is with the senatorial class and the armed forces, as Tacitus clearly reveals. ((1958a) 445)

---

[8] Syme archive, Bodleian Library, Oxford: MS *The* Germania *of Tacitus*, pp. 44 and 53–4. Syme's conclusions about the nature of the *Germania* and Tacitus' limitations in it are still evident in Syme (1958a) 126–9, but there the criticism of Tacitus is replaced by the explanation that the historian, 'at the threshold of a magnificent achievement', was still honing the skills of inquiry and research.

[9] Cf. (1958a) 274 'The hunt for historical sources, often a pretext for frail hypothesis or tenuous argumentation, must here avow its affinity to guess and fancy'; also 291 '[T]he historian generally selects a single source and adheres to it closely; he abbreviates rather than supplements; and, if he alters, it is style not substance that is modified. In this dogma there are manifold attractions: the scope of historical inquiry can be narrowed on the plea of precision, the idiosyncrasy of a writer dismissed as irrelevant or barely existent'.

Crucial in such an approach to Roman history was an understanding of the political careers and family connections of the members of the Roman aristocracy. The complexity of the problem was the same for the modern historian as for his ancient counterpart:

> So many names and agents, such is the nature of senatorial annals ... For all his alertness, Tacitus was often baffled. Senators keep turning up (old families or new) whose importance depends upon their previous rank, alliances or actions. Not all were common property to the contemporaries of Tacitus, for many families had lapsed and perished in the course of the century.
>
> ((1958a) 379, 384)

Therefore, the prosopography of the Roman aristocracy that is the outstanding characteristic of Syme's work was not an end in itself, although his seemingly superhuman recall and precise control of the most arcane facts about the Roman aristocracy garnered from countless texts and inscriptions remains Syme's most impressive mental achievement. In Syme's work, prosopography was an analytical tool that rendered Roman politics comprehensible through the identification of those in power and their alliances. '[I]f the facts are properly set forth, they often arrange themselves in significant relationships. Not a mere catalogue of persons and families, but the development of a system of government and the process of change in the upper stratum of society' (Syme (1979) 539).

Syme's social history was not that of the demographers with their abstract calculations and deductions based on the meagre evidence for the populations of the Roman empire. Commenting on the greatest social historian of the ancient world, Syme said of Rostovtzeff and his *Social and Economic History of the Roman Empire* (1926): 'That great work ... would have benefited if the author had properly exploited Tacitus for the social history. Many of his generalizations are vague and vulnerable' ((1958a) 445 n. 1). Syme had little interest in the anonymous masses of antiquity, and if pressed on the issue would admit that they bored him.[10] The statement is not one of class prejudice, but rather an assertion of his Tacitean perspective: 'The lower classes had no voice in government, no place in history' (Syme (1939) 476). The senatorial class and the Principate that evolved from it were the controlling forces in Roman history. It was a perspective that Syme believed fundamental to understanding Tacitus:

> Preoccupation with the fate of noble Roman families does not have to be excused in an historian. If the old names appealed to sentiment and memory, they were also the substance of Roman annals, continuous from the Republic

---

[10] Alföldy (1983) 17.

> to the monarchy of the Caesars ... At Rome men and families had always mattered more than rules and institutions ... Oligarchy is the enduring fact of all Roman history, whether Republican or imperial, and constant in most things, save in its composition. The recruitment of that oligarchy, its titles to rank, its behaviour and its vicissitudes, such is the constant preoccupation of the historian Tacitus.   ((1958a) 562–3, 570, 583)

And Syme did not hesitate to defend it as his own view:

> Dynastic and family politics are only one aspect of the principate of Caesar Augustus. And these inquiries may incur dispraisal or censure as being a narrow theme, occupied with tedious pieces of information about names and personas, consuls and commanders of armies. On the contrary, this is the stuff and matter of political and social history ... [F]amilies and individuals illuminate the transition from Republic to Principate.   ((1984) 935–6)[11]

Both Tacitus and Syme viewed Roman history in personal terms, their outlook 'based on a profound interest in human beings and their relationships, against the background of their social environment in all its complexity'.[12]

But this focus on the personalities and lust for power in the Roman aristocracy had consequence. Narrative history as Tacitus (and Syme) practised it became the study of the dark side of humanity, sombre and pessimistic in its quest to 'unmask the guile of political managers and unravel the complexities of human nature' (Syme (1958a) 202). Ambition, deceit and violence ruled Roman affairs, and the few heroes in Tacitus were those senators who could retain their Republican honour (*dignitas*) in an age of autocracy and flattery (*adulatio*). Syme's heroes were the Roman historians Sallust, Asinius Pollio and Tacitus himself, writers who had the requisite 'maturity, penetration and ferocity' to pursue history rather than the historical mythology of Livy or the antiquarianism of Varro ((1958a) 202). Syme's own sharp judgement on men and affairs in *The Roman Revolution* resulted in Arnaldo Momigliano's labelling its author a 'moralist historian',[13] and many will agree. Yet Syme recognised the risks of moralising. Writing of Sallust some years after Momigliano's review, Syme noted that the ancient historian revealed 'the struggle for power behind the words and pretexts ... If his standpoint seemed to become moral rather than political, that was not unmixed gain for an historian' ((1958a) 204).

---

[11] Also Syme (1979) 711.
[12] E. Badian in Syme (1979) xiii, whose judgement on Syme is here extended to include Tacitus.
[13] Momigliano (1940) 75.

In addition to his view of the proper subject of history, Syme was also deeply influenced by Tacitus in the way he wrote history. Syme shared the ancients' view that history was a literary art and that 'style' (to use Syme's term) was integral to historical narrative. This view, unusual if not anachronistic for a 'modern' historian, may be explained by Syme's deep love of literature (especially poetry, which he could recite in many languages) and extraordinary talent with languages. As an undergraduate at Oxford he won three University prizes for composition in Latin prose, Greek prose and Greek verse (he had only begun studying ancient Greek four years before), and he could converse and correspond fluently in a number of modern languages (Turkish among them). Syme's linguistic talent is on full display in the ninety-five appendices in the second volume of *Tacitus*, many of which deal with recondite details of style and language and are impressive in their learning and accuracy even by the high standards of classical philology.

As has been repeatedly noted since the publication of *The Roman Revolution*, Syme's own style of writing history was clearly inspired by that of Tacitus in the *Annals*. From 1939 on, Syme's prose betrays a Tacitean development from an artfully concentrated, direct narrative of abrupt and short sentences with liberal use of asyndeton and parataxis to an increasingly opaque and elliptical mode of expression that occasionally dispensed with verbs and could leave the reader puzzling over its precise meaning ('Intrigue had been active, and eager partisans.').[14] While it is clear, especially in his later work, that Syme employed 'style' for effect, it is also clear that he considered such style essential to history properly composed:

> Narrative is the essence of history. To tell a story properly calls for speed and variety. Those virtues are inherent in the style of Tacitus. He never allows the action to flag or stagnate. Narrative records and explains what happened – imagination compels it to be seen and shared. An artist has free scope with description – he can choose, add, and invent. ((1958a) 193)

Style in history is essential because it is the means by which the skeleton of the historian's 'facts' is brought to life through imagination. History is a story and the historian an artist. Tacitus 'writes with that imagination which is the soul of history as it is of poetry'. The ancient historian shared a sombre, violent imagination with an older contemporary, the epic poet Lucan: 'Tacitus is a poet and a dramatist, not different in that from other historians (such as deserve the name), but better' (Syme (1958a) 363, 143, 546). This link between style and imagination in writing history might illuminate Syme's own evolution as a stylist. In the last two decades of his

---

[14] Syme (1958a) x.

career, as his prose seemed to become a caricature of itself, Syme had also became increasingly interested in the links between history and forgery and fiction. In a monograph on Julius Caesar that he seems to have been working on when he died, Syme maintained that the characterisation of Caesar in Shakespeare was as helpful – or more so – to the historian as the ancient biographies of Plutarch and Suetonius, the inspiration and imagination of the dramatist being of more historical use than the fictional anecdotes of biography.[15] This is not to suggest at all that Syme saw no distinction between history and fiction. But, where the facts and certitude ended, the historian had the duty to employ conjecture that found its origin in historical imagination, for without conjecture 'history is not worth writing, for it does not become intelligible' (Syme (1958a) v). Such conjecture was the art of the historian and as with any art, for it to be effective, it had to be presented with style.

Furthermore, Syme believed style was a function of genre and so he did not see the evolution in style in Tacitus as necessarily a chronological development. The Ciceronian tone of the *Dialogus* and the encomium of the *Agricola* could be explained as well by the demands of the genres as by any hypothesis of an early style of Tacitus.[16] The majesty of historical narrative in the *Histories* and *Annals* required something quite different:

> The effects to which the Tacitean idiom aspires are no mystery – the writer will be swift and splendid, intense and majestic. All manner of devices contribute. Tacitus likes his words to be hard and fierce, heavy and ominous ... Verbal disharmonies reflect the complexities of history and all that is ambiguous in the behaviour of men ... His theme was savage and sinister, with no place for hope, ease or happiness ... Tacitus took possession of the Latin language, bent it to his will, and pushed to the utter limits all that it knew or promised of energy, gravity, and magnificence. ((1958a) 341–2, 347–8, 358)

This effect of genre on style is evident in Syme's own work. For more than a decade before the publication of *The Roman Revolution*, Syme had been publishing scholarly articles and chapters for the *Cambridge Ancient History*, all written in a lively and incisive manner. But nothing in his previous work prepared the reader for the distinctive style and tone of *The Roman Revolution*. The reader was forewarned in the preface:

> No less than the subject, the tone and treatment calls for an explanation... The design has imposed a pessimistic and truculent tone, to the almost complete exclusion of the gentler emotions and the domestic virtues. Δύναμις and

---

[15] On the 'late Syme' and fiction, cf. Wiseman (1998) and Griffin (2005).
[16] Syme (1958a) 198, 672, 711 (citing the arguments of F. Leo and E. Norden).

Τύχη are the presiding divinities. The style is likewise direct and even abrupt, avoiding metaphors and abstractions. ((1939) vii–viii)

The posthumous publication of Syme's *The Provincial at Rome*, the manuscript of which was completed a year or so before Syme began writing *The Roman Revolution*, now makes it clear that the style of the latter work was not new with that work but had been developed some years before. Syme had waited until he undertook a comprehensive historical narrative of a crucial topic to employ a majestic style inspired by Tacitus but uniquely his own.

'Narrative is the essence of history.' This proclamation raises a question. Why did this master of the art compose only one extended piece of historical narrative, *The Roman Revolution*? After a decade of publishing only reviews owing to his war service, Syme began in 1949 to publish at an increasingly prodigious rate with books that analysed Roman authors, the Roman elite and Roman institutions, always accompanied by a steady flow of articles, many of which are small gems of historical narrative in their own right. But Syme never again undertook a work of narrative history on a large scale.

According to Syme, the writing of *The Roman Revolution* was begun in the summer of 1936 and the manuscript was submitted to Oxford University Press in September of 1938. Therefore, this detailed and complex piece of scholarship was written in an astonishingly short time. As immediate stimuli to his thinking, Syme cited the 'fraud and nonsense' he saw coming in 1937 with the celebration of the bimillenary of Augustus' birth. In addition, there was the publication of the Soviet constitution in 1936, a document that Syme was surprised to see was accepted as credible by people who should have known better and which lent new perspective on the nature of the constitution of Augustus.[17] *The Roman Revolution* was published in September of 1939, a few days after war was declared. Syme spent the first two years of the war in government service at the British embassies in Belgrade and Ankara, and then for three years he was Professor of Classical Philology at the University of Istanbul, 'under circumstances never quite explained'.[18] Although he was hard at work on various projects, Syme published nothing but reviews between 1939 and 1949, and by the late 1940s he seems to have begun the work that would lead to *Tacitus* in 1958. By the

---

[17] Syme archive, Bodleian Library, Oxford: notes from lectures entitled 'Rom. Hist. 50 or 60 Years Ago' and 'Forty Years On'.

[18] Birley in Syme (1999) xiii, whose introduction is very informative on Syme's unpublished work from his years in Istanbul. Although it is generally assumed that Syme's position in Istanbul involved intelligence work, he himself never spoke of it; cf. Bowersock (1993) 549–51.

mid-1950s, owing to the profound impact of *The Roman Revolution*, Syme was recognised as one of the greatest living Roman historians, and comparisons were already being made with Mommsen himself, who had won the Nobel Prize for Literature in 1902 for his Roman history.

Syme, a self-conscious literary artist, must have sensed how much his own historical genius in *The Roman Revolution* owed to the time and circumstance of its composition, and that he could never compete with his own accomplishment in narrative history. Therefore he chose to exercise that genius in other areas of Roman history. Syme said of Gibbon and his great work: 'He was fortunate in discovering a theme of high import that was congenial to his tastes and not beyond his talent' ((1984) 970). Such fortune is not likely to occur more than once in a lifetime.

The subject of Syme and Tacitus goes beyond simply noting how Tacitus fundamentally influenced the way Syme thought and wrote about Roman history. Issues of an epistemic character are involved, especially with Syme's *Tacitus*. It is fair to say that our understanding of Tacitus, who he was and why he wrote, is in significant part due to Syme's own analysis of him; much that is generally accepted by scholars about Tacitus is due to *Tacitus*. The problem is then compounded by the fact that in *Tacitus* there is a fair amount of complementary and complimentary projection: the Tacitus that emerges from *Tacitus* has features that were characteristic of Syme himself.[19]

Syme was a notoriously private individual who avoided self-advertisement and even self-reference to an extraordinary degree. In personal correspondence he avoided the use of the first-person pronoun (the 'odious pronoun'[20]) and simply referred to himself as 'this person'. Although congenial and sociable, he remained slightly distant and something of a mysterious personality even to those who knew him best and longest. Although we know virtually nothing of Tacitus the man, Syme detected a personality remarkably like his own. 'A proud reserve was congenial to his nature – or had become so ...Tacitus ... expresses an almost morbid fear of ostentation and *iactantia* [boastfulness].... It is not easy to nail down this elusive and complex character' (Syme (1958a) 540, 547). What Syme had to say of what

---

[19] Momigliano (1961a) 55 refers to a blending (*Verschmelzung*) of the characters of Syme and Tacitus; Griffin (2005) 32: 'In *Tacitus*, Syme is virtually indistinguishable from Tacitus himself.' Griffin (1999) 144–7 suggests another dimension to the relationship by drawing a parallel between the ancient rivalry of Tacitus and Pliny the Younger and that of their respective champions in twentieth-century Oxford, Syme and Pliny's commentator A.N. Sherwin-White.

[20] Syme (1958a) 304.

he supposed was a lengthy period of preparation and study before Tacitus sat down to compose the *Histories* could well apply to his own experience with *The Roman Revolution*:

> His reticent and austere character, his loathing for self-advertisement permit a deduction. He would hesitate to challenge publicity unless he had a substantial contribution, both ready and in reserve ... [E]ver conscious of the effort of style, [he was] a writer who could summon the unfailing resources of wide reading, who had formed the habit of documentary inquiry, and who was ferociously accurate in small details. ((1958a) 119, 541)

There are other revealing parallels. Syme was convinced that Tacitus had come to realise that he had made a mistake in beginning the *Annals* with the death of Augustus. The year AD 4 would have been more appropriate for Tacitus' purposes.[21] In a similar way, in a talk given forty years after the publication of *The Roman Revolution*, Syme claimed that its point of inception was mistaken. Instead of beginning in 60 BC with 'the end of the Free State', he too should have gone back some years and started his account with the death of Sulla in 78, or possibly back to 91, the year of the tribunate of Drusus the Younger and the outbreak of the Social War.[22]

Syme was careful to avoid polemic or scholarly rancour.[23] His scholarly opponents were often challenged anonymously and the criticism was frequently indirect. Syme detected the same trait in Tacitus: '[H]e eschews elaborate refutation, with names and dates and all the paraphernalia, of other men's mistakes. Tacitus is content with a hint, or a typical example' ((1958a) 378).

Prefaces to an ancient historical work were and are important. They gave the ancient writer an opportunity to assert his veracity and objectivity, and for the modern reader they often provide the only evidence about the origin, biography and personality of the ancient historian. Tacitus' prefaces demonstrate an essential line of development from the relatively long, rhetorical and personal preface of the *Agricola* to the impersonal and almost antirhetorical preface of the *Annals*.[24] 'Tacitus gives very little away. His prefaces are splendid and formal. What assures their value is brevity, point and impersonality' (Syme (1958a) 520). The prefaces of Syme's works show a similar development from the conventional to the idiosyncratic. The preface

---

[21] Syme (1958a) 368–74, 431; (1984) 928.
[22] Syme archive, Bodleian Library, Oxford: notes from a lecture entitled 'Forty Years On', where his notes have 'Point of Inception, always *the* problem'. Momigliano (1940) 78 discussed the issue in his review of *The Roman Revolution*.
[23] Only the German Wilhelm Weber elicited Syme's severe and constant rebuke in print; but he could be sharp in reviews.
[24] Janson (1964) 71.

to *The Roman Revolution* is a standard statement of the book's topic and approach and it closes with the standard list of acknowledgements to other scholars and friends. The preface to *Tacitus*, a long and complicated work, has only one sentence of acknowledgement that mentions three people. A startling statement precedes it. 'Nor, in making the written text fit for publication and compiling the vast index, can aid or alleviation be recorded from any academic body, from any fund or foundation dedicated to the promotion of research in history and letters' ((1958a) v–vi). This cryptic proclamation seems to be targeted at some audience, but the details remain a mystery (Syme was extremely frugal, and to have paid out of his own pocket for the preparation of the manuscript would have rankled).[25] This most private of men came to use a preface in a subtle way that revealed or alluded to aspects of his own life. The preface to *History in Ovid* contains a homily to Wolfson College, Syme's academic base after his retirement from Brasenose College and his professorship in 1970: 'a community whose indulgence abates the distempers that encroach upon the evening of life'. The significance of his sentiments there only becomes evident if one knows that owing to college rules that did not allow retired members to maintain their rooms in Brasenose, Syme was 'homeless' for some years before he could take up residence in Wolfson since the college buildings were not ready for occupation until 1974. The poet Ovid, often a companion on Syme's frequent and long travels, had become a particular consolation during the years of academic wandering that intervened, and, although he had been exiled to 'the northern outskirts of Oxford' (as he described Wolfson), Syme, unlike the ancient poet, was supremely happy in his new home.[26]

It is striking that Syme leaves his discussion of the life and personality of Tacitus to the end of *Tacitus*, and the ancient historian's identity is revealed only in the last chapter of that long work. He turns out to be a provincial, a native of Narbonese Gaul, and a *nouus homo*, a 'new man' whose ancestors had held no high magistracy at Rome:[27]

> It was a good thing for a historian to be a *novus homo* ... The judgements of the *novus homo*, like his status, derived from his own efforts. In pride of achievement, putting himself on a level with the older stocks when they first won rank by merit, he might look their descendants in the face – or pass them by ... When Tacitus wrote, colonials and provincials from the Latin West occupied the place of the Caesars. There was only one higher pinnacle: literary

---

[25] Fergus Millar (*per litteras*) points out that Syme's statement here may simply have been a slight parody of such acknowledgements in other books: 'I am sure that he never made any formal application to any foundation'.
[26] Griffin (2005) 33.
[27] Syme (1958a) 611–24; Syme here builds on the argument of Gordon (1936).

renown. To that also the epoch of Tacitus and Hadrian might confidently aspire. Men and dynasties pass, but style abides.   ((1958a) 582, 624)

In fact, we know virtually nothing about the person or life of Tacitus. Previous to Syme, theories about the origin of Tacitus ranged from an attribution of high aristocratic pedigree (because of the name Cornelius) to a servile origin as a freedman. It is not surprising that Syme's identification, based on learned assessment of meagre evidence and nomenclature, has won wide assent, and the latest edition of the *Oxford Classical Dictionary* confidently pronounces him a native Gaul. In such an identification, however, the ancient and modern historian meld one last time, and in a startling way. Each had come from the frontier of Empire to settle in the intellectual capital, and each won admiration and renown through the practice of the literary art of Roman history. Although he spent the whole of his adult life in England, Syme retained his New Zealand citizenship and the dedication in *The Roman Revolution* is to his parents and fatherland (*parentibus optimis patriaeque*). While he lived among the English academic aristocracy, it is generally agreed that by his own volition and reserve Syme was never fully a part of that group. He remained, as he envisioned Tacitus at Rome, a proud outsider.

Tacitus was more than an influence on Syme. Along with Gibbon, the ancient historian was his model and inspiration. If at times Syme's analysis of Tacitus blended into mild projection, it is testimony to Syme's conscious adherence to a tradition. In his manuscript on Julius Caesar, left incomplete at his death, Syme said of Mommsen's portrait of Caesar in his *Römische Geschichte*, 'It is a brilliant literary artifact, composed with passion and enthusiasm – and with style in accord.'[28] It is a statement that well describes Syme's own historical art, and explains why the works of Syme, along with those of Tacitus and Gibbon, will remain fundamental reading for anyone with a serious interest in Roman history.

FURTHER READING

No full biography of Syme exists, although there is a plan for one by an author in New Zealand. The illuminating memoir of Bowersock (1993), based on personal acquaintance, communication with Syme's family and the use of his papers, is the best account of his life. Devine (1989) provides an affective portrait of Syme in retirement at Wolfson, along with a comprehensive bibliography. The publication of the first two volumes of Syme's papers in 1979 (under the editorship of E. Badian) elicited admiring, thoughtful critiques of Syme's achievement (Bowersock (1980), Millar (1981), Alföldy (1979) and (1983)). The assessment of that achievement has

---

[28] Syme archive, Bodleian Library, Oxford: MS entitled 'Caesar'.

continued since his death with Wiseman (1998) and Griffin (2005), and analyses of Syme's scholarly legacy have been provided by German scholars or those of European background (Galsterer (1990), Linderski (1990), Christ (1990) and Alföldy (1993)). Thanks to the diligent editorial work of A.R. Birley, five more volumes of Syme's *Roman Papers* have been published, and he has edited two posthumous volumes by Syme, *Anatolica: Studies in Strabo* (Oxford 1995) and *The Provincial at Rome/ Rome and the Balkans 80 BC–AD 14* (Exeter 1999).

CHRONOLOGICAL TABLE

Historical events	Author dates
BC	BC
	?35 Sallust dies; Livy starts his history
31 Battle of Actium	
AD	AD
14 Augustus dies	
14–37 Tiberius *princeps*	?17 Livy dies
	30 Velleius' history published
	35 Servilius Nonianus consul
37–41 Gaius Caligula *princeps*	
41–54 Claudius *princeps*	
	43 Curtius Rufus consul
54–68 Nero *princeps*	
	56–8 Tacitus born
	65 Lucan and Seneca forced to commit suicide
	66 Petronius forced to commit suicide
68–9 Galba *princeps*	68 Silius Italicus consul
69 'Year of the Four Emperors' (Galba, Otho, Vitellius, Vespasian)	
69–79 Vespasian *princeps*	
	?70 Suetonius born
	76–7 Tacitus marries Agricola's daughter

Chronological table

Historical events	Author dates
77–84 Agricola governor of Britain	
79–81 Titus *princeps*	79 Pliny the Elder dies in eruption of Vesuvius
81–96 Domitian *princeps*	?81 Tacitus *quaestor Augusti*
	?85 Tacitus tribune of the plebs
	86 Martial starts publishing his epigrams
88 Domitian's Secular Games	88 Tacitus praetor
	92 Statius' *Thebaid*
93 Agricola dies	
	?95–6 Quintilian's *Institutio Oratoria*
96–98 Nerva *princeps*	
	97 Tacitus consul; ?starts his *Agricola*
98–117 Trajan *princeps*	98 Tacitus' *Agricola* and *Germania* published
	100 Pliny consul, writes *Panegyricus*
	101 Silius Italicus dies
	102 Martial's last book of epigrams; ?Tacitus' *Dialogus*
	103–4 Frontinus dies
	106–7 Tacitus writing the *Histories*
112 Trajan's Forum dedicated	112–13 Tacitus proconsul of Asia
113 Parthian war; Trajan's Column dedicated	?113 Pliny the Younger dies
	115 Tacitus writing the *Annals*
117 Hadrian becomes *princeps*	

ABBREVIATIONS AND BIBLIOGRAPHY

Abbreviations

References to Tacitus' text are abbreviated as follows:

A.   *Annals*
Agr. *Agricola*
D.   *Dialogus*
G.   *Germania*
H.   *Histories*

Other abbreviations of ancient works generally follow those in the *OCD*. References to the fragmentary Roman historians are given according to the editions of Peter (1967) and Cornell *et al.* (forthcoming) in that order (e.g. Cato fr. 77P = 81C).

Most scholarly works, apart from certain standard forms of reference that are listed below, are referred to by author's name and date, e.g. Syme (1984); full details may be found in the Bibliography.

Dates are AD unless stated otherwise.

ANRW *Aufstieg und Niedergang der römischen Welt*, ed. H. Temporini and W. Haase, Vols. 1.1–2.37, Berlin and New York 1972–96
CIL *Corpus Inscriptionum Latinarum*
ILS *Inscriptiones Latinae Selectae*
OCD *The Oxford Classical Dictionary*, ed. S. Hornblower and A. Spawforth, rev. 3rd edn, Oxford 2003
OLD *Oxford Latin Dictionary*, ed. P.G.W. Glare, rev. repr., Oxford 2004
RE   *Paulys Real-Encyclopädie der classischen Altertumswissenschaft*
RG   *Res Gestae Diui Augusti*, ed. J. Scheid, Paris (Budé) 2007
RIB *Roman Inscriptions of Britain*, ed. R.G. Collingwood, R.P. Wright and R.S.O. Tomlin, rev. repr., Stroud 1995
SCPP *Senatus Consultum de Cn. Pisone Patre*, ed. Eck *et al.* (1996) (references are to lines)
TLL *Thesaurus Linguae Latinae*

Bibliography

Adams, J.N. (1972). 'The language of the later books of Tacitus' *Annals*', *CQ* 22.350–73
   (1973). 'The vocabulary of the speeches in Tacitus' historical works', *BICS* 20.124–44
Alföldy, G. (1979). Review of Syme (1979), *AJAH* 4.167–81
   (1983). *Sir Ronald Syme, 'Die römische Revolution' und die deutsche Althistorie.* SHAW, Phil.-hist. Kl. 1. Heidelberg
   (1993). 'Two *Principes*: Augustus and Sir Ronald Syme', *Athenaeum* 81.101–22
   (2004). 'Marcus Cornelius Nigrinus Curiatius Maternus: Neues und Altes zum Werdegang eines römischen Generals', *Revue des Études Militaires Anciennes* 1.45–62
Allison, J.W. (1999). 'Tacitus' *Dialogus* and Plato's *Symposium*', *Hermes* 127.479–92
Ammirato, S. (1594). *Discorsi ... sopra Cornelio Tacito*. Florence
Anderson, B.R. (1991). *Imagined Communities: Reflections on the Origin and Spread of Nationalism*. Rev. edn. London and New York
Ando, C. (1997). 'Tacitus *Annales* VI beginning and end', *AJP* 118.285–303
Antón Martínez, B. (1992). *El Tacitismo en el siglo XVII en España. El proceso de recepción*. Valladolid
Apsler, A. (1947). 'Writers from across the sea', *College English* 9.1.19–24
Ash, R. (1998). 'Waving the white flag: surrender scenes at Livy 9.5–6 and Tacitus, *Histories* 3.31 and 4.62', *G&R* 45.27–44
   (1999a). *Ordering Anarchy: Armies and Leaders in Tacitus' Histories*. London
   (1999b). 'An exemplary conflict: Tacitus' Parthian battle narrative (*Annals* 6.34–35)', *Phoenix* 53.114–35
   (2003). '"aliud est enim epistulam, aliud historiam ... scribere" (*Epistles* 6.16.22): Pliny the historian?', *Arethusa* 36.211–25
   (2006a). *Tacitus*. London
   (2006b). 'Following in the footsteps of Lucullus? Tacitus' characterisation of Corbulo', *Arethusa* 39.355–75
   (2007a). 'Victim and voyeur: Rome as a character in Tacitus' *Histories* 3', in Larmour and Spencer (2007) 211–37
   (2007b). *Tacitus Histories Book II*. Cambridge
Aubrion, E. (1985). *Rhétorique et histoire chez Tacite*. Metz
   (1991). 'L'*eloquentia* de Tacite et sa *fides* d'historien', *ANRW* 2.33.4.2597–688
Badian, E. (1966). 'The early historians', in T.A. Dorey (ed.), *Latin Historians* 1–38. London
Baldwin, B. (1979). 'The *acta diurna*', *Chiron* 9.189–203
   (1983). *Suetonius. The Biographer of the Caesars*. Amsterdam
Barnes, T.D. (1977). 'The fragments of Tacitus' *Histories*', *CP* 72.224–31
   (1998). *Ammianus Marcellinus and the Representation of Historical Reality*. Ithaca, NY
Barton, T.S. (1994). *Power and Knowledge: Astrology, Physiognomics, and Medicine under the Roman Empire*. Ann Arbor, Mich.
Bartsch, S. (1994). *Actors in the Audience. Theatricality and Doublespeak from Nero to Hadrian*. Cambridge, Mass.

Bastomsky, S.J. (1988). 'Tacitus, *Histories* IV, 73–74: a unique view of Roman rule?', *Latomus* 47.413–16
Baumann, U. (2006). 'Frühnationalismus und Freiheit. Fichtes Berliner Perspektiven einer deutschen Republik', in U. Baumann (ed.), *Fichte in Berlin. Spekulative Ansätze einer Philosophie der Praxis* 177–97. Hanover-Laatzen
Baumstark, A. (1875). *Ausführliche Erläuterung des allgemeinen Theiles der Germania des Tacitus*. Leipzig
Baxter, R.T.S. (1971). 'Virgil's influence on Tacitus in Book 3 of the *Histories*', *CP* 66.93–107
 (1972). 'Virgil's influence on Tacitus in Books 1 and 2 of the *Annals*', *CP* 67.246–69
Beard, M. (2003). 'The triumph of Flavius Josephus', in Boyle and Dominik (2003) 543–8
Beck, H. and Walter, U. (2001–4). *Die frühen römischen Historiker*. 2 vols. Darmstadt
Beck, J.-W. (1998). *Germania – Agricola: zwei Kapitel zu Tacitus' zwei kleinen Schriften: Untersuchungen zu ihrer Intention und Datierung sowie zur Entwicklung ihres Verfassers*. Hildesheim and New York
Benario, H.W. (1964–5). 'Recent work on Tacitus (1954–63)', *CW* 58.69–83
 (1969–70). 'Recent work on Tacitus: 1964–8', *CW* 63.253–67
 (1977–8). 'Recent work on Tacitus: 1969–1973', *CW* 71.1–32
 (1986–7). 'Recent work on Tacitus: 1974–1983', *CW* 80.73–147
 (1995–6). 'Recent work on Tacitus: 1984–1993', *CW* 89.91–162
 (2004–5). 'Recent work on Tacitus: 1994–2003', *CW* 98.251–336
 (2007). 'Tacitus in America', in R. Bedon and M. Polfer (eds.), *Être romain: Hommages in memoriam C.M. Ternes* 57–67. Remshalden
Bennett, J. (2001). *Trajan: Optimus Princeps*. 2nd edn. London and New York
Benze, R. (1936). *Nationalpolitische Erziehung im Dritten Reich*. Berlin
Bergmann, B. and Kondoleon, C. (eds.) (1999). *The Art of Ancient Spectacle*. Washington, DC
Berry, D.H. (2008). 'Letters from an advocate: Pliny's "Vesuvius" narratives (*Epistles* 6.16, 6.20)', in F. Cairns (ed.), *Hellenistic and Augustan Latin Poetry, Flavian and Post-Flavian Latin Poetry, Greek and Roman Prose* [= *PLLS* 13] 297–313. Cambridge
Bews, J.P. (1972–3). 'Virgil, Tacitus, Tiberius and Germanicus', *PVS* 12.35–48
Billot, F. (2003). 'Tacitus responds: *Annals* 14 and the *Octavia*', *Prudentia* 35.126–41
Bird, H.W. (1969). 'L. Aelius Sejanus and his political significance', *Latomus* 28.61–98
Bireley, R. (1990). *The Counter-Reformation Prince: Anti-Machiavellianism or Catholic Statecraft in Early Modern Europe*. Chapel Hill, NC
Birley, A.R. (1975). 'Agricola, the Flavian dynasty, and Tacitus', in B.M. Levick (ed.), *The Ancient Historian and his Materials. Essays in Honour of C.E. Stevens on his Seventieth Birthday* 139–54. Farnborough
 (1999). *Tacitus: Agricola and Germany*. Oxford
 (2000a). 'The life and death of Cornelius Tacitus', *Historia* 49.230–47
 (2000b). *Onomasticon to the Younger Pliny*. Munich and Leipzig
 (2005). *The Roman Government of Britain*. Oxford

Birley, E. (1953). *Roman Britain and the Roman Army: Collected Papers*. Kendal
Blake, M.E. and Bishop, D.T. (1973). *Roman Construction in Italy from Nerva through the Antonines*. Philadelphia, Pa.
Bo, D. (1993). *Le principali problematiche del Dialogus de oratoribus*. Hildesheim
Boccalini, T. (1656). *I Ragguagli di Parnasso: or, Advertisements from Parnassus*. Trans. Henry Carey. London
Boesche, R. (1987). 'The politics of pretence: Tacitus and the political theory of despotism', *History of Political Thought* 8.189–210
Bond, H.L. (1960). *The Literary Art of Edward Gibbon*. Oxford
Bonner, S.F. (1949). *Roman Declamation in the Late Republic and Early Empire*. Liverpool
Borchardt, F.L. (1968). 'Etymology in tradition and in the Northern Renaissance', *JHI* 29.415–29
Borzsák, S. [=I.] (1968). 'P. Cornelius Tacitus', *RE* Suppl. 11.399–416
   (1982). 'Alexander der Grosse als Muster taciteischer Heldendarstellung', *Gymnasium* 89.37–56
   (1994). 'Laus Caesaris. Ein Epigrammzyklus auf Claudius' britannischen Triumphzug', *AAntHung* 35.117–32
Botero, G. (1589). *Della Ragion di Stato, libri dieci, con tre libri delle cause della grandezza e magnificenza della città*. Venice
Bowersock, G.W. (1977). 'Gibbon on civil war and rebellion in the decline of the Roman Empire', in Bowersock *et al.* (1977) 27–35
   (1980). 'The emperor of Roman history', *New York Review of Books* 27 no. 3 (6 March). 8–13
   (1993). 'Ronald Syme, 1903–1989', *PBA* 84.539–63
Bowersock, G.W., Clive, J. and Graubard, S.R. (eds.) (1977). *Edward Gibbon and the Fall of the Roman Empire*. Cambridge, Mass.
Boyd, C.E. (1916). *Public Libraries and Literary Culture in Ancient Rome*. Chicago
Boyle, A.J. and Dominik, W.J. (eds.) (2003). *Flavian Rome: Culture, Image, Text*. Leiden
Bradley, K.R. (1978). *Suetonius' Life of Nero. An Historical Commentary*. Brussels
Braund, D.C. (1985). *Augustus to Nero: A Sourcebook on Roman History 31BC–AD68*. London and Sydney
   (1996). *Ruling Roman Britain. Kings, Queens, Governors and Emperors from Julius Caesar to Agricola*. London
Brilliant, R. (1984). *Visual Narratives*. Ithaca, NY
Brink, C.O. (1950). 'A sixteenth-century editor of the *Annals* of Tacitus', *CR* 64.120–2
   (1951). 'Justus Lipsius and the text of Tacitus', *JRS* 41.32–51
   (1989). 'Quintilian's *De causis corruptae eloquentiae* and Tacitus' *Dialogus de oratoribus*', *CQ* 39.472–503
   (1993). 'History in the *Dialogus de oratoribus* and Tacitus the historian', *Hermes* 121.335–49
   (1994a). 'Can Tacitus' *Dialogus* be dated? Evidence and historical conclusions', *HSCP* 96.251–80
   (1994b). 'A bipartite stemma of Tacitus' *Dialogus de oratoribus* and some transmitted variants', *ZPE* 102.131–52

Briscoe, J. (2005). 'The language and style of the fragmentary republican historians', in Reinhardt *et al.* (2005) 53–72
Brock, R. (1995). 'Versions, "inversions" and evasions: classical historiography and the "published" speech', *PLLS* 8.209–24
Brunt, P.A. (1984). 'The role of the senate in the Augustan régime', *CQ* 34.423–44
  (1988). *The Fall of the Republic and Related Essays*. Oxford
  (1993). 'Cicero and historiography', in P. A. Brunt, *Studies in Greek History and Thought* 181–209. Oxford (= *Miscellanea di studi classici in onore di Eugenio Manni* (Rome 1980) 1.311–40)
Burke, P. (1969). 'Tacitism', in Dorey (1969a) 149–71
  (1990). 'Stoicism, scepticism and reason of state', in J.H. Burns (ed.), *The Cambridge History of Political Thought, 1450–1700* 479–98. Cambridge
Butterfield, H. (1955). *Man On His Past*. Cambridge
Calder, J. (1997). *The Nine Lives of Naomi Mitchison*. London
Campbell, D.B. (1986). 'The consulship of Agricola', *ZPE* 63.197–200
Canfora, L. (1979). *La Germania di Tacito da Engels al nazismo*. Naples
Cartledge, P. (1977). 'The enlightened historiography of Edward Gibbon, Esq.: a bicentennial celebration', *Maynooth Review* 3.67–93
  (1989). 'The "Tacitism" of Edward Gibbon (two hundred years on)', *MHR* 4.251–70
  (1995). 'Vindicating Gibbon's good faith', *Hermathena* 148.133–47
Casson, L. (2001). *Libraries in the Ancient World*. New Haven and London
Castelli, E. (2006). 'The ambivalent legacy of victims and victimhood: using early Christian martyrs to think with', *Spiritus* 6.1.1–24
Caterall, J.L. (1938). 'Variety and inconcinnity of language in the first decade of Livy', *TAPA* 69.292–318
Champion, C. (1994). 'Dialogus 5.3–10.8: a reconsideration of the character of Marcus Aper', *Phoenix* 48.152–63
Champlin, E. (2001). 'Pliny's other country', in M. Peachin (ed.), *Aspects of Friendship in the Graeco-Roman World*. JRA Suppl. Series 43.121–8. Portsmouth, RI
  (2003). *Nero*. Cambridge, Mass. and London
  (2006–7). *Tiberiana 1–4*. Princeton/Stanford Working Papers in Classics (www.princeton.edu/~pswpc/papers/authorAL/champlin/champlin.html)
Chaplin, J.D. (2000). *Livy's Exemplary History*. Oxford
Charlesworth, M.P. (1927). 'Livia and Tanaquil', *CR* 41.55–7
Chassignet, M. (1996–2004). *L'annalistique romaine*. 3 vols. Paris
Chausserie-Laprée, J.-P. (1969). *L'expression narrative chez les historiens latins. Histoire d'un style*. Paris
Chilver, G.E.F. (1979). *A Historical Commentary on Tacitus' Histories I and II*. Oxford
Christ, K. (1990). 'Ronald Syme (1903–1989)', in K. Christ (ed.), *Neue Profile der alten Geschichte* 188–247. Darmstadt
Claridge, A. (1993). 'Hadrian's Column of Trajan', *JRA* 6.5–22
Clarke, K. (2002). '*In arto et inglorius labor*: Tacitus' anti-history', in A.K. Bowman, H.M. Cotton, M. Goodman and S. Price (eds.), *Representations of Empire: Rome and the Mediterranean World* 83–103. Oxford
Classen, C.J. (1997). *Zu Heinrich Bebels Leben und Schriften*. Göttingen
Clemm, G. (1881). *De breuiloquentiae Taciteae quibusdam generibus*. Leipzig

Cole, T. (1992). 'Initium mihi operis Servius Galba T. Vinius consules ...', *YCS* 29.231–45
Coleman, K.M. (1990). 'Fatal charades: Roman executions staged as mythological enactments', *JRS* 80.44–73
Cooley, A. (1998). 'The moralizing message of the *Senatus consultum de Cn. Pisone Patre*', *G&R* 25.199–212
Cornell, T.J. et al. (forthcoming). *The Fragments of the Roman Historians*. Oxford
Costa, C.D.N. (1969). 'The *Dialogus*', in Dorey (1969a) 19–34
Courbaud, E. (1918). *Les procédés d'art de Tacite dans les 'Histoires'*. Paris
Courtney, E. (1980). *A Commentary on the Satires of Juvenal*. London
  (2003). *The Fragmentary Latin Poets*. Rev. edn. Oxford
  (2004). 'The "Greek accusative"', *CJ* 99.425–31
Craddock, P.B. (1972). *The English Essays of Edward Gibbon*. Oxford
  (1982). *Young Edward Gibbon: Gentleman of Letters*. Baltimore, Md. and London
  (1989). *Edward Gibbon: Luminous Historian 1772–1794*. Baltimore, Md. and London
Crook, J.A. (1995). *Legal Advocacy in the Roman World*. Ithaca, NY
Dammer, R. (2005). 'Wenn das Temperament mit einem durchgeht...Marcus Aper im *Dialogus de oratoribus*', *RhM* 148.329–48
Damon, C. (1994). 'Caesar's practical prose', *CJ* 89.183–95
  (2003). *Tacitus: Histories Book I*. Cambridge
Damon, C. and Takács, S. (eds.) (1999). 'The *Senatus Consultum de Cn. Pisone Patre*', *AJP* 120.1–162
Dangel, J. (1989). 'Les discours chez Tacite: rhétorique et imitation créatrice', *Ktema* 14.291–300
Davies, J.P. (2004). *Rome's Religious History: Livy, Tacitus and Ammianus on their Gods*. Cambridge
Degel, F. (1907). *Archaistische Bestandteile der Sprache des Tacitus*. Nuremberg
Delpuech, P. (1974). 'Entre l'offensive et la démission: Corbulon et l'impérialisme tacitéen', in *L'idéologie de l'impérialisme romain*. Publications de l'Université de Dijon 46.91–107. Paris
De Mattei, R. (1963). *Il Pensiero politico di Scipione Ammirato*. Rome
  (1979). *Il Problema della ragion di stato nell' età della Controriforma*. Milan and Naples
DeRousse, P. (2007). 'A textual problem at Tacitus *Annals* 2.88.1', *Mnemosyne* 60.651–61
Devillers, O. (1994). *L'art de la persuasion dans les Annales de Tacite*. Brussels
  (2003). *Tacite et les sources des Annales*. Louvain, Paris and Dudley, Mass.
Devine, A.M. (1989). 'Sir Ronald Syme (1903–1989): a Roman post-portem' and 'Sir Ronald Syme and *The Roman Revolution*', *AncW* 20.67–76 and 77–92
  (2004). 'Syme, Ronald (1903–89; Kt 1959)', in R.B. Todd (ed.), *The Dictionary of British Classicists* 3.941–5. Bristol
De Vivo, A. (1980). *Tacito e Claudio: storia e codificazione letteraria*. Naples
Dominik, W. (2007). 'Tacitus and Pliny on oratory', in W. Dominik and J. Hall (eds.), *A Companion to Roman Rhetoric* 323–38. Oxford
Dorey, T.A. (1969a). *Tacitus*. London
  (1969b). '*Agricola* and *Germania*', in Dorey (1969a) 1–18

Draeger, A.A. (1882). *Über Syntax und Stil des Tacitus*. 3rd edn. Leipzig
Duff, A.M. (1958). *Freedmen in the Early Roman Empire*. Corr. edn. Cambridge
Duff, T. (1999). *Plutarch's Lives: Exploring Virtue and Vice*. Oxford
Dugan, J. (2005). *Making a New Man: Ciceronian Self-fashioning in the Rhetorical Works*. Oxford
Dunkle, J.R. (1971). 'The rhetorical tyrant in Roman historiography: Sallust, Livy and Tacitus', *CW* 65.12–20
Dupont, F. (1985). *L'acteur-roi ou le théâtre dans la Rome antique*. Paris
Du Pont, O. (2005). 'Robert Graves's Claudian novels: a case of pseudotranslation', *Target* 17. 2.327–47
du Toit, L.A. (1977). 'Tacitus and the rebellion of Boudicca', *AClass* 20.149–58
Dyson, S.L. (1970). 'The portrait of Seneca in Tacitus', *Arethusa* 3.71–83
Earl, D.C. (1961). *The Political Thought of Sallust*. Cambridge
Eck, W. (2002a). 'Cheating the public, or: Tacitus vindicated', *SCI* 21.149–64
  (2002b). 'An emperor is made: senatorial politics and Trajan's adoption by Nerva in 97', in G. Clark and T. Rajak (eds.), *Philosophy and Power in the Graeco-Roman World: Essays in Honour of Miriam Griffin* 211–26. Oxford
Eck, W., Caballos, A. and Fernández, F. (1996). *Das Senatus Consultum de Cn. Pisone Patre*. Munich
Eliot, J. (1879). *The Monarchie of Man*. Ed. A.B. Grosart. London
Epstein, S.J. (1992). 'More speech and allusion in Tacitus' *Annals* XIV', *Latomus* 51.868–71
Evans, J.A.S. (1973). 'The shadow of Edward Gibbon', in P. Fritz and D. Williams (eds.), *City and Society in the Eighteenth Century* 247–57. Toronto
Fabia, P. (1929). *La Table Claudienne de Lyon*. Lyon
Fagan, G. (2002). 'Messalina's folly', *CQ* 52.566–79
Fairweather, J. (1981). *Seneca the Elder*. Cambridge
Feeney, D. (2007). *Caesar's Calendar: Ancient Time and the Beginnings of History*. Berkeley, Los Angeles and London
Feldherr, A. (ed.) (2009). *The Cambridge Companion to the Roman Historians*. Cambridge
Ferri, R. (1998). 'Octavia's heroines: Tacitus *Annales* 14.63–64 and the *Praetexta Octavia*', *HSCP* 98.339–56
Fest, J. (1996). *Das Gesicht des Dritten Reichs*. Munich (first publ. 1963)
Feuchtwanger, L. (1935). 'The purpose of the historical novel', available on the website of the Feuchtwanger Memorial Library at the University of Southern California: www.usc.edu/libraries/archives/arc/libraries/feuchtwanger/writings/historical.html (first published as 'Vom Sinn des historischen Romans', *Das Neue Tage-Buch*)
  (1937). *The Pretender*. New York
  (1942). *Josephus and the Emperor*. New York
Fichte, J.G. (1968). *Addresses to the German Nation* (ed. G.A. Kelly). New York and Evanston, Ill.
Fink, G.-L. (1987). 'Von Winckelmann bis Herder. Die deutsche Klimatheorie in europäischer Perspektive', in G. Sauder (ed.), *Johann Gottfried Herder, 1744–1803: Vorträge der neunten Jahrestagung der Deutschen Gesellschaft für die Erforschung des achzehnten Jahrhunderts* Bd. 9. 156–76. Hamburg

Fitzgerald, W. (2001). 'Oppositions, anxieties, and oppositions in the toga movie', in S. Joshel, M. Malamud and D. McGuire (eds.), *Imperial Projections: Ancient Rome in Modern Popular Culture* 23–49. Baltimore, Md. and London
Flach, D. (1973). *Tacitus in der Tradition der antiken Geschichtsschreibung.* Hypomnemata 29. Göttingen
Fletcher, G.B.A. (1964). *Annotations on Tacitus.* Brussels
  (1969). 'On some passages in Tacitus, *Histories* II', *Latomus* 28.42
  (1971a). 'On the *Annals* of Tacitus', *Latomus* 30.146–50
  (1971b). 'On some passages in Tacitus, *Histories* I and II', *Latomus* 30.383–5
  (1982). 'On some passages in Tacitus, *Histories* III and IV', *Latomus* 41.647–53
  (1983). 'On the *Annals* of Tacitus again', in C. Deroux (ed.), *Studies in Latin Literature and Roman History* 3.299–324. Brussels
  (1985a). 'On some passages in Tacitus, *Histories* 5', *LCM* 8.95–6
  (1985b). 'On the *Histories* and *Germania* of Tacitus', *SIFC* 78.92–100
  (1985c). 'On Tacitus, *Annals* 1 and 2', *LCM* 10.27–8
  (1986a). 'On the *Annals* and *Agricola* of Tacitus', *SIFC* 79.68–76
  (1986b). 'On the *Histories* of Tacitus again', *LCM* 11.98–100
Flower, H.I. (1996). *Ancestor Masks and Aristocratic Power in Roman Culture.* Oxford
  (2006). *The Art of Forgetting: Disgrace and Oblivion in Roman Political Culture.* Chapel Hill, NC
Foertmeyer, V.A. (1989). 'Tourism in Graeco-Roman Egypt', diss. Princeton University
Fortier, P.A. (1967). 'Gobineau and German racism', *Comparative Literature* 19.341–50
Foucher, A. (2000). *Historia proxima poetis. L'influence de la poésie épique sur le style des historiens latins de Salluste à Ammien Marcellin.* Brussels
Fowler, R.L. (1996). 'Herodotus and his contemporaries', *JHS* 116.62–87
Fox, M. (1996). *Roman Historical Myths: The Regal Period in Augustan Literature.* Oxford
Frazer, R.M., Jr. (1966). 'Nero the artist-criminal', *CJ* 62.17–20
Frenzen, W. (1937). 'Germanenbild und Patriotismus im Zeitalter des deutschen Barock', *Deutsche Vierteljahresschrift für Literaturwissenschaft und Geistesgeschichte* 15.203–19
Frier, B.W. (1999). *Libri Annales Pontificum Maximorum: The Origins of the Annalistic Tradition.* 2nd edn. Ann Arbor, Mich.
Furbank, P.N. (2004). 'On the historical novel', *Raritan* 23.3.94–114
Furneaux, H. (1896, 1907). *The Annals of Tacitus.* Vols. 1–2. 2nd edn. Oxford
Fussell, P. (1987). 'The caricature scenes of Robert Graves', in H. Bloom (ed.), *Robert Graves: Modern Critical Views* 111–27. New York
Gabba, E. (1981). 'True history and false history in classical antiquity', *JRS* 71.50–62
Galsterer, H. (1990). 'A man, a book, and a method: Sir Ronald Syme's *The Roman Revolution* after fifty years', in K.A. Raaflaub and M. Toher (eds.), *Between Republic and Empire. Interpretations of Augustus and his Principate* 1–20. Berkeley

Garber, J. (1989). 'Trojaner – Römer – Franken – Deutsche: "Nationale" Abstammungstheorien im Vorfeld der Nationalstaatenbildung', in K. Garber (ed.), *Nation und Literatur im Europa der Frühen Neuzeit* 108–63. Tübingen
Garson, R.W. (1974). 'Observations on the death scenes in Tacitus' *Annals*', *Prudentia* 6.23–31
Gärtner, H.A. (1983). 'Massilia et l'*Agricola* de Tacite', in *La Patrie gauloise, d'Agrippa au IVe s.* Actes du colloque de Lyon 1981.89–97. Lyon
Gay, P. (1966). *The Enlightenment: An Interpretation*. Vol. I. New York
  (1974). *Style in History*. New York
Geiser, M. (2007). *Personendarstellung bei Tacitus: am Beispiel von Cn. Domitius Corbulo und Ser. Sulpicius Galba*. Remscheid
Ghosh, P.R. (1983). 'Gibbon's Dark Ages: some remarks on the genesis of the *Decline and Fall*', *JRS* 73.1–23
  (1991). 'Gibbon observed', *JRS* 81.132–56
Gibson, B.J. (1998). 'Rumours as causes of events in Tacitus', *MD* 40.111–29
Gilmartin, K. (1973). 'Corbulo's campaigns in the East', *Historia* 22.583–626
  (1975). 'A rhetorical figure in Latin historical style: the imaginary second person singular', *TAPA* 105.99–121
Gingras, M.T. (1992). 'Annalistic format, Tacitean themes and the obituaries of *Annals* 3', *CJ* 87.241–56
Ginsburg, J. (1981). *Tradition and Theme in the Annals of Tacitus*. New York
  (1986). 'Speech and allusion in Tacitus, *Annals* 3.49–51 and 14.48–9', *AJP* 107.525–41
  (1993). '*In maiores certamina*: past and present in the *Annals*', in Luce and Woodman (1993) 86–103
  (2006). *Representing Agrippina: Constructions of Female Power in the Early Roman Empire*. Oxford
Giua, M.A. (2003). 'Tacito e i suoi destinatari: storia per i contemporanei, storia per i posteri', in A. Casanova and P. Desideri (eds.), *Evento, racconto, scrittura nell' antichità classica* 247–68. Florence
Goddard, J. (1994). 'The tyrant at table', in J. Elsner and J. Masters (eds.), *Reflections of Nero* 67–82. Chapel Hill, NC
Goldberg, S.M. (1999). 'Appreciating Aper: the defence of modernity in Tacitus' *Dialogus de oratoribus*', *CQ* 49.224–37
Goodyear, F.R.D. (1968). 'Development of language and style in the *Annals* of Tacitus', *JRS* 58.22–31 (= Goodyear (1992) 125–37)
  (1970). *Tacitus*. *G&R* New Surveys in the Classics 4. Oxford
  (1972, 1981). *The Annals of Tacitus*. Vols.1–2. Cambridge
  (1992). *Papers on Latin Literature* (ed. K.M. Coleman, J. Diggle, J.B. Hall and H.D. Jocelyn). London
Gordon, M.L. (1936). 'The *patria* of Tacitus', *JRS* 26.145–51
Gowers, E. (1993). *The Loaded Table: Representations of Food in Roman Literature*. Oxford
Gowing, A.M. (2005). *Empire and Memory: The Representation of the Roman Republic in Imperial Culture*. Cambridge
  (2007). 'The imperial Republic of Velleius Paterculus', in Marincola (2007) 411–18

Graves, R. (1965). *I, Claudius, from the Autobiography of Tiberius Claudius, born BC 10, Murdered and Deified AD 54*. New York (1st edn 1934)
   (1966). *Claudius the God and his Wife Messalina*. London (1st edn 1934)
   (1998). *Goodbye to All That*. Intro. Paul Fussell. New York (1st edn 1929; rev. edn 1957)
Gray, V.J. (2007). *Xenophon on Government*. Cambridge
Green, C.M.C. (1993). 'De Africa et eius incolis. The function of geography and ethnography in Sallust's *History of the Jugurthine War (BJ 17–19)*', *AncW* 24.185–97
Griffin, M.T. (1976). *Seneca: A Philosopher in Politics*. Oxford
   (1982a). 'The Lyons tablet and Tacitean hindsight', *CQ* 32.404–18
   (1982b). Review of Ginsburg (1981), *JRS* 72.215–16
   (1984). *Nero: The End of a Dynasty*. London
   (1986). 'Philosophy, Cato, and Roman suicide', *G&R* 33.64–77 and 192–202
   (1990). 'Claudius in Tacitus', *CQ* 40.482–501
   (1994). 'Claudius in the judgement of the next half-century', in V.M. Strocka (ed.), *Die Regierungszeit des Kaisers Claudius (41–54 n. Chr): Umbruch oder Episode?* 307–16. Mainz
   (1995). 'Tacitus, Tiberius and the principate', in I. Malkin and Z.W. Rubinsohn (eds.), *Leaders and Masses in the Roman World* 33–57. Leiden
   (1997). 'The senate's story', *JRS* 87.258–61
   (1999). 'Pliny and Tacitus', *SCI* 18.139–58
   (2005). ' "Lifting the mask": Syme on fictional history', in R.S.O. Tomlin (ed.), *History and Fiction. Six Essays Celebrating the Centenary of Sir Ronald Syme (1903–89)* 17–39. London
Gudeman, A. (1914). *P. Cornelii Taciti, Dialogus de oratoribus*. 2nd edn. Leipzig
   (1928). *Tacitus De vita Iulii Agricolae and De Germania*. Boston
Guicciardini, F. (1994 [1530]). *Ricordi* (ed. G. Masi). Milan
Hahn, E. (1933). 'Die Exkurse in den Annalen des Tacitus', diss. University of Leipzig
Hammer, D. (2008). *Roman Political Thought and the Modern Theoretical Imagination*. Norman, Okla.
Hansen, M.H. (1993). 'The battle exhortation in ancient historiography: fact or fiction?', *Historia* 42.161–80
Hanson, W.S. (1987). *Agricola and the Conquest of the North*. London
   (1991). 'Tacitus' *Agricola*: an archaeological and historical study', *ANRW* 2.33.3.1741–84
Hardie, P.R. (1992). 'Tales of unity and division in imperial Latin epic', in J.H. Molyneux (ed.), *Literary Responses to Civil Discord* 57–71. Nottingham
Hartog, F. (1988). *The Mirror of Herodotus*. Trans. J. Lloyd. Berkeley, Los Angeles and London
Haß-von Reitzenstein, U. (1970). *Beiträge zur gattungsgeschichtlichen Interpretation des Dialogus de oratoribus*. Cologne
   (1986). 'Aktuelle Probleme der Dialogus-Rezeption: Echtheitserweise und Lückenumfang', *Philologus* 130.69–95
Haynes, H. (2003). *The History of Make-Believe: Tacitus on Imperial Rome*. Berkeley, Los Angeles and London

Heldmann, K. (1982). *Antike Theorien über Entwicklung und Verfall der Redekunst.* Munich

Henderson, A.A.R. (1984). 'From 83 to 1983: on the trail of Mons Graupius', *Deeside Field Club* 18.23–29

(1985). 'Agricola in Caledonia: the sixth and seventh campaigns', *Echos du monde classique/Classical Views* 29.318–35

Henderson, J.G.W. (1989). 'Tacitus/The World in Pieces', *Ramus* 18.167–210 (revised in Henderson (1998) 257–300)

(1998). *Fighting for Rome: Poets and Caesars, History and Civil War.* Cambridge

Herdmann, F. (1990). *Montesquieurezeption in Deutschland im 18. und beginnenden 19. Jahrhundert.* Hildesheim and New York

Herzog, P.H. (1996). *Die Funktion des militärischen Planens bei Tacitus.* Frankfurt

Heubner, H. (1963). *Tacitus: Die Historien.* Vol. 1. Heidelberg

(1968). *Tacitus: Die Historien.* Vol. 2. Heidelberg

(1972). *Tacitus: Die Historien.* Vol. 3. Heidelberg

(1976). *Tacitus: Die Historien.* Vol. 4. Heidelberg

(1982). *Tacitus: Die Historien.* Vol. 5. Heidelberg

(1984). *Kommentar zum Agricola des Tacitus.* Göttingen

(1994). *P. Cornelii Taciti Libri Qui Supersunt.* Vol. 1, *Ab Excessu Diui Augusti.* Rev. edn. Stuttgart and Leipzig

Himmler, H. (1974). *Geheimreden 1933 bis 1945 und andere Ansprachen* (ed. B.F. Smith and A.F. Peterson). Frankfurt

Hinds, S. (1998). *Allusion and Intertext. Dynamics of Appropriation in Roman Poetry.* Cambridge

Hoberman, R. (1997). *Gendering Classicism: The Ancient World in Twentieth-Century Women's Fiction.* Albany, NY

Hobsbawm, E. (1992). 'Introduction: inventing traditions', in E. Hobsbawm and T. Ranger (eds.), *The Invention of Tradition* 1–14. Cambridge and New York

Hoffer, S.E. (1999). *The Anxieties of Pliny the Younger.* Atlanta, Ga.

(2006). 'Divine comedy? Accession propaganda in Pliny', *JRS* 96.73–87

Hollis, A.S. (2007). *Fragments of Roman Poetry c. 60 BC–AD 20.* Oxford

Hölzle, E. (1925). *Die Idee einer altgermanischen Freiheit vor Montesquieu.* Munich

Horsfall, N. (1985). 'Illusion and reality in Latin topographical writing', *G&R* 32.197–208

(1993). 'Empty shelves on the Palatine', *G&R* 40.58–67

(2006). *Virgil, Aeneid 3: a Commentary.* Leiden and Boston

Hurley, D.W. (2001). *Suetonius: Divus Claudius.* Cambridge

Hutchinson, G.O. (1993). *Latin Literature from Seneca to Juvenal.* Oxford

Huzar, E. (1984). 'Claudius – the erudite emperor', *ANRW* 2.32.1.612–50

Jacobi, R. (1993). 'Eine unbeachtete Germania-Reminiszenz bei Ambrosius', *RhM* 136.376–7

Janson, T. (1964). *Latin Prose Prefaces.* Stockholm

Joachimsen, P. (1970a). 'Tacitus im deutschen Humanismus', in N. Hammerstein (ed.), *Gesammelte Aufsätze* Bd. 1.275–96. Darmstadt

(1970b). 'Der Humanismus und die Entwicklung des deutschen Geistes', in N. Hammerstein (ed.), *Gesammelte Aufsätze* Bd. 1.325–86 Darmstadt

Joannou, M. (1999). *Women Writers of the 1930s: Gender, Politics and History*. Edinburgh
Jones, B.W. (2000). *Suetonius: Vespasian*. London
Jones, P.J. (2005). *Reading Rivers in Roman Literature and Culture*. Lanham, Md.
Jordan, D.P. (1971). *Gibbon and his Roman Empire*. Urbana, Ill.
Joshel, S.R. (1997). 'Female desire and the discourse of empire: Tacitus' Messalina', in J.P. Hallett and M.B. Skinner (eds.), *Roman Sexualities* 221–54. Princeton, NJ
  (2001). '*I, Claudius*: projection and imperial soap opera', in S. Joshel, M. Malamud and D. McGuire (eds.), *Imperial Projections: Ancient Rome in Modern Popular Culture* 119–161. Baltimore, Md. and London
Kajanto, I. (1970). 'Tacitus' attitude to war and the soldier', *Latomus* 29.699–718
Kaster, R.A. (2001). 'Controlling reason: declamation in rhetorical education at Rome', in Y.L. Too (ed.), *Education in Greek and Roman Antiquity* 317–37. Leiden
Keitel, E. (1978). 'The role of Parthia and Armenia in Tacitus *Annals* 11 and 12', *AJP* 99.462–73
  (1984). 'Principate and civil war in the *Annals* of Tacitus', *AJP* 105.306–25
  (1986–7). 'Homeric antecedents to the *cohortatio* in the ancient historians', *CW* 80.153–72
  (1987). 'Otho's exhortations in Tacitus' *Histories*', *G&R* 34.73–82
  (1991). 'The structure and function of speeches in Tacitus' *Histories* I-III', *ANRW* 2.33.4.2772–94
  (1992). '*Foedum spectaculum* and related motifs in Tacitus *Histories* 2–3', *RhM* 135.342–51
  (1993). 'Speech and narrative in *Histories* 4', in Luce and Woodman (1993) 39–58
  (1995). 'Plutarch's tragedy tyrants: Galba and Otho', *PLLS* 8.275–88
  (2006). '*Sententia* and structure in Tacitus *Histories* 1.12–49', *Arethusa* 39.219–44
  (2008). 'The Virgilian reminiscences at Tacitus, *Histories* 3.84.4', *CQ* 58.705–8
Kenney, E.J. (1974). *The Classical Text*. Berkeley
Kersnowski, F. (1989). *Conversations with Robert Graves*. Jackson, Miss.
Keynes, G. (1980). *The Library of Edward Gibbon: A Catalogue*. 2nd edn. Dorchester
Kirchner, R. (2001). *Sentenzen im Werk des Tacitus*. Palingenesia 74. Stuttgart
Klingner, F. (1958). 'Tacitus und die Geschichtsschreiber des 1. Jahrhunderts n. Chr.', *MH* 15.194–206
Koestermann, E. (1955). 'Die Majestätsprozesse unter Tiberius', *Historia* 4.72–106
  (1958). 'Die Feldzüge des Germanicus 14–16 n. Chr.', *Historia* 7.429–79
  (1963–8). *Tacitus: Annalen*. Vols. 1–4 (1963, 1965, 1967, 1968). Heidelberg
Kohl, A. (1959). *Der Satznachtrag bei Tacitus*. Würzburg
Kohn, H. (1949). 'Arndt and the character of German nationalism', *AHR* 54.787–803
Köhnken, A. (1973). 'Das Problem der Ironie bei Tacitus', *MH* 30.32–50
Komnick, H. (2001). *Die Restitutionsmünzen der frühen Kaiserzeit*. Berlin and New York

Kra, P. (2002). 'The concept of national character in 18th-century France', *Cromohs* 7.1–6

Krapf, L. (1979). *Germanenmythos und Reichsideologie. Frühhumanistische Rezeptionsweisen der taciteischen 'Germania'*. Tübingen

Kraus, C. S. (1994a). *Livy Ab Urbe Condita Book VI*. Cambridge

(1994b). ' "No second Troy": *topoi* and refoundation in Livy, Book V', *TAPA* 124.267–89

(1998). 'Repetition and empire in the *Ab urbe condita*', in P. E. Knox and C. Foss (eds.), *Style and Tradition: Studies in Honor of Wendell Clausen* 264–83. Stuttgart and Leipzig

(2005). 'From *exempla* to exemplar? Writing history around the emperor in imperial Rome', in J. Edmondson, S. Mason and J. Rives (eds.), *Flavius Josephus and Flavian Rome* 181–200. Oxford

(forthcoming). 'Historiography and biography', in A. Barchiesi and W. Scheidel (eds.), *The Oxford Handbook of Roman Studies*. Oxford

Kraus, C. S. and Woodman, A. J. (1997). *Latin Historians*. *G&R* New Surveys in the Classics 27. Oxford

Krauss, F. B. (1930). *An Interpretation of the Omens, Portents, and Prodigies Recorded by Livy, Tacitus, and Suetonius*. Philadelphia

Krebs, C. B. (2005). *Negotiatio Germaniae. Tacitus' Germania und Enea Silvio Piccolomini, Giannantonio Campano, Conrad Celtis und Heinrich Bebel*. Hypomnemata 158. Göttingen

(forthcoming). *The Most Dangerous Book: Tacitus' Germania from the 15th to the 20th Century*. New York

Kroll, W. (1927). 'Die Sprache des Sallust', *Glotta* 15.280–305

Krusch, B. (1933). *Translatio sancti Alexandri, filii Felicitatis, Wildeshusam anno 851*. Nachrichten von der Gesellschaft der Wissenschaften zu Göttingen, Phil.-Hist. Kl. 405–37. Göttingen

Kuntz, F. (1962). *Die Sprache des Tacitus und die Tradition der lateinischen Historikersprache*. Heidelberg

Labuske, H. (1989). 'Die Römer am Kimbern Kap', *Klio* 71.138–45

Laederich, P. (2001). *Les limites de l'empire: les stratégies de l'impérialisme romain dans l'oeuvre de Tacite*. Paris

Laird, A. (1999). *Powers of Expression, Expressions of Power: Speech Presentation in Latin Literature*. Oxford

Laistner, M. L. W. (1947). *The Greater Roman Historians*. Berkeley

Larmour, D. H. J. and Spencer, D. (eds.) (2007). *The Sites of Rome: Time, Space, Memory*. Oxford

Lauletta, M. (1998). *L'intreccio degli stili in Tacito. Intertestualità prosa-poesia nella letteratura storiografica*. Naples

Laurens, P. (1979). 'Rome et la Germanie chez les poètes humanistes allemands', in J.-C. Margolin and J. Lefebvre (eds.), *L'humanisme allemand*. XVIIIe colloque international de Tours 339–55. Paris

Lausberg, H. (1998). *Handbook of Literary Rhetoric: A Foundation for Literary Study* (ed. G. A. Kennedy). Trans. M. T. Bliss, A. Jansen and D. E. Orton. Leiden

Lausberg, M. (1980). 'Caesar und Cato im *Agricola* des Tacitus', *Gymnasium* 87.411–30

Lenchantin de Gubernatis, M. (1940). *Cornelii Taciti Libri Ab Excessu Divi Augusti I–VI.* Rome
Lendon, J.E. (1997). *Empire of Honour: The Art of Government in the Roman World.* Oxford
Levene, D.S. (1993). *Religion in Livy.* Leiden
  (1997). 'Pity, fear and the historical audience: Tacitus on the fall of Vitellius', in S. Braund and C. Gill (eds.), *The Passions in Roman Thought and Literature* 128–49. Cambridge
  (1999). 'Tacitus' *Histories* and the theory of deliberative oratory', in C.S. Kraus (ed.), *The Limits of Historiography: Genre and Narrative in Ancient Historical Texts* 197–216. Leiden
  (2000). 'Sallust's *Catiline* and Cato the censor', *CQ* 50.170–91
  (2004). 'Tacitus' *Dialogus* as literary history', *TAPA* 134.157–200
Levick, B.M. (1978). 'Antiquarian or revolutionary? Claudius Caesar's conception of his principate', *AJP* 99.79–105
  (1982). 'Morals, politics and the fall of the Roman republic', *G&R* 29.53–62
  (1990). *Claudius.* London
  (1999a). *Vespasian.* London
  (1999b). *Tiberius the Politician.* 2nd edn. London
  (2000). *The Government of the Roman Empire: A Sourcebook.* 2nd edn. London
Lichocka, B. (1974). *Justitia sur les monnaies impériales romaines.* Warsaw
Liebeschuetz, W. (1966). 'The theme of liberty in the *Agricola* of Tacitus', *CQ* 16.126–39
  (1979). *Continuity and Change in Roman Religion.* Oxford
Lightfoot, C.S. (1990). 'Trajan's Parthian War and the fourth-century perspective', *JRS* 80.115–26
Linderski, J. (1990). 'Mommsen and Syme: law and power in the principate of Augustus', in K.A. Raaflaub and M. Toher (eds.), *Between Republic and Empire. Interpretations of Augustus and his Principate* 42–53. Berkeley
Lintott, A.W. (1972). 'Imperial expansion and moral decline in the Roman republic', *Historia* 21.626–38
Lipsius, J. (1589). *Politicorum, siue civilis doctrinae libri sex.* Leiden
Löfstedt, E. (1933, 1942). *Syntactica.* 2 vols. (Vol. 1, 2nd edn). Lund
  (1958). *Roman Literary Portraits.* Oxford
Logau, F. von (1984). *Sinngedichte.* Stuttgart
Lovelace, J. (2003). *The Artistry and Tradition of Tennyson's Battle Poetry.* London
Lowe, E.A. (1980). *The Beneventan Script: A History of the South Italian Minuscule.* Vols. 1–2. 2nd edn by V. Brown. Rome
Luce, T.J. (1986). 'Tacitus' conception of historical change', in I.S. Moxon, J.D. Smart and A.J. Woodman (eds.), *Past Perspectives: Studies in Greek and Roman Historical Writing* 143–57. Cambridge
  (1991). 'Tacitus on "History's Highest Function": *praecipuum munus annalium* (*Ann.* 3.65)', *ANRW* 2.33.4.2904–27
  (1993). 'Reading and response in the *Dialogus*', in Luce and Woodman (1993) 11–38
Luce, T.J. and Woodman, A.J. (eds.) (1993). *Tacitus and the Tacitean Tradition.* Princeton, NJ

Lund, A.A. (1991a). 'Zur Gesamtinterpretation der "Germania" des Tacitus', *ANRW* 2.33.3.1858–988

(1991b). 'Kritischer Forschungsbericht zur "Germania" des Tacitus', *ANRW* 2.33.3.1989–2222 and 2341–82

(1995). *Germanenideologie im Nationalsozialismus. Zur Rezeption der Germania des Tacitus im 'Dritten Reich'*. Heidelberg

Macaulay, T.B. (1854). 'von Ranke', in T. B. Macaulay, *Critical and Historical Essays Contributed to the Edinburgh Review* 3.99–146. 8th edn. London

Mackay, C.S. (2003). '*Quaestiones Pisonianae*: procedural and chronological notes on the *S.C. de Cn. Pisone Patre*', *HSCP* 101.311–70

Mair, J. (1939). 'New novels', *New Statesman and Nation*, 7 October 1939

Malcolm, N. (2004). 'Hobbes, Thomas (1588–1679)', in H.C.G. Matthew and B. Harrison (eds.), *Oxford Dictionary of National Biography*. Oxford

(2007). *Reason of State, Propaganda and the Thirty Years' War: An Unknown Translation by Thomas Hobbes*. Oxford

Malissard, A. (1991). 'Le décor dans les "Histoires" et les "Annales". Du stéréotype à l'intention signifiante', *ANRW* 2.33.4.2832–78

Malloch, S.J.V. (2004). 'The end of the Rhine mutiny in Tacitus, Suetonius, and Dio', *CQ* 54.198–210

(2005). 'The date of Corbulo's campaigns in Lower Germany', *MH* 62.76–83

Malvezzi, V. (1635). *Discorsi sopra Cornelio Tacito*. Venice

Marchesi, I. (2008). *The Art of Pliny's Letters: A Poetics of Allusion in the Private Correspondence*. Cambridge

Marincola, J. (1997). *Authority and Tradition in Ancient Historiography*. Cambridge

(1999). 'Tacitus' prefaces and the decline of imperial historiography', *Latomus* 58.391–404

(2007). *A Companion to Greek and Roman Historiography*. Oxford

Martin, R.H. (1967). 'The speech of Curtius Montanus: Tacitus, *Histories* IV, 42', *JRS* 57.109–14

(1969). 'Tacitus and his predecessors', in Dorey (1969a) 117–47

(1981). *Tacitus*. London (rev. 1989, 1994)

(1990). 'Structure and interpretation in the *Annals* of Tacitus', *ANRW* 2.33.2.1500–81

(2001). *Tacitus: Annals V & VI*. Warminster

Martin, R.H. and Woodman, A.J. (1989). *Tacitus: Annals Book IV*. Cambridge

Martyn, D. (1997). 'Borrowed fatherland: nationalism and language purism in Fichte's addresses to the German nation', *The Germanic Review* 72.303–15

Marx, F.A. (1937). 'Tacitus und die Literatur der *exitus illustrium uirorum*', *Philologus* 92.83–103

Masters, J. (1992). *Poetry and Civil War in Lucan's Bellum Ciuile*. Cambridge

Mattern, S.P. (1999). *Rome and the Enemy*. Berkeley

Mattingly, H. (1926). 'The restored coins of Trajan', *NC* 61.232–78

(1948). *Tacitus on Britain and Germany*. Harmondsworth

(1966). *Coins of the Roman Empire in the British Museum*. Vol. 3, *Nerva to Hadrian*. Repr. London (first publ. 1936)

Mayer, R. (2001). *Tacitus: Dialogus de Oratoribus*. Cambridge

(2003). 'Pliny and *gloria dicendi*', *Arethusa* 36.227–34

(2005). 'The impracticability of Latin "Kunstprosa"', in Reinhardt *et al.* (2005) 195–210
Mehl, A. (1974). *Tacitus über Kaiser Claudius: Die Ereignisse am Hof.* Munich
Melliet, L. (1619). *Discours politiques et militaires, sur Corneille Tacite.* Lyon
Mellor, R. (1993). *Tacitus.* New York and London
 (1995). *Tacitus: The Classical Heritage.* New York
 (1999). *The Roman Historians.* London
Mendell, C. W. (1911). *Sentence Connection in Tacitus.* New Haven
 (1954). 'Leidensis BPL. 16. B. Tacitus, XI–XXI', *AJP* 75.250–70
Mendell, C. W. and Hulshoff Pol, E. (1966). *Annales (XI–XVI) et Historiae.* Leiden
Mertens, D. (2004). 'Die Instrumentalisierung der "Germania" des Tacitus durch die deutschen Humanisten', in H. Beck, D. Geuenich, H. Steuer and D. Hakelberg (eds.), *Zur Geschichte der Gleichung "germanisch-deutsch": Sprache und Namen, Geschichte und Institutionen. Ergänzungsbände zum Reallexikon der germanischen Altertumskunde* 34. 37–102. Berlin and New York
Millar, F. (1967). 'Emperors at work', *JRS* 57.9–19
 (1981). 'Style abides', *JRS* 71.144–52
 (1992). *The Emperor in the Roman World (31 BC–AD 337).* 2nd edn. London
Miller, N. P. (1956). 'The Claudian tablet and Tacitus: a reconsideration', *RhM* 99.304–15
 (1961–2). 'Virgil and Tacitus', *PVS* 1.25–34
 (1964). 'Dramatic speech in Tacitus', *AJP* 85.279–96
 (1968). 'Tiberius speaks: an examination of the utterances ascribed to him in the *Annals* of Tacitus', *AJP* 89.1–19
 (1969). 'Style and content in Tacitus', in Dorey (1969a) 99–116
 (1975). 'Dramatic speech in the Roman historians', *G&R* 22.45–57
 (1987). 'Virgil and Tacitus again', *PVS* 18.87–106
Mitchison, N. (1923). *The Conquered.* London
 (1924). *When the Bough Breaks and Other Stories.* London
 (1929). *Barbarian Stories.* London.
 (1948). *The Blood of the Martyrs.* New York (1st edn 1939)
 (1979). *You May Well Ask: A Memoir. 1920–1940.* London
Momigliano, A. D. (1940). Review of Syme (1939), *JRS* 30.75–80
 (1947). 'The first political commentary on Tacitus', *JRS* 37.91–101 (= Momigliano (1977) 205–29)
 (1954). 'Gibbon's contribution to historical method', *Historia* 2.450–63 (= Momigliano (1966) 40–55)
 (1961a). Review of Syme (1958), *Gnomon* 33.55–8
 (1961b). 'Historicism in contemporary thought', *RSI* 73.104–19 (= Momigliano (1966) 221–38)
 (1961c). *Claudius: The Emperor and his Achievement.* Repr. with additions. Cambridge
 (1966). *Studies in Historiography.* London
 (1977). *Essays in Ancient and Modern Historiography.* Oxford
 (1994). *Studies on Modern Scholarship* (ed. G. W. Bowersock and T. J. Cornell). Berkeley and London
Mommsen, T. (1919). *Römische Geschichte.* 5th edn. Berlin

Montefiore, J. (1996). *Men and Women Writers of the 1930s: The Dangerous Flood of History*. London and New York
Morello, R. (2002). 'Livy's Alexander digression (9.17-19): counterfactuals and apologetics', *JRS* 92.62-85
Morello, R. and Gibson, R.K. (eds.) (2003). *Re-Imagining Pliny the Younger. Arethusa* 36.2
(forthcoming). *An Introduction to Pliny the Younger*. Cambridge
Morford, M. (1990). 'Tacitus' historical methods in the Neronian books of the *Annals*', *ANRW* 2.33.2.1582-1627
(1991). 'How Tacitus defined liberty', *ANRW* 33.5.3420-50
(1993). 'Tacitean *prudentia* and the doctrines of Justus Lipsius', in Luce and Woodman (1993) 129-51
Morgan, M.G. (1992). 'The smell of victory: Vitellius at Bedriacum, Tacitus *Histories* 2.70', *CP* 87.14-29
(1993). 'The unity of Tacitus, *Histories* 1, 12-20', *Athenaeum* 81.567-86
(1994). 'Rogues' march: Caecina and Valens in Tacitus *Histories* 1.61-70', *MH* 51.103-25
(1996). 'Cremona in AD 69. Two notes on Tacitus' narrative techniques', *Athenaeum* 84.381-403
(1997). 'Caecina's assault on Placentia. Tacitus, *Histories* 2.20.2-22.3', *Philologus* 141.338-61
(2005). 'Martius Macer's raid and its consequences: Tacitus, *Histories* 2.23', *CQ* 55.572-81
(2006). *69 AD: The Year of Four Emperors*. Oxford
Morris, J.M. (1969). 'Compositional techniques in *Annals* XIII-XVI', diss. Yale University
Mosse, G.L. (1985). *Toward the Final Solution: A History of European Racism*. Madison, Wis. (first publ. 1978)
(1998). *The Crisis of German Ideology. Intellectual Origins of the Third Reich*. New York (first publ. 1964)
Muhlack, U. (1989). 'Die "Germania" im deutschen Nationalbewußtsein vor dem 19. Jahrhundert', in H. Jankuhn and D. Timpe (eds.), *Beiträge zum Verständnis der Germania des Tacitus* Part 1.128-54. Göttingen
Münkel, G. (1959). 'Redner und Redekunst in den historischen Schriften des Tacitus', diss. University of Würzburg
Murgia, C.E. (1980). 'The date of Tacitus' *Dialogus*', *HSCP* 84.99-125
(1981). 'The length of the lacuna in Tacitus' *Dialogus*', *California Studies in Classical Antiquity* 12.221-40
(1985). 'Pliny's Letters and the *Dialogus*', *HSCP* 89.171-206
Murgia, C.E. and Rodgers, R.H. (1984). 'A tale of two manuscripts', *CP* 79.145-53
Murison, C.L. (1991). 'The historical value of Tacitus' *Histories*', *ANRW* 2.33.3.1686-713
(2003). 'M. Cocceius Nerva and the Flavians', *TAPA* 133.147-57
Nippel, W. (2003). 'Einführung', in *Edward Gibbon: Verfall und Untergang des römischen Imperiums bis zum Ende des Reiches im Westen*, Vol. 6, 7-102 (with bibliography, 103-14). Munich

Nisbet, R.G.M. and Hubbard, M. (1970). *A Commentary on Horace Odes 1.* Oxford
Noè, E. (1984). *Storiografia imperiale pretacitiana. Linee di svolgimento.* Florence
Norden, E. (1920). *Die germanische Urgeschichte in Tacitus Germania.* Leipzig and Berlin
  (1923). *Die germanische Urgeschichte in Tacitus Germania.* 3rd edn. Leipzig
Oakley, S.P. (1997). *A Commentary on Livy Books VI–X.* Vol. 1. Oxford
  (1998). *A Commentary on Livy Books VI–X.* Vol. 2. Oxford
  (2005). *A Commentary on Livy Books VI–X.* Vol. 4. Oxford
Oestreich, G. (1982). *Neostoicism and the Early Modern State.* Cambridge
Ogilvie, R.M. and Richmond, I. (1967). *Cornelii Taciti De Vita Agricolae.* Oxford
O'Gorman, E. (1993). 'No place like Rome: identity and difference in the *Germania* of Tacitus', *Ramus* 22.135–54
  (1995). 'On not writing about Augustus: Tacitus, *Annals* book I', *MD* 35.91–114
  (2000). *Irony and Misreading in the Annals of Tacitus.* Cambridge
  (2006). 'Alternate empires: Tacitus's virtual history of the Pisonian principate', *Arethusa* 39.281–301
Oliver, R.P. (1951). 'The first Medicean manuscript of Tacitus and the titulature of ancient books', *TAPA* 82.232–61
Olshausen, E. (1987). 'Tacitus zu Krieg und Frieden', *Chiron* 17.299–312
Oniga, R. (1995). *Sallustio e l'etnografia.* Pisa
Packer, J.E. (1997). *The Forum of Trajan in Rome: A Study of the Monuments.* Vols. 1–3. Berkeley and Los Angeles
  (2001). *The Forum of Trajan in Rome: A Study of the Monuments In Brief.* Berkeley, Los Angeles and London
Pagán, V.E. (1999). 'Beyond Teutoburg. Transgression and transformation in Tacitus *Annales* 1.61–62', *CP* 94.302–20
  (2002). 'Actium and Teutoburg: Augustan victory and defeat in Vergil and Tacitus', in D.S. Levene and D.P. Nelis (eds.), *Clio and the Poets* 45–60. Leiden
Paparelli, G. (1950). *Enea Silvio Piccolomini – Pio II.* Bari
Parker, G.R. (2008). *The Making of Roman India.* Cambridge
Paul, G.M. (1991). 'Symposia and deipna in Plutarch's Lives and in other historical writings', in W.J. Slater (ed.), *Dining in a Classical Context* 157–69. Ann Arbor, Mich.
Paul, U. (1936). *Studien zur Geschichte des deutschen Nationalbewusstseins im Zeitalter des Humanismus und der Reformation.* Historische Studien CCXCVIII. Berlin
Pelling, C.B.R. (1993). 'Tacitus and Germanicus', in Luce and Woodman (1993) 59–85
  (1997). 'Biographical history? Cassius Dio on the early principate', in M.J. Edwards and S. Swain (eds.), *Portraiture in Ancient Literature* 117–44. Oxford
  (2002a). *Plutarch and History.* London
  (2002b). 'Speech and narrative: Herodotus' debate on the constitutions', *PCPS* 48.123–58
  (2004). 'Plutarch', in I.J.F. de Jong, R. Nünlist and A. Bowie (eds.), *Narrators, Narratees, and Narratives in Ancient Greek Literature. Studies in Ancient Greek Narrative*, Vol. 1, 403–21. Leiden and Boston

Perl, G. (1990). 'Tacitus' *Germania*', in J. Herrmann (ed.), *Griechische und Lateinische Quellen zur Frühgeschichte Mitteleuropas bis zur Mitte des 1. Jahrtausends u. Z.* Vol. 2. Berlin

Perret, J. (1950). *Recherches sur le texte de la "Germania"*. Paris

Peter, H. (1967). *Historicorum Romanorum Reliquiae*. 2 vols. Repr. Stuttgart

Petersen, C. and Ruth, P.H. (1934). *Ernst Moritz Arndt: Deutsche Volkwerdung. Sein politisches Vermächtnis an die deutsche Gegenwart*. Breslau

Petersmann, G. (1991). 'Der "Agricola" des Tacitus. Versuch einer Deutung', *ANRW* 2.33.3.1785–806

Pigoń, J. (1992). 'Helvidius Priscus, Eprius Marcellus, and *iudicium senatus*: observations on Tacitus, *Histories* 4.7–8', *CQ* 42.235–46

Plass, P. (1988). *Wit and the Writing of History: The Rhetoric of Historiography in Imperial Rome*. Madison, Wis.

Pocock, J.G.A. (1999–2003). *Barbarism and Religion*. Vol. 1, *The Enlightenments of Edward Gibbon, 1737–1764*; Vol. 2, *Narratives of Civil Government*; Vol. 3, *The First Decline and Fall*. Cambridge

Poignault, R. (2001). 'Les fleuves dans le récit militaire tacitéen', *Latomus* 60.414–32

Poliakov, L. (1977). *The Aryan Myth: A History of Racist and Nationalist Ideas in Europe*. Transl. E. Howard. Repr. New York

Pomeroy, A.J. (1991). *The Appropriate Comment: Death Notices in the Ancient Historians*. Frankfurt

(2006). 'Theatricality in Tacitus's *Histories*', *Arethusa* 39.171–91

Purcell, N. (1986). 'Livia and the womanhood of Rome', *PCPS* 32.78–105

Questa, C. (1967). *Studi sulle fonti degli Annales di Tacito*. 2nd edn, rev. repr. Rome

(1998). *L'Aquila a due Teste*. Urbino

Quint, D. (1993). *Epic and Empire: Politics and Generic Form from Virgil to Milton*. Princeton, NJ

Rae, P. (2003). 'Proleptic elegy and the end of Arcadianism in 1930s Britain', *Twentieth-Century Literature* 49.2.246–75

Raepsaet-Charlier, M.-Th. (1991). 'Cn. Iulius Agricola: mise au point prosopographique', *ANRW* 2.33.3.1808–57

Rankin, H.D. (1965). 'On Tacitus' biography of Petronius', *C&M* 26.233–45

Rawson, E. (1979). 'L. Cornelius Sisenna and the early first century BC', *CQ* 29.327–46

Rehm, R. (1994). *Marriage to Death: The Conflation of Wedding and Funeral Rituals in Greek Tragedy*. Princeton, NJ

Reinhardt, T., Lapidge, M. and Adams, J.N. (eds.) (2005). *Aspects of the Language of Latin Prose. PBA* 129. Oxford

Reiss, S. (2006). 'Fichte in Berlin. Öffentliches Engagement und Arbeit am System', in U. Baumann (ed.), *Fichte in Berlin. Spekulative Ansätze einer Philosophie der Praxis* 9–46. Hanover-Laatzen

Reynolds, L.D. (1983). *Texts and Transmission: A Survey of the Latin Classics*. Oxford

Reynolds, L.D. and Wilson, N.G. (1991). *Scribes and Scholars: A Guide to the Transmission of Greek and Latin Literature*. 3rd edn. Oxford

Rich, J. (2009). 'Structuring Roman history: the consular year and the Roman historical tradition', in J.D. Chaplin and C.S. Kraus (eds.), *Oxford Readings in Classical Studies: Livy* 118–47. Oxford
Ridé, J. (1977). *L'image du Germain dans la pensée et la littérature allemandes de la redécouverte de Tacite à la fin du XVIe siècle*. Vols. 1–3. Lille and Paris
Ries, W. (1969). *Gerücht, Gerede, öffentliche Meinung: Interpretationen zur Psychologie und Darstellungskunst des Tacitus*. Heidelberg
Riess, W. (2003). 'Die Rede des Claudius über das *ius honorum* der gallischen Notabeln: Forschungsstand und Perspektiven', *REA* 105.211–49
Rives, J.B. (1999). *Tacitus, Germania*. Oxford
Rivet, A.L.F. and Smith, C. (1979). *The Place-Names of Roman Britain*. London
Robbert, L. (1917). 'De Tacito Lucani Imitatore', diss. University of Göttingen
Roberts, M. (1988). 'The revolt of Boudicca (Tacitus, *Annals* 14.29–39) and the assertion of *libertas* in Neronian Rome', *AJP* 109.118–32
Robinson, R.P. (1935). *The Germania of Tacitus: A Critical Edition*. Middletown, Conn.
Roller, M.B. (2001). *Constructing Autocracy: Aristocrats and Emperors in Julio-Claudian Rome*. Princeton, NJ
  (2004). 'Exemplarity in Roman culture: the cases of Horatius Cocles and Cloelia', *CP* 99.1–56
Römer, F. (1976). *P. Corneli Taciti Annalium Libri XV–XVI*. (WS Beiheft 6.) Vienna
  (1991). 'Kritischer Problem- und Forschungsbericht zur Überlieferung der taciteischen Schriften', *ANRW* 2.33.3.2299–339
Römer, F. and Heubner, H. (1978). 'Leidensis redivivus?', *WS* 91.159–74
Rose, D. (1994). *Die Thule-Gesellschaft*. Tübingen
Rostagno, E. (1902). *Taciti Codex Laurentianus Mediceus 68.I[–II] phototypice editus*. Vols. 1–2. Leiden
Rubiés, J.-P. (1994). 'Nero in Tacitus and Nero in Tacitism: the historian's craft', in J. Elsner and J. Masters (eds.), *Reflections of Nero: Culture, History, and Representation* 29–47. Chapel Hill, NC
  (1995). 'Reason of state and constitutional thought in the Crown of Aragon, 1580–1640', *Historical Journal* 38.1–28
Russell, D.A. (1979). 'De imitatione', in D. West and T. Woodman (eds.), *Creative Imitation and Latin Literature* 1–16. Cambridge
Rutledge, S. (1998). 'Trajan and Tacitus' audience: reader reception of *Annals* 1–2', *Ramus* 27.141–59
  (1999). '*Delatores* and the tradition of violence in Roman oratory', *AJP* 120.555–73
  (2000). 'Plato, Tacitus, and the *Dialogus de oratoribus*', *Latomus* 254.345–57
  (2001). *Imperial Inquisitions. Prosecutors and Informants from Tiberius to Domitian*. London
Ruysschaert, J. (1949). *Juste Lipse et les Annales de Tacite. Une méthode de critique textuelle au XVIe siècle*. Louvain
Ryberg, I.S. (1942). 'Tacitus' art of innuendo', *TAPA* 73.83–404
Sage, M.M. (1990). 'Tacitus' historical works: a survey and appraisal', *ANRW* 2.33.2.851–1030 and 1629–47

(2000). 'Roman visitors to Ilium in the Roman imperial and late antique period: the symbolic functions of a landscape', *Studia Troica* 10.211–31

Sailor, D. (2008). *Writing and Empire in Tacitus*. Cambridge

Salmon, J.H.M. (1980). 'Cicero and Tacitus in sixteenth-century France', *AHR* 85.307–31

Santoro L'Hoir, F. (2006). *Tragedy, Rhetoric, and the Historiography of Tacitus' Annales*. Ann Arbor, Mich.

Šašel Kos, M. (1990). '*Sententiae* in the *Agricola* of Tacitus', *Živa Antika (Antiquité Vivante)* 40.83–109

Savage, J.J. (1938–9). 'Germanicus and Aeneas', *CJ* 34.237–8

(1942–3). 'Germanicus and Aeneas again', *CJ* 38.166–7

Schäfer, E. (1977). 'Domitians Antizipation im vierten Historienbuch des Tacitus', *Hermes* 105.455–77

Schama, S. (1995). *Landscape and Memory*. London

Schaps, D. (1979). 'The found and lost manuscripts of Tacitus' *Agricola*', *CP* 74.28–42

Schardius, S. (1673). *Schardius Redivivus sive Rerum Germanicarum Scriptores varii olim a D(omino) Simone Schardio in quatuor tomos collecti*. Vol. 1. Gießen

Schellhase, K.C. (1976). *Tacitus in Renaissance Political Thought*. Chicago and London

Schillinger-Häfele, U. (1965). 'Claudius und Tacitus über die Aufnahme von Galliern in den Senat', *Historia* 14.443–54

Schmal, S. (2005). *Tacitus*. Hildesheim, Zurich and New York

Schmaus, H. (1887). *Tacitus, ein Nachahmer Vergils*. Bamberg

Schottelius, J.G. (1900). *Neu erfundenes Freuden Spiel genandt Friedens Sieg*. Halle (first publ. 1648)

Schwindt, J.P. (2000). *Prolegomena zu einer Phänomenologie der römischen Literaturgeschichtsschreibung von den Anfängen bis Quintilian*. Göttingen

Scramuzza, V.M. (1940). *The Emperor Claudius*. Cambridge

Seager, R. (2005). *Tiberius*. 2nd edn. Malden, Mass.

See, K. von (1986). *Deutsche Germanenideologie vom Humanismus bis zur Gegenwart*. Frankfurt (first publ. 1970)

Seelentag, G. (2004). *Taten und Tugenden Traians. Herrschaftsdarstellung im Principat*. Hermes Einzelschriften 91. Stuttgart

Segal, C. (1981). *Tragedy and Civilization: An Interpretation of Sophocles*. Cambridge, Mass.

Seif, K.P. (1973). *Die Claudiusbücher in den Annalen des Tacitus*. Mainz

Sheehan, J.J. (1981). 'What is German history? Reflections on the role of the nation in German history and historiography', *Journal of Modern History* 53.1–23

Sherwin-White, A.N. (1966). *The Letters of Pliny*. Oxford

Shochat, Y. (1981). 'Tacitus' attitude to Otho', *Latomus* 40.365–77

Shotter, D.C.A. (2000). 'Petillius Cerialis in northern Britain', *Northern History* 36.189–98

(2002). 'Roman Britain and the "Year of the Four Emperors"', *Trans. Cumberland Westmorland Antiq. Arch. Soc.*, 3rd ser. 2.79–86

Shumate, N. (1997). 'Compulsory pretense and the "theatricalization of experience" in Tacitus', in C. Deroux (ed.), *Studies in Latin Literature and Roman History* 8.364–403. Brussels

Sinclair, P. (1995). *Tacitus the Sententious Historian: A Sociology of Rhetoric in Annales 1-6*. University Park, Pa.
Skinner, Q. (2002). *Visions of Politics*. Vol. 2 *Renaissance Virtues*. Cambridge
Skovgaard-Petersen, K. (1995). 'Tacitus and Tacitism in Johannes Meursius' *Historica Danica* (1630-38)', *SO* 70.212-40
Smallwood, E.M. (1966). *Documents Illustrating the Principates of Nerva, Trajan and Hadrian*. Cambridge
(1984). *Documents Illustrating the Principates of Gaius, Claudius and Nero*. Rev. repr. Cambridge
Smart, S. (1989). 'Justus Georg Schottelius and the patriotic movement', *MLR* 84.83-98
Smiles, S. (1994). *The Image of Antiquity: Ancient Britain and the Romantic Imagination*. New Haven and London
Smuts, M. (1994). 'Court-centred politics and the uses of Roman historians', in P. Lake and K. Sharpe (eds.), *Culture and Politics in Early Stuart England* 21-43. London
Sörbom, G. (1935). *Variatio sermonis Tacitei aliaeque apud eundem quaestiones selectae*. Uppsala
Soverini, P. (2004). *Cornelio Tacito: Agricola*. Alessandria
Spitz, L.W. (1957). *Conrad Celtis. The German Arch-Humanist*. Cambridge
Sponagel, L. (1939). *Konrad Celtis und das deutsche Nationalbewußtsein*. Bühl
Stackelberg, J. von (1960). *Tacitus in der Romania. Studien zur literarischen Rezeption des Tacitus in Italien und Frankreich*. Tübingen
Stadtwald, K. (1996). *Roman Popes and German Patriots. Antipapalism in the Politics of the German Humanist Movement from Gregor Heimburg to Martin Luther*. Geneva
Stegner, K. (2004). *Die Verwendung der Sentenz in den Historien des Tacitus*. Stuttgart
Suerbaum, W. (1990). 'Zweiundvierzig Jahre Tacitus-Forschung: Systematische Gesamtbibliographie zu Tacitus' Annalen 1939-1980', *ANRW* 2.33.2. 1032-1476
Syme, R. (1939). *The Roman Revolution*. Oxford
(1955). 'Marcus Lepidus, capax imperii', *JRS* 45.22-33 (= Syme (1970) 30-49)
(1958a). *Tacitus*. Oxford
(1958b). 'Obituaries in Tacitus', *AJP* 79.18-31 (= Syme (1970) 79-90)
(1958c). 'The senator as historian', in *Histoire et historiens dans l'antiquité*. Fondation Hardt Entretiens 4. 185-212. Geneva (= Syme (1970) 1-10)
(1959). 'Livy and Augustus', *HSCP* 64.27-87 (= Syme (1979) 400-54)
(1960). 'Roman historians and Renaissance politics', in *Society and History in the Renaissance: A Report of a Conference Held at the Folger Library on April 23 and 24, 1960* 3-12. Washington, DC (= Syme (1979) 470-6)
(1964a). *Sallust*. Berkeley, Los Angeles and London
(1964b). 'The historian Servilius Nonianus', *Hermes* 92.408-14 (= Syme (1970) 91-109)
(1970). *Ten Studies in Tacitus*. Oxford
(1974). 'History or biography: the case of Tiberius Caesar', *Historia* 23.481-96 (= Syme (1984) 937-52)

(1977). 'Liberty in classical antiquity', *Memoirs of the American Philosophical Society* 118.8-15 (= Syme (1984) 962-8)
(1978a). *History in Ovid*. Oxford
(1978b). 'Mendacity in Velleius', *AJP* 99.45-63
(1979). *Roman Papers*. Vols. 1-2. Oxford
(1984). *Roman Papers*. Vol. 3. Oxford
(1986). *The Augustan Aristocracy*. Oxford
(1988). *Roman Papers*. Vol. 4. Oxford
(1999). *The Provincial at Rome/Rome and the Balkans 80 BC–AD 14*. Exeter
Tabacco, R. (1985). *Il tiranno nelle declamazioni di scuola in lingua latina*. Turin
Talbert, R.J.A. (1984). *The Senate of Imperial Rome*. Princeton, NJ
Theissen, W. (1912). *De Sallustii, Livii, Taciti digressionibus*. Berlin
Thomas, R.F. (1982). *Lands and Peoples in Roman Poetry: The Ethnographical Tradition*. Cambridge Philological Society Supplement 7. Cambridge
 (2004). 'Torn between Jupiter and Saturn: ideology, rhetoric and culture wars in the *Aeneid*', *CJ* 100.121-47
Tiedemann, H. (1913). *Tacitus und das Nationalbewusstsein der deutschen Humanisten am Ende des 15. und Anfang des 16. Jahrhunderts*. Berlin
Till, R. (1943). *Handschriftliche Untersuchungen zu Tacitus Agricola und Germania*. Berlin
Timpanaro, S. (2005). *The Genesis of Lachmann's Method*. Ed. and Trans. G.W. Most. Chicago
Todd, M. (2003). 'Anti-Calvinists and the republican threat in early Stuart Cambridge', in L. Knoppers (ed.), *Puritanism and its Discontents* 85-105. Newark, Del.
 (2004). 'Dorislaus, Isaac (1595-1649)', in H.C.G. Matthew and B. Harrison (eds.), *Oxford Dictionary of National Biography*. Oxford
Townend, G.B. (1964). 'Cluvius Rufus in the *Histories* of Tacitus', *AJP* 85.337-77
Tresch, J. (1965). *Die Nerobücher in den Annalen des Tacitus: Tradition und Leistung*. Heidelberg
Trüdinger, K. (1918). *Studien zur Geschichte der griechisch-römischen Ethnographie*. Basle
Tuck, R. (1993). *Philosophy and Government, 1572-1651*. Cambridge
Turner, A.J. (1997). 'Approaches to Tacitus' *Agricola*', *Latomus* 56.582-93
Ullmann, R. (1927). *La technique des discours dans Salluste, Tite-Live et Tacite*. Oslo
Urban, R. (1979). 'Tacitus und die *Res gestae divi Augusti*', *Gymnasium* 86.59-74
Utard, R. (2004). *Le discours indirect chez les historiens latins: écriture ou oralité?* Louvain
Vacher de Lapouge, G. (1899). 'Old and new aspects of the Aryan question', *American Journal of Sociology* 5.329-46
Van den Berg, C.S. (2006). 'The social aesthetics of Tacitus' *Dialogus de oratoribus*', dissertation, Yale University
Vazsonyi, N. (1999). 'Montesquieu, Friedrich Varl von Moser, and the "National Spirit Debate" in Germany, 1765-1767', *German Studies Review* 22.225-46
Verbrugghe, G.P. (1989). 'On the meaning of *annales*, on the meaning of annalist', *Philologus* 133.192-230
Vessey, D.W.T.C. (1971). 'Thoughts on Tacitus' portrayal of Claudius', *AJP* 92.385-409

Vick, B. (2003). 'The origins of the German Volk: cultural purity and national identity in nineteenth-century Germany', *German Studies Review* 26.241–56
Vielberg, M. (1987). *Pflichten, Werte, Ideale: eine Untersuchung zu den Wertvorstellungen des Tacitus*. Hermes Einzelschriften 52. Wiesbaden
Viereck, P.R.E. (1961). *Metapolitics: The Roots of the Nazi Mind*. Rev. edn. New York
Viroli, M. (1992). *From Politics to Reason of State: The Acquisition and Transformation of the Language of Politics: 1250–1600*. Cambridge
Voet, L. (1980–3). *The Plantin Press (1555–1589)*. Vols. 1–6. Amsterdam
Volpilhac-Auger, C. (1985). *Tacite et Montesquieu*. Oxford
  (1993). *Tacite en France de Montesquieu à Chateaubriand*. Oxford
Voss, B.-R. (1963). *Der pointierte Stil des Tacitus*. Orbis Antiquus 19. Münster
Walker, B. (1952). *The Annals of Tacitus*. Manchester
Wallace-Hadrill, A. (1983). *Suetonius: The Scholar and his Caesars*. London
Watson, P.A. (1995). *Ancient Stepmothers: Myth, Misogyny and Reality*. Leiden
Weaver, P.R.C. (1972). *Familia Caesaris: a Social Study of the Emperor's Freedmen and Slaves*. Cambridge
Wellesley, K. (1954). 'Can you trust Tacitus?', *G&R* 1.13–33
  (1969). 'Tacitus as a military historian', in Dorey (1969a) 63–97
  (1972). *Cornelius Tacitus. The Histories Book iii*. Sydney
  (1986). *Cornelii Taciti Libri Qui Supersunt. Tomus I, Pars Secunda: Ab Excessu Divi Augusti Libri XI–XVI*. Leipzig
  (2000). *The Year of the Four Emperors*. 3rd edn. London
Welwei, K.-W. (1995). 'Verdeckte Systemkritik in der Galbarede des Tacitus', *Gymnasium* 102.353–63
Wharton, D.B. (1997). 'Tacitus' Tiberius: the state of the evidence for the emperor's *ipsissima verba* in the *Annals*', *AJP* 118.119–25
Whitehead, D. (1979). 'Tacitus and the loaded alternative', *Latomus* 38.474–95
Wiedemann, T.E.J. (1993). 'Sallust's *Jugurtha*: concord, discord and the digressions', *G&R* 40.48–57
  (1996). 'Tiberius to Nero', in A.K. Bowman, E. Champlin and A. Lintott (eds.), *The Cambridge Ancient History*, 2nd edn, Vol. 10, 198–255. Cambridge
Wilkes, J. (1972). 'Julio-Claudian historians', *CW* 65.177–192, 197–203
Wilkinson, L.P. (1963). *Golden Latin Artistry*. Cambridge
Willems, A. (1880). *Les Elzevir*. Brussels (repr. 1962)
Williams, G.W. (1978). *Change and Decline. Roman Literature in the Early Empire*. Berkeley
Wills, J. (1996). *Repetition in Latin Poetry: Figures of Allusion*. Oxford
Winkler, M. (2001). 'The Roman empire in American cinema since 1945', in S. Joshel, M. Malamud and D. McGuire (eds.), *Imperial Projections: Ancient Rome in Modern Popular Culture* 50–76. Baltimore, Md. and London
Winterbottom, M. (1964). 'Quintilian and the *vir bonus*', *JRS* 54.90–7
  (1972). 'The transmission of Tacitus' *Dialogus*', *Philologus* 116.114–28
  (1975). 'The manuscript tradition of Tacitus' *Germania*', *CP* 70.1–7
  (1982). 'Cicero and the silver age', in W. Stroh *et al.* (eds.), *Eloquence et rhétorique chez Cicéron* 237–66. Geneva
  (2001). 'Returning to Tacitus' *Dialogus*', in C.W. Wooten (ed.), *The Orator in Action and Theory in Greece and Rome* 137–55. Leiden

Wirszubski, C. (1950). *Libertas as a Political Idea at Rome During the Late Republic and Early Principate.* Cambridge
Wiseman, T.P. (1991). *Flavius Josephus: Death of an Emperor.* Exeter
  (1998). 'Late Syme: a study in historiography', in T.P. Wiseman, *Roman Drama and Roman History* 135–52. Exeter
Wolfson, S. (2008). *Tacitus, Thule and Caledonia. The Achievements of Agricola's Navy in Their True Perspective.* BAR British Series 459. Oxford
Womersley, D. (1988). *The Transformation of the Decline and Fall of the Roman Empire.* Cambridge
  (1994). *The History of the Decline and Fall of the Roman Empire.* Vols. 1–3. London
  (1997a). *Edward Gibbon: Bicentenary Essays.* Oxford
  (1997b). *Religious Scepticism. Contemporary Responses to Gibbon.* Bristol
Woodman, A.J. (1975). 'Velleius Paterculus', in T.A. Dorey (ed.), *Empire and Aftermath: Silver Latin II* 1–25. London
  (1977). *Velleius Paterculus: The Tiberian Narrative (2.94–131).* Cambridge
  (1979). 'Self-imitation and the substance of history', in D. West and T. Woodman (eds.), *Creative Imitation and Latin Literature* 143–55, 231–5. Cambridge (= Woodman (1998) 70–85)
  (1983a). 'From Hannibal to Hitler: the literature of war', *University of Leeds Review* 26.107–24 (= Woodman (1998) 1–20)
  (1983b). *Velleius Paterculus. The Caesarian and Augustan Narrative (2.41–93).* Cambridge
  (1988). *Rhetoric in Classical Historiography.* London and Sydney
  (1989). 'Tacitus' obituary of Tiberius', *CQ* 39.197–205 (= Woodman (1998) 155–67)
  (1993). 'Amateur dramatics at the court of Nero: *Annals* 15.48–74', in Luce and Woodman (1993) 104–28 (= Woodman (1998) 190–217)
  (1995). '*praecipuum munus annalium.* The construction, convention and context of Tacitus, *Annals* 3.65.1', *MH* 52.111–26 (= Woodman (1998) 86–103)
  (1997). 'Tacitus', in Kraus and Woodman (1997) 88–118
  (1998). *Tacitus Reviewed.* Oxford
  (2004). *Tacitus: The Annals.* Indianapolis, Ind. and Cambridge, Mass. (rev. edn 2008)
  (2006a). 'Mutiny and madness: Tacitus *Annals* 1.16–49', *Arethusa* 39.303–29
  (2006b). 'Tiberius and the taste of power: the year 33 in Tacitus', *CQ* 56.175–89
Woodman, A.J. and Martin, R.H. (1996). *The Annals of Tacitus Book 3.* Cambridge
Woolliscroft, D. and Hoffmann, B. (2006). *Rome's First Frontier. The Flavian Occupation of Northern Scotland.* Stroud
Worden, B. (2006). 'Historians and poets', in P. Kewes (ed.), *The Uses of History in Early Modern England* 69–90. San Marino, Calif.
Yakobson, A. (1998). 'The princess of inscriptions: *Senatus Consultum de Cn. Pisone Patre* and the early years of Tiberius' reign', *SCI* 17.206–24
Yarrow, L.M. (2006). *Historiography at the End of the Republic. Provincial Perspectives on Roman Rule.* Oxford
Zimmermann, M. (1889). *De Tacito Senecae Philosophi Imitatore.* Breslau

INDEX LOCORUM

Tacitus

Agricola

(1.1) 19, 47, (2.1–3) 311, (2.1) 11, (2.2) 11, (2.3) 192, (3.1) 31, 187, 192, (3.3) 31, (4.2–3) 7, (4.3) 192, (5.1) 36, (7.1–2) 87, (9.3–4) 51, (10–12) 61, 98, (10.3) 17 n. 2, 23, 28, (10.4) 53, (13.1) 17 n. 2, (14.1–2) 205, (18.5) 50, (18.6) 51, (21.1–2) 57, 260 n. 25, (28) 54, (30.3–5) 305, (30.4–5) 197, (30.5) 1, 58, 197, 198, (35.3) 34, (36.3) 56, (38.2–4) 52–3, (42.3–4) 309, 314, (42.3) 193, (42.4) 51, 143, 152, 192, (44.2) 154, (44.5) 31, (45.1–2) 147, 151, 186

Annals

(1.1–10) 266, (1.1.1) 100, 104, (1.1.2–3) 24, 101, 182, (1.1.3) 103, 176, (1.2.1) 101, 260 n. 25, (1.2.2) 173, (1.3.1–5) 102, (1.3.5–7) 110, (1.5.4) 104, (1.6.3) 260, (1.7.1) 189, (1.9–10) 105, (1.53.5) 200, (1.61.2) 4, (1.63.1–2) 234, (1.63.3–68.5) 232, (1.64–8) 235, (1.65.1) 199, (1.65.7) 249, (1.69.3) 17 n. 2, (1.73.1) 162, (1.73.2) 35–6, (1.74.3) 34, 36, (1.74.5) 190, (1.75.1) 187, (1.77.3) 188, (1.81.1) 176, (1.81.2) 188;

(2.5.2) 6–7, (2.6.3–4) 235, (2.14–21) 236, (2.14.3) 199, (2.15–21) 233, (2.20.3) 199, (2.22.1) 6, (2.23–4) 196, (2.23.2) 5, (2.24.1) 6, (2.39.2) 2, 25, (2.43) 177, (2.45.3) 1, (2.52.5) 193, (2.53–82) 177, (2.53–4) 111, (2.59–61) 111, (2.69.2–3) 3–4, (2.87) 188, (2.88.1–3) 152, (2.88.1) 8–9;

(3.1–19) 177, (3.3.2) 9, (3.7–19) 10, (3.16.1) 10, 179, (3.18.4) 169, (3.19.2) 302, (3.26–8) 172, (3.26) 172, (3.30.2) 17 n. 2, 22, 173, (3.47.3–4) 189, (3.55.4) 173, (3.55.5) 42, 168, (3.58.3) 36, (3.60–3) 187, (3.65.1–2) 188, (3.65.1) 12, 87 n. 11, 175, 274, (3.65.3) 187, (3.66) 19, (3.76) 147;

(4.1) 22, (4.1.1) 62, 152, 165, 182, (4.1.2) 170, 172, (4.6.1) 166, (4.6.2) 185, (4.10–12) 156, (4.20.2–3) 193, (4.20.3) 169, 172, (4.32–3) 136–7, 231, (4.32) 20, (4.32.1–2) 226, (4.33) 172, 174, (4.33.1) 259, (4.33.2) 175, (4.33.3) 121, 226, 231, (4.33.4) 37, 154, (4.34–5) 258, (4.34.3) 17 n. 2, 23, (4.34.4) 17, 17 n. 2, (4.35.5) 12, 21, (4.46–51) 234–7, (4.53.2) 17 n. 2, 156, (4.56) 19, (4.57) 164, (4.57.1) 198 n. 14, (4.58.2–3) 170, (4.61) 42 n. 34, (4.64.1) 171, (4.67.2) 152, (4.72–3) 237;

(5.1.1–4) 113, (5.5) 243, (5.6.1) 243, (5.9.2) 156;

(6.2.3–4) 190, (6.7.4) 176, (6.14.2) 205, (6.19.2–20.1) 153, (6.19.2) 37, 161, (6.20.2) 153, 170, (6.21) 170, (6.22.1) 169, (6.22.3) 170, (6.22.4) 170, (6.23–4) 153, (6.24.3) 37, (6.25) 113, (6.27.4) 193, (6.31–7) 232, (6.38.1) 226, (6.48.2) 166, (6.50.2) 36, (6.51.3) 165;

(11.3.1) 203, (11.11.1) 37–9, 149 n. 5, (11.16–21) 237, (11.18.3) 154, (11.20.3–21) 27 n. 33, (11.23–25.1) 124–6, (11.23–4) 180–1, (11.24.5) 125, (11.27) 156;

(12.31.1–40.5) 120, (12.35.3) 37, (12.40.5–41.1) 121, (12.43.1) 171, (12.43.2) 169, 172, (12.52.3) 200, (12.64.1) 171;

357

INDEX LOCORUM

(13.1.1) 127, (13.3-4) 213, (13.4.2) 185, (13.20) 157, (13.20.2) 8, 17 n. 2, 18, 28, (13.21.2-5) 213, (13.49.1-4) 190;

(14.1.1) 205, (14.1-10) 128, (14.2) 157, (14.2.1) 18 n. 2, (14.2.2) 18 n. 2, 28, (14.5.1) 169, (14.10) 22, (14.12.1) 191, (14.12.2) 171, (14.17.1) 153, (14.19) 18 n. 2, 27, (14.22.4) 170, (14.27.2) 36, (14.29-39) 230, (14.43-4) 190, (14.49.1) 191, (14.64.3) 188;

(15.1-17) 227-9, (15.6.4) 229, (15.7) 171, (15.16.1) 18 n. 2, (15.20.1-22.1) 191, (15.34.1) 198, (15.37.4) 196, (15.41.1) 36, (15.47) 171, (15.49.1) 157, (15.51.1) 157, (15.52.2-3) 157, (15.53.3-4) 158, (15.53.3) 17 n. 2, (15.61.3) 18 n. 2, 28, (15.65) 134, (15.73.1-2) 177, (15.73.2) 157, (15.74.3) 4, 9;

(16.4.4) 154, (16.6.1) 154, (16.16) 11, 136-7, (16.16.2) 141, 170, 174, (16.21-35) 191, (16.29.1) 249, (16.33.1) 171, (16.35.1) 316

Dialogus

(1.1) 74, (1.2) 77, (7.1) 204, (9.6) 33, (12.1) 33, 82, (12.2) 82, (12.6) 17 n. 2, (16.4) 83 n. 23, (18.3) 83 n. 23, (23.2) 17 n. 2, 27, (36.1) 32, (40.2) 80

Germania

(1.1) 63, (1.2) 63, (2.1) 153, (2.2) 289, 299, (3.2) 67, (4) 281, 282, 293, 297, (5.2) 153, (6.4) 287, (9-10) 282, (12.1) 297, (13-14) 298, (13.3) 298, (14.1) 287, (17.1) 60, (19.1) 36, (27.1) 200, (27.2) 62, (28.1) 17 n. 2, 22, (32) 198, (33.2) 48 n. 2, 65, (34.2) 67, (35.1-2) 68, (37) 287, (37.2) 64, (37.3) 64, (41.1) 63, (46.3-4) 153, (46.3) 69

Histories

(1.1.1) 22, 24, (1.1.2) 150, (1.1.3-4) 147, (1.1.3) 39, 87, 176, (1.1.4) 31, (1.2.1) 58, 225, (1.2.3) 202, (1.3.2) 169, (1.4) 175, (1.4.1) 19, 169, (1.10.3) 171, (1.15-16) 90, 214, 215-18, (1.15.1) 216, (1.16.1) 90, (1.16.4) 187, (1.18.1) 171, (1.18.3) 151, (1.22.2-3) 170, (1.29-30) 221, (1.29.2-30.3) 214, (1.34.1) 150, (1.37.1-38.2) 214, (1.37.1) 218, (1.44.2) 91, (1.47.1) 200, (1.49.4) 202, (1.51.1) 62, (1.80-5) 90, (1.83-4) 159, (1.83.2-84.4) 214, (1.85.3) 160, (1.86.2-3) 171;

(2.7.2) 200, (2.13.2) 93, (2.38.2) 169, 172, (2.42.2) 198, (2.76-7) 219-21, (2.78.1) 170, (2.91.2-3) 191, (2.99.2) 37, (2.101.1) 176;

(3.22.2) 155, (3.25.2-3) 93, (3.25.2) 7, 155, (3.25.3) 202, (3.28) 7, 17 n. 2, (3.28.1) 156, (3.31.3) 34, (3.38.4) 36, (3.46.1) 88, (3.51.1) 92, (3.51.2) 7, 19, (3.63.2) 196, 202, (3.65.2) 37, (3.72.1) 170, (3.74.1) 37, (3.75.1) 154, (3.84.4-85) 207-11;

(4.1.1) 96, (4.4-5) 191, (4.4.3) 191, (4.6.1) 191, (4.6.2) 192, (4.8.2-3) 159, (4.8.2) 261 n. 28, 186 n. 11, (4.8.4) 187, (4.11.1) 201, (4.13.2) 96, (4.26.1-2) 171, (4.38.1) 183, (4.40-4) 221-3, (4.42.2-6) 187, (4.43.1-44.1) 192, (4.43.1) 17 n. 2, 18 n. 2, (4.43.1) 28, (4.49.1) 36, (4.70.3) 200, (4.78.2) 169, (4.81.3) 155 n. 18;

(5.2-13) 97, (5.23.2) 248

Other authors

Accius (204R³) 129 n. 8
Albinovanus Pedo (1 Courtney = 228 Hollis) 67
Ammianus Marcellinus (31.16.9) 241 n. 2

Caesar (*B Gall.*7.77) 58
Cato (*Orig.* 2P = 2C) 47, (77P = 81C) 19
Cicero (*Arch.* 1) 285, (*Brut.* 45) 80, (*De Or.* 2.63) 175, (*Off.* 2.41-2) 173, (2.49-51) 77, (*Rep.* 1.65, 69) 172, (*Tim.* 44) 33
Curtius Rufus (7.11.4) 51, (9.9.1) 51

INDEX LOCORUM

Dio (39.50.4) 54, (56.43.4) 185, (57.7.1, 57.19) 182 n. 21, (62.12) 230, (62.13.4) 130, (63.27–9) 141, (64.20.1–3) 209 n. 39, (66.20.2–3) 53

Ennius (*Ann.* 206–7 Sk) 82

Fronto (p. 108 VDH²) 41 n. 27

Herodotus (4.22–5) 69
Horace (*Carm.* 1.3.21–4) 67, (1.37.9–10) 196, (3.6.1–20) 170, (*Epist.* 2.1.34–49) 83 n. 23, (2.1.76–8) 83 n. 23, (2.1.160) 82

Jerome (*Comm. Zach.* 3.14.1–2) 86 n.5, 241
Juvenal (1.162–7) 37 n. 15, (2.159–61) 56, (4.46) 36, (8.13) 36, (13.171–3) 36, (15.112) 56

Livy (*praef.* 4) 64, (*praef.* 9) 48, (1.41) 104, (1.57.10) 114, (4.3–4) 181, (5.22.8) 65, (8.13.14–15) 1 n. 2
[Longinus] (*Subl.* 26.2) 154 n. 13, (44) 73 n. 1
Lucan (1.128) 306, (2.40–2) 89
Lucretius (5.1105) 173

Ovid (*Met.* 14.166) 60

Pliny the Elder (*HN* 2.18) 90, (3.39) 57 n. 32, (4.102) 55, (7.76) 35 n. 12
Pliny the Younger (*Ep.*1.6) 32–3, (1.9) 35, (1.9.3) 34, (1.9.5) 34, (1.9.7) 34, (1.20) 33–4, (1.20.12) 33, (2.1.6) 31, 48, (2.11.1) 79, (5.8.12) 85, (5.13.8) 10 n. 31, (6.16.22) 174, (7.33.1) 23 n. 19, 31, (7.33.3) 10, (9.10.2) 33, 245, (9.14) 42, (9.19.5) 28 n. 35, (9.23.2–3) 79 n. 14, (9.27) 87, (10.8) 36
Plutarch (*Galb.* 23.2) 215, (27.4) 92, (*Mor.* 410A, 419E) 51, (856C) 160
Polybius (1.1.2) 175, (6.10–18) 184, (10.21.8) 176

Quintilian (10.1.101–4) 26, (10.1.101) 17, (10.1.122) 78, (10.7.26) 33

Sallust (*Cat.* 6.1) 104, (6.6–7) 173, (8.5) 285, (53.1) 50, (54.2–6) 51, (54.6) 51, (*Hist.* 1.88) 97 n. 37, (4.69) 58, (*Iug.* 4.5–6) 178, (17–19) 98, (95.2) 19, (113.1–3) 22
Scriptores Historiae Augustae (*Tac.* 10.3) 42, 241
Sempronius Asellio (1P = 1C) 19, 175
Seneca the Elder (*Controv.* 1 praef. 6–7) 73 n. 1, (10.3.5) 89, (*Hist.* fr. 1P = 2C) 27
Seneca the Younger (*Cons. Marc.* 1.2–4) 27, ([*Epigr.*] 69–70) 93, (*Epist.* 90) 172
Sidonius (*Epist.* 4.14.1, 22.2) 243
Silius Italicus (1.475–6) 37, (3.597) 56, (5.197) 37, (9.137–8) 37, (11.1–3) 62, (16.514) 37, (17.416–17) 56
Sophocles (*Ant.* 801–5) 131, (850–2) 132, (944–87) 131
Statius (*Ach.* 1.888) 37, (*Silv.* 5.1.88–93) 56, (5.2.8–10) 36, (5.2.54–6) 56, (5.2.142–9) 55, (*Theb.* 3.74) 36, (8.665) 36
Suetonius (*Calig.* 6.2) 182 n. 21, (*Claud.* 21.2) 28, (*Galb.* 17) 215, (20.2) 92, (*Ner.* 34.1–4) 130, (40–7) 141, (*Tib.* 12.3) 36, (28) 4 n. 7, (39) 182 n. 21, (61.1) 28, (68.4) 36, (*Vit.* 16–17) 206–11

Thucydides (7.44.1) 155

Valerius Flaccus (1.398) 37, (2.654) 37
Varro (*Ling.* 5.7.1) 62
Velleius (94–125) 25, (112.7) 2, (126–30) 25, (129.3) 2, 3–4, (131.1–2) 26

INDEX LOCORUM

Virgil (*Aen.* 3.594) 60, (6.756–9) 62, (6.853) 6, (7.37–40) 62, (8.96) 5, (9.230) 5, (10.103) 5, (10.803) 5–6, (11.587) 65, (12.36) 5, (12.646) 142, (12.647) 6–7, (*Georgics* 1.474–5) 64, (3.544–5) 1

Non-literary

CIL (6.41106) 80 n. 16, (13.1668 = *ILS* 212) 124, 180–1, (col. 1, lines 8–40) 125
P Oxy. (2345 recto) 6, 6 n. 15
Senatus Consultum de Cn. Pisone Patre (lines 165–8) 178

GENERAL INDEX

(Dates are AD unless stated otherwise)

ablative case 205, 206, 210
abstract nouns 201
accusative of respect ('Greek accusative') 37, 60
acta diurna 9, 9 n. 30
acta senatus 4, 4 n. 7, 8 n. 23, 8–10, 178, 180, 190 n. 20
adulatio 185, 188, 189, 193, 321
Agricola 48–58, 152, 154, 260, 263, 309, 314
Agrippa Postumus 2–3, 4, 5, 25, 105, 260
Agrippina the Elder 107, 109, 112, 113, 148, 189
Agrippina the Younger 17, 17 n. 2, 117, 118, 120, 123, 127–30, 143, 169, 182, 213
Albinovanus Pedo 67
Alexander the Great 51–2, 68
allusion 1–7, 14, 25, 32–7, 43, 47–8, 50–1, 60, 65, 67, 74, 80 n. 17, 81, 104, 114, 131 n. 12, 196, 229
Ammianus Marcellinus 241
Ammirato, Scipione 262–3, 264
amplitude of expression 204, 205 n. 34, 275
anaphora 199
annales, annals 18 n. 4, 18–19, 21, 21 n. 13
annalistic format 100, 115, 119 n. 16, 120, 122, 127 n. 2, 182, 183
annalists 17, 18–21, 29
Annius of Viterbo 284
antithesis 199, 200
Antonia the Younger, mother of Germanicus 111
Aper, M. 74–84
aphorisms *see* epigrams
'appendix' sentences 205–6, 210
apud 8–9

Aquilius Regulus, M. (suff. date unknown) 75, 77, 222
archaeology 52, 55, 58, 59
archaisms 196
Arminius 1–5, 152, 232, 234, 288
Arndt, Ernst Moritz 281, 292, 293
Arulenus Rusticus, Q. (suff. 92) 47, 140, 312, 314
Asinius Pollio, C. (cos. 40 BC) 17, 17 n. 2, 78, 83, 303, 321
assonance 210
astrology 169, 170, 183
asyndeton 135, 197, 199, 200, 322
audacia 67
Aufidius Bassus 26, 27, 59
Augustus 23, 25, 28, 42, 101–4, 106, 114, 165, 184, 259, 260, 263, 265, 318, 324, 326
authority (of author) 39, 149, 155, 156, 164
Aventinus, Johannes 286

Batavian revolt 88, 96–7
Beatus Rhenanus 249, 284, 288
Bebel, Heinrich 285
beginnings 96, 100, 113, 114, 120, 121, 148, 182, 183
Beroaldus the Younger 244, 248
Berosus 284
biography 206–211, 318
Biondo, Flavio 275
Boccaccio 244
Boccalini, Traiano 264–5
book divisions 182–3, 243, 248
Botero, Giovanni 261
Boudicca (Boadicea) 230, 305, 307, 316
brevity 197, 275, 322
Brink, C.O. 251

361

GENERAL INDEX

Britain, Britons 50–8, 120–2, 151, 226, 230–1, 304, 305, 306
Britannicus 128, 304
Burrus, Sex. Afranius 128, 130, 131, 182, 182 n. 21

Caesar 17, 17 n. 2, 22, 50–1, 59, 203, 227, 229, 323, 328
Caesennius Paetus, L. (cos. 61) 228
Calgacus 57, 151, 197, 305, 307
Caligula 49, 64, 108, 178, 182, 184
Calpurnius Piso, C. (suff. date unknown), Neronian conspirator 133–4, 139–40, 157, 158, 164, 170, 177
Calpurnius Piso, Cn.(cos. 7 BC) 9–10, 118 n. 12, 177–80, 190
Calpurnius Piso Frugi Licinianus, L. 90, 150, 151, 187, 214, 215–18, 221
Campano, Giannantonio 284
Capitol 91, 96
Cara(c)tacus 120–3, 305, 307
Cassius Severus 76, 78
catalogues 62–3, 66–70
Catherine de' Medici 258
Cato the Elder 18, 19, 47, 78, 83, 120, 196
Cato the Younger 50–1, 141 n. 41
Celtis, Conrad 285
Chamberlain, Houston Stewart 289, 294, 295
Charles I, king of England 266, 267
Charles VIII, king of France 254
chiasmus 64, 202
Chifflet, Claude 250
Cicero 7, 19, 21, 24, 49, 73, 74, 77, 78, 80, 81, 83, 172, 173, 175, 203, 205, 212, 254, 275, 285, 318, 323
civil war 86–99, 90 n. 22, 100, 111, 112, 131, 131 n. 13, 137, 174, 225, 259
Claudius 28, 38–9, 116–26, 169, 179, 180–1, 182, 185, 301
closure *see* endings
Cluverius, Philippus 289
Cluvius Rufus (suff. date unknown) 8, 17, 18 n. 2, 28, 157
codex Aesinas 53, 65, 246–8, 251, 299
Coelius Antipater 3, 19
commentarii 29
comparison (*comparatio*, synkrisis) 92, 105, 107
Corbulo *see* Domitius Corbulo
Cornelius Sisenna, L. 7, 17, 17 n. 2, 19–20, 92
Cornelius Sulla Felix, Faustus (cos. 52) 133

Corvey 244
Cosimo I, grand duke of Tuscany 262
counterfactual history 90
Cremutius Cordus, A. 17, 21, 23, 26–7, 226, 258
Croce, Benedetto 277
Crosland, C.A.R. 13 n. 40
Curiatius Maternus 74–84
Curtius Montanus 221–3
Curtius Rufus, Q. (suff. 44) 24, 27 n. 33, 51, 196, 197
cycles of history 90, 101, 106, 108

Darré, Walther 296, 298
dating, consular 100, 121, 182
Decembrio, Pier Candido 246, 247
declamation 76, 199, 202
delatores 76, 77, 78, 190, 192, 221, 222
Demetrius of Tarsus 51
Demosthenes 212
Devereux, Robert (2nd earl of Essex) 266
diction *see* vocabulary
Dictys of Crete 246, 247
didactic mode 62–3
digressions 63–6, 97, 120, 120 n. 20, 234
Dio 130, 141, 185, 194, 230
Domitian 26, 38–9, 47, 56, 70, 72, 80, 85, 87, 88, 88 n. 12, 89, 152, 184, 192, 194, 222, 309, 311, 313, 315, 318
Domitius Corbulo, Cn. (suff. 39) 17, 17 n. 2, 121, 123 n. 29, 126 n. 41, 139, 143, 154, 226, 227–9
Donatus 242
Dorislaus, Isaac 267
Drusus Caesar (cos. 9 BC) 64, 67, 71, 102, 109, 110
Drusus Caesar (cos. 15 21), son of Tiberius 108, 156, 166, 182, 182 n. 21, 189
Drusus Caesar, son of Germanicus and Agrippina 113, 153, 189

Egypt 112
Eliot, Sir John 267
Elizabeth I, queen of England 266
enargeia see vivid writing
endings 89, 96, 148, 182, 188 n. 16, 202
end-of-year notices 120 n. 20, 132
England 266–7, 306
Ennius 18, 82
epigrams 51 n. 8, 65, 71–2, 167, 196, 199, 202, 202 n. 28, 210, 253, 255, 263, 270
Eprius Marcellus, T. (suff. 62, 74) 76, 77–8, 159, 186 n. 11, 187, 192, 222, 261

362

Erasmus 249
ethnography 59–72, 97, 112
exempla 93, 94, 94 n. 33, 95, 124–6, 142, 142 n. 44, 181

Fabius Justus, L. (suff. 102) 31, 74, 74 n. 2, 77
Fabius Pictor, Q. 18–19
Fabius Rusticus 8, 17, 18 n. 2, 23, 28, 157
'fact and impression' 160–6
Fannia, wife of Helvidius Priscus 313
Ferguson, Adam 277
Feuchtwanger, Lion 312–16
Fichte, Johan Gottlieb 289, 292
France 254, 257, 262, 263, 288–91
freedmen 116, 118, 119, 185
freedom *see libertas*
French Revolution 272
Fronto 41
Fulda 242, 243, 246, 281
    Rudolf of 245, 282

Gaius *see* Caligula
Galba 42, 90, 150, 170, 171, 187, 214, 215–18
Galerius Trachalus, P. (cos. 68) 78
Gaul 306, 327
Germanicus 4, 5–7, 68, 105, 107–12, 116, 127, 162, 163, 165, 177–9, 182, 226, 232–7, 302
Germany, Germans (ancient) 60–72, 232–7
    (early modern, modern) 280–99
gerund, genitive of 198 n. 18
Gibbon, Edward 174, 269–78, 317, 325, 328
gnomic utterances *see* epigrams
Gobineau, Arthur de 293
gods *see* religion
Goebbels, Josef 312
Goethe 292
Göring, Hermann 296
Granius Marcellus, M. 34, 35
Graves, Robert 300–4
Grotius, Hugo 268
Guarnieri, Stefano 246
Guicciardini, Francesco 255–8, 261, 263, 265
Günther, H.F.K. 281, 296

Hadrian 26, 191 n. 23
Heidegger, Martin 289
Heine, Heinrich 280, 281, 292
Helvidius Priscus 28, 47, 187, 191, 222, 313
Henty, G.A. 307

Herder, Johann Gottfried 291
Herennius Senecio 47, 312
Herodian 194
Herodotus 17, 69, 103 n. 9, 148, 174, 227
Hersfeld 242, 245, 246, 247, 281
hexads 89
Himmler, Heinrich 287, 296, 297, 299
historic present 209
historiography, Latin 3, 5, 7
Hitler 295, 306
Hitler Youth 296, 297
Hobbes, Thomas 268
Holy Roman Empire of the German Nation 280, 282
Horace 67, 82, 83, 170
Hume, David 269, 271, 276
hypophora 125

imitation *see* allusion
intertextuality *see* allusion
Ireland 306
Italy (early modern) 254, 255, 262, 263, 283–4

Jahn, Friedrich Ludwig 293
James I, king of England 265, 266
Jerome 241
Jesi 246–8
Jews 97–9
Julius Caesar *see* Caesar
Julius Civilis, C. 88, 96, 98, 226
Julius Secundus 74–5
Junia, wife of the tyrannicide Cassius 148, 155
Justus Lipsius 242, 249, 253, 259–61, 271, 288
Juvenal 36, 56, 82

landscape, terrain (foreign) 234–7
language *see* vocabulary
Lausanne 270
Lebensraum 287, 298
Leo X, Pope 244, 249
Lepidus, M. Aemilius (cos. 6) 193
Lex Papia Poppaea 173
libertas 64, 80, 81, 139, 148, 151, 173, 185–94, 266, 274, 290, 311
libraries 40, 42, 43, 241
Lipsius *see* Justus Lipsius
Livia, wife of Augustus and mother of Tiberius 42, 105, 107, 108, 113–14, 182, 303

GENERAL INDEX

Livy 1, 17, 17 n. 2, 22–4, 25–6, 48, 49, 64, 86, 100, 103, 103 n. 9, 104, 114, 120, 195 n. 2, 196, 197, 203, 213, 225, 227, 229, 236, 266, 272, 303, 318, 321
'Longinus' 73
Lucan 14, 18 n. 3, 60, 89, 306, 322
Lucian 41
Lucretia 114
Lucretius 62, 173
Luther, Martin 254

Machiavelli, Niccolò 255, 258, 260, 262, 270
maiestas 162
Malvezzi, Virgilio 263–4, 266, 267
manuscripts 242–8, 250
  'First Medicean' (M1) 243–4, 249, 251
  'Second Medicean' (M2) 244–5, 251
  Leidensis 245, 251
  see also codex Aesinas
Marcus Aurelius 273
Maroboduus 1–4
Marius Priscus 79
Memmius Regulus, P. (suff. 31) 132, 190, 194
Messalina 117–18, 120, 156, 182
metaphor 1–2, 3, 4, 14, 90, 90 n. 22, 93, 137, 197, 298
metus hostilis 96
Mitchison, Naomi 306–11
moderatio, modestia, modus 187, 192, 193
Mommsen, Theodor 317, 325, 328
Mons Graupius 50, 52, 56, 197, 305
Montaigne 258
Monte Cassino 244
Montesquieu 271, 275, 277, 289–91
Mucianus, C. Licinius (suff. 64(?), 70, 72) 219–21, 222, 223
Muretus (Marc-Antoine Muret) 250, 254

names 101, 108
Narcissus 118, 128
National Socialism 280, 281, 286, 292, 295–9, 312
Necker, Suzanne (*née* Curchod) 273
Nero 26, 28, 117, 119, 127–43, 148, 157, 170, 182, 184, 185, 213, 306, 307, 311
Nerva 31 n. 1, 47, 85, 87, 88 n. 12, 90, 150, 187, 194
Netherlands 255, 257
Niccolò Niccoli 244, 245

Norden, E. 295
Nuremberg race laws 296

obituaries 91, 105, 105 n. 18, 113, 114, 115, 119, 132, 165, 182, 182 n. 21, 184, 185 n. 7, 189 n. 19, 193
Ocean 5, 67–8, 71
  see also rivers
Octavia, wife of Nero 130–2, 182, 188
Odysseus 67, 112
openings see beginnings
oratory 59, 61, 73–84
  see also speech(es)
Otho 90, 150, 159, 170, 214, 218
Ovid 82, 327
oxymoron 200

parataxis 322
Parthia 40–1, 227, 232
Pascal 275
Pasquale, Carlo (Pasqualius) 258
personal pronouns 152–4
Petil(l)ius Cerialis, Q. (suff. 70, 74) 55, 193, 226, 230
Petronius 136
Piccolomini, Enea Silvio 283, 296
Pichena, Curtius 242, 244, 250, 251
Piso see Calpurnius
Pliny the Elder 7, 8, 17, 17 n. 2, 27, 55, 59, 89, 156, 157, 158, 164
Pliny the Younger 10, 23 n. 19, 28 n. 35, 32–5, 43, 48, 79, 85, 87, 88 n. 12, 174, 245, 265
Plutarch 8, 41 n. 29, 51, 92, 160, 163 n. 44, 215, 323
poetic colour 196
  see also allusion
Poggio 244, 245, 247
Pollio see Asinius Pollio
Polybius 17, 172, 175, 176, 184, 213
Pomponius Secundus, P. (suff. 44) 82, 83
Poppaea Sabina the Elder 117
Poppaea Sabina the Younger 130, 131, 132
Poppaeus Sabinus, C. (cos. 9) 234–7
portents 169, 171
Posidonius 59, 172
primitivism 60, 66, 153
prodigies 120, 120 n. 21, 170, 171
proleptic notices 116 n. 2
prosopography 320
Puteolanus 248, 251
Pytheas of Massilia 54

Quintilian 17, 26, 33, 76, 78, 79, 83, 195, 202

'reason of state' 261, 262, 263, 264, 265, 266, 270
religion 11, 168, 183
reprehensio 165 n. 47, 166 n. 49
Res Gestae (of Augustus) 28
Rhenanus *see* Beatus Rhenanus
ring composition 103, 117, 117 n. 8
rivers 63
  see also Ocean
Robertson, William 269, 272, 276
Rosenberg, Alfred 292, 296
Rubellius Plautus 133, 139
rumours 150, 160, 163, 176, 209, 302
Ruysschaert, J. 250

Sallust 17, 17 n. 2, 19, 22–4, 49, 50–1, 96, 104, 120, 131 n. 12, 173, 178, 195, 196, 197, 213, 222, 266, 285, 318, 321
Sallustius Crispus, C., courtier 260
Savile, Henry 266
Saxons 282
Sejanus 22, 104, 113, 123, 131 n. 12, 138 n. 33, 148, 152, 156, 165, 170, 182, 182 n. 21, 189, 190, 258, 263, 267
Sempronius Asellio 19, 175
senate 184–94, 258
Senatus Consultum de Cn. Pisone Patre 9–10, 14, 177–80, 183
Seneca the Elder 27, 73, 89
Seneca the Younger 14, 128, 130, 131, 134, 136, 140, 182
sentence structure 12 n. 38, 14, 94, 94 n. 32, 135, 197–206, 210
  balance or parallelism in 199, 200, 210
  periodic 203, 204
  see also 'appendix' sentences
sententiae see epigrams
Septimius Severus 276
Servilius Nonianus, M. (suff. 35) 18 n. 2, 26, 27
seruitus, seruitium 185, 187, 188, 192, 193, 266
Shakespeare 323
Sidonius 243
Silius Italicus (suff. 68) 37, 56
sources 3, 5, 7–10, 14, 156, 157, 229, 269, 318
Spain (early modern) 254, 259, 262, 263

speech(es) 1, 4, 57, 124–6, 159, 178, 180–1, 190, 195, 197, 199, 201, 203, 212–24, 230
Statius 36–7, 55, 56
Stoicism 168, 168 n. 2
structure 60–3, 88–90, 100, 103, 119–23, 127, 182–3, 214, 225
style 12–13, 14, 22, 24, 49, 59, 70, 74, 83, 180, 195–211, 275, 322, 323
  changes of in Tacitus 14, 195
  pointed 195, 199–203
subjunctive, second-person 70 n. 26, 150, 154, 154 n. 13
Suetonius Paulinus, C. (suff. 43 (?)) 230–1
Suetonius Tranquillus, C., biographer 4 n. 7, 8, 28, 35–6, 92, 130, 141, 194, 206–11, 215, 323
Syme, R. 12–13, 317–29
syntax 211

Tacitism 26–7
Tacitus
  career 37–9, 40, 43, 149, 176
  dates of works 31, 48, 74 n. 2, 241
  early printed editions 248–51, 253
  editio princeps 248
  Nachleben 278
  philosophy of history 168–73
  political theory and thought 172, 253–68
  praenomen 243
  'voiceprint' 148, 153, 157, 158, 161 n. 35, 187
Tennyson 305
testimony, eye-witness, oral etc. 9, 57, 59, 86, 179
thaumata 69, 70
theatricality 143
  see also tragedy
Thrace, Thracians 234
Thrasea Paetus, P. Clodius (suff. 56) 47, 78, 135, 190, 314, 316
Thucydides 17, 213, 227, 317
Thule 52–4, 56
Tiberius 2, 3–4, 4 n. 8, 6–7, 25–6, 28, 42, 77, 102, 103, 104–15, 148, 161, 162, 163, 164, 165, 166, 170, 173, 177, 178, 179, 182, 184, 185, 187, 234, 256, 259, 260, 263
Tigellinus 131, 133, 182, 182 n. 21, 307, 310
Titus 42, 54, 56, 88, 89
tragedy 92, 129 n. 8, 131, 131 n. 14

Trajan 23, 26, 31, 31 n. 1, 39–43, 48, 49, 80, 85, 85 n. 3, 88, 88 n. 12, 90, 125, 150, 187, 191 n. 23, 219
   Column 40–1
   Forum 39
   restored coinage 41–2
   translation 13
tricolon 204, 274
Trucculensis portus 52–3
Trüdinger, K. 295
tyrants 138 n. 33, 256

uariatio 14, 198, 199, 210, 211
uirtus 49, 51, 185, 191 n. 22

Valerius Flaccus 37
Valerius Maximus 95
Varro 321
Velleius Paterculus 2 n. 4, 2–5, 24–6, 249
verbs, omitted 198, 198 n. 14, 198 n. 15, 210, 322
Vespasian 88, 89, 90, 170, 171, 173, 187, 191, 219–21
Vettius Bolanus, M. (suff. 66 (?)) 36, 55, 56, 193
Vibius Crispus, L. Junius (suff. 61, 74, 83) 76, 77–8

Victoria, queen of England 305
Vindelin de Spira 242, 248
Vipstanus Messalla 7, 75–84, 155
Virgil 1–7, 14, 60, 62, 64, 66
Vitellius 196, 203, 206–11
vivere civile 254
vivid writing 61, 68, 70 n. 26, 117, 120, 121, 128, 149, 154, 209, 210
   see also historic present; subjunctive, second-person
vocabulary 4 n. 8, 5–7, 7, 14, 195–7, 211
Vologeses 228
Voltaire 271, 275

Wagner 294
warfare 225–38
Wimpheling, Jacob 285
women 107–14, 116, 123, 128–32, 131 n. 12, 134
wonders *see thaumata*
Woolf, Virginia 301
word play 202

Xenophon 17, 227

zeugma 198

Cambridge Companions To ...

AUTHORS

Edward Albee edited by Stephen J. Bottoms

Margaret Atwood edited by Coral Ann Howells

W. H. Auden edited by Stan Smith

Jane Austen edited by Edward Copeland and Juliet McMaster

Beckett edited by John Pilling

Aphra Behn edited by Derek Hughes and Janet Todd

Walter Benjamin edited by David S. Ferris

William Blake edited by Morris Eaves

Brecht edited by Peter Thomson and Glendyr Sacks (second edition)

The Brontës edited by Heather Glen

Frances Burney edited by Peter Sabor

Byron edited by Drummond Bone

Albert Camus edited by Edward J. Hughes

Willa Cather edited by Marilee Lindemann

Cervantes edited by Anthony J. Cascardi

Chaucer, second edition edited by Piero Boitani and Jill Mann

Chekhov edited by Vera Gottlieb and Paul Allain

Kate Chopin edited by Janet Beer

Coleridge edited by Lucy Newlyn

Wilkie Collins edited by Jenny Bourne Taylor

Joseph Conrad edited by J. H. Stape

Dante edited by Rachel Jacoff (second edition)

Daniel Defoe edited by John Richetti

Don DeLillo edited by John N. Duvall

Charles Dickens edited by John O. Jordan

Emily Dickinson edited by Wendy Martin

John Donne edited by Achsah Guibbory

Dostoevskii edited by W. J. Leatherbarrow

Theodore Dreiser edited by Leonard Cassuto and Claire Virginia Eby

John Dryden edited by Steven N. Zwicker

W. E. B. Du Bois edited by Shamoon Zamir

George Eliot edited by George Levine

T. S. Eliot edited by A. David Moody

Ralph Ellison edited by Ross Posnock

Ralph Waldo Emerson edited by Joel Porte and Saundra Morris

William Faulkner edited by Philip M. Weinstein

Henry Fielding edited by Claude Rawson

F. Scott Fitzgerald edited by Ruth Prigozy

Flaubert edited by Timothy Unwin

E. M. Forster edited by David Bradshaw

Benjamin Franklin edited by Carla Mulford

Brian Friel edited by Anthony Roche

Robert Frost edited by Robert Faggen

Elizabeth Gaskell edited by Jill L. Matus

Goethe edited by Lesley Sharpe

Günter Grass edited by Stuart Taberner

Thomas Hardy edited by Dale Kramer

David Hare edited by Richard Boon

Nathaniel Hawthorne edited by Richard Millington

Seamus Heaney edited by Bernard O'Donoghue

Ernest Hemingway edited by Scott Donaldson

Homer edited by Robert Fowler

Horace edited by Stephen Harrison

Ibsen edited by James McFarlane

Henry James edited by Jonathan Freedman

Samuel Johnson edited by Greg Clingham

Ben Jonson edited by Richard Harp and Stanley Stewart

James Joyce edited by Derek Attridge (second edition)

Kafka edited by Julian Preece

Keats edited by Susan J. Wolfson

Lacan edited by Jean-Michel Rabaté

D. H. Lawrence edited by Anne Fernihough

Primo Levi edited by Robert Gordon

Lucretius edited by Stuart Gillespie and Philip Hardie

David Mamet edited by Christopher Bigsby

Thomas Mann edited by Ritchie Robertson

Christopher Marlowe edited by Patrick Cheney

Herman Melville edited by Robert S. Levine

Arthur Miller edited by Christopher Bigsby (second edition)

Milton edited by Dennis Danielson (second edition)
Molière edited by David Bradby and Andrew Calder
Toni Morrison edited by Justine Tally
Nabokov edited by Julian W. Connolly
Eugene O'Neill edited by Michael Manheim
George Orwell edited by John Rodden
Ovid edited by Philip Hardie
Harold Pinter edited by Peter Raby (second edition)
Sylvia Plath edited by Jo Gill
Edgar Allan Poe edited by Kevin J. Hayes
Alexander Pope edited by Pat Rogers
Ezra Pound edited by Ira B. Nadel
Proust edited by Richard Bales
Pushkin edited by Andrew Kahn
Rilke edited by Karen Leeder and Robert Vilain
Philip Roth edited by Timothy Parrish
Salman Rushdie edited by Abdulrazak Gurnah
Shakespeare edited by Margareta de Grazia and Stanley Wells
Shakespearean Comedy edited by Alexander Leggatt
Shakespeare on Film edited by Russell Jackson (second edition)
Shakespeare's History Plays edited by Michael Hattaway
Shakespeare's Last Plays edited by Catherine M. S. Alexander
Shakespeare's Poetry edited by Patrick Cheney
Shakespeare and Popular Culture edited by Robert Shaughnessy
Shakespeare on Stage edited by Stanley Wells and Sarah Stanton

Shakespearean Tragedy edited by Claire McEachern
George Bernard Shaw edited by Christopher Innes
Shelley edited by Timothy Morton
Mary Shelley edited by Esther Schor
Sam Shepard edited by Matthew C. Roudané
Spenser edited by Andrew Hadfield
Laurence Sterne edited by Thomas Keymer
Wallace Stevens edited by John N. Serio
Tom Stoppard edited by Katherine E. Kelly
Harriet Beecher Stowe edited by Cindy Weinstein
August Strindberg edited by Michael Robinson
Jonathan Swift edited by Christopher Fox
J. M. Synge edited by P. J. Mathews
Tacitus edited by A. J. Woodman
Henry David Thoreau edited by Joel Myerson
Tolstoy edited by Donna Tussing Orwin
Mark Twain edited by Forrest G. Robinson
Virgil edited by Charles Martindale
Voltaire edited by Nicholas Cronk
Edith Wharton edited by Millicent Bell
Walt Whitman edited by Ezra Greenspan
Oscar Wilde edited by Peter Raby
Tennessee Williams edited by Matthew C. Roudané
August Wilson edited by Christopher Bigsby
Mary Wollstonecraft edited by Claudia L. Johnson
Virginia Woolf edited by Susan Sellers (second edition)
Wordsworth edited by Stephen Gill
W. B. Yeats edited by Marjorie Howes and John Kelly
Zola edited by Brian Nelson

TOPICS

The Actress edited by Maggie B. Gale and John Stokes
The African American Novel edited by Maryemma Graham
The African American Slave Narrative edited by Audrey A. Fisch

Allegory edited by Rita Copeland and Peter Struck
American Modernism edited by Walter Kalaidjian
American Realism and Naturalism edited by Donald Pizer

American Travel Writing edited by Alfred Bendixen and Judith Hamera

American Women Playwrights edited by Brenda Murphy

Ancient Rhetoric edited by Erik Gunderson

Arthurian Legend edited by Elizabeth Archibald and Ad Putter

Australian Literature edited by Elizabeth Webby

British Romanticism edited by Stuart Curran

British Romantic Poetry edited by James Chandler and Maureen N. McLane

British Theatre, 1730–1830, edited by Jane Moody and Daniel O'Quinn

Canadian Literature edited by Eva-Marie Kröller

Children's Literature edited by M. O. Grenby and Andrea Immel

The Classic Russian Novel edited by Malcolm V. Jones and Robin Feuer Miller

Contemporary Irish Poetry edited by Matthew Campbell

Crime Fiction edited by Martin Priestman

Early Modern Women's Writing edited by Laura Lunger Knoppers

The Eighteenth-Century Novel edited by John Richetti

Eighteenth-Century Poetry edited by John Sitter

English Literature, 1500–1600 edited by Arthur F. Kinney

English Literature, 1650–1740 edited by Steven N. Zwicker

English Literature, 1740–1830 edited by Thomas Keymer and Jon Mee

English Literature, 1830–1914 edited by Joanne Shattock

English Novelists edited by Adrian Poole

English Poets edited by Claude Rawson

English Poetry, Donne to Marvell edited by Thomas N. Corns

English Renaissance Drama, second edition edited by A. R. Braunmuller and Michael Hattaway

English Restoration Theatre edited by Deborah C. Payne Fisk

Feminist Literary Theory edited by Ellen Rooney

Fiction in the Romantic Period edited by Richard Maxwell and Katie Trumpener

The Fin de Siècle edited by Gail Marshall

The French Novel: from 1800 to the Present edited by Timothy Unwin

German Romanticism edited by Nicholas Saul

Gothic Fiction edited by Jerrold E. Hogle

The Greek and Roman Novel edited by Tim Whitmarsh

Greek and Roman Theatre edited by Marianne McDonald and J. Michael Walton

Greek Lyric edited by Felix Budelmann

Greek Mythology edited by Roger D. Woodard

Greek Tragedy edited by P. E. Easterling

The Harlem Renaissance edited by George Hutchinson

The Irish Novel edited by John Wilson Foster

The Italian Novel edited by Peter Bondanella and Andrea Ciccarelli

Jewish American Literature edited by Hana Wirth-Nesher and Michael P. Kramer

The Latin American Novel edited by Efraín Kristal

The Literature of the First World War edited by Vincent Sherry

The Literature of World War II edited by Marina MacKay

Literature on Screen edited by Deborah Cartmell and Imelda Whelehan

Medieval English Literature edited by Larry Scanlon

Medieval English Theatre edited by Richard Beadle and Alan J. Fletcher (second edition)

Medieval French Literature edited by Simon Gaunt and Sarah Kay

Medieval Romance edited by Roberta L. Krueger

Medieval Women's Writing edited by Carolyn Dinshaw and David Wallace

Modern American Culture edited by Christopher Bigsby

Modern British Women Playwrights edited by Elaine Aston and Janelle Reinelt

Modern French Culture edited by Nicholas Hewitt

Modern German Culture edited by Eva Kolinsky and Wilfried van der Will

The Modern German Novel edited by Graham Bartram

Modern Irish Culture edited by Joe Cleary and Claire Connolly

Modernism edited by Michael Levenson

The Modernist Novel edited by Morag Shiach

Modernist Poetry edited by Alex Davis and Lee M. Jenkins

Modern Italian Culture edited by Zygmunt G. Baranski and Rebecca J. West

Modern Latin American Culture edited by John King

Modern Russian Culture edited by Nicholas Rzhevsky

Modern Spanish Culture edited by David T. Gies

Narrative edited by David Herman

Native American Literature edited by Joy Porter and Kenneth M. Roemer

Nineteenth-Century American Women's Writing edited by Dale M. Bauer and Philip Gould

Old English Literature edited by Malcolm Godden and Michael Lapidge

Performance Studies edited by Tracy C. Davis

Postcolonial Literary Studies edited by Neil Lazarus

Postmodernism edited by Steven Connor

Renaissance Humanism edited by Jill Kraye

The Roman Historians edited by Andrew Feldherr

Roman Satire edited by Kirk Freudenburg

The Spanish Novel: from 1600 to the Present edited by Harriet Turner and Adelaida López de Martínez

Travel Writing edited by Peter Hulme and Tim Youngs

The Twentieth-Century English Novel edited by Robert L. Caserio

Twentieth-Century English Poetry edited by Neil Corcoran

Twentieth-Century Irish Drama edited by Shaun Richards

Victorian and Edwardian Theatre edited by Kerry Powell

The Victorian Novel edited by Deirdre David

Victorian Poetry edited by Joseph Bristow

War Writing edited by Kate McLoughlin

Writing of the English Revolution edited by N. H. Keeble

Printed in Great Britain
by Amazon.co.uk, Ltd.,
Marston Gate.